ADVANCE PRAISE FOR *I SAW THE ANGEL OF DEATH*

"The testimonies included in this book, available for the first time in English translation, describe the experiences of Jews of eastern Poland from September 1939 through 1943. The authors, among the small percentage of Polish Jews to survive the Second World War, were 'lucky' to avoid falling victim to the Nazis by being punitively deported eastward by the Soviets instead. Mainly civilians, these individuals, adults as well as children, describe their difficult lives and their struggles to remain alive in Soviet camps and special settlements. [This book] provides invaluable insight into an understudied aspect of the Polish and Jewish experiences of World War II."

—KATHERINE R. JOLLUCK,
senior lecturer, Department of History, Stanford University

"The importance of publishing for the first time the complete 'Palestinian Protocols' in English cannot be overestimated. These firsthand depositions, testimonies, and statements of 171 Polish Jews, caught in the firestorm of the Nazi and Soviet occupations of Poland, 1939–41, are precious documents of Holocaust and gulag history. They also underline the fierce determination of Polish Jews to survive despite murderous attacks by the Germans, frightening obstacles to flight to the east, and internment in Soviet special camps, where they were brutalized beyond imagination. Only the Sikorski-Maisky agreement of July 1941 made possible the amnesty of tens of thousands of Polish Jews, including most of these Polish Jews, and their fraught transfer to Tehran and then to Jerusalem, where their statements were collected. Documenting the trials of the survivors in their own words is a fitting testimony to those millions of Polish Jews who perished."

—NORMAN M. NAIMARK,
Robert and Florence McDonnell Professor of East European Studies,
Stanford University, and senior fellow, by courtesy, Hoover Institution

I Saw the Angel of Death

I Saw the Angel of Death

Experiences of Polish Jews Deported to the USSR during World War II

Edited by ***Maciej Siekierski*** and ***Feliks Tych***

Translated by ***Karolina Klermon-Williams***

HOOVER INSTITUTION PRESS
STANFORD UNIVERSITY STANFORD, CALIFORNIA

With its eminent scholars and world-renowned library and archives, the Hoover Institution seeks to improve the human condition by advancing ideas that promote economic opportunity and prosperity, while securing and safeguarding peace for America and all mankind. The views expressed in its publications are entirely those of the authors and do not necessarily reflect the views of the staff, officers, or Board of Overseers of the Hoover Institution.

hoover.org

Hoover Institution Press Publication No. 724

Hoover Institution at Leland Stanford Junior University, Stanford, California 94305-6003

Translation of *Widziałem Anioła Śmierci: Losy deportowanych Żydów polskich w ZSRR w latach II wojny światowej* (Rosner i Wspólnicy, 2006) by Karolina Klermon-Williams, with review by Irena Czernichowska, funded by the Suzanna Cohen Legacy Foundation, whose mission is to honor the precious legacy of courage and resilience demonstrated by survivors of the Shoah, through the preservation, publication, and teaching of their remarkable stories.

First printing 2022
28 27 26 25 24 23 22 7 6 5 4 3 2 1

Manufactured in the United States of America
Printed on acid-free, archival-quality paper

Library of Congress Cataloging-in-Publication Data
Names: Siekierski, Maciej, editor. | Tych, Feliks, editor.
Title: I saw the Angel of Death : experiences of Polish Jews deported to the USSR during World War II / edited by Maciej Siekierski and Feliks Tych.
Other titles: Widziałem anioła śmierci. English | Hoover Institution Press publication ; 724.
Description: Stanford, California : Hoover Institution Press, [2022] | Series: Hoover Institution Press publication ; no. 724 | Translation of: Widziałem anioła śmierci. | Includes bibliographical references and indexes. | Summary: "Personal testimonies reflect the experiences of Polish Jews whose towns were occupied by German and Soviet forces during World War II and who were deported and imprisoned in Soviet camps"—Provided by publisher.
Identifiers: LCCN 2022005982 (print) | LCCN 2022005983 (ebook) | ISBN 9780817925048 (cloth) | ISBN 9780817925062 (epub) | ISBN 9780817925086 (pdf)
Subjects: LCSH: World War, 1939–1945—Deportations from Poland. | World War, 1939–1945—Prisoners and prisons, Soviet. | World War, 1939–1945—Personal narratives, Polish. | World War, 1939–1945—Personal narratives, Jewish. | Jews, Polish—Soviet Union—Biography. | Poland—History—Occupation, 1939-1945.
Classification: LCC D810.D4 W5413 2022 (print) | LCC D810.D4 (ebook) | DDC 940.53/438—dc23/eng/20220214
LC record available at https://lccn.loc.gov/2022005982
LC ebook record available at https://lccn.loc.gov/2022005983

Contents

Foreword

The Hoover Institution is honored to partner with the Suzanna Cohen Legacy Foundation to publish this translation of the testimonies in *I Saw the Angel of Death* (first published by Rosner i Wspólnicy in Warsaw in 2006). As noted in the superb introductions by Dr. Feliks Tych, director of the Jewish Historical Institute from 1995 to 2006, and Dr. Maciej Siekierski, senior curator emeritus of the Hoover Institution Library & Archives, the collections that house these testimonies are full of extraordinary and harrowing first-person accounts of thousands of victims of the Soviet communist and Nazi fascist regimes.

As a library and archive, our mission is to collect, preserve, and make available the most important material on war, revolution, and peace in the twentieth and twenty-first centuries. For over sixty years, the testimonies of these Jewish victims of the Soviet gulag have been preserved in our archives. Some had been published earlier in Hebrew, Polish, and English, but this edition is the first scholarly English translation of what were known as the "Palestinian Protocols"—accounts of Jews who were released from the brutality of the gulag after the Sikorski-Maisky agreement, and who then escaped to the Middle East.

The English-language publication of *I Saw the Angel of Death* is yet another example of the scholarship, persistence, and dedication of Dr. Maciej Siekierski, who championed its publication for many years. Under Dr. Siekierski's leadership, the Eastern European collections at Hoover grew to be among the most important in the world. An archive can have the most important collections in the world inside its doors, but the key is for those collections to reach a broad public. With this publication, we continue Herbert Hoover's vision for the institution that bears his name—that it be "more than a mere library." And indeed, this book will allow a new generation of scholars, students, and wider audiences to read and understand the horrific experiences of Polish Jews under Nazi and Soviet occupations.

Many people helped make this project possible. I would like to thank Kim Dana Kupperman of the Suzanna Cohen Legacy Foundation; translator Karolina Klermon-Williams; Gerardina Małgorzata Szudelski, Nicholas Siekierski, Irena Czernichowska, and Jean Cannon of the Hoover Institution Library & Archives; copy editor Beverly Michaels; and Barbara Arellano, Alison Law, and Danica Michels Hodge of the Hoover Press. I also offer gratitude to Andrzej Rosner of Rosner i Wspólnicy for his assistance.

Documents speak through those who read them. May you and others have this opportunity to read, remember, and never forget.

Dr. Eric Wakin
Deputy Director
Research Fellow
Director of Library & Archives
Hoover Institution, Stanford University

Note on the Translation

This book has been translated as closely as possible from the Polish edition, *Widziałem Anioła Śmierci: Losy deportowanych Żydów polskich w ZSRR w latach II wojny światowej* (Warsaw: Rosner i Wspólnicy, 2006). Adjustments to make the text more legible to readers of English have been added in brackets [like this]. Question marks in brackets indicate a lack of clarity in the original material, such as locations or facts that could not be verified. Some footnotes have been added to provide additional context. As in the text, any notes added to the English edition have been provided in brackets. Some footnotes from the original edition have been combined or replaced by definitions or dates added directly to the text, in brackets.

Certain place-names have been provided with various spellings, reflecting the original protocols, or testimonies. These spellings have largely been preserved. Dates in the protocols are also kept as they appear in the original documentation, with the day preceding the month.

The glossary draws on many definitions from the Polish edition but has been entirely revised for readers of English. The indexes have been fully revised.

Polish Jews
Prisoners of Soviet Camps

Feliks Tych

The collection of documents presented here has extraordinary value in terms of both information and insight. It consists of personal testimonies of victims—taken shortly after the events they describe, when memory was still fresh—who were among the more than one hundred fifty thousand people, Polish citizens, who were deported, imprisoned, and killed during World War II by Soviet authorities.

How this collection of testimonies was created and how it made its way to the Hoover Institution, the co-publisher of this volume, is described in the adjoining introduction by Dr. Maciej Siekierski, curator of the East European Collection at Hoover.

Actually, these documents include (in varying degrees) the experiences of Polish Jews under both occupations: Soviet and German. Occasionally there are texts that pertain more to the German occupation than to the Soviet occupation and the Soviet Union. Nevertheless, generally only introductory fragments of the testimonies describe the first months or weeks after the German invasion of Poland. It was during exactly this time, which has been less documented and is not as well known as the later period (beginning in the second half of 1941), that Nazi Germany began, according to its own terminology, "the final solution to the Jewish question." The fragments dealing with the beginning of the German occupation give concrete information about the extreme brutality and cruelty of the behavior of the Germans, including the Wehrmacht, toward the Jews, from the first days of the occupation: the burning alive of large groups of Jews in the synagogues, frequent instances of tearing out of beards together with the skin, beating, compulsory cleaning of latrines with bare hands and other maltreatment, and tens of other painful torments. Besides confiscations and contributions, there was also widespread "private" robbery by soldiers and officers of all branches of the German military. The farther to the east, the greater was the cruelty of the German military and police formations in the just-occupied territories.

For the Jews this was the first well-remembered lesson, as it was at the root of their decision to escape to the East, which saved the lives of many. On the other hand, for the Jews who remained under German occupation, the memory of the first weeks or months was eclipsed by later events, the time of genocide.

It was this savage behavior of the German invaders, from the beginning of the occupation, that explains why about 300,000 Polish Jews from various political and social sectors—from the poor to the well-to-do, from leftists to rabbis—escaped from the German occupation to the East. For Polish Jews there was essentially no other escape route than to the East. Most likely less than twenty thousand of them were able to escape into Hungary or Romania.

Relatively few Jews sought safety in the East because of any leftist, pro-Soviet convictions. For the great majority of the refugees the reason was much simpler—this was simply a choice of the lesser evil, and as it seemed initially, a temporary asylum.[1] The circumstances of reaching a decision, whether to remain under German occupation or to escape to the East, were in some regions especially dramatic, because between September and October 1939 the boundary between the two occupations, German and Soviet, was not yet finally delineated. The secret protocol of the decision for the fourth partition of Poland, appended to the Ribbentrop-Molotov Pact of August 23, 1939 (de facto Hitler-Stalin pact), initially provided that the territories of the Second Polish Republic to the east of the Narew-Vistula-San line, thus most of Lublin province, would go to the USSR. It was not until the signing of the September 28, 1939, German-Soviet Boundary and Friendship Treaty that the German-Soviet boundary was set on the Bug and San rivers. In exchange for the territories between the Vistula and Bug rivers (this took place in October 1939), the Germans agreed to the future Soviet occupation of Lithuania. Between September

1. See Daniel Boćkowski, *Losy zydowskich uchodzcow z centralnej i zachodniej Polski przebywajacych na Kresach polnocno-wschodnich w latach 1939–1941,* in *Świat niepożegnany: Żydzi na dawnych ziemiach wschodnich Rzeczypospolitej w XVIII–XX wieku*, ed. Krzysztof Jasiewicz (Warsaw: Instytut Studiów Politycznych PAN and Oficyna Wydawn. RYTM; London: Polonia Aid Foundation Trust, 2004), 91–108.

and October, some towns and villages changed hands twice, which intensified the suffering and the confusion of the Jewish population. "And when the Russians began to retreat one day"—recalls a witness, the son of a rabbi from Siedlce—"most people went with them, including my father, who knew that [even though], as a rabbi, he would suffer with the Bolsheviks, he [still] would prefer to go to Siemiatycze rather than stay with the Germans."[2]

In Żółkiewka, in the province of Lublin, during a three-day interlude between the withdrawal of the Red Army and the second occupation of the town by the Germans, the local population organized a pogrom against the remaining Jewish population (those who had not left town along with the Soviet administration) in retaliation for the Jews' supposed collaboration with Soviet authorities and murdered twenty Jews.[3] Similar tragedies took place elsewhere. The suffering of the Jews intensified with the change of the occupying force, not only in the summer of 1941, but as early as the fall of 1939.

The use of the expression "supposed collaboration" in the context of the events in Żółkiewka is not intended to deny instances of such collaboration with the Soviets, as there were many of them. Rather this expression notes the widespread and long-lived legends, with frequent instances of generalizing these attitudes and exaggerating their extent still practiced by some historians.

Many Jewish refugees, after only a few months of experiencing life under Soviet rule, tried to return to their homes under German occupation. This was encouraged in part by the Soviet authorities' announcement that the refugees could sign up for such a return. Indeed, a certain number of ethnic Poles were allowed to do so. Jews, on the other hand, were generally not allowed back by the Germans. What was worse, this very registration to return home to the German occupation became a trap for tens of thousands of Jews, as those who had registered for return soon constituted a significant number of the people deported to Siberia, and consequently of the authors of the testimonies published here. It is possible that the release of a certain number of ethnic Poles for return to the General Government was a move aimed at enticing others into this trap. Jews who refused to accept Soviet passports (Soviet citizenship), or

---

2. See Protocol 131.
3. Chaim Zylberklang, *Z Żółkiewki do Izraela* (Lublin: Julian Grzesik, 2003), 27.

who were considered "bourgeois," or "socially dangerous elements," or were active members of Jewish political parties, or who in general belonged to social elites, provided more targets for Soviet repression.

Besides reporting experiences under German occupation and first contacts with the Soviet system, the documents here also include a third, very important, though only briefly described, layer of information. They draw a broad picture of prewar Jewish society in Poland. They speak about how this society supported itself and how it lived, functioning in the economic, political, and spiritual space assigned to it. Indeed, nearly every text includes in the very beginning information about the place of residence, close family members and their occupations, and how the family supported itself, as well as the family and social status of the individual witness. In this respect these are not monothematic documents, dealing only with martyrdom. Even though the witnesses' experiences in Soviet camps and prisons usually occupy the central place in their testimonies, the information pertinent to this subject flows logically from the situations and events preceding imprisonment or deportation, and in some way also from the information about their situation or status during normal—that is, prewar—times.

It is exactly these three historical layers that combine to produce the dramatic effect of the testimonies. What needs to be added here is the finale, which was the difficult and long road (sometimes thousands of kilometers), frequently marked by the deaths of close family members, from the "amnesty"—that is, the release in late summer of 1941 of Polish citizens from camps, prisons, and *spetsposelki*—to the place of their evacuation from the USSR, via Persia—to Palestine.[4]

Finally, the fourth layer: Polish-Jewish relations in these tragic circumstances. Besides the experience from occupied Poland and the USSR, the testimonies occasionally include little-known facts from other territories, describing the solidarity of Poles and Polish Jews in their common suffering. One of the testimonies, for example, reports that branches of the Polish

4. *Spetsposelki* is an abbreviation from "special settlements," the official name of informal forced labor camps, settlements created for deportees in uninhabited, forested areas in the Siberian taiga, where the deportees had to build primitive barracks or dugouts for themselves from the materials found in the forest. The principal occupation of the deportees was the production of lumber for the needs of the Soviet economy, or the construction of roads. See glossary: *posiolek*.

YMCA, present during the war in Romania, were issuing documents to Polish Jewish refugees, which made it more difficult for the Romanian authorities to identify them as Jews; and that this activity was on a substantial scale.[5]

In the case of Polish-Jewish relations on the territory of the USSR, the testimonies speak of a wide range of attitudes. These documents speak of solidarity between ethnic Poles and Polish Jews in prisons, camps, and *spetsposelki*, of mutual assistance; but also recount examples of antisemitism shown by Polish fellow inmates. It is striking that frequently examples of this are brought out in the testimonies of children, who earlier, in Poland, shielded by family and school, had not been consciously affected by these attitudes. Only here, thousands of kilometers from Poland, in orphanages, shelters, and schools created by local representatives of the Government of the Republic of Poland in exile, did they experience prejudice for the first time. Generally in such situations, Polish teachers came to the rescue, and this is gratefully acknowledged in the testimonies.[6] Where did these unfriendly attitudes of their Polish classmates come from? They could only have been acquired from the family home. Also, during recruitment to the Anders Army, Jewish draftees or volunteers were more frequently rejected by the draft boards, usually at the request of Soviet officers participating in these boards, but also very frequently by their Polish members. The same applied to the evacuation of civilians and children. Sometimes only the intervention of a high-ranking Polish officer made it possible to change a decision.[7] In this context, the positive role of Gen. Zygmunt Bohusz-Szyszko is noted in many testimonies, as someone who frequently corrected his subordinates' negative decisions regarding Jews. The picture presented in Wiktor Sukiennicki's report, engaging and adding much to the subject of our publication, which is presented as an appendix to the documentary part of the book, requires some revision in the light of these

---

5. See Protocol 316.

6. See also Daniel Boćkowski, *Czas nadziei: Obywatele Rzeczypospolitej Polskiej w ZSRR i opieka nad nimi placówek polskich w latach 1940–1943* (Warsaw: Wydawn. Neriton, 1999).

7. On this subject, for example, please see the reminiscences of a rabbi in the Anders Army, who earlier shared the experiences of Polish and Polish-Jewish deportees and political prisoners in the USSR: Pinkas Rosengarten, *Zapiski rabina Wojska Polskiego* (Warsaw: Pamięć Diaspory, 2001), 70–90; also Tomasz Gąsowski, *Pod sztandarami Orła Białego: Kwestia żydowska w Polskich Siłach Zbrojnych w czasie II wojny światowej* (Krakow: Księgarnia Akademicka, 2002), passim (as well as a bibliography on the topic). See also Yisrael Gutman, "Jews in General Anders' Army in the Soviet Union," *Yad Vashem Studies* 12 (1977): 231–96.

testimonies.[8] The report provides information on the difficulties facing Polish Jews from the Soviets at the time of the release of Polish citizens from camps, prisons, and *spetsposelki*, during recruitment to the Anders Army, and during the evacuation from the USSR. It also recounts generally successful interventions by Polish authorities on behalf of Jewish citizens of Poland when the Soviets discriminated against them. However, from the testimonies published here, it appears that the difficulties facing Jewish citizens of the Second Polish Republic during recruitment to the Anders Army were frequently the result of the negative attitudes of some Polish officers and NCOs toward Jews volunteering for service with the Polish forces.[9] Undoubtedly military recruitment boards were struggling with very serious substantive problems, which influenced the recruitment process. These were connected with the limited provisions supplied by the Soviets to the Polish Armed Forces and other structural conditions of the whole operation, as well as the physical condition of the recruits, preference for those with prior military experience, etc. Nevertheless, the existence of antisemitism among a certain portion of soldiers, NCOs, and officers is confirmed by General Anders's order of November 14, 1941, directed against manifestations of antisemitism in his army, commanding equal treatment of Jews in all military units under his command.[10]

* * *

The testimonies of Jews saved from the hell of Soviet prisons, camps, and *spetsposelki* that are published here come from religious Jews who use Yiddish on a daily basis as well as from assimilated Jews; and from people of various ages, from twelve-year-old children to adults. The testimonies were given by witnesses of different levels of education, representing very diverse social

8. This report (in Polish) titled "The matter of Jewish citizens of Poland in the light of official documents and practice of the Soviet authorities" was prepared on August 11, 1942, for the use of the Polish Government-in-Exile by Dr. Wiktor Sukiennicki (1901–1983), lawyer and political scientist, acting professor of law at the Stefan Batory University in Wilno, and professor at the Academy of Political Studies in Warsaw, member of the Scholarly Research Institute of Eastern Europe in Wilno, at the time of the writing of the report, counselor of the Embassy of Poland in the USSR, then located in Kuybyshev, later director of the Study Center of the Ministry of Information of the Polish Government-in-Exile.

9. See Rosengarten, *Zapiski rabina*, 81–83.

10. Rosengarten, *Zapiski rabina*, 139.

classes and political preferences, and from nearly all regions of the Second Polish Republic. A lot of information is repeated in these documents, and on occasion even literally, especially as pertains to the circumstances of arrest and the conditions of transportation to the place of detention. This repetition points to the scale of the phenomenon and to the uniformity of the procedures used by the Soviet political police, as well as to the centralized character of the activity. Nevertheless, each of the testimonies also contains information that is unique, pertaining to the experiences of a given family or individual. It is the sum total of these experiences that represents the whole phenomenon.

It is clearly evident from the testimonies presented here that most people who came into contact with the Soviet prison and camp system did not survive this experience. It was not uncommon that from a family of several people only one member survived. The rest died from starvation, cold, work exhaustion, or epidemics caused by the deplorable sanitation and nutrition, both during the long transport and in the camps or *spetsposelki*.

Many testimonies speak of the religious persecutions conducted by Soviet camp administrators, which were acutely felt by the Jews, as well as about the openly antisemitic attitudes of Soviet authorities toward Jewish deportees.[11] This also worsened the situation of the prisoners. "Out of the 600 Jews who arrived in the camp," recalls one of the witnesses, "150 died from hunger and 50 from other diseases."[12] Another witness relates: "Our family was made up of five children, three of whom died in Russia," and another one will testify: "Seven of us left Poland, [while] three died of hunger and diseases."[13] Not uncommonly, death—by that time caused not so much by cold and overwork, but principally by typhus, exhaustion, hunger, and lack of medical care—caught up with the deportees even after the amnesty, after release from the camp or *spetsposelok*, on the road to the much longed-for evacuation from the USSR.

If it were not for the pact between the Polish Government-in-Exile and the Soviet government (the so-called Sikorski-Maisky agreement), signed in London on July 30, 1941, leading to the amnesty decree of the Supreme Soviet of the USSR of August 12, 1941, ordering the release of all Polish citizens

11. See, for example, Protocols 132 and 136.

12. See Protocol 126.

13. See, respectively, Protocol 112 and Protocol 127 (testimony of a fifteen-year-old boy; his parents and one of the siblings died).

imprisoned in the USSR (which was also a Polish precondition for signing the pact)—as well as the Polish-Soviet agreement of August 14, 1941, on the formation of the Polish Armed Forces in the USSR (commonly referred to as the Anders Army)—probably very few of the victims would have left these camps and *spetsposelki* alive. "None of us would have survived if the Amnesty hadn't saved us."—declares one of the witnesses.[14]

Higher chances of survival were associated with only those Polish Jews who either volunteered for work inside the USSR before the German attack on the USSR on June 22, 1941, and did not refuse to accept Soviet citizenship ("passport"), and those who remained free in Eastern Poland, annexed by the USSR in the fall of 1939, and managed to escape east ahead of the Soviet-German front.

When the Germans attacked the USSR on June 22, 1941, those Polish Jews who found themselves in the territories of the Second Polish Republic occupied by the USSR after September 17, 1939, and who did not manage to run east ahead of the front line, became, like virtually all Polish Jews under German occupation, victims of the Nazis' "final solution to the Jewish question"—that is, genocide—which was intended to include all the Jews of Europe. Many of them were murdered in the summer of 1941, well ahead of the Jews of the General Government, whose total extermination began in March 1942.

In spite of great casualties among the Polish Jews who found themselves in the hands of the NKVD during World War II, the majority of them managed to escape German genocide on Soviet territory. Some of them survived under conditions as dramatic as those described in testimonies published here; others in the severe conditions of Soviet wartime "normality," which was shared by most of the ordinary citizens of the USSR.

The number of Polish Jews who managed to survive World War II in the USSR is much greater than the number who managed to survive the German occupation in hiding, with false papers, in the guerrilla units, in concentration camps, in labor camps, or in other circumstances. Frequently they owed their survival to the brave assistance of their non-Jewish fellow citizens. It is estimated that of the c. 350,000 Polish Jews who survived the Holocaust (of the 3.3 million prewar Polish Jewish population), 250,000 survived in the USSR.

---

14. See the glossary and the appendix with the aforementioned report by Wiktor Sukiennicki. See Protocol 316 for the witness statement.

Had it not been for the inhuman conditions of life in the camps and penal settlements, the number of Polish Jews who survived in the USSR would have been much higher.

The documents in this volume clearly indicate that the Soviet camp system, the infamous gulag archipelago, was in essence genocidal. They also show the mechanism of this genocide. It was based not on the use of gas chambers or mass executions, the principal instruments of genocide utilized by the Third Reich. In the USSR, where group (though rarely mass) executions were in certain periods a daily occurrence, the main instruments of genocide were different. They consisted of the devastating prison and camp regime that exposed people to deadly hunger, cold, and overwork, and to conditions favorable to the emergence and spread of contagious diseases. Stalinist genocide was generally based on the regime's contempt for human life, its "own" people as well as "others," on a war against its own society and, at the same time, against those whom it considered its enemies.

* * *

An explanation of less widely understood terms and foreign words appearing in the text is included in the glossary, which appears on page 885. Foreign terms that appear only once are explained in the footnotes. The footnotes also include brief biographical notes for some of the personal names appearing in the testimonies. This rule is applied sparingly because of the economy of space in our publication. The main criterion was the rank of a given person. The pages where these biographical notes are found are marked in bold type in the index of names.

The texts of the testimonies are published without any omissions and in the linguistic style in which they were recorded. Because some of the witnesses testified in Yiddish, it is not impossible that mistakes in proper names were sometimes the fault of the recorders (as well as the translators from Yiddish to Polish). In those instances where the publishers were able to correct the incorrect spellings of places, institutions, or foreign words, they have done so in the notes. However, in cases where it was not possible to identify and correct the place-name, they have put a question mark next to the name in square brackets. The original numbering of the protocols has been preserved. Gaps in the numbering are the result of gaps in the Stanford collection.

Information Center.[5] Jewish subjects in the CIW, at least until the fall of 1943 when she transferred to the Documents Bureau, were handled by Dr. Teresa Lipkowska, Kuybyshev secretary and cipher operator to Ambassador Kot. She was an extraordinary woman of aristocratic descent, sister-in-law of General Kazimierz Sosnkowski, who herself had lived through two years of Soviet prisons and camps. She was a woman of great sensitivity, a Catholic in love with Jewish culture, a collaborator with the Zionist movement and its military arm Irgun, led by Menachem Begin. It was probably she who initiated the CIW's collecting of Jewish testimonies "from the inhuman land" published in this volume.[6] The Military Documents Bureau, which in September 1943 was moved to Jerusalem, also became active in creating Jewish documentation. Here the principal specialist in these matters was a law graduate of the Jagiellonian University, a prewar Zionist leader, Dr. Menachem Buchweitz (Buchwajc). Buchweitz was the author of a special thirty-three-item "Jewish questionnaire," which was distributed in the summer of 1943 among Jewish soldiers, whose ranks were already thinning as a result of desertion, after the army reached Palestine. Later in the Documents Bureau, Buchweitz authored an extensive unpublished report titled "Polish Jews under Soviet rule," based principally on the testimonies collected by the CIW.[7] Thanks to people like Lipkowska and Buchweitz, cooperation between the Center for Information

5. The CIW was also known by its English acronym PIC (Polish Information Centre M.E.). The archives of the CIW did not survive. Some miscellaneous materials belonging to the CIW were left behind in the basement of the monastery on a Mamilla street in Jerusalem. Sometime during the early fifties, Menachem Buchweitz went through these deteriorating remnants, sending the books to the Eastern Institute "Reduta" in London. A file of CIW correspondence with the Ministry of Information, which survives in the Ministry's archives (HIA-MINF, box 71, folder 4), does not pertain to the program of Jewish testimonies. The Anders Collection preserves the original "Protocol establishing the form of cooperation between the Polish Army and the Center for Information in the East with regard to gathering of materials pertaining to the Soviet occupation and Soviet Russia," signed on April 15, 1943, by General Anders and Jan Tabaczyński. This protocol does not mention Jewish subjects as topics for joint study (HIA-Anders, box 76, folder 74).

6. After the war, Lipkowska remained in her second homeland (Teresa Lipkowska, "*Dlaczego zostałam w Izraelu*," in Zamorski, *Dwa tajne biura*, 124–27). Teresa Lipkowska died in 1991 in Israel.

7. Groups of Jewish statements and questionnaires are located, for example, in box 57 (50 copies), box 59 (85 copies), and box 61 (30 copies) of the Anders Collection. The report "Polish Jews" is in box 72, file 29, of the Anders Collection. In box 43 of the same collection is Buchweitz's manuscript (in Polish) "The Jewish question in the Soviet Union" (eight pages). After the war, Buchweitz fought for the independence of Israel, and later was a judge and professor of law.

in the East and the Documents Bureau, at least on the level of gathering Jewish documentation, developed successfully despite fundamental political differences separating the initiators of the CIW and the Documents Bureau, Minister Kot and General Anders.

The CIW began recording Jewish testimonies, commonly called "Palestinian Protocols," in the spring of 1943, after the departure of Minister Kot from Jerusalem and his move to London to take over the Ministry of Information and Documentation, where he replaced Stanisław Stroński. Testimonies were written down on the basis of oral statements, first manually and later copied on a typewriter and numbered. Some of the testimonies, especially those of children, were written down in Yiddish, then translated into Polish, copied by hand, and finally typewritten. The unnumbered testimony of Chaim Besser of Łuków (born in 1927) is the only surviving such example.[8] A CIW official encouraged the youngster to recall details by a promise of sweets.[9] It is impossible to state categorically that unauthorized changes or deletions were not made during the translation and copying, since the protocols are not authorized originals but typewritten copies. Nevertheless, the surviving testimonies, frequently critical of Poles and Polish authorities for their antisemitic prejudice, suggest that CIW officials did not censor the statements. The Ministry of Information and Documentation archives preserve most of the cover letters accompanying the successive mailings of the protocols from the director of the CIW Tabaczyński in Jerusalem to Minister Kot in London. From them we know, for example, that Protocols 43–45 and 47–55 were carried in the mail of General Sikorski and that they were destroyed during the Gibraltar crash of July 4, 1943. Copies of these numbers were re-sent on August 19. The cover letters suggest that the CIW collected statements until at least the fall of 1944 and that the project included at least 332 witnesses. In November 1944,

8. Zachary Baker, [Reinhard Family] Curator of Judaica and Hebraica Collections at the Stanford University Libraries, has read all three versions of Chaim Besser's testimony and decided that the translation is accurate but does not quite reflect the style and the personality of the author of the testimony in Yiddish (letter of Z. Baker of April 23, 2004).

9. This information came from Ofer Zimmerman, the son of Chaim Cymmerman (letter of May 17, 2003). Chaim remembered that the conversation took place about four to five months after his arrival in Palestine, in a house near Dizengoff Square in Tel Aviv, not in the Jerusalem office of the CIW (Valero House, Bezalel Street). Chaim testified in Yiddish, and a man took down the statement. Unfortunately, the chocolate turned out to be only a ploy.

Professor Kot was recalled from the Ministry of Information, and his portfolio was given to Adam Pragier, which suggests that the Palestinian Protocols project was connected with the tenure of Stanisław Kot. In London, the principal recipient of the protocols, after Professor Kot, was the director of the Study Center of the Ministry of Information, Professor Wiktor Sukiennicki, former counselor in the Polish embassy in Kuybyshev and author of the August 1942 report "The matter of Jewish citizens of Poland in the light of official documents and practice of the Soviet authorities," which is published in this volume. Unfortunately, occupied with work on the "plebiscite" and then with the Katyn investigation, Sukiennicki did not manage to fully utilize the materials sent to him.[10] Some of them were incorporated into individual country reports on the Soviet occupation in Eastern Poland. Others, perhaps those that included more detailed information on crimes, were sent to the Ministry of the Interior. Unfortunately, they did not survive in the archives of the Interior Ministry in the Polish Institute in London, nor in that portion of the archive transferred to the Hoover Institution.[11]

Jewish testimonies recorded by the CIW, or the so-called Palestinian Protocols, made their way to the Hoover Institution in 1959 together with the archives of several official institutions of the Second Polish Republic, as a deposit of Minister Aleksander Zawisza. During the next twenty years this deposit was known as the Hoover Institution's Polish Government Collection (PGC). After the period of the deposit expired, the PGC materials were processed and divided into a number of separate collections corresponding to institutional divisions of the Second Polish Republic, including the Ministry of Information and the CIW, as its subordinate agency. The Palestinian Protocols escaped the attention of researchers using the PGC collection in the

---

10. The protocols were preserved along with the manuscript list of the statements, which notes key details about their authors—place of residence, age, where deported, etc. It is possible that this represents an early effort at processing this material. Though he worked at the Hoover Institution after the war, Professor Wiktor Sukiennicki did not resume his research on the deportees. His postwar years were spent principally on the political history of the Eastern Borderlands during World War I. He finished his work and died in California in April 1983. The book appeared in two volumes under the title *East Central Europe during World War I: From Foreign Domination to National Independence*, edited by Maciej Siekierski, preface by Czesław Miłosz (Boulder, CO: East European Monographs, 1984).

11. The Jewish files in the Interior Ministry collection at the Polish Institute and Sikorski Museum do not include any testimonies of deportees, according to Mr. Andrzej Suchcitz's letter of September 2004.

Hoover Institution. In 1987 they were found by the author of this introduction, curator of the European collections, and noted in his review of sources on Polish-Soviet relations in the archives of the Hoover Institution.[12] He also sent copies of eight protocols to Norman Davies, who published them in English translation by Joanna Hanson, in his book about the Jews of Eastern Poland during World War II.[13]

The next publication of some of the protocols was completed in 1994 in Poland. Henryk Grynberg, after receiving some photocopies of the protocols from his California acquaintances, selected seventy-three testimonies of children and had them published by the Polish journal *Karta*. The same book was republished the following year in a Hebrew translation in Jerusalem and three years later in English.[14]

Our publication offers the first scholarly edition of all of the surviving Palestinian Protocols of the Center for Information in the East. The documents are held now in boxes 123 and 124 of "Poland. Ministerstwo Informacji i Dokumentacji Records, 1939–1945" of the Hoover Institution Archives. There are 161 of them, including one unnumbered (Chaim Besser) and two separate but complementary testimonies by the same person (Estera Barasz). In addition to these, in the archives of the Documents Bureau of the Second Polish Corps (Anders Collection), ten more CIW protocols were found, which are no longer available in the Ministry of Information papers. These are the copies of Protocols 20, 25, 26, 46, 52, 215, 216, 219, 223, and 232.[15] Thus, we are publishing here 171 separate texts of Jewish testimonies.

---

12. Maciej Siekierski, "Hoover Institution's Polish Collections: An Overview and a Survey of Selected Materials on Polish-Soviet Relations," *Polish Review* 33, no. 3 (1988): 325–32.

13. These were Protocols 28, 32, 41, 128, 176, 215, 251, and 259. Norman Davies and Antony Polonsky, eds., *Jews in Eastern Poland and the USSR, 1939–46* (London: School of Slavonic and East European Studies, University of London, 1991), 301–60.

14. Henryk Grynberg, *Dzieci Syjonu* (Warsaw: Wydawnictwo "Karta," 1994; Hebrew edition, Jerusalem: Yad Vashem, 1995; English edition [*Children of Zion*], Evanston, IL: Northwestern University Press, 1997).

15. Protocols 20, 25, 26, 46, and 52 are in box 59, and 215, 216, 219, 223, and 232 are in box 46. Besides these, the Anders Collection includes a significant number of copies of other CIW protocols, which are also available in the Ministry of Information collection. This is undoubtedly a good example of close cooperation of the civilian Center for Information in the East and the secret military Documents Bureau.

Testimonies

Protocol (unnumbered)[1]

Testimony of **Chaim Besser**, born 1927 in Łuków, Lublin voivodeship. Father: Icchak. Mother: Miriam. Brothers: Lejb, Szlojme, Aron. Sisters: Chaja and Itte. The father owned a shoe store in Łuków.

On a Friday morning, German planes bombed the Łuków rail station. Many people died. A few days later the Jewish district was bombed as well.

After a week of war, I left with my family for the town of Stoczek, where we stayed for six days. When we heard gunshots we hid in the apartment. We thought that there was fighting between the Poles and the Germans taking place nearby. Soon, the Germans arrived in town and knocked on the doors shouting: "*Juden heraus*!" We went out onto the street [and] lined up. A few Jews were shot. We were told to gather the most essential things and leave town.

The town was burned down after we left. We spent all night in a barn and returned to Łuków in the morning. The Germans took us from Łuków to Mińsk Mazowiecki to work for two weeks.

When we heard that the Muscovites were [about to] enter Łuków, we returned. The Soviet army arrived a few days later. When the Russians left after another six days, we went, with [my] father and brothers, to Brześć. In Brześć we were asked if we wanted to go to work in Russia. We agreed.[2] We left for the town of Tołoczno [Talachyn; Polish: Tołoczyn] in the Vitebsk Oblast, where we worked in a shoe factory for six months. We couldn't make ends meet there so we returned to Baranowicze. In Baranowicze there operated a German commission.[3] We registered to return home.

---

1. [This unnumbered protocol is the only protocol that has been preserved as a manuscript. The version here is from a slightly redacted translation of the typescript version that appears at the end of the testimonies. For additional information on the transcription and translation of the protocol, see the chapter in this volume by Maciej Siekierski.]

2. In areas occupied by the Red Army, a campaign of voluntary departures for work within the USSR was taking place.

3. At the end of 1939, the USSR made an agreement with the Third Reich to resettle mainly Germans to areas occupied by the German army. [The agreement] also covered certain categories of refugees, allowing them to return to their original places of residence. For the enactment of the agreement, mixed Soviet-German commissions were put in place, registering and assessing the people expressing an interest in resettlement.

After two months, one Friday night, we were woken up, a search was carried out, [then] we were driven out of town and loaded into dark freight train cars. We traveled like cattle for five days. [We] weren't given food. The train only stopped in Sverdlovsk. We were given bread and tea. From Sverdlovsk, we traveled to Tavda on the same train. And from Tavda, by river, it took five days to the Tos camp, Sverdlovsk Oblast, Taberinskij district.[4]

We stayed in barracks, fifty families to one, for two days, and were then taken to work. Father went to the forest and received four rubles after eight days. One of my brothers mowed hay fields for pennies. [Anyone] who asked how we were to make ends meet was arrested. In the winter, we worked the forest in temperatures of −50°C [−58°F]. Anyone who had anything sold it to survive. The answer to our complaints was: "Work." One [of the people] who worked with me died. We cried at assemblies and the commandant shouted: "You have to get used to this. You're staying here forever. Forget about Warsaw."

After fourteen months a commission arrived; we were given Polish passports and released.[5] We had no money for travel and [had to] walk the three hundred kilometers to [the town of] Tavda. In Tavda, we registered with the authorities and went to the city of Turkestan. Work began again in Stalin's kolkhoz [collective farm]. We worked all day for three hundred grams of black flour divided among five people.

My brothers: Szlojme, age twenty, and Aron, age eighteen, lay ill at home for five days. Then the hospital took them away. One of them died on the way to the hospital; the other one passed, too, in the hospital. I was left in the kolkhoz with one other brother and our father. We knew we would die. And we went back to Turkestan and carried bricks in a brickyard. We earned two rubles and three hundred grams of bread per day. I was then taken to a Polish orphanage where they gave me food and clothes. After two weeks, I was taken along with the others to Ashgabat. I stayed in a Polish children's home for four weeks.[6]

And then we left for Iran with the Polish army.

---

4. Tabory district [original Polish correction: Taboryski rejon].

5. Refers to the so-called Amnesty for Polish citizens based on the decree of the Supreme Soviet of the USSR from 12 August 1941, which was a result of the Sikorski-Maisky agreement signed in London on 30 July 1941. See also F. Tych's introduction and the glossary: Amnesty.

6. Polish children's homes in the USSR: a network of orphanages created by representatives of the Polish Government-in-Exile in different regions of the USSR. See glossary.

Protocol 27

Testimony of **Dora Werker**, age forty-eight, from Raszub [?]. Owner of a haberdashery store. Arrived in Palestine with daughter Rut, age sixteen, from Russia via Tehran, in February 1943.

On Tuesday 29 August 1939, a bomb exploded in a rail station in Raszub, wounding and killing tens of people.[7] It turned out that the bomb was inside a suitcase that a German spy left in the station waiting room. Panic swept the city. The possibility of war started to be taken seriously. The following day, our decorator, a German, walked into our shop where he'd worked for years and arrogantly stated that he no longer wished to work for Jews, [and] that he was to be paid what he was owed. Fearing vandalism, my husband paid up everything the man demanded.

After the decorator left, some office and shop girls, Germans, gathered and proclaimed that the shop belonged to them and that they would not work for Jews anymore. Seeing what was afoot, my husband hired a truck, filled it up with the merchandise, and the whole family drove to Kraków in that truck.

We arrived in Kraków on the day the war broke out. We bought a horse and a cart there and made our way to Tarnów, where my parents lived. The roads were full of soldiers and civilians; we were bombed and shot at from machine guns. Planes came down low above us. We got to Dębica with difficulty. The bombardment was so severe there that our cart driver, a peasant, said he would not take us further. Left with no choice, we stopped at a cottage that had been abandoned by the owners and spent the night there. On the way, planes bombed us. We hid underneath a freight car to avoid the rifle shots. A family with a nine-year-old boy hid with us. The child leaned out from behind the cart, a pilot spotted him, aimed, and killed him on the spot. After a long journey we arrived in Złoczów.

In Złoczów

We wanted to stay in Złoczów for a few days and then set off again, but the children fell ill and spent three weeks in bed with a high fever so that we

7. The actual place-name has not been identified. The only event similar to the one described occurred on Monday 28 August 1939 at the rail station in Tarnów.

couldn't dream about further journey. Meanwhile, the Bolsheviks entered Złoczów, and the Germans Tarnów. We were advised to get to Tarnów since the Germans were allowing people to leave for Palestine. I received a letter from [my] mother saying that the situation in Tarnów wasn't bad, [and] that we should try to come her way. Since a registration[8] to leave began in Złoczów, we stated that we wanted to go to Tarnów.

Before the arrival of the Bolsheviks, food prices rose immediately. Houses, shops, and factories were nationalized. The bourgeoisie, the merchants, and the middle classes were thrown out of their homes. One day, a regulation was issued proclaiming the Polish currency void, so that there was nothing with which to pay for bread. Arrests began. The wives of Polish soldiers, the formerly rich, and also those who signed up to leave for the German-occupied territory were arrested. [People] spent the nights outdoors, afraid of sleeping at home. Every morning I wrote out a sign on the windowpane. This way, my husband knew he could return home, that I had not yet been arrested.

Deportation

My husband got pneumonia from sleeping outdoors. As he lay in bed with a 40°C [104°F] fever, at twelve at night on 28 June 1940, there was a knock on the door. The owners did not want to open up, so the members of the NKVD forced their way in and broke into the apartment.[9] They were two civilians and one policeman. They asked if Werker lived here. One of them shouted: "You want to go to the Germans—get dressed." I started crying and begging them to leave the ill one be, I showed the doctor's note, but to no avail. They carried my husband out and laid him into the car, allowing us to bring fifty kilograms of luggage. They made an inventory of the rest of the things [and] promised they would sell them and return the money to us. We were all sent to the station. We spent the night on the floor [there]. Only in the morning were we loaded into carriages. Fifty people to one. We started in an unknown direction.

8. Registration: an operation of registering people to return to former places of residence carried out by mixed Russian-German commissions. See glossary.

9. NKVD: The People's Commissariat for Internal Affairs, a political police force of the USSR operating under this name in the years 1934–46. Successor to the OGPU, antecedent of the KGB. See glossary.

There was only one bunk between eight people in the car. We all sat on the floor—women, men, and children. The carriage doors were locked. A hole in the floor served as a toilet. At each station we were given water, a portion of bread and fish soup came daily. We were constantly told when being passed the food: "You're going home."

We didn't know where we were being led throughout the journey. We weren't let out at stations. I begged for a doctor for my husband. After examination, we asked the doctor where we were headed. His response was that one [should] work a lot in Russia but talk little.

On the train I got to know two Christian families who traveled with us. One of them was [Jan] Kwapiński, the former mayor of the city of Łódź, with his wife and children.[10] Kwapiński had been wounded in his arm when he had tried to cross to Romania via Zaleszczyki. The doctor didn't want to assist him, saying that he would be fine. The second was Antoni Pająk, an MP for PPS.[11] In our car there also traveled Dr. Ettingier, Mrs. Wilczek, Milano, and others.

In the Labor Camp

We rode through Kiev, Kharkiv, Saratov, Potolinsk,[12] Tomsk, Irkutsk, Odinski district.[13] The journey lasted a few weeks until we reached a wild Siberian steppe. We got off the carriages and were taken to a labor camp surrounded by wire. We were given bread once a day and nothing cooked with it. After two weeks we were loaded up and taken to the Nirezna *posiołek*.[14] We were supposed to stay for good there. The *posiołek* consisted of earth, water, and woodland. There was nowhere to sleep. We slept under the open sky. There were 450 of us, including fifteen Polish families. Soviet exiles occupied a few old huts. The *posiołek*'s commandant was a deportee himself. The following day we were

10. Jan Kwapiński (1885–[1964]): PPS [Polska Partia Socjalistyczna; English: Polish Socialist Party; PSP] and union activist, mayor of Łódź in 1939, escaped to the East after the entry of the German army. Imprisoned by the Soviet authorities, released in October 1941. A delegate of the embassy of the Polish Government-in-Exile in Tashkent. A member of the Government-in-Exile in London from 1942.

11. Antoni Pająk (1893–1965): former legionnaire, executive PPS activist, MP of the Republic of Poland. When escaping east from the Germans fell into Soviet hands in Skałat and was deported. Escaped the USSR in 1942. Held various positions in the Polish Government-in-Exile.

12. Could refer to Semipalatinsk.

13. Should be: Ust-Ordynsky district [Polish: Ust-Ordyński rejon].

14. *Posiołek* (Polish, from the Russian *posiolek*): a settlement, often an informal labor camp. See glossary.

told that whoever wanted to could erect himself a barracks. Since wood was plentiful, the work began and the barracks were erected, with twenty people occupying each. My son was a mechanic and was given machinery work in a gold mine. He worked thirty-six hours without rest. For [those hours] he received [part of text missing] thirty rubles. The Russians envied his high earnings, as such a quota was [normally] paid with ten rubles. The first two hundred rubles he earned were not paid to him on account of, it was explained, the cost of electricity and the rent for the barracks. Because of our proximity to the mine, we could use electric lights. I was exempted from work on account of the fact that my husband chopped wood in the forest. He worked from five in the morning to seven in the evening but couldn't fulfill his wood quota. He earned around a ruble a day.

Life in the Camp

There was a kitchen in the *posiołek* where once a day one received soup and groats, and once a week a reindeer cutlet. In the barracks there stood a stove. In the evenings, when everyone returned from work, wet rags were hung out to dry. The air was insufferable. The clothes were so wet that they didn't manage to dry out overnight and had to be put on damp for work in the morning. At night it was so freezing inside the barracks that [our] hair would freeze to the blankets. Hands, noses, and ears were frostbitten on a daily basis. Twice weekly, propagandist assemblies took place. Our commandant, Akarukow, and his deputy, Jarosław, comforted us by saying that we would never get out of Siberia, and since we had no homes of our own anymore, we should work busily for the good of our new motherland—the Soviet Russia. Both commandants were antisemites. They wouldn't give Jews passes to go to the second *posiołek*, where the gold mine workers lived whom it was always possible to sell some of our clothing, and to buy something to eat with the money. They said that Jews were speculators, that they conned Russians. They did give out leave passes to the Poles.

The Kwapiński and Pająk families lived in our barracks too, with whom we grew extremely friendly. Seeing that I would not be able to deal with the commandant, I had an idea to promise him a bribe. That helped. I got the pass and went to the second *posiołek*, where I sold some junk—and this repeated regularly.

In that region the summer lasts only two months. The nights are light, white. All the barracks were full of bedbugs. The wood that we carried from the forest was rotted and served as a perfect hiding place for bugs of all sorts. The bite of a [tick] causes skin inflammation and ulcers. Once this bug bites into the skin you can't get it out without tweezers.[15] We were also tormented by mice. Clothes were hung high up out of fear of them. They fought among themselves at night, often ending up in between sleeping people. Fighting them was impossible. My son made a trap and caught twenty mice within an hour. The battle against bedbugs and mice lasted until the morning, making it difficult to sleep. In May 1941, all of the men from our *posiołek* were taken to build a railway. After a month, when the German-Russian war broke out, they were brought back with a statement that, as "harmful elements," they could not be trusted with the railway work.

We, the women, were prohibited from visiting the second *posiołek*, communicating with the Russians [or] selling things. Trading could only take place through the commandant. He himself made estimates and payments. Naturally, these sales were worthwhile to no one.

Kwapiński and Pająk Arrested

The second *posiołek* was eight kilometers away in a town called Otkrytoye. There the mine specialists, as well as Poles, lived. It was difficult to get there. Temperatures reached −70°C [−94°F]—anyone making the journey had to bandage themselves up, otherwise they might freeze to death. There was a radio station and two newspapers in that *posiołek*: *Prawda*[16] and a local paper. Sometimes we received mail from our relatives, parcels, and money. The post office was located in the Otkrytoye *posiołek*. We decided to appoint someone as a postman so that they would bring us the mail and the parcels. Jan Kwapiński was chosen for this honorary position. Every day on his way to the post office he would first have to get the commandant's permission. Once, in April 1941, when Kwapiński went to see the commandant for the permission, he was told to wait. He waited half a day until an order from the NKVD in Aldan arrived

15. Note: The original text refers to this insect as "a type of bedbug." However, the need for removing it with tweezers suggests the author may have meant ticks.

16. [*Prawda* (Truth): Newspaper published by the Front for the Rebirth of Poland, a clandestine anti-Fascist organization formed in 1941 by a group of secular Catholics.]

ordering his arrest. A strict search took place in the barracks. Mrs. Kwapińska was body-searched and told that her husband would not come back again. No one was allowed to leave or enter the barracks. During the search they took off Kwapiński his gold watch and all documents. Pająk and six other people were arrested alongside Kwapiński. They were only arrested so that no one would say that Jews were favored.[17]

After two months' prison Kwapiński came back to the *posiołek*. It was in July,[18] already after the Amnesty.[19] He said he had stayed in a separate cell and was given a slice of bread to eat per day. He was interrogated day and night. Every day and every night he would get woken and taken to the judge. The cross-examination lasted for hours. The procedure was repeated twice every night.

After his return from prison, Kwapiński received a telegram from Moscow with a permission to come [there]. Indeed, he left with his family and promised to help us.

About the Amnesty

In July [1941],[20] representatives from the NKVD arrived and told us we were free. The commandant gave everyone a certificate valid for three months and we had to choose the direction of travel. We decided to go to Samarkand. As there was no railway there, we got a cart on the commandant's intervention and went toward Otkrytoye. It wasn't possible to find a place to stay overnight. Somehow we managed to get set up at a Russian woman's place; we slept on the floor for five rubles a night. We weren't allowed to stay there longer and we went to Odan.[21]

---

17. For more detail of Kwapiński's arrest, see his memoirs: Jan Kwapiński, *1939–1945: Kartki z pamiętnika* [Pages from the diary] (London: Wydawn. Światowego Związku Polaków z Zagranicy, 1947), 32–37.

18. The author's memory fails her here. The Amnesty act was issued by the Soviet authorities on 12 August 1941.

19. Amnesty; here: release from prisons, camps, and other places of forced deportation within the territory of the Soviet state of Polish citizens on the basis of a decree of the Supreme Soviet of the USSR from 12 August 1941. See glossary.

20. The Amnesty was actually declared on 12 August 1941.

21. Here and henceforth likely refers to the town of Aldan [Polish: Ałdan].

In Odan [Aldan]

Odan is a town with small wooden houses. Despite the fact that the whole population works at the gold mine, the quality of life is very poor. At every step one comes across people from the NKVD guarding the mine treasures. It was with difficulty that we got a room at a local hotel. The furniture in the room consisted of a bunk, a table, and a bench. In the hotel restaurant one could get sour cabbage soup and some beetroot. Bread and meat were out of the question. After a few days we went to Tynda by truck. It is a small rail station from which one can go to Novosibirsk. The station is no more than a hut. We slept on benches in barracks. We only just managed to push onto [the train]. In Novosibirsk they wouldn't let us out of the station so we stayed on the concourse waiting for the next train to arrive.

We wanted to go to Tashkent, but other difficulties awaited us. The ticket had to be stamped at the counter. Thousands of people waited in line in front of the cashier's counter waiting to get their tickets stamped. We gave the cashier a hundred and he stamped our tickets straightaway. We went to Tashkent on the first train. We rode for three days and three nights. We arrived in Tashkent but were not allowed to enter the city as refugees were not allowed in the first-line cities. We stayed in the station. Our biggest worry was protecting the last of our belongings since, in the station, people had pillows stolen from underneath their heads. In this typical country of theft, the Soviet Russia, the laments of the robbed rung out over and over. Despite watching out we had our suitcase stolen. When my husband went to report it to the police he found out that an hour earlier a high-ranking state official had a suitcase with ten thousand rubles inside of it stolen. Everyone had to be searched but the suitcase was never found. There was no accommodation to be found close to the station. We didn't want to enter the café as it was full of Uzbeks, half-feral people who might just have ripped the suitcases from our hands. So we slept in a garden close to the station. My daughter fell ill with appendicitis. I continued to sleep in the garden with the sick child. The child got sicker and sicker, and I fruitlessly begged people to allow me into their homes—putting up a refugee was punishable by five years' prison. Besides, the locals did not want to let Jews in. Only when I said I was a Christian did I get a corner in some hut for twenty rubles.

Meanwhile, Kwapiński arrived in Tashkent. He was organizing a Polish delegation[22] and a Help Committee and employed my husband as a delegation official, but despite this, it was difficult for us to get registered in Tashkent. Finally, we got a small room and arranged it somehow but continued to sleep on the floor as there was no furniture in it. I had to leave my daughter in the hospital. I was worried about the local hospital full of people with typhus and managed to get into the Red Cross hospital after Kwapiński's intervention. She was operated on by Professor Orłow and after two weeks I signed her out. We spent six months in Tashkent. We moved to Samarkand along with other Polish officials when the delegation changed its office. There we got a small room in the "Krasny Oktiabr" hotel. My husband claimed that the delegation did not differentiate between Jews and Poles. But Jews would not be accepted into the army. Kwapiński intervened and my son, Zygmunt, was accepted into a regiment stationed in Kermine. General Bohusz[23] advised that my son not come to Kermine because of a terrible typhus epidemic there, from which thousands of Poles were dying. [Instead], from Kermine he went to London where he's currently serving as a pilot in the Polish army. After [my] son's departure we stay in Samarkand for three weeks. We heard that transports were being sent to Persia. We were also told that the last transport was to leave within days. We quickly packed up our things and went to the station. We waited at the station for two days so that, when we got to Kermina,[24] it was too late. The transport had left.

My Husband's Death

It was impossible to get food in Kermine, even with money. No one wanted to [let us] register. The fear of the NKVD was even greater there than elsewhere. We were watched at every step. Seeing that a transport wasn't forming, my husband went back to Samarkand to his old post in the delegation. We stayed in Kermine. Two days later my husband fell ill and couldn't leave the bed anymore. Unable to manage on his own, he sent a man to Kermine to get us. I

22. After the establishment of diplomatic relations between the Polish Government-in-Exile and the USSR government in July 1941, a Polish embassy was opened in Kuybyshev, with regional delegations. See glossary: delegation.

23. Zygmunt Bohusz-Szyszko (1893–1982): general, Chief of Staff of the Polish army in the USSR.

24. This way of spelling Kermine [Kermina] is found in many deportee testimonies.

myself soon suffered an attack of kidney stones then but taking no notice of it, left [my] daughter to watch over our things and went to Samarkand. I found my husband gravely ill with typhus.[25] He was taken to the hospital where he died on 10 May.

There were plenty of ill people, infected doctors in the hospital. The nurses treated the patients brutally. They stole the food the patients were sent. I visited the head doctor on the day of my husband's death. He told me to pray to God for his life. I sent a telegram to my daughter so that she would come. She couldn't get a ticket. She made it to the funeral thanks to Lt. Anenek.

My husband was buried in a Jewish cemetery. The delegation gave me a sheet and a shirt in which he was buried. This much remained from his riches. Alone and without means of supporting myself, I went to the delegation, and thanks to Prof. [Marian] Heitzman, a docent at Kraków University, my daughter was able to take my husband's position in the delegation. She received five hundred rubles per month and provisions.

Arrest of the Delegation Members

One day, Prof. Heitzman was called in to the NKVD and [a] swarm of NKVD agents [was] sent [to raid] the delegation's offices. A thorough search took place, all of the documents were taken, the office was sealed and the officials arrested.[26] They arrested the [main] delegate—Prof. Heitzman, his deputy—Eng.[27] Kazimierczak,[28] the head of the passport office—Kowal, and the clerks. My daughter happened to not be in the office, which is why she wasn't arrested. After the delegation was shut down we were left with no means of supporting ourselves. The situation of the Polish refugees was worsening [and] we escaped to Kermine. There, a transport began to be formed again. The Russians caused

25. [The author specifies the disease in question as "tyfus plamisty" (*typhus exanthematicus*), which is the type caused by the bacteria *Rickettsia prowazekii*. It is referred to in English-language literature as "epidemic 'louse-borne' typhus," or "spotted typhus." There are numerous other references to typhus epidemics in the testimonies, and since historical references to non-specific typhus in English literature are generally considered to be this condition, the term "typhus" has been used. "Tyfus brzuszny" (*typhus abdominalis*) has been translated as "typhoid fever."]

26. Refers to May 1942. The NKVD carried out numerous arrests among the workers of the delegations then, accusing them of espionage. Most were released after a few months.

27. [Polish: "inż.," from *inżynier* (literally, *engineer*), a title specifying a type of a science/engineering degree in Poland. The English abbreviation will be used going forward.]

28. See Kwapiński, *Kartki z pamiętnika*, 51–52.

difficulties for Jews, not allowing them to leave the country. Thanks to our protections and contacts in the delegation, we were registered. Two days before the departure our tickets were taken away [and] we were told: "You're Jews, you cannot come." I went to the group's commandant, Major Dziurzyński, but my pleadings were for nothing. Even Poles with Jewish-sounding names encountered difficulties, [where] only baptism certificates helped. I went to a captain I knew, Baron Silesia, who, although always polite [in the past], did not want to help me this time. I registered with the garrison commandant, Col. Janusz. He was genuinely moved by my story, the loss of my husband the delegation member, and the fact that my son was in the army, and said that if nothing else works, he'll put us down as his own: mother and daughter. Col. Janusz's intervention worked after all and I was finally allowed to join the transport. Colonel Janusz turned up at the station to say goodbye to us in person. We traveled for three days to Krasnovodsk. From there, via Pahlevi and Tehran, we came to Palestine.

Protocol 28

Testimony of **Jachiel Szajnblum**, age forty, born and resident in Przemyśl. Official of a state grain enterprise. Arrived in Palestine via Tehran in May 1942.

The Przemyśl Massacre

The Germans entered Przemyśl in the first days of September 1939. On the first day the Jewish shops were robbed. Then, after a few days, they herded civilians into the empty shops and photographed them to have documents [proving] it was the local civilians and not the soldiers who stole Jewish property.

The Germans stayed in Przemyśl for eleven days. Two days before departure they organized a hunt for people, for Jews, men, grabbing them on the streets. It was called that they were being captured for forced labor but they were led to a cemetery close to the village of Pikulice. There they were told to dig graves, and then were all shot. So that those killed couldn't be identified, hydrochloric acid was poured over the faces of all the dead. Thus six hundred Przemyśl Jews were massacred. Among them Rabbi Hersz Glazer, Rabbi Zajdel, Dr. Pinser, Eng. Szifer, [Mojżesz] Grosman, Dienstag, Sztejner, Bakin,[29] Deutsch, Hirsz, Zalcberg and son, Edward Kunke, Sofer and his two sons-in-law, and plenty of refugees who had sheltered in Przemyśl. This atrocity was made known by the Christian inhabitants of Pikulice who brought the message to the city right after the crime had taken place. Women, wives, mothers, and children went to the cemetery, where they identified, by their clothing, those who were killed. The burial was taken care of by the shochet[30] and mohel,[31] Nehamia Rosenblum. All were buried in the same grave.

The day before leaving the city, the Germans picked up a few Jews, gave them bottles of kerosene and forced them to pour them over the Torah scrolls in the synagogue and set them on fire. In the same way, the Jews were forced to set fire to all of the synagogues.

---

29. Most likely refers to Izrael Bakun.
30. Shochet: a person who performs ritual slaughter of animals, ensuring it is kosher. See glossary.
31. Mohel: a person who performs ritual circumcisions. See glossary.

The Arrival of the Russians

The Russians occupied Przemyśl on 20 September. Their first decree was for the occupants of the houses by the San River to vacate their homes. Przemyśl was split into two parts. On one side the Germans, and on the other the Bolsheviks were in charge.[32] At first we thought we might somehow be able to coexist well with our new overlords. Trading began, goods went up [in price], people made money. Despite high food prices, almost everyone could afford to buy enough to eat one's fill. But this situation lasted only a month. Afterward, the Russians started throwing people out of their homes. The first victims were the so-called bourgeoisie and the middle classes, that is to mean Jews. Naturally, the non-Jewish bourgeoisie weren't respected either. Then there began a series of arrests. The president of the Hitachdut;[33] Chaim Elisze, who later lost his mind in jail; the chairman of the Revisionists,[34] Dr. Babad; and many Polish officials, activists, and merchants were arrested. The number of arrested Jews turned out to be higher than that of the Poles because [the latter], seeing what was afoot, crossed over en masse to the German side.

The Ukrainian Soviet Elections

The elections were free and democratic [on paper], but in fact people were all but forced to vote for the people written out on the electoral list.[35] Only one list existed. The polling stations were equipped with buffets and loudspeakers, one could eat one's fill, listen to music, and take something nice back home.

---

32. [The author is referring to the practical result of the secret nonaggression agreement between the USSR and Nazi Germany known as the Molotov-Ribbentrop Pact. In this accord, Hitler and Stalin divided Poland into spheres of influence, increasing territories for each country. This agreement, made before the war began, was broken in June 1941 when the Nazis invaded the USSR.]

33. Hitachdut: Zionist Labor Party Hitahdut. Formed in 1920. After the war, in 1944, it briefly resumed its activities; disbanded by the authorities of the Polish People's Republic in 1949.

34. Revisionist Zionists: a revisionist faction of the Zionist movement led by Vladimir Ze'ev Jabotinsky [Polish: Władimir Zeew Żabotyński]. See glossary.

35. In October 1939, in the Soviet-occupied territories of the Republic of Poland, elections to the People's Assemblies of Western Ukraine and Western Belorussia [Belarus], called a plebiscite, took place. On 29 November 1939, a citizenship decree was issued recognizing all persons present in those territories between 1 and 2 November 1939 as Soviet citizens. Many refugees and Eastern Borderlands inhabitants resisted the issuing of Soviet identity cards (so-called passports), risking repressions from the NKVD. See glossary: elections.

Who wasn't eager to take part in the election was visited at home and had it made clear to them that it would be better for them if they voted.

Nationalization

Immediately after the elections the nationalization of town houses, businesses, and factories began. Every ten houses were joined into one block and in charge of that block was a commissar. There was an administrator in each house. The administrators reported to the commissar, and the collected rent money went to the housing office.

Factories, workshops, and shops were assigned commissars too. They were outsiders in part, who nonetheless ran the business according to the Soviet rules. Immediately afterward an order was issued forcing everyone to work. Anyone who didn't work risked jail for sabotage. Older Jews, unable to do physical work, were given caretaker jobs, and one worked not eight hours but as much as the commissar of the given business had assigned to one. After work assemblies took place, attendance at which was compulsory, where a "*politruk*"[36] lectured in propagandist Soviet studies.

Around the new year of 1940, the passport issue started becoming a topic [of concern].[37] Many Jews didn't want to take a Soviet passport and crossed over to the German side. The stubborn ones were visited at night, told to pack up their things, and taken to Siberia in freight cars.

Passportization[38] took place in the following way: special operatives drew up lists of names of the occupants of each house and gave them to the passport office. There were many illegals and unregistered in each house. It was possible to find out from the drivers which district the "purge" would take place in. The illegals would leave the apartments for the night then. Unable to find the wanted ones, the NKVD officials began arresting children and women—as hostages. This way [they] managed, most of the time, to force people to report.

36. *Politruk* (Russian): an officer for political affairs. See glossary.

37. According to the decree of the Supreme Soviet of the USSR from 29 November 1939, persons present on the territory of the Western Belorussia [Belarus] and Western Ukraine between 1 and 2 November 1939 automatically obtained the citizenship of the Soviet state. At the beginning of 1940, forced issuing of Soviet passports began. See glossary: passportization.

38. Passportization: the campaign of forcing the Eastern Borderlands inhabitants to accept USSR passports in the first half of 1940, and then in March 1943. See glossary.

They were sent to Siberia with their families. It happened that only the women and children were sent away and the men couldn't be found.

A Greeting from Bukovina

In February 1940 we received first messages from Chernivtsi, the capital of Romanian Bukovina, which the Bolsheviks occupied at the time.[39] There the NKVD came upon an evil idea: it was announced that all those who wanted to go to Palestine, or had relatives there, should register with the NKVD. A few hundred people turned up. They were registered and assured that they'd be on their way within a few days. When they were released home with this message, a few thousand Jews came to register. One night those registered were woken up and taken to Siberia in locked freight cars. It was also said that the Bolsheviks, right after they assumed control [of the city], forbade the Chernivtsi residents from showing themselves on the streets. All houses, shops, and workshops were closed. It was so that people wouldn't hide their belongings. Then came the work order. Who couldn't show how they were supporting themselves were arrested and sent to Siberia.

Conscription

In March 1940 there came a mobilization order for men between twenty-two and twenty-three years of age. The recruits were sent to the Finnish front. Later, the age limit was extended to thirty-five.

Escape from Przemyśl

In June 1940, along with [my] wife, I escaped from Przemyśl to Lwów where my brother-in-law, Ajzyk Goldberg, lived, who had had his factory taken away by the Bolsheviks, and been arrested. After long efforts he managed to be freed and get a worker's position in his own factory. With nowhere to go, after a few days' stay in Lwów I went to my brother in Boreszów. [Since] my brother had been ruined by the Bolsheviks, I packed up my things and went to my father-in-law's [place] in Kołomyja. [My] father-in-law was an owner of a large wine warehouse in the market square. The Bolsheviks took away his shop and threw him and his family out on the street. Not having a Soviet passport, I was afraid of registering in

39. A mistake on the part of the author: Northern Bukovina was given to the USSR in June 1940.

Kołomyja, especially since upon registration it was checked what one did for a living, where one worked, and from where and with what intention one had arrived. Eventually, however, I had to go to the police. That same night I was woken up, told to pack up my things, and taken to the station. My wife was spending the night in a different apartment and knew nothing about the fate that awaited me.

In the Carriage

The train I was loaded onto was made up of a few tens of freight carriages and one refrigerated one—for the bodies [of those] who died on the way. In the carriage, seventy men were placed [and] instead of benches, two levels of bunks were put in. We stood at the station for twenty-four hours, being given nothing to eat. Only before we set off were we given rusks and soup. We began the journey, which lasted thirty-six days. On the way we stopped at different stations, sometimes for a few hours at a time, sometimes longer than a day. We were fed rusks and soup. Throughout the journey we didn't wash or shave. We relieved ourselves in the carriage. Lice began to eat us alive. The straw we slept on rotted, and we decided to steal some fresh straw at one of the stations. On the way we came upon similar trains with Russian deportees. Their carriages were sealed shut and people were begging for a piece of bread. In this manner we reached Suslonger in Mari ASSR [Autonomous Soviet Socialist Republic], where we stopped for a full twenty-four hours. Then we were told to get out of the freight cars and divided into groups. Altogether there were 3,600 of us. My group consisted of 250 people. We were taken to a forest. We walked all day toward our destination. Since there were few barracks, we slept 250 to one. Seventy-five people slept in one file on each of the three bunk rows. Each barracks was numbered, surrounded by wire, and closely guarded. The following day we were taken to our place of work a few kilometers away. I feigned illness, hobbling on one leg, so that they sent me only as far as one kilometer from the barracks.

Work in the Forest

Each of us had to cut down twenty-two trees per day. No one could fulfill those quotas.[40] I cut down five trees a day with great effort. We were given

40. Production quotas, also called "norms," were set for all work carried out by inmates. Meeting or failing to meet the quotas determined the amount of food, which was measured out in kettles.

two hundred grams of bread to eat in the evening and two hundred grams in the morning. In the evenings they also gave us soup. Those who managed to fulfill the quotas were given eight hundred grams of bread and better soup, but there were few who managed it.[41] Some played around and included the trees cut the day before, or two days before, in [their tallies]. This way they fulfilled the quotas and got a higher bread ration. Drivers and mechanics were picked out of our group and assigned to better jobs. The guards watching us didn't live or eat better than us. At any rate, the watch was unnecessary as there was nowhere to escape to. Around us there stretched a primeval forest. We didn't know where we were, in which part of the world. We had to clear the way to work ourselves out of the forest thickets. We worked from five in the morning until five in the afternoon. We ate only twice a day. The trees were so thickset and tall that they covered up the sky. The forest was covered with a damp darkness. We didn't know either who took the cut trees out of the woods or when.

Typhus Epidemic

After a few months an awful typhus epidemic broke out among the deportees. Out of our group, the typhus claimed a few hundred [lives]. We didn't have medical assistance, [only] some poorly qualified feldsher[42] who didn't have any medical supplies to help. The ill and the infected slept alongside the healthy. We warmed our cold bodies against their bodies, hot with the disease. The dead were simply buried in the sand. With a piece of wood the sand would be shoved aside, the body laid down and covered up. The following day it was no longer known where the deceased had been buried.

41. The kettles varied, but in general: Kettle 1 was for those who accomplished more than 50 percent and less than 100 percent of the quota and consisted of 14–18 ounces of bread daily and very thin soup three times daily. Kettle 2 was for those who accomplished 100 percent of the quota and consisted of 21–26 ounces of bread daily and very thin soup daily and a spoonful of barley or groats at night. Kettle 3 was reserved for Stakhanovites, those workers who accomplished more than 100 percent of the quota, and consisted of 26–42 ounces of bread daily, soup, and groats three times daily and probably fish and a white roll at night. Kettle 4 was for those with "soft jobs" (nonphysical labor) and consisted of 28 ounces or more of bread and three full meals daily. The punishment kettle was for those who accomplished less than 50 percent of the quota and consisted of 10.5–14 ounces of bread and one meal of the worst quality soup, daily.

42. A type of often unlicensed healthcare professional operating throughout the Russian Empire and the Soviet Union—a physician's assistant prototype, often relied on in times of physician scarcity and in rural and underserved areas. Many feldshers served as army medics.

In the winter the temperature reached –50°C [–58°F]. We worked even in –46°C [–50.8°F]. It was better to work in the forest than stay in the barracks, where the air stank and it was difficult to breathe. All this time we didn't undress. Didn't wash. Didn't shave. We had long beards and looked like savages. Only when the epidemic broke out, something resembling a bathtub was arranged in the barracks, but it was difficult to wash in it. [This is because] the water was constantly frozen [and] to wash oneself carried the risk of pneumonia.

All of us had our hands and feet frostbitten. Many had frostbitten noses that would crumble off. There was no water to drink. The water pipes froze constantly. We took turns [bringing] water in. The wellspring lay a few kilometers from the barracks. More than one of us froze[43] on the way to get the water. Instead of makhorka [low-grade tobacco], we smoked grass and roots.

Amnesty

We lived like this until December 1941, until the message about the Amnesty arrived. We went to the head of our group and told him that we'd like to join the Polish army. He told us to fill out an application and put off making a decision from one day to another, and tried to influence us so that we'd stay put and not leave the Soviet paradise.

In the meantime, one of us fell gravely ill, and because it was after the Amnesty, he was driven to the hospital in the main town of the region. When he returned after a month, he brought us [news] about the war, the Amnesty, and the creation of the Polish army.[44]

We slowly began the escape from the barracks and the forest. I and my companion, Elijahu Stahl, pretended to be ill and were sent to the hospital in Jaszkar Ala.[45] We arrived in the city at night. Because there are no hospital admissions at night, we went to the town's president, who arranged accommodation for us at a certain Maria Tichonowna Kazarnawa's.

---

43. It is unclear whether the author means a loss of life here (that is, froze to death).

44. Polish army in the USSR: a military force formed pursuant to the Sikorski-Maisky agreement of 30 July 1941 about the establishment of diplomatic relations between the USSR government and the Polish Government-in-Exile. See glossary.

45. Yoshkar-Ola [Polish: Joszkar-Oła].

In the Siberian House

The woman lived in a small room where there were three beds. She lived with three children, two of them were married. The whole family slept in one bed. In the room's corner there lived three lodgers: engineer Piotr Wolkow—a Komsomolets[46] who worked in an ammunition factory, Wiera Kristirin from Kursk and Liowa Mezakow from Jurno [?]—both school friends who worked in the ammunition factory after the outbreak of the war.

There were a few ammunition factories and a large airport [nearby] in this town. The factories were underground. There were many soldiers and recruits in town, who were trained and sent to the front from here. The engineers and specialists slept in one bed, without sheets, on bare boards, covered in their own torn coats. Their clothes, covering, were [more patch than cloth]. As there was no room for us, we were shown to the inglenook,[47] where we slept for a few months. [This is because] we went to the hospital the next day, but since there were no free spaces, we were told that as long as we could stand on our own two feet, we were not hospital candidates.

In the meantime, my companion really did fall ill with typhus. Even with a fever of 39°C [102.2°F] they did not want to admit him to the hospital. He continued to sleep in the inglenook with me. Later, when [his] temperature went over 40°C [104°F], he was admitted, and recovered two months later.

The town of Joszkar [Yoshkar-Ola] was made up of a few streets. The paths [were] made out of wood. We met many refugees there, among others Dr. Cinder, Dr. Frisz, and Dr. Szafir from Kraków, Messingier from Katowice, Countess Urbanowska from Sokal, the wife of Col Hubert, with daughter, from Częstochowa, Potok, the owner of the "Potokal" factory in Trzebinia, the lawyer Głogowski and judge Hauber from Kraków, Organg from Jarosław, Szmajder from Krynica. We were all looking for a way to get out of there.

We Take Up Trading

I traded bread. I was given a permit to buy two kilos of bread; I would write another zero and receive twenty [instead]. Naturally, I sold some of the bread.

46. A member of the communist youth organization Komsomol: the acronym of first parts of the three words Kom (Communist) So (Soviet) Mol (Youth).

47. A nook by a stove.

For a reel of thread bought for five rubles from deportees who had got it in a parcel, we got twenty rubles in the kolkhoz. I traded bread for makhorka. I paid thirty rubles for a glass of makhorka. We bought shirts, coats, and underwear off soldiers and sold them in the kolkhoz. At the market, one paid sixty rubles for a bucket of frost-damaged potatoes, for meat—four hundred rubles per kilo, twenty rubles for a liter of milk, for onions—eight rubles per six. Kolkhoz members were reluctant to sell for money and bartered instead. For my torn coat I got five kilos of pork, which I sold, buying myself a new coat with the money. The state, the commandant said, turned a blind eye to this profiteering, only noting the names of the traders, with whom it would settle accounts after the war. Prof. Mezakow told me while the Komsomolets was not home how bad things were in Russia. He already experienced life abroad but couldn't cope. He often asked me for a piece of bread.

My hostess is a wife of a deportee. Her husband is in prison for counterrevolution. She received a letter from him saying that he was ill with *cynga*[48] from malnourishment and that he doubted that they would ever see each other.

New Journey

On 19 March, I met with my companion, [and] we falsified the passes they had refused to give us. I write in this document that I was going to Bukhara for work. Refugees paid thousands of rubles for a piece of paper like that. Since they wouldn't sell me a ticket, I sneaked onto the train and traveled to Kazan [without a ticket] for thirty-six hours. I spent two days in the station; there was nowhere to go in town. I met Poles who lived [and] survived in terrible conditions. I also met Poles who had deserted from the Soviet army. I ate dry bread I had brought with me on the journey. From Kazan I went on to Ruzayevka. I roamed the streets for two days, sleeping at the station; I got [some] hot water with difficulty [but] a place for the night was out of the question. However, because I offered dry bread crust to some woman, [she and her family] let me spend the night in their room.

From Ruzayevka I traveled to Kuybyshev; the journey took two weeks. I got off at a station before Kuybyshev because I knew that there was very strict document control in Kuybyshev.

---

48. Scurvy. See glossary: *cynga*.

In Kuybyshev

I walked alongside the train tracks toward the city. They didn't want to let me into the station without a delousing confirmation. There was a bad case of typhus there. The next day I washed, shaved, burned all [my] rags, and went out into town. All my luggage now consisted of one empty food tin and a wooden spoon. With this luggage I went to the Polish embassy. I was received by the secretary, Mr. Aleksander Miszek. I didn't say I was from Przemyśl as a rumor had been going round that everyone from Eastern Galicia was automatically a Soviet citizen. I didn't say that I was a Jew either because I had also heard by then that Jews weren't accepted into the Polish army. I said that I was a Catholic and that I came from Kraków. I was sent to the military attaché [and] from there to the captain, who told me that Jews were not admitted into the military. Only after lengthy pleading was I given a piece of paper [telling me] to report to the [collecting] point with. Poles received a lot of help in Kuybyshev; I was given nothing. I set off onward. They wouldn't let me into the station when I arrived at the assembly point. I wandered around all day until I got into the assembly point. There I was told again that Jews were not accepted. I said I was a Catholic, Kazimierz Chamicki, was let in then and I stayed for a few days in the camp.

I went in front of a draft commission which operated out of a train carriage. The doctor didn't examine anyone. There officiated: Major Barycki on the Polish side and a Russian major on the Soviet side. I presented my document, wasn't asked any questions, was immediately accepted. The Russian said I could go to a kolkhoz and gave me the address of [it].

They didn't want to keep me any longer at the assembly point [so] I went to the station again. I waited for a train with the Polish army. I waited for two days at the station without food and without drink, then it turned out that there was no room on the train. I grabbed onto the accordion-like connection between two carriages and got to Kermine this way. There I was caught by the transport manager, who said he would hand me over to the Russian police if I didn't get off. I got off, and traveled again in the night holding onto a different train until the Abszbabach[49] station.

49. Should be: Ashgabat [Polish: Aszchabad].

There the Bolsheviks organized a reception for the Polish transport, and since I was starving, I joined the feast without much thought. After the reception I went to Krasnovodsk with the army, where I took advantage of another elegant lunch. The port from which the army was leaving was surrounded by wire and guarded by the Soviet police; documents were carefully checked and I [obviously] wasn't on the transport list.

I begged the Poles and the major to take me. The answer was the same everywhere: "We're not taking Jews." Seeing what was afoot, I sneaked out over the fence. I was spotted by some Pole, Sanacki, whom I knew from one of my journeys. He took me to the NKVD and exclaimed: "He's not one of ours." I begged the NKVD to let me go free or release me into the hands of the Polish gendarmerie. I asked the Polish gendarme with tears in my eyes to release me from the Soviet hell. He replied: "Go to the commanding officer." I was taken to the same major. I kissed his hands and feet, begged by everything that is holy, beseeching him to allow me on the ship since I was already here after such a long journey. He took pity on me and allowed me to load my luggage in. I worked for three even though I was very weak. At night, when the ship was in the middle of the sea, it dawned on me that the Soviet paradise was far away behind me. Not being a part of the transport, I went from Pahlevi to Tehran. Since I didn't have a penny to my name, was naked and barefoot, I pulled out three gold crowns from my teeth, got forty-six tomans[50] [for them], and survived for a few days this way. After a month's stay in Tehran, I came to Palestine.

50. Iranian unit of currency.

Protocol 31

Testimony of **Eliezer Helfman**, age fifteen, from Izbica, Lublin district. Whole family, consisting of six children, parents, and a stepchild, had been sent to Russia.

We lived in Izbica. My father was a tanner and earned well. Until the outbreak of the war there lived 1,200 Jewish families in Izbica.

The first week of the war passed calmly in our little town. It was only in the second week that the bombing started. My mother was baking bread at the time. She left everything and we fled to the woods. The next day the Germans arrived. Three tanks and a lot of motorbikes. Everyone took cover. There wasn't a living soul out in the streets. One shochet, Chaim Falek, a forty-something Jew, was closing the gate to his house. The Germans shot at him and killed him. His son served in the Polish army and fought in many battles. He returned home [in one piece]. Outside town, in the mountains, lights burned. The neighboring villages were on fire. The Polish army resisted the Germans for another six hours.

In Izbica the Germans summoned all men and told them to stand with their hands raised above their heads for a whole hour. Then an officer came and said to disperse. Suddenly that officer noticed a huge Jew, very tall. That Jew was called "Josek's son" in town. The whole family were tall like that. They were the town's favorites. The officer shot and wounded the giant. They treated him in a hospital afterward, but he died, even though he was taken to the hospital in Zamość. The whole town cried over the loss of a beautiful and healthy boy. The Germans stayed in Izbica for twelve days. Among the Germans there were also Austrian soldiers who comforted the Jews by saying that soon the Russians would come. The Bolsheviks arrived on Thursday [and] the Jewish population breathed a sigh of relief. They were received in a friendly manner. Some Jewish youths joined the militia and wore red bands. The militiamen helped looking for weapons. The Bolsheviks took away away the landowners' cattle and drove it away in trucks. The Russians stayed for only eight days [and] then left, saying they would return. They advised the Jews to come with them. They said that no one would hurt us in Russia. You'll become Soviet citizens, they said. Around a hundred families decided to follow the Bolsheviks. We, too, went after them. We were taken in cars to Włodzimierz and took some things with us.

We spent nine weeks in Włodzimierz. Refugees arrived in town also [and] it got crowded. The Russians announced that workers were needed for a coal mine deep inside Russia. They advised for people to report voluntarily because if not, they would take them by force. We registered voluntarily to go deep into Russia. We were allowed to bring all our belongings, were taken by car to the station and loaded onto a train going toward Łuck. We arrived in the town of Azditisz [?].[51] It was a nice town where only Jews lived. There was a Refugee Assistance Committee there. We were treated well and fed for free for four months. Then, NKVD officials arrived from Moscow and said that there was no room in Russia for idlers. They carried out a registration and examined everyone. My father avoided the examination, he hid. But he had to register in the end. All refugees were captured and loaded onto trains. We were taken to the city of Gorky.[52] It was wintertime, there were small stoves burning in the trains. We spent three months in Gorky.

Again, NKVD agents arrived and told us to get to work. Russia is big, we must help build it. Who doesn't register for work voluntarily will be sent to Siberia with criminals. We signed up voluntarily. We went to a big village of Pravdinsk, next to Gorky. The village had eighteen thousand residents. Our refugee group was made up of ninety-five people. There were a few Poles and a few Ukrainians. The NKVD agents said that in Russia everyone had the same rights.

For three days we were fed for free, and then, were told to work. There was a paper factory in the village employing twelve thousand workers. The refugees were told to carry blocks of wood two cubic meters in size. The older ones assembled the paper. The children studied at school. I turned thirteen at the time.

Father earned 150 rubles—its worth was two dollars. [He] brought home bread from the factory. Mother would wait in lines to get provisions. The lines were long, sometimes a thousand people waited in them. The Russians often gave up their place for Mother. They said: "You've suffered enough from the

51. Perhaps: Arzamas in Gorky district.

52. Up until 1932, and currently: Nizhny Novgorod.

war." Bread was brought to our house. And sweets for the children. There was a huge workers' canteen by the factory but the food there was *treif*[53] so my father could not use the canteen.

After three months, there appeared posters on the walls announcing that refugees shouldn't receive any benefits any longer. They were already Soviet citizens. Things began to get worse for us then. We stood in lines all night. People often fought in the lines. After a full night of waiting one would leave without bread.

We understood that we couldn't stay in Russia or we'd starve. We wanted to get to Wołyń where, we heard, life was easier. We sold a few things to be able to get to Wołyń. The journey to Wołyń led through Moscow. To get to Moscow one had to have a special permit from the head of the village. Whoever asked for this permit was, as punishment, sent to Siberia. We went to Moscow illegally, not by train but by ship. We bribed the cashier, paying him an extra five rubles per ticket. We waited for the ship for a long time, suffering from hunger. We spent three days in Moscow. We slept on the street. The shop displays were full of everything, even products from abroad. Just like in Poland before the war. We got our outbound tickets easily and traveled toward Kiev.

It was summertime. Lots of refugees slept in the streets in Kiev. All—Ukrainians, Jews, Poles—wanted to go back home, even though the Germans were in power there. Letters arrived saying life was easier there than in Russia. Later it turned out that thanks to the Russian-German agreement only Ukrainians were allowed to return.[54] Some Jews with non-Jewish surnames would sneak out and return to the German-occupied territories.[55] In Kiev refugees were being registered again, many signed up to go back home. One day, at one o'clock at night, the NKVD organized a roundup among the refugees and took them away in cars. You want to go to Wołyń, be my guest—an NKVD official told us. We thought, based on his calming words, that they were indeed giving us a chance to return home, but after a few minutes we found ourselves

53. Nonkosher. See glossary: kosher.

54. The author likely meant Germans here.

55. The agreement on the matter of resettlements excluded, on demand from the German side, Jews from the group allowed to return to the German-occupied territories. However, a small number of Jews returned to their old places of residence this way. However, the registration lists containing the names of people of Jewish origin who had been rejected by the commissions were used by the NKVD for mass deportations to labor camps and *specposiołki*, which took place in June 1940.

in jail with a few thousand refugees. We were surrounded by a strict police guard. We waited like that for many hours. It was a night of fear. One of the refugees tried to hang himself. Alarm was raised, he was narrowly rescued. That same night a registration took place again and a large number of refugees were sent to Wołyń.

We breathed a sigh of relief after passing Shepetivka, the Russian border. There one could already get sugar, bread, and other products. There, one could live. We traveled around ten days. We went through Kowel, Równe, and Ludmir,[56] returned home and settled in the same apartment as before. The luggage we left at the station. One night an NKVD representative arrived and told us, shouting, that they would send us to Siberia, to [ASSR] Komi. We cried, telling him about what we had suffered. Clearly, this moved him. We were taken to the station, had our luggage inspected and nothing suspicious was found. We were taken home and left under house arrest. But a few days later another NKVD agent appeared and took us to the station. A large group of refugees had gathered in the station. They were divided into four groups. Each group traveled in one hundred carriages. We waited at the station from Friday to Sunday. We were allowed to bring food.

An NKVD representative said, "You want to go to Germany? You shall . . ." We did indeed think we were returning to Poland but it turned out that we were going deep into Russia. The carriages were locked, no one was allowed out. Armed guards traveled inside the freight cars. This way we got to Siberia. We stopped at the station of Asina[57] in the Novosibirsk Oblast. Thirty people rode in each carriage so that three thousand disembarked from one hundred freight cars. Many were sick and weak after the journey. The Russian Red Cross helped the sick.

We waited at the station for two hours. Other trains were arriving. There were already fifteen thousand refugees in Asina. One doctor from Warsaw died. We were given twenty dekagrams of bread per day. Every crumb was cherished. Women cried because they couldn't feed [their] children. We had heavy hearts.

The rail line came to an end in Asina. The closest settlement was three hundred kilometers away. We were loaded onto a ship. The ship was for

56. Ludmir: the name for Włodzimierz Wołyński used by Polish Jews.

57. Asino. It appears in the protocols in different spellings, e.g., Asina, Assino, Assnina.

700 people but 2,500 refugees sailed on it. [People] lay in the cabins, one on top of another. We sailed down the wide river for [some text missing] days. There was no bread, we were fed herring, two kilos per day. Many people fell ill on the journey. A forest stretched down both sides of the river. From time to time we would see strewn-around barracks. They comforted us saying this journey from hell would be over soon.

We disembarked in Tygielder,[58] where we stayed for two weeks, sleeping in tents that were rotted through. It was raining buckets and [our] belongings, protected with such difficulty throughout the journey, rotted. The men were sent out to work. [They] rode by cart for thirty-five kilometers to log trees in the forest. Mosquitos bit relentlessly [so that] people swelled up. The women rebelled to have us moved to a better place and got their way. We were sent to Tszed,[59] in the taiga. The rich refugees rode on carts, the poor went on foot. Money means a lot even in Russia.

Tszed was a huge labor camp with four large barracks. Only one commander, a Russian man, was present in the camp. The Russian deportees were sent to a different place. What caught our eye in this settlement was a huge cemetery where thousands of Trotskyists had been buried and which made a huge impression on us.[60] We [knew] what awaited us.

In Tszed there was a branch of the Red Cross which took care of the sick. Immediately the next day we were ordered to work. We had to build barracks for ourselves. We made huts out of young trees as there were no trees [suitable] for planks. Naturally, those were no protection from the rain. One Jew, an eighty-year-old elder from Włodawa, died on the first day while chopping trees. There was no school. Small children worked too. For two weeks of work one received sixty rubles. The workers received, through ration cards, a kilo of bread, soup, and one kilo of beans a week as well as half a liter of oil and a piece of soap. The camp's commander asked in one of his speeches that we get to work and build a settlement so that we're happy there. My father and some other Jews [page missing].

The commander announced that if he saw Jews at prayer one more time, he'd put them in jail. [This is because] praying is forbidden in the Soviet

58. Teguldet, a town in the vicinity of Asino.

59. Here and henceforth refers to a camp called Czet'.

60. Trotskyists were members of the Communist Party accused of forming an opposition.

Union. A similar announcement caused a revolt among the pious Jews. The NKVD arrested a few and deported them to a different place. This agitated everyone even more. The Trotskyist cemetery, located next to our barracks, kept telling us: "to try is futile."

There lived 150 Poles in our *posiołek*, but they didn't get mixed up in our affairs and we, trusting them, did not let them in on anything. Our barracks were abuzz. We made contact with two more camps: Buchtaiłow and Zawod, and we readied for a mass escape. We made a few hundred cartson wheels out of wood—no one knew about them. We would carve a wheel out of a block of wood. The Poles were not involved in this work but did not betray us. One day there was a Soviet holiday. The NKVD chief and his deputy got drunk. We used that moment and set off on the way. [Our] belongings were loaded on the carts. The women tied the children to their backs and the crowd, made up of twelve thousand people, set off, at night and on foot. We walked quietly on forest paths and managed to make twenty kilometers.

Suddenly, NKVD agents arrived on horseback. They cut us off. An NKVD representative gently advised us to return. He promised better work conditions and more food. He promised us the moon but the crowd did not move. The women were particularly stubborn. The NKVD arrested around twenty men but that didn't help. The crowd did not want to go back.

We stood by the water. A huge Russian cargo ship came close. The refugees pushed their way onto the ship and chased away the sailors and the captain. Around 1,500 refugees found themselves on the ship. They were going toward Omsk. The ship sailed downstream for half a day. It was chased by Soviet motorboats. [It] had to turn back. Six airplanes appeared, circling above the crowd of refugees. They shot upward from the planes to scare people. The Russians brought in cannons. The refugees said they were not afraid—death was better than this life. The revolt lasted four days. The NKVD pursued negotiations, scared [us], threatened, made promises. The provisions ran out. There was nothing to eat. The refugees surrendered and returned to Asina. We were treated better. They fed us much better: pasta, potatoes, and even those who didn't work were given food. This lasted six weeks. Then it got worse again. Another revolt was being planned. This time they planned to kill the commander and escape for good. The NKVD noticed that we were up to something. The camp was liquidated and the twelve thousand refugees sent away in different directions.

Our group was sent to the Sverdlovsk Oblast. The journey took two weeks. Our group was made up of 1,500 people. They were settled in Serov and Saswa[61] alongside 350 others. We lived there for an entire year. There was a factory—a sawmill—in Saswa where special planks for train carriages were made, and many refugees were employed [there]. There were many Jews among the NKVD agents. Some spoke Yiddish. We traded with them, selling watches and buying other things. The Russians [in] the NKVD had nothing to do with it. The head of the factory was one Goldberg, a converted Jew. Five thousand people worked in the factory. They paid well, especially for the production of ammunition boxes. One got two hundred rubles per month [and] a kilo of bread cost one ruble. You got good soup at a special canteen for a few kopecks. Apart from that, each refugee got half a *morga*[62] of land, where onions, potatoes, and sunflowers were grown. We also picked blueberries in the woods, and [other] berries. We sold the berries and got manufacture for them. Our situation improved a lot. The refugees built a few big, light, beautiful barracks. We painted them blue-and-white as a sign that we remembered Palestine. The commander was very happy with us. Foremen were brought who taught [us] craftsmanship. The camp was surrounded by wire and guarded; it was forbidden to leave it but within [its] boundaries we enjoyed relative freedom. The women tried to get chickens and goats but were not given them. We learned about the German-Soviet war from the Poles. Then, large demonstrations took place with singing, the commander got soundly drunk, and the workers were given better food on the first day of the war. The bread portions were doubled. Things were going well for us in the camp. We were told that it was much worse in others.

Then the Amnesty happened. The commander gave us passports [and] bread for the road, and we were released from the camp. We were also told that we could go wherever we wanted. [Our] group made up of five families—thirty-five people—hired a freight car to Bukhara. Each one paid fifty-five rubles for the train ticket.

From Bukhara some refugees went to kolkhozes. My father and older brothers got work in a tannery. Father was an excellent craftsman. He introduced

---

61. Likely: Sosva [Sośwa]. Appears in other protocols as Saswa, Sozwa, Soszwa.

62. *Morga*: a unit of land area measurement equal to approximately 0.56 hectare.

new tanning methods in the tannery which had been unknown there, and used chemicals. At first Father earned well but later the workers began to grumble about the new order. Father got angry and we left for Tashkent. In Tashkent it was difficult to get food, even with money. We were exhausted. Father died from hunger. Mother fell ill and died also. Seven of us had set off on the way and there were two left of the whole family. Me and my brother Abraham returned to Bukhara. We were accepted into an orphanage. Out of three hundred children, one hundred died. Forty-seven Jewish children survived. The Polish army took us to Tehran.

Protocol 32

Testimony of **Mordechaj Mowszowicz**, age nineteen, born in Iwie, by Lida. Father: Chaim Israel, insurance agent. Mother: Rachel. Lived in Nowogródek, 45 Piłsudski Street. Arrived in Palestine in 1942.

Our town was bombed by the Germans on the first day of the war outbreak. There were lots of casualties. A few houses were demolished. On 17 September 1939, the Soviet army began its march on Poland. That same day the Bolsheviks occupied Nowogródek. Almost all the residents stayed in town, which was only abandoned by the police officers and former state officials. In the first period the Bolsheviks treated people in a friendly manner, they gave out free papers and cigarettes and organized cinema performances. Only later did they get down to business. A decree came out that said that no goods could be stored, that everything one had in one's shop had to be sold. As a result, all the stores were empty within a few days. After some time, the nationalization of homes, shops, factories, and workshops began. A number of cooperatives were created and people began to get used to the Soviet order.

Arrests

Soon the new authorities began a series of arrests. Lists were drawn up of settlers, former Polish legionaries who had received land from the government, families of police officers, former military personnel and officials whose husbands had run away. All those were arrested and sent to Siberia. Among the arrested there were: Benjamin Efron—a Revisionist[63] accused of holding discussions with the Communists, Akiba Kasmaj—a merchant who was arrested with his brother and elderly mother. Kahan, a tailor, who sewed military uniforms and was in contact with the military because of it, was also arrested.

Elections

Ninety-nine percent of the population took part in the elections to the Western Belorussian Soviet.[64] Only a small number of risk-takers voted against

63. Supporter of the so-called Revisionist, right-wing part of the Zionist movement.

64. The Soviets staged elections to Moscow-controlled Supreme Soviet (Council) of the newly created provinces of Western Ukraine and Western Belorussia [Belarus] to legitimize the Soviet rule.

the state list. Those who didn't take part in the elections, or who expressed negative views about it, were arrested within a few hours and deported. Buffets were set up in the polling stations where one could get free sweets and white bread rolls. Buffets were [even] organized at all the pre-election rallies to draw in the public. After the elections, labor offices were set up. The head of the office was a Communist from Russia, and his [deputies were] one Szapiro and Nacumowski, a teacher. The former bourgeoisie were not given work. Generally, the worker's past was the primary consideration during work assignment.

My father was assigned work in a certain group (*artel*).[65] He then worked in that *artel*'s office but his earnings were not enough to live on [and] we had to sell various things from the house. I went to school. There were two Polish and two Russian gymnasia.[66] The former Hebrew Tarbut[67] school was changed into a school where the language of instruction was Jewish, but the headmaster remained the same, Sztejnberg.

Passportization

At the end of 1939, a decree was issued about identification cards. During the issuing of passports, various categories were differentiated. Landowners or landowners' sons received passports with the number thirteen. Other "suspicious elements" received a passport with a number eleven. Owners of such identification papers were not allowed to live in big cities of the first and secondary category. Former social activists and officials, among them also rabbis, were given passports for three months only. Later they had those passports changed for five-year [ones]. At the beginning of 1940 a conscription was announced for those born in 1919. Later the mobilization was extended to the older years too. The conscripts were sent to regiments. They all received mobilization cards that stated that when the war breaks out, they will be sent to the front.

---

65. *Artel* (Russian): a craftsmanship cooperative. See glossary.

66. Gymnasium (Polish: gimnazjum): a type of secondary school in some European countries, typically preparing students for university. In the prewar school system primary school lasted seven years, but if a student wanted to continue the education, he/she could be admitted to gymnasium after six years. The higher school was divided into a four-year gymnasium (*gimnazjum*) and a two-year lyceum (*liceum*), after which the matriculation exam was taken.

67. Tarbut: a Jewish cultural and educational association for the development of Hebrew schooling. Active in Poland and a few other countries. See glossary.

The Countryside

Unlike other regions, we did not have kolkhozes created and the trading of food articles took place normally for a year and a half, that is, from the outbreak of the war with Germany. The peasants would bring, as ever, eggs, cheese, butter, milk, and vegetables to the town market, and who had any money bought as much as they wished.

The trade in old clothes and old items was blossoming. The peasants who brought their products to town would buy [those] items. We were not in want of bread. There was no sugar, one had to wait in line for hours to get a little bit of [it]. There was no order in the lines, those who had waited all night [might have got] nothing and others, having got into the shop in an illegal way, left having stocked up on everything.

Cultural Life

As was the case in all lands occupied by the Bolsheviks, almost every day there took place rallies, meetings, and factory assemblies where people were taught about the Soviet order. Religious life stopped. The youth took advantage of the freedom and the ability to get around religious prohibitions. [Two] synagogues were turned into a warehouse and a workshop. One of the churches was turned into a community center and a cinema was set up there.

The German-Russian War

On 22 June [1941] an unexpected German attack on Russia took place. A great panic broke out and all those able to carry a weapon, except for those with mobilization cards, were called up. People escaped the town on foot, on carts, on bicycles. It was said in town that the Germans were already by Lida.

Our family, made up of [six] people—the parents, my brother, who had returned from captivity, thirteen-year-old sister, myself, and my younger brother—waited for the space on a truck that had been promised to us. We had already packed up our stuff. We didn't get a space on the truck though. Me and my brother decided to flee on bicycles. However, at the last moment, in spite of the fact that our parents did not oppose our departure, my brother backed out of it because he felt bad about leaving our defenseless family behind. They tried to convince me to go. I was to go to Mińsk, my brother lived there who studied at a technology school.

On Tuesday 24 [of June] at seven in the morning before the evening [?] I left my family home. My neighbor came with me. The road to the former Polish-Soviet border, Stołpce, was dark with fugitives: trucks, carts, bicycles, people on foot. The road was being constantly bombed by the Germans. Their airplanes came down low, just above the heads of the refugees. The pilots shot from machine guns. We hid in the forest, avoiding the road. This way we got to Stołpce. But there we were not allowed through because we had Belorussian passports. We spent the night in the woods and only the following day sneaked across the border. I rode four hundred kilometers on a bike. On 26 June, at night, I arrived in Mińsk but the city had already been burned down. The sky glowed red; we were not allowed into the city. With nothing to be done, we continued on in our journey. On the way we came upon wounded people and saw hundreds of dead ones. No one even thought about burying the dead, the traffic moved between the piles of corpses. Some were only gravely wounded; some woman begged for help but no one answered her. At a station after Mińsk, the first transports for the homeless were organized. Each train consisted of between eighty and a hundred carriages, in each carriage people were pushing and suffocating. Me and my neighbor got onto one such carriage with our bikes and set off on the way. We got no food and the crowding was unbearable. At some stations we were taken to a canteen where we were given a bit of soup and a piece of bread. We didn't have money on us. My fortune consisted of one hundred rubles. I laid my only hope in the bicycle, which I intended to sell in Russia for a large sum, but that hope evaporated.

"Paratroopers"

As our train waited at the station, two NKVD agents entered our carriage and asked if there were any strangers there, because German paratroopers were spotted descending at the station before Homel. They split up and ran off into the area and there was a suspicion that they got on the refugee train. My neighbor, who had changed into a leather jacket at the station, aroused suspicion of the traveling refugees. What's more, we had the bikes with us. We were immediately arrested, had our bicycles taken away, and were led to a police station. On the way our documents were inspected. It turned out that they had no suspicions around us; we were sent back to the refugee train but had to leave the bikes at the station. Thus we lost the bicycles, which we had intended to sell in Russia, and which were our only wealth.

However, we were not completely free of the NKVD agents' suspicions. Because of this, we were placed in a carriage with thieves and other criminals. Two NKVD members were added for company, who took us to a police station, again, in Mogilev.

The journey to Mogilev, in one carriage with the criminals, turned out to be a real hell. We were robbed of everything and only some of [our belongings] were returned to us after an intervention by the train manager. We trembled in fear ahead of the interrogation in Mogilev but it turned out that the agents disappeared, at which point we tried to get into the refugee carriages but were not let in. This way we rode for five weeks with the criminals toward Uzbekistan. On the way my face swelled up from a blow that, along with the hunger and the filth, exhausted me once and for all.

At one of the stations our transport, made up of eighty carriages, was split into two and sent off in two different directions. We went to Saratov. We were unloaded at the Kirillov station. [From] Kirillov we were sent to the Orion Sikowka kolkhoz on trucks. There we were given ration cards for bread and soup. A special commission made decisions about work assignments. I was assigned to the tractors. For two weeks I learned how to drive a tractor and then, as a professional driver, I was sent to the Saratov kolkhoz. From time to time I would go out to the train station, hoping I would meet someone I knew, because I felt abandoned and lonely. Indeed, I once met three boys from Nowogródek. They were going to Tashkent. I suggested that they take me with them. They didn't want to agree so as not to make their group, traveling illegally with no permit, bigger. When a train to Tashkent came into the station, all three of them sneaked into a carriage, and I followed them. In that group there was one well-known Communist, who played an important role in our town since the beginning of the war. I was very confused as to why he was escaping and received an answer stating that he did not want to go to a kolkhoz and be exploited by the Uzbeks. There were many like him. In Tashkent it transpired that the city was full of fugitives and the authorities were not letting any more in. We got off a few kilometers before the station and went toward the city on foot. I found myself in Tashkent in August 1941. It was so overcrowded that it was impossible to find a roof over one's head or a place to rest.

On every street, square, and in every garden there were people camping who ate, slept, fell ill, and even died under the sky. There was no help organized for [these] desperate humans. I had the luck of meeting an acquaintance from our town who pointed me toward the kolkhoz Zwycięski Oktober,[68] where there was a vacancy. He promised me that with his help I would attain bearable standards of living at the kolkhoz. There was nothing left for me to do but accept his offer.

In the Kolkhoz

Five hundred people lived at the Zwycięski Oktober kolkhoz. Clay huts without floors or windows, set up in a very rough-and-ready way, served as accommodation. There weren't even [any] stoves. It was already winter, so that all the kolkhoz members would warm up by the so-called "sandals." In the middle of the hut there was an opening that was filled with firewood and lit. The opening was covered with a rag, which could be used to warm one's legs. In such a hut there was also a primitive [writing illegible]. In the first instance I worked on a machine used for spraying plants to destroy harmful pests. It was a job with a lot of responsibility for which I received three hundred rubles per month. Apart from this I received three hundred grams of bread.

I Become a Trader

I grew sick of my job very fast and decided to take up trading. The kolkhoz manager revealed to me that every day there were a few liters of milk left over in the kolkhoz, which could be sold. I found a companion and together we drove the milk to Tashkent, where we sold it for a large profit. In a short time we earned enough to buy planks for bunks to sleep on. We also exchanged the milk for "trader's bread." It was the first category of bread that could not be bought on the market and was intended for the privileged. We traded in other things too: rice, flour, soap, and meat. But the most important trade was the milk one, which was a difficult kind of work. A vat containing twenty liters of milk had to be carried into town for five kilometers, through mud and snow. More than once I would slip on the way and spill all the milk. Sometimes the milk went sour. Later we became milk suppliers to a military school, where

68. "Victorious October."

we delivered seventy liters of milk per day. From that business we made a few hundred rubles. This lasted until March 1942.

Mortality among the refugees increased. Typhus, dysentery, and malaria caused devastation. I heard that the Polish army was being formed [and] went to Łukowaja,[69] where the Poles' assembly point was located.

The chief at the assembly point did not want to admit me to the army. I went to a second place, to Kermine, hoping that maybe they would accept me there. Thanks to the protection of my acquaintance from Nowogródek I went in front of the commission but while Poles, even the infirm ones, were admitted into the army, I, with the best health conditions, was classified as category E. In despair, I went to the barracks and begged Captain Buzek from Nowogródek to help me get into the army because I had heard a transport was being organized going out of Russia.[70] Captain Buzek said that now, after the commission, he couldn't do anything. But I did not give up and went to the station from which the transport was to depart. I met there a policeman I knew, one Skraczek, who was the manager of the transport. I ran up to him, begged him. He advised that I get into a carriage from the other side of the tracks. I did so. With me there got into the carriage my two companions: Grisza Cukierman and Chaim Lewin. Cukierman was spotted [and] thrown off the train, what happened to him—I don't know. Lewin, however, thrown off once, got into another carriage. This transport, which left Krasnovodsk for Pahlevi was the last Polish transport leaving Russia. On the ship there was no difference made between Jews and non-Jews. During the loading of the ship there was a lot of hurry and no one paid attention to documents. Even though we were not on the list, an additional list was created at the last minute. This was taken care of by the captain's wife, who treated us very kindly. Our ship journey fell during Pesach.[71] With my last coins I bought myself a bottle of wine. From Pahlevi I went to Tehran, and after two months, found myself in Palestine. During the whole time I spent in Russia I looked, in vain, for my brother, a talented man of letters who wrote for the Polish-Jewish press. I don't know what happened to him.

---

69. Correctly: Lugovoye [original Polish correction: Ługowaja].

70. See the glossary: evacuation of the Polish army.

71. Pesach, Passover: Jewish holiday observed in the month of Nisan (March–April). In 1942 [it] fell on 2–9 April. See glossary.

Protocol 36

Testimony of **Zwi [?] Elsana**, age fifteen, daughter of Henoch and Pesi. Born and resident in the town of Kurzan [?], by Łomża. Arrived in Palestine with her brother Nisan, age twelve, in February 1943.

My father was an affluent man, the owner of a candle factory and a big wholesale food warehouse. There were five children in the house. On 2 September 1940[72] our town was cruelly bombed by German pilots. Next to the town there were barracks with a lot of military personnel. The Polish authorities ordered the evacuation of all people. We didn't even get a chance to take anything with us. We escaped to Wodowa [?], but when the Germans entered it and the persecution of Jews began we went to Ostrów Mazowiecki,[73] where our cousin lived.

The Massacre in Ostrów

We settled in Ostrów quite well. The Bolsheviks occupied the town. Then the Germans came. But it was expected that the Germans would leave and the Bolsheviks would come back again. We waited for a whole month in Ostrów. The Germans organized pogroms of Jews, and the Poles helped them. Many Jews left town and crossed over to the Russian side. The weak, the ill, and families with small children stayed in town and waited for things to change for the better.

One day, after a month of our stay in Ostrów, a decree came out calling all Jews to gather in a square outside town, from where they would be taken toward the Soviet border. Everyone gathered. My father was not in town at the time, which is why he was late to the assembly point. When he went to the square, sounds of heavy gunfire came from it. We hid in the basement of an abandoned house. This saved us from death. All the Jews, gathered in the square in the number of six hundred, were shot dead. Many were buried half-alive. The square where the massacre took place and where the mass grave of the six hundred Jews was located was paved with asphalt and assigned to become a bus station.

72. An error, of course; refers to September 1939.

73. Correctly: Ostrów Mazowiecka.

We spent two days hidden in the basement. We didn't have anything to eat, not even water, so we sneaked out of our hiding place at night and escaped toward the Russian border, which we crossed successfully. We found ourselves in a little town. We spent two weeks in Zambrów. There were many refugees in town and it was impossible to find a place for the night. We slept in the synagogue. We decided to flee to the small town of Boćki, where the local rabbi was a relative of my father. We thought that we might [be able to] settle there. Nine months we lived in this small town. Father did not take part in the elections and didn't want to take a Soviet passport. He said that he wouldn't take a Soviet passport because he had left his wealth in Poland. Since the town was small, and the power lay in the hands of local Communists, we weren't afraid that anything bad would happen to us. In February 1940 a regulation was announced about the registration of those Polish citizens who wanted to go back to the German occupation. Since messages were coming in from that side that things had got better and people were earning their keep quite well, and here things were getting worse, Father registered. Two months went by. In June 1941, in the middle of the night, there was a knock on the door.[74] We were all told to get dressed and pack up some of our things. Soldiers with rifles stood under the window and told us that we were going to Baranowicze, where an exchange of citizens took place. In the market square there had already gathered many people from Wyszków and Międzyrzec. We were loaded onto trucks and driven to the train station. There we were put into freight cars, forty people to each, as well as the luggage. It was terribly cramped. Only ten people used the bunks. The cars were sealed and the journey began, which took a month, until we got to Arkhangelsk.

In the *Posiołek*

Immediately the next day after we arrived in Arkhangelsk we were sent to a *posiołek*. We lived in barracks, fifty people to one: Poles, Jews, and Byelorussians [Belarusians]. The Jews often asked to be put in separate barracks but the request[s] were fruitless. We suffered a lot at the hands of the non-Jews, particularly from the Byelorussians. We were insulted, humiliated, and sometimes

74. The event refers to June 1940.

even beaten. No one dared to complain to the commandant as no good fate would meet them.

We worked in the forest. The work consisted of cutting down trees, loading them up onto wagons, and cutting off the branches. I, too, sawed trees. My quota was eight cubics [cubic meters] per day, in reality I would cut only one. For this we, children up to the age of sixteen, were given four hundred grams of bread daily, and those adults who met their quotas—eight hundred grams of bread daily. We were supervised by a brigade leader [who] constantly rushed us to work and never let us catch our breath. We worked from eight in the morning till eight in the evening. Very often the brigade leader would wake us in the night when it was freezing, tell us to get up and to load the tree trunks onto wagons. After some time, a tree trunk fell onto Father's leg. Father fell gravely ill and lay in the barracks for a few weeks, suffering terribly. There was no medical assistance. The leg continued to swell up. We asked for Father to be taken to the hospital but did not get a response to our requests. When Father's condition became more dangerous, we decided to organize a strike. My older sister, Zlata, told the *posiołek* commandant that if they didn't take Father to the hospital, we wouldn't go to work, even if they shot at us. We didn't go to work. For two days we got no food. The commandant threatened us with severe punishment, but we didn't let him intimidate us. On the third day Father was taken to the hospital.

Father stayed in the hospital for six months. We very rarely got messages from him. In vain did we beg the commandant to let us visit the sick man. The commandant told us openly that he used such methods as punishment for our strike. We were so distraught that we lost all hope of seeing Father alive. But God helped [us], Father came back healthy from the hospital and got to work. After six weeks the whole family fell ill with a terrible illness called *cynga*. Our blood turned into matter. The whole body resembled an open wound. The body lacked fat and vitamins [and] we could not get those. We suffered terribly. Bits of [our] bodies would simply fall off. After a few weeks the illness matured. At first, we still had a bit of money and bought [extra] food from the kolkhoz members. But the savings ran out and we began to sell clothes to buy milk, which saved us from illness. For some time we also received parcels from relatives in Belorussia, and this saved our lives. But the sending of parcels stopped. We were hungry and in rags. Our lives ceased to mean a lot to us.

Sister's Arrest

As I pointed out, my sister, Zlata, was the organizer of our family strike. Although we won the strike and Father was taken to the hospital, there was no avoiding punishment. The commandant may have even forgiven us for it but others started to copy us and a series of strikes began in the *posiołek*. Anyone who had some grievance reacted to it with a strike, and the commandant suspected my sister of organizing those strikes.

One time, at three at night, [my] sister was woken up and told that she was under arrest. She was placed in a disciplinary cell, a small, narrow cell where there was nothing except for a bench. The cell was ridden with insects and mice. She wasn't given food. She stayed like that for twenty-four hours. During the day she would be sent to work in the forest, and after her return from work she was kept in the cell. Of the quotas she would fulfill, only 25 percent was counted. This lasted for two months until she fell ill with typhus. Only then did they allow her to be taken into the barracks. We all became infected, but they didn't want to take us to the hospital—still for that same offense. Our neighbors fled from the barracks out of fear of being infected. We all recovered, but from that time on Mother began to spit out blood. Her heart hurt. We felt that she would not last long. We stayed another year and a half in the *posiołek*, and were then sent to a different place. There were many Poles there who treated us very kindly. They helped us get settled and gave us useful pieces of advice. The *posiołek*'s commandant was a Russian, an enemy of Poland, [who] abused Poles. He insulted them, teased them, told them ten times a day that there would be no Poland and that they would always remain in Russia. We would come to assemblies, where all had to be present, to listen to the commandant [and] it wasn't allowed to complain about anything. On the Day of Atonement in 1940 the Jews decided not to go to work [but] spend their time praying.[75] The commandant brought in NKVD agents who wanted to arrest us. Later, however, they received a delegation and apologized to it. This cost us three men's suits: two for the agents, one for the commissar.

---

75. Yom Kippur: the Day of Atonement, one of the most important Jewish holidays, which fell on 12 October in 1940. See glossary.

The Outbreak of War

Immediately after the outbreak of the Soviet-German war in June 1941 a commission arrived with the NKVD chief, which told us that from that day on we were allies, which is why we should work even more zealously for the common interest. In the initial period we did not notice any changes in relation to us. We continued to work hard, were given measly bread rations, only we were insulted less and treated more nicely during work. Only after the Amnesty was announced did a Polish commission arrive which took us under its wing. Food and clothes were brought in which were only used by the Poles, Jews weren't given anything. Then we were told that all Polish citizens were being sent to Kazakhstan. We received a referral to Ural'sk but were sent to Bukhara. We were loaded into carriages and sent on the way. The journey from Arkhangelsk to Bukhara took seven weeks but we felt well during that journey. Whenever the train stopped at a station, our fellow travelers ran to the other carriages and always returned with a haul: flour, sugar, meat, and canned foods. We would throw ourselves on those products like mad people because we had not eaten anything like it for two years. The Bolsheviks noticed how we ate and conducted a search in the carriage, but all the provisions were already in our stomachs. One Pole was arrested for the fact that a little sugar had been found on him. As a result, all stations were notified to beware because a train carrying criminals was on its way. In Bukhara we were ordered to go to work in a kolkhoz, but we knew [what we risked doing so]. We asked the Polish delegation for advice; we were told to make efforts, officially, to be sent away, but to avoid the kolkhoz in reality. We didn't want to register, which is why we slept at the station, since no one in the city wanted to let us into their home.

One night the Uzbeks took us to a kolkhoz by force. The kolkhoz was called "Janko Tarma" and was located not far from Bukhara. At first we received four hundred grams of flour per day for the work [but] later they didn't give us anything. We lived off grass and roots. We lived in a small clay hut and slept on bare ground. We suffered like this for three weeks. The kolkhoz manager, seeing how we were suffering, gave us a pass to go to Bukhara. In Bukhara the situation was even worse than before. Apart from [Polish] refugees, masses of refugees were pouring in from all of Russia, from Russian cities being evacuated. People were [living] out in the streets. With no other choice, we turned to an Ewakpunkt[76] and asked for a *komandirovka*[77] [to go to] a kolkhoz. We were sent to a kolkhoz Mołotow Number 1. There was no room for us there. We went to the Mołotow Number 2 kolkhoz. There too they didn't want to let us in. We wandered like that from kolkhoz to kolkhoz and everywhere we received the same response: "There is work—accommodation there isn't." Three times we returned to the Mołotow kolkhoz and finally went back to Bukhara, deciding to stay in the city. After many weeks of suffering, we managed to find an "apartment" in an old, cluttered stable, for which we paid sixty rubles per month in rent. We suffered a lot at the hands of the stable's owner and his son, a common thief. One day he stole a coat from Father and when Father demanded its return, [the landlord's son] beat him badly. Father went to the NKVD with a complaint. The investigation took months. Father was summoned for an examination a few times. The thief returned the coat after [his] first examination.

We Trade

We had nothing to live on and decided to take up trading, even though this was harshly punishable. There was no other way. We traded foodstuffs: bread, rice, sugar, and flour. The older family members bought the products and we, the children, sold them. Father knew a warehouse worker in a large cooperative, who gave him a few tens of kilos of bread per day. We paid thirty rubles per kilo for the bread, while the official price was 1.05. We sold the bread for thirty-five to forty rubles per kilo. Bread was the main trade product, but the warehouseman introduced us to another warehouseman who supplied us with rice, sugar, meat, black flour, and white flour. Our earnings were not bad. We had a lot of mishaps. I myself got arrested maybe ten times while carrying the goods on the tram and in the cinema, where the trading took place. At the *cyrkul* [militia station] I was beaten, kept throughout the day, and had the goods confiscated once or twice. They wanted to get out of me who had supplied me with the products. Despite the beatings I did not reveal my address and concealed the fact that I had parents. Since I looked sickly, I passed for a seven- or eight-year-old child; I was let free.

---

76. Likely refers to a bureau for the relocation of refugees from the German-occupied areas.
77. *Komandirovka* (Russian): a business assignment/trip; here: a referral. See glossary.

The situation in the city continued to worsen. The influx of refugees increased. People escaped en masse from the kolkhozes to the city. People were lying down out in the streets, in the gutters. They were trampled on like insects. People were dying from hunger in the streets, but no one paid them attention and they didn't even get funerals organized for them. The corpses were thrown into containers with rubbish. Awful epidemics went around: dysentery, malaria, typhoid fever, and typhus. There were no spaces in the hospitals; medicines couldn't be obtained even with money. Although a doctor from the Polish delegation came, he was powerless without medicines. The most terrifying was the dysentery epidemic, whose cause was determined by the doctors to be eating *makuchy* [oil cakes]. There were two oil mills in the city producing oil for the army. Civilians baked cakes from the residues of the rapeseed pressing. In our town cows ate it. We paid between two and three rubles per cake.

Our Casualties

The first casualty was my brother, ten-year-old Sender. He fell ill with dysentery. He lay ill at home. After eight days he was taken to the hospital, where he died. For a large sum of money we recovered the body of the dead [boy] and buried him in a Jewish cemetery. Three weeks later, Mother fell ill with dysentery. We managed to place her in a hospital. She died one day later. We wanted to bury Mother but were told that the body had been buried at night, in an unknown place.

In the Orphanage

After Mother's death, Father began making efforts to have me and my brother admitted to the Polish orphanage. After long efforts I got in, along with my brother, to the Polish orphanage. Father and my two sisters lived in the city. We didn't see either Father or the sisters again because we left for Persia two weeks later. I will never forget those two weeks spent in the orphanage. We suffered a lot at the hands of the Polish children who kept shouting: "Jews off to Palestine." The thick soup was only given to the Polish children, and we received a bit of *wodzianka*.[78] We were constantly hungry, and even though the

78. Thin, watery soup; a typical camp fare.

commission had recommended a special diet for us, we weren't given anything to eat. From Bukhara we went to Krasnovodsk and from there to Pahlevi. There, a commission of English doctors examined us, of whom one, when he saw me, exclaimed: "Who is this you've sent us? Corpses or children?" I was sent off to the English Hospital for a fattening treatment. There I came back to health. I was sent to Tehran, where I lived in camp number 1, along with Polish children. Then I got into a Jewish orphanage, [to be] in the care of Sochnut.[79] We were fed well but looked ragged. Transports of clothes from America and India came, which were divided between the Poles. The worse stuff was given to the Jews. Out of this worse stuff the orphanage staff picked out the best bits for themselves, and the children were left with rags. Throughout my whole stay in Tehran I wore a night shirt, only one day before departure I got a torn dress. I begged to be given a toman to send a letter to Father. They took my letters and promised they would send them off. I didn't get a response, however. Other children who received money from America, and the Polish children who were given stamps, received replies from their relatives in Russia. I spent eight months in Tehran, then I went to Karachi, from where I undertook a long and exhausting journey to Palestine.

79. Sochnut (Jewish Agency): a nongovernmental organization created through a mandate of the League of Nations in 1922 for the purposes of representation of Jews to the mandate powers in Palestine and to the League of Nations. Currently the executive arm of the World Zionist Organization. See glossary.

Protocol 37

Testimony of **Judyta Patasz**, age fifteen, daughter of Fiszel and Chaja. Resident in Goworowo, by Łomża. Father was a craftsman; she had six siblings. Arrived in Palestine via Tehran in February 1943, with a sister and two brothers.

On 6 September 1939 the Germans entered Goworowo. The town had been bombed two days before the arrival of the Germans. All residents fled, hid in the neighboring villages. We took necessities with us and escaped to the countryside. We spent a few days there. Father returned home before Saturday arrived. After entering the town the Germans took all the men between 17 and 40 years of age and sent them for forced labor in East Prussia. The day after they arrived in town the Germans shot at houses for no reason. One hundred and fifty people were killed then. Most of the houses in town, and the synagogue, were burned down. The Germans could not be bothered to look for the men who were hiding, so they would burn down a house along with those hiding in it. We lived in the town for two weeks. Father and my older brother hid in the basement. When we ran out of food in the house, we all sneaked out of town at night and went, by night, toward the border, to Białystok.

In Białystok

The border between the Russian- and German-occupied lands was open at that time. No one bothered us when we crossed it. We easily crossed over to the other side of the Bug River. We found a small apartment, and since Father had nothing to live on, he took up trading. [My] older brother helped him. They traded in manufacture, salt, watches, and anything they could. The Bolsheviks bought everything. Russian soldiers would come to our apartment and buy whole deliveries of goods. Father said that we would survive the war easily this way.

Passports

I remember that Father came home one day and told us about the passing of a new law. We all got frightened because we knew it meant another flight and hiding again. Father told Mama that everyone had to take a Soviet passport, and that meant that we would never again return home and would have to remain in Russia always. I don't remember how Mama replied, I only remember that Father added that he would not take such a passport. A few days later, Father returned home happy and told Mother that bureaus have been opened on the main street where registrations were being taken for those who wanted to return home, or who had relatives in Wilno [Vilnius] and wanted to go to Lithuania. Mother was awfully glad because our eldest sister lived in Wilno. The following day Father registered us all to go to Wilno. Almost every day Father would tell us about new prohibitions, about arrests, about the rich being thrown out of their apartments, about the seizing of shops and factories. The trading stopped—there was nothing to trade in. Father complained that there would be nothing to eat. Who traded was taken to jail, and Father was worried that he would be met with the same fate. One time, Father came back from town and said that you couldn't walk around with parcels because agents searched people on the street. Then, me and my little sister Bela, who was ten, told Father to take us with him. Children were not searched. Thus we became merchants. Father took us to the place where merchandise was bought and showed us where it was sold. Later we managed without [his] help. We became the family breadwinners. This lasted until June 1940. One night there was a knock on the door and we were told to open up. A few military men ordered us to get dressed, pack up our things. We were taken to the station in cars.

Deportation

Twenty of us were placed in a small freight car. In the big carriages there traveled between fifty and sixty people. The car was sealed and sent on its way a few hours later. We didn't know where we were going. Father looked out through a crack and wanted to guess the direction of [our] travel. Mother cried and despaired. It was difficult to stand the heat in the freight car. There was no toilet. We, the children, were embarrassed to relieve ourselves in front of the adults, and so we ripped off the doors of the carriage. At each station we would run out to go to the toilet and to get water. No one guarded us. We traveled for eight days; after eight days we were told at some station that we were getting off. We got out of the cars. Father told us that we were in the Arkhangelsk Oblast, at the station of Siktifkar.[80] The station was located seventy kilome-

80. Correctly: Syktyvkar [original Polish correction: Syktywkar]. Appears in other testimonies as Syktyfar, Siktifrak, Siktifar, Syktyfkar.

ters away from the city. We were not allowed inside the city. Tractors arrived, we were divided into groups and taken, on the tractors, to *posiołki*. We were placed in the *posiołek* of the second precinct.

In the *Posiołek*

In the *posiołek* there stood barracks, in each barracks there lived thirty people. Inside the rooms, bunks had been installed instead of beds. After the exhausting journey in the freight cars we slept like logs on those bunks. It was only later it turned out that there were bedbugs in the bunks that wouldn't let us sleep. They were horrible bedbugs, massive, that didn't even run when they were being set on fire. We demanded new bunks. I remember that the older people announced that if they weren't allowed to sleep at night, they wouldn't go to work in the morning. New iron beds were brought in for everyone. The barracks were lit with small lamps at night but after some time the wicks, kerosene, and glass ran out so that we only burned wooden logs.

At Work

The next day we were sent to work. I was twelve and had to work too. My quota was sixty roots per day; children didn't saw trees but worked pulling out the roots. Naturally, I could not manage such hard work. Anyone who made the quota got eight hundred grams of bread per day; anyone who didn't—only six hundred. One had the right to buy soup in the canteen. Apart from the bread we received a few kopecks. Even though Father and Mother and [my] brothers worked, we struggled so much that we couldn't all afford to have soup. In winter, during a freeze of –60°C [–76°F], Mother and I were excused from work. From the *posiołek* to the place of work one had to walk for ten kilometers. Our destitution was grave. We all had to eat the bread earned by Father and [my] brother. Soup was a faraway dream. Very often after work everyone was called in to assemblies where a *politruk* would exhort people to work more diligently. We talked between ourselves that they made us work a lot, but eat little. It wasn't allowed to go to the second *posiołek* without a pass. It was punishable by jail. Many people were arrested, locked up in disciplinary cells without bread or water. There was no soap in the *posiołek*. Luckily we had some soap with us brought over from Białystok. During Pesach of 1941 [12–19 April], not having any matzos, we ate bread. Father fasted for whole days because he didn't want to eat bread. Only in the evening, very exhausted, he could be convinced to have a nonkosher meal. He complained at it and whined all night.

After the holidays Mother fell ill with pneumonia. There was no doctor in the *posiołek*. In the second *posiołek* there lived a feldsher. Since Father and [my] older brother had to go to work every day, I became Mama's nurse. After long pleading I managed to get a permit to bring in the feldsher. He found Mother's condition dangerous. I burst into tears, fell to his feet so Mother would be taken to the hospital. He replied that there were no room in the hospital, and that he would come to us every day. He told me to give Mother a cupping treatment. Since I didn't have any cups, I used three glasses that we had brought from Białystok. Instead of alcohol I used a bit of kerosene the commander gave me. Mama's condition worsened by the day. I found out that, a few tens of kilometers from our *posiołek*, there was a hospital where Polish doctors practiced. I received a pass from the commander, went to the village, and told the Polish doctor about Mama's dangerous condition. I was given a card for Mother to be taken into the hospital. With this card I ran to the commander so that he would let Mother be transported to the hospital. It wasn't easy. "In Russia horses are harder to come by than people," he replied. Only after I burst into tears did I receive the promised horse.

Mama Dies

The following day I harnessed the horse to a cart; [my] father and brother were at work in the forest. With other children's help, we moved [my] sick Mama with difficulty onto the cart and set off on the way. After a few kilometers' journey, Mother died on the cart. Seeing that Mama was dead, I turned back and went, with my dead Mama, to the *posiołek*.

The following day, [my] father and brother were released from work. We found an empty space, dug a hole, and buried Mother. On a tree that stood nearby we carved out an inscription. This was in June 1941. After Mother's death all of the household responsibilities fell on me. I had to take care that the small children had something to eat, sew and patch up our rags, wash the underwear, clean the room. Two weeks later we were moved to a different *posiołek*, fifteen kilometers away. There I worked digging up tree trunks. Bread was given out on ration cards. One could also get two hundred grams of sweets per month on a card. In the *posiołek* we could move about freely and do the shopping in the nearby kolkhozes. The kolkhoz members commanded high prices—five rubles for rotted potatoes, forty rubles for a glass of milk. In the kolkhozes there lived exiled Russians, former kulaks.[81] They had enough to eat, their own cattle and poultry. They had enough to sell products. They sold not for money, however, but for clothes. Among the kolkhoz members there were many dissatisfied people who longed for an outbreak of war to find a chance to escape. Us they assured that we would not get out of Siberia and that we would be buried here. They said these things when no one could hear because they were afraid of the NKVD.

The Outbreak of War

We were notified about the outbreak of war between Germany and Russia by the commander and the feldsher. At a special assembly we were exhorted to work intensely for the common interest. Our situation did not improve. We weren't given more bread but had to work hard. We decided not to work on Yom Kippur [1 October 1941]. Everyone gathered together and the prayers began. Meanwhile, the NKVD arrived and called on us not to miss work during holidays. They could just about excuse the older people who wanted to pray, but not the youth who should have been working. When this speech didn't help, we started to be threatened with punishment and a tribunal. Who stood twice in front of the tribunal had 25 percent taken off his work pay, who stood in front of the judge for the third time received a harsher penalty. Mrs. Ita Pruszyńska was locked in a work camp for fifty days. Unafraid of punishment, we did not stop the prayer. The next day I was referred to the tribunal along with the adults. I wasn't punished, however, since I was a minor.

The Amnesty

Right after Yom Kippur we were informed about the Amnesty for Polish citizens. Everyone [was] to receive a certificate allowing them to travel to small

81. A peasant in Russia wealthy enough to own a farm and hire labor. Emerging after the emancipation of serfs in the nineteenth century, the kulaks resisted Stalin's forced collectivization, but millions were arrested, exiled, or killed. During World War II, kulaks were among the first to be deported from Eastern Poland into the forced labor camps of the Soviet Union. In the Bolshevik ideology, kulaks were characterized as having excessive wealth and were a class enemy against whom all forms of state repression were justified.

cities, since refugees were not allowed in big cities. But not everyone could leave. A few families stayed because they didn't have a penny to their name. Our journey to Tashkent took six weeks. Father fell ill on the way. [My] brother and three sisters went to a kolkhoz, I stayed with the sick father who couldn't walk—and to the kolkhoz one had to get to on foot. We were put up in a teahouse.[82] Father died at night. In the morning, savage Uzbeks came, grabbed Father's body, and drove it away. I wasn't allowed to go with, so I don't know where Father has been buried. After Father's death I went to the kolkhoz, to my siblings. The kolkhoz was called Kidil-Juldus and was located ten kilometers from the city. We all worked picking cotton there. For this work we received four hundred grams of flour a day. I made dumplings with this flour and cooked them in water. This was our morning and evening meal. The houses in the kolkhoz were made out of clay, they leaked in the rain. We literally lived in the mud.

The Third Casualty

A month later [my] brother fell ill. He dragged himself home with his last bit of strength and lay down on the floor. I was released from work to take care of [my] sick brother. I went to the doctor but did not find him home. This repeated for eight days until I was finally able to find a doctor. [My] brother was treated by the feldsher who lived in the kolkhoz. It was only the doctor who prescribed that [my] brother be taken to the hospital. The hospital was located at a twenty-five-kilometer distance from the kolkhoz. Brother died two days later. When I came to find out how [he] was doing, I was told that he had died that night. I sat down in front of the hospital and cried bitterly over my fate. I waited all day to see my brother to the cemetery. In the evening they told me that the funeral had already taken place. They didn't want to show me where the grave was.

After [my] brother's death I became, as the oldest one, a caretaker to three children, for whom I was to replace a father and a mother. I wanted to go back to the kolkhoz but I could not find the way to it. I wandered around all day and returned to the hospital in the evening. It took a few days before someone from the kolkhoz came and drove me to my three little orphans. It

82. Text: "czajna," originally corrected to *czajnia*; Russian: *chainaya*.

was wintertime, awfully freezing. Children were excused from work [and] I became the only family breadwinner. After some time, me and my sister Bela fell ill with typhus. We were sent off to Tashkent, to a hospital. I recovered after five weeks. While I was ill the other children, Abraham and Zwi, simply went hungry. They wandered around the kolkhoz and didn't even complain to anyone. Only after a few days did they run, crying, to the kolkhoz commander complaining that they hadn't eaten in a few days. He gave them a *lepyoshka*[83] each and said that anyone who doesn't work, doesn't eat. After my return from the hospital I was signed off work for fourteen days. Despite this, they didn't want to give me my flour ration. I managed, with difficulties, to haggle some measly flour rations for the children. With no other choice, I returned to work after a few days. After work I tended to the household, cooked dumplings. In the summer I worked with the children. Even little five-year-old Zwi had to work. He stayed close to me and I was careful that he was busy with work when the supervisor came close. During harvest time the work was easier.

I found out that there was a Polish orphanage in Tashkent. At first, they didn't want to accept any of us. Only after long pleading did they take two of the younger children—Abraham and Zwi. Abraham escaped after a few days, saying that the Polish children made his life hell. He was beaten and insulted. The youngest one, on the other hand, stayed, and went to Persia with the first transport. Only later, when a Jewish woman took over the running of the orphanage, were we all taken in. We stayed there for three weeks. Only ten children, full orphans, went to Persia, the rest stayed behind. We were told we were going to India. We went to Ashgabat, and from there to Tehran. I didn't know where my brother was. Only after a few days was I informed that my brother was in Tehran. All four of us found ourselves together, which was a great fortune. In Tehran we were fed well but had nothing to put on our backs. We still wore rags. Six months later we came to Palestine.

83. A Central Asian flatbread similar to a naan.

Protocol 38

Testimony of **Leon Klajman**, age twenty-seven, born and resident in Łódź. Arrived in Palestine in 1943 via Tehran.

In the first days of September 1939, when the Germans were nearing Łódź, I left my hometown. The roads were full of refugees. German airplanes came down low over the roads and shot at the escapees from machine guns. There were a lot of dead and wounded people on the roads. German colonists threw stones at us, blockaded the roads and wouldn't let us escape. In the village of Witki the colonists shot at us. It wasn't possible to get water for the wounded in the village, let alone any rest. We ran on ahead. In Łowicz we saw a hospital ablaze, full of casualties. Ninety kilometers past Rawa [Mazowiecka] we came upon a German military unit, which stopped and searched us, and took away everything each of us had on them. A boy who'd had three spent rifle shell casings found on him was killed on the spot. We ended up in jail. It was so crowded [there] that one couldn't breathe or move. Children cried from hunger and fear. We thought our final hour was approaching.

German Sadism

The Germans released all Poles [and] Ukrainians from among those arrested. We Jews were held. When the Germans noticed that most [of us] were beginning to faint from hunger and thirst, they threw a few pieces of bread between us to tease our appetite, and so that we would fight over [it]. They also put in a pot with potatoes that would have been enough to feed [only] a tenth of those arrested. Indeed, fights broke out. One would rip a morsel of bread from another's mouth. The Germans watched this spectacle, splitting their sides. One Austrian officer would often come to our window. You could see that our suffering did not please him—unlike the Germans. I chose an appropriate moment and began to complain to him. I looked very young then. I cried and kept repeating how I'd left my old and sick mother, for whom I was the only provider, at home. I begged him to release me from jail. I had a diamond ring with me that I'd managed to hide during the search. I took a risk and showed that ring to the officer. He turned red but responded in a cool manner: "We'll see [about it] tomorrow." I didn't sleep all night with anxiety—[this was because] I didn't know whether the officer would free me or report me. Best case, they would take away the ring. What danger would come after? I'd certainly heard plenty about German cruelties. Just in case, I prepared for the bad and the good. I found my brother in the mass of arrestees and said goodbye to him. We both cried, fearfully awaiting the dawn.

The diamond, however, clearly kept the Austrian officer up. In the morning he called me, took the ring, and told me leave the camp quickly. I was afraid of going to Warsaw on my own so I turned back onto a road leading to Łódź. I'd hardly walked up eight kilometers when I fell into German hands again. It was outside the village of Głuchów. I was arrested and placed in the local monastery. As in the first camp, there were many people there, and just as in the other one we were thrown pieces of bread like starving dogs. The arrestees threw themselves on [the bread] and fought over a piece until blood was drawn. In Głuchów, moreover, the Germans amused themselves in yet another way. Every now and again they raised the alarm, shouting "Gas attack," and everyone rushed like mad toward the exit, trampling and hitting one another. The Germans would calmly watch the spectacle. When that whole mass [of people] banged on the front door, shots would ring out. As before, when they all rushed ahead toward the exit, so then, frantic with fear, they would start hiding in corners. A game like this would normally cost a few human lives. After some time young girls and children began to be released. The examinations were carried out by a young Polish lieutenant who had been taken prisoner. Only cripples, women, children, and adolescents were released. I lied, saying I was sixteen, and was let go. All those who had been released went to Będzin and only from there to Łódź, on carts. We paid three thousand zlotys for the cart; however, some arrestees still went on foot. The pleasure of riding [in] the cart did not last long. As soon as we left the town we came across a few German soldiers. We were told to get off the cart. They shot at us with handguns, aiming at the legs. Those who got away in one piece reached Łódź by back roads.

In Łódź

In Łódź the Germans had taken over completely. Each day brought with it new atrocities and new murders. Sixty-three Jews were dragged out of the Astoria café. Two were spared, so they could dig the graves, the rest shot. The following day one of those two lost his mind. One Jaskowicz was shot on the spot, along with his children, at 9 Piotrkowska Street because he didn't open the door to two German soldiers quickly enough. One tailor was killed for no reason. A well-known baker, Jelin, was killed at 24 Piotrkowska Street. Human life began to depend on a German soldier's whim. [They] robbed without mercy, tortured with no reason. On 11 October the Germans hanged two Poles and one Jew in the town square in Bałuty. The hanged [men] were left on the gallows for twenty-four hours, and the residents of Łódź forced to go and look at them. On 24 December, the yellow badge decree came out.[84] The constant terror and everyday murders made life in the city a living hell. We thought about how to escape from that hell. I went from Łódź to Warsaw by train, from Warsaw to Siedlce, and from there to the Bug River by cart. I made it across the Bug, which was the Soviet border at the time. Twice the Bolsheviks caught me and sent me back on my way. Only by the third time did I manage to avoid the border guard and reach Białystok.

In Białystok

Białystok was full of refugees. People slept in synagogues, in the station, and up against fences. By day the streets were swarming with people. Outside the local municipal office there were long lines of people waiting for ration cards for lunch and for bread. I roamed around from one place to another and didn't have any accommodation. It was cold [and] snow had already fallen. I fell ill and wandered around with a fever that knocked me off my feet. There was no way of getting into the local hospital, where doctors from Warsaw were working. The beds were taken and patients were lying even in the corridor. I could see I would not get into the hospital so I began to try [to get] a place to sleep for a few days.

How I Voted

Half-conscious, I wandered around from one place to another. I looked for people I knew and offered all the money I had until I found a corner in some room. I had a high fever. The illness overwhelmed me so much that I didn't

84. That is, the compulsory marking of Jews with a yellow six-pointed star. See glossary: yellow badge.

know anything about the plebiscite that was announced by the Bolsheviks at that time, or about the fact that the residents of Białystok and refugees decided to boycott the elections.[85] Late in the evening, two civilian NKVD agents came into the room where I lay suffering. I didn't know what they wanted from me. I thought they wanted to take me to the hospital, [but] my illness did not interest them at all. They asked why I wasn't going to vote. "You can see that I'm ill," I replied. Immediately, a ballot box appeared next to me. An envelope was placed in my hand. Without thinking about what I was doing, I dropped the envelope into the box. I lay ill for a few weeks. When I returned to health I started to think about what to do with myself. There was no work to be had in town, and trading was very dangerous. [My] money dwindled by the day. I was at risk of hunger. I decided to get through to Lida, and from there to Lithuania. Lithuania was a neutral country. One could make contact abroad from there. There was enough food there. I went to Lida. In Lida, at the station, I met a smuggler. He told how he had smuggled people across the border in summertime. Since he liked the look of me, he demanded a thousand rubles from me to take me across border. I believed him. I didn't know the addresses of [any] other smugglers. He showed me a place where I was to wait for him [until] he had put together a group of people wanting to cross. The smuggler turned out to be a trickster. He collected the money and never showed again. With no other choice, I had to return to Białystok. In Białystok I came upon the famous registration. Although I didn't want to go back to the Germans, staying in Białystok and accepting Soviet citizenship seemed to me a worse fate. I would never have [been able to see] my parents. They would lock me up in the Soviets[86] like in prison and I'd never see those close to me again. I decided to register to return.

Deportation

For some time after the registration one would walk around as if in a dream, thinking about returning home. On 21 June 1941, at night, NKVD agents accompanied by a Soviet soldier turned up at my place, told me to pack up my

85. The plebiscite was the elections to the People's Assemblies of Western Ukraine and Western Belorussia [Belarus] in the autumn of 1939. See glossary.

86. [Soviet republics.]

things and took me to the police station.[87] The day before the Bolsheviks requisitioned all the cars, droshkies, and platform trucks. It was clear something was being prepared. Fear of the unknown and curiosity took over Białystok. One wanted to read from the face of one's neighbor what it was that awaited us. Various speculations were whispered [from one ear to another]. Unrelated to this, a few days before, a citizen exchange transport had left for the German border. The transport was mostly made up of Germans who lived in the Polish territories occupied by the Bolsheviks. The number of Poles and Jews was minimal. People comforted each other [saying] that any day now the second fugitive transport would depart. Only the violence with which the Bolsheviks treated the refugees caused worry. In the evening the streets swarmed with cars, droshkies, and platform trucks. Everyone was taken to the station on trucks, and there, loaded onto freight cars, sixty people to [one]. Where were they taking us?—there was no one to ask. The Bolshevik soldiers did not answer questions. I had already seen, from afar, what a deportation to Siberia meant. The previous year my brother had been sent into the depths of Russia. A student of the Technical School, he had planned to continue his studies in Russia and registered to work there. The workers were welcomed with music in Russia, but instead of a technical school, he was sent to a coal mine. He wasn't used to that work and didn't know one had to avoid the gas that the coal released. He got poisoned and stayed in a hospital for three months. My brother's turns of fate taught me not to look at a journey to Russia through rose-tinted glasses.

Meanwhile, new transports of people continued to arrive. The cars filled up. Crying, screaming, and complaining came out of [them]. Families wanted to travel together in the same carriage. Children looked for [their] mothers, and mothers for [their] children. The soldiers stood like stones at the doors and didn't want to listen to any complaints. A day passed by like this. Only those who had provisions with them ate. People begged for a piece of bread [and] argued over bunks. [They] were sleep-deprived and tired; it was extremely hot. People argued and even fought, and didn't notice when the train started. We traveled for fifteen days. Every night at two o'clock the soldiers brought us soup, bread, sometimes a piece of meat. We napped on the bunks. A hole in

87. The forthcoming events suggest this to have been June 1940.

the car floor was used instead of a toilet. We got used to children's screaming. We didn't know where we were going. Only on the fifteenth day did we arrive in Kotlas, six hundred kilometers from Kirov.

Siberia

We are deep in Siberia. [In] Kotlas there is no room for us in the barracks and so they take us further on, on a ship on the river. Food rations are becoming stingier. The crowding is horrendous, and Siberian mosquitos are simply biting off pieces of our bodies. For nine days all we saw was water and woodland steppes, [until] we arrived in Madz [?]. The part of Siberia where we are is four times the size of Poland and inhabited by only 319,000 people. Deportees, on the other hand, number three million here. In some labor camps a hundred thousand people are at work, and around the camps stretch kilometers of forests untouched by humans.

Our labor camp is located seventy kilometers from the main city of Siktifar,[88] 1,500 kilometers from Kirov. In the middle of huge woodlands there stood two wooden barracks. Each barracks was made up of twelve rooms, in each room there lived more than twenty people. There were 150 of us deportees, and to begin with, we slept on the floor. Only later did they allow [the] carpenters from among [us] to build bunks, but we weren't given [any] bedding, not even a blanket to cover oneself with. The cold at night, despite it being summertime, was already difficult to bear, so that even after the three-week journey we couldn't, out of cold, fall asleep on the floor. There was enough food, however, especially for those who had money. A kilo of bread cost one ruble, and a bucket of potatoes between eight and nine rubles.

In the Forest

After five days we were sent to work. I worked sawing wood. We labored between eight and nine hours and walked four kilometers to [get to] work. Work began at seven o'clock. People used to physical labor were paid pretty well. They got between ten and fifteen rubles a day and could live well on that. But I, unused to physical work, earned only half a ruble per day. It was enough for half a kilo of bread. Intellectuals with higher degrees fared even worse.

88. In the original an erroneous name for Syktyvkar [original Polish correction: Syktywkar].

Eminent doctors from Warsaw had been deported to our labor camp, like Dr. [Stanisław] Frank, Dr. [Abram] Kobryner, and Dr. [Jakub] Szpilman; lawyers—[Beniamin] Lewin, Rybak; a man of letters Leo Finkelstein, Jehoszua Trunk, Krakowiak, Fendzar, and others. They earned a lot less than I did or didn't earn at all. In winter, the temperature in our area reached −55°C [−67°F]. At −45°C [−49°F] we had to go to work. Diligent workers would receive warm clothing from the commandant; we, however, wore our own clothes and had our feet, hands, ears, and noses frostbitten. It was even worse in the summer. One couldn't stave off [all] the flies and mosquitos so that on the way to work, one had to tie a rag around one's head. [Our] hands swelled from the bites [and] blisters formed. I fell ill. I swelled all over and developed a heart problem. It didn't help me get signed off work. I was given easier work, working with Leo Finkelstein removing bark from the trees. The intelligentsia with higher degrees—except the doctors Kobryner, Frank, and Szpilman, who were allowed to practice in the hospital in Siktyfer[89] (Kobryner became the head doctor at the hospital)—were accommodated in one room. They kept together. After work they often talked and had discussions, and more than once the commandant asked them what topics they were discussing in their room. The commandant was very careful not to allow us to have meetings. It was even forbidden to pray together. He was worried that if people got together, they would look for ways to get out of hard work and that, in his view, was sabotage. He himself, however, often organized assemblies where he kept [trying to] convince us that the forest belonged to us, that the huge stretches of Siberia were our property, that our homeland was the USSR. People would avoid those meetings however they could but would gather readily for group prayers. Someone would keep watch outside the barracks in case the officials should notice.

Arrests

In our labor camp there lived three snitches, [who were] bribed by the commandant with easier work and better pay. The snitches repeated everything that happened in the camp to the commandant. This way the commandant knew that prayers had taken place on Yom Kippur [and] that on Pesach people

89. [Syktyvkar.]

had gathered in one room for a Seder feast.[90] He also knew about the discussions taking place in the intelligentsia room, and who took part in [them]. The intelligentsia knew about the snitches and the eavesdropping outside their room. Sometimes they would find strewn-around papers, [proof] that a search had taken place in their absence. They paused the nightly talks for some time but their desire for discussion and conversing won out. One night, thirty-two NKVD members arrived at the labor camp and immediately made their way to said room, woke up the occupants, carried out a search so thorough that they even pulled the floorboards up, and arrested all twenty-four [people], except for Trunk. Those arrested were sent to prison in Siktyfar.[91] This prison is infamous. Most arrestees do not return. Well-known politicians and the Communist Party members are serving their punishment there. There are also Zionist activists, locked up during different stages of the revolution. Every five years they are called for new interrogations [where it is demanded] that they abandon their beliefs. Stubbornly, however, they do not give up their ideology, and return to prison for another five years. Our arrestees were accused of sabotage and preparing for a breakout. But there was no way to escape from the camp—one would die in the woods or on the steppe. Even our foremen, who are locals, are afraid of going deep into the forest. There is no railway at all in the area. Our Syktyfar, the main city, has no rail connection and [is connected] to the world only through a waterway. These arguments, however, did not prevent the accusation. Every night they were taken for an interrogation. They were cross-examined, threatened with further deportation, [and] finally all released except Leo Finkelstein and Rybak the lawyer. My wife, already post-Amnesty, went to Syktyfar and saw Leo Finkelstein being led under the supervision of NKVD agents. He looked awful, he had death in his eyes. Before the war he had suffered from a heart condition. He used a moment when the agents were busy and begged my wife to get people from the camp to write applications to support his case, or he would be killed. He was being taken to a court to Kartgeraz [?]. He was freed, along with Rybak, only one year after the Amnesty. We, however, in the camp, wrote to all the Soviet authorities with requests for his release. Because I had worked with Finkelstein in the forest, I

90. Seder: an evening meal on the first days of Pesach. See glossary.
91. [Syktyvkar.]

was called in for interrogation. I gave statements under oath. In vain did they try to get [evidence for the prosecution] from me. This arrest was the most prominent event in the camp and was talked about constantly. It was the only topic livening up our hard and dreary lives. In our camp there was a rabbi from a small town located on the Polish-Soviet border. His son was an NKVD official, but despite this, couldn't get his father out from the camp, and [could] only send him food parcels. Parcels from the Bolshevik-occupied lands, from Russia itself, and most importantly from America, kept us alive. Those who received them shared [them] with the others. Clothes were sold and bread and potatoes bought with the money. Makhorka was cheap in the camp. One got as much of it as one wanted, whereas in other areas of the USSR a packet of makhorka cost more than a loaf of bread. Clothes, on the other hand, were impossible to get. People wore rags, and the only non-torn clothes were worn by the members of the NKVD, because they took bribes.

Bribes and Theft

Theft and bribes are an everyday occurrence. He who dares object to this custom is kicked out of the unit in question because he disadvantages the rest of the thieves. Back in Białystok, where I worked in a state vegetable co-op, where lines formed to wait for a kilo of potatoes, my colleagues would force me to take home a bag of potatoes. An engineer I knew worked in a factory employing two thousand workers. He dug in his heels and wouldn't lie to say that twenty-eight thousand kilowatts of electric power had been used above the norm. He didn't want to sign a fraudulent statement and so he had to leave the work at the factory. In our camp, false quota statements were commonplace. Theft and bribery are systemic in Russia.

After the Amnesty

After the Amnesty I went to Syktyfkar.[92] I settled there and lived off the sale of my possessions. I looked for an opportunity to get through to Koltas on a barge and go by rail from there. The barges had been requisitioned for the army. I went from place to place in a small boat, and after two months' journey, arrived in Uzbekistan. I worked in a Kyrgyz kolkhoz for two months.

92. [Syktyvkar.]

I received five hundred grams of flour per month. Continuing to sell [my] things, I arrived in Tashkent. It's impossible to describe the hunger [there]. One paid 150 rubles for a kilo of bread. People lost their minds from hunger, they dropped like flies from starvation and typhus. When the evacuation of the Polish army was announced, I claimed to be a Catholic and gave a fake name. We didn't think they would [treat people differently] based on faith. But a Polish officer openly said that the army was not a charity and that only Poles would go. Panic broke out among the Jews. It was difficult to understand how, [somehow], all the Jews [could be] infirm and all the Poles healthy. We felt the old whiff of antisemitism. A Soviet colonel, a Jew, intervened and put forward a list of Jews who were to go with the army. I, however, was not on that list. I had to go as a Christian, with a fake passport. In Tehran I was accused of giving a false name. I gave the reason for my deed [and] was spared punishment. This way I came to Palestine.

Protocol 39

Testimony of **Rojza Lauterbach**, age thirty-eight, born and lived in Tarnów. Arrived in Palestine in February 1943 from Russia via Tehran.

In September 1939, I and my husband, a lawyer from Tarnów, arrived in Lwów. With me there was also my younger married sister, Perla Gotlieb, wife of a Polish officer who had been mobilized. We lived together in Lwów. It was easy to find an apartment. We got a room in a beautiful six-bedroom apartment at Mrs. Kapeluk's on Paderewski Street. We had brought food products from home with us: forty kilograms of sugar, butter, jams, and masses of cigarettes. My husband, who had a talent for learning languages, began to learn Russian. There were no prospects of finding work. One day the Bolsheviks searched our landlady's apartment, confiscated 240,000 zlotys, gold coins, silver, gold objects, and valuable furniture. The most beautiful room in the apartment was taken up by a Soviet major from the Red Army. He was from Winnica, and his wife was a Catholic. We became good friends with them and spent time together. The major often got into discussions with my husband. The major's wife brought us food products from the co-op for the army, gave us tickets to the Ukrainian theater and to the opera that came to Lwów from Kiev. The major was delighted that we liked the opera, and that we spoke flatteringly of the Red Army.

Plebiscite

It was in the period before the plebiscite. The Bolsheviks undertook a huge propaganda campaign and praised life in the Soviet territories. In the local Soviet cooperatives one could get anything one wanted. Members of the Red Army and the NKVD treated the public particularly kindly. Since no one thought that the plebiscite would have any impact on the future, one went lightheartedly to the ballot box and dropped the paper in. The Bolsheviks did not check whether those voting were refugees or permanent Lwów residents. They wanted to gather the largest possible amount of votes. In our apartment, the harmonious coexistence continued. The major's kindness was so great that he began to look for a job for my husband. My husband, already knowing a bit of the Russian language, got the job of a bookkeeper at the Georges hotel,[93] with rather decent pay, thanks to [the major]. Immediately after the plebiscite, food products evaporated from the cooperatives. The lack of sugar, salt, and kerosene [could be] felt. All night, lines [of people] stood in front of shops. One had to buy products from backstreet sellers and pay ten times the [normal] price. Homes and shops were nationalized. The influx of refugees increased. One couldn't get a place for the night even with money anymore, and the discontent among the people grew by the day.

We too, despite having some food reserves, began to feel homesick. We couldn't stop longing [to see our] old father whom we had left there, [our] friends and family. [My] husband [would sigh], yearning for his old post. So, when the Russian-German commission arrived in Lwów, with offices on Orzeszkowa Street, and posters appeared in town about the registration to return home, 95 percent of refugees, we among them, registered to leave. The major almost cut [all] ties with us—he had given my husband a job that paid pretty well, and now [the man] wanted to go back to the Germans because he didn't like the Soviets? He didn't want to accept Soviet citizenship? The major and his wife avoided us. My sister and I were not much bothered by this situation. But my husband, always among the Bolsheviks and knowing of their sensitivities, stopped spending nights at home and stayed at the villa of his boss, the director of the Georges hotel. Unrest began in the city. Polish officers and military families were arrested and sent to Siberia. I was worried about the fate of my sister, the wife of an officer. The thought of being separated from each other haunted us.

Exile

On 29 June the Bolsheviks ordered an emergency drill in Lwów. Everyone had to stay at home that night. In our apartment only the major was missing. We felt that something wasn't right. [He] always spent the nights at home. At eleven at night there was a knock on the door. A few NKVD members, armed to the teeth, appeared. They told us to get dressed and pack a few essentials. "Where are we going?" "You'll see." We were told to bring warm clothing and watched as if we were under arrest. They took us to a huge truck where four armed soldiers awaited. They helped us get onto the truck and load the

93. Hotel George, the most elegant hotel in prewar Lwów.

suitcases, and looked over our documents by the light of a small electric lamp. They left me and my husband in the truck and told my sister to get into another one, for those who were companionless. My husband resisted, [saying that] [my] sister had come with us and belonged to our family. They said that she needed to go to a police station first, where she could be accompanied by my husband. Before she managed to get out, however, the truck took off. We were devastated. It turned out that my sister managed brilliantly. She was in our carriage within an hour. It transpired that they weren't able to verify her identity. At the Lwów police station, under the eye of the NKVD, she wouldn't allow herself to be examined by a clerk, and demanded to be taken to the chief of the NKVD. She wouldn't give her surname or address, and because they didn't know what to do with her, they took her to the chief. She told the chief how brutally the agents had treated her and complained that it was pointless to tear her away from the family. The chief began to make excuses in front of her. In response, she asked for a gun: "Torn away from home and family [I] have no reason to live." That statement made such an impression that the chief ordered an NKVD officer to drive her to the station. The streets of Lwów looked like a military camp. Trucks filled with crying and screaming people sped down the streets. The station was madly busy. Groups of people arrived and departed. The din, the screaming and the crying made one's head explode.

Thirty-three of us sat in a freight car. In our car there was also a rabbi with a daughter and a son, [and] also Polish and Ukrainian families. The cars stood on the sidetrack all day under military guard, and one couldn't wander off from one, even to go to the toilet. It was terribly hot, people were suffocating in the carriages, and flies tormented us. We weren't given food [and] had to share our supplies with those who had brought nothing with them. At night, the cars set off on the way. You could have lost your mind from [all] the screaming and crying that rose up, which the rattle of the train could not drown out. People tried to jump out of the carriage [and] the guards struggled to cope with them. Only late at night did things calm down. People napped on the bunks after the experiences of the previous twenty-four hours. At two o'clock at night we were brought hot soup and a portion of bread each. Some couldn't eat out of exhaustion, others [were so hungry they] burned their lips. We traveled for twelve days and nights. It seemed to us that we would be listening to the cars' rattling forever, that we would forever remain in [this] muck and mud. We didn't have any water to wash our hands with; the clothes would stick to our bodies. On the thirteenth day we were far beyond the Urals and arrived in Altynay in the Sverdlovsk Oblast. Getting off the carriage was a joyous sensation to us.

New People, New Adventure, and New Climate

Deep woodland around, anywhere you look—woods and [more] woods. At the station in Altynay we were able to wash. Three hundred people were loaded onto a smaller train and sent to their destination. In a cut-down clearing in the forest stood three wooden barracks. In each barracks there were between thirteen and fifteen rooms, and in each room twelve beds. Fifty Russian deportees, sentenced to exile by the Soviet courts, lived there. Some of them managed to settle fairly well there: they had a cow, a horse, a goat, and rams, and the land they worked on belonged to them. In one of the barracks there was a drying room. We were placed in one room and allowed to rest. Mosquitos kept us from sleeping. There were countless bedbugs. [Our] tired eyes fell shut in vain—we tossed from side to side, eaten by insects whose bites hurt like being stabbed with a knife. On the third day my husband went to the *posiołek*'s commandant, Romanow, also a deportee, who was charged with production of counterfeit money. He wore an NKVD uniform, however, [and] likely not as a result of good deeds. He treated my husband very kindly. He advised that we move to another room, uninhabited up to that point. We were the subject of general envy. Among us there were a pharmacist from Katowice and the wife of the former editor of *Nowy Dziennik*,[94] Berkelhammer,[95] with a seventeen-year-old son. All of these people didn't have the courage to make a complaint, and looked at us with envy as we moved from the barracks to a shed. The shed stood in front of the command residence and had once been used as a workshop for cart repair. We tidied and cleaned it up, making it habitable. We spent [our] two days of rest on hard work. I was so preoccupied with the house cleanup that I forgot to go to the command office opposite and register for work. Although I did remind my husband about that duty, he laughed at me. "Every day without work is a day won," he would say. The shed began to look like a home.

---

94. *Nowy Dziennik* [New Journal]: A Zionist Polish-language journal that appeared daily in Kraków 1918–39.

95. Wilhelm Berkelhammer (1889–1934): editor of *Nowy Dziennik* from 1925 until his death.

My husband and sister went to the commandant to be assigned work. The work consisted of cutting down trees. The timber was taken out of the forest on a small train. A special brigade took the bark off the trees, others dug up roots, others still chopped the branches—[the latter] was considered the work for the weak. My husband was given harder work, [my] sister—lighter. At six in the morning everyone had to be at the assembly point. The foremen would set off for work with the group. Arriving ten minutes late was punishable by a write-up and a court case. *Progul*[96] was punishable. This was most often the loss of between 15 and 25 percent of one's pay. Second offense was punishable by deportation for hard labor. On the first day [my] sister and husband, despite working intensely all day, did not meet their quotas. After some time [my] husband would make 10 percent of his quota. He barely made fifteen rubles per month, while a hard worker received five hundred rubles for their quota. Despite these poor achievements at work, we would both return home half-dead, our hands covered in blisters, and exhausted, collapse on the beds. We were too exhausted to sleep.

But my sister got lucky. The next day the canteen cashier had a day off and my sister covered for her. My sister had worked as a cashier in Tarnów for a big Polish company, so the canteen work was a piece of cake for her. The Russian woman worked slowly and often made mistakes. My sister got through the work quickly. Around that time the chief of the *lesprotarg*[97] came to [visit] and seeing my sister at work, decided that she would stay at the register for good—and this way my sister got a decent job. It was the same job she'd performed at home, and much easier too. One of her duties was to work out how much bread everyone was to get with their meal. A large portion of white bread cost fifty-seven kopecks, black—thirty kopecks, and the same for groats.

To avoid overcrowding, lunches were split across three groups and everyone had their set hour. The workers in the forest ate lunch at twelve, others at different times. Not only was [my sister's] work easy, she was also able to help us. When [her] husband returned from work, she would sneak him the best pieces of meat and soup and various treats. She brought sugar, white bread, and rusks home, and bought products from the cooks. From one cook, a drunk, she would buy white flour, eggs, and meat. My husband, on the other hand, did not

96. *Progul* [Polish: *progul*]: Russian term for lateness or absence at work. See glossary.

97. *Lesprotarg*: a state enterprise for timber trade. See glossary.

fare well despite the fact that he was virtually the only one in the labor camp who knew written and spoken Russian, and wrote letters and telegrams for everyone. A lawyer by trade, he would always find a way to write letters in code and find the right [arguments] for the applications written to the commandant or the central authorities. People would gather in our apartment after work, also because it was nicer to spend the time there than in the barracks rooms. The commandant did not like these gatherings that took place in front of his house. However, he didn't dare say anything. In the letters that went through his censorship process, and in the applications, he recognized my husband's handwriting. He looked for a way to put a stop to the matter. At that time, the quota percentages among the well-to-do people who received parcels from home, or bought food with secret money, began to fall. Work was approached reluctantly and carelessly. [Those people] didn't care about their earnings—to the poor, however, despite their having no strength, a fifteen-ruble monthly payment meant a lot. They would sell the shirt off their back for milk and meat.

Overall, the work results in our camp were lamentable and the commandant began to suspect that my husband was convincing people to sabotage the work during the meetings at our apartment. He started to bully [my husband:] he would send him out for the hardest work, to the most faraway places—in rain, mud, frost, and snowstorms. At –55°C [–67°F] he ordered him to remain in the forest for ten hours. My husband got used to that work and performed it skillfully—then, the commandant moved him to a different one. He took his revenge so far that he took away [my] sister's cashier job and sent her to the forest. He also began to pick on me personally and all of us began to feel like hunted animals at home.

The Sabotage Charge

One day, [my] husband got injured at work. He was bedridden for some time [and] was then given easier work. Suddenly, the NKVD summoned him. He was told to sign a statement. He demanded to read it first. "Do you not believe the NKVD?" "I do, but I want to read it." "In that case we'll send the statement off without a signature." "There's nothing I can do about that." A few days later my husband was summoned for an interrogation in Altynay. The judge asked what antics my husband had been engaging in in the *posiołek*. He replied [saying] he didn't know anything [about it]. He was shown the NKVD statement He had been accused of stirring the *posiołek* workers up to sabotage. He was accused of cutting his leg himself to get out of hard work. The judge believed my husband's explanations and told him that the trial would take place in Suchlar,[98] thirty-five kilometers from Altynay. My husband asked the judge to call the foreman as a witness, who would assess his fitness for work. At the trial, [my] husband repeated the same thing. The foreman was called [but] despite this, [my] husband was punished for *progul* by having his monthly earnings reduced by 25 percent for four months. The news of this lenient sentence caused great joy. The commandant took it as a slap in the face. At the time, there was a bookkeeper vacancy at the *lesozagotowka*[99] and my husband was the only one who could be recommended for that work. He earned 250 rubles per month. Then the commandant began to persecute me. As I mentioned, I hadn't registered for work at the beginning [as] I was taking care of the household. One day, when I was still in bed, Salomon, the pharmacist from Katowice entered my room. The pharmacist acted as a doctor in the *posiołek*. I grew embarrassed and said that I was unwell. Since only those with a temperature over 38°C [100.4°F] were exempt from work, he told me that I could be punished harshly, and that I was to register for work. When I complained about my throat, he added that he would need to report the case to the health commission. Should the commission decide that I'm simulating illness, I would be punished severely. I didn't know whether someone had sent the pharmacist on purpose, or whether he came of his own accord—and whether I should go in front of the commission. We didn't know what to do. In the meantime, the doctor arrived and I was called in for an examination. I complained of a sore throat. I was told to go to a hospital for an examination with a specialist. Thus I was released from work and waited until a group of us formed to go to the hospital for examination. In the meantime, winter came and there was no way of going into town. The commandant ordered me to go to work.

Russian-German War

Meanwhile, news had spread that the commandant had been mobilized for the army. Everyone rejoiced. The foremen breathed a sigh of relief. They became

---

98. Perhaps: Sukhoy Log.

99. *Lesozagotovka* (Russian): forest logging enterprise. See glossary.

gentler at work. No one had grasped that the commandant's mobilization was one of the signs of a forthcoming war. On 22 June we were working as normal, and no one was expecting any sensational news, when a Red Army officer arrived and said that war had broken out, and that all Russian deportees were mobilized. [Everyone descended] on the radio in the *posiołek*. When the message about the Amnesty arrived, everyone left work; only my husband continued to work. All deportee accounts had to be settled. [My husband] worked nights, knowing that people were waiting for their pay to be able to leave. The foremen promised higher pay and easier work, as well as contracts for further work. But no one wanted to stay. To tie oneself to the Bolsheviks with a contract is to become a slave. We had no money other than that earned by my husband and sister, which is why we couldn't set off. We received a letter from Salomon, the pharmacist at the Prawda kolkhoz. He advised [my] husband to accept the post of a bookkeeper at the kolkhoz.

Two weeks later, we accepted the pharmacist's advice and went to the kolkhoz. He hadn't lied. The Prawda kolkhoz was indeed a rich [one]. It was made up of four hundred people, nothing was lacking there, and we had everything we wanted. Immediately after our arrival, the kolkhoz management told my husband to take the products he required, and he came back home bringing white bread, cream, honey, and eggs. Our apartment consisted of a room and a kitchen. My husband worked as the head bookkeeper. All products leaving and entering the kolkhoz had to be logged by him. Naturally, it was impossible [for] him not to bring things home. Apart from the apartment, he received three hundred rubles per month. Despite [all] this, we were very sad. It seemed to us we were blocking our way home with our own hands. We reproached ourselves for not taking the chance to leave Russia. After seventeen days, to the astonishment of the kolkhoz members, we left [the kolkhoz]. We went to Tashkent. At the time, one could still get white bread and grapes in Tashkent. We had nowhere to spend the night. We spent five days in the station waiting room and went on to Bukhara.

Bukhara was full of refugees. There was nothing to eat. People slept in the streets and there was a typhus epidemic. One hundred and fifty people died daily. We slept on the floor during the six months we spent in Bukhara. We paid ninety rubles per month to a certain Jew for the right to sleep on the floor. At night, we waited in lines for bread and potatoes. We sold our clothes.

Anyone who was registered at the magistrate received four hundred grams [of bread] per day, but for that same piece of bread one paid fifty rubles on the black market. In Bukhara, my sister fell ill. We were worried about typhus, however, it turned out it wasn't typhus after all. Half of the people who had lived with us in the *posiołek* died of typhus. The son of Mrs. Berkelhammer, her seventeen-year-old only child, died after eight days of illness, and the sight of the lonely woman broke our hearts. When a branch of the Polish delegation was opened in Bukhara, [people] weren't allowed in the building for fear of typhus. Thousands of people waited outdoors for nights and days—dirty, ragged, and hungry—waiting to have their cases examined. Most supplicants didn't receive anything, and some of those who belonged to the delegation and mediated between it and the claimants—among them Jews—sold, at black market prices, what was intended for the poor. The Bukharan Jews are very poor. They themselves don't have anything to put on their backs and one couldn't count on their help. Our reserves were slowly running out and we were at risk of starving to death. I won't forget the day when the post office delivered a letter to us from [my] brother-in-law, the Polish officer. He wrote that he was free, was with the newly created Polish army, and was on his way to us. We couldn't contain our happiness. He arrived shortly afterward. My brother-in-law and my husband went to Guzar, where the Polish army was being formed, and we received a military family allowance. But we couldn't go to Guzar as we didn't have a *komandirovka*. It wasn't possible to be seen by the delegate. We waited for days in line in front of the delegation. Finally, thanks to the protections [afforded to us], we obtained this document. It had to be certified by the police. When we went to the police station, our certificate was torn up. Furious, we entered the delegation building. The delegate heard us out, gave us a different piece of paper, and told us to leave without getting a certification from the police. In Kogon we waited in front of the ticket office all day. Only the porter took pity on us and brought [us] the tickets. We went to Guzar. As the wives of Polish officers we received five hundred grams of bread per day and other products. Life went on as normal. After five months, along with the wives of all the officers, we went to Krasnovodsk and from there to Pahlevi.

Protocol 40

Testimony of **Chaim Dawid Cwiebel**, age sixteen, son of Jehoszua and Saba. Born in Kraków and resident there at 36 Dietl Street. Arrived in Palestine via Russia and Persia in February 1943.

One year before the war my parents moved to Rozwadów, where my grandfather, my mother's father, had died. We went to inherit [what he had left us]. There were seven of us at home: Fryda, age twenty-four, Szmuel, age twenty, Chaja, age nineteen, Icchak, age eighteen, Gołda, age seventeen, me, age fifteen, and [our] little twelve-year-old sister. My father was the owner of a haberdashery store and earned well. On Friday 1 September 1939, the station in Rozwadów was bombed. One wave of airplanes would arrive [as] another left. In the morning, a military train made up of eight carriages was bombed. The entire train was shattered into pieces; there were many killed and wounded. The bombardment lasted a whole week. On Thursday, airplanes approached from [all] four sides and bombed the city so much that all of the houses were burned down. It was said that in Stalowa Wola a German plane had been shot down. Dr. Tarłow, a lawyer by trade, became the defender of the COP;[100] he led the defense. Two days later a secret radio transmitter was found at the apartment of the main COP commandant. A few hours later he was hanged in the woods. They left the hanged man on the tree for a few days. A piece of paper was pinned to him: "This is how a spy dies." People talked about how lots of spies were found in Tarnobrzeg and in Sandomierz. Among those killed by the bombing were many civilians. On Sunday the Polish army began to evacuate towns. During the evacuation, Jewish shops were robbed. My paternal uncle, Benjamin Band, had all of [his] bicycles taken from a storehouse. When the plundering was over, a Jewish officer appeared and tried to establish order. Up until Thursday anarchy reigned. The bombardment stopped. On Thursday the Germans surrounded the railway but did not yet enter the city. Having heard about the Germans' approach, we escaped to the countryside, to Wisznica, where our relatives lived. Father did not want to spend Saturday

100. COP [Polish: Centralny Okręg Przemysłowy; English: Central Industrial District; CID]: the largest industrial investment in the interwar period, a grouping of arms industry factories. See glossary.

in the countryside, where there was no synagogue, and returned to the city on Friday. We found our apartment looted. The furniture had been broken into pieces, so we had to sleep on the floor. That same Friday the city was bombed once more. Among the victims was Jozéf Goldman from Janów Lubelski, a relative of ours, a refugee who had sought a safe place in Rozwadów. Order was kept by a police force made up of Jews and Poles. This lasted until Rosh Hashanah.[101]

Germans in Rozwadów

On the second day of Rosh Hashanah the Germans arrived in Rozwadów. First of all, they searched all the apartments and found a few hidden soldiers, whom they took prisoner. That same day the Gestapo issued a decree ordering all shops to be opened, and anyone who didn't open [their] shop would be sentenced to death. Immediately after the shops were opened, the German soldiers began to steal the goods. German officers burst into the clothing shop of Zysel Zylber and began to carry away ready-to-wear clothes. Having plundered the store, they told the owner to turn to Minister Beck, who would reimburse [him for] the losses.[102] An older German with a gun in his hand came to our apartment and asked: "Do you have underwear?" Father replied: "You'll get this underwear without a gun." The German grew visibly embarrassed and left, taking nothing. After some time, an announcement appeared on the walls in the city calling all Jews to gather in the main square at eight in the morning. When all the Jews had gathered, a body search was conducted on each, everything one had on them was taken away, they were all beaten and kicked out to the other side of the San River, to the Bolsheviks. Many Jews hid and didn't come to the square. We too were among them. We hid in the basement, where we spent two days. When things quietened down, we left our hiding place and set off on our way. Father intended to go to Łuków. On the way we changed direction and went toward Lwów. We walked down back roads, avoiding the main road where the Germans would beat the Jews they came across. Outside Tarnogród, airplanes flew over our heads and shot at fugitives. Three people

101. Rosh Hashanah: Jewish New Year. In 1939 the holiday fell on 14–15 September. See glossary.
102. Józef Beck: foreign minister of the Second Polish Republic in the years 1932–39.

from our group were killed. Hiding in the woods, we avoided death by the skin of our teeth.

We Sneak across the Border

Walking down [those] back roads, we arrived in Nowy Dzików, where there were Germans. We arrived in town at dawn. All day we hid in the woods for fear of the Germans. At sunset we went toward a small bridge that served as the Soviet border. On the bridge we came upon two Bolshevik guards with dogs. We begged them to let us across the border, explaining that we could not go back because the Germans would kill us. Only when they received two gold watches did they leave their posts. In a group of forty we went over to the Soviet side. From there, after a few kilometers' journey, we got to Rawa Ruska. We spent two days in that town. It was full of refugees; one couldn't find a place to spend the night. The pavements were blocked by people and boxes. Every two hours freight trains would come and take refugees to Lwów. We arrived in Lwów on one of those trains. After arriving in Lwów, seeing that we wouldn't find an apartment in the city full of refugees from all of Poland, we decided to move to Szczerzec, where Father's sister lived. We arrived there in the evening. [My] aunt was very happy when we arrived, as she didn't think she would see us alive. We rented an apartment and settled in the small town. Thanks to the help of [my] uncle Jankiel Adel, who was the president of the local borough, my father managed to make the acquaintance of a baker, Sinowidzki, who supplied bread for the army, and used this acquaintance to gain responsibility for delivering wood to the bakery.

I and my older brother took up trading. We traded vodka, almonds, and other products, which we'd transport from Lwów into town and the other way round. One day we were caught in Lwów while transporting 120 liters of vodka on a tram. We didn't want to reveal where we had gotten the vodka. The tram was stopped and we were taken to the police station, but I escaped on the way. My brother was kept in jail until midnight. I ran off to an acquaintance, Benjamin Filer, who supplied our goods. He went to the NKVD where he knew a Russian Jew, and with him to the police. There he received a check for the vodka for the sum of two hundred rubles. [My] brother was released. It wasn't easy to trade in Lwów. The slightest offense was punishable by a harsh prison term. An acquaintance of ours, Josel Kieszenbojm from Rozwadów, was sentenced to five years in prison because he'd had a dollar found on him. Another acquaintance, whose name I don't remember, also got five years in jail for selling matches. Despite this, we continued to trade because it was difficult to support ourselves with only Father's earnings. This lasted until June of the year 1940.

Passportization and Registration

At that time a decree was issued that everyone was to apply for a Soviet passport. Bureaus were opened, too, where one could register to return home, to the Germans. Since Grandfather's assets were located in Rozwadów, we decided to register. On Friday 1 June 1940, Father brought a wagon of timber into town. After the freight car was unloaded, NKVD agents appeared and told us—the kids who were helping with the loading—to clean it. We didn't understand what that meant, but after a few hours [we] understood who we were cleaning the car for. At midnight two policemen arrived at our apartment. [My] father and brother hid in the loft. The policemen, guns in their hands, told us to bring [our] things and come with them. We said that [my] father and brother were in Stryj. [My] father and brother, seeing what was happening, left their hiding place, as they didn't want to become separated from us. The policemen flew into a rage, forbade us from bringing our belongings, and rushed us to the station. They loaded us into the freight car that we ourselves had been cleaning in the morning. Father managed at the last moment to convince the guards to let him take [some] things. The carriage was sealed and we were driven to Stryj under convoy. We waited at the Stryj station for two days. Other carriages were attached to ours. There were seventy of us. It felt terribly stuffy when we set off on the remainder of the journey. We went toward Lwów and Kiev. In Kiev we waited at the station for a few hours. At the station, Ukrainian Jews sold us white challahs they had brought in under their clothes. Then we traveled through Ufa, Omsk, Novosibirsk, and Tomsk, all the way to Asina.[103]

In our carriage there were two bunks for thirty people; the others lay on the floor on top of one another. At stations we were let out, under convoy, to use the toilet. In Asina we got out of the car. We were accommodated in

103. Here and henceforth an erroneous inflection of the town name Asino.

barracks, a hundred people in each, and the next day we were split into groups and sent to work. [My] two older brothers worked in the local sawmills for eight hours a day, where they earned thirty kopecks each. [My] father, who was over sixty, was exempted from work. And we, as small children, did not work either. [My] sister Chaja, a corset maker by trade, got a job in her trade. She worked for the wives of officials, engineers, and other important people. Thanks to the fact she had brought a suitcase with accessories with her, she could fulfill orders. We lived in Asina for six weeks. Sleeping at night was out of the question. The barracks were infested with bedbugs, and outside it was freezing. We decided to go on strike until we are moved to different barracks. A few NKVD-ers turned up, an investigation was organized, and a few people were arrested as the ringleaders of the strike. Then we were split up and sent off to *posiołki*.

In the *Posiołek*

We were sent to the Dak *posiołek* and put ten to a "room," that is, the barracks was divided into segments with [hanging] sheets. In the *posiołek* we had iron beds and small boards instead of mattresses that were surprisingly comfortable to sleep on. [My] two older brothers worked in a nail factory located in a small town of Revda. At first they made between seventy and eighty rubles per month, then, as Stakhanovites, they got to between two and three hundred rubles monthly.[104] [My] father and mother did not go to work. Chaja continued to work in her trade. We bought meals from the local shops. We got bread, without restrictions, for one ruble per kilo. I chopped wood for the commandant of the *posiołek*, and for my own needs. Close to Revda a new city was being built—Sotsgorod, where there were fully modern homes intended for high officials. Polish and Russian deportees were hired for the building work. In our *posiołek* there were five hundred Jews and one Pole. Of the Jews I remember: Baruch Wajnman with [his] wife from Rozwadów, Szloma Gusbojm from Krasna, Mansztajn, Haber, and Feidt.

The *posiołek* was located on one side of a railway track, on the other side there was a settlement for exiled Bolsheviks. The Russian deportees had settled

104. Stakhanovite [Polish: *Stachanowiec*]: a productive, diligent worker, from the name of A.G. Stakhanov (Stachanow), initiator of the work competition movement in the USSR. See glossary.

there for good, had their own homes, cows, and poultry, but lived in great poverty. In [one of their] rooms there was nothing but a bed [and] a table knocked together from planks of wood. They wore old, padded jackets, rotted through from the rain. Only after the arrival of the Polish refugees did they equip themselves with clothes they bought in exchange for food products. They weren't allowed to have any relations with us and were terribly scared of [having a] conversation. With me, a child, they let themselves get into longer talks. They asked me if it was true that in Poland all people are well dressed and that there is a wardrobe in every house where various clothing is hung. In Sotsgorod a big three-story building for a hospital was being finished. Two weeks before the outbreak of the Russian-German war, I fell ill with malaria. I was taken to the hospital, where I stayed for two weeks.

Yom Kippur in the *Posiołek*

I was treated well at the hospital [and] left fully recovered. I will never forget the Day of Atonement holiday in the *posiołek*. We decided not to work. Naturally, we didn't inform anyone about this, knowing ahead of time that we would not be excused from work. On the morning of Yom Kippur [12 October 1940] none of us moved [to go to work]. We decided to gather for communal prayer. The commandant came and asked why we weren't going to work. When we told him that we were observing the Day of Atonement that day, [he] grew very angry. He returned half an hour later in the company of a few NKVD agents, to whom one Maniek Ajmer from Rozwadów explained, in Russian, the meaning of that holiday. After conferring together they told us that there were no holidays in Russia, only working days. If we didn't want to work, they would consider us to be sabotaging work and sentence us to jail time. Our representative replied that we were prepared to bear any sacrifices, but that we weren't going to work. After a short while Maniek Ajmer and some other people, thought to be the organizers, were arrested. They were taken to Sverdlovsk, where they spent three months. After returning from the Sverdlovsk prison they told us there was a rabbi from Sverdlovsk there, who had been sentenced to death by the Bolsheviks. During the interrogation they subjected him to horrendous torture, trying to extract statements on where other rabbis and shochets were in Russia. But the rabbi did not turn anyone in.

The Outbreak of War and the Amnesty

A few days later, when the Russian-German war broke out, the commandant summoned us to a meeting, where we were told we had to work and fight for the common cause. But the amount of work did not decrease and we began to feel the shortage of bread. The local shops were immediately emptied of all food products. In October, a taxi arrived in our *posiołek*. A Polish and a Russian officer got out of [it]. We were informed about the Amnesty and allowed to go anywhere we liked as long as we avoided big cities. We went to Chalkovo, where we could find neither bread nor a place to spend the night. We set off for Tashkent. Tashkent was full of refugees, and they didn't want to let us into the city. We stayed in the station nights and days and went to Bukhara after some time. They didn't want to let us into Bukhara either. Only when [my] brothers got jobs in a brick factory did we gain the right to stay in the city. Thanks to [my] brothers we could also buy four hundred grams of bread per person. Since [my] brothers' earnings weren't sufficient, [my] sister began to work in her trade again, and I took up trading. I traded tea, makhorka, bread, and almonds. I bought these products from the local shop. I made friends with the manager of a cooperative who let me have two kilos of bread, one hundred grams of tea, and a box of almonds per day. A packet of tea I had paid fifty rubles for I would sell for sixty rubles; for bread I asked double. One day I was caught in the street by policemen when [I was] carrying a packet of almonds. As I was being examined, the policemen ate all my almonds. Then I was taken by the scruff of my neck and thrown out. Seeing that I was under observation I decided to give up street trading. Instead, customers would come to my home. We were earning more by then and decided to rent a room. It was a simple stable for which we paid one hundred rubles in rent. From the Polish delegation in Bukhara we received two hundred rubles per month for the whole family, as well as half a kilo of flour for each person per month. Clothes we did not receive. The Poles got clothes and underwear. At the delegation there were also Jews working, among them Szlomo Bester from Kraków. In Bukhara there also was a rabbi from Trzebinia, Weisenfeld,[105] one of the most prominent

105. Dow Berysz, son of Jakub, Wajdenfeld (1881–1965): rabbi of Trzebinia from 1923 until the war. Founder of the Kochaw Mi Yaakow yeshiva. Escaped to Lwów at the outbreak of war; deported to Siberia; left for Palestine in 1946.

gaons[106] in Poland. We recited daily prayers together in his apartment. Rabbi Kaner from Kraków was there also.

After Easter, my twenty-one-year-old cousin, Eliezer Cwiebel,[107] fell ill with dysentery. He died in the hospital a few days later. A month later, Mother fell ill and died in the hospital two weeks later. After Mother's death, my brother Icchak fell ill and also died in the hospital. We buried [my] mother and cousin in the Jewish cemetery in Bukhara. But where [my] brother is buried I do not know. Initially, Father fell ill with dysentery too. At first we didn't want to send him to the hospital, but seeing the danger of the situation, we decided to send him there. He died after a few days and we don't know where he's buried, as the hospital did not release the body. After Father's death I was admitted to a Polish orphanage. [My] other brothers and sisters did not want to be separated from one another. The youngest sister, [a] deaf-mute, was accepted into a shelter by the Bolsheviks. After a month's stay in the orphanage, thirty of us children were sent to Ashgabat. One of the boys got drunk and engaged in such outrageous antics that the commandant of the orphanage, a Polish officer—Koenig—said that because of [that boy], the whole group would not go to Persia. Only when our arrival was ordered from Persia were we sent abroad—without papers, which an officer had to return for. In Mashhad, on the Persian side, they took in all of the Polish children and told the Jewish ones that they would send them back to Russia. We were completely distraught and cried bitterly, [but then] an officer, a Polish Jew, came and comforted us, reassuring us we would go to Tehran. I arrived in Tehran in September. I was taken into a Jewish orphanage. I spent seven months there. Lessons took place once a week. We weren't allowed in the city. We weren't given clothes either. Only on the eve of our departure were we dressed and sent to the station. I came to Palestine in February via India.

---

106. Gaon: title bestowed upon rabbis of excellence known for [their] authority and learnedness. See glossary.

107. A different spelling of the surname has been preserved here to match the original [source].

Protocol 41

Testimony of **Chawa Kestenbojm**, age forty, from Lwów. Wife of engineer Kestenbojm, a lieutenant in the Polish army. Arrived in Palestine with two children, ten-year-old Arie and seven-year-old Sulamit, via Tehran, in 1943.

A few days before the outbreak of war, in August 1939, my husband, as a lieutenant in the Polish army, was mobilized. Later, when some of the Polish army crossed the Hungarian border, my husband got to Hungary and was interned there. He is in an internment camp in Hungary to this day. On Friday 1 September Lwów was bombed for the first time. The townspeople were so convinced that they were anti-aircraft exercises that no one took cover in shelters and my neighbor, Salka Wiszniak, [even] stood on the balcony and watched the airplanes. She was hit in the head by a bullet shard and died a few hours later. Only after some time did we realize that [we've been visited] by German airplanes. The bombardment lasted a few days. Seeing that it was becoming stronger by the day, I went, on 9 September [and] on almost the last train leaving Lwów, to Podwołoczyska, a small town located on the Soviet-Polish border where my mother and sisters lived.

In Podwołoczyska

After arriving in Podwołoczyska I had a lot of trouble registering because the local authorities explained it was a town located in a borderland area. In vain did I explain that I was a wife of a Polish officer who was at the front, and a daughter of Podwołoczyska citizens. It didn't help at all. The chairman of the county board told me to leave town immediately. After returning home I suffered a gallstone attack and it was out of the question for me to leave. Meanwhile, the Soviet army crossed the border and took Podwołoczyska on 17 [September 1939]. Before the army's entry the town was shot at from all sides. Everyone thought that it was the Germans shooting, and that the Polish army, in town at the time, was moving toward the Soviet border. Only the first Russian tanks put this misunderstanding to bed.

Bolsheviks in Town

The Bolsheviks treated the people in town very politely. The shops were slowly opening, the town took on a normal appearance. After a few days, however, searches, arrests, and nationalizations began. Everything was nationalized: homes, factories, shops. My mother had her home taken away, my sister—a sawmill. They began to throw the former bourgeoisie out of [their] apartments and requisition [those], without offering any [others] in exchange. Poles and Jews began to slowly leave town, and I, too, decided to return to Lwów.

In Lwów

At the end of October 1939 I returned to Lwów. My five-bedroom apartment had already been requisitioned, taken by the Bolsheviks. In one room lived my brother, Józef Grynhalt from Kielce, who had come to Lwów during my absence and settled in [the] apartment. After long efforts I managed to get the apartment back. With nothing to live on, I sublet the apartment to refugees, living in one of the rooms myself. My husband had been the co-owner of the company Fizan, a sausage factory, and the owner of the Delfinger i Sp.[108] depot, as well as the co-owner of many other factories. After the nationalization of those firms, I was left with no means of making a living. I sold various items in the house to have money for bread for my children.

Elections and Sovietization

In January 1940, elections to the Ukrainian Soviet and passportization took place.[109] Assemblies took place in every house, urging people to take part in the elections and accept [Soviet] passports. These meetings took place in my apartment, as it was the biggest one in the building. In these meetings, the speakers would stress that we were Soviet citizens. Despite [this] mad propagandizing, many people boycotted the elections and didn't want to exchange [their] passports. Meanwhile, registration offices for those who wanted to return to the German-occupied lands were opened. Thousands of Jews and Poles registered, [then] were arrested sometime later. Some of the Poles were released, but all of the Jews were sent to Siberia. At the end of February 1940,

108. i Sp.: i Spółka, a type of legal entity (& Co.).

109. The elections to the Ukrainian People's Assembly took place not in January 1940 but on 22 October 1939.

I was summoned to the NKVD and asked where my husband was. Since I received letters from [my] husband, I replied that he was a Polish officer and that he was in an internment camp in Hungary. They also asked me who lived in my apartment. Some instinct told me to keep secret the names of my flatmates, and I replied that I lived alone.

Deportation

On the night of 12 April there was a knock on the door. Four agents with handguns burst into the apartment. Everyone present was ordered to stand still with their arms raised. A detailed search was carried out and some plans were found in between the papers. "These are war plans," they cried. In vain did I [try to] explain to them that my husband was an engineer and the plans are a part of his work. They concluded that they'd found important documents, told us to get dressed and bring a few small things with us, and told us they were planning to take us out of Lwów to a different city. They took no account of the fact I had a 40°C [104°F] fever and my doctor neighbor had said I was not to leave my bed. In vain did I ask that the children be left at home. We were led, twenty-nine of us, into a freight car. The car was sealed. After twenty-four hours we started off in an unknown direction.

In the Carriage

There were two bunks inside the car, one above the other, where sixteen people slept—the rest had to stand between the bunks. During the journey we were let out of the car three times. A hole in the carriage floor served as a toilet. The passengers in our carriage were almost exclusively women and children, families of soldiers. We traveled for eighteen days toward Lwów, Kiev, Tashkent. Upon arriving in Tashkent, however, they didn't want to allow us into the city, [so] we went to Kazakhstan, to Alma-Ata. We weren't allowed to disembark there either, so we went to Ayagoz in the Semipalatinsk Oblast. It was the last train station [on the line]. We got out of the freight cars and [were] driven off in different directions on trucks. I was sent to Farm Number 3, 150 kilometers from the train station—a farm known as Tikibulak. We arrived on 1 May. The settlement was covered in flags. We were led to a May Day assembly. We were spoken to beautifully in a language we didn't understand. The speakers were Mongols.

At the Farm

In the settlement there were three barracks with no windows, no doors, and no floors. We lived thirty people to a room. After three days of rest we were summoned to work. The work consisted of grazing cattle [and] bringing in barrels of water from the river located a few kilometers from the farm. We, however, were not allowed to use that water, which was brought in exclusively for the livestock. We received a flask of water per day and suffered with thirst. We were also used for agricultural labor—weeding gardens, etc. We worked from seven in the morning until eight in the evening, and sometimes would even be woken up at four in the morning and rushed to work. Our warden, Alzajew, was very strict. The savage Kazakh treated us brutally. We didn't get money for the work. We received a few grams of bread daily and soup. Those working in the haying brigades [and some others] were fed better. The parcels I received from my family in Lwów, as well as trading of the odds and ends I had with me, kept me alive. With money, one could get flour, potatoes, and milk at the neighboring farm. At first a pood[110] of flour cost forty rubles, later its price jumped up to 350 rubles. I baked flatbreads myself with [this] flour over the flames. When there was no firewood I also baked the cakes in the sun. Sometimes, a Kazakh woman would bake me some bread in exchange for some [old] rag. The Kazakhs lived in clay huts without doors or windows. Holes in the clay served as front doors. In summer, after the haying, the Kazakhs, along with [their] families and livestock, set off for the steppe. They lived there in tents until winter came. During high heat, when the Kazakhs sought to cool down on the steppe, we stayed behind in the clay huts, and since there was no work, busied ourselves with preparing firewood for the winter. We gave away the better pieces of wood to our landlords, with the scraps left over to us.

A cattle disease called *bruculas* [brucellosis] was widespread in the area. It meant the cattle were rotting alive. Among the people, syphilis was widespread. Most of the Kazakhs were syphilitics. Among the refugees there was a dysentery epidemic. There was no doctor in the area. The doctor who would sometimes come from the hospital located twenty-five kilometers away knew little about this disease. One day I was so weakened from the dysentery that

110. Weight unit introduced in the Russian Empire in 1835, still used in the 1930s as a grain measuring unit; equal to approximately 16.38 kilograms.

I couldn't go to work. This was during the sheepshearing time. The warden asked me why I wasn't going to work. When I told him I was sick I was sentenced to twenty-five lashes. The warden himself carried out the punishment. He beat me over the back with a stick. I lost consciousness after the first strikes. After a few days a health commission arrived, to whom I complained about the bad state of [my] health. I was sent to the city of Urzhar to another commission, which exempted me from work and gave me an appropriate certificate.

I Become the Farm Doctor

Since I was left without a job and had many medical supplies that had been sent to me in parcels from Lwów, and because I knew the rules of administering first aid, I became, as it were, the doctor to the suffering refugees. At first, out of envy, I was threatened with being reported for illegally treating the sick, but after digestive problems and dysentery began to spread, [my position] was accepted, and the doctor who came from the city—after I taught him to use percussion on an ill person and examine him—started to take me with him to medical council meetings. Officially recognized as a *medrabotnik* [health care worker], I now received bread and water which I didn't have to carry myself. On 17 June 1941 I had a serious gallstone and kidney attack. I went to the NKVD and asked them to let me live in the city as I needed medical care. I went to the city with [my] children, where for forty rubles per month I rented a clay hut without doors and windows. I lived off selling things. One could get everything for undergarments and bed linen, which were in short supply in the area.

The Outbreak of War

On 22 June posters were put up in the city exhorting people to work harder and to make sacrifices for the good of the homeland under threat. The situation at the farm, where I went every day as a *medrabotnik*, worsened considerably. The Kazakhs lost their trust in the refugees, won over with such difficulty. They treated them like enemies. At the farm lived 120 Polish families and four Jewish ones. Only after the announcement of the Amnesty did our situation improve markedly. A few days later, NKVD agents arrived at the farm, ordered everyone to hand over the Russian passports valid for five years, and gave us pieces of paper with certifications allowing us to travel across all of Russia.

Not knowing where to go, I decided to stay put. Others decided the same. The work got easier. The warden did not wake us when he wished. One worked eight hours per day; the sick were released from work; we were given freedom of movement. This lasted until January 1942.

Off and Away

On 2 January, along with Mrs. Finkel from Lwów, wife of a Polish officer, I went on foot to Ajasir, where the train station was located.[111] We stopped there to find out where the Polish headquarters were, because [text missing] worked there. On 2 April we found out that Mrs. Finkel's husband was in Uzbekistan. We set off on our way to [see] him. The Poles welcomed us cordially. We were given bread, soup, and a place to stay the night. The wives of the men who did not serve in the army were helped by the Polish delegation, which provided them with clothing, flour, and rice. A kitchen was opened for the poorest. The military wives received help from the army. At first they didn't want to grant me an allowance; later I received 250 rubles per month. I could not get anything with this money since a pood of flour cost one thousand rubles.

First Transports

When the first Polish army transports to Persia began to depart, I started making efforts to join one. I was promised that I would leave with the first transport. Then I was told that the NKVD were not letting Jews go. I sought protections. The military families who had been with me at the farm submitted a statement that, were it not for my medical assistance, they would have died from lack of care, but that didn't help. A certificate confirming that I came from Kraków rather than Lwów, which the Bolsheviks had no issue with, did not help either. I went to Dr. Stiel from Lwów, whose husband[112] had died along with ten thousand Polish officers in Smolensk, and who was obligated to me. I went with her to General Szyszko-Bohusz, who solemnly swore that I would leave with the first transport. I was convinced that this promise would be fulfilled. But Captain Raczkowski, the guardian of the military families,

111. Likely refers to Aysary in Kazakhstan.

112. There is no person of this surname on the list of Katyń victims. It's possible [the author is referring to] a person with the surname Stein: Reserve Lieutenant Leon Stein (1895–1942) indeed died in Katyń.

said that he would not sacrifice his twenty-year military career to save Jews. Everywhere I was advised to get baptized. With no other solution, I went to Major Trzeski,[113] a priest, who issued baptism certificates to many Jews and saved more than one this way. I told him that I did not want to be baptized as I was ill and weak, afraid of death, and wanted to die as Jewish woman. He gave me an officer's word that he would do everything to get the children and me out of Russia. Half an hour before the departure of the transport, the aforementioned Father Trzeski came to my apartment and told me to come with him to the station. This way I got to Tehran. In Tehran, in camp number 2, no difference was made between Poles and Jews. I fell ill and stayed in a hospital for two months. On 16 January I left Persia for Palestine.

113. Refers to Father Włodzimierz Cieński from Lwów, chaplain of the Polish army in the USSR.

Protocol 43

Testimony of **Adela Weinling**, born in Kraków, age twenty-eight, graduate of the Faculty of Philosophy of the Kraków University. Arrived in Palestine in February 1943 from Russia via Tehran.

In the summer of 1939, my married sister lived in a summer resort outside Lublin. I intended to go to [see] her and had even sent my things ahead already. Immediately after the outbreak of war I went to my sister to bring her home from there. Everyone thought it was safer [around] Lublin than in Kraków and encouraged me to go to Kraków [to] bring in [my] parents. Thus during the outbreak of the war, I was traveling between Lublin and Kraków, until one day I got stuck in Zamość.

Germans in Zamość

On 13 September the Germans entered Zamość. It was on a Friday,[114] before the holiday of Rosh Hashanah [14–15 September 1939]. The Jews were praying in the synagogue, as is usual during holidays, and the Germans did not prevent them from carrying out prayers. [They were] an Austrian group. They were even nice to women. When they bothered a woman they would ask if she was married, and if she was, would not bother her anymore. An Austrian officer, accommodated in the same apartment as I was, insisted that I accept a hundred cigarettes from him, which by then were difficult to obtain in Zamość. When we talked of the Nazi cruelties out loud, he said, war will be war. One could gather that he himself wasn't a great supporter of Hitler. Life in the city carried on normally. There were no robberies or assaults. Shops were open [and] peasants came to town to do [their] shopping. In the city only a few arrests were carried out, and it sometimes happened that the soldiers would bother Jews. After two weeks, other German units and people from the Gestapo arrived.[115] Everything in town changed. The soldiers robbed the Jewish shops of anything they could and broke into apartments by force. At night there were screams, during the day Jews were grabbed [to be sent for] forced labor during which

114. 13 September 1939 fell on a Wednesday rather than Friday.

115. The author is likely referring to the Einsatzgruppen, the German paramilitary death squads.

people were beaten so badly that no Jews dared show themselves on the streets anymore.

This didn't last long as the Bolsheviks entered Zamość. The Bolsheviks' entry seemed like salvation to the tortured Jews. Shops opened up again in town, the Russian soldiers bought everything, and incredible sums were paid for watches. The fate of my parents in Kraków kept me awake. I went to Rawa Ruska, which was also under Russian occupation at the time. There, the Russian soldiers behaved differently than in Zamość. They took a watch from my friend in the street. I complained at the Bolshevik commandant's headquarters. At the headquarters I was told to wait in the courtyard under a tree. They advised that I sneak out so that I would not be accidentally hit by a stray bullet. I listened to this good advice and did not wait for the return of the watch. I was arrested outside Rawa Ruska when crossing the border. Instead of Kraków, I went to Lwów after [my] release and stayed there for ten months.

In Lwów

During the plebiscite people were afraid to not vote. It was [well] known that the consequences would be felt by everyone. [The authorities] knew how to deal with inconvenient people. In May [1940] the Bolsheviks opened bureaus to register people who wanted to return to the German-occupied lands. Despite the fact that I really wanted to be with [my] parents, I could not bring myself to return to the Germans. Neither did I want to accept Soviet citizenship. It was difficult to decide which was worse. Meanwhile, my sister and brother-in-law from around Lublin also came to Lwów. Life became easier. We lived together, received letters with fairly encouraging [news], and unable to take a decisive step, missed the registration deadline. Therefore I didn't have Russian citizenship and wasn't registered for a return home. A few weeks went by like this. One day two policemen stopped me in the street and asked me for documents. Since I didn't have any documents, they wanted to take me to the police station, but I refused. I knew that, as a single person, [I would be sent] into the depths of Russia. Arguing with them, I reached my home and ran into the apartment. The policemen followed. My brother-in-law came to my defense, and they went away. I don't know if it was them who sent the NKVD agents to us. The fact was that, in the afternoon, an officer arrived in the company of a few soldiers. The officer was very polite. He [tried to] convince me to accept Russian citizenship and left me in the house. I understood that although I saved myself from danger twice, I wouldn't manage it anymore. At night, Bolshevik soldiers arrived at the house, told us all to get dressed and pack our things and took us to the station. We were put inside freight cars. This was on 22 July. It was extremely hot. Eighty people were placed in one carriage. There were many children. People fought for spaces. [They] were dirty, sometimes [wearing] ragged [clothes]. It was possible to take a chance and flee. The guards let [us] off the cars at fixed times to relieve ourselves and [to go] to the buffet. We had nowhere to hide in Lwów and that's why we stayed put. We tried to disinfect the carriage. We poured *lizol* [disinfectant] over it, but the disinfection did not make the dirt disappear. In our car there traveled a paralyzed woman, who not only needed to be attended to, but who couldn't by any means move from [her] spot. It was a pity to see how she suffered. The Orthodox Jews recited prayers in the carriage. Later, when in the neighboring car a woman died of pneumonia, prayers for the dead were said in ours. It was so stuffy and so cramped one could lose one's mind. Arms and legs grew weak. One's head spun. The clamor was such that we couldn't hear one another. We didn't get anything to eat for thirty-six hours. The scariest, however, was the thought of the journey to Siberia.

Deportation

The carriage started only the following night. After ten days' journey we arrived at the Volga River. We were taken to the port on trucks and boarded a ship. We traveled for eight or ten hours. On the riverbank sawmills worked busily. We were set ashore in an area where, apart from the forest and the water, there was nothing. We continued ahead on a light train, in small open-air carriages. The sparks from the steam engine burned our clothes. The surroundings were charming: woodland, fields, and meadows around, a forest on the horizon, tempting with [the promise of] coolness. At dusk, mosquitos started to bite us mercilessly. Children cried in pain, and the further [we went], the more mud and mosquitos [there were]. Anxiety crept in. We didn't know how to deal with the wicked insects. Suddenly, the train [stopped] and we [were] given the order to get off. We'd gone past those beautiful surroundings yet had to settle in a swamp. Who gave that sadistic order and what [had we done to] deserve being eaten alive by mosquitos? We began to protest. We wouldn't move from our spots. Children wailed loudly and [their] cries confirmed our conviction about the justness of our rebellion. The policemen didn't know what was going on, or were themselves perhaps moved by our lot, and stayed quiet. Night fell; it got cool. The forest grew scary. We didn't move. Was this the last station of the light railway? We didn't know. We sat down like stones, only the children crying. I don't know how long it lasted. For a second time there sounded the order: "Get off." Some fell to the policemen's feet begging not to be left behind but the policemen were helpless. An order is an order.

The crowd began to revolt. Outraged voices rose up. It seemed as if the rebels might break the train apart at any moment. Suddenly, the policemen started to throw [our] boxes out of the carriages. An outcry spilled out. Women sobbed and threw themselves on the policemen but they, oblivious to everything, [continued to] throw the luggage into the mud. People ran after their things, collecting valuable belongings in the dark. The fear of losing what one had overcame everyone, and [people began to jump] off the cars into the mud. The policemen walked us to the forest where there stood ten barracks. They helped us carry [our] things, and as if wanting to apologize, sent us to a canteen for a meal. We were given hot soup, grouts, fish, *kompot*,[116] and sweet tea. There were three hundred of us. Everyone got a bed to sleep in after eating. Four people stayed in one room. Without even looking around to see who our neighbors were, we threw ourselves on the beds. The night was horrendous: we were tormented by vicious mosquitos, vicious bedbugs, and vicious mice. One couldn't get rid of them. Tired to the point of exhaustion, we couldn't sleep a wink. Before, we had still believed we could make it in this forest somehow, but then we understood that it was impossible.

After five days of rest the commandant of the *posiołek* split us into two groups: a female one and a male one. The commandant himself took us to work in the forest. Those in charge of us consisted of: the NKVD commandant, two policemen, one warden, and two foremen. All of them went to the woods with us and showed us what each of us was to do. We wrapped our faces and hands in rags so we wouldn't get bitten by mosquitos. A mosquito bite caused ulcers and unbearable pain. We worked without respite. Our hands swelled even though we didn't achieve much. After work we were cramped and

116. A sweet beverage made by boiling fruit in water, sometimes with sugar or raisins as sweetener.

stiff. We had to put up not only with the hard work, but also with the snitching of one Polish girl, a servant, who would constantly accuse us of sabotage and contemptuously refer to us as "intellectuals." Many of us fell ill. But only those whose temperature was higher than 38°C [100.4°F] were released from work. If it wasn't for the fact that we received food parcels from my father in Kraków, we would not have lasted a month there. We received money from acquaintances in Lwów, the bread was cheap, makhorka plentiful, and somehow we managed to get by. It was worse when winter came. We didn't have warm clothing. The temperatures reached –65°C [–85°F], at –45°C [–49°F] we had to work. There existed special types of winter labor. I, for instance, worked digging up moss from under the snow that reached up to my ankles. I would return from work frozen stiff from the cold. However, we felt better in the winter than in the summer. In the winter it was warm in the barracks, we would visit one another and talk, whereas in the summer the mosquito scourge would not let us be. People fell ill a lot in our labor camp. *Cynga* in particular was widespread. Teeth would fall out, limbs fall off—we lacked vitamin C and couldn't get it from anywhere. It was impossible to get something as basic as camphor, and many died because they couldn't be given a camphor injection. Death in the camp was awful, and more awful still to those who knew that the person could [have been] saved with simple remedies. Two children died in our labor camp of angina, also because of the lack of medicine. We wrote to the NKVD headquarters [and] a commission was sent to us, but nothing beyond that. There were plenty of informants among us, [so that] one had to weigh each word.

Observant Jews were afraid to pray. Celebrating Pesach was banned and we had to work on Yom Kippur. The pious ones prayed in the woods. As a result of denunciations, they were taken to the [camp] court.[117] Every Sunday was our day off, we could walk around and pick berries in the forest. We were scared of going deep into the woods. One woman got lost and never came back. In winter there were wolves in the forest that would come near the kolkhoz.

The kolkhoz was poor. The peasants wanted to buy clothes from us but had nothing [to pay with]. They thought that they [would be able to] get

117. Prisoners were subject to the jurisdiction of special camp courts. In each camp operational divisions were organized to eliminate hostile activities carried out by prisoners within the camp.

our clothes in [any way they chose]. We were objects of awe to the peasants. Until then, they had not seen a European. Despite this I noticed an antipathy toward Jews. The word "Jew" is banned in the Soviet areas but the rural children would throw stones at us and use other insults. The peasants are pious. In every house above the stove there are icons and a cross. The older generation goes to Orthodox churches. The youth liked to talk with us but were afraid of [keeping in] contact because of a ban by the NKVD. Despite the fact that the country, the people and their customs were very interesting, we were so concerned with our situation that we couldn't think of anything other than ourselves. We boycotted the assemblies organized by the commandant, we didn't want to believe or hear about the better pay that was being promised us. Our only hope was the parcels from home.

German-Russian War

We found out about the outbreak of war straightaway. We thought that it would effect an improvement to our situation at once. We didn't wait long. Everyone was released. One could go where one wanted and settle where one wished. The commandant warned us of hunger and poverty and advised us to stay put. We didn't want to hear about staying in the camp and set off toward the warmer parts of the Soviet Union. We went by light rail, ship [and] train, lived in a station for two weeks, until we arrived in the Kazan area. The biggest scourge of the journey were thieves. They would steal boxes, clothing, everything they could get their hands on—you had only to look away from [your] things for one moment to find them gone. When [you were] buying tickets, it would transpire at the cashier's window that you'd had the money taken out of your bag. Women cried [and] ran to the NKVD to complain, and when there was nothing else to do, one would sell whatever one had with them to [be able to] travel onward. Trade flourished at stations. [Things were] sold and bought. The middlemen made loads and were ruthless when they saw someone selling the very clothes they were wearing. People sold [their belongings] to buy a piece of bread or a ticket. No one knew what pity toward [another] human meant; trading took place without scruples. On the road in Saratov we met Polish soldiers. They promised they would try to procure a ship for us for our onward journey. Indeed, a ship was delivered, but we sailed on it in absolutely hellish conditions. The crush and stale air were unbearable. Typhus claimed casualties daily. The people in charge tried to keep an order of sorts, [but] in vain. On the way we also had a basket with provisions stolen. The police were in cahoots with the thieves and deliberately pointed us toward false leads.

After some time we arrived in Kazan.[118] It seemed to us that it would be better to live closer to the border, where it was possible to get out of Russia more easily. But seeing that there was no hope of leaving, we went to Tashkent. We lived in a square close to the city [center?]. There we slept, cooked, and even washed [our] undergarments. Every day there were cases of illness and getting into a hospital was out of the question. Waiting one's turn in line for the hospital was itself a sure way of catching an illness. The hospital was so overfilled that the doctors didn't know what everyone was ill with. My brother-in-law was ill with pneumonia, and the doctors would treat him for typhus. In one square in Tashkent there lived Polish and Russian refugees, Jews, Ukrainians, and so on. Bread was impossible to get. We went to the kolkhoz Luczerski. It was an Uzbek kolkhoz. They treated refugees cruelly. They stole from [them], exploited them, bought everything [off them] for peanuts. We couldn't get work. Chronic starvation set in. After a few weeks' stay at the kolkhoz we went to Vrevskoye. There was a Polish outpost there and my brother-in-law signed up for the army. They didn't want to admit him, a Jew. We were certain we would remain in Russia forever. Among the military personnel I came upon the father of one of my students from Kraków. He tried to do everything he could so that we could leave. Every day we received a different message: [that] we were going, [that] we were not going. Once we were crossed off the list when we were ready to set off. One day, in the last moment before the train's departure, we were informed that we were going. All Jews were treated this way.

In Persia I fared well. I worked as a modiste [milliner] and earned excellent [wages]. All of us fell ill in Persia from overeating, as our bodies had gotten used to starvation. It took a long time for us to return to a normal state. With a group going to Palestine, we left too.

118. It follows from the testimony that this should refer to Kogon (Kagan) rather than Kazan.

Protocol 45

Testimony of **Edmund Finkler**, age thirty-nine, born and resident in Lwów. Officer in the Polish army, former legionary. Arrived in Palestine from Russia with his wife, Franciszka, age thirty, and daughter, Regina, age twelve, in August 1942 [February 1943].

On 27 August 1939 I was mobilized and assigned as an officer to the 40th regiment. I took part in the defense of Warsaw[119] and fell into German captivity on 29 September. I was sent to a prisoner of war camp in Kalwaria[120] by Żyrardów, camp number 1 for officers.

The attitude of the Germans toward Polish officers, of whom there were 630 in the camp, was not bad. We were fed twice a day, received two hundred grams of bread daily and fifty grams of margarine with each meal. It was a synthetic margarine made from coal and everyone fell ill with dysentery after eating it. Everyone was so weak they could barely stand up straight.

I Escape from the Camp

At two o'clock at night on 7 October, I and two of my friends, Lieutenant Bolski and Second Lieutenant Smirski, also from Lwów, crawled out on all fours from the barracks, and unseen by anyone, reached the fence. We dug underneath the fence, broke the wire, and got out of the camp. The Germans noticed our escape. Heavy gunfire began, first from rifles and then from machine guns. Miraculously, we avoided the bullets and escaped.

We got as far as Częstochowa. In the city, Jews were allowed to show themselves on the street only until seven in the evening. Thus, we spent the night in a field by the city. Only at dawn did I reach the city [and] found an engineer acquaintance who gave us civilian clothes and some money. We set off toward Kielce [and] Kraków. [All of us] avoided people. We hurried toward Przemyśl to reach the Soviet border, and from there go to Lwów, where my wife and child lived. At the border I was arrested and put in jail. My companions had

119. The siege of Warsaw began on 1 September 1939 and was fought between the Polish Warsaw army and the invading German army. During the siege, more than ten thousand citizens perished and more than fifty thousand were wounded before the lack of supplies forced a surrender on 28 September 1939.

120. Likely refers to Góra Kalwaria.

more luck and crossed the border easily. I was in jail with seventy-nine other people in one cell. There were women, children, elderly, and ill people there—all sentenced for illegal border crossing. Meanwhile, through the prison caretaker, I managed to send a letter to my lawyer, Karol Tauber, asking him to intervene in my case. After a short time I escaped from the prison.

Escape

My escape took place as follows: there was no kitchen in the prison. We received meals from a committee organized by Jews and Poles who sent in kettles of soup every day. One day a boy who brought the soup to the prison approached me [and told me to] stand in for him, to carry the soup, [while] he remained in the prison. It was a good chance to escape but I didn't want the boy to risk [any] unpleasantness. To that he replied that he intended to escape anyway, [and] that the caretakers knew him as the one who delivered meals and would let him out of prison without a word. I left the prison with a kettle in hand. After some time I met the boy who set me free in the committee kitchen. I stayed in Przemyśl for a few hours and went to Lwów.

In Lwów

I arrived in Lwów on 20 November. [My] wife and child had not had messages from me since the beginning of the war and were convinced I was already dead. My return, then, caused enormous joy and sensation among [our] friends. A few days later I got a job as the director of a sports club, Spartak. Arrests began in the city. They arrested, among others: Major Filip Friedlender, president of the local borough; the lawyer Ajnikler; the leaders of Bund[121]—Emanuel Szerer,[122] Mar, et cetera; the president of the city [docent Stanisław] Ostrowski;[123] professor Roman Rencki,[124] professor [Aleksander]

121. "Bund": General Jewish Labor Bund (Polish: Powszechny Żydowski Związek Robotniczy), an international Jewish socialist organization founded in the Russian Empire. The Polish fraction was active in the interwar years. See glossary.

122. Emanuel Scherer (1901–1977): politician, union activist, publicist, member of the "Bund" Central Committee.

123. Stanisław Ostrowski (1892–1982): dermatologist, docent of medical sciences, president of the city of Lwów. Imprisoned in the Soviet labor camps in Siberia. Left USSR with the Polish army after the Amnesty. Fought in the Second Polish Corps. Settled in Great Britain after the war.

124. Roman Rencki (1867–1941): doctor, professor at Lwów University. Murdered by the Germans in July 1941.

Damaszewicz;[125] clergyman Trzenski (Cieński); Lieutenant Śniadowski [?]; [and] members of the sports club Jutrznia. The Polish and Jewish intelligentsia, former bourgeoisie, and those politically engaged, as well as people who had been denounced, were arrested.

Elections

The elections to the Western-Ukrainian Soviet were to take place in a free and democratic manner. Everyone would choose whomever they wanted—that's what was announced. In reality, however, people were forced to vote for candidates featured on an official state list. I decided not to vote. However, at ten thirty at night a car pulled up in front of my house. Two local Communists entered my apartment and asked why I hadn't taken part in the elections. I said that I didn't know the candidates and that I couldn't vote for people I knew nothing about. They started to explain to me that in the Soviet Union everyone had to have trust in the party candidates. Debating didn't help much, me and my wife were almost violently dragged to the polling station. At the polling station my presence was met with joy. The "politicians" who were present there called out: "He was convinced after all." I was given a piece of paper. Unseen, I slipped it into my pocket and dropped an empty paper into the ballot box.

Meanwhile, the nationalization of private businesses took place. They started to kick the bourgeoisie out of their apartments. Because of the influx of refugees, the lack of houses and food was noticeable in the city. Black market trade flourished. Everyone traded in everything they could. Clothing new and old, dollars, zlotys, watches [and] food products were the most popular items. The former bourgeoisie who had nothing to live off were the sellers, the buyers—the "new overlords." The Bolsheviks helped the black market grow. Ragged and deprived of the most essential things, they bought everything for any price, officials as well as military personnel—they were the best customers. Watches were particularly popular. Within a short amount of time the city was completely emptied of goods. The smuggling of products from the German occupation began. Even though smuggling was

125. Aleksander Domaszewicz (1887–1948): noted neurosurgeon, at the time a docent of the Jan Kazimierz University in Lwów.

very dangerous and punishable by many years of prison, people desperate for income took it up.

Arrested

On 4 January 1940 at one o'clock in the afternoon, when I returned home from work for lunch, a few civilian-dressed agents stopped me. They checked who I was and told me to get into a car. I was taken to the NKVD [and] kept for thirty-six hours. I was beaten and tortured to have a statement squeezed out of me. During that time I wasn't given anything to eat. I wasn't given water either. They asked me where the weapons were hidden as they suspected I belonged to a secret military organization. They tried to force me to reveal the surnames of other members of [that] organization. I said that I did not belong to any organization, that I didn't know anything about any weapons [and] that I didn't know what they wanted from me. During the interrogation I fainted a few times. They would throw a bucket of water over me, and when I came to, the tortures would begin again. After thirty-six hours of examination, I was taken to a military prison [and] put in cell number 21.

Professor Schorr

Cell 21 was tiny. There were thirty people in there. Among them there were the chief rabbi of Warsaw, the well-known scholar and professor at Warsaw University Dr. Mojżesz Schorr;[126] Bund activist Wiktor Alter; the senator and professor Stanisław Głąbiński,[127] leader of National Democracy;[128] and other personages making up Poland's intellectual elite. I spent a few days with Professor Schorr. Despite his advanced age, he was constantly taken to exhausting interrogations and beaten. He would be woken up in the middle of the night, taken for an interrogation for many hours and brought back

126. Mojżesz Schorr (1874–1941): historian, orientalist, full professor at Warsaw University, senator of the Republic of Poland, rabbi of the Great Synagogue of Tłomackie [Street]. Arrested on 10 October 1939, died 8 July 1941 in the camp of Posty [camp not listed in any sources] in Uzbekistan.

127. Stanisław Głąbiński (1862–1943): professor of economics, one of the leaders of National Democracy (ND), deputy prime minister of the Polish government in 1923. Likely died around 1943.

128. National Democracy (Polish: Narodowa Demokracja; ND; Endecja, phonetically from the "ND" abbreviation): Polish nationalist political movement active from the end of the nineteenth century until the end of the Second Polish Republic.

only in the morning. He was being accused, as he would later recount to us in the cell, of being one of the supporters of the bourgeois government and the counterrevolution leaders. I spent ten days in the same cell as Professor Schorr. I admired his spirit. Despite [his] suffering, he would not be broken—after the interrogations he came back calm and full of dignity. By chance the leader of the Endecja was in the same cell. The representative of the Jewish people and the former antisemite became so friendly with each other that they slept on the same bunk. After ten days Professor Schorr was taken out of our prison, and I never saw him again.

With Wiktor Alter

One day, yet another fellow sufferer was brought into our cell. We didn't know him, but his demeanor suggested he must have been someone notable. Professor Głąbiński wasn't in the cell at the time. When he returned he was greatly excited at the arrival of Wiktor Alter and said that since his companion, Professor Schorr, had been taken away, he would now share his bunk with Wiktor Alter. The Bund leader stayed in our cell for a few days in total. He had only been brought in to challenge a few Bund activists from Lwów who denied their involvement with the party. After each confrontation [he] came back very upset, grinding his teeth and clenching his fists. He would tell [us] about the inhuman treatment of the prisoners, about the beatings and insults dished out to them during the confrontations and the interrogation. During one of the examinations he was asked for his opinion on the Russian-German pact. Alter replied saying that he considered the pact a betrayal of workers' interest [and] that Hitler was the number one enemy of the proletariat. The chairperson berated him with vulgarities for his audacity to speak this way about Russia's ally. He was beaten so badly then that he fell unconscious, and only regained consciousness a few hours later. Despite the suffering [inflicted on] him, the Bolsheviks failed to break the man's spirit. He believed, and always repeated, that a different time would come, that the future would be better. In the middle of [one] night Alter was taken from the cell and I never saw him again. The clergyman Trzenski [Cieński?], chaplain of the Polish army, was also beaten during examinations. I spent nine months in cell 21. I was then moved to cell 64, where I remained until trial.

The Trial

On 18 October 1940 my trial in the military court took place. At the judges' table, three judges and a prosecutor who had come in specifically for the trial from Russia took their places. The prosecutor asked me various questions. Did I belong to a secret Polish military organization, was I an active member, had I fought with weapons against Russia. To all questions I answered "No," still maintaining that I didn't know anything about any military organization. Seeing that they weren't achieving anything, the prosecutor demanded that the testimony be read out of Henryk Pisarski, member of the Jutrzenka Club,[129] who testified during an interrogation that I and a collection of other people belonged to a secret Polish military organization in Lwów. Pisarski was sentenced to death and the sentence was carried out in Lwów. The prosecutor called upon my feelings as a Jew, told me I was on the brink of death—why would I lie in a moment like this? Pisarski had confessed, why wouldn't I? Seeing I had nothing to lose, I replied that I had known Pisarski from sports organizations, [that] I knew he was an honest man and never lied, but that I didn't know the circumstances under which he had given [this] evidence. Perhaps he was beaten and tortured during the interrogation and had the testimony forced out of him. The court and the prosecutor were furious when they heard what I said. My defense counsel was a lawyer from Lwów, Sawicki, a good friend of mine. He couldn't, however, say what he wanted to say in his defense speech. When the court went to deliberate [my] lawyer said to me: "How gladly I would swap places with you . . ."

Sentencing

The deliberation took ten minutes. I was sentenced to death. However, owing to various extenuations my sentence was changed to ten years in prison. On 23 February I was driven, along with a few other prisoners, to the Kharkiv prison. I was put in a small cell where 150 people were locked up. The conditions were dire. Among the arrestees there were many people who were half-conscious, not quite with it. Some were rotting in front of our eyes from dirt and disease. The smallest disagreement resulted in fighting. Among the prisoners I met many Poles from the intelligentsia. After a seven-day-long stay in that

---

129. "Jutrzenka" was a Jewish minority Polish football club during the interwar period.

hell I was sent to the camp of Buchta Borodka, where thousands of convicts served their punishment.[130] The authorities' attitude toward the incarcerated was inhuman. People were beaten for the most trifling misdemeanor. We were starved systematically. We were given two hundred grams of bread and a bit of water daily. Besides this, we had to work in a quarry for fourteen hours a day. In the camp there were many Russians. The Russian convicts exiled to forced labor treated the Poles with hostility. They beat us, robbed us, and called us names like "Polish overlords." [And] woe unto one they knew was a Jew. Their antisemitism surpassed everything I had known about antisemitism. Complaints to the warden didn't help. The warden, himself an antisemite, always sided with the Russians. After a complaint like that the situation would become unbearable. No one stood up in our defense. I spent a [some text missing] month in the camp.

After a month, in a freight car, I was sent to Magadan in the Kolyma Oblast. In Magadan we were loaded onto a ship. We sailed for nine days. It was horribly freezing—[the temperatures] reached −90°C [−130°F] [?]. We were given a piece of bread once a day. On the ship there were six thousand people—Poles, Jews, and Russians. We lay on top of one another. Apart from the human cargo the ship was carrying iron cases and barrels, carefully guarded by the Russians. It was said that they contained ammunition and explosive materials. We slept on top of those cases and barrels that stood on the deck. At night shouting could be heard—it was the convicts fighting over a space on top of a barrel. The weak would lie on bare floors, in between the barrels, the strongest—the Russian convicts—would always win the places on [top]. We didn't have warm clothing and it sometimes seemed that we wouldn't survive the freezing cold night. Almost everyone had their feet, hands, ears, and noses frostbitten. Normally, a ship takes seven days to make the journey, but because ours was carrying particularly heavy and valuable cargo, we were moving very slowly. At every stop it was thoroughly checked that all the cases and barrels were all right and that nothing was missing. Only on the tenth day did we arrive in the empty wilderness of Staraja Dreszwa,[131] located not far from the islands of Berenga [?].[132]

130. Likely refers to the town of Buchta in the Chita Oblast.
131. Piestraja Dreszwa [?].
132. Likely refers to the Bering Strait.

In the Far North

We found ourselves in a desert: frozen-through earth and the sky was all we could see. We put up the tents that had been brought, and in [our] drill clothing, slept in those tents in temperatures of –60 to –70°C [–76 to –94°F]. We worked on the construction of a road leading to a lead and gold mine. We worked eighteen hours out of twenty-four and received three hundred grams of bread per day as well as soup, sometimes salted fish. After a month we all fell ill with bloody dysentery. Instances of death were a daily occurrence. What the dysentery didn't accomplish, hunger did. Eighty percent of those who had arrived at that cursed place perished. The tents emptied out. Of the two thousand people most were Lwów residents, deported there during my time—157 survived. Our management was made up of NKVD members with disciplinary sentences. The lower-ranking officials were Russian deportees, most often habitual criminals who tormented and beat us. The management did not react to [those] cruelties. The only law was the law of the taiga. Any official could punish the slightest misdemeanor with death. This power was readily used. Every day Polish citizens were killed, and our every move was closely watched. We couldn't move around freely without permission. We couldn't walk away to relieve ourselves without permission. Since everyone was sick with dysentery, and the caretakers were reluctant to allow a few minutes' break from work, it's not difficult to imagine how that ended . . .

The freezing temperatures did their thing. Trousers would freeze to our bodies. After [our] return to the tent they had to be torn off, often with the skin. We were wounded and suffering constantly with those injuries. We were cut off from the world. We didn't know what was happening in the world [and] none of us believed we would return to the [land of the] living . . . Only in mid-July 1941 did one of the caretakers, relatively more human than the rest, tell us about the outbreak of the German-Russian war. Then we were told about the Polish-Soviet pact.[133]

Amnesty

On 23 August 1941 we were all summoned and told we were free. We embarked on a ship and ten days later arrived in Vladivostok. In Vladivostok,

---

133. See the glossary: agreement.

an American consul took care of us, gave us food [and] money and set up a special Polish camp for us. From Vladivostok I went to the Polish army, to Bazaluk.[134] In Bazaluk I became the chief of the local officer school and the person in charge of physical education at the Polish army. I was assigned to the team of General Anders.[135] In February 1942 I arrived in Tashkent, where I remained until August. From there I went to Persia. I was discharged from the army, and from there, after unexpectedly finding my wife and daughter in Tehran, I arrived in Palestine with my family in February 1943.

134. Here and henceforth an erroneous name for the town of Buzuluk [original Polish correction: Buzułuk].

135. Władysław Anders (1892–1970): general, in the years 1941–42 commander of the Polish army in the USSR; later commander of the Second Polish Corps in the West.

Protocol 47

Testimony of **Maria Rudnicka**, age twenty-five, from Warsaw. Father owned a tenement house. Lived until February 1940 in Poland under German occupation. Because of the worsening conditions of the Jewish populace, decided to cross the Soviet border to meet her fiancé, who had escaped Warsaw in September 1939.

Investigation and Arrest

On 6 February 1940 I stood on the bank of the Bug River by the bridge. I had made an appointment there with a smuggler who was to take me and one more person across the frozen-over Bug. On the Soviet side all three of us were stopped. We were taken to Brześć, and on the way the soldiers asked me if I had [any] watches on me, stopping a few times to hold negotiations about these watches. Unfortunately, I had no watches, and so was taken to the garrison. Over a few nights I was examined in a horrific manner: I'd be woken up at night, left alone in a room for hours, not allowed to fall sleep, and when I was completely exhausted and upset the interrogation would begin. I was accused of having crossed the border for espionage purposes. I didn't want to rat out the smuggler and said he was my fiancé. However, I didn't know the smuggler's personal details—didn't know how old he was, what his name was, where he was born—so my testimony was very poor. One of the examining magistrates wanted to help me, which is why he put the smuggler's testimony in front of me during the examination. I couldn't read Russian, however, and only noticed how old [the smuggler] was. The investigation dragged on. Every night the same procedure would be repeated—every night I was brought to mental exhaustion. Those sleepless nights and interrogation were causing me to lose consciousness [so] I decided to confess to everything. There were many women with me in the cell and the same thing was happening to them as to me. The [effects of the] interrogation led to them signing whatever statement [was put in front of] them. The interrogation was carried out by many judges. Every day a new one would arrive and start the interrogation anew. Only later did I realize that the different magistrates were in collusion, and as one conducted the interrogation, the other checked whether the testimony matched the previous one. Normally, the examination would be halted and the judge would leave the room under some pretext. It turned out that he would listen to the rest of the interrogation that followed from across the wall. I am of the opinion that these methods meant that there was no person facing charges in the Soviet territories who did not give a statement that the NKVD wanted.

Eventually I was told that I was only accused of illegal border crossing. A special court in Moscow sentenced me to three years in prison and I was to serve this sentence in a camp outside Moscow.

One day, I was loaded onto a freight car alongside refugees and a horrendous journey that took five weeks began. Within the first few days we were all already covered with lice. We didn't get [any] water to wash with, there wasn't even enough drinking water. We went to the toilet in the car so it's no wonder that not before long all the train passengers began to fall ill. A typhus epidemic took hold. Only when we arrived at the hub station of Orsha did I notice that our train was not the only one. From Orsha, rail tracks diverge to all parts of Russia. At the station there were lots of trains with deportees—several tens of thousands of [exiles]. I [suddenly] felt gravely miserable. It dawned on me that I would never get back out into the world and would forever remain in this foreign land. People who had died of typhus were being carried out of the freight cars. The survivors looked like cattle being led to slaughter. I'd never seen such a hopeless sight. The GPU could not feed everyone.[136] The deportees cried from hunger. A basket of bread and salted fish were thrown into the carriages but only the strongest would get their hands on them. After a meal like that we'd be dying of thirst. Cries and complaints went up to heavens but the guards were heartless. Instead of water we got vulgar insults. The dirt in the train cars was indescribable. [We] no longer looked like human beings. Our clothes were torn and stained. All those who had entered the train as civilized people now looked like a bunch of beggars. Smokers suffered greatly—they would have given [their] life for a cigarette. They had to make do with inhaling the cigarette smoke from the guards. Individual people were picked out from the train cars and put together into groups. I was sent to Kazakhstan, the Doliński [?] area.

---

136. GPU: in the years 1922–34 the name of the Soviet security authority. The author of the testimony means the NKVD. See glossary.

In the Labor Camp

Steppes stretched around us. There were no normal settlements here, only work camps for deportees. One camp was located ten kilometers from another and at night only tiny lights on the horizon were visible. I was placed in a mixed camp made up of seven hundred women and three hundred men. The barracks were small and dirty. There weren't even [any] bunks. We slept on the floor, covered up with any old thing since no sheets were provided. On the first day I got to taste the reality of [life in] the camp: I was robbed. I found out that here in the camp you had to keep all of your belongings on you, otherwise you would end up with nothing. Complaining wasn't allowed, as the so-called *bytoviki*[137] and Russian women would beat [you] up in that situation. The task of a deportee was to turn the empty steppes into fertile fields. To that purpose, dams had to be built to stop the water that ran off from the melting snow and the overflowing river. The water reservoir was to be used for irrigating the future gardens. Dams were built there from sand and clay, which dam was called a *platyna*.[138] The dam was to be two-and-a-half kilometers long and had to be finished by spring. The work was hard. [We] got so little to eat that [we] simply didn't have enough energy to work. A piece of damp bread and two bowls of watery soup—that was [our] daily meal. Immediately after [our] arrival we were fed and even given meat. But after the temperatures reached −50°C [−58°F], [the authorities] stopped feeding us well. The warden's excuse was that we worked poorly. Our camp resembled the Tower of Babel. Here one could find deportees from all the nations that make up the USSR. And of different ages. My neighbor was a seventeen-year-old girl serving the third year of a sentence for prostitution. She was a professional thief. There were a few Jewish girls from Poland, too, who had escaped to Russia in 1934, and in 1937, during the purge, had been sentenced to labor camp.[139] One of them had been sentenced to eight years in prison for writing letters to her mother in Wilno [Vilnius]. They didn't change their views—they just thought that Russia had gone down the wrong path. So-called *volnonaemnye*, that is, those

137. *Bytoviki* (Polish: *bytowik*, *bytowicy*; Russian: *bytoviki*): people convicted primarily of petty crimes; in camp jargon, people from pathologically criminal environments.

138. Actually *plotina* [original Polish correction: *płotina*].

139. Refers to a wave of mass repressions to which Communists from Poland were subjected in the USSR in the years 1937–38.

who remained in the camp after finishing their sentences, also worked here. Normal work hours were from five in the morning to one at night. At night one worked by the light of special lamps. The work consisted of flattening earth mounds using a press. When, after three months of work, I caught the sight of myself in a mirror I found by chance, I didn't recognize myself. I now looked like all the [other] women in the camp. I fell ill with *cynga* due to malnutrition. My legs swelled. Sores covered my arms and legs, and when winter came, with temperatures of –50°C [–58°F], and I couldn't continue working, I no longer received food. Some women gave themselves to the warden and got lighter work, a warm barracks, and better food for it.

Demoralization

Overall, the camp was hugely demoralized. Russian women are generally quite depraved. They resemble men. They work like men, and do work intended for men. There are no favors for women that [we know] in Europe. A woman is a workhorse. The men disregard her. The Polish women were hugely popular and the wardens often forced them to perform various immoral acts. This caused jealousy among the Russian women, who tormented the Polish women at every step: [the Poles] were denounced, given the hardest jobs, stolen from. Not all Polish women agreed to the propositions from the wardens, who had most often been recruited from among criminal deportees. Pity the woman who resisted a warden's will. She would be given the worst and the hardest work and bullied in sophisticated ways. One who agreed to a warden's demand, on the other hand, would immediately get easier work, for example in an office, the laundry room, and the kitchen. Officially, any relations between women and men in the camp are strictly forbidden—despite it, there were many children born in the camp, so that they had to separate out special areas for them. When, during winter months, the food rations became more and more scant, many women gave up [their] moral values and gave in to the officials, in exchange for which they received soup from the first kettle intended for the Stakhanovites. The Russian women had lost all of [their] feminine qualities because of the harsh living conditions. Among Russian women, lesbian love [has become] increasingly popular. In our camp there were plenty of such female couples. Women in such pairs who played the role of the man wore men's clothing. It was a phenomenon so common one did not give it any attention. Its cause was the desperate loneliness of the deportee women, who were treated like male convicts. The women simply longed for friendship and kindness, but the men always picked the European women who, despite the hard work, retained small parts of their charm. The men, *bytoviki*, terrorized [the women] who resisted. One day, the *bytoviki* were playing cards. The stakes were as follows: whoever lost had to beat up a woman picked by the victor. That same day a woman was beaten. The people in charge did not react as they were afraid to mess with the *bytoviki*. How much [they] were afraid of the *bytoviki* is proven by the following fact: in the camp there was a young female thief who had been serving a sentence since the age of eleven. She stole from me my last undergarments, my toothbrush, and soap. When I recognized that she was wearing my underwear, the warden advised that I not bring in a complaint, as I would not get the underwear [back] and would get beaten up.

During the winter a typhus epidemic broke out in the camp. The mortality rate was immense. In the spring I was sent to another camp in the same district, called Tsardas.[140] The work conditions were the same [there]. Thanks to the protections [I had been afforded] I was given lighter work.

After the Amnesty

Immediately after the Amnesty, all Polish citizens were pulled from the camps and put together into one brigade, but the authorities didn't want to release us from the camps until harvesttime. The last two months we worked without quotas and without wages. In December we, the Polish citizens, were told to pick a place we wanted to go. We were encouraged to go to the factory town of Yuzhny Kazakhstan, where we'd be given work. The whole group agreed to go, but how surprised we were when, on getting there, we found merely a rail station in place of a factory town. There were no factories there; they existed only in plans. We lived for five weeks in that station, without food or anywhere to rest our heads. I eventually went to Turkestan, where I met [some] friends, and where I spent seven months. I worked in factories, in a kolkhoz, anywhere I could. Many a night I spent sleeping on the street, hungry and ragged, and eventually I didn't even have the strength to work. Meanwhile, my brother,

140. Likely refers to the camp of Płasina Dzardas.

who I didn't know had been deported, was looking for me everywhere. He was already a member of the Polish army and came to Turkestan to get me. He took me to Dzala-Bat.[141] His unit received an order to move to Iraq. At the same time, I found out that Jews were only allowed to bring immediate family, but not sisters. I was not on the evacuee list. My Polish name and surname saved me at the last minute. It cost me a lot of health and effort to receive a permit to go to Palestine where, I knew, I would forget about all of my horrendous experiences.

141. Correctly: Jalal-Abad [original Polish correction: Dżałał-Abad].

Protocol 48

Testimony of **Wanda Ludmir**, age thirty-three, born in Tarnów, resident in Jarosław. Arrived in Palestine from Russia via Tehran in February 1943.

Already on 1 September 1939 at eight in the morning the bombing of the city had begun. Four houses were destroyed, and I, along with [my] husband and six-year-old son, fled to Lubaczów to relatives. There were lots of military personnel on the roads, and behind them the civilian population was trying to escape. Carts, cars, military columns, all mixed up into one panic-stricken mass. One blocked another's way in the disarray. The army could not move around freely as the civilian vehicles were in their way. The civilians' escape was being hindered by the army. This chaotic mass [of people] became an excellent target for German pilots. Parents lost sight of their children; luckily, children wore medallions on their necks with inscriptions of their names and where they came from. Children would locate their parents only months later. We arrived in Lubaczów safely. The next day this town too was bombed. My husband did not want to stay in his relatives' house and ran around the city like mad. First, he hid in a house close to the synagogue, then he thought [his] shelter wasn't safe enough. He ran out into a field and waited there until the bombing stopped. Indeed, it turned out upon our return to town that the three houses we were supposed to have used as shelters had been bombed. There were many casualties, and only my husband's intuition saved us. To stay in Lubaczów was pointless. We didn't know where to run to. By an odd twist of fate I ran into my brother and brother-in-law in the main square, driving their own car. They didn't have gasoline, however, so we had to abandon the car after five kilometers' drive and go on foot for four kilometers to the Ukrainian village of Zaliski.[142]

In the Ukrainian Village

I settled in a peasant's hut with my husband and child, and my brother-in-law and brother [lived] in another one. At first they wouldn't be let into the house. They had to pay an overinflated sum to stay the night. We had more luck: we

142. Likely refers to the village of Zalesie, by Lubaczów.

came across an honest old peasant, [and] met his son, a judge, who took us to his place. The young judge said that I reminded him of his first fiancée. And he brought us flowers and milk for our child. Throughout the eight days we spent in the countryside he could not stop showering us with gifts. But we wanted to carry on. We heard that the Germans were burning [firebombing] villages from airplanes and we were afraid that they would occupy the village any day. The judge [tried to] calm us, reassured us that there were agreements between the Germans and Ukrainians, and that Ukrainian villages would not be burned down. The Ukrainian youth served in the German army. German planes dropped pamphlets telling people to wear headwear, hats, and scarves that would signal that they were Ukrainian. The judge told my husband to put on a white blazer and a hat, and a white scarf [for] me, and assured us that we could stay in the village in peace. My brother and brother-in-law were like cats on hot bricks. Every night they would go out on the road looking for a chance to leave. They would ask [soldiers] to take them in army cars and begged us to come with them. During that time there was more and more trouble on the roads. One couldn't get a peasant cart even with money. The peasants did not want to risk [their] horses. They hid them from the army. Women would pay in diamonds for a horse and cart, so it was in vain that we waited on the road from Tuesday to Saturday for a cart. The Polish army was exhausted and weary by then. Some soldiers no longer wore uniforms, only [carried their] weapons and [wore] civilian clothing. Others were in uniforms but without weapons. Getting into a military car was out of the question. On Saturday night, however, we managed to find a cart. My boy refused point-blank to get on the cart. He threw himself on the ground, cried, and ran around to stop us from going. We had to stay thanks to him [because] this saved our lives. The cart that my brother-in-law and brother traveled on was attacked by a band of robbers. A fight broke out between those traveling on the road and the bandits, which my brother, brother-in-law, and sister-in-law took advantage of and hid in a cabbage field. Meanwhile, the Polish army arrived, dispersed the bandits, and thinking that the rest of [them] were hiding in the field, threw a hand grenade toward those hiding. The grenade exploded right next to them.

We, however, stayed in the countryside. The Germans kept their promises with regards to the Ukrainians and did not bomb the village. Even the German units marching from Lubaczów to Rawa Ruska bypassed the village, and the young judge, who found a hiding place for us in his house should the Germans go looking for Jews, did not [have to] use it as the village was calm, and we lived as if in a paradise. Only when the Germans came close to Rawa Ruska did we leave for Jarosław. The judge's father, an old Ukrainian peasant, harnessed horses to a cart, and we set off. On the road there marched German soldiers. We had to stop in the middle. The German army walked on and on. Only in the morning did the road clear and we set off again. Midway to Jarosław on the river we saw a demolished bridge, and a temporary [one] constructed by the Germans. The guard on the bridge would not let us cross. We pretended not to understand what he was saying to us. The Ukrainian peasants truly did not understand the guard's words. But [they] had heard us talk with German soldiers on the way and asked us to mediate between them and the guard. A German soldier approached us and advised us to wait until he took over the watch so that we could cross the river. We continued on despite the fact that the roads were full of [soldiers]. Before reaching Jarosław we had to stop. They weren't letting [anyone] into the city. The Germans were catching Jews for [forced] labor. I knew nothing about this practice and almost fainted on seeing my husband led along with a group of Jews. I thought I would never see him again. They were taken to Jarosław and told to carry rails. [My] husband took advantage of the fact that the work site was located close to our home and ran off after five minutes. I only got home at two in the afternoon.

In Jarosław

The city was full of [soldiers and] trucks. Despite this, after weeks of wandering we were happy to be returning home. We had enough food products [and] lived the kind of life we did before the war. We had a nice apartment; my husband was an clerk in an English export firm and earned well. An Austrian officer who stayed in our apartment conducted himself very well. He spent evenings with us, brought chocolate for the child and told us about the fighting outside Rawa Ruska that he had taken part in. Out of politeness he didn't even ask for the key to his room to lock [the door]. He would move the table against the door and place [his] handgun on top of it. The worst was the hostage situation. The military authorities took hostage six of the most respected citizens: the president of the local borough, Melech Reiss, Merbojm, Pataszer, Erlich, my husband, and Rosenblum, the richest man in town. Abraham Erlich hid in the basement with a small window onto the street. Since they threatened to arrest the whole family if he were not to be found, [his] wife revealed his hiding place. The poor man lost his mind out of fear and took his life a few weeks later in Przemyśl. By chance, Merbojm's elder son came [to visit] from Kraków. When the police arrived, he was in the bathroom. Hearing voices in the adjoining room he asked who was there. He was arrested and never heard from again. It was said that afterward they found the mutilated bodies of Melech Reiss, Merbojm, and young Rosenblum in the woods. Pataszer, who had his teeth knocked out by the Germans, was released, [as well as] the old Rosenblum and the deranged Erlich.

They could not find my husband. The Austrian officer staying with us helped him hide. Polish snitches from the dregs of society would denounce him, but during the searches I hid him first in the laundry basket, and then in a three-door wardrobe in the child's room. The Gestapo officer could read from my pale face that [my] husband was hiding in the house—[he] looked in the bed and in other hiding places. I quickly opened up the doors of all the wardrobes except the one where my husband was hiding. I then asked loudly: "Shall I open this one?," to which he replied: "No need." This way I saved my husband.

Tragic news came in from other cities. We heard about the Przemyśl massacre, about the murder of 680 Jews in Lwów, about children who had to dig their parents' graves, and about Jews who were drowned in barrels in the river.

Exile

All of those pieces of news caused a terrible panic in the city, and when the hostages who were still alive were released on a Friday and told to cross the San River over to the Russian side, [people] began to talk about how all of Jarosław's Jews would meet the same fate—and that was indeed the case.

On Sunday morning an order came out for all Jews to gather in the courtyard of the officers' casino, [from] where they were escorted across the San. My husband did not want to report to the assembly point. We made it to the river, located fifteen minutes from the city, on our own, via back paths. We were led by our two Ukrainian clerks. We were all carrying boxes. An officer on horseback rode up in front of us. He stopped the horse. He didn't understand what was going on when he saw me wearing an old coat and [my] husband dressed as a peasant. We didn't look like Jews. He asked: "What is happening, are they expelling our own from the city too?" "I'm a Jew"—I replied from a distance. He followed us with his gaze and said nothing. When we reached the viaduct and looked over the road underneath, fear shook us. I will never forget that image: quietly, with their heads down, a crowd of exiled Jews walked on. They walked two abreast, carrying bundles on their backs, holding children by the hand. Behind every tenth Jew there walked a German soldier with [his] bayonet drawn. German civilians stood on the viaduct and photographed the crowd of the outcasts. Shame and pain prevented me from continuing on. My heart ached, and what hurt the most was the calmness of those civilians, pointing [their] cameras. I said in Polish, as it turned out they were not Germans: "Enjoy yourselves, enjoy—your time will come too." My husband dragged me away and we went on. Our Ukrainian clerks walked us all the way to a small village, seven kilometers beyond the San. One of them had parents in that village. But the Ukrainian police would not allow us in. In other villages the exiled Jews were beaten. We went like this from village to village until we reached Lubaczów and could breathe a sigh of relief. Lubaczów was a somewhat neutral place, designated as a border town and full of Ukrainian gangs. There was a danger of an attack or a robbery at every step, but the Bolsheviks were already in town and we felt safe. We didn't want to stay there—the border was close and we feared that the Germans could move [it].

In Lwów

We arrived safely in Lwów. It was raining buckets [and] I waited with our child on the street for [my] husband to organize a room for us. I had heard that [my] brother-in-law and brother were in Lwów but I didn't know their address. As I stood there with my child, soaked through and shivering, someone came up to me and asked if I'd only just gotten there and whether [I] needed anything. I asked him about a hotel or a room in a family home. "I'm the owner of the biggest hotel in town," he replied. "I had leased it five years ago, but I understand that one can't get a room in Lwów these days. Allow me to [take you there.]" He could see that, as a woman, I couldn't really accept this invitation. He left me in the street and came [back] with his wife. At that moment my husband turned up with the news that he had not found a room. We accepted the invitation. We spent the whole day at the Zylbergs'. We felt bad to be [relying on] the hospitality of strangers, but were not able to get a room, even with money. The Zylbergs sublet us a room in their beautifully finished apartment, where we stayed for a long time. After some time, someone on the staircase asked me if I was looking for a room. I said that I was. It turned out he was a Communist from Lwów who had requisitioned an empty four-bedroom apartment in the same building, a part of which he wanted to give up to me. Naturally, I accepted the offer. In this apartment lived the Communist from Lwów, ourselves, and three Czech Jews, driven from the Sudetes by the Germans, as well as four Communist refugees. The kitchen and other amenities belonged to everyone, and I started cooking. One Ukrainian, an acquaintance of my husband who was employed by the Bolsheviks in the Soviet-Ukrainian Cultural Institute, and who wanted to return to Jarosław, gave up his job to my husband. [My] husband earned three hundred rubles per month. We had butter, meat, and eggs brought over from Lida, and life with the Bolsheviks went on normally. I found [my] brother and brother-in-law. They had become large-scale merchants [in town]. They earned a lot of money and rented a villa outside Lwów. My parents, who had stayed in Tarnów and had to deal with the Germans' persecutions, fared badly.

During the plebiscite many did not vote. Smugglers and capitalists were arrested. Things turned for the worse when one had to decide [whether] to accept Soviet citizenship. My husband, as a Bolshevik clerk, was ready to acquiesce to it, but I objected. I could not make peace with the thought that I would never see [my] parents, that I would always remain in a country that I would not be able to leave. Because of me my husband gave up the Soviet passport, and this came back to haunt us terribly. At first, unmarried people were sent away from Lwów. [Those people] would not sleep in their homes at night. They were locked inside shops, in basements, and on roofs, slept in the fields. Then a rumor spread that it would be all the men, after all, who would be sent away, leaving the women and the children. The men, fathers of the family, [had to then] spend their nights like the unmarried did. My husband did not want to leave home. "If we are to be deported, let them deport us together."

We Leave Lwów

On 21 June [1940], the Lwów NKVD requisitioned all available vehicles in town. [We knew] that something was brewing. At night, four policemen entered [our apartment], asked if we had Russian passports, and released the Communist who presented a Russian identity card. The next day we were ordered to go the police station and bring luggage up to a hundred kilos in weight. I insisted that I bring everything I had saved from home, and the NKVD agent allowed [it]. We loaded [our belongings] up onto a cart and went to the police station. We came upon thousands of people there. It's difficult to imagine the chaos there and how many people were sneaking away. My husband had a chance to get out but did not do it on account of the family. We sat there from five in the afternoon until nine in the morning. We were taken to the train station on trucks and placed thirty-six to a carriage. Our friends brought bread, butter, and vinegar to us at the station. The vinegar in particular turned out to be useful during the journey. It served as a disinfectant, particularly against lice, of which there were lots in the car. The train was a few kilometers long. One couldn't see the end of the train, which stopped only at small, side-route stations. The doors and windows were locked—[people] fought like mad for a space by the window. They fought similarly for a space on the bunks, a piece of bread, and a bit of water. Everyone slept on the bare floor. The dirt [and] the heat riled people into madness. In our train there were also carriages with Russian arrestees. [We] reached Cherdyn in Ural. The group, made up of four hundred people, was taken across the mountains and rocks, deep into the country. We traveled through the mountains for three days and three nights. We weren't given anything to eat throughout the journey. On the morning of the fourth day we pulled up at the Niares River. Swarms of mosquitos hovered above it—they looked like fog. We burned fires to get rid of them. The Niares River, which flows into the Kama River, is located in the very center of the Urals. Forest, water, and sky—that was all that we saw around us. We were put up in the small houses of the Niares village, seven families to one small room, and rested there after the two-week-long journey. We were split up according to the size of everyone's family. We lived and worked in that village. We often went to work in the forest and survived this difficult period. After the outbreak of the Russian-German war, and the Amnesty for the Polish citizens, we went to Tashkent and from there, via Persia, to Palestine.

Protocol 49

Testimony of **Maria Mandelbrot**, age thirty-two, born and resident in Warsaw. Graduate of the Warsaw Conservatory; wife of journalist Lejb Mandelbrot. Arrived in Palestine via Russia and Persia in April 1943.

I escaped Warsaw on 17 October 1939. It was after Warsaw's capitulation, after the German airplanes destroyed a third of the city and thousands of casualties from among [its] citizens were buried. I spent three weeks in occupied Warsaw. The persecution of Jews shook me up so much I decided to leave the city at all costs. My husband fled Warsaw on the night of 6 September. I was left alone. After receiving the information that my husband was in Wilno, I decided to [join] him. I went from Warsaw to Siedlce. The city was in ruins. The remaining residents wandered around the ruins of buildings, [of] their apartments. From there I went to the Bug River. I crossed the Bug, went to Białystok, where I stayed for a day, and from there set off toward Lida and Bieniakoni. With a smuggler's help I crossed over to the Lithuanian side, and this way, reached Wilno.

With the Lithuanians

I met my husband in Wilno. This was at the time when the Russians gave Wilno to the Lithuanians.[143] On that day, the Lithuanians organized a pogrom of Jews during which many were killed and many wounded. The pogrom lasted three days. Jews did not come out into the streets, hiding in their houses. Only on the third day did the authorities put things in order and life returned to normal. The Lithuanians brought in a number of strict registration bylaws, the aim of which was to make life difficult for the refugees escaping the German or Soviet occupation. It was said that those who couldn't produce a receipt for residence registration by 28 October would be sent away from Lithuania. This caused panic among the refugees, [who] began to look for ways of obtaining such documents. The Lithuanian police readily accepted bribes and issued the aforementioned [receipts] in exchange for money. After a month, another

143. Wilno was occupied by the Red Army on 17 September 1939. On 27 October 1939, as a result of an agreement between the Third Reich and the USSR, the Soviet army left the city and the following day, 28 October, the Lithuanian army entered.

decree came out [stating that people] had to obtain special refugee passports. People stood in long lines for hours in the freezing cold in front of the police station. The refugees had only light clothing with them and many had their hands and feet frostbitten during [this] wait for a passport. The police officers had the authority to tell the refugees where they were allowed to live. The aim was to send them away from Wilno and spread [them] among small Lithuanian villages. Since no one knew the Lithuanian [language] and everyone wanted to remain in Wilno—which we considered a Polish city—bribes of a few hundred *litai* per person again showered [the authorities]. Many refugees arrived much later from the areas occupied by the Soviets—they would spend months in the hospitals having their limbs, frostbitten during border crossing, treated. They could not count on being allowed to stay in Lithuania. Many of them were sent back to the Soviets, where they landed straight in prison. Generally, however, the well-to-do managed somehow. The Lithuanians tried to destroy any traces of Polishness in Wilno. The streets were given Lithuanian names. People were beaten for speaking Polish in the streets. The Polish theater was closed. In churches, priests were not allowed to give sermons in Polish. The Jewish refugees were supported by [the] Joint[144] in Wilno. More than a hundred accommodation points were set up for the refugees in the city. Clothes were distributed; special workshops produced clothing and shoes for the refugees. Without [the] Joint's help, tens of thousands of refugees would have died from hunger and cold. My husband, as a journalist, received special help from [the] Joint. This lasted until 14 June 1941.[145]

Bolsheviks in Wilno

All kitchens were closed when the Bolsheviks arrived in Lithuania. All accommodation points were also closed. Journalists, fearful of persecution, went into hiding in small Lithuanian towns and looked for work to [be able to] obtain food products. We left for Kaunas. My husband, speaking [a few] languages, got a job at one of the co-ops. I, a pianist, got work too, and we managed

144. Joint American-Jewish charitable organization—Joint Distribution Committee—supporting Jewish communities affected by poverty. See glossary.

145. Error on the part of the author of the testimony: should be 14 June 1940. The Red Army entered Lithuania on that day. During July and August, the incorporation of Lithuania into the USSR took place.

to settle decently. My husband, however, was constantly worried he would be called to account for his political past. Many refugees, before the foreign consulates were closed, received visas for various countries: America, Palestine, and Japan. My husband did not want to go to the Japanese consulate as it was said that all those with visas would be deported to Siberia. In fact, the visa holders went abroad, and we remained in the Soviets. In 1941 my husband registered to leave Russia despite not having [any] visas. We registered on the basis of a telegram we received from Dr. Mozes[146]—director of ŻAT, where my husband worked[147]—in which he said he was sending us an American visa. The visa, however, did not arrive.

Arrest and Deportation

At the beginning of June 1941, apartment searches began. Above all, [it was] those who had registered to leave and those who didn't have Soviet passports [who] had [their] apartments searched. Every day we expected a visit from the police, and indeed, on the night of 14 June I heard voices in the backyard. My husband was asleep [and] I didn't want to wake him. I thought that maybe they weren't here for us. There was a knock on the door. I opened it in [my] nightgown. Four NKVD agents, guns in hand, burst into the apartment. My husband woke up. They didn't let him move. He sat in bed with his hands raised. Two agents undertook a search, throwing all [our] papers around. [The other] two watched us. We were given fifteen minutes to pack [our] things. We were loaded onto a truck and driven away, picking up other people on the way. This way we got to the train station.

Parting with [My] Husband

At the station my husband was told to take his things. Since our belongings were packed together, I was told that my husband was only leaving for a few minutes. He took the suitcase with him. Meanwhile, I was loaded into

146. Mendel Mozes (1885–1966): director of the Jewish Telegraphic Agency (JTA; Polish: Żydowska Agencja Telegraficzna; ŻAT). On 5 September 1939 he evacuated from Warsaw with [his] family, and via Wilno, the USSR, and Japan, made it to the United States in 1941.

147. ŻAT (Polish: Żydowska Agencja Telegraficzna): Jewish Telegraphic Agency (JTA). Active in Poland until September 1939. After the war, briefly recommenced activities in 1944 in the liberated parts of the country. Nowadays, JTA provides a press information service in Yiddish to Jewish publications around the world, identified by the abbreviation ITA (Jidisze Telegrafen Agentur).

a freight carriage. I saw my husband being loaded into another one. I calmed down because I thought we were going on the same train, only in different cars. Only later did I notice that the other carriage was being separated from the train, and our train [then] set off. I saw [my] husband from afar, inside the freight car at the station. To this day I have never seen him again.

Inside the Carriage

The carriage was small. There were tiny windows at the top. The doors were sealed. There were thirty people inside. The stuffiness was incredible. My neighbors were a Lithuanian minister with his wife, the wife of another minister with two daughters, a Lithuanian painter with his daughter, a Jewish homeowner, a merchant, et cetera. In the car there were two bunks, on which only ten people could sleep—the others [slept] on the floor. It was horrendously hot [and] there was no water. We drank dirty water. Because of that water and the dirt an epidemic of bloody dysentery broke out that spread among all the passengers. People relieved themselves in view of others. At first [they] were terribly embarrassed and hung a piece of a cloth sack from the ceiling but the sack was too short and one could [still] see the back parts of the body through it. Later, the embarrassment was forgotten, and human dignity lost. At first the car was under convoy and the doors sealed. After a week it was permitted to open the doors. We were also allowed to leave at stations to go to the toilet. We received three hundred grams of bread per day and soup. Soup was always given at night.

We traveled for two weeks inside the freight car. We went from Kaunas, via Barnaul, to the Altai Krai. We, the women traveling in the carriage, comforted each other [by saying] that our husbands were following in our footsteps. I did not want to permit myself the thought that I would not see [my] husband again. Only after arriving in Barnaul, where we were split into groups, horrible scenes played out. There were no husbands [to be seen]. The women were in hysterics, children's cries went up to the heavens. I had four rubles on me. I was wearing a summer dress and open sandals—that was the entirety of my wealth. Despairing, I went to the warden and asked if my husband would be coming here. He laughed and replied: "One does not ask about such things in Russia. Our people do what they deem appropriate." I burst into tears, thinking I would lose my mind. I was taken back to the group and sent all the way to the river, from where we went to Kamen[148] by ship. The journey down the Ob River took eighteen hours. I was consumed by deep melancholy: I didn't eat, didn't drink. I stared ahead unseeing. Twice I attempted suicide, twice I was convinced not to by the wife of the Lithuanian minister, who was in the same situation as me.

In Exile

After [our] arrival, we waited a whole day for the warden to come, who was to split the work among us according to professions. It took a few hours for the list to be put together. Some people were sent to the woods, others remained in the city. I was left in the city. I thought I would find some work to do with music. We were accommodated in two barracks—damp, without doors [or] windows. We slept on the stone floor. They wouldn't even give us straw. When we'd finally settled down on the floor, the warden walked in and rudely ordered us to move up, as there were others still to arrive in the barracks. We were given three days to rest. After three days some were sent to a brick factory, some to clothes-making workshops. I was given a job in a factory [producing] shoelaces and wool hats. I was a top worker [but], despite being held up as an example [to others], I didn't receive a penny for three months. Because I went continually hungry, I sold [my] gold watch and took up trading.

Trading

I worked eight hours a day. The rest of [my] time I devoted to trading. Since I didn't have my own things to sell, I took in items from people I knew, to resell on their behalf, and sold those. My clients were the wives of pilots, high-ranking NKVD officials. At first I went around to [their] houses. Then they would come to me. After some time I bought myself felt boots, a dress, and a wool sweater. When I saved up a few rubles, I went to the warden and asked him to let me live by myself. Along with another woman I rented a room for fifty rubles a month. My landlord was a bookkeeper. He also had a piece of land and a cow—he fared rather well. He told me how well one had lived in this city before the Bolsheviks, and how, now, the entire population complained about the regime. He also told me that a series of arrests had taken

148. Full name: Kamen-na-Obi [Polish: Kamień na Obi].

place in the city a few months back, and that there wasn't a single home from which no one had been taken. [No one knew] what they had done with those arrested. Apparently, they had been sent to [work] drying the taiga. The men were taken, the women left behind. People in town would say: "Someone is killed every night." My apartment was located opposite the prison, where people were arriving all the time. The prison was huge and consistently overcrowded. No one was allowed to approach the prison; it was surrounded by a powerful guard. The biggest scourge of those three months was the agricultural work. Every Saturday and Sunday we were sent to kolkhozes located ten kilometers from the city, to help the kolkhoz members with agricultural work. The journey was difficult—during rainy periods the mud reached [our] knees. You had to pull [your] legs from the mud with [your] hands. In the kolkhozes there was no space to sleep—we slept out in a field, in the rain. Neither was there [any] bread in the village, so we had to go hungry throughout Saturday and Sunday. The first time I came to work in a kolkhoz I fainted from exhaustion and hunger. I couldn't work [and] was taken back to the city. I decided I would not go to the kolkhoz anymore, and even though the commandant threatened me with jail, I never again worked the fields.

A Pianist Again

After three months, an artistic troupe from Leningrad arrived in Kamen. Passing by the theater, I heard the sound of music. I decided to go [inside]. Without saying anything to anyone, I got on the stage, sat at the piano, and began to play. The stage manager, hearing my playing, ran up to me and asked me to stay with them. I said that I was in exile and could not do anything without NKVD's permission. He arranged for an appropriate permit. I worked in that theater until the beginning of January, and I earned very well. When the news of the Amnesty for Polish citizens spread, I immediately procured a certificate and left for Barnaul on a ship.

On the Ship

There were also Russian recruits [traveling on the ship]. The lice and the stench were unbearable. The recruits stole from one another, and since they were also being served vodka, got drunk and had knife fights. With nowhere to hide from them, I went to the NKVD cabin where four agents were staying, and without any shame, asked them to let me stay in their cabin. They agreed to it. Staying in the cabin of the "powers that be," I got the chance to listen to a few judgments they passed for minor misdemeanors. Every hour soldiers would turn up with complaints: one had been robbed, another beaten up. They were told: "Watch your stuff," or "Punch him in the mug too." Then they would turn to me: "See what people [they are]? Going to the front [yet wasting time on] stupidities." I replied: "They're fighting out of despair." When I arrived in Barnaul it was late autumn. It was warm outside, raining. I came across thousands of Poles waiting for trains going south, where the climate was milder. In Russia they don't allow you to wait at the station. Half an hour before the train departure they open the ticket windows [and] only the strong [manage to] get tickets—the weak wait their turn for days. Miraculously, I got into the train through a window. Inside the carriage people were lying on top of one another. Everyone was dressed in rags. Women wore undergarments and aprons on their heads in place of scarves. Their legs were wrapped in rags too. I traveled ten days to Tashkent. We were warned that they weren't letting [people] into Tashkent. I carried on and [later] returned to Tashkent.

In Tashkent

The city was full of refugees: Poles, Ukrainians, and people of other nationalities. Not only apartments and houses were full of people but also the streets. The mortality rate was horrifying. Every day hundreds of people who had died of typhus, dysentery, and starvation were picked up off the streets. I lost my documents, and because of it, was left not only without a portion of bread but also at risk of arrest. I was stopped a few times and had to sign [a document stating] I would leave the city within twenty-four hours. I slept out on the street for five weeks since no one wanted to let me into [their] apartment without documents. I would ride the tram until two o'clock at night, then pretend I was waiting for a phone call at the post office. I was completely exhausted and hungry. I wasn't receiving bread and could not buy it myself—I would pass out from hunger a few times a day. Only when the spring came did I sell my wool suit jacket and bought myself [some] raisins that I swallowed straight without washing. From this, I got typhus. They didn't want to admit me into a hospital.

I was lying on the road with a 40°C [104°F] fever. This was in May 1942. I stopped an army car going to Jang-Jul[149] and asked the driver to take me with him. He left me in the middle of the road. With my last strength I walked to town, [arriving at] twelve at night. In town I went to the Polish delegation, where they gave me a few injections and took me to the hospital. I stayed in the hospital for three months—twice ill with typhus and once with pneumonia. At the hospital I received letters from [my] husband sent to me by the Polish delegation. He was in the Jambul district. After leaving the hospital I was accommodated in a Polish camp where the attitude toward Jews wasn't the best. We were treated like second-class people and had great difficulties made for us when [trying to get] out of Russia. In the first and second transports there were no Jews. I was only sent to Pahlevi in the third transport. Ill with dysentery, I was taken in a sanitary vehicle to Tehran. I spent eight months there working as a pianist in a hotel. I didn't fare badly [and] began to be myself [again]. On 21 April 1943 I flew out of Tehran by plane and that same day arrived in Palestine.

149. Should be: Yangiyul [original Polish correction: Jangi-Jul]. Appears in other testimonies as Jang-Jul, Jang-Giul, Jang-Iul.

Protocol 50

Testimony of **Jozef Hurwicz**, son of Jehoszua and Sara. Born in Wieliczka near Kraków. Father was the owner of a flour shop. The boy arrived [in Palestine] from Russia via Tehran with his eleven-year-old brother, Mosze, in February 1943.

My father was an affluent man. We had our own tenement house and a large wholesale flour warehouse. Our family was made up of three children, of whom I was the eldest. My other brother, thirteen years old, stayed in Russia with [our] parents. In September 1939 at seven in the morning the train station located three kilometers from town was bombed by the Germans, and during the days that followed our town was bombed [too]. The German planes wanted to destroy the salt mines under Wieliczka. On Monday 4 September we decided to flee from home. We were joined by our paternal uncle, aunt, and children. We hired a cart, loaded [our] things up, and set off on our way. Outside town we had our cart requisitioned for the Polish army and had to go on foot, carrying heavy bundles on [our] backs. At night we came across two Polish soldiers who chased us off the road into the woods, saying our bundles made us targets for the German planes. Throughout the journey we walked on, tired and depressed. The small children could barely drag themselves behind the grown-ups. Only the following night, at one o'clock, did we arrive in Bochnia. At that time the city was bombed. German planes came down very low, dropped incendiary bombs, and shot at civilians with machine guns. We barely managed to hide in a bombed-out house and we stayed there until evening. When things calmed down, Father went into town. He bought a horse and a cart and we set off.

We didn't know which way to go. Wherever we got to it seemed to us the Germans would enter straightaway, as if they were pursuing us. On the way we were in danger because the German pilots circled right above the heads of refugees and shot at roads. People fell like flies. We avoided death by a miracle [and] reached Białogóra [?]. The town was up in flames. Every house was on fire. The relatives we were counting on had fled and we had nowhere to go. The Germans were not in town yet. We hid in an abandoned house and lived there for two weeks, unable to continue because of tiredness. On Sunday, after Yom Kippur [24 September 1939], the Germans entered the town and immediately Jewish [suffering] began. People were captured for [forced] work, told to clear debris and sent to [do] other dirty work. The theft of Jewish goods began, and the local people were outstandingly helpful to the Germans in this work. We decided to go back to Wieliczka—since we were under German occupation anyway, we would be better off at home. We traveled a ways until we found ourselves [near] Leżajsk. From there we went up toward the San River where we had to cross a bridge. But the German guard only let Christians cross the bridge, [and] stopped Jews from entering. A few Christians were having a friendly conversation with the German guard. They pointed out who was to be allowed across the bridge and who was not and helped to torment the terrified Jews. We waited until the evening, rented a boat, and tried to get to the other side of the river. All of a sudden, we saw a German plane flying right above our heads. My aunt got so frightened that she dropped [her] one-year-old baby from her hands and it fell into the water. My father was a good swimmer—[he] jumped into the water and rescued the baby. After many adventures we got to Leżajsk, where we spent the night. The next morning we learned that an order had come out for all Jews to gather at the market square at twelve noon. Suspecting that nothing good would come from it, we left all our belongings and escaped town toward Wieliczka. We did not recognize [our] hometown; it was completely ruined. The Jews had fled, many of [them] murdered by the Germans. Among those killed were five of our relatives. There was no point staying in town [so] we set off ahead.

We struggled along for a long time until we reached the town of Sieniawa. There were neither Germans nor Russians there. Order was being kept by a citizens' militia made up of Christians and Jews, and refugees were treated badly. [The militia] wouldn't let refugees stay in the city; they were afraid of food shortages. The residents who gave shelter to refugees risked harsh penalties. We stayed in a peasant hut outside of town. A few days later the Bolsheviks entered town and the situation improved. However, [our] father had nothing to do in this small town. We went to Rawa Ruska where Father's acquaintances—merchants and friends—were. We stayed in Rawa Ruska for six weeks. Father took up trading and we made a living. However, we didn't fare that well. We lived two families to one small room; we had no sheets, clothing, or household amenities. All of that we had abandoned during the journey. Since we had close relatives in Skole, we turned to them. We rented an apartment [and] bought some furniture; Father began trading flour. The trading was difficult but we earned [our] keep. The Bolsheviks were taking away all the houses and shops. They treated the rich in an awful way. They threw them out of [their] homes, took their clothes away, left them almost naked, didn't allow them to work. Observant Jews could not take on work because of Saturdays. The town was destitute. The passportization began [and] everyone was forced to take a Soviet passport. Father could not get used to the new order; he missed home, where he had left—buried in the basement—money and merchandise, and he decided not to pick up a passport, knowing that by doing so he'd be blocking his way home. Many refugee families did the same.

Registration and Deportation

After New Year 1940 a decree was issued [stating] that whoever wanted to return to the German-occupied territories should register with the NKVD. At first no one trusted this registration and only a few families, mainly Christians, registered. That first group was indeed taken over to the German side. Seeing that registering brought solid results, we decided to register too. My father foresaw, however, that this decision would take a dreadful toll on us. In April it was already being discussed openly that those who didn't have Soviet passports and who registered to return to the Germans would be deported into Russia. In May they started sending off unmarried men. Father was afraid to sleep in the house and thought about leaving town and going to Lwów. One Friday at the end of May, two officials from the magistrate entered our apartment. There was no one at home except Mother and [my] youngest brother. They asked Mother why we wanted to go to Germany. Mother replied that we had long since given up that intention and that Father regretted having registered, which [he did only because] he'd been talked into it. The officials wrote down Mother's statement, and she thought that our case had been successfully taken care of. She begged Father to spend the night at home. Father, however, would not be convinced. One night, at two o'clock, there was a knock [on the door]. Four NKVD agents appeared with guns in their hands. One of them stood by the door, another by the window. The other two forced us to pack up [our] things and announced that we were going to Germany. We were then taken to the station and loaded into a freight car in which there were a hundred people. We were terribly anxious because of Father's absence. At dawn I managed to get out of the carriage [and go] into town. I found Father and brought him to the station. Mother fainted at the sight of [him]. It took us an hour to bring her around. The train commandant patted Father on the back, calling him a *molodetz*[150] for voluntarily reporting for the transport.

The long and arduous journey began. At first we weren't given food. We ate the provisions we had brought from home. When those provisions ran out, we were each given a piece of moldy bread with water. Everyone got dysentery from that bread. In the car there was a hole in the floor instead of a toilet, but because of the illness it was difficult to get to. Small children went to the toilet on the floor. One could suffocate from the stench. Every moment someone else would faint. A few people died on the train—the train would stop [and] they would be buried in a field by the rail embankment. We traveled [through] various cities. We stopped for the longest time in Kiev. The local Jews wanted to give us food but the guard[s] didn't allow it. We rode for four weeks until we reached Assino,[151] Sverdlovsk Oblast. There we were let out of the freight cars and taken outside the city where there stood old, rotted barracks. In the barracks people lay on top of each other. We received two hundred grams of bread per day. Our biggest scourge was bedbugs, whose bites left holes in the body. They bit [us] not only in the barracks but even when we slept outside.

Hunger Strike

Our group was made up of six hundred people, mainly Jews, very few Poles. Weeks went by; we weren't given work [and] suffered from hunger. We didn't know what to do with ourselves. We turned to the warden, who said: "Rest up a bit more." One day a letter arrived for one of our group from an acquaintance who had been deported to the Arkhangelsk Oblast. In the letter he told of a strike organized by the deportees to get better work conditions. The letter made a huge impression and we decided to announce a hunger strike. The strike lasted three days. During that time a lot of people escaped from the labor camp. The NKVD sent guards on horseback to watch us. On the third day, everyone gathered to stage a demonstration. We shouted until the warden arrived and said that he was sending us to *posiołki*, where we would have enough of everything.

---

150. *Molodetz* (Polish: *mołodiec*): a term of praise similar to "well done," "good man," etc.

151. Correct name: Asino.

In the *Posiołek*

We were assigned to the Szlaczynsk *posiołek*. The *posiołek* was located in the forest. It was made up of small huts that had ten people living in each. Our family got one of those little houses. No one was forced to work if they weren't registered to work. But those who did work risked a fine or even jail time for being late. My parents, not wanting to work on Saturdays, said that they wouldn't register for work. Father would say that, for observing the Sabbath, God would help him and not let the family die of hunger. Indeed, parcels and money began to arrive from our relatives in Western Galicia, which we lived off of for a long time. When the parcels ran out we would sell some of [our] things. For Pesach [12–19 April 1941] we received matzo and even festive lard. Father got arrested a few times and was sentenced to a few days in jail for trading. Overall, our situation was much better than that of those who worked. Father, having quite a lot of spare time, taught us Talmud,[152] because his greatest concern was that we grow up to be pious Jews.

Outbreak of War

We lived peacefully like this until 22 June 1941, the outbreak of war.[153] That day all nonworker privileges were revoked, and [we were told]: "Anyone who doesn't work doesn't eat." The flow of parcels from our relatives stopped, too. With no other choice, Father and Mother went to work in the forest. Soon we were moved to a different *posiołek* where there were more kulaks. One could buy milk, flour, and eggs from them. Children would pick berries in the woods. [My] parents worked hard: [their] hands were swollen from work; however, they never fulfilled their quotas. As a result, part of their bread ration was deducted.

Amnesty

One day, when Father arrived to work in the forest, the foreman told him: "I'll tell you a piece of good news after work today"—and told him after work the happy news about the Amnesty for Polish citizens. A few days later a commission made up of NKVD members and Polish officers arrived. We were told

152. Talmud: a collection of treatises, commentaries, legal articles, and religious tradition. Made up of the Mishnah (oral law) and the Gemara (rabbinic discussions). See glossary.

153. Invasion of the USSR by the Nazis.

that we were free and [that] we could go wherever we wanted. We said we wanted to go to Tashkent because we'd heard one could get bread and oranges there, like in Palestine. We set off on the way and reached the station of Shalashinsk [?]. A few families rented a wagon, we got onto it as if [we were] princes, [and] didn't allow in anyone we didn't know. We reached Tashkent after six weeks of journeying. They didn't want to let us into the city. Thousands of refugees were wandering around and sleeping in the streets. The city of Samarkand was overfilled too, like Tashkent. Finally, we got to Bukhara. We went weak at the knees. To get a roof over one's head was out of the question. People were dying in the streets from hunger and from typhus. In exchange for a watch Father managed to get a basement room and we moved in there. Father started trading and earned a little.

During that time my brother Naftali fell ill with typhus. Even though his condition was not grave, he spent six weeks in a hospital. Then Mother fell ill, I fell ill, and the whole family went through typhus. Only [our] uncle and [his] two-year-old child were left in the house, and when we were discharged from the hospital, [he] and the child were taken [there]. At that time a Polish delegation that helped refugees opened up in Bukhara. We found someone we knew among the officials, and thanks to this, received an allowance that came to three hundred rubles per month. A few months later I fell ill again with typhoid fever and dysentery. My seven-year-old cousin fell ill with me. We were in the hospital together and she practically died in my arms. My brother Mosze fell ill with tuberculosis, and thanks to the efforts of the Polish delegation, was admitted to a Russian sanatorium. When his health improved, he was sent off to a Polish children's home, where he spent two months.

One day Father came home and told [us that] children from the orphanage would be evacuated to Persia. I really wanted to go with them. I went to the station, ostensibly to say goodbye to my little brother. We swapped our hats. Wearing a beret with a Polish eagle, I got into a carriage and went to [Kogon].[154] In [Kogon] they checked the children and discovered I didn't belong to the group. I begged to stay on the train but it didn't work—I was thrown out of the carriage. Some Polish soldier, seeing me cry, promised that he would push

154. The original erroneously refers to the town of Kazan and has been corrected in this instance; it should be Kogon, near Bukhara [Polish: Kagan]. An identical error appears in other testimonies.

me onto the carriage at the last moment, when the train started. He did as he promised. Unfortunately for me there was a delegate in that carriage. He stopped the train and kicked me out of the car. I returned to Bukhara from [Kogon]. Father, hearing my story, turned to the delegation and begged that [my brother Naftali and I] be admitted to a Polish children's center. But my mother wanted at all costs to keep one child with her, and Naftali, my brother, was a very spoiled child and could not do without Mother's care. At the center I found out that a transport was leaving in five days' time, but [that] it would only be taking Polish children. Indeed, the Polish children were separated out and the Jewish ones left behind. Because the list was short by four children, four Jewish ones were taken. I was one of them and I was taken to the station. I spent four weeks in a Polish camp in Pahlevi. Then I went to Tehran. Because I was in such poor condition that I could barely stand up straight, I was sent to an English sanatorium where, after four weeks, I came back to health. After leaving the sanatorium I spent two weeks in camp number 1 with Polish children and two weeks in camp number 2, for Jewish children only. In camp number 2, to my great joy, I [found] my brother Moszele. Finally, the end of our suffering had arrived. My little brother and I arrived together in Palestine via Karachi.

Protocol 51

Testimony of **Regina Treler**, age thirty-four, born in Kraków. Wife of lawyer Emmanuel Treler. Teacher of Polish at the Hebrew Gymnasium in Kraków. Arrived in Palestine on 7 January 1943.

Before the war I became the commandant of a block of houses, appointed by the Air Defense,[155] and I was on duty on 1 September. At six in the morning, two hours after the Germans had crossed the border, Kraków was bombed. People did not escape to shelters—on the contrary, they ran out into the streets, curious to watch the maneuvers of "our" airplanes. Because of this there were many killed and wounded. Only after a few hours did the Air Defense commandant have us warn the people, before more bombing by the Germans. On Sunday morning, on the third day of the war, panic took over the city. The men fled toward Wołyń and Lwów. It was said in the city that the Germans were approaching at high speed. My husband could not decide at first whether to leave the city or not. However, since he was actively engaged in an anti-Hitler committee, and also held the position of a secretary of the Revisionist Organization,[156] we decided to leave Kraków and go toward Tarnów.

Journey

We were nearing Bochnia when the city was bombed. We hid in the famous Niepołomicki Forest, which was simply jammed with the army and civilians. Everyone sought shelter from the airplanes. One basically [had to] walk on top of [other] people. Small children cried and the elderly moaned. After one of the alarms we got out of the woods to continue on our way. Meanwhile, a new airplane squadron arrived. They flew so low that I saw the pilots, despite [my] poor eyesight. With no other choice, we returned to the forest and continued the journey at night. After more wandering around, with no drink or food, we arrived in Kałuszyn. The town was full of refugees and army people. The people had no idea about the barbaric deeds of the Germans until our stories caused panic in town. In the evening, when all the refugees set off on

155. Referred to as OPL (Obrona Przeciwlotnicza) in the original.
156. Refers to the Revisionist Zionist organization. See glossary: Revisionist Zionists.

their way, the Kałuszyn residents joined us. We bought a horse and a cart in Kałuszyn and went toward Tarczyn. [Some of] our relatives and friends lived there. We left our horse on the way, as it was exhausted and could no longer pull us, and harnessed up another [one] to the cart. On the way we came across not only abandoned horses but also empty cars with pieces of paper with the owners' surnames stuck on them. Since [my] husband got a bit of gasoline, we moved our things into an abandoned car, left the horse and the cart, and continued on. The roads were so crowded that one could not move around freely. We drove slowly. Meanwhile, German planes continued to bomb us. It was difficult to hide in the car [so] we left the mechanical vehicle and continued on in an abandoned cart we found by the road. After fourteen days' journey we arrived in Tarczyn. We found the town in ruins. The residents had run off in different directions. We did not find our friends. We rested in an abandoned house after the long journey. The next day we bought another horse and went toward Równe. When we arrived in town, the first Russian tanks appeared.

Bolsheviks in Równe

It was on 17 September. In the beginning, the local people welcomed the Russians in a friendly manner. Not only Jews came out into the street to welcome the Soviet army, but also Poles [who] crowded the town in numbers. It was generally believed that the Russians were not arriving as occupiers but [that] they were rushing to help Poland, to give her assistance in the fight against the German invaders. It turned out differently. The Russians immediately assumed civil powers through the local Communists and the [newly] arrived NKVD members. Arrests began of Polish officers, officials, police officers, social activists, etc. The city ran out of bread. One would wait nights in line for a piece of bread. Although kitchens were opened for refugees, not everyone could get soup [from them] because the local Communists carefully checked the backgrounds and previous beliefs of the refugees. My husband, as a well-known Revisionist, had to hide, as many of his associates were in prison. We decided to go to Lwów, thinking that it would be easier to hide from the NKVD in a big city. I went to the NKVD with a request for permission to go to Lwów, supporting my desire to leave with the fact that I had many relatives and friends in Lwów. I received the permit and we went to Lwów by train.

In Lwów

In Lwów we stayed at a relative's place at 35 Skarbkowska Street. The winter was hard. It was impossible to get fuel [for heating]. A cartful of firewood cost five hundred rubles. Food was difficult to obtain. In the city, filled with refugees, people simply slept on the streets. We didn't get any messages from [German-occupied Poland.] We didn't know what was happening with our relatives. Only when the first people from Kraków arrived were we told that it wasn't too bad on the German side, and that people over there worried about [us]. Many people returned across the border illegally. In December we were told that the border near Przemyśl, Rawa Ruska, and Brześć would be opened up for some time and those who wanted to could return home. We decided that [my] husband would stay in Lwów, and I [would] go to Kraków to see what the reality was—or, alternatively, return to Lwów with [our] belongings. I received a permit to cross over to the German side in Równe, from the commission that held office there. Full trains were departing in the direction of the German border. Miraculously, through a window, I got into a carriage, but before the train started [my] husband ran into the station, pulled me out of the carriage and said that at the border they were letting through Poles [but] arresting Jews. [My] husband wasn't earning anything. We lived off a money transfer paid into our account in Kraków and smuggled to Lwów.

Elections

In December elections took place for the Western-Ukrainian Soviet.[157] Everyone had to vote. People were dragged out of [their] homes, passersby were stopped in the street, and anyone who didn't want to vote was threatened with deportation to Siberia. With no other choice, we had to vote but we dropped in blank papers. After the elections, regular registrations took place where various questionnaires were filled [out] and [where people were] photographed. We didn't know what the purpose of them was. In the meantime, searches [and] arrests were taking place. They were looking for Polish officers, officials, [and] police officers, and arresting Jews and Poles—then, they were all deported. My husband looked for a job in his trade. He found out that anyone

157. The elections took place on 27 October 1939.

who wanted to practice law had to fill in a questionnaire including questions about the applicant's political past. My husband gave up the legal [profession].

The black market boomed. Despite penalties, persecution, and arrests, [people] continued to trade. I sent a letter to Mama in Kraków to [get her] to send me a few watches. Our servant brought me these watches, which I sold for good profit. In the summer, the situation in the city with regard to basic supplies improved. Cooperatives [and] state shops opened up where one could get food.

Registration Again

At the end of March 1940, news spread that sixty thousand refugees could return to the German side. It was said that this only applied to Poles. Despite this, Jews registered en masse. In the first transport that left in May, Jews were taken too. No more transports left and it was said that those registered were to be deported. Meanwhile, news had come about the arrests of all registered men in Przemyśl. Since we didn't know which registration this concerned, my husband went into hiding and didn't sleep at home.

Mobilization

At the beginning of June [1940], men between the ages of eighteen and forty-five were mobilized. My husband received a mobilization order. He went in front of the commission, showed a document [confirming that] he was a refugee [and] was set free. I didn't sleep at home but at [my] sister-in-law's; her husband worked, had a work card, and thus did not fear arrest. The situation worsened by the day. The searches were often repeated. Even the workers, if unable to produce a document immediately, were arrested. We decided to return to our apartment and prepared for [the worst].

In Exile

It was on 30 June [1940], at two o'clock at night, when there was a knock on the door and two policemen entered. [They] told us to pack our things, and during their search, stole a gold watch from me. They drove us to the station, loaded us into a freight car, and after forty-eight hours of waiting at the station we set off toward Kiev. Relatives brought food to the carriage for us.

My brother, an educator [and] an auditor at academic courses, comforted us [by saying] they were sending us—so he'd heard—not far from Lwów, from where he would try to bring us [back]. The cars were sealed and we set off. We couldn't all fit on the two bunks in the carriage. People slept on the dirty floor. We weren't allowed out at stations. We were given a piece of bread, and at night, [some] soup. It was possible to buy fruit from peasants during the journey. Within a short time everyone suffered from an upset stomach.

From Kiev we went to Trzubak-Sar,[158] a Tatar republic. We traveled for fourteen days. In Trzubak-Sar we were loaded onto barges and sailed down [the] Volga to a place from which [we traveled] by light railway for twenty-four hours to Madar, which was located in the Mari El Republic, whose main city is Yoshkar-Ola. It was a place hidden in deep forests, a place of exile for Russian kulaks who, after having served their punishment, settled down and built their lives there. Each had his own hut; single people lived in barracks.

We received eight hundred grams of bread per day. One could buy soup from the local kitchen with one's own money, but we did not take advantage of this benefit since the soup was inedible.

At first we weren't forced to work. The warden warned us that we would eventually have to start working. As my husband had fallen ill with rheumatism, I registered to work in his place. [The camp] authority consisted of a commandant in charge of political matters. He was a representative of the NKVD who had at his disposal only one policeman. Work was managed by the warden and a secretary. The assignment of work and accommodation and the issuing of bread [ration] cards were among his responsibilities. After a few days of rest the men were told to go to work in the forest, and the women in the laundry. I worked as a laundrywoman. The laundry was located in the forest. A cauldron stood there; one had to light a fire underneath it, and in this cauldron we would do the laundry. We did the washing for the warden and the locals, who paid the warden [for it]. A few pieces of soap had to last us a whole month. After a few months the laundry was closed down as there was no [more] soap, and the women were sent to work in the forest. My husband had to go in front of a medical commission, which, after an examination, gave him an exemption from work for four months. After some time a typhus epidemic

158. Here and henceforth should be: Cheboksary [original Polish correction: Czeboksary].

began to spread among us. Seventy percent of the people fell ill with typhus; others got malaria. There was no doctor. No one was sent to the hospital. The only medicine was quinine tablets. Only when fatalities began did they start sending people to the hospital. During the winter months we did not go to work. We didn't have warm clothing and the frosts were horrendous. We were virtually starving, as without work we received no food. Food parcels that our relatives from Lwów sent to us saved us from starvation. In March 1941 an order came for everyone to report for work, even children. We were split into three categories. The physically healthy chopped wood. The weaker loaded the wood onto wagons, and women and children cut off branches and tore up roots. When we finished the work we were sent to a second station, twelve kilometers away. We would leave for work on Monday morning and return on Saturday evening. The road was hard, muddy. We almost drowned in the mud. In the whole area there were fifty thousand deportees [and] eighty-five stations, [within an] eighty-kilometer [radius?]. One could get bread and soup in the canteens in the workplace. This cost a hundred rubles per month, while my husband earned sixty rubles per month. After we were allowed to communicate with the kolkhoz, we would swap clothing for food. A night blindness epidemic spread. The men suffered from it. It meant that one could not see anything at night. We were tormented by mosquitos and the rags we tied around our heads did not help.

Outbreak of War

The commandant notified us about the outbreak of war on the same day.[159] He told us not to rejoice just yet as we would never leave this place. Despite this our situation did improve [and] we believed that salvation would come. We lived in this anticipation until the end of August. During that time a commissar arrived [at the camp] and passed out passes [allowing us] to leave. We said we wanted to go to Tashkent but the commandant said they would not let us in there. We gave the [name of] the city of Shymkent, in the south of Kazakhstan. The commandant tried in vain to convince us to stay, scaring us [with tales] that the city was besieged by refugees from Ukraine. We thanked him for his advice and set off on the way.

159. That is the German invasion of the USSR on 22 June 1941.

New Misfortunes

We sold [our] old stuff, hired a cart, and went to Kosmodemyansk. There we waited for a ship that was to leave toward Kuybyshev. We slept outdoors for four nights and then traveled for five days until we arrived in Kuybyshev. We weren't allowed into the city [that was] overflowing with refugees. We went to Sichan [?] but there, too, it was impossible to find either bread or a place to stay the night. I found a solution to that, however. I gave a waitress at the train station two silk dresses and got fifteen kilos of bread for it. With these food reserves we undertook the fifteen-day-long journey to Turkestan. At the station we met [some] acquaintances who advised that we go not to Tashkent but to Shymkent [because] the NKVD did not want to register refugees [in Tashkent].

In Turkestan

The town of Turkestan looks like a European village. There isn't a single house made of brick there. The huts are shaped out of clay, without doors and without windows. For a small room in a hut we paid forty rubles per month. My husband worked as a loader. He would load goods onto a wagon [and] earn three rubles per day, which was enough for bread. We sold off the rest of [our] belongings. After two months my husband lost his job and we were left with no livelihood. It was only in January 1942 that bread ration cards were introduced. Since we had nothing to eat, I turned to the Selsoviet[160] and tried to get a job as a housekeeper. In February all the Polish women had [their] bread cards taken away. We were told to go to a kolkhoz. Even though they told us that people were dropping like flies in the kolkhozes, we had to go [there] regardless. Our landlords did not know that we were Jews. The antisemitism was horrendous. Landlords kicked lodgers out onto the street as soon as they found out they were Jews. My landlord was an escort guard and supplied the railway workers with food. Because he made little [money] and had to make it up with theft, he would take my husband with him so that he would help him in this work. My husband carried parcels for him in which there was vodka, kielbasa, flour, bread, etc. Half of these parcels were shared with us by

160. Selsoviet [original Polish text: Selsowiet, corrected to Sielsowiet]: formally the lowest level of a local government, a rural authority; in reality an organ of state administration.

their owner. In the city, speculative businesses developed. Dollars were traded, whose main recipients were reportedly NKVD agents.

My husband went to Tashkent where there was a Polish army camp, and where he was told that Jews were not accepted in the army. In March we received a telegram from Kuybyshev, from the Polish embassy, in which we were informed that [our] certificate for departure to Palestine had arrived. Our friend, Dr. Marek Kahan, who had gone to Kuybyshev, took our papers and promised to sort out our departure. Meanwhile, universal mobilization of Polish citizens was announced. My husband went in front of a Russian commission which deemed him capable of serving and sent him to Czag-Bag,[161] to a Polish camp. From there he was sent to Persia after a few days. After my husband's departure, Marek Kahan came to [see] us and brought us our papers. In possession of a Palestinian and Persian visa, I began to try to obtain permission to leave. Meanwhile, a Polish outpost opened up [in the city]. Delegate Bohdan Kościałkowski promised to help me obtain an exit visa. The NKVD told me that to obtain a departure visa I needed a document certifying "*vidnazhitelstvo*,"[162] which I did obtain after long efforts. During that time my Persian visa expired. Distraught, I went to the delegate, who took my passport and went with it to Kuybyshev. I lost the allowance from the delegation because I was told that my husband had gone away not as a [soldier] but on a civilian list. Delegate Kościałkowski, whom I met at the NKVD [offices], gave me a certificate of an escort of goods traveling to Turkestan, and this way I reached the city.

In Turkestan, a horrific typhus epidemic had taken hold. Thousands of people died daily. It was said that refugees would be sent to kolkhozes. The workday was upped from ten to twelve hours. Since many people did not want to work, mobilization for compulsory labor was announced. Seeing that I might get stuck at a kolkhoz somewhere, in July 1942, along with a few women, I boarded a train going toward Jang-Giul.[163] At the first station it transpired during a check that we were all traveling without documents, but I managed to

161. Correctly: Chok-Pak/Tschok-Pak [original Polish correction: Czok-Pak].

162. *Vid na zhitelstvo/vidnazhitelstvo* [Polish transliteration: *Wid na żytielstwo/widnażytielstwo*]: identity document and a residence permit. See glossary.

163. Incorrect spelling of Yangiyul [Polish: Jangi-Jul]. Appears in the protocol as Jang-Giul, Jang-Jul.

reach the city after all. I went to the Polish delegation, told them everything, and asked for advice. I was told that I was not a wife of a Polish [soldier] and therefore they could not help me. In despair, I went to the private apartment of Dr. Jenicz. He told me not to worry about anything, and to get on a train carrying people out. That I did. I tried to get into one of the carriages. They threw me out, explaining that I was coming from a region that had no agreement with Russia, and that the Russians did not admit citizens from those areas. At the station were General Szyszko-Bohusz and a Russian Colonel Tishkov. I told the general my story—he wanted to help me but couldn't. Then I turned to the Russian colonel, and when I showed him the documents he said, "You're a Polish citizen, get in the carriage." At a distance stood two rabbis. I didn't know their names. At the last moment they were crossed off the list and at risk of being left in Russia. Having seen the result of an intervention in my case, they turned to the colonel and began to cry. He looked through their documents and told them to board the train. From Jang-Jul I went to Krasnovodsk, from there to Pahlevi, where I met my husband wearing a Polish soldier's uniform. He serves in the Polish army to this day. In Tehran I obtained an Iraqi visa, and through Baghdad, came to Palestine.

Protocol 53

Testimony of **Mordechaj Szmulewicz**, age fifteen, son of Izrael and Adela. Resident in Łódź, 276 Piotrkowska [Street]. Arrived in Palestine in February 1943 via Russia and Persia.

My father was the owner of a textile factory. Our factory was located at 220 Piotrkowska Street and employed more than a hundred workers. Apart from this we had a goods warehouse at 15 Południowa Street. My father was a religious man and raised me and my sister Chaja in the same spirit.

When the war broke out we were living in Łódź. The Germans took over Łódź on Friday 8 September. At four in the afternoon they entered the magistrate, ordered the dark coverings to be taken off the streetlamps and the city was light again. The neighborhood where we lived was home to many Germans with whom we were on friendly terms. From the day the Germans entered the city, they stopped greeting us in the street. My father tried on the eleventh, a Monday, to get to the factory, but the porter by the door said that the foreman, who was German, had said not to let [my] father into the factory anymore. This way Father['s] factory was taken away. A few days later there was a search in our apartment. The Germans looked for money, jewelry, and hidden merchandise. But they didn't find anything. Then the foreman from the factory, along with a Gestapo [officer], came by our apartment and demanded the keys to the shop. Father calmly gave over the keys, and like this, we were left with nothing.

We stayed two months in Łódź under the German occupation. I heard it being discussed that the Germans were grabbing Jews off the street for forced labor, beating and torturing them. It was said, too, that men were pulled out of [their] homes and not allowed to return. There was also a story [about how] fourteen Jews were pulled out of a café on Piotrkowska Street and killed on the road. Among those killed was an acquaintance of my father, Bister, former owner of a stocking factory, and Szafir, also a factory owner. Father decided to escape to Warsaw with the family. We stayed in Warsaw for a short time. We didn't come across any of the people we knew. Most of the houses were in ruins and we couldn't find a place to sleep. A few days later we left for Małkinia. At the station in Małkinia the Germans surrounded our train [and] pulled the men and the women out of it separately. The Germans formed rows and let the Jews pass between them. They hit them over the heads, searched them, [took] everything. [Eventually] they let us out into an empty field on the other side of the station. We spent two days in the "no-man's-land" and waited for the Russians to open the border. On the third day, at night, the border was opened and we crossed over to the other side. We went to Białystok.

In Białystok

We arrived in the city in the evening. We spent the whole night in the station along with a thousand refugees. At dawn we went out looking for people we knew and met Father's cousin. He advised that, instead of going to the city, where it was hard to find an apartment, we go to the town of Ignacik [?]. We went there but found no place [to stay] and returned to Białystok. Since it was difficult to get an apartment in the city, we settled in the suburb of Zwierzyniec. Father, an excellent textile specialist, began to look for work in his trade, but was told that the bourgeoisie were not given employment. In one place he was offered the opportunity to become a loader. He agreed to it and earned eight rubles per day. He worked as a loader only for a few months. One day his work was terminated because he didn't have a Soviet passport. In May and April of 1940 a registration took place in Białystok for those who wanted to return to the German side. My parents who, when escaping from Łódź, had left my little seven-year-old sister, Chaja, with [her] grandparents, decided to return to Łódź.

Father Deported

One day, when Father was to make his way to Kowel with a load of goods, he was arrested at the station and asked for documents. Asked about a Soviet passport he responded that he had registered to go to Łódź to [his] child. He was arrested and sent away. To this day I don't know whether he's alive [or] where he is. [We] haven't had any news from him. Two weeks later on a Friday evening there was a knock on our door. Mama was sure that it was Father [who] was knocking and quickly opened the door. Four NKVD agents entered the room, and when [she] asked what they wanted, answered: "You're going to [join] your husband." Mother was overjoyed and told me to get dressed quickly. We took a few things and went to the station. We were loaded into a freight car; the doors were sealed. It wasn't until the evening that we left Białystok. There were fifty of us in the carriage. We almost suffocated from the stench. Luckily, we had brought some food from home with us, and Mother had drops that stopped her from fainting. Unable to stand the miasma any longer, we decided, along with other kids, to break down the carriage doors. We pulled out a bar from the car and pried the door open, and this way a bit of fresh air got in. We traveled for two weeks. On the way and at stations we came across masses of people who extended their hands and asked us for bread. We came across other trains too. Mother ran up to the window as if she was crazy and cried to me: "Look, there's your father." Every two days we received a piece of bread and some soup.

In Arkhangelsk

After two weeks we arrived in Arkhangelsk. From there we were driven ninety kilometers on trucks until we reached a *posiołek* in the forest. We spent the night there. We were given soup [made] from fish scales to eat. At four in the morning we were woken up. We were told to go on foot all the way to the river. We waded through the river—the water was up to our necks. At the other bank there was a barge. We went on that to some village where we waited for a few days again. Then our belongings were loaded onto carts and we followed [the carts] on foot for a few hours. The carts ran on wooden rails, with which the whole road was laid out. Around us stretched a forest, partially cut down, but with stumps [still] standing, which is why the carts had to go on rails. After eighteen kilometers' journey we arrived at a place called Paszta Niżniaja Kirza Uczastok Pojaminka, District 118.

The place was in the middle of a dense forest and surrounded by barbed wire. In the four corners there were sentry posts for guards who had watched the political prisoners who formerly lived in this *posiołek*. Those prisoners had been sent away to various districts before our arrival. The barracks were spacious but low. They were maybe half a meter tall.[164] We saw holes cut out in the floor that served as toilets for the prisoners. Having looked at the barracks we knew that we wouldn't be able to live there. I went into the woods, looking for some solution. I found an ax on the ground. We got to work. We cut

164. Could be a typo for *półtora* (1.5 m).

down some trees and started putting up a barracks. When the work was done, we made ourselves wooden beds, and three families settled in that barracks. At first there was enough bread because not all refugees have arrived yet, and we collected bread for everyone. Later, when the next transports arrived, there were thirty people living to a barracks. When everyone arrived, we were given saws and axes, and sent to work in the forest. It was a wild and huge forest. It was easy to get lost in it. First it had to be cleared of weeds [and] shrubs so that we could get to the trees. Clearing the forest was hard work. Our hands and feet were lacerated, and when we were pulling out the roots, weird worms and insects would jump out of the earth and bite and sting wherever they could.

After a few days of work people began to resist. They said that they wouldn't work if they didn't get a larger portion of bread. NKVD agents silenced the rebellion. But people shouted that they wanted to return home, to which the agents responded that once the whole forest had been cut down, they would be sent home. After the NKVD's visit the bread portions were increased to one kilo per day. Nonworkers received five hundred grams. We also got fifty grams of groats, ten grams of herring, thirty grams of peas, fifty grams of corn. We were supposed to be given these portions every day, but in reality, received them once per month. There was no kitchen. We cooked outdoors but the wood was wet and didn't want to light, so the food was smoky and inedible. We decided to eat the peas and the groats raw. From this we got dysentery. There was no doctor [in the camp]. They would call in a doctor for the gravely ill but it took weeks for him to arrive. There were no medicines, nor were there bandages for dressing open wounds. Winter came. No one had warm clothing. Rebellions, demands for warm clothing and medicine, began again. Seeing that our work was poor, they sent a group of Russian exiles to help us. In response to our demand for warm clothing they said: "If you don't want to work, the Russians will work in your place; they don't get cold because they work really fast." As a result of the strike, a few people were arrested. They were deported and we never again heard anything about these persons.

[My] mother, who was ill, was exempt from work. I was not forced to work either. Seeing that there wasn't a lot of stuff left for us to sell, I went to the foreman to get work. He gave me a horse harnessed to a sled. Another sled was tied to [that one]. I would go to the forest and move the timber to the tractors that took it to the river. The horse was weak; it would stop on the way and didn't want to pull the load. The foreman gave me a piece of iron and showed me how to beat the horse so it wouldn't stop on the way. But when we were going uphill I had to push the sled myself. Three times a day I went to the forest for the timber. The foreman considered me a top worker. I earned enough, and we got by without selling [our] belongings. I worked like this for a few months. Then when the snow melted, I was given different work: burning branches in the forest. I became a brigade leader and had five people under me. I had to watch my group and make sure they fulfilled their quota. We worked by the hectare. A hectare of branches had to be burned daily. Despite [our] best efforts, we could not do more than a hectare a week. It hindered [us] that we were only given one pack of matches per day and we struggled because the branches were wet. The work weakened me greatly and I was then given different work: pulling bark off trees. During that work [I] was almost killed by a falling tree.

Outbreak of War

We found out about the outbreak of war[165] only after some time. The foreman urged us not to abandon the work. He promised to send us to a better *posiołek* where we'd get better food, but we didn't want to hear of it and began to settle our accounts. Deductions were made for accommodation [and] wood and we [ended up having] to pay out more than we earned. We stopped working and received only two hundred grams of bread, with no soup.

On the Way Back

We began to leave the forest. We loaded [our] belongings onto carts that rode on wooden rails. [The rails] broke and [our] belongings tipped over. One such cart, loaded with belongings, fell on top of me and almost killed me. We went to Niżnia Kawsza [Nizhnia Kavsha?], from there to the river. We stayed on a ship moored there for eight days. I had enough bread, because I delivered bread for all of our group. I filled in a higher requirement than there were people, and this way obtained more bread. But when the ship set off there was nothing to eat. I poked about the ship until I found a bread storeroom. I waited until the supervisor opened the room, grabbed a loaf, bit into it, broke off a half, and ran off with [it]. We traveled on the ship for a few hours in total,

165. See the glossary: German-Soviet war.

and after arrival, were taken to a *posiołek*. Recognizing that we would not fare well there, I went to the commandant and asked him to send us to *posiołek* number 1 where, I had heard, the situation was better. He gave me a cart and a horse. I loaded up our belongings. The commandant taught me how to drive that [kind of] cart. This way [we found ourselves] in *posiołek* number 1.

After arriving I introduced myself to the new warden. As it was dark and Mother suffered from night blindness, I left her on the cart and went to the camp by myself and brought [back] bread for [her], then an iron bed for us. I placed [it] in our room, lit a lamp, and with the ax [I had] found in the forest, with which I never parted, I chopped up [some] branches, made a fire, and prepared coffee we had brought from Białystok. When everything was ready I took Mama off the cart, put her onto my back, and took her to the room. We had a feast. After eating I unharnessed the horse, fed it, and wanted to lie down to rest. But the commandant turned up, [and] told me to harness up the horse and go to the old *posiołek* to bring more people. I took bread with me too and went there and back. It was already four in the morning. The commandant told me that if I went for a third time I would get a double portion of food. Without thinking too long, I went for the third time. I drove like this [for] a few weeks, there and back. I was the highest-earning man in the *posiołek*. I got 150 rubles per month. When the first snow fell, I carried timber again. Mother worked in the *posiołek*. We had enough food and money [and] didn't need to sell anything. I then got a job transporting food supplies. From each item I carried I received a kilogram [for myself], so that not only did I have enough food, but [I] could also help others.

When I heard that people were going to the south of Russia, we decided to abandon everything and also leave. We traveled for three months by train, as far as Chelyabinsk. We had enough bread throughout the journey. On our documents it was marked when we received bread. I would erase [the note] using fresh bread, fill in a date and get bread for a second time. They spotted this and [started writing] the dates in ink. I went to the NKVD and started crying, [saying] we'd lost our documents. I was given a different piece of paper, and this way got bread twice. In Turkestan we weren't allowed to get off the train. I didn't want to go farther, as I'd heard they were sending [people] to faraway kolkhozes. Only when I was assured that we'd be sent to a kolkhoz located twenty kilometers from the city did we agree to carry on. During the first week in the kolkhoz I got into a bag of flour straightaway and skimmed off eight kilograms for us. Mother started baking *lepyoshki*.[166] We worked picking cotton and got four hundred grams of flour a day for it. After a month's stay at the kolkhoz, [my] mother fell ill with typhus. The *predsedatel* [person in charge][167] did not want to give me a cart to take [her] to the hospital. However, I took [her] to the city myself. In the meantime, they wanted to send us to a different kolkhoz. I said I wouldn't move until [my] mother returned from the hospital. Seeing that [this wouldn't work], I escaped from the camp to Turkestan. Meanwhile, Mother left the hospital. We decided to approach the delegation [for help]. We spent a whole night on the stairs leading up to the delegation. In the morning we made it inside, and despite our pleading, were given only fifteen rubles in assistance. Realizing that we would starve, Mother went to the NKVD and asked that we be sent to a kolkhoz. We were sent to [one located] eight kilometers from the city. Every new arrival received eight kilos of flour. We took those eight kilos, sat around at the kolkhoz for a day, and ran off to the city. We sold the flour for fifty rubles a kilo. Then I went to the NKVD and said I wanted to [go to] a kolkhoz. At the other kolkhoz we got four kilos of flour. I sold it in the city.

In possession of some cash, we rented a room. [My] mother went to [work in] an oil factory, and I decided to go to a Polish children's center. They didn't want to accept me because I was fourteen. I said that I was ten years old [and] that my parents had died, and because of that they took me in. Mother, having found out I'd been admitted to an orphanage, was angry with me for leaving her alone. I told her I would try to send her parcels from there. I fared well at the orphanage. The manager did not let the children beat me or call me names like "Jew." When they began to register children to leave, I went to the delegate and asked him to send me away too. He promised that, even though they weren't taking Jews, he would try to send me. A few days later our transport left. During the journey the Polish children bullied me a lot. I didn't say goodbye to [my] mother; I only saw her once during my stay in the orphanage. I was afraid they would find out I wasn't a full orphan and throw me out of there. What happened to her I don't know. From Turkestan, via Pahlevi, I went to Tehran and to Palestine.

---

166. A type of flatbread typical of Uzbek cuisine.

167. Polish original: *predsedatiel*.

Protocol 54

Testimony of **Naftali Gutman**, age sixteen, from Jarosław. Son of Ariel and Chaja-Estera. Arrived in Palestine in February 1943.

My father was the owner of a paper depot in Jarosław, the only one in the industry in the whole area. We had our own house and the paper depot. At home there were seven of us siblings, of whom only I survived. When the war broke out the city was bombed. On the first day we had thirty-five casualties. On Sunday, rumors were spread that the Germans were approaching. My father, as a well-to-do man who was well known in the city, was afraid that the Germans would take him hostage, [and] escaped along with my older brother, Jozef, [and] crossed the San River, presuming that the Germans would [not follow]. For two weeks my father and brother wandered around various villages and towns, and before Rosh Hashanah [14–15 September 1939], they returned home, telling of how the Germans had taken over all of Poland, that there was nowhere to escape to; and if [Father] were to die, he'd prefer to die in his own home. We spent ten days under own [?] occupation. During that period the Germans and Ukrainians stole everything they could from the Jews. In other depots, when they couldn't take the goods with them, they would destroy them on the spot. They grabbed people off the streets for work. They made Father clean toilets with [his] bare hands all day long.

Before Yom Kippur [23 September 1939], they began to round up Jews in the street and force them across to the other side of the San; then they would also say that anyone attempting to return would be shot on the spot. One of the first ones to be kicked over to the other side of the river was my brother Józef. We hid, thinking that this situation would pass and that we'd be able to stay [in town]. On Tuesday[168] 27 September [1939], the German commandant of the city issued a decree that all Jews had to leave the city within four hours and cross over to the other side of the river, to the Bolsheviks. Death awaited anyone who remained in the city. A great panic broke out. [People] began to pack up [their] belongings, bury jewelry and precious objects in the ground; and we, since we [already] had all of [our] valuables buried,

168. 27 September fell on a Wednesday.

were not able to find them in such a short time. At the appointed time, all the Jewish people—women, children, the elderly, and the sick, loaded up with heavy bundles—found themselves on the riverbank ready to set off on [their] journey. The Germans and the Ukrainians on that same riverbank took away everything [the Jews] had with them and let [them] pass only with small bundles. My brother Józef awaited us on the other side of the river. He told us that, upon learning about our exile, he had prepared a room for us in the village of Szusk,[169] not far from the river. We spent four days in that village.

Recognizing that it was pointless to remain in the countryside, we went to the town of Sieniawa, where our uncle, a poor teacher, lived, [and he] shared with his rich relative[s] everything he had. We spent two months in Sieniawa. [My] father began to look for work. As he couldn't do anything in his line of work, he traded whatever he could: sugar, flour, shoes, and dollars. But that wasn't enough to live on; there was a large family to feed. Father decided to move to Lwów at the first opportunity. We waited a month, until the railway was repaired, and went to Lwów. We arrived in Lwów in October. The city was full of refugees. It was impossible to find a room. We spent the first eight nights in a beth hamidrash,[170] but [my] father knew some merchants with whom he [used to trade]. We got a room in the suburbs. We were loaned a bit of money and started to get by reasonably well. One day, [my] father had his merchandise confiscated. He was locked up for three days, then released with the understanding that if he were caught once more, he'd be sent to Siberia. We did not recognize Father when he returned from his three days in jail. That same day he had a heart attack and we decided to stop him from trading [again]. We would take it upon ourselves to earn money. As well as my brother Józef, who had been trading for a long time already, I too went out into the city carrying a box. I found a few brushes and a box for the polish [and] became a shoe shiner. For cleaning shoes I received two, three, up to five rubles. I earned sixty rubles per day on average, and on public holidays even a hundred. In April [1940] the passport regulation came out. Even those who received the passports did not have full rights; they were sent off to small towns. [My] father kept thinking about returning home, where he had left his

169. Likely refers to the village of Szówsko on the San in the vicinity of Jarosław.

170. Beth hamidrash: Jewish house of prayer and learning. See glossary.

fortune, and did not want to take a Soviet passport. When the registration began for a return to the German-occupied lands, Father was first to register, convinced that he would be able to make it to Jarosław.

Deportation

We spent six months in Lwów. We settled down somehow, didn't go hungry. We thought we would survive here until the end of the war. On 29 June 1940 a decree came out about blackouts. In the city they explained that the reason for the blackouts was the war with Romania;[171] in reality, however, during those dark evenings a purge of undesirable elements took place. At three o'clock at night there was a knock on our door. Four people entered, two [of them] soldiers with rifles, told us to pack [our] belongings, and said that we were going to Germany. Outside there was a truck waiting that took us to the railway. We were pushed into a freight car in which there were seventy people, and the train was made up of fifty carriages. Most of the deportees were Jews, the rest—Poles. We waited in the station for twenty-four hours. We weren't given food or drink. Finally the train took off. We traveled through Dubno, Równe, Shepetivka, Kiev, Kuznetsk to Chelyabinsk. We were given two hundred grams of bread per day, sometimes soup. We weren't allowed to get off at big stations to get water. We bought bread there. In Kiev, for instance, we bought a six-kilo loaf from a Jewish woman. Before leaving the woman whispered to Father that, although the bread cost twenty rubles and she'd gladly have given it to the deportees for free, she wasn't allowed to do it. She asked that [my] father share the bread with others.

In the Coal Mine

After ten days we arrived in Chelyabinsk. We got off the train, loaded our belongings onto carts, and following the carts on foot for twenty kilometers, went to the town of Kapuńsk.[172] We were accommodated in barracks, thirty people in each. After a few days' rest we were sent to work. [My] father, mother, brother, and sister worked in the mine. [My] mother and sister loaded

171. Likely refers to the operation of takeover of Northern Bukovina.

172. Here and henceforth refers to the town of Kopeysk [original Polish correction: Kopiejsk] in the vicinity of Chelyabinsk.

coal onto wheelbarrows and pushed the wheelbarrows all the way to the elevator. The work took place two hundred meters underground. The workday was twelve hours long. For this work [my] mother and sister got four rubles per day, and [my] father and brother five rubles. Adults got eight hundred grams of bread per day, children—four hundred. The [work in the] mine was extremely rigorous. For being late five minutes one had 25 percent of [one's] earnings taken off; being late twice was punishable by arrest and a few months of jail. There were state shops there where one could get everything for a cheap price. Children had to go to school. I didn't want to study in a Soviet school, did not do [my] homework, pretended to be an idiot, and when [all] punishments proved fruitless, I was kicked out of school. We received parcels from relatives and this saved us from hunger. In the autumn, during a rainy period, the mines were flooded with water. No one worked [and] we began to suffer hunger. In those days we received only five hundred grams of bread per day. Because our family was among the best workers, we received a number of privileges, such as the right to buy a newspaper or a cinema ticket. The warden treated us well. There was only one day on which the whole family missed work: it was the day of Yom Kippur [12 October 1940]. Father said that there was no way he would agree for us to work on the Day of Atonement. The next day the warden told us that the only reason he wasn't charging us with sabotage was our honest work.

We're Free

On 22 June [1941] the war broke out, and that was when an NKVD representative came into the mine, gathered all the workers, and said that victory over the enemy depended solely on our work, and that we would get a bonus for overproduction. Hard days of grueling labor began. The NKVD-ers rushed us and wouldn't let us catch [our] breath. When they came home, [my] parents were deathly exhausted. This didn't last long. In August, the Amnesty for Polish citizens was announced over the radio. [The Polish citizens] could go wherever they wanted. That same day we abandoned [our] work and left for Uzbekistan. From the town of Kapuńsk [Kopeysk] we went to Chelyabinsk and waited for a train there for a week. As it was impossible to get a train in a normal way, we rented a carriage along with a few [other] families and set off for Tashkent, via Oranienburg.[173] The journey took four weeks. In Tashkent, we weren't allowed in the city, which was overflowing with refugees. People were lying outside on the pavement—we had no choice but to carry on.

We went to Leninowód.[174] Since during the journey we had decided not to go to Parugan,[175] which was far from the [city] center, we stayed in Leninowód. They didn't want to register us and no one wanted to let us into [their] apartment. We roamed the streets, and recognizing that nothing good would come of it, went to the NKVD with a request that we be sent to a kolkhoz. We were sent to the kolkhoz Maksym Gorky. We were very unhappy in that kolkhoz. We worked with cotton from morning to evening and received four hundred grams of flour per day for it. We lived in kibitkas [primitive huts] with the Uzbeks so that we wouldn't be able to rebel.

We worked so hard that Father and Mother fell ill and went into convulsions from hunger. They couldn't be taken to a hospital and were only taken into town after some time. After a day's stay in the hospital, Mother passed away. This was in June of the year 1942. Two days later Father died, and then [my] sister. I don't know where they were buried. My younger sister fell ill with asthma [and] spent eight months in the hospital. She was then sent to a Russian orphanage, where she spent three months. My sister Dina and I fell ill with dysentery. We were taken to the hospital. [Dina] died a few days later. When I recovered, I decided not to go back to the kolkhoz again—I would rather have died out on the street.

Good people took an interest in my fate. One Mrs. Jakubowicz from Łódź registered me as her son, and this way I received a [ration] card for bread. She worked in a shoe factory, and thanks to her I got a job. One day she told me she was going to Jang-Giul[176] and that she intended to leave Russia with the Poles. I asked her to take me with her; she refused, saying it would be difficult for her to obtain a permit for two people. Without much thinking, I wrapped my feet in rags and sold my shoes for 120 rubles. With this money I went to Jang-Giul. I found Mrs. Jakubowicz there and was put on the Jewish list with her. I knew,

173. [This location has not been found. Perhaps Orenburg?]

174. Here and henceforth an erroneous name for the town of Leninabad [nowadays: Khujand].

175. Likely refers to the town of Fergana.

176. Here and henceforth an incorrect spelling of the name of Yangiyul [original Polish correction: Jangi-Jul].

however, that they weren't allowing Jews to leave Russia. Mrs. Jakubowicz returned to the shoe factory. I stayed in Jang-Giul and decided to leave with the Polish children. I was starving and managed to beg a piece of bread from a Polish soldier who was standing guard. I told him my story. The soldier intervened for me and I was taken into an orphanage. I stayed there a few days, and along with a children's transport, went to Pahlevi. I spent a month in an English sanatorium for my health to improve. From there I went to Tehran and arrived in Palestine in February [1943].

Protocol 55

Testimony of **Nachman Elbojm**, age sixteen, yeshiva [Jewish secondary school] student in Baranowicze. Arrived in Palestine from Tehran in February 1943.

Before the outbreak of the war I was a student at the Baranowicze Yeshiva. On Thursday night [31 August], [people] said in Baranowicze that war had broken out. We were told to go home on Thursday. I left in the early evening and arrived in Otwock at six in the morning on Friday. My mother lived in a guesthouse in Otwock [and] I intended to spend the night in that guesthouse. I was witness to the first German air raid of the Jewish orphanage of CENTOS.[177]

First Attack on Otwock by German Airplanes

When I was walking from the station to the guesthouse where Mother lived, an air raid alarm sounded. Despite the early hour the streets of Otwock were full of people. Everyone had come out on the street to find out the [latest] news. Despite the alarm no one was running to shelters because they thought it was a test alarm. They calmly looked up at the airplanes flying low over the town.

When I came close to the guesthouse, I heard three explosions. It became clear to me that bombs had gone off in the neighborhood. Awful screams and cries rang out. I went to see what had happened, alongside other curious people. We walked up to the CENTOS building. It was terribly crowded. The building lay in ruins. One part of the building was on fire because the Germans had dropped incendiary bombs, too. From the building came the wailing of injured children. The emergency help arrived quickly [and] the personnel and the neighbors took part in the rescue. By the time the Otwock fire service arrived, eight dead children and twenty-three injured ones, gravely or more lightly, had been pulled from the rubble. Jews, oblivious to danger, threw themselves into the fire and pulled out the wounded children. Before they managed to put out the fire, German airplanes appeared. Despite the alarm

177. CENTOS [Polish: Centralne Towarzystwo Opieki nad Sierotami]: Central Society for the Care of Orphans, also referred to as The Association of Societies for the Care of Jewish Orphans. See glossary.

that was rung, no one stopped the rescue operation. This time the planes did not drop bombs. Otwock also tallied ten heart attack victims. In our guest-house one Gitla Fajzenfeld from Częstochowa died of fright.

I Return to Warsaw

On Sunday morning we received a message that Warsaw had been bombed also. Thousands of people descended on the rail station. Mother and I went to Warsaw. We didn't have provisions prepared, as Mother hadn't been at home. I had to look for food [items], which is why I was out in the streets all the time when Warsaw was being bombed. I happened to be near the post office where I was supposed to get sugar. Houses were burning. I pulled sacks of sugar and rice from the burning houses alongside other people and was given [some] sugar and rice in a bag for it. During the bombing and the siege of Warsaw we changed apartments a few times. Two apartments were destroyed but we survived the disaster[s] in one piece.

Captured for Forced Labor

On the second day of the *Kuczki*[178] holiday I went with Father to Pawia Street to Rabbi Kaminker, to pray there. Since there was no place for praying in the Nalewki district, a line formed on Pawia Street in front of the rabbi's house. Suddenly, like a bolt from the sky, there appeared a group of German soldiers [who] surrounded us. Around twenty people were taken to the parliament building to work. We worked very hard. At dusk we wanted to go home but it was only in the evening that our suffering [truly] began. As it was a holiday, observant Jews were wearing silk gabardines. The Germans began to mock us. They ordered us to sing and hit one another; Father was told to beat me. They pulled hair out of my father's beard. Then, without food or drink, we were locked inside the parliament building, in the basement. We spent three days in that basement. We cut each other's beards so that they couldn't torture us any-more. After three days of hard labor, we were harnessed to carts like horses and told to carry rubble. In the end they set us free, but on the way, every German we came across tormented us.

---

178. *Kuczki*: name used in Poland for the holiday of Sukkot (see glossary), observed two weeks after the Jewish New Year. In 1939 the holiday fell on 28–29 September. See glossary.

I Become a Tradesman

After this first experience I lay in bed for eight days. Father was afraid to go out in the streets. I became a tradesman. I went to my paternal uncle Mosze Elbaum[179] who had a small tricot factory at number 9 Nalewki. I took some merchandise from him and started to trade it in the street. One day [some] Germans stopped me and asked about the price of tricot undergarments. I said half of what I had paid for it myself. The Germans beat me up terribly and took away all of the merchandise. They demanded that I give them the address of the factory. I let myself get beaten but did not tell the address. I didn't have [money] to pay for the goods and was ashamed to go to [my] uncle. At home, we began to go hungry. We decided that all the men should go to Białystok. But we didn't have [money] for the cost of [their] travel. I started trading sweets and cigarettes in the streets.

Pogrom at Number 9 Nalewki

Every day it was becoming more difficult to trade—more difficult to live. Groups of German soldiers went from shop to shop, from factory to factory. One day I went to my uncle, [at] 9 Nalewki, for advice regarding the journey to Białystok. As it was seven o'clock, when Jews weren't allowed to walk in the streets, I stayed the night. At dawn I heard horrific screams. I went up to the window and saw a group of youths fighting among themselves. Soon they dispersed, and left on the ground was a man in the uniform of a Polish police officer. It was later said that this policeman was associated with a band of thieves who had fought over [their] loot. Soon, a large number of Gestapo members arrived [and] surrounded the entire yard, but we managed to escape over the roof to the attic of the neighboring house. We saw from the roof how fifty-seven people, the inhabitants of the house, were taken outside. They were all innocent people. The Germans shot them all dead.

We Go to Białystok

Recognizing that we would not last long under the German occupation in Warsaw, we decided—[my] father, [my] uncle, and myself—to leave. We went

179. This is the way the name had been noted in the original.

through Kałuszyn, Siedlce [and] Mordy all the way to the Bug River. German soldiers collected a high payment from every Jew crossing the bridge. Moreover, I saw how the Germans took away everything of any value. From us they didn't take anything. On the contrary, they showed us the stuff they had stolen and even asked if we wanted any [of it]. We thanked [them] for [their] kindness. As soon as the boat with the passengers pulled away from the bank in the dark of night, the Soviet guard fired rockets all around our boat. We thought we were done for. But the journey was concluded safely and we avoided the patrol when disembarking. We didn't know which way to go, and in small groups, followed a small lit lamp. We went through swamps, pulling one another from the mud. We worried someone might drown. We wandered like this for half the night, unable to find a dry spot. Luckily, there was no patrol. We were, however, terrified and dispirited, since we weren't able to pull one youngster from Warsaw, Kalman Berliner, out of the swamp, and he drowned. We couldn't get this loss out of our heads. Later we came upon Soviet soldiers whom we managed to convince by begging to let us go free. After long suffering we eventually arrived in Białystok, where we had friends. In Białystok I became a real tradesman. At first, I smuggled sugar, rice, [and] flour from one town to another. I [not] only earned a living but also sent money to Warsaw to my mother and aunt. Because restrictions on traders began, we decided to sneak over the Lithuanian border.

During the crossing of the Soviet-Lithuanian border, in January 1940, we put up with a lot of suffering. We were arrested a few times but made it to Wilno eventually. Straightaway I located the head of the Baranowicze Yeshiva, Rabbi Wasserman, and asked him to take me on again to study, as I didn't want to become a smuggler. The rabbi lived in Troki, outside Wilno. Immediately after the occupation of Lithuania by the Bolsheviks, persecutions of rabbis and religious people began. My [teacher] was arrested and I do not know what happened to him. Rabbi Rapaport, the other director of the yeshiva, was arrested too. What happened to him nobody knows. Their wives and children are in Dzhambul. The Yeshivites split into groups and settled in various small towns.

Deportation

On 15 June 1941,[180] on a Saturday in the middle of the night, when we were all asleep, half-starved, a large NKVD group entered, bursting into our room by pulling the doors off with [their] gunstocks. They started to swear at us and force us to hurry. Two students ran off. They were shot at. Most of my friends were taken into the depths of Russia [and] to this day I don't know what happened to them. I managed to sneak out of the room and run off to Father, who lived in Šiauliai. The same thing as [had happened] in Troki and Wilno happened to the most respected Jews in Šiauliai. Rabbi[s] Sender, Lubkin, and Lejzerowicz were deported [and their fate remains unknown]. A large number [of deportees] died during the journey from hunger or diseases.

War Outbreak and the Kolkhoz

I lived in Šiauliai with [my] father and uncle until the outbreak of the Soviet-German war. On 23 June [1941] we went to the station, which was overtaken by a terrible panic. Tens of freight cars were waiting in the station. [Those who wanted to], got on [the train] and set off without a destination or a plan. The train was constantly bombed by the Germans. In such conditions, without food or drink, our evacuation train traveled through Połock, Rybnik [likely Rybinsk], and Ewaszana [likely Kineshma] in the Gorky district.[181] We were assigned to the Woroszyłow kolkhoz and told to pick moss in the forest. We received little food for it, went hungry, and [yet were] ordered to work twelve hours a day. Out of eighty-four Jews, half fell ill. Many died. We escaped to town, and then to Sawaslek,[182] where we were given work in a garden, but the food situation was still poor. After the holidays, when the cold started to be a problem and we got increasingly colder in [our] summer clothes, we decided to escape to the south of Russia. We went to the warden and asked for [our] accounts to be settled for the time we had worked. We were laughed at. We fled to the neighboring town, sold everything we had, and half-naked, set off for Tashkent. The road led to Midan [?]. We came across a group of older Jews there who had lived in that city since the time of the revolution. The Jews, who to this day are covertly loyal to religion and Jewish rituals, helped us a great

180. Error on part of the author: refers to the year 1940.
181. Up until 1932 and currently Nizhny Novgorod.
182. Perhaps Shileksha [original Polish suggestion: Szileksza].

deal. We then went to Gorky, where we stayed for a few weeks and suffered a great deal.

I Lose Father

In Gorky a tragedy befell me. After three days of starving, I went to the town square to sell a few ladies' stockings to buy myself some food. I sold the goods, bought the bread, and was happily on my way home. I found neither [my] father nor [my] uncle in the house. All of my efforts to find out what had happened to them were fruitless. They had vanished from the face of the earth. I went on my own to Kuybyshev [until 1935 and currently Samara] and from there to Tashkent. The journey took a very long time. I traveled without a rail ticket, slept at stations, and often heard insults on the streets, like *bosjak* [bum].[183] My situation only improved [when I got to] Tashkent. I met a Jew from Moscow; he took me to his home, gave [me] clean underwear—that man truly saved my life. He was a well-known activist and had a lot of influence with the Soviets, and it was he who opened my eyes to everything. He gave me various items to sell. [Through whatever I sold in Tashkent]—army boots, stockings, socks, sugar, rice—I had enough food. This lasted a few months. I saved a bit of money and decided to find [my] father and paternal uncle at all costs. But it's difficult to find anyone in Russia. I fell ill with typhus. The illness put an end to all of my plans. I spent thirty-three days in the hospital. When, weakened after the illness, I left the hospital, it turned out that my [savior] had left for Moscow. I had no roof over my head; I slept in the street, as they wouldn't let me stay in the station. I roamed the streets of Tashkent for a few days without a crumb of bread, until I made the acquaintance of one Jewish photographer in the city. He took pity on me [and] saved my life—he took me home with him. I am certain that were it not for the photographer I would have died of hunger in the streets, like so many other refugees.

I Find Father

My father and uncle, like myself, looked for me everywhere. This went on for half a year. My uncle, who was traveling via Tashkent to Samarkand, found out that I was in Tashkent. And I found out that Father had gone to Tashkent. We

183. *Bosjak*/*bosiak* (from Russian *bosoi*: barefoot): hobo, bum, ragamuffin.

looked for one another for two days in vain. We met by accident in the street. I don't have to tell how much we cried during that meeting. My father and uncle told me what they had lived through during that half year. From Gorky they went to Astrakhan, passing by Stalingrad.[184] They wouldn't let them through to Astrakhan. They waited by the river for three days and suffered terrible destitution. In Astrakhan they waited in line for hours for a piece of bread. In one small room, forty people slept. They were allowed to sleep two out of twenty-four hours, taking turns. Eventually, the police told all the outsiders to leave and threatened [them] with deportation to the north. The news about the Amnesty for Polish citizens was miraculous for me. My father and uncle decided to join the Polish army. They made their way to Samarkand and found out during the journey that I was in Tashkent. I took up trading again and supported all three of us for some time. Then we went to Samarkand. I found out that they had opened an orphanage in Samarkand for Polish children. I tried in vain to get into this orphanage. When I learned that Polish children would be evacuated to Persia, I signed up [to be added] to the evacuation list. One Polish lieutenant told me that I would go with the next transport. I begged him for such a long time that he took pity on me and sent me off with the first transport. From Persia I came to Palestine.

184. Before the October Revolution, Tsaritsyn [Carycyn], and after 1956, Volgograd [Wołgograd].

Protocol 56

Testimony of **Chana Gelernter**, resident in Warsaw at number 20 Nowolipie. Arrived in Palestine via Tehran in 1943.

When the war broke out I was at the *hakhsharah* in the Hashomer Hatzair kibbutz in Lublin.[185] During the first days of the war the kibbutz was closed down. Most of the kibbutz members went to Wołyń, Równe, Kowel, Łuck. I stayed in Lublin and moved in with my distant relatives. The bombing of Lublin lasted two weeks, day and night. There were lots of casualties from among the Polish and Jewish people. Many homes were demolished.

Germans in Lublin

During [their] first stay in the city the Germans pulled many Jews and Poles out of [their] homes and took them to army barracks located outside the city. On the way they beat the Jews horribly. Those few hundred people in the barracks were declared to be hostages. All Jews were ordered to deliver the keys to the factories and shops to the commandant's headquarters within two weeks. The Jews were split into categories. They were assigned to various [types of] work in different camps located on the Bug River, where fortification[s] were being built. After some time, it was ordered that the yellow badge be introduced. Hard times began for the local Jews. Frequent searches came with beatings and abuse. Then, all Jews were kicked out from the central streets. Trade ground to a halt. Poverty increased. A Jewish council was formed whose role it was to provide help to refugees.

Refugees

At the beginning of the year 1940 trains with Jews displaced from Łódź, Kalisz, and other cities arrived in Lublin daily. Those masses of refugees worsened the existing destitution. Typhus began to spread and the mortality among the Jewish population went up considerably. Local social activists devoted their time

185. *Hakhsharah* (Hebrew) was a professional training [program] for future Jewish pioneers in Eretz Israel led by the Zionist youth movement Hashomer Hatzair (Young Guard). See glossary.

to working with the refugees. All Jewish political parties joined in. A clothing collection began.

The Germans closed down Jewish schools, but children studied illegally. Then, huge groups of Jews from Austria arrived in Lublin. It was said that a Jewish reserve would be formed in Lublin—at the same time, however, illness [rates] were increasing. All factories, schools, [and] synagogues were turned into hospitals. There weren't enough pairs of hands to tend to the ill. The most necessary medical supplies ran out, as well as . . . plots in the cemeteries. A harsh winter arrived. People, hungry and ragged, dropped like flies from the cold. Moreover, the Germans began to send over large groups of Jews [and] Polish prisoners of war to Lublin. Only one transport was released. Others were sent as forced labor on the fortifications, where people worked for fifteen hours a day. After two prisoners escaped, the Germans stripped thirty soldiers naked and ordered them to stand outside like this for six hours in freezing temperatures. Fifteen people died. It was announced that should an escape occur, they would kill a hundred Jews for each fugitive. The following day three [people] ran away. The Germans killed thirty-three soldiers. The Germans forced observant Jews to dance half-naked with women in the streets.

Smuggling across the Border

Recognizing that the situation was becoming increasingly worse, I decided to cross over to the Soviet side. Before that, however, I went to Warsaw to say goodbye to my parents. I went from Lublin to Warsaw on foot. From time to time I managed to cover a few kilometers on a peasant's cart. In Ryki, a German soldier stopped me and took me to [his] commandant. I saw myself how the commandant tortured a young, pretty Polish girl in my presence. When the commandant was done with the girl, he asked the soldier what contraband [he had brought him], and pointed at me. The soldier replied that he had found a Jewish girl atop a cart. The commandant ordered for me to be bathed and brought to him. I was saved by a miracle because the commandant had a few Polish women with contraband brought to him. The Germans paid [me] no attention and I escaped. After four days' journey I arrived in Warsaw. I found [my] parents in a horrific state. Mother had gotten a concussion from the difficult experiences, and Father was paralyzed. I wanted to abandon my journey to Russia but Father convinced me to go.

In Białystok

After two days' stay in Warsaw I went, via Małkinia, to the Soviet border and got to Białystok after many difficulties. I spent a few days on the streets without a roof over my head. Only later did I find a small corner in a school, for three hours of the night in total. But I was happy, remembering everything I had lived through with the Germans. I arrived with a group of young Jewish and Polish girls from secondary school. We were starving. We received a ruble per day and had to live off that. And it's a lot more difficult to study when one is hungry. We wanted to open up a dormitory for our friends. We forced our way into a premises which we wouldn't leave, even though it had been requisitioned for the army. The issue of the dormitory became an issue of life [and death] because we had nowhere to spend the night, and sleeping in the station and in other lice-infested places was no longer feasible. One day they even tried to throw us out of the station. We resisted. A bloody fight ensued. The authorities were represented by three men—we were forty girls. They announced they would come the next day. We locked ourselves inside the building, put up barricades, and decided that we wouldn't let ourselves be thrown out. NKVD-ers came in a big group, didn't try to talk with us, they just hosed us with water from fire hoses. As a result of the fight, eight girls were injured and we were kicked out of the building. We announced a hunger strike [and] didn't eat anything for three days. The Soviet school office, however, deemed our allowance sufficient and the gymnasium was closed down.

Soviet Passports

It was demanded that we become Soviet citizens. We didn't want to consent. Some registered for a return to Poland. They were immediately arrested and sent to Siberia. Another group, myself among them, received passports with paragraph 11.[186] In accordance with the regulation[s] we had to leave Białystok and go to Rusiniec. I struggled a great deal. [It was the old story]: hunger and sleeping in stations. More than once I thought about suicide. I got a job by chance. I chopped wood for a bakery. It was during winter, [and] my earnings were such that I got enough bread to fill me up at the bakery and a warm spot by the oven for sleeping. All the bakery workers slept there. The wages amounted to

186. This paragraph forbade living in larger cities and their surroundings.

ninety rubles per month. I worked hard but was happy that I had [something to] eat, and I became a subject of envy from my girlfriends. They would come six kilometers on foot to see me so that I would offer them a piece of dry bread. I stole that bread for my visitors. I worked in the bakery for five months. I put aside four hundred rubles—this way I was able to finish gymnasium. I received my secondary school certificate on 16 June 1941. I got an office job but it lasted a very short time, only three months, because the Russian-German war broke out.

Russian-German War

Along with a group of my girlfriends I went to Mikaszewicze. German airplanes were bombing the town. Hundreds of people died in front of our eyes. We decided to evacuate. We went to Kiev via Żydkowo.[187] The journey was horrendous. The train was constantly under fire from the German planes. We saw that two Soviet [forces] whose role it was to defend Belorussia [Belarus] and Ukraine, had been bribed, and the whole army capitulated along with the ammunition, tanks, and the heavy artillery. During the journey my friend Rywka Goldkorn had her hand[188] cut off by a piece of bomb shrapnel. Finally, we got to Kiev. In Kiev there was a horrific panic, such that the image of the first days of the war in Poland seemed idyllic compared to the hell I came across there. The city looked like a huge refugee camp. All the roads were densely filled with refugees who were arriving here from Ukraine and Belorussia. There were thousands of refugees in a huge botanical garden: Jews, Poles, Ukrainians, Belorussians [Belarusians], Lithuanians, Latvians, and others, who were afraid of the Germans. We slept outdoors. A female committee whose role it was to look after the refugees was not able to deal with the task.

Fugitive Wedding

During those horrendous days I met a friend from my youth, Sewek Altbaum from Warsaw, and we got married. A few days later, in that same garden, I found my brother Aron Gelernter. During the Germans' bombardment of Kiev my brother was killed. I escaped to Voronezh with my husband. In Voronezh we made our way to a kolkhoz where both of us worked very hard.

187. Likely refers to the town of Zhytkavichy [original Polish correction: Żytkowicze].
188. This could refer to either her arm or her hand (the Polish word can mean both).

The kolkhoz managers exploited refugees cruelly. Despite [our] hard work we were constantly starving. I fell ill with dysentery. I had to [return to] work before I recovered. We received an order to take part in the haymaking. The point was [to get it done quickly] because the enemy was approaching.

My Husband's Death

We worked in the Voronezh kolkhoz until December. In times of freezing cold the work was unbearable. In [those times] all our limbs would get frostbitten and we weren't allowed to fall sleep so that we wouldn't freeze during sleep. There were a few such incidents. Since the enemy was approaching Voronezh, it was decided that we would be evacuated to the Urals. With empty stomachs, in open freight cars, in temperatures of −40°C [−40°F], we were sent to Siberia. To warm up, we would dance the hora [Israeli dance] for days and nights on end. We did everything possible to not fall asleep but it was in vain. Out of our group, fifteen people froze to death during the journey. The dead bodies were thrown out of the window during the journey. My husband was suffering terribly. Both of his feet were frostbitten. Thus we arrived in Karasu in Turkestan where I carried my husband, who was unable to walk, for eighteen kilometers. I took him to the hospital. His condition was grave. I myself got busy with work on cotton plantations. After work I visited my husband in the hospital. My husband suffered for a few weeks in the hospital. The support [he received] was poor. He would wait entire days for a doctor, and it's no wonder his condition worsened under such conditions. He died on 20 March 1942. [My] husband's death shook me horribly. I was in an altered state [of mind]. I asked to be given lighter work, but my requests were fruitless. I got the response that during war everyone had to work equally. Antisemitism was rife in the Uzbek kolkhoz. Everyone, young and old, exhibited hatred toward Jews. The Uzbeks are bad people by nature. They don't understand what it means to give someone a piece of bread, or even a bit of water.

After the Amnesty

After the Amnesty I went to Dzidabar.[189] I turned to the Polish delegation so that they would help me. I didn't receive help because I was a Jewish woman.

189. Could be Jalal-Abad in the Dzida region, Kyrgyzstan.

I then went to Kyrgyzstan, where I was sent for hard labor in a coal mine, and there I miscarried. I couldn't even rest one day because I risked starving to death. I found out that the Polish delegation readily provided assistance to Poles. I went to Dzidabad [?] and registered as a Christian. Immediately I received help and clothing. With an aching heart, I pretended to be a Christian for entire months. I arrived in Tehran also as a Christian. There, I told the camp manager who I was. He replied that he had known from the first moment that I was a Jewess, but that to avoid causing me problems, he pretended not to know about it.

Protocol 58

Testimony of **Dawid Zylkiewicz**, Warsaw, 12 Zamenhof Street, born in 1915. Jazz musician in Adria café in Warsaw. Came to Palestine from Russia via Tehran.

At the outbreak of the war, I was taking leisure time in Urle outside Warsaw. On Friday 1 September [1939] I went to Warsaw by train. At the station I came upon thousands of reserve soldiers who were hurrying to the assembly point. The station manager could not manage—he couldn't find cars for everyone. The atmosphere was spirited, army songs were sung. We got to Warsaw before the evening. I went to the 3rd police district. I found thousands of reservists there. I was sent to Cytadela with the others. We all slept under the open sky. There wasn't [enough] clothing for everyone, let alone guns. I was sent to Mińsk Mazowiecki to the second regiment. I was known as a good shot and an excellent jazz musician. I had to wait a long time, however, for a gun and bullets. Finally, I got a gun and was sent to the front. I fought in the section between Kałuszyn and Mińsk Mazowiecki and then, when we retreated, took active part in the defense of Warsaw.

Defense of Warsaw

By a stroke of luck, the commandant of my regiment assigned me to an outpost by the Zenit rocket battery on Jasna Street by Adria, where I had entertained Warsaw as a member of an orchestra for many years. I was decorated by the command for shooting down two German planes that were circling over Warsaw. I did everything I could to shoot on target. I cared particularly strongly about shooting well when I found out that the house where my parents lived at 13 Zamenhof Street had been bombed and 120 people [ended up] under its rubble. Unfortunately, our fight did not last long. When I found out about the city's capitulation and the surrender of the army, I escaped home so I wouldn't fall into the enemy's hands.

After Capitulation

After the capital's capitulation I was overcome by heavy apathy. I was afraid to go out in the streets. I had seen tens of Jews who'd had [their] beards cut off by the Germans, along with parts of their faces. I was afraid of encountering such a scene. However, when the bread ran out at home I had to go out into the streets. It was the holiday of Sukkot[190] when the first field kitchen arrived. Magnanimously, the Germans wanted to hand out soup to the hungry people. Thousands of Poles and Jews stood in line in front of the kitchen. Before anything else happened, the Germans pulled the Jews out of the lines and beat them terribly. The rest of the Jews ran off. The Germans forced the Polish policemen to beat old Jews, and when the Jews came to after the beatings, they forced them to [attack] the policemen. I will never forget the horrendous scenes that played out in the Saski Garden. During the street roundup a few Jews hid in the Saski Garden. Two managed to hide [and] the Gestapo were furious. They closed all the garden gates and started herding all the people inside the garden into the building of the Summer Theater. There, body searches were carried out. Since I had on me a [membership] card of the Polish Musicians' Association, and [because] the surname Zylkiewicz did not sound Jewish, I was released. But I won't forget what they did to the others. Two Jewish girls were thrown into the pond. We stayed, me and four other men, until the evening and tried to search the pond. We pulled both girls out dead, there was no way of saving them. We laid them on the grass next to the water and pinned a piece of paper to them with writing in Polish: "Shame on you, wretched murderers of two Jewish girls." The next day the Germans closed down the Saski Garden.

Horrific Scenes

I saw many a thing, lived through many a scene. But there are some images I could never forget in my life, even if I wanted to. On the one occasion I happened to be at my brother-in-law's. The Germans paid a visit to a leather merchant to carry out a search. There were six of them. They took everything that was of any value. By chance, the Germans stopped by the apartment adjacent to the leather merchant's, [that of] Rabbi Gutszechter. It so happened that they found the old man, a well-known figure in Warsaw, during [his] studies of the Talmud. They were a little abashed at first—the elder's dignified person made an impression on them. But soon the abashment disappeared, and they

190. Sukkot: holiday observed in the month of Tishri (September–October) to commemorate the wanderings of the Israelites in the desert after they left Egypt. In 1939 the holiday fell on 28–29 September. See glossary.

carried out a search. They took jewelry and valuable objects [that had been] given to the rabbi as deposits by others. With feigned politeness they turned to the rabbi and told him that they wanted to rejuvenate him. In vain did the rabbi's son-in-law, Dawid Szapiro, plead with the Germans to have mercy on the old man. For the intervention [fragment of text missing] Finally, they ordered the rabbi to take the Pentateuch [Torah] out of the Ark,[191] lay it out on the floor [and] strip naked; they forced the seventy-year-old elder to dance over the Pentateuch for half an hour. The old man was drowning in tears. The Germans paid it no attention, [they] cut off his beard, and having taken everything he owned, walked away from the apartment.

Desecration of Synagogue

It was three weeks after *Kuczki* that the Germans burst into the synagogue at 44 Miła. They said they had received a message that there was gold inside the Ark. Ten Jews who were present in the synagogue at the time—as it was a Saturday—were held. After carrying out a search and after it transpired that nothing has been found, they forced those praying to walk on all fours from the synagogue to the cemetery and to bark like dogs on the way. This scene had an unimaginable effect on [the city's] Jews. On the way, [the Germans] captured all the Jews they came across and made them walk on all fours and bark too.

From the first moment they entered Warsaw the Germans forced Jews to sing Jewish songs during forced labor. The Jews, out of despair, sang songs about the Messiah. It became a habit for the Germans to demand that the exhausted Jews sing that song. No matter how much I tried to avoid falling into the hands of the Germans, I did not succeed. One day they carried out a search in our house at 13 Zamenhof Street. Despite the fact that the house was half-collapsed, the Germans came there and took even the oldest people for forced labor. I found myself in a group made up of forty people. They took us to the Citadel, and during the work, we were beaten terribly for the slightest misdemeanor. I did not avoid a beating either. They beat one on the back most often, injuring the lungs. After a short time they had to release half of the people as unfit for work. They beat my companion, Szymon Zajdman from

---

191. Ark of the Covenant (Aron Hakodesh): in a synagogue, a chamber or cabinet on the Eastern wall of the temple where the Torah scrolls are stored.

13 Zamenhof, for so long that he dropped dead on the spot. After four days of work at the Citadel, when I returned home, I decided to flee from the Germans. I wanted to go to Russia. The journey to the Bug River was not easy—a truly hellish [one].

German Provocation in Węgrów and Sokołów

On the way to Węgrów I was crossing through [some] woods. In the woods there prowled a gang of bandits, attacking and robbing passersby. I clearly [managed to convince] them that I was a poor peasant, because they let me pass freely, and this way I made it to Węgrów. That same day the Germans released a decree [announcing] they would shoot at every Jew and Pole they came across in the streets together, and that every act of Polish-Jewish collaboration would be punished with death. This was because the Germans had found out that Jews and Poles supported each other. To foment hatred toward Jews, the Germans hit upon the idea of a wicked provocation. They forced a group of Jews to go into a church and foul the altar. Then they made Poles remove that waste, at which point it was announced that the Jews had committed [this] blasphemy. They did the same in the Great Synagogue, forcing Poles to foul it, and Jews to take the waste out. When I was passing [through] Sokołów four days before Pesach [23–30 April 1940], I found not one Jew on the streets anymore. I went through Rybki [Rybienko, a holiday village on the left bank of the Bug] with the last Jewish droshky driver and it was he who told me about the atrocities that Jews had lived through over the past few days. The Germans killed a Christian child and left it in the Jewish cemetery. Then the gendarmerie conducted an investigation that concluded that the child had been killed by Jews. The Jews of Sokołów and the president of the local borough, Morgenstern, wanted to get in touch with the priest and warn him of the German orchestration of [this] ritual murder. But the Germans arrested the president of the borough, along with [his] family. Tales of the murder were spread successfully.

My personal experiences began in the village of Rybki on the bank of the Bug. The Germans, despite the fact that they themselves readily smuggled passengers across the river, instructed the Polish fishermen to command very high rates for transportation. I was prepared for it. That's why, instead of [crossing to] the other side of the river I fell into the hands of a German gendarme, who took me to the commandant's headquarters. I was beaten cruelly there. I was set free when a group of nine Poles, led by a priest, was brought in. When the search of the nine Poles began, I was still lying on the floor half-conscious, and crawling on my stomach, [tried to] get out of the room, but I did hear the commandant shout angrily: "Polish pigs, you're smuggling Bolsheviks." Then I saw how the Germans made the eight Poles and the priest get into a boat at noon, after which they signaled to the Russian side and gunshots [enveloped] the boat from both sides. The boat capsized. I don't know what happened to them then as I and a few other Jews, who almost met with the same fate, ran off out of fright. One thing I do know is that [some] fishing boys who were great swimmers came to the rescue of the drowning Poles. I heard later how the boys cried because they didn't manage to save anyone. In the evening, thirteen of us Jews, including one woman and four children, walked toward a boat as if we were walking to our own deaths. But there was no other solution. Ten minutes later we were on the other side of the river. When we arrived at the Soviet border, the patrol soldiers were boasting about how they had shot nine Polish spies inside a boat.

At the Bolsheviks'

We went to Białystok via Siemiatycze. Everywhere we came across terrible destitution. At the station I saw thousands of refugees, among them many acquaintances. I couldn't understand why those people were unhappy and were trying to return to Poland. After some time I did understand. Here, too, human life meant little. I did not get work in my trade, despite the ostentatious fanfares greeting the new arrivals. So, after a month of journeying by Soviet railways to Lwów, Równe, Łomża, I registered to return to Warsaw. The following incident, [which was] typical, happened to me. An acquaintance of mine introduced me to an official at the NKVD who demanded a bribe of two thousand rubles from me, in exchange for which he wanted to take me to German-occupied Poland. I did not have that kind of money on me. The NKVD took money from many people and I doubt that they kept their promises. I only know that the NKVD representative who sat on the mixed Soviet-German commission[192] had with him a registration list of those who wanted to return [to past places of residence, and instead] were sent to Siberia.

192. Mixed Russian-German commissions for resettlement, appointed on the basis of the agreement between USSR and the Third Reich at the end of 1939. Their aim was to resettle Germans residing in the Soviet occupation zone to regions under German rule. See glossary.

I knew about the deportations that were taking place and didn't return home for the night. I suffered for three weeks. Nevertheless, I was arrested. I was sent off to Białystok [and] placed in the factory of the Becker company, where there were already thousands of Poles, Ukrainians, and Belorussians [Belarusians]. We were given hardly any food, except for herring soup. I was held like this for a month until, one night, we were taken to a camp. There we slept on bare ground in unsanitary conditions. I spent three months in the camp in Sosnówka. There were people there I knew: editor of *Kurier Czerwony*,[193] Fryt [likely Stefan Frycz], with his wife, and the lawyer [Władysław] Kahan. At first we had parcels delivered, but then that too was banned. We were starving. Finally we were taken, a few thousand [of us], to a train station, where we waited for three days, locked in freight cars, almost without food and drink. In the cars there were holes in the floor that were used instead of a toilet, despite the fact that women, children, and men rode together. Before the departure we were counted carefully; the number of passengers was written down on a small plate hung by the freight car and we were counted thoroughly [again] at each station. The train advanced slowly, at times it waited at stations for hours on end. It was a horrendous journey. Not only were we not given food, but we were beaten. We had an arrangement, however, where if they started beating someone, such a racket and screams of "Don't beat [us]" would rise up inside the freight car that the Bolsheviks, afraid of Soviet citizens finding out how refugees were being treated, would cease the beating.

We traveled through Mińsk, Orsha, Smolensk, Moscow. On the way to Orsha the refugees tore a few planks out from the floor and eight [of them] escaped as the train was moving. When we were counted and it turned out there were eight missing, the terrified NKVD-ers ran out into the street, captured eight passersby, loaded them into our carriage, and deported them alongside us. This way the escape was kept from those in charge. The NKVD agents persecuted us terribly. A Polish lieutenant did something that got him in trouble and was locked in a freight car with fourteen prostitutes from Lwów for it. Thus we reached [the Autonomous Soviet Socialist Republic of] Komi, where I was to serve a six-year sentence that followed from various offenses

193. *Dobry Wieczór–Kurier Czerwony* [Good Evening–Red Courier]: *Kurier Czerwony* was a pro-Jewish afternoon journal published 1921 [1922?]–39 by Warsaw-based Dom Prasy SA. It merged with *Dobry Wieczór* in 1932.

investigated during two trials. We went to Komi on barges, and to Kotlas by rail. Then we were taken to the locality of Zemlaga by cars. There, we were washed and sent off to oil wells. At first we were fed well. Warden Krafczun and Warden Bustrycki were carrying out a detailed registration of specialists. It turned out that in our group there were a few professors, lawyers, engineers, doctors, journalists, and artists. We thought that this registration would yield appropriate results. However, all the qualifications were good only for work in the forest. We were split into brigades. *Czerwonoarmiejcy*[194] who looked after us had the right to shoot us for the slightest misdemeanor. Alongside me worked—beyond their capacity—Lieutenant Przeczelewski, Captain Doctor Rogowski, Captain Regina, Lieutenant Unsz, Janek Feldman. Despite working, we were fed poorly. All this accomplished was an increase in bribes. Even though theft was punishable by death, people stole as much as they could.

Amnesty

Warden Krafczun told us about the Amnesty. He implored us to stay in the camp, promised better meal[s]. Only a small group stayed. We were sent to Syktyfar [Syktyvkar].[195] I signed up for the army. The Bolsheviks gave out permits to leave without difficulty. There was no difference made between a Jew and a Pole. [At the time when] we went to sign up, Jews were only made to wait and come back a few days later. After some time, they began to cause difficulties for the Jews, and even persecuted them. Because there were a large number of Jews in the Polish army, a few high-ranking officers came forward with an initiative to split us into special formations and send [us] off to Koltubanka. There, a regiment was formed with Jewish officers, and at [its] helm stood Colonel Kołodek and Major Durko. It has to be said that [these] two leaders looked after us like fathers [look after] their own children. Many Jews were saved thanks to them. The Jewish regiment was dissolved and incorporated into the Polish army. I arrived in Tehran along with the army.

---

194. A collusion of Polish and Russian; from *krasnoarmeytsy* (members of the Red Army) but with "red" replaced with the Polish equivalent.

195. Original Polish correction: Syktywkar.

Protocol 62

Testimony of **Etka Gutfrajnd**, age twenty-nine, owner of the guesthouse Paradis in Krynica. Arrived in Palestine in 1943, from Russia via Tehran.

Until the outbreak of the war I lived in the health resort of Krynica and was the owner of the guesthouse Paradis. A few days before the war, the mood here was already full of anxiety. Krynica is located close to the border and the resort visitors were departing quickly. On the morning of 1 September 1939 we heard a few powerful explosions. At first, we got terribly frightened, thinking that a bomb had exploded somewhere, but we were told that the mineral springs had been blown up. The same thing happened to the machines in the health center. The management of the health resort fled immediately.

Before leaving, people destroyed everything they could. Director Nowotarski, afraid that he would not be able to save the cash register, burned all of the banknotes. He told me about this himself when I met him in Lwów. The guesthouse owners also escaped, although it was difficult for them to part with Krynica, where they have been living for many generations. People left their riches and fled wherever their feet would take them. During [my] flight I met all of the guesthouse owners: Fajwel Stempel, owner of the guesthouse Trzy Róże [Three Roses], Doglender, Herbert Willi, Fogel, Hercog, etc.

Awful Devastation in Krynica

The Germans, as soon as they entered Krynica, started to loot and haul away to Germany everything that had any value at all, even bathtubs and sinks. It was announced that for disclosing the whereabouts of director Nowotarski one would receive a reward of twenty-five thousand marks. Jews and Poles deliberately misled the Germans, pointing to various false places where the director was supposed to be. Among the guesthouse owners from Krynica there was one Hasid from Kalisz, a learned man, Reb Mendel Bek.[196] He did not want to part with Krynica or with his two large tenement houses, for which he had worked his entire life. His undoing was the surname Bek, [also] the surname of

196. Hasid (Hebrew): observant Jew, normally tied to the "court" of his Tzaddik, seeking full communion with God through song, dance, and prayer. See glossary.

the Polish foreign minister. Local rabbis allowed Jews to cut off [their] beards for fear of persecutions. And for this reason, Bek cut off his beard too. A piece of information found its way into German hands that Foreign Minister Beck was hiding in Krynica. Again it was announced that the [person] who revealed Minister Beck's hiding place would receive a reward of twenty-five thousand marks. Mendel Bek became frightened and tried to sneak over to the Slovakian side, over the mountains. A German patrol caught him, told him to stop, and shot him. The Germans organized [what was] a true pogrom in Krynica for both the Polish and the Jewish population. Among the many physicians killed there were the well-known gynecologist Dr. Dukit, hairdresser Szweczkensztul, Dr. Szwarc, and others. Later, the Germans expelled all the Jews from Krynica, the health center was closed down, and all the guesthouses were turned into Soldier's Houses. Then Krynica was incorporated into Slovakia. We had intended to leave Krynica much earlier, but didn't do so for particular reasons. The summer before we had turned the house into the guesthouse Paradis, and [eleven] days before the outbreak of war my son was born, so that a mere three days before the outbreak of war we were celebrating my son's bris.[197] Weak after the birth and with a baby, I couldn't allow myself to travel into the unknown. Later, however, we understood that there were no impossible things. Human life meant nothing to the Germans. [They] would kill innocent people in front of our eyes. That's when we decided to escape. We took hardly anything with us. The most important treasure was [our] child. We walked more than we drove. Using roundabout roads we reached Nowy Sącz, and from there [we went] via Tarnów, Radomyśl, Kolbisze [and] Sokal to Swinok[198] on the Russian-German border. On the eve of the Day of Atonement we crossed the German-Russian border. Barely alive, we found ourselves in the town of Swinok and went straight to the synagogue to thank God for saving [us]. We stayed in the town for a few weeks. During that time we received the news that many of our friends and relatives had gone to Lwów, where it was possible to settle down somehow. Without thinking long [about it], we went to Lwów. It turned out that literally all of Krynica was indeed living in Lwów, with the exception

197. Brit milah, bris: ritual circumcision of a Jewish boy on the eighth day after birth.

198. The author of the testimony had confused the directions and the locality names. The likely escape path led through Kolbuszowa, Sokołów Małopolski (not Sokal), and Sanok (not Swinok), where they crossed the occupation zone border.

of those killed by the Germans. We started to trade and earned pretty well. In Lwów I found director Nowotarski who was hanging around the city, ragged and hungry. A guesthouse owner from Krynica, Mr. Fogel, had a restaurant in Lwów, and he invited Eng. Nowotarski over to his [place] and fed him for free for a long time. Later, the owners of the Jewish guesthouses pooled together a bit of money, bought clothing and shoes, and gifted all that to the director. He was very moved by the gift and said he would never forget it as long as he lived.

Meanwhile the Soviet regime worsened by the day, and masses of refugees started being sent away. On Friday 30 June [?] 1940 announcements appeared in the streets of Lwów in Russian, Jewish, Polish, and Ukrainian that all refugees who wanted to return to their homes should report to the mixed Russian-German commission in order to register. Already tired of smuggling, having forgotten about what the Germans had done, we registered, like other refugees, to go back. That same day, after we had registered, the city was surrounded by the Soviet army [and] NKVD agents, who went from home to home. My husband, who took cover, came out of his hiding place when he heard my laments as they were pulling me out of the house. This was a true blessing for me, as [otherwise] I would have been sent off alone and would never in [my] life have found my husband, just as it happened with many other women. We were taken to the station, where there stood a train made up of freight cars. In each car they put forty people: men, women, and children together. Without a toilet, without water, in inhuman conditions, we traveled for four days. We were certain that we wouldn't make it to our destination. After four days we received [our] first piece of bread. After ten days' journey we arrived in the Sverdlovsk Oblast. Then, by light rail, we reached the camp of Rotkies [?]. There we were registered, and everyone between the ages of sixteen and fifty was sent to work in the forest. We were assigned to the labor camp 145 in Soszwa [Sosva (Polish: Sośwa)], Sverdlovsk Oblast. At first, even though I was busy with the baby, they did not want to exempt me from work. I was given very little to eat. We were exhausted. My husband and I went through serious [bouts of] dysentery and typhus. After all, we ate wild berries and grass. The Soviet warden who watched over our group, which was made up of a thousand people, did not want to release us from work at first. We were only excused when we were very dangerously ill.

There, too, human life carried little importance. Hundreds, [including] a lot of [our] friends, died in front of our eyes. We didn't cry over anyone anymore. Often the living envied the dead. Those with small children fared the worst. One's heart broke at the sight of the little ones starving, without [even] a little milk and sugar. We couldn't manage at first; however, I was then exempted from work as the mother of a small child, and my husband became the manager of the kitchen and a cook. Our situation improved markedly then. He would bring home a bit of everything. He made friends with the commissar, the main supplier of products. He would give him larger receipts than what the deliveries amounted to, and in exchange for this the commissar turned a blind eye to items being taken away. This way we were fed perfectly. I stayed at home and took care of the child, who was sick for a year and a half. All this time I missed my siblings and parents terribly; they, like us, had been deported. I didn't know where they were. I could have helped them. As I received a message one day that my parents were not far from the place we were, I went to [see] them. I found them all together: [my] father, mother, sister, brother-in-law, and [their] small children. They were in a dire situation. I helped them with a generous hand. I couldn't, however, feed them to their hearts' content. I gave them a whole pack of old clothes, which they sold. I spent a few weeks with them. When their situation improved a little, most fell ill with typhus. Of my loved ones, my father died of typhus.

I returned to my husband distraught, but that same day was arrested by NKVD agents. I was suspected of espionage. One can understand how I felt reading my indictment. I thought I would easily manage to prove the truth, since how could they believe that a Jewish woman would want to deliver messages to the Germans. But I wasn't allowed [to say] a word. My husband gave a gold watch to a person who needed to be given [a bribe], and this way, I was acquitted and released from jail.

Amnesty

We were informed about the Amnesty immediately and told that we were free and could go wherever we wanted, with the exception of cities of the first and second category, that is, Moscow, Kharkiv, Kiev, etc. The Russians urged us to stay. We were well-off and [debated] whether to go. My husband was still the manager of the kitchen and we were doing well. However, two reasons convinced us to leave. One was the mindless accusation of espionage [leveled at me], the second the fact that absolutely all the refugees were leaving. We decided to leave. We found ourselves outside of Tashkent, in a place where a Polish outpost was located. There, my husband, who had a lot of experience already of how a communal kitchen is run in Soviet Russia, opened a canteen for refugees. The Polish authorities were very happy with my husband's work, so Dr. Jenicz assured us immediately before the registration that he would evacuate us. We saw, however, that the attitude of the Poles toward Jews was worsening by the day. Jews were bullied during army recruitment; it was made difficult for them to have their children accepted into children's centers. We were very bitter, just like other Jews. Noticing that Jews were being crossed off of the registration list, a delegation that my husband was also part of turned to General Szyszko-Bohusz to [ask that] some number of Jews be taken out of Russia too. There were rabbis on the list who should be saved above all. General Szyszko-Bohusz said that the Polish government would like to save the largest number of Jews possible, but [that] the NKVD would not agree to it.[199] The same delegation went to the leader of the NKVD and heard, to its astonishment, that the NKVD had nothing against Jewish refugees leaving Russia with the Poles. The delegation immediately went to General Szyszko-Bohusz and [recounted] what the NKVD leader's response had been. Since the situation had become uncomfortable, the Polish authorities had to agree to send fifteen rabbis. My husband's surname was added among them, and this way, we got out of Russia.

199. The right to leave the USSR was ensured for Polish citizens, and because the Soviet authorities limited claims to Polish citizenship exclusively to people of Polish nationality, the option of joining the Polish army and to leaving the USSR with the Polish military was closed to Jews.

Protocol 64

Testimony of **Szmul Zyfberfajn [?]**, age thirty-three, from Warsaw. Came to Palestine from Russia.

Two weeks after the Germans occupied Warsaw, on 15 October 1939, I made it over to the Soviet side along with my companion. In Warsaw, one could feel the heavy hand of the Gestapo. Constant roundups in the streets and the insecurity of existence poisoned our every moment. Once I was captured for [forced] labor, [and] returned from it covered in blood and completely dejected. I decided to escape, and since leaving by train was a danger to [one's] life, my companion and I got onto bicycles and set off on the way. We covered over eighty kilometers per day [and] found ourselves in Białystok after a few days. The city was full of refugees. Białystok had never seen this many people. Because of the unprecedented crowding there was great chaos. The Soviet authorities were preparing for the plebiscite[200] and the big events [around it]. That is why I immediately got a job illuminating city squares and lighting up specially built propaganda towers. All of the electrical technicians and decorators who found themselves in the city got work for good pay. But then, when the celebrations ended, we all lost [our] jobs and were left without means of support. The city was in such disorder that not a single factory was operating. The reasons for it were the fact that the Germans had taken some of the machinery away, and [also] partly because the Bolsheviks could not organize the work. I got tired of wandering the streets without a roof over my head and starving—and my mother had stayed in Warsaw [when] I had left my home there. Many refugees decided to return, as they had no more energy to wander the streets without work.

In the second half of December I returned to Warsaw. Immediately I knew that I wouldn't be able to live there. Deadly danger[s] lurked on every corner. People were still being rounded up for forced labor, fifty innocent Jews were killed at Nalewki, and the fear of further executions overcame [everyone]. After three days spent in Warsaw, I escaped to the Soviet side again. I preferred to

200. On the incorporation of Western Belorussia to the Soviet Socialist Republic of Belarus, and thereby to the USSR.

live on bread and water if only I would not see the Germans. Again, I returned to Białystok and again was left without a job. Every day, trains with refugees would leave for Russia. I too wanted to register for work, but the messages coming from the cities took away my desire to leave. On 20 June 1940 there arrived in Białystok a few thousand "catchers" from the NKVD, who began a true hunt for refugees. [The refugees] were caught in the streets [and] in apartments; families were separated; children didn't know where their parents were, and when they went to obtain that information, they too were captured and loaded into a train. I was in hiding for eight days. On the ninth day I left my hiding place to wash and that's when I was arrested. The agent [claimed] he only wanted to check [my] documents and that he would send me home straightaway. Everyone was reassured this way, [but] I knew that I would not ever return home.

I was kept in jail in Białystok for three months. To begin with, I was locked up along with two thousand other people in a large hall of a factory that was closed. It was easy to get out of [there], but the NKVD came up with a good idea: we were fed well, much better compared to how we ate on the outside. Since there was no work at all, we would ask ourselves what exactly we would escape for, and to where. However, for the good food we had to pay. We began to be registered and sorted [into groups]. Then the exit[s] were guarded by the military. There were two thousand people inside the hall. Sitting down was out of the question; we were so tightly huddled that it was impossible to raise [one's] hand. People became agitated, bumped into one another. It was worse at night. There was no way to lie down anywhere. Anyone who fell asleep upright and lay down on the floor in their sleep immediately had a few others on top of them who wanted to sleep lying down. This exhausting situation lasted for nine days that seemed to us like nine years.

One night we were rushed out of the hall and to somewhere beyond Białystok, on foot. Police, NKVD agents, and police dogs surrounded us. All it took was to step out of line for the dogs to jump on you and bite. Someplace outside Białystok we were put into barracks surrounded with barbed wire, which made up a concentration camp. We lived there for two months. The camp was surrounded by watchtowers. There was no way of escaping. Unexpected searches were carried out a few times a day—each barracks had its leader from among the arrestees who had to report the number of arrestees present in the barracks to the policemen. At night we were woken up to check that no one had escaped. This could happen twice in a night. We were half-deranged. No one understood what [all] this was about, why exactly these constant checks [were necessary]. One young man, a Czech Communist, who had a few books with him, cried all day and transcribed books in his spare time. Some seventy-year-old elder wrote a song about the bombing of Warsaw and composed the music [to go] with it. Generally speaking, people were acting crazy. Often, when the prisoners would beg for water, the guards would beat us and swear. People would talk gibberish. Among us there was one real madman caught during a manhunt in the streets. This sick man behaved relatively more normally than all [the rest] of us. He comforted everyone and calmed [them] down. One official of the Poale Zion [Zionist Workers' Party (Polish: Poalej-Sion)], which had its office in Warsaw at 14 Pawia Street, always repeated the same sentence: "Stalin has killed more people than he has hair on [his] head," or shouted: "Out with the Soviet Bereza Kartuska."[201] One night one of the prisoners cut his veins with a shaving knife. He was [a man] from Łódź whose name I unfortunately don't remember. No one noticed the suicide. At the time, the NKVD agents had just come in for a *proverka* [inspection (Polish: *prowierka*)]. The barracks commandant reported the number of arrestees. They started counting and noticed the [man] lying in the corner of the barracks. They kicked him, told him to get up, finally dragged him away and [left] a stream of blood underneath him. They understood that it was suicide. One of the agents ran up to the barracks leader and [kicked] him in the stomach with [his] boot, making him fall unconscious. He was accused of having known about the suicide. They took him with them and he returned a few days later, beaten and broken. He didn't want to say anything [about] what they had done to him. A few days later he was taken away again and never returned again.

A week later, trucks arrived and took us all away. We were loaded like this: we would sit facing each other, as close as if we'd been pressed together. This way a large number of people could fit [inside]. Bundles were placed on our backs, everyone was covered with a tarp, and this way, we reached Białystok. The passersby could not even make out that there were people riding on the

---

201. Bereza Kartuska: Polish camp for political prisoners operating in the years 1934–39.

trucks. When the truck drove over a bumpy road, people would fall on top of each other and many would faint. Exhausted and broken—spiritually and physically—we were placed in a Polish prisoner of war. The camp was located inside a monastery. I was in a cell with 554 people. The cell was fourteen meters long and twenty wide. The floor had been paved with asphalt; the windows [had] no glass. To lie comfortably on the floor was out of the question. One slept on one's side, went to the toilet in a bucket that was emptied once every twenty-four hours alongside [others]. Everyone was infested with lice. We did not get water to wash with. We received a meal once a day that consisted of soup and a piece of bread. The bread was divided as follows: pieces would be torn off a loaf and distributed. We didn't get bowls for the soup [and] had to procure dishes ourselves; many ate the soup out of the spittoons they found in the convent, or out of wooden boxes, or rusty food tins. I spent a month in that camp. We were again loaded onto trucks, the same way as the first time, and sent to a prison in Białystok. According to the protocol we had to be shaved and undergo a disinfection, but this was abandoned as the water pipes were not working. We were taken to the station in small prison cars, and [covered] with [the same] lice, loaded onto *teplushki*.[202] This was at the end of August 1940. In the cars, the same procedure as in the camp was repeated. Twice a day the arrestees were counted [and] the walls of the cars inspected [to check] that they were sturdy enough. Holes in the floor of the cars served as toilets. Once a day we were given moldy bread. After all the searches no one had a pocketknife [left]. The bread [had to be] torn piece by piece and eaten quickly to stop it from becoming the neighbor's loot.

After three weeks we arrived in Kotlas. There, as it turned out, was the central point from which people were sent to work camps. Our group was taken to a special place for disinfection to be carried out. From behind the barbed wire I heard the Jewish tongue and spotted a Jew with a long beard. We started a conversation with him. It turned out that he was the uncle of my party associate, Frydrych, who lived in Warsaw at Nowolipki. He was a Jewish colonist from Crimea. He had gotten ten years' deportation for some minor misdemeanor. He told me that Kotlas was known as the island of tears. Here people

202. *Teplushka* [original Polish transliteration: *tiepłuszka*): freight wagon with a heater, a so-called *koza*.

lost all hope, because not a single Soviet citizen had [managed to return] home from here. After a few days in jail in Kotlas, where the newly arrived prisoners were robbed of the remains of their belongings, the refugees were loaded onto five large barges. The barges were attached to a steamship and we set off on a six-day journey. One barge was filled with black rusks and water. The rusks were distributed by criminal offenders, *bytoviki*, who made fun of our naivety. Along the banks stretched primeval woods. The ship made stops in certain places. One barge would be detached and the rest would carry on. We went all the way to a point called Ustwik.[203]

The first person I got to know in that place was a professor from a Moscow university. He had lectured at the university for thirty years. He received a sentence of ten years hard labor for maintaining correspondence with foreign countries.

Ustwik was a transit point. We were loaded into cars and sent off to a place [called] Kniaź Fagar.[204] This was in December. It was horribly freezing. We were half-naked and not prepared for the harsh winter. From Kniaź Fagar we traveled 220 kilometers on open platform train cars to Ukhta, ASSR [Autonomous Soviet Socialist Republic] Komi. Human strength must [truly] be limitless, [given that] the entire transport did not die from the freezing temperatures and hunger. Ukhta is known for [its] oil and radium mines. We reached a camp surrounded by wire. A small gate through which only one person could go at a time served as the entrance. The gate was guarded by a soldier. I arrived in the camp without [any] belongings—I had been robbed clean. I did, however, manage to hide a watch. The soldier at the gate took away that watch from me and didn't want to give it back. I had nothing to eat out of; dish[es] were not provided [and] we ourselves had to procure a food tin that served as a plate and a mug. The cook told me I was lucky to have found myself in a good camp. My work consisted of digging up potatoes that had been left in the ground since fall. I dug [through] the soil with my bare hands. We worked twelve hours a day to dig up the largest [possible] amount. I met a Jew from Mińsk who'd been sentenced for profiteering. The Soviet Jews were ashamed of speaking Jewish. They tried to use incorrect Jewish language that proved

203. Here and henceforth refers to the camp of Ust-Vym [original Polish correction: Ustwym].

204. Correct name of the locality: Kniaz-Pogost [original Polish correction: Kniażpogost]. Appears in other exile testimonies as Kniaź Fagar, Kniaź Hagaz, Kniaź Fagas.

that they'd been assimilated and that they had nothing to do with the Jewish populace.

In our camp there were 3,500 people working. It was a so-called economic-technical station, whose role it was to serve the city. People operating the power plant, the oil distillery, the bathhouses, [and] the sawmill were recruited from among the prisoners. I ended up [there] thanks to the fact that I was an electrical technician and a mechanic. After a few days a geological group was set up whose task it was to research how far the alabaster fields surrounding the city stretched. The group was made up of thirty people under the leadership of a supervisor, a geologist and engineer who had been sentenced in the year of 1937, during a purge, to ten years' prison. His coworkers were thieves and crooks. We mostly went by car, then the tents and the pickaxes were moved into a boat. The boat, pulled by horses, went upstream up the river. Our expedition was to [last] half a year. At rest stops, we slept under the open sky. In the prearranged spot we started to cut down trees to build ourselves a settlement. I fell ill at that time. My legs swelled. I was sent back to the station. I lay ill with *cynga* for a few weeks. Thanks to the protection of the engineer I got into a local power plant, in place of a worker [who had been] killed. I worked ten hours a day, without a day's rest, and my work pleased the warden very much. It was decided that I would stay there for the whole year. Women worked equally to men in the camp. They were exploited in a merciless way and all, in the number of seven hundred, were ill with tuberculosis.

After six months I received a judgment sentencing me to three years in prison as a dangerous member of society. Meanwhile, the Amnesty arrived. All the Poles were gathered in one place. We waited for the formalities to be taken care of. For now, everyone did their duties, but we received wages and worked eight hours a day. My papers got lost and I was sent back again to the station. As there were eighty such [people] with missing papers, for the time being we were placed in isolation cells so that we wouldn't be [mixing] with Russians. During the day we worked for twelve hours. During our stay in the cells we had everything stolen from us. Eventually our papers turned up and the NKVD told us to go to Totskoye, Chkalov Oblast,[205] where the Poles'

205. Both Totskoye and Chkalov were in Orenburg Oblast, located along the evacuation routes; Totskoye was one of the main recruitment and evacuation collecting centers. The author appears to have confused the region with the name of the place.

assembly point was located. We thought that after all the suffering they would accept us into the Polish army. But immediately, at the first station, where an *eszelon* [special purpose army transport unit] was forming, Polish officers began their antisemitic antics. It had been decided that each Polish citizen who was released was considered to be a soldier, and that the *eszelon* was a part of the army. However, Jews were not allowed into the train car at the station. Thanks to the intervention of Major Durko, a certain number of Jews got into the army. There used to be a Russian war camp in Totskoye inside horse stables [converted] into barracks. We were naked, ragged, and barefoot. There had been no food in three weeks. We suffered from hunger and cold living in the stables. Tattered and hungry, we were grouped into divisions of artillery, infantry, and tankers. The division was called the 21st regiment Dzieci Warszawy [Children of Warsaw]. A penal company was formed where only Jews were sent. The regiment commander was Felsztyn, a baptized Jew who used to be called Feldstein.[206] The commander of my battalion was Captain Przybylski.

206. Tadeusz Felsztyn (1892–1962): colonel in the Polish army; died in emigration in Great Britain.

Protocol 65

Testimony of **Józef Rosenberg**, age fifteen, from Krzeszów by the San, Lublin voivodeship. Arrived in Palestine via Tehran on 19 February 1943.

Before the war we lived in Krzeszów. My father, Nechemia, was the owner of a mill. He died from hunger in Russia. In Krzeszów there lived 150 Jews among a total population of six thousand. The local peasants worked manufacturing baskets, which they transported to Rudnik, and from there the baskets were exported to America. After the outbreak of the war, terrible fighting took place around the town. Nearby is Stalowa Wola, full of the military. The Polish army had its positions on the hill of Frycz, and the Poles shot at the Germans from above and set explosives under a bridge on the San. So that they could see the Germans better, the Poles burned down the town. The people were informed about this [and] left their homes and hid in the neighboring woods. On the second day of Rosh Hashanah [15 September 1939], the Germans took over the town. [They] dropped a floating bridge across the San and crossed the river in fifteen minutes. The Jews hid [in] peasant [homes]. Then the Bolsheviks came. The Poles, hiding in the forests and the hills, started shooting. The Russians and the Germans didn't know what to do with themselves. The Bolsheviks shot at the Germans, and the Germans at the Bolsheviks. Only later did Russian tanks arrive and a battle against the Poles took place between Krzeszów and Biłgoraj. It was more of a slaughter than a battle. It lasted all of twenty minutes. The Bolsheviks took the remains of the Polish unit prisoner.

My father left the forest for the town and made his way to his apartment. Suddenly, shooting could be heard in town. Some Poles were shooting at Germans from [their] hiding places. The Germans took their revenge on Jews. An order was issued [that said] if a Jew is found being harbored by a peasant, the whole village will be burned down. Despite this, one Polish peasant harbored our entire family. One day, German soldiers knocked on [the door of] our cottage and demanded to stay the night. The peasant hid us all in the cellar. It then turned out that those soldiers were Czechs [actually Sudeten Germans] and [that] they behaved very respectably. My father came out of the hiding place and told them openly that the town had been burned down and he had to live in the country. Father talked with the Czechs in a friendly manner; they gave him some food for the whole family from their provisions. Father learned from the Czechs about the terrifying atrocities the Germans had committed in our town. Despite this, we left [our] hiding place and returned home. We learned that many of our friends had been killed. Among them was Zyndel Manes—a glassworker. The Germans captured the son of the rabbi and one Izrael, Mosze Burstein—a merchant, and ordered them to dig graves for themselves. They killed Burstein. Then they said: "It's a waste of a bullet for the other Jew, we could use him as a laborer"—and spared his life. He later escaped to Russia with the rabbi. I don't know what happened to them. A few Jewish women were also killed, among them Mrs. Roza Bokser. The Germans tore off her finger along with the ring, she was raped and murdered. This happened two days before the Russians' arrival.

When the Russians entered the town, the Jews left their hiding places to meet them. The Russians treated the people well, generally. They ordered the mills to be opened and distributed bread. They confiscated cattle from landowners and shared the livestock out among the poor. One of the landowners did not want to give up his herd and made threats with a gun. A Russian soldier threw a grenade into his house and destroyed the apartment. Corpses were dug out of the fresh graves located in the middle of town; the Jews were buried in the Jewish cemetery. The funerals of the killed Poles, Germans, and Russians lasted eight days. Germans were the most numerous of those killed. The Bolsheviks carried out a propaganda campaign in town and told stories [about] how good [things were] in Russia. Many people signed up to the Red militia. All of a sudden, we learned that the Russians were leaving town. All the Jews in town ran off with the Bolsheviks. People escaped on foot, bundles in hand. On the way, signs of [earlier] fighting were visible. One could see lots of killed, decomposing horses, and the stench in the area was unbearable. We walked some thirty-three kilometers, until [we got to] Biłgoraj. We came upon thousands of refugees in town. A light railway took us to Kowel. In Kowel, refugees roamed the streets. It was already cold by then. Later the Russians requisitioned public buildings for refugees. Batei hamidrash were also requisitioned. We spent nights in a beth hamidrash along with the Polish refugees.

We spent six weeks in Kowel. We saw that there was no point in staying in the beth hamidrash. Father had a brother in Russia and we decided to go to [be with] him. Along with the whole family, we registered to go to Russia. [We had to] wait in line for three days and nights to register.

We went by rail all the way until Złoty Gosz, in the Poltava guberniya.[207] Most of the town's residents were Jews. The town president was a Jew, too—Jarszewski. The Russian Jews greeted the refugees at the station with music and gave us food [and] drink and shared out clothing among us. We were allowed to rest for two weeks. Then we were sent to a kolkhoz outside town. One day, when Father was praying in ritual robes, the camp warden asked him: "Why aren't you working? Manna does not fall from heaven these days, one has to have strength in [one's own] hands." Father replied that he had no strength to work. Once the kolkhoz had belonged to Jews, a few hundred [of them] worked there. When we arrived, there were only forty families left who occupied the highest positions, while the simple work was done by Russian peasants. We were told that the kolkhoz was superbly organized and that's why talented Jewish workers were sent to another kolkhoz for administrative work. The earth was fertile there; the kolkhoz abounded in amazing orchards. The kolkhoz's administrative office was located in a building that was once a synagogue. Children had to go to school, but we were not allowed to go to a Jewish school because we knew the Jewish language anyway. We had to learn the Russian and Ukrainian languages.

When Father stopped working, they didn't want to give us food in the kolkhoz. He was sent off to a Seniors' Home located four kilometers from the city. It was a special colony for one hundred elderly people. Among them there lived three Jews. The home's managers were Jews. People were fed their fill but the food wasn't kosher. At first, Father was given kosher food—there were even matzos for Pesach—but when the war broke out between Russia and Germany only *treif* food was given. In the home there was a clubhouse, a reading room; there was a radio. Five children lived in the Seniors' Home with their parents. My older brother had turned eighteen but forged [some] papers to be able to stay with the family. Small children were taken to school on sleds, the older ones walked. We were given food to [take to] school. We learned the Ukrainian and the Russian language. Older children studied for seven hours, younger—four. The head of the school was a Jew, the teachers

207. Likely refers to the locality of Zolotonosha [original Polish correction: Zołotonosza].

[were] Christians. We lived like this for three months. After the outbreak of the war with Finland[208] the situation changed for the worse. A shortage of food products was noticeable in the city. Lines formed in front of shops and people often fought over bread. Huge posters hung by the stores with an appeal to the people to allow refugees to go into the stores without waiting in line. I made use of this privilege as a refugee and bought food for my teacher.

We heard that it was possible to return home, and despite the fact that Germans were there, we registered to go. Many Jews registered with the warden, wanting to return home. One of the most important reasons was the lack of kosher [food] in Russia. During the first Easter we received matzo. The Jews thought that [in the German-occupied lands] they wouldn't be prevented from [celebrating] holidays. I didn't want to go back because I had gotten used to the school and felt good there. I had made friends with the town president, Jarszewski, whose son studied with me at school. I often went to their house. Mr. Jarszewski would say: "This is how the refugees are repaying Russia for the good welcome they experienced. The Russians will be offended and take revenge on them." Father, however, forced the whole family to return to Kowel. We had no money. The Germans were not letting either Jews or Poles across the border, only Ukrainians. In Kowel there were three thousand Jewish refugees who were waiting to return to the Nazis. A group of women and children went to the NKVD, cried and wailed that they had no more energy to travel. The group were told to select a delegation. Two children were picked from among them, me and the son of lawyer Majerowicz. We said we wanted to return to our homes and that we wouldn't accept Russian passports. We were arrested and my father received an order to leave town within twenty-four hours. The next day the army surrounded all buildings where refugees were living and everyone was ordered to make their way to the station. The refugees were told they were being taken to the Nazis but were [actually] taken to Russia. After a long journey we arrived in the area of the city of Assina [Asino], Novosibirsk Oblast. The journey took eight weeks. We arrived on [the day of] Pentecost of 1940.

There were six thousand of us, Jews and Poles. Most were Jews. In the work camp, malaria was widespread, as it was surrounded by swamps. We lived in

208. The USSR's war against Finland, started by the USSR, lasted from 30 November 1939 until 13 March 1940.

tents, but [even so], bedbugs tormented us. Many refugees lost their minds, unable to stand the suffering. Children received forty dekagrams of bread each, adults a kilo of bread per day. You could fill holes with that bread, that's how claylike it was. One day, thirty children died. We thought that not a single one of us would survive. Again the women and children organized a demonstration. The NKVD-ers dispersed the demonstrators. Parents ran off as they were afraid of jail. Children were not scared and stayed. My friends were arrested: Icchak Haber, Chaim Zylber, Naftali Rosenberg, and Sonenstern. We were asked by the NKVD what it was we wished for. We said we wanted to go back home, since children were dying here. We were sentenced to [stay in] a punishment cell, weren't given food. It was cold and dark in there. At night we pulled off the gate and escaped. After four weeks' stay at the camp, a thousand people were sent to the village of Shalashinsk, Sverdlovsk Oblast. The journey took a month. The refugees were split into groups. We got there before Rosh Hashanah [3–4 October 1940]. My father and brother worked as glassworkers. There were only a few barracks in the village. A few refugees tried to escape. They were deported far away to Siberia. We spent ten months in Shalashinsk. There was one Pole with us. The commandant of the camp turned out to be a German exile. He was a horrible antisemite and [he] tormented Jews. We earned forty kopecks per day, for which one could get half a kilo of bread. We didn't go hungry. We worked cutting down tree stumps for steam engine fuel. Children worked too. On Yom Kippur [12 October 1940] Father did not want to go to work, and he was arrested. He was released a few months later. Mother fell ill from anxiety.

In the neighboring village, laborers worked loading goods onto trains. There one earned five rubles per day. We went to that village but weren't allowed to work. One day the camp warden, the German, called us all up and threatened, in his speech, that if we didn't work more, we would perish miserably. He shouted: "There is enough land to bury you—[you] Jewish crooks." He ordered us to sign a pledge that we would work more. Then, one Jew said: "If all Jews are crooks, then your Kaganowicz[209] is a crook too, and your entire country is made up of crooks." What it came to was that a case was brought

---

209. Łazar Kaganowicz (1893–1991): Bolshevik activist, member of the administration of the CPSU (Communist Party of the Soviet Union; Polish: Komunistyczna Partia Związku Radzieckiego; KPZR), performed a variety of party and state functions, removed from those positions in 1957.

against the camp warden, the German, for persecuting Jews, and he was sentenced to exile.

In the camp there was a school made up of four grades. But the older children could not study because they had to go to work, and the younger ones did not go to school because they had no shoes. During the summer we received parcels from Ukraine. The new foreman turned out to be much better, and we earned between two and three rubles per day. Sometimes I would be sent off somewhere [else] and would earn extra [money]. I became a cart driver. The foreman gave me a horse [and] I carried wood from the forest—it wasn't hard work. My two brothers also got horses, and this way we earned five rubles per day together. With this money we could support ourselves well. We did, however, have large expenses, because Father's stay in the hospital had to be paid for, and that cost 120 rubles per month. We worked hard, without any hope for the future [or] any possibility of improving our life. We decided to get through it somehow. We cleared a piece of the forest and turned it into a field: we planted onions and cucumbers, beets, grain, and potatoes; we made hotbeds. We worked until late at night. But we could not enjoy our garden, because we were sent away again, 150 kilometers away. We arrived in the settlement of Nizhny Tagil and were forced to work straightaway. I made friends with the brigade leader. He told me that a special type of wood was required for the production of gunstocks. I looked in the woods for two days until I found such a tree. As a reward I received a special bonus: a thousand packs of makhorka, a real treasure. In the forest, wood was chopped for railroad ties. One earned 250 rubles per month. Workers received fifty dekagrams of bread per day, nonworkers—forty. The German-Soviet war broke out. We received papers allowing [us] to leave. We went to Serov. For a pack of makhorka, one got forty rubles. I cashed some in [and got] a few thousand rubles this way. But one could not get an apartment [even] with money.

Mother fell ill. The illness was exhausting our financial resources. We decided to go south. We went to Samarkand. The journey took three weeks. Train after train departed; it was impossible to find a space in a carriage. The Polish government helped with obtaining food. One day, the Russians told us that we were to go to Kazakhstan. On the second day an order came for us to leave the train. Our group was sent to the kolkhoz Mołotow. At first, everyone was given twenty dekagrams of flour; after two days only ten dekagrams each was given. Everyone fell ill with typhus. Among the ill was our compatriot, Jehoszua Majmon, who was written about in the papers before the war. He had a rabbinic ordination but did not want to remain a rabbi. He had received a huge dowry and an inheritance in America. He was working on an invention in the field of magnetism. Many states wanted to buy that invention from him but he wanted to sell it only in America. He told us how the Polish government offered him two million zlotys for this invention, but he did not want to sell so as not to increase unemployment. He intended to go to America and had found rich [business] partners. Jehoszua Majmon fell ill from hunger. One night he fainted, and I went to get the doctor in a windstorm. The doctor did not want to come, and only gave [me some] medicine. The distance to the doctor's was two kilometers. The windstorm got stronger and I lost all strength. As if in a dream, I felt myself freezing. I could not move. Luckily, my teacher spotted me from afar, woke me up from my sleep, [and] ran to get my brothers. I was taken home on a stretcher. I was revived with difficulty. Only then did I remember that I'd had the medicine for Mr. Majmon on me but had lost it along the way. We tried to save the sick man then but did not succeed. Jehoszua Majmon died. His children are in Palestine. We warmed [some] water, washed down the body of the deceased, dressed him in clean undergarments,[210] and buried him in the Christian cemetery on the kolkhoz. There were Uzbeks present at the funeral. With a four-year-old child, I said Kaddish [mourning prayer].

The news that our father had died in town was kept from us. [We were told] he had gone to look for work in Bukhara. My brother found work in the stables; Mother fell gravely ill. The kolkhoz manager told us to look for somewhere else to stay. We didn't receive food. We hunted dogs and killed them, ate grass and mushrooms. Once my brother managed to get a loaf of bread, but as he was bringing it home, he was robbed on the way. We left the kolkhoz and made our way to Samarkand on foot. Mother was admitted to the hospital [and] the children told the Polish delegation that they were orphans. Along with [children from] the orphanage we arrived in Zyrbuliak [?], outside Kermine, where the Polish army was. Malaria and dysentery had taken

210. The burial custom among observant Jews involves the washing of the body and clothing it in clean white linen. It is usually performed by the Chevra Kadisha, or burial society. Both linen and the Chevra were, naturally, unavailable in the camps.

hold there, but slowly the situation was improving. Mother stayed in Russia [while] we were brought to Palestine. Of the people I remember, I want to mention one Mendel Weiss, who was an actor and a writer. He comforted us in sad moments, writing and producing songs about refugees. He managed to get himself a German passport, as he thought that Germans were allies to Russia, and [that] he would get privileges this way. He was arrested and I do not know what happened to him. In Uzbekistan, many refugees wanted to get into a prison as there [you had] a roof over [your] head and were fed. But the Russians quickly recognized this refugee [trick and] acquitted everyone.

Protocol 66

Testimony of **Emma Lewinówna**, age twenty-three, from Radom. Daughter of a physician. Arrived in Palestine via Russia from Tehran in February 1943.

We left Radom on 5 September 1939 with the whole family and [some] friends, which made up a party of twelve people altogether. Because of the lack of gasoline, we decided to go on a cart. My parents had particular reasons to fear the arrival of the Germans, as my mother was the chair of the Women's Zionist Organization and of the Anti-Hitler Committee. Father, a well-known physician in Radom, was also active in a string of social organizations. We took few belongings but had quite a lot of money and jewelry on us. We set a course to the east, toward Kowel, where we had family. The journey to Lublin took two days. We were being constantly bombed on the way, and when we arrived in Lublin the city was in flames. Father had a brother in Lublin—we settled at his [place] but staying in that city was becoming impossible. We decided to set off for Kowel. We spent eight months in Kowel, living almost normally and without any financial constraints, as apart from the money reserves we had brought with us, Father was the head of a railway polyclinic. He stayed in that post until the time of deportation. My brother studied medicine in Lwów.

When the deportation took place—which I shall not describe in detail as it occurred under the same conditions as for everyone [else]—that is, we did not want to take Soviet passports and were told one night to get out of Kowel—our family told [my] brother to hide in Lwów in order to avoid our fate. We traveled for fourteen days altogether toward Voronezh, Omsk, Novosibirsk, and Tomsk. It was a high-speed train that hurtled ahead, stopping hardly anywhere. We didn't suffer from hunger as we'd brought provisions with us. We immediately designated my father as the transport doctor, [which is] why we traveled in the so-called doctors' train, a passenger carriage with open doors, unlike the other carriages, which had their doors sealed. One hundred kilometers beyond Tomsk, where the railway line ended and the taiga began, the train stopped and we were told to disembark. We spent two days under the open sky before being moved to the Assina [Asino] *posiołek*. It looked like a huge concentration camp surrounded by barbed wire, with guard outposts in every corner. Russian exiles had lived there before. Now no one with a Soviet passport was allowed to enter. It happened by chance that twenty-six doctors lived in that camp—from among them I remember the familiar name[s] of Dr. Glass [either Jerzy or Mieczysław Glass] from Warsaw, Dr. Talerman and wife, Dr. [Izaak] Milejkowski, Dr. Kielerwurm from Radom, Dr. [Jakub] Zylberstein, lawyer Grynstein, etc. The overall number of deportees in that place came to 25,000. Naturally, it was difficult to get them settled straightaway—they lived out in the open on the streets, and it was the rainy season at the time. After some time, small transports were sent off across the river to the forest. My father worked as a doctor from the very beginning and fared relatively well.

I Become a Waitress

I was immediately employed as a waitress in the NKVD canteen. I earned 125 rubles per month, apart from upkeep, plus I had the privilege of [being allowed to] bring soup home. It was a canteen intended exclusively for NKVD officials and wardens, and when I was hired I had to swear to be bound by strict secrecy with regards to everything that happened there, starting with the dishes served [and] ending with [any] conversations overheard. In the canteen itself there were two halls, number 1 and number 2, where the menu types were kept strictly separate. Hall number 1 was intended exclusively for the wardens. Every day meat, tea with sugar, and other "luxuries" were served there. Perhaps because there were no alcoholic beverages served at the canteen, not once did anyone address me in an inappropriate or truculent manner. Only female refugees, most often young girls, worked in the canteen. From among the civilian population, no one was allowed to approach the area where the canteen was located—a permit was needed to enter and to leave.

Soviet Women

While only refugee women were waitresses, only Russian ones worked in the kitchen. I had conversations with them many times during the breaks in between meals, and was on friendly terms with more than one of them. From these conversations I concluded that, despite the fact that a Russian woman benefits from all equal rights privileges, she is deeply degraded, and our European relations seem to her an unattainable paradise. Not only is she treated badly by men, [as is customary] in the East, but frequent changes in the objects of [her] love result in the fact that often she does not know who the father of her child is. Although the Soviet courts always take the side of the woman, and award her, with great ease, child support from anyone she indicates, the amount of money paid by the alleged father to the mother absolutely does not solve the difficulties of raising and feeding a child. That is because, in Russia, given the vastly inflated prices and the difficulty of obtaining products, money has minimal [value]. The issue is that most often the woman complains about the lack of a home, lack of family atmosphere and kindness and male protection, which, in Russia, takes on not only an emotional form, but is primarily expressed in a fierce struggle to provide food, clothing, etc. for the child. A divorce costs fifty rubles in Russia, a wedding—three rubles. Both one and the other take place without any formalities and with great ease.

I Change Jobs

I spent eight months in the NKVD canteen, and both I and the whole family were faring well, as we consistently received parcels from Radom and were sent both food and clothing. Despite this, I decided to change jobs, as [this] type of work did not suit me. I had an education in nursing from Poland and a lot of passion for that work. Thanks to Father's influence I got into a hospital, where I worked in the infectious diseases department for typhus, malaria, and venereal diseases. Our hospital, intended for refugees and run by refugee doctors, made such a name for itself locally that we had people brought in from Tomsk for operations. What plagued us the most was the lack of medicines. The lack of disinfectants prevented the containment of the typhus epidemic [despite] the doctors' greatest efforts. However, refugees received medicines in the parcels arriving from Poland. The local people, on the other hand, were deprived of everything. The economic situation of the refugees, compared to [that] of the local people, was excellent. We were 100 percent better clothed and often better fed than the locals, which caused widespread envy. How low the living standard was, even among the privileged Soviet citizens, is shown by the fact that during my visit to the apartment of an NKVD chief, I noticed that his universally known [life of] luxury meant one iron bed, a table, and two chairs in one room. What a wardrobe is no one knows in Russia. During conversations with the local citizens I often heard complaints about the regime, and a belief that the war would turn things around for the better in some way.

Antisemitism

It was a disappointment and a surprise for us to note the antisemitism in Russia. Because I didn't look Jewish, I often heard from the locals' mouths that Jews were the cause of the war and that Jews occupied all the high positions. Very often I came upon situations where peasants didn't want to sell to Jews or buy from Jews. My work, [though] poorly paid, had the benefit of my working in a warm, heated place, and it seemed to be that I was somehow doing my duty for my unfortunate brothers.

Cultural Life

The cultural life in the *posiołki* was concentrated in the clubhouse. From time to time a Soviet traveling troupe would come; films were often screened that I did not go to see, as they were exclusively of a propagandist nature. The concerts, on the other hand, were of high quality. In conversations with the artists I often heard complaints, even though they were the most well-off people in Russia. When I told them how artists lived in Poland, they didn't want to believe me. Inside the barracks literary evenings and discussions also took place—not interesting, because [they were] supervised. Our only pleasure was finding release in memories. In our *posiołek*, 30 percent [were] Poles, particularly the intelligentsia, clerks from Pomorze.

Father Arrested

My mother was the leader of the barracks and her role consisted of having to check every day whether everyone was present and whether they went to work. One day, when a policeman came to Mother for the report and [she] was not at home, the policeman brutally awoke Father, who had returned from a nighttime operation. Father took offense, in response to which the policeman hurled insults at him, like "Polish pig," as a result of which Father was accused of resisting the authorities and sentenced to a month in jail. After an intervention, he was locked up for only five days in total. But only Father was so lucky. I had acquaintances who returned from jail half-deranged. One day there was a revolt among the women demanding better conditions, and a hundred people were arrested then and sent off to prison.

After the Amnesty

After the outbreak of the [German-Soviet] war, my brother came to [see] us from Lwów. He was fleeing from the Germans and had crossed the front lines on foot. Throughout the entire journey across Russia he was brilliantly helped by the authorities of different universities. Because he had a Soviet passport, he wasn't allowed to stay with us, so he went to Tashkent. As a Soviet citizen he should have reported to the Soviet army, but he reported to the Polish army [instead]. After the announcement of the Amnesty we left for Tashkent. The journey took a whole month. I remember that our biggest scourge was the stamping of tickets at every station, which was indeed a truly hellish idea of Soviet bureaucracy. Fifty kilometers from Tashkent, my father became the head doctor of a maternity hospital. My brother and I, working at the hospital, fell ill with typhus but recovered after four weeks.

In the Polish Army

Since I've heard numerous complaints [stating] that the sole cause for not accepting [Jews] into the Polish army was the antisemitism of the Poles, I want to state that I saw with my own eyes how, in the mixed commission made up of Bolsheviks and Poles, a Bolshevik commissar wrote down on my cousin's document: *Yevreyev ne nado* [No Jews needed]. I heard how General Szyszko-Bohusz explained that the exclusion of Jews was the result of the Soviet authorities' ban, and that according to the agreement, the Bolsheviks were only permitting native Poles to leave Russia, and not minorities such as Ukrainians, Jews, or Belorussians [Belarusians]. I personally never saw signs of antisemitism in the army where my brother and father served. I was close friends with Mrs. Szumacher, the wife of a Jewish actor who, along with [Szymon] Dżigan, also a well-known Jewish actor, was arrested by the Bolsheviks in Russia.[211] Szumacher and Dżigan had Soviet passports, had

211. Szymon Dżigan (1905–1980) and Izrael Szumacher (1908–1961) were a widely known duo of comedians and Jewish cabaret actors. [Note: Dżigan's surname is spelled both with and without the diacritic in the testimony; these inconsistencies have been preserved.]

appeared in Soviet films, and—it was said—had pro-Soviet inclinations. One day, [while] on a journey along with the leader of the seventh division, they found out about the evacuation of the Polish army and asked to be accepted [into it]. They were admitted, and even though their activities with the Soviets were known in the army, enjoyed great popularity. Mrs. Szumacher worked at the command center of the garrison, by the headquarters, and wrote poems for the community center. On the day of the evacuation, Szumacher and Dżigan were pulled off the train as Soviet citizens, and what happened to them no one knows.[212] Szumacher was badly ill with dysentery; his wife and child stayed in Russia, not wanting to abandon him.

212. They were deported to Kazakhstan. Returned to Poland in 1947 as repatriates, emigrated to Israel in 1949.

Protocol 69

Testimony of **Roza Buchman**, age forty-three. Husband owned the Korona tannery in Radom. Arrived in Palestine in 1943 via Tehran.

My husband was the director of a huge tannery in Radom employing a few hundred workers. My parents lived in Warsaw, where I would come to stay for longer periods very often. My son, Mieczysław, currently nineteen years of age, and daughter, Hanna, currently twenty-one, were studying in Polish schools in Radom. We didn't know anything about the planned evacuation of officials when, on 6 September [1939], [our] chauffeur came in and told us that all our vehicles, including the factory trucks, had been requisitioned, and that [the cars were going to be used to] evacuate the county prefect and [his] family, as well as all the state officials, including the caretakers and the janitors with [their] children. They didn't want to take us with them, [even] though my husband held a leading position in Polish industry and could be in great danger if Radom were to be occupied. The chauffeur, however, made it a condition that he would not go without us, so that the officials had to relent. We found ourselves [part of] a group of six official cars, with a small amount of belongings we had taken from home. We also managed to take our friends, Dr. Szenderowicz and his wife, with us. We traveled toward Lublin. A few times the leader of the transport, a Polish official whose surname I do not remember, got out of the car and tried to kick us out of [ours], arguing that only official persons had the right to evacuate. I sat next to the chauffeur, and were it not for my firm and determined stance, we would have been left out on the road. On the way, we stopped in the village of Wołki, twenty kilometers from Włodzimierz. The local Jews helped us, just like Czech colonists did in the villages we passed on the way. The prefect's cars ran out of gas. Our chauffeur had a hidden supply of gasoline, and this way we were all saved. After arriving in Kowel we realized that we could not stay there any longer, and wanted to set off for somewhere else. However, before we had decided where to go, the Bolsheviks arrived. On the first day they started disarming Polish officers and taking their uniforms away. The officers resisted, there were a few instances of suicide. One Jew opposite us, an officer, shot himself in the street. After two weeks' stay in Kowel, we set off for Białystok, firstly because we all suffered from some odd mania for traveling, and we could not stay put; secondly, to be closer to Warsaw.

"Good Germans"

There began to be restrictions, persecutions of the rich, arrests of officials in Białystok—the atmosphere worsened by the day. My husband suffered terribly and said that if he were to die, he would prefer [to do it] in his own home rather than in a strange city with the Bolsheviks. News was coming in from the German-occupied territories [saying] that the persecutions had died down a little, [that] there was enough food and [that] people were becoming used to the new order of things. Since all of our assets were located on the German side, we thought about how to save some of them. I received a message that my parents in Warsaw had been killed by a bomb in their apartment. I wanted to go to [visit their] graves at all costs. Since a woman was in less danger, I decided to go. A smuggler took me across; this was quite easy at the time. Warsaw made a harrowing impression on me. Ruins of homes, immeasurably despondent people, all of this got me in such a mood that I decided to go back to [my] family. Before that, however, I had to take some things from my apartment in Radom. Between Warsaw and Radom there shuttled the private car of a certain engineer from Warsaw, whose female friend worked for the Germans and had obtained a permit to drive a car. This journey cost quite a lot—[in the car] there traveled myself and my brother-in-law and one more lady. By chance, none of the passengers looked like Jews. This saved us, because a German patrol stopped us on the road, looked through the driver's documents, and even though everything was in order, the driver-engineer was punched between the eyes so [hard] that he lost consciousness. This was the first encounter of German brutality in my life. It made a shocking impression on me. With a trembling heart, I entered my Radom apartment, which had been requisitioned by the Germans, not knowing what awaited me there. In my apartment three judges of the Supreme Court, Austrians, [and] two secretaries had been accommodated.[213] One room was taken by my brother and

213. Possibly three Austrian judges and two secretaries, but this is unclear; similar lists (mostly of persons) exist in other testimonies where it is not always clear which elements the descriptors refer to.

[his] wife. Imagine my surprise when I found all [our] belongings in place. The Germans called me *Gnaedige Frau* [madam], brought home sardines and wine, and asked me to have lunch with them. They let me take everything out of the apartment: carpets, crystal, silver. They only asked that I leave them the net curtains. Sure enough, I left them an empty apartment. I hid all of the stuff in the factory or with Polish neighbors.

In the Factory

In our factory, the German-appointed commissar was a Pole. His attitude toward me proved that he really wanted to garner my favor. He asked that I cooperate with him "for the good of Poland"—as he claimed. He sent letters to [my] husband asking that he return to the factory and take over its management. I was prepared to stay and write to [my] husband [asking him] to return, when the following incident took place in our home. During this idyll[ic time] with the Germans, the Gestapo burst into the bedroom and started brutally pulling the men out of their beds, thinking they were my husband and brother, [both of] whom they wanted to apprehend for forced labor. It turned out, however, that they were the Supreme Judges of the German court, and before the situation was straightened out, the German officials got [their] taste of a roundup. I knew that they were against brutal methods themselves.

Return to Białystok

On the way back I spent a week in Warsaw. I bought a great deal of things—stockings, fabrics, which were scarce under the Soviet occupation. However, the smuggler, whom we paid an overinflated sum to take us, tricked us and took us to a customshouse. There, a very scrupulous search was carried out. Fearful for my life, I did not claim [the] sacks and suitcases that contained [my] fortune. I had five-hundred-zloty banknotes sewn in in my garters. The body search was carried out by men—Germans—in a brutish way. They did not realize that I was a Jew, and thanks to that, I got out of the [situation] in one piece. I returned to Białystok, but my husband did not want to hear about staying with the Bolsheviks. He set off for the German-occupied Poland, to Radom, to establish what the chances were to return. I was left alone with the children in Białystok. Letters arrived from [my] husband [saying] he was working in his factory, that he was being treated well, that he earned well. He intended to bring us to [join] him.

Exile

I waited impatiently for him to send someone for me, or to come himself. The children went to school. We lived with our friends in [their] private apartment [and] did not suffer hunger. In the meantime, the famous voting took place [and] the passportization, which, naturally, we wanted nothing to do with. Like a bolt from the blue the news came to us of the deportation of Polish citizens to Siberia. We were living our lives in a state of security when—as was the case with others—NKVD agents visited us. I will not describe how much we suffered during [this] journey to an unknown hell. I had enough money and belongings with me to not be afraid of destitution; however, in fear of the Bolsheviks, I did not take with me the half a million rubles I had in Białystok. Food was brought to the station to us by [our] acquaintances. Inside the car, however, nothing could be bought with money. We traveled for two weeks to Arkhangelsk and Vologda.

Siberia

The 220 of us were placed in the Zawidowo *posiołek*, in barracks, eight people to a room. As I had two children, I used the excuse of having to do housework and did not work in the forest like everyone else. I worked hard at home, trying to keep up maximum [levels of] hygiene and prepare, where possible, meals out of the scarce [and] poor-quality products that one could get in the area. My husband sent me parcels and money from Radom. The parcels were so bountiful and numerous that the postal officials claimed they took up the entire transport. Where I could, I shared with neighbors. As it was, the people who lived with us were simple people, only Jews with the exception of a few Poles. The men worked in the forest, the women most often in the laundry [and] sometimes in the forest. After three months we were moved to another *posiołek*, Tochonino. There was a small town with a school nearby, which it was very difficult to get into. Only the son of our doctor was accepted there. Our cultural life, very pitiful, developed in the so-called "red *ugolok*,"[214] where there

214. *Krasnyj ugolok*/*ugołok*: a community center of a propagandist nature.

were a few Russian propaganda books, a Russian propaganda film from time to time, and from time to time a propaganda lecture. My daughter worked in the forest—she sawed wood or cut down grass in a swampy area. My son worked in the forest—he was an exemplary worker [and] exceeded his quotas, [earning] around five hundred rubles per month.

Courts in *Posiołki*

One of the most horrendous scourges in the *posiołek* was the justice system. Two civilians would arrive, and the only offenses considered were [those of] *progul*, that is, being late for work or missing it. The punishments were disproportionately high for the wrongdoing. Being late was punishable by jail time. One of our neighbors, a young girl, was sentenced to four months in jail for lateness. When she returned to the *posiołek*, it turned out she [had gone insane]. Naturally, she did not say what had been done to her in prison.

Soviet-German War

The outbreak of war did not improve our situation in the *posiołek*, and for me, it was a real disaster. Not only did the supply of parcels cease, but I lost contact with [my] husband, from whom I never again, to this day, received [any] messages. Since the children were earning money and I had quite a few belongings, I was not at risk of hunger. However, I had to constantly fight for the children like a lioness. They were being given work that could destroy their health. For months, the boy worked transporting tree trunks [by river], standing in water. For that reason, when we received the news about the Amnesty, we immediately left on a peasant's wagon for Kotlas where, paying eighty rubles per head, we got into an *eszelon* going toward Kuybyshev. On the way we had to get off in the town of Katakurga,[215] as they were not letting [people] into Kuybyshev. We rented an apartment, or rather a hovel, where we stayed for half a year. This was a time of horrific devastation among refugees caused by epidemics. We picked lice off ourselves by the handful. I had a friend who worked in a sanitary center, who supplied me with a little bit of disinfecting products. Naturally, I cleaned from morning to evening. Apart from that I went to the market every

---

215. Here and henceforth the author of the testimony incorrectly names the town of Kattakurgan [original Polish correction: Katta-Kurgan].

day to sell things, a bit at a time, for which I would buy—at massively inflated prices—bread, onions, and olive oil. This concern for giving the children [all] possible vitamins and my excessive attention to hygiene meant that none of us fell ill with any epidemic illness, even though two people in our room were ill with typhus. From Katakurga we went to Kermine where—I had heard—the Polish army was forming. There was no talk of evacuation yet at the time. My son reported to the army, led exclusively by [his] sense of duty. He stated this to the captain, who took him on. In Kermine, however, they crossed all Jews off the lists of army [recruits]. After what we had suffered through, and after the hopes around the formation and the future of the Polish army, [this] was a painful disappointment for us, and for my son simply a profound blow.

Evacuation

We looked for a way to get out of the Soviet hell, and we knew they were closing the last escape route in front of us. Only illegal means were left. A friend of mine, a lieutenant, put me down as his wife, and this way myself and my children got on the military family list. We thought we would be evacuated alongside the others. Imagine our surprise when, [though] added to the list one day, we were crossed off from it the day before the transport's departure. My daughter made friends with a young Polish lieutenant, who treated her with genuine special regard and even suggested marriage. Thanks to him she got into the house of Major X, a softhearted man who received many refugees, offering [food] from his officer's table to the hungry. When, covered in tears, I found out from the transport officer that the only thing that could save us was a declaration by trustworthy people that we were not Jews, we decided that [my] daughter would ask the major for such a declaration. Breaking his officer's word of honor, in defense of three people's lives, Major X testified in writing that he knew us to be an evangelical family. Despite this, when the approached hour to add us to the list, the Polish official wondered whether our names—Roza, Mieczysław, and Hanna—were Polish enough, and it took long persuading by the major to knock those suspicions out of [the official's] head. It is therefore an untruth, which I am noting, that the Bolsheviks caused Jews problems when leaving Russia. Most of the time everything depended on the Polish officials. And it is only thanks to their ill will that hundreds of Jews perished in Russia. I was also witness to a situation where one Polish manager of an *eszelon* threw Jews out of the train car who had already passed the mixed Polish-Bolshevik commission and could have confidently boarded the ship. These were symptoms of strong antisemitism, which existed alongside manifestations of high humanitarianism on the part of the Poles, as was the case in our situation and many other instances. We arrived in Tehran, where we were placed in a camp and [where my] son was immediately accepted into the Polish army. My daughter worked as a waitress and I as the person in charge of the house of a Persian man until the time when we left for Palestine.

Protocol 70

Testimony of **Jechiel Tennenblum**, age forty-five, from Łódź. Arrived in Palestine via Tehran on 18 February 1943.

I escaped from Łódź on the night of 5 September of the year 1939. I rode in a car along with Dr. Jeżewski, a captain in the Polish army. [We had] a small Red Cross banner waving on our car, and this way reached Warsaw safely. Passing by Łowicz and by Sochaczew, we saw both cities in flames—the result of relentless German bombing. Unable to pass by these cities, we turned back toward Grodzisk, and after a thirteen-hour journey, arrived in Warsaw. We spent the night [there]. That night the bridges on the Wisła River were bombed. We hired a tractor, attached a platform to it, and at night, [with] a group of twelve people, made it across the bridge with the army. It was difficult to move around. We were [only] allowed to go [at a speed of] fifteen kilometers per hour. We traveled by night and hid in the woods by day, afraid of the bombing. Garwolin stood ablaze. We went toward Lublin. Entire neighborhoods were on fire in Lublin. We intended to go toward the Romanian border. However, on hearing about the difficulties of border crossing, we set off for Równe. The journey to Równe took eleven days.

Bolsheviks in Równe

A few kilometers before the city we came upon a marching Soviet army. A patrol stopped us and asked if we had [any] weapons. One of our group, [the] lawyer Tykociński, surrendered his handgun. We were searched and set free. In the city there were sixty thousand refugees. It was impossible to find a place for the night, or a piece of bread. Finally, we were put up in a loft. A few days later it was announced that all refugees had to register and that we wouldn't be allowed to live in the large cities. The lack of foodstuffs was noticeable. Long lines stood in front of the shops [selling] bread; one would wait for hours to get a loaf of bread. After a few days' stay in Równe, I received a permit to leave for Lublin, as the Bolsheviks were not aware that the Germans were in Lublin. I didn't know about it either—I was only told about it on the way—[and] I abandoned my journey. In those days, refugees could go to Wilno readily, but most left for Lwów. I too decided to go to Lwów. From Lwów I began to try to make contact with Łódź. I had left my fifteen-year-old daughter there with [my] brother-in-law. [My] wife and older son had been surprised by the war [while they were] in France. I sent a special emissary to Łódź with a letter and received a response that [my] daughter wasn't doing too badly, that she was attending a gymnasium, and that it was said around Łódź that I had supposedly been killed on [my] journey.

During the same time, I turned to the French consul in Kiev and told him that I had left my foreign-travel passport, along with a visa to leave for France, back in Łódź, and that my son Eliahu, student at a Polytechnic in Paris, was there. For years I had been in constant trade contact with the French rubber and motorcycle industries, and I had requested a French visa for these reasons. Three weeks later I received a response from the consul in Kiev [saying] they would soon send me the appropriate documents and were prepared, in the meantime, to act as a go-between in [my attempts to] establish contact with my wife and son. After fourteen days I received a letter from the consulate with a letter from my wife and son attached, informing [me] that they were in good health. Forms from the embassy were attached to the letter, after whose completion I was to receive the visa. Meanwhile, a second letter from [my] wife arrived, reassuring me that I would soon come to France. My son, as it turned out, was already serving in the air force of the Polish army. Soon afterward I received a message that my daughter was in Radom with my brother-in-law, Ginzburg. They were doing well and advised that I come to Radom also.

In April I received a letter from the embassy. I was informed that the passport was ready, told to send fifty rubles for the visa, and asked which direction I wanted to go in—Italy or Odessa. The ambassador wrote that he would try for an exit visa from Russia for me. Before the formalities concluded, France fell. There was no way of leaving [and] I had to stay in Lwów.

In Lwów

In Lwów I lived in constant fear; I did not know what to do with myself. I did not want to go back to the Germans. In Lwów, I risked being deported to Siberia. We were watched at every step. We had to agree beforehand what we would talk about, because a government agent suddenly encountered could ask what we were discussing. Everyone was forced to take a Soviet passport. Most Jews did not want to agree to it. In the end, not even those who were keen received the passports. [Those with jobs] would get a passport, and jobs were held by those who had got the passports. In May a decree came out about the registration for a return home. Long lines formed in front of the registration bureaus. Jews with families were registered, [but] only unmarried Poles. However, only some of those registered were sent to Germany. After the first transport was sent off, the border was closed and no one else was able to return home. Many people had themselves smuggled to the German-occupied territories.

Manhunts and Arrests

On 24 June 1940, the newly arrived NKVD agents from Kiev started carrying out manhunts, arresting a few thousand people, in particular single ones, and sending them deep into Russia. After a few days, at two o'clock at night, three NKVD agents entered my apartment. One of them told me to get dressed, another was spreading out my belongings. I had at home a few diamonds, rings, a gold watch, and a fountain pen. They took everything, including the money, and left me a mere sixty kopecks. When I was dressed, I asked where they were taking me. They said, to a police station. They listed everything they had taken from me on a piece of paper. I was so agitated I did not even notice what I was signing. It turned out that in the protocol they had listed metal rings instead of rings with diamonds. They didn't let me take any belongings with me. The owner of the place I was staying at entreated them to allow me to bring a rucksack with undergarments. I was then taken to the police station. In vain did I ask for an audience with the police superintendent. I wanted to explain that I had not registered because I had a French passport. I had no chance to explain myself, however, and after spending three hours at the station, I was taken into the prison in Brygidki alongside a few hundred other people. There were thousands of people in the prison courtyard. There were tables set against the walls at which everyone was registered and logged. We were led to cell number 11.

In Prison

The cell could fit ten people at the most, but eighty-seven were [put] in it. It was so hot that we all stripped naked. There wasn't even room to sit down. We weren't even given any food or water in the first two days, only later did we get some watery soup and a slice of bread. Of the large number of arrestees,

55 percent were Jews. In our cell there was also a well-known industrialist from Łódź, Naftali. Generally, the intelligentsia predominated: lawyers and teachers and doctors. Among us there was also a lawyer from Toruń, Senator Jeżewski. After a few days' imprisonment we were told that a warden would come and that we were not allowed to call him "comrade" since, being imprisoned, we were second-class citizens, [and that] he was to be referred to as *Citizen*. As was the custom, in order to leave the cell to use the toilet, one had to turn to the cell leader, whom we had chosen from among us and who was responsible for everything that went on. The cell leader would knock on the door three times, but the custodians were not always there, which meant that one would go to the toilet in the cell. We could go to the toilet once a day and in groups of ten people. According to the regulations we were allowed a fifteen-minute-long walk. In reality, however, we were taken out twice in the course of two weeks. The walk took place in the courtyard, where the bathing area was located as well. Before we managed to undress we'd already be called back upstairs, so that we walked around dirty and infested with lice. After ten days a dysentery epidemic spread in the cell. There was no doctor. Everyone treated themselves with the resources they had. After some time we were told that we could write applications to the authorities to relax the prison regimen. An improvement to the conditions meant seventeen people being taken out of the cell, so that it was now possible to flip from one side to the other at night. Seventeen days later a colonel from the NKVD came to us and asked about the conditions in the prison. Senator Jeżewski, who knew Russian, asked for a less strict [regimen]. To this, the colonel responded, with a laugh, that soon we would be taken back to Germany.

Investigation

During the entirety of my stay in prison there wasn't a single night when someone would not be summoned for an interrogation. One day I myself was summoned, too. In the room I was led into there were four tables—behind them sat higher-ranking NKVD members. I was asked: "When did you leave home? Why did you leave? Have you crossed the border? Have you registered to return? What do you do currently? Do you have a Soviet passport? How are you supporting yourself? What are your relations with foreign countries?" I answered all questions. When I was accused of lying, I became agitated and said they wanted to set me up me deliberately. I never went to cabarets and I don't even know where the market is. I spoke so loudly that other judges became interested in my case. After the investigation the judge said that he was crossing out the charge of illegal border crossing, but that I would be answering [the accusation of] not accepting a Soviet passport. I did not want to sign the protocol. He said, however, that I was only facing a fine of a hundred rubles and two weeks in jail, and [that] it was possible he would release me. I did well in signing the protocol, as others, more stubborn, were called for interrogation every night and tortured until they signed. After being examined by a doctors' commission and having my fingerprints taken, I was sent back to the cell.

Deportation

After three weeks, on 2 August, we were ordered to pack [our] belongings, and gathered out in the yard. There were a few thousand [of us]. We were told to strip naked, despite the fact that there were houses around us that people were looking out of. We had to raise our hands up and come up like this, one by one, to the tables, where the NKVD would look inside our mouth[s and] nose[s] using a small electric flashlight, order [us] to do squats—all this to check that we didn't have any valuables on us. Then our belongings were inspected. All pieces of paper, documents, letters, [and] photographs were torn up and [we] were sent off to the train station in groups of thirty. We were placed inside freight cars, eighty-five people in each, and remained in the station for twenty-four hours. We didn't get food before the departure. During the journey we were given soup and bread. The soldiers would check to see if anyone was trying to rip out a plank from the train car to escape. After eleven days' journey we were told to get off. We did not know where we were. After a five-kilometer walk, we were brought to a camp. The labor camp was surrounded with barbed wire [and] there were guard outposts on four sides. We were placed in barracks, three hundred people in each. There were bunks there made of wood planks. Mice and rats scampered around at night, lice were eating us [alive], but we grew used to it. On the walls we found writing in Polish: "No one will get out of here alive." We understood that we weren't the first refugees who had found themselves in this camp. In eighty-seven barracks there were 2,040 people, out of whom 90 percent were Jews. In the labor camp there was an administrative office and a hospital with a feldsher, but no medicines. On the second day we were visited by the "management." We were told that brigades would be formed, with brigade leaders at their helm. The brigade leader would need to know the Russian language and be energetic. The leader would receive the work instructions. We couldn't move around freely in the camp; we could only go to the toilet. We were led to work under convoy at five in the morning, to a forest four kilometers away from the camp. There we were busy sawing trees, loading wood, and building a railway embankment. At first we worked for twelve hours, then work [hours] were extended to between sixteen and seventeen a day. For our work we received five hundred grams of black bread in the morning, and at lunch and in the evening watery soup. It was difficult to wait up for the evening meal, which sometimes appeared at two o'clock at night, so that, exhausted, we would give up. The young and healthy worked above [their] quotas to get more bread, but the wardens, seeing that the quotas were being achieved, increased the amount of work [required]. After two months, the record-holders died from being overworked. At work we were not allowed to catch a breath; we were rushed and beaten. Writing letters or receiving parcels was not allowed, so we did not know what was happening in the world. Only someone with a 39°C [102.2°F] fever was allowed to complain of bad health and get exempted from work. A legal apprentice from Nowy Sącz by the name of Fisz tried to get an exemption from work as he had a fever of 38.7°C [101.66°F]. This was not an [accepted] temperature according to regulations, [so] he did not get an exemption, caught a cold, and died of pneumonia. Many people among us swelled up from hunger. There were many instances of suicide by hanging, [wrist-]cutting or throwing oneself into a well that was inside the camp. We were not allowed to take part in the funeral of the first victim. The guards laughed and said, "You will all die here." The dead were left out in the snow. The winter lasted ten months, the summer—two. During the thaw we found the decomposing corpses of our companions. It wasn't until a few religious Jews bribed the guards [that they let us] bury the dead.

During the first six months 150 people perished. In January 1941 a commissar from Moscow visited us to investigate the causes of this horrific mortality. Everyone was examined and the camp was closed down. Of the 2,040 people brought into the camp, fifteen healthy ones were taken out; five hundred were deemed invalids. I was sent to the labor camp number 5. Here the regime was milder. Russian exiles lived here. They received better food and worked less. Here we wove slippers and laid ropes. The quotas were eight slippers and fifty meters of rope. The preparatory work was not easy—one would stand in water up to [one's] knees and cut down branches. With my best intentions I fulfilled 6 percent of the quota. We were woken up at dawn and told to carry wood to the administrative office. We were given huge bundles of wood and chased with sticks to [make us] carry them more hastily. If someone collapsed on the way, they became a victim of the dogs. We were beaten with sticks on the stomach and kidneys and told to run in water up to our knees. We were called Polish spies, Polish parasites, and threatened with extermination. At first, horses would pull the small wagons with the timber; then eight people were ordered to do that work. Let the fact that the shoe and rope transports were left at the rail station until they rotted be proof of how urgent our labor was. We threw them away like rubbish afterward.

War Outbreak and the Amnesty

At the beginning of June[216] we found out about the outbreak of war. Our situation did not improve—only in August were we gathered and told that we were allies, and that we should increase production. Our workday was increased by two hours. We were so [badly] tormented and tortured after the Amnesty [that] no one thought they would get out alive. From 23 August onward they began to release us, fifty people per day. I was released in the third group. Only after my release did I find out what the place of my ordeal was called: Sucha Bezwodnaja,[217] Gorky Oblast. We traveled forty kilometers on foot to the center of Sucha Bezwodnaja. There I learned that of the 2,040 people exiled to the labor camp, 460 had survived. Of those, many more died during the journey. I decided to go to Sigral [?]. I received a rail ticket and fifteen rubles per day for food. The journey took twelve days. I was hungry and sold the remnants of my clothing on the way. In Sigral [?] I turned to the Housing Committee and said that I wanted to join the Polish army. After four days' stay in the city we went to Buzuluk. Polish officers awaited us there. We were received well, settled in barracks, underwent a health inspection, and were deemed capable of

216. Likely July 1941. The German-Soviet war broke out on 22 June 1941.

217. Correctly: Sukhobezvodnoye [original Polish correction: Suchobiezwodnoje] in the Gorky Oblast.

army service. In the camp there were thirty thousand people. After six weeks, 350 people, Poles and Jews, were discharged from the army. We were sent to Tashkent and told that the Russian Government had taken it upon itself to cover [our stay in] a sanatorium until we returned to health. Hearing that they were taking us to kolkhozes, we did not want to get off the carriage. We reached Kogon. There we were chased off the train [and] left in an empty field. When we sat down in the field, they tried to chase us away from there by pouring water [over us]. We lay in the water. Many caught a chill and died; many went to kolkhozes. I stayed out in the field for two weeks and eventually went to Bukhara. I lived in Bukhara for almost a year, living off the assistance of [my] friends. The mortality was so great there that there wasn't enough room in the cemetery—it stood at 90 percent [capacity]. On 1 August 1942 I went to Jang-Iul [Yangiyul (Polish: Jangi-Jul)]. I had been trying to leave with the Polish army and managed to go with the last transport. I spent four months in Tehran, got a certificate there, and went to Palestine.

Protocol 74

Testimony of **Nachum Teper**, age fifteen, from Nachal [?] by Lwów. Arrived in Palestine from Tehran.

My father, Szmul Abraham, was a quality controller. His job was to estimate the [yield of a] forest. In our town there lived three thousand people. The Germans bombed our little town on 8 September 1939. Fourteen German airplanes took part in the bombing, and it was a special miracle that there were no human casualties. The Germans entered the town on Rosh Hashanah [14 or 15 September 1939]; they wanted to gain popularity among the people and the German soldiers would give out cigarettes in the street. After five days the Poles took the town back by force. It was said that during the attack on our town three German generals were killed, because there was a command headquarters in town. One day, a German car with a colonel burst into town. The Poles threw a grenade at the car and demolished it completely.

The next day the Germans entered the town again and burned it down completely as punishment. Only three houses were left. The Germans took special revenge on Jews, killing three of them. Among these killed was Nachman, a cattle trader who ran to save his belongings during the fire in town and was shot. Lajbisz Załking died as a martyr: he decided to save the Pentateuch from the synagogue; the Germans locked him in the synagogue and set [it] on fire. He and a few other Jews were burned to death along with the holy books. Before setting the town on fire, the Germans plundered the warehouses and took away all the food products. A few days later the Bolsheviks arrived. The local Communists helped the Bolsheviks in searching for weapons. The Poles were very upset with them. Then the Germans returned again. Some of our friends warned us that the Polish people were hostile to Jews because of the Jewish Communists who were helping the Bolsheviks in confiscating arms. Our Polish friends advised people to leave town, since acts of revenge could be carried out. We let [other] Jews know about this, and five hundred people, almost all of the Jewish population, left town and went toward Rawa Ruska. There we lived for eight months under Bolshevik occupation. The Bolsheviks demanded that we take on Russian passports, but we knew that refugees had it bad in Russia, as messages were coming in from those who had voluntarily reported to work in Don-Basen [Donbas].[218] They all escaped later, ragged and hungry. After returning to Rawa they would tell horrible stories about the conditions of [their] stay in Russia. Generally they had to keep quiet, because those who talked fell into the hands of the NKVD. The NKVD began the registration [of refugees], asking people the question: "Do you want to return to the Germans, or stay in Russia?" We replied that we wanted to [go] home, despite the fact that there were Germans at home. One Friday evening there was a knock [on our door] and we were told to get dressed. We weren't allowed to bring [any] belongings. The NKVD-ers told us that we were going home, loaded us onto buses, and took [us] to the station. On the train there were already two thousand people. We traveled for two weeks. We managed to bring food for the journey. The journey was very difficult.

The train stopped at the station of Wartoga[219] in Siberia, close to huge forests. The Bolsheviks said to us: "You are the bourgeoisie. You have to work. You will stay here until death." We all worked: Father, Mother, sisters, and brothers. Our family was made up of eight people and everyone worked, so we were able to survive. Each of the adults earned eighty kopecks per day, but with that money you could buy at most a box of matches. The last time we were leaving Russia, a box of matches cost only five rubles.[220] The refugees were split into groups, three hundred people in each. In our transport there were lots of Poles. The Poles were afraid that they would be deported far away, to more dangerous districts, and that's why they pretended to be Jews; they stayed with us and shared our fate. We mostly lived off forest berries to begin with. We received only four hundred grams of bread per day. The attitude toward us was very strict. We weren't allowed to write letters to Lwów. Only later did they let us write to Lwów, [and] from there we received help. Committees were formed in large Galician towns [and] parcels were sent to refugees who had been deported deep into Russia. The parcels we got from the committee well and truly saved us. Life was very hard. We slept in barracks, eighty people in each. Russian peasants had been kicked out of there to make room for refugees. They convinced the peasants that we were savages; it was forbidden for them

218. Donets Coal Basin [Polish: Donieckie Zagłębie Węglowe]. See glossary: Donbas.

219. Possibly Vorkuta [original Polish correction: Workuta].

220. Perhaps: kopecks? The author likely alludes to the fact that prices were less inflated outside of the camp.

to speak with us or come to the village. There was no well in the *posiołek*—we would carry water from the river. Bread we received from a neighboring village at first, and later we baked it ourselves. The Bolsheviks opened a school for children in the village of Stieklarka [?], located one kilometer from the village where we lived. The refugees built a barracks for the school on their own out of cut timber. Two female Russian teachers arrived. Children up to sixteen years of age had to go to school. We studied for four hours a day, but it was so rainy and muddy in the autumn that the children could not come to school, as they didn't have shoes. The NKVD threatened the parents with punishment if the children weren't sent to school.

We really liked both of the Russian teachers. They had a lot of patience and helped the children to learn. They knew the Polish language and German. The children grew really attached to them. The observant Jews tried to open a cheder [religious school for younger boys] but the NKVD did not allow it. We were not allowed to hold communal prayers either. But one was not disturbed when praying separately. My father tried to encourage us to pray, but was told that if they found out he was forcing children into prayer he would be severely punished.

The refugees worked hard in the forest sawing wood and producing planks. On their own they built a clubhouse for themselves, where [they] spent time free from work. The hospital was located at a distance of eighteen kilometers from us. There were many ill and many died, among them Mrs. Karman from our town—she was forty and died from hunger. By chance we found out about the agreement between Russia and Poland.[221] A Jew from Kiev sent us a parcel, and inside the parcel he put a newspaper with news about it. The commandant had known about it for two months but hid that information from us. The food situation was still difficult. The cooks stole everything. We went on strike and did not go to work. They threatened that if we did not return to work they would not give us any food at all. We dug our heels in and replied that we had no intention of dying, that we wanted to leave here. The strike dragged on. Two older NKVD leaders arrived and called a meeting in the clubhouse. During long speeches we were told that we were free, and that as Polish citizens

221. Agreement, here: the so-called Sikorski-Maisky pact. Agreement signed on 30 July 1941 in London between the prime minister of the Polish Government-in-Exile, General Władysław Sikorski and the USSR ambassador in London, Ivan Maisky [Mayski]. See glossary: agreement.

we had the right to evacuation. They advised us, however, to stay in Russia. Evacuation was a dangerous thing; the Germans were bombing the evacuation trains. We replied that we wanted to get out of there. To this they [responded] that it was the rainy season then, and that cars could not drive on the waterlogged roads. We decided to go on foot and file a complaint with the Polish consulate. Eventually we were allowed to leave. The NKVD-ers changed—we were allowed to bring everything with us, were paid everything we were owed for work, [and] given two days' worth of bread as well as tractors for the journey. But because of the mud, we had to push the tractors ourselves. We barely made it to the rail station. There we were told to buy train tickets to the nearest hub. A rail ticket cost 118 rubles. Since there were eight of us, we needed a thousand rubles. We said: "You brought us in without a ticket so take us out without a ticket too." An order arrived for us to be thrown out of the station, as we were hindering traffic. It so happened that Lieutenant Epstein from Kraków was at the station at the time, and he advised us to send a telegram to the Polish agency in Buzuluk to complain about how they were treating us. Eventually we won. An order arrived from Moscow that we should be fed and loaded into the carriage. We received a notice saying that we were Polish citizens, and had the right to travel and live anywhere in Russia with the exception of the large cities. On the way we were given bread.

We made it to Tashkent. Our permit was good for a journey to Bukhara. We arrived in Tashkent on the holiday of Rosh Hashanah [22–23 September] of the year 1941. We had to get off the train and spend the night in the station. The crowding at the station was such that when we were leaving the next day, we could not get into a carriage together. The family lost each other. We lost sight of Mother and [my] two small sisters. We found them two days later. We arrived in Kogon. We were not allowed to go to Bukhara and were told to make our way to the evacuation point. We did not have permission to live in Bukhara, a large city. We were told to go to a kolkhoz. But we carried on toward Bukhara. We went by cart and reached the city this way. We rented a room for thirty rubles per month from an Uzbek man. At first it was very cheap, and later, with the arrival of refugees, the prices rose and resentment of the new arrivals increased. Our Uzbek landlord, worried that we were unregistered, told us to register with the police. Thanks to the help of the Polish agency we were not kicked out of the city. We came across Jews from Bukhara who knew the Hebrew language. But they could not help us much, since the rich had long since been deported, and the poor had nothing to eat themselves. They welcomed us very warmly regardless. We prayed alongside them. They were very happy to meet Jews, and worried that because of us the prices were rising, and concurrently, the hostility of the population toward refugees.

Unregistered refugees did not receive a food ration card. Hunger took hold and a typhus epidemic broke out from which thousands of people were dying. In March 1941[222] Father and I fell ill with typhus and were taken to the hospital. We lay in the corridor for three days. We got back from the hospital before Pesach [2–9 April 1942]. There was no matzo [and] we had to eat bread. However, the Polish government made efforts so that refugees would get matzo. We received 270 grams of bread per person per day. But the lines in front of the shops were so long that, tired out by hunger and illness, we could not get in. Others got [things] straightaway and then sold [them] on the black market. After typhus, an epidemic of typhoid fever and dysentery broke out in the city. The starved refugees were eating green plums chased with water. Many died. My mother fell ill with typhoid fever and lay for three days without care or medicine. There were no doctors. The Russian doctors had been mobilized to the front, and there were only dentists left in the hospital. We cooked cabbage for Mother, since there was no other food. One day I went by the hospital and asked my sister how Mother was doing. To this, my sister replied: "Say Kaddish for Father." When I returned home after finishing the prayer, I found out that Mother was dead. We buried Mother in the Jewish cemetery. We sewed a burial shirt from bedsheets. We sold off [some] belongings and paid 150 rubles for a plot in the cemetery. That same week on Friday we were robbed. They took Mother's jewelry and all of our things from us. We were left without parents and without money.

We reported to the delegation so that we would be admitted to an orphanage. We [stayed in] a children's care center. We were happy there. We received three hundred grams of bread and a bowl of soup every day. We shared the bread with [our] older siblings even though we risked a severe punishment for it. One day we were told that we were going to Iran. We gathered up bread for the older siblings who had to remain in Bukhara—we were scared that

222. From the course of the testimony it follows that this refers to March 1942.

the center manager would find the bread and accuse us of theft. We told her the truth. She was not a good teacher. She gave larger bread portions and better beds to Polish children than to Jewish children. But this time she was understanding because we told her the truth. At the station, refugees were saying goodbye to us, jealous of the fact that we were getting out of Russia. We went to Krasnovodsk, where there was neither tea nor water for three days. We drank seawater, salty and reeking of oil. On board the ship Kaganowicz, after a twenty-four-hour journey, we arrived in Pahlevi, where the Polish Red Cross awaited us. The children were split up into the healthy and the sick. We snatched away four sick children so that they could come with us to Palestine. The Persians welcomed us with great hospitality. They gave us [sweet] biscuits and water, which was the most important [thing] for us. In the camp, the Polish and Jewish children lived separately. At first the Polish children teased the Jewish ones, but this slowly ceased. We lived in a tent for three weeks. I fell ill with [an eye problem] and was treated. We received amazing food: bread, eggs, milk, cocoa, and cooked meals. We were also given tomans for small expenses. We bathed in the sea. We were returning to health. One transport left for Palestine via India. I was on the list of children but didn't want to go without [my] four-year-old little sister. I waited three weeks. Finally, we left. I was afraid during the journey. We traveled over high hills and descended into valleys, and I saw one Russian car crash. Before [we got to] Tehran the water in the radiator ran out and we couldn't carry on. Luckily we were stopped near a Polish camp. Army cars took the children. We found ourselves in camp number 3. It was said that they would send us to Africa. We were afraid of another [long] journey, but a representative from the Agency [Jewish Agency (Sochnut)] came [and] took three hundred children who were intended for departure to Palestine. When they asked me in Russia where I came from I would say . . . from iron. Now, in Palestine, I want to learn a trade, to become a self-sufficient man.

Protocol 76

Testimony of **Mosze Gliksberg**, age seventeen, from Różana. Son of Szmul Jakob and Judyta. Arrived in Palestine via Tehran in February 1943.

In January 1939 I lived in Warsaw, where I studied at a yeshiva and lived in a boardinghouse by the yeshiva. On Friday, 1 September, when the war broke out, all pupils went to their homes; but many, like myself, could not return home because of a disruption of the railway lines, and had to stay in Warsaw during the bombardment. As I found out later, our family left home on 2 September, evacuated by the Polish authorities. The army was concentrated in Różana; the civilian population had to leave town and the surrounding areas. Our family made its way to the small town of Długosiodło, where our relatives lived. There they already came upon Germans, and stayed until the time when the Germans chased all the Jewish inhabitants out of town. They escaped to Dąbrowa and from there to Białystok.

I Go to My Parents

During the bombing of Warsaw I fell ill with pneumonia. Strangers took care of me. When I recovered, I was so weak that I could not undertake the journey to find my parents. Not until three weeks after Sukkot did I set off on my way, and [I] made it to Maków [Mazowiecki], where my relatives lived. The journey, on a peasant's cart, took two days, but I will never forget what I experienced there. After a few kilometers of travel, Germans stopped the cart, which was carrying eight Jews, among them two women and a thirteen-year-old boy. The Germans beat up the Jews in a horrific way and then chased them into the courtyard of a mansion house, where we had to load sacks onto trucks. There were another few hundred Jews there, from the neighboring towns. Everyone had to, without help from [others], hoist up sack[s], and a few Jews who wanted to help the weaker ones were shot on the spot. In the evening, when we finished work, we were set free. A few tens of carts were going toward the Soviet border. The Germans stopped us a few times, taking everything we had on us. Once, Gestapo [officers] stopped our carts, pulled one Jew off each cart, took [them] to a nearby forest, and killed [them]. [The rest of] us they ordered to carry on ahead without looking back, otherwise we were threatened with death. Gravely frightened, I made the journey to Maków [Mazowiecki]. I thought I would find Bolsheviks there, but it turned out that there were Germans there. I found out from relatives that my family was in Białystok. I wanted to set off straightaway, but my relatives stopped me and informed [my] parents that I was with them. I spent four weeks in Maków, living through all the suffering with [other] Jews. Jews were rounded up for forced labor, beaten; many did not return as they were shot during work; others escaped to the Russian side. I wanted to do the same, but my relatives would not allow it. Only after a month did my sister come to Maków and take me to Białystok.

In Białystok

My parents were in a dire financial situation. All that was left of [our] wealth was some leather that Father had taken from home. We lived in a small room in Zwierzyniec. The household was provided for by my sister, who smuggled foodstuffs from Białystok to Lwów. My father would not touch the smuggling [business]. We received Soviet passports with paragraph number 11, which were valid for three months. Father did not register to leave for Germany, telling everyone that he did not believe it, that it was a joke on the part of the Bolsheviks. When the decree came out for all refugees to leave Białystok, we too received an order to go to Iwie, outside Lida. We lived in Iwie until 28 June 1940. There were a few hundred refugees in town to begin with, who dispersed as there was nothing [there] to live off. Only between fifty and sixty families remained. Father traded in leather [and] shoes, and my sister continued to go to Lwów, and this way we survived somehow.

In Exile

On Friday 28 June 1940, in the middle of the night, our house was surrounded by the NKVD. We were woken up, told to pack up [our] belongings, [and] rushed to the station. My sister was not at home. The NKVD-ers assured us that we were going to Lida [and that] all refugees were escaping the small town. Fifty refugees were led to the station of Gawja [?], where we were put in freight cars and taken to Lida. We thought that they would release us, but it turned out that they attached our car to a huge train carrying refugees. There were only twenty-three of us in the carriage, whereas in each of the other cars there were eighty people. We set off into the unknown. Once a day we received bread and soup. We reached Mołodeczno and moved to Russian freight cars traveling on wide rails. We rode for three weeks in horrendous conditions—everyone fell ill during the journey—until we arrived in Kotlas. There we got off and were carried onto barges on the River Dvina [Polish: Dźwina]. A few thousand people sailed on two barges. The young and the strong took up spaces, [while] families with children could not make it onto the barges. An order came out [stating] that if everyone was not on the barges within five minutes, [they] would be thrown on by force, without luggage, and the barges would leave. Panic broke out, children and parcels were thrown, children were trampled. A few children drowned. The screams went up to the heavens. Finally everyone found themselves on the barges, which left the next day in the evening. We traveled for thirty-six hours to the village of Szeftria.[223] There we disembarked. We were a group of a few thousand people, Jews and Christians. We were sent out to *posiołki*. We had neither food nor money with us. All of our money had stayed with the merchants in Iwie, and because we left abruptly, we did not cash in our accounts. Father asked for bread for the children. The warden replied: "Go to the shop and buy [some]. Take [your] shoes off, sell them and you'll have bread." Father cut off a small piece of leather from the reserves we were carrying with us, and we got bread for it. We were put onto a sled attached to a tractor and traveled through a thick forest. Children and women rode on the sleds; men went on foot. The sled tipped over. One lady from Wieluń was killed on the spot. The transport leader was not bothered by it and decided to carry on ahead, leaving the killed [woman] behind. We protested and it was decided that I and one [other] woman would stay to guard the dead woman until a cart arrived from the *posiołek* to take [her] away. I spent the whole night standing guard. Only in the morning did the cart arrive. We placed the corpse onto it and we set off for the *posiołek*. The road was muddy, the girl who was leading the horses did not have enough strength. We tipped over a few times before we arrived at the *posiołek*, where the dead woman was buried.

In the *Posiołek*

The *posiołek* was made up of a few barracks split into small rooms full of bedbugs and fleas. The sanitary conditions were horrendous. The *posiołek* was

223. The name or location of this village could not be confirmed.

inhabited by settlers—Poles who had been exiled here from the Borderlands. They greeted us in an awful manner and said they would not allow Jews in. The Poles' resistance worked and the warden decided that we had to go back to Szeftria. The seven-kilometer-long journey took a whole night. We arrived in the evening. We were put up in a bakery where there was no bread, only bedbugs. Father went to an Ewakpunkt [evacuation point] and told [them] how we had not been allowed into the *posiołek*. The warden assigned us to the *posiołek* Zorawi. With nowhere to go, Mother went to the *posiołek* straightaway with the children, while Father and I stayed behind to guard [our] belongings. The next day we received a letter from Mother [telling us] to be careful, as the road led through a river, and at night, a few carts had tipped over and children had drowned. Our friend, Lajbel Cywiak from Różana, had thrown himself in to help them but could not save all of them. Finally, we arrived at the *posiołek*. In our barracks lived the following families: Zelman Rozenfeld from Brześć, Jozef Fil from Różana, Krankenberg from Wyszków, and the widow Morgenstern, with two children, from Długosiodło. My sister and I went to the forest to pull the bark off trees. We earned fifty kopecks per day. One day, when the warden caught me picking berries, [he] beat me, and as punishment, Father and I were to receive [only] three hundred grams of bread per day, while others received six hundred grams. I said that I would not go to work regardless and that, according to the regulations, I was under no obligation to work as a youth. The warden took me to the commandant of the *posiołek*, [and] it was confirmed that indeed I did not need to work, but my sister and father were sent to work, while Mother—being sick—was exempted.

Sister Saves Us

Free from work, I took care of the household. We had in [our] provisions forty kilos of wholemeal flour, a few kilos of rice, [and] some potatoes, and this saved us. As I mentioned, my older sister had been traveling when we were sent away from Iwie. On returning home, she learned of our fate and begged the NKVD leader to send her to us. She was told that this was impossible because our address was unknown, and she could only go after the first letter [had been received]. She was told that no more people would be deported. She was offered a job as a bookkeeper in an *artel*, which she accepted. She earned four hundred rubles per month. Immediately after arriving at the *posiołek* we sent a telegram to our sister, and received a response [explaining] that she was sending us money and parcels. During [our] exile we received a few hundred food parcels from her, and that saved us from death from starvation. My other sister and my father, as workers, each received a kilo of bread per day, other family members half a kilo each. Small children picked berries and mushrooms in the woods—state offices paid a ruble for a kilo of berries, two rubles for a kilo of mushrooms. Generally speaking, our situation in the *posiołek* was not the worst. Even so, everyone was ill with *cynga* because of the lack of vitamins. Pneumonia and dysentery were common illnesses. I remember friends who perished in the *posiołek*: Tauba Kronenberg from Wyszków, Menachem-Jechiel Morgenstern from Długosiodło. We buried them near the barracks.

Strike

The work in the forest was very hard. One worked twelve or fourteen hours a day. The work was not paused even during heavy frost. Eventually everyone lost their patience and declared a strike. A numerous NKVD group came [to the *posiołek*], an investigation was carried out, twenty people were arrested, handcuffed, and taken to jail. A few families were sent off to a different *posiołek*. A canteen was opened—this was the only result of the strike. My sister got a job as a secretary to the commandant. She had to log the quotas, log whether everyone went to work. Apart from this, among her duties was keeping the commandant's administrative office clean. On Pesach 1941 [12–19 April], we received thirty kilos of matzo, raisins, wine, [and] lard, and potatoes picked fresh from the field from my sister. The children wished Pesach would last all year. The Bolsheviks, wanting us to stay put, assigned us land which we dug up. We planted vegetables—potatoes, carrots, and cabbage—and when the war broke out and we stopped getting parcels from [my] sister from Iwie, this vegetable garden kept us from going hungry.

Amnesty

After the announcement of the Amnesty for Polish citizens, a high-ranking NKVD official arrived [at the *posiołek*], and in his speech, asked us to stay, in exchange for which he committed to giving us land, seeds, and tools, and promised that they would not take away [our] Polish citizenship. We did not want to hear of this proposition—having been cut off from the world for so long, we were afraid that we would stay there forever. We were given papers to go to Barnaul, had a cart hired for us, [and] were taken to a ship. We went to Kotlas [and] hired a freight car, in which we went to Tashkent. In Kogon, the train stopped. Because of the freezing temperatures the locomotive could not be fired up; I had my feet frostbitten and could not put [my] shoes on. I was taken to a doctor and the doctor issued a certificate [stating] that I could not continue on the journey. We stayed in a field under the open sky.

In Bukhara

Somehow, we made it to Bukhara. We were the first Polish refugees who arrived in this city. We got an apartment. Everything was cheap in Bukhara: bread cost one ruble per kilo, and six children from our home would go to [stand in] line and bring back six kilos of bread. A kilo of flour cost twenty kopecks, soy—six rubles, a kilo of prunes—thirty rubles, watermelons—one ruble a piece. After three months the prices went up so much that a kilogram of flour jumped up to a hundred rubles. Of bread we received only four hundred grams, and only on [ration] cards. Only registered people received bread, and we were among them. We received an order to leave the apartment. We moved to a stable, where all of us fell ill, and my sister Ester died. Then everyone was ill with dysentery and gastritis. We could barely stand up.

Protocol 77

Testimony of **Gitla Rabinowicz**, age seventeen, born in Siedlce, daughter of Rabbi Jechiel, known as the Rabbi from Biała. Arrived in Palestine via Russia and Tehran in February 1943.[224]

My father, known as the Rabbi from Biała, had many followers both in town and in other areas of Poland. We had our own house in Siedlce, built for Father by the followers. It was a beth hamidrash full of valuable books and next to the beth hamidrash there was our private apartment. In Siedlce and nearby, a lot of Polish army troops were stationed; ditches and trenches had been dug there [and] there was preparation for resistance.

The Germans bombed Siedlce very abruptly, and when the front was approaching, the town was shot at by heavy artillery. The order of the bombardment was as follows: at eight in the morning, surveillance airplanes would arrive and they were shot at by the Zenit artillery; around nine o'clock, bomber airplanes would arrive and the bombardment would last until eleven. The same would be repeated after lunch. The town was on fire. People escaped [their] homes, as it turned out that basements turned into graves for the unlucky ones. People lay down flat on the streets, in the field, [they] looked for shelter under trees; some fled to the country, and when they returned during a pause [in the bombardments], they often found no trace of their homes. The number of casualties among the civilian population was huge. During this bombardment, 2,500 people were killed in the period between 1 and 11 September. It was months before those killed were pulled from under the rubble. On Saturday 9 September at nine in the morning, we ran away from our home during the bombardment: Father, Mother, and five children, of whom I was the eldest. We ran ahead without an agreed-upon destination until we fell into trenches that had been prepared by the local people for defense. When [things] calmed down, it turned out that we no longer had a roof over our heads. Our whole house with our belongings—books, antiques, and family heirlooms passed down from generation to generation—had been burned down.

224. [Gitla Rabinowicz appears to be the sister of Jakub Rabinowicz, whose testimony is recorded in Protocol 131.]

No one, however, thought about their own fate in that moment; the whole town was burning; the neighborhoods inhabited by Jews were especially damaged. We looked for shelter in the neighboring village. We thought that the Germans would not want to waste bombs on pitiful peasant huts inhabited by poor people. After a few hours' escape we arrived in the village of Cieplin [Ciepielin or Ciepliny?], where people did not want to let us in at first, explaining that the influx of refugees would invite the enemy's attention. Only after an intervention by [some] well-known and valued citizens did the peasants open up the barns, where we [managed to] settle reasonably. An awful panic prevailed. Parents lost their children, husbands their wives, people were looking for each other in the barns and the stables. But even in this village we could not rest. Here, too, the German bombs reached us—there was a large number of casualties among the civilian population.

Germans in Siedlce

On Monday 11 September, the Germans occupied Siedlce. We had noticed since the morning that the Germans weren't bombing the city and the area. Later we saw the Polish army run away. A lot of the civilian population escaped too, particularly youths, but families with small children could not entertain the idea of running away. We returned to Siedlce before the evening. The devastation was horrific; whole streets had disappeared. The returnees settled in the remaining houses. We were put up in some small apartment. We thought of the coming day with fear.

On the third day the Germans started a manhunt for Jews. They pulled all the men out of the houses and sent them to prison. In one prison cell there were between two and three hundred people. They were held for forty-eight hours without food and drink, had their clothes torn off them, were beaten and tortured, and then set free. A few days later an order was issued for all men to gather in the square, and those who were found at home would be shot. When everyone gathered in the square, the military commandant of the town said that all men were being deported to a concentration camp in Węgrów, and ordered everyone to quickly set off on their way; whoever stayed behind would be shot. The crowd began the journey to Węgrów. My father was among those people, too. He was an older man who suffered from heart [problems], and [he] knew that he would not make it to Węgrów, but would collapse after two kilometers.

There was nothing else awaiting him but a German bullet somewhere outside the town, where he wouldn't even be buried. If they killed him in town, he could count on the Jews to organize a proper funeral for him. When the crowd found itself in a narrow street, Father ran off and hid in the entrance of one of the houses. A German soldier shot at Father but missed. With the cry of "Shema Yisrael,"[225] Father ran to the attic and hid in between pieces of junk. The German [went] after him, looked around in all directions, but did not notice him and returned to the street. Father stayed in the attic all night long, afraid of moving from [his] spot. The next day the occupant of that house arrived and told [us] what had happened to Father. It's difficult to describe our joy when we heard that Father was alive and in town, when we had presumed that [he] was no longer among the living. As a few bakers remained in town who had been left [there] by the Germans to bake bread, Mother went to one of them, borrowed a baker's outfit, and in this disguise, Father returned home. During the holiday of Rosh Hashanah [14–15 September 1939] there were only a few Jews left in Siedlce who gathered in our apartment to recite prayers. After two weeks, all the Jews were released from the camp in Węgrów [and] returned to town.

Russians in Siedlce

On 18 September the Soviet army occupied Siedlce, but announced the following day that they had no intention of staying there; anyone who wanted to could go to Russia or to the lands occupied by the Bolsheviks. After five days the Russians left town and the Germans entered. Along with the Russians almost all of the civilian Jewish population left, [and] many Poles. We left with the Bolsheviks too. We went to Baranowicze to be with our relative, a rabbi. We spent eight months in Baranowicze. With nothing to live on, we had to take up trading. They didn't want to give us Soviet passports because Father was considered a nonuseful element. Without a Soviet passport we had to register to go to Lithuania, thinking that we would reach Palestine from there.

Deportation

After a few months—it was on a Friday night at eleven o'clock—NKVD-ers came to our apartment and asked us if there were any weapons [there]. They

225. Shema Yisrael (Polish: Szema Israel): one of the main prayers of Judaism. See glossary.

carried out a thorough search, gave us ten minutes to pack our belongings and took us to the station. They loaded us into a freight car, and after twenty hours of waiting in the station, our refugee train set off for Russia. We traveled for eight days. We went by Mińsk, Moscow, Sverdlovsk,[226] until [we got to] the station of Tavda. There is a town near a river by the same name. We were taken to the river, loaded onto barges, and two days later, set down in a primeval forest in the district of Tawarsk.[227] In that district there were a few *posiołki* for deportees. Our *posiołek* was called Czasz.[228] There were three hundred of us and only six Polish families. We settled in barracks; mosquitos, ants, and other insects I had not known until then welcomed us. They tormented us terribly. We were swollen; the climate was humid and heavy. We worked in the forest cutting down trees, pulling out roots, weaving baskets. Generally speaking, this was a rich *posiołek*: [it] had a mill, a power station, a brick factory, a post office, and a school. At first, we received a kilo of bread per day; later the portions were reduced to six hundred grams. During that time the commandants and wardens changed. Observant Jews suffered the most, because they did not want to work on Saturdays [the Sabbath]. Apart from my father, there was in the *posiołek* a shochet from Siedlce with his family. Father and the shochet were called "popes," [and] they were constantly summoned for interrogation, accused of encouraging the Saturday rest. Every Saturday was marked by interrogations and discussions, but in the end, those who didn't want to did not work Saturdays.

Day of Atonement and New Year

Before the Holidays[229] the commandant summoned Father, implored him not to disturb the work, and told him that if he wanted to pray, let him pray on his own, and that [the commandant] understood the religious needs of a "pope." The Stalinist constitution does not prevent anyone from performing their religious rituals but does not allow religious propagandizing. Besides, gatherings of refugees in large groups was strictly forbidden in the *posiołek*.

226. Until 1924, and currently, Yekaterinburg.

227. Likely: Tabory.

228. Likely: Czet'.

229. In 1940 New Year fell on 3–4 October and the Day of Atonement fell on 12 October. See glossary.

Father said that he would definitely not propagandize anyone, but could not guarantee that people would not come to him for the holiday prayers of their own will and need. On the first day of the holidays, thirty people gathered in our barracks and prayers commenced, as [they would] at home. Children were put out as guards to signal the approach of the NKVD. In the middle of the prayers, five NKVD-ers burst into our barracks with the commandant; Father, the shochet, and one other older bearded Jew were arrested. The arrested were led through the *posiołek* like criminals; Father was pulled by his collar. He was taken for an interrogation but later released. The warden threatened Father with the gravest punishments if he did not cease his harmful activities. The arrest of Father in the middle of the prayer [and] his being treated like a criminal made such an impression on the Jews that the next day everyone, even the secular Jews, abandoned [their] work in protest and turned up at our barracks for the prayers. The commandant came to the barracks, noted down a few tens of surnames, and it ended with a few tens of people being disciplined in punishment cells. Before Yom Kippur, the commandant turned up at Father's place and told him that since he was seeing religious enthusiasm among the Jews, he would release everyone from work on the day of Yom Kippur.

Fourteen people escaped from the *posiołek*. Various epidemics were spreading; everyone was dejected. Families did not live together. No one believed they would get out of there alive. Generally, there was no hunger there—everyone received parcels from relatives [and], besides, trading took place with the Russian exiles who had already settled down in their homesteads. We would get bread, and even chickens, for any old rag. On Pesach [12–19 April] in 1941 we received matzo, lard, raisins for wine, and even festive dishes from Belorussia [Belarus]. In addition to this, Father opened a matzo bakery and supplied the neighboring *posiołki* with [matzo].

Outbreak of War and Amnesty

The regime became stricter when the [German-Soviet] war broke out. The workday was extended by two hours, the amount of bread was reduced, [and] everyone was forced to work. The flow of parcels from outside stopped. We found out about the Amnesty at the end of August. Higher-ranking NKVD officials came to us and a propaganda campaign was begun to make us stay. The commandant told us about the danger[s] and the difficulties of a journey to the south of Russia, particularly for families with small children. Only a few listened to him. The shochet with his family stayed—he received a dessiatine[230] of land where he worked with the children, and from the letters we later got from him, it appeared that his situation was much better than the situation of those refugees who left for the south of Russia. We hired a cart, went to the city of Tavda, and from there, traveled by train for four weeks. It was a horrendous journey; we were standing more than we were sitting. Sometimes we would wait at one station for forty-eight hours. It was difficult to get a piece of bread; there were epidemics on the train and all the children under four perished. Finally we arrived in Turkestan. After long efforts we got a clay hut [to live in]; we were starved and exhausted. We had nothing to sell or to [use to] buy bread. Typhus did not spare anyone. We all fell ill one after another [and] stayed in a hospital for a few weeks. The mortality rate was terrible. Many of our acquaintances died, among them many well-known rabbis. After leaving the hospital we had to go to a kolkhoz, where we worked with cotton. Weakened, we were often not able to report for work, and were not given bread then. We sold our last pillow [and] our last shirt—we were naked and in rags. He who has not experienced hunger does not know the feeling. When hunger tormented us greatly, Mama would always find some shirt, go to the market with it, barely dragging her feet, and bring back bread. The children would huddle around her when she returned and [she] would split the bread into portions. They swallowed those measly portions within one moment and still called out: "Mama, I am hungry." At that time, Father received a pass to go to Palestine. He spent entire days at the delegation trying to get out of Russia with the army transports, but it was not working. They didn't want to accept Jews, and even the wives of Jewish military men had to stay in Russia. As I was blond and did not look like a Jewish girl, I managed to get into a Polish children's center, and thanks to this, I saved myself [and got] out of Russia. Later, my father managed to place my three brothers in a Polish [orphanage] and they arrived with the last children's transport [to] Tehran, where they are until this day. From Jangi-Jul I traveled to Krasnovodsk as a daughter of a Polish army man. I will never forget what they did for me. From Krasnovodsk I went to Pahlevi and from there to Tehran. I came to Palestine with a group of children from Tehran.

230. A tithe: a one-tenth part of a land.

Protocol 79

Testimony of **Boruch Flamenbaum**, age fourteen, from Biłgoraj, son of Abraham and Sara. Arrived in Palestine from Russia via Tehran in February 1943.

My father was a forest administrator. We were well-to-do people. We had a three-story tenement house. I was an only child. Our house stood in front of a convent. Then the war broke out and the bombing of the town started, including the convent. Immediately after the first air raid, on Wednesday[231] at eleven in the morning, we escaped to the apartment of our paternal uncle Jona Akierman, a lawyer who lived in the far end of town. During that first air raid, in which ten airplanes took part, the town was terribly bombed; many houses burned down [and], opposite us, one bomb destroyed half a house. Stones flew around in the air in the streets and the only good fortune was that many bombs fell onto a field. After the first bombing there were no human casualties in town. We lived in town with Uncle. We stayed under shelter, afraid of sticking [our] head[s] out into the street. The bombings continued. The heaviest air raid was on the fourth [of September], on Monday. Despite the alarm, Father ran out into the street to see what was happening. On hearing that the synagogue, the beth hamidrash, the mikvah (ritual bath), and the neighboring houses were burning, Father ran to see what was happening to our house. He saw our house all up in flames.

Since we weren't sure of our safety at [our] uncle's either, we decided to go to the country. On the way we heard an alarm, hid in a potato field, and saw how German airplanes flew very low above the field and hunted down individual people with machine guns. Some peasant lying right next to me was killed. When we got to the first village, one boy said that Jews weren't allowed in the village, but the older peasants opened up a barn for us and we spent the night there. The next day we returned to town, and because all of our belongings were hidden away in the basement that [had managed to] avoid destruction, we took with us all the valuable items we could find. Out of a few hundred houses in our town, there were only twenty left. We settled in the remaining houses; in each room there lived a few families. The town was

231. Error in the text. Refers to Saturday 2 September 1939.

left to fend for itself. The police and the fire brigade had already left town on Friday, on the second day of the war.[232] Hoodlums started plundering. On Saturday 9 September, the Germans dropped bombs on the bridge so that the Polish army could not escape. One bomb fell into a house and killed a hundred people, among them my cousin, Berysz Flamenbaum, age twelve. A piece of shrapnel fell into the house where we were hiding [and] tore out the side wall, but luckily no one was hurt. We could not leave the house because everything around was on fire. We lay down next to one another, stretched out on the floors and scared to death. The shooting and the bombing lasted all of Saturday and Sunday nights. After each device that exploded nearby we would call out "Shema Yisrael," believing our last moment was approaching. Things only quieted down on Monday.

Germans in Biłgoraj

The Germans entered the town from one side, and on the other side, in a small woodland, the Poles were hiding. A battle started. [It] lasted the whole day. We didn't know if the Polish army had managed to escape. The Germans led many prisoners through the town. On Monday the Germans' rule began. When they spotted a Jew with a beard they would set his beard on fire, tear the hat off his head, and beat him; they took Jews for [forced] labor, told them to sing, dance, and fight with each other, pummel and insult one another. Small Polish boys would run with the German soldiers and point to where the Jewish apartments where located, where the Germans would enter and take everything they found. On holidays we prayed in a private house under the protection of a guard.

Bolsheviks Approaching

The Germans left town after the holidays. When the last of [them] were leaving town, we saw groups of Polish [soldiers] running across town. As the Polish soldiers ran through town, all at once a German army car arrived with a German officer in it. A Polish soldier shot and wounded the officer. When the Russians occupied the town, they drove the wounded German officer to a hospital. For four days the town was left to fend for itself, to be plundered by bad

232. Friday was the first day of the war.

elements. A citizens' militia was put together made up of Jews and Christians. The Bolsheviks were in Biłgoraj for eight days altogether. In that time, they bought all of the food; soldiers in coats carried piles of herring, [something] they clearly had not eaten in a long time. They didn't do anything bad to anyone; officers would talk to everyone they came upon on the street. The town was busy.

Germans Again

After the Bolsheviks' departure, order was kept by the citizens' militia again until the Germans arrived. In the first days the Germans behaved decently. They pretended they didn't see Jews. The Jews talked among themselves, [saying] that the Gestapo, who were the cruelest, had not yet arrived. Indeed, a few days later the Gestapo arrived and got started on the Jews. They went around to Jewish apartments, stole everything they could, beat Jews for no reason, and made threats that worse was still to come. Every morning at six they ran around the Jewish apartments and shot at the windows so that everyone would run out of the apartments, at which point they would round up the men for [forced] labor. The work consisted of building a road, and they kept the Jews until ten in the evening, even though Jews were only allowed to walk around town until seven. The unlucky ones stayed in the ditches until morning. Father was also caught for [forced] labor. He was taken to a big square. They told him to pick up rubbish and this work lasted all day long. When it got dark and Father said that he wanted to return home, they beat him up thoroughly. Father said that he would report to work voluntarily the next day. He was given a piece of paper and was no longer captured for work [forcefully]. He went of his own accord every day, barely standing up on [his] feet; at night he wailed in pain, and recognizing that he could not bear it anymore, we decided to escape town.

On the Trail

Many Jews had fled from town before us. Rich people who had money escaped; the Germans had constantly blackmailed them and extorted big sums of money from them under various pretexts. It was in the middle of October when Father hired a cart [and] loaded it up with the belongings we had gotten out of the basement at night, and we went toward Tarnogród. There were Germans there too, but not as bad as the ones [in our town]. Jews were allowed to trade, [and] they weren't rounded up for work because the local municipal office supplied a set number of workers every day. Knowing already that the same thing would eventually have to happen here as it had [in our town], we left the city and went to Sieniawa, which was on the Russian side. We hired guides and set off across the border. On the other side of the border we were met by Bolsheviks; the smugglers disappeared [and] we were left alone with the patrol. They did not want to let us through. We implored them until they took us to the guard post. We spent the night there, and the next day, they took us to jail in Sieniawa. We spent the whole night in jail without food and without drink; Father was released after an investigation. We went to see acquaintances of ours who nonetheless advised us to leave there as soon as possible and go to a big city. We went to Lwów. We did not stay for long in Lwów—we could not find a place for the night and we went [on] to Radziłów. There we rented an apartment and Father got a job as a bookkeeper in a carpenters' cooperative. Overall, we didn't fare badly. We had enough food, but Father was teased in the cooperative for not being one of their people. Father avoided ceremonies [and] assemblies, where Stalin was constantly praised. They could not fire him, however, because he was a great bookkeeper and had become indispensable. Father often said that the air in there made him choke, and that he would rather be under Hitler than deal with the harassments of the Communists. Father did not take part in the elections. He did not want to get a Soviet passport either, and when the law came out about the registration, he registered to return home. After some time, we heard that they were deporting all unmarried refugees to Russia.

In Exile

A few days later—it was a Friday—there was a knock at our apartment door at night. We knew who would enter, because we had heard during the day that there were hundreds of freight cars for refugees waiting at the station. The NKVD-ers asked us why we wanted to go back home and took us to the police station. Father asked why we needed [our] belongings—to this they replied that they could be left behind. Instead of the police station, we were taken to the rail station. We came upon thousands of people at the station; everyone was put inside freight cars and the sealed cars were left at the station.

After twenty-four hours the train started, and when we stopped for the first time it turned out that we were at the station of Równe. We slept on the floor because there was [only] one bunk in the carriage; there was no toilet either. We children went to the toilet through a crack [in the floor] and the older [people] negotiated with the soldiers so that they would be allowed to leave at stations. It happened very often that people, particularly women, went to the toilet where they were. One can imagine the stench inside the carriage. We had enough bread. At some stations we were allowed to open the doors of the car, and we would then exchange bread for milk, eggs, watermelons, and once for oranges.

We traveled for six weeks until we arrived in Assina [Asino], Novosibirsk Oblast. There we got off the train [and] were placed in barracks. The crowding was awful. After a few days we were led to a river. We saw people lying down by the river, under the open sky. We came across our uncle there, the lawyer Akierman, who had been there a few days already, and [who] went on ahead [of us] on a ship the next day. A few days later, we went to Teguldet on a different ship. There our belongings were loaded onto carts and we went on foot until we reached our destination. After a few days' stay in the village, we were again loaded onto carts and driven through a thick woodland to a forest. The cars drove on planks because the ground was muddy, and we had to work there [in those conditions]. Our supervisors comforted us: "You'll get used [to this]; and if not, you'll kick the bucket." We traveled like this for forty kilometers to Czeta.[233] In the middle of the forest there was a *posiołek* where one thousand people lived, Jews and Poles. After a few days' work Father became a brigade leader, and later he worked in the administrative office. We received two kilos of bread for three people. Every month we got half a kilo of pasta, half a liter of olive oil, some sugar, herring, fish, and salted meat. Father fell ill after six months, and since everyone was being sent to Sverdlovsk,[234] we had to stay behind on account of Father. The doctor who was called did not want to come because he said he did not have [any] medicines. After Father recovered, five hundred new people arrived in the *posiołek*, among them Russian exiles. Kitchens were built and Father continued to work in the office. We

233. Location of the Soviet forced labor camp Czet'.

234. Until 1924, and currently, Yekaterinburg.

received less bread and none of the other products at all, and weren't paid any wages.

We were released after the announcement of the Amnesty for Polish citizens. Father was paid what he was due for four months [of work] and we went to Teguldet. A ship had left two hours earlier. We had to wait for two weeks, under the open sky, in the rain, until by chance, we [were able to get to] Assina on a small barge. It was already cold then [and] we did not have warm clothing. We could not get onto any train. Along with a few other families we went in a specially rented train car to Samarkand. They didn't want to let us into the city—[they] threw us out of the train cars into a field and we lived outdoors for two weeks. Father and Mother fell ill with typhus; I also fell ill. After a few weeks we all recovered; then I had malaria. Father went to the Polish delegation in Samarkand and when a Polish children's center opened, [and] Father got a job there, I too was placed there. Two months later, along with a group of Polish children, I went to Palestine via Tehran.

Protocol 82

Testimony of **Szloma Zdrojowicz**, resident of Łódź, age forty-two.

I escaped from Łódź on 5 September 1939. The [fact of] the Germans' approach was noticeable in the behavior of the German population of the city, who became immediately emboldened. I remember an incident where an eight-year-old German boy attacked a doctor on the street and tore the mustache from his face along with a piece of skin. On 5 September, in the morning, we sent our servant to the shop. She returned with the news that the shop was closed and that thousands of people could be seen on the streets escaping the city. I, my wife, and my brother-in-law Dobrzyński with [his] wife ran out into the street. We saw a veritable procession of refugees: they were leaving the city with bundles and suitcases, or [even] with nothing. We allowed ourselves to be swept up by the crowd. We sent the women, whose situation was not as dangerous as ours, back to the house, and left the city ourselves [to go] toward Brzeziny. Five kilometers from that town we were spotted by German airplanes. The airplanes came down so low that we could clearly see the pilots. We had machine guns aimed at us. Hundreds of refugees, especially women and children, were killed. I avoided death by a miracle.

In the villages of Jeżów and Lipiny, German colonists shot at refugees from machine guns. Everywhere along the way, towns and villages were burning. Brzeziny and also Rawa [Mazowiecka], where we arrived on Wednesday, were in flames. We walked on without stopping. On Friday we arrived in Warsaw.

We found tipped-over trams and dug-up telegraph poles, as well as a demolished road. The bombardment lasted day and night. I found myself on Grzybowska Street, close to a basement where a lot of women and children had been buried under the rubble. I helped to bury the dead. When I heard that the Bolsheviks had taken over Białystok, I decided to smuggle myself to Białystok, where my uncle lived, via Małkinia.

I spent forty-eight hours in the buffer zone with hundreds of refugees, sleeping under the open sky. Tens of children died there [and] were buried on the spot, but despite this, the Bolsheviks did not want to allow the refugees in. I decided to smuggle myself through in a roundabout way, and along with a few daredevils, managed to outsmart the vigilance of the Bolshevik guard. My uncle, Jabłoński, was the owner of a large haberdashery shop in Kościuszko Square in Białystok. He readily hired me as help. My wife, too, made it to Białystok with the help of smugglers. Unlike other refugees, we experienced neither hunger nor destitution there—we fared well.

The Bolsheviks in Białystok ordered elections to the Soviet,[235] and forced even the people who were [still] in the station, having only just arrived, to vote. Afraid of reprisals, I, too, voted—admittedly, I don't know who for; I dropped into the ballot box the piece of paper that was put into my hand. After the plebiscite the prices of food products and clothing went up noticeably. One stood for hours in line to get a loaf of bread. In our shop, the shelves had been emptied of merchandise. The difference between our prices and [those] in the market was tenfold. Whereas in the market one paid between fifty and sixty rubles for warm undergarments, [in our shop] they cost between seven and eight. For this reason, the market traders stocked up in our shop. Lines formed; soldiers bought everything they could—as a result, the shop was emptied of goods. Naturally, no new merchandise arrived. I understood that there was no point in working for my uncle anymore. We also knew about the "happiness" awaiting us in the Soviet paradise. On [my] wife's persuasion, we decided to get across to Lithuania. To investigate the danger of the journey, I went alone at first toward Woronowo. The rabbi from Woronowo allowed Jews to travel on a Saturday so that they could escape the Bolsheviks. That same rabbi was later arrested by the Russians for providing assistance [to people being] smuggled to Lithuania. In Ejszyszki, Jews helped us, when they could, to get across the border. This was at the end of 1939. The freezing temperatures outdoors burned [our] ears and noses, [but] I made it to a hut of a Jewish peasant in Ejszyszki. I was welcomed warmly, and on Sunday morning, dressed as a peasant, made it across the border. The Lithuanians asked me about [my] passport. I got out of it somehow, and it wasn't until I was on a bus traveling to Wilno that I was taken off [it] for not having papers. I bribed my way out of the hands of the Lithuanian police and then, on a peasant's cart, traveled the seventy kilometers that separated me from Wilno. I got by somehow. An uncle, a rabbi in Alytus [and] later the head of a yeshiva in Chicago, helped

235. See the glossary: elections.

me. My uncle's family members who had remained in Lithuania helped me, as did a cousin who lived in Wilno. I ate at a refugee kitchen, not wanting to be a burden on [my] relatives. My wife fared worse. As she was smuggling herself toward Święciany, she was arrested by the Bolsheviks at the border. Luckily, I had sent her a telegram from Wilno before that [which said that] our child was dangerously ill. She showed this telegram to the border authorities. When she was caught for the second time crossing the border illegally, she was chased for fourteen kilometers on foot to the city and locked up in a cell. She was kept in jail for so long that she got encephalitis. She spent months in a hospital in Święciany without regaining consciousness, fighting death. When she recovered, the Bolsheviks guarded her so that she wouldn't try to go to Lithuania. She settled in a small town and made a living by going to Lwów from time to time to sell a few old things. One time she found herself in Lwów during a time when refugees were being sent to Russia. She hid, waited out the dangerous period, and came to Wilno when the Bolsheviks were already positioned in Lithuania.

In the meantime, I prepared all the papers necessary to leave and turned to the NKVD asking for a departure visa. I did not get this visa. I got a job in Lithuania. Close to Klaipėda was the largest textile factory in Lithuania, which produced linen and employed around 1,500 people. The job had the advantage of allowing [me] to think about escaping: from Klaipėda it was easy to get out to Sweden. I worked in that factory from the beginning of the year 1941 until the start of the German-Soviet war. It was a few days before the outbreak of the war. We were not expecting anything when NKVD agents arrived in the factory. Given ten minutes to prepare for the journey, we were led to the station with a group of local residents. We went to Šiauliai. As we waited in Šiauliai to carry on with the journey, the war broke out. The panic that arose in the city was immediately felt at the station. German airplanes bombed the station. We sat locked inside freight cars from which we were not allowed to move. There were forty-two people inside the car. Among them were a well-known Lithuanian-born Polish woman doctor with [her] son and daughter, a Polish pharmacist, a Polish official, and a number of Jewish merchants, all suspected of [having] German sympathies. Fear and helplessness brought us all together, we regarded each other like doomed souls. Finally, the train started. We did not, however, go the route of Wilno-Mińsk, but went via Jelgava[236] toward Velikiye Luki, Rzhev, Yaroslavl, Kazan, Sverdlovsk, Novosibirsk. The journey took three weeks. During the journey our train was bombed many times. Particularly severe bombardments took place along the section of Velikiye Luki and Rzhev, so that arriving in Siberia, in regions remote from the war, seemed like a blessing to us. From Novosibirsk we traveled six hundred kilometers by water and then by trucks all the way to Lesnoi Zavod number 2. It was a Russian village, consisting of wooden huts. My wife and I rented a room from a peasant with our own money. Those who didn't have money lived in barracks, between forty and sixty people in each. We worked in the local forests. We cut down trees, sawed them up, and loaded [them] onto trucks. We earned between four and five rubles per day and ate in a canteen where, for two to three rubles, one [could get] soup and groats. My wife, being in a blessed state, was exempted from work. Other women, [those] who had close relations with NKVD officials, received easy dispensation from work too.[237] They had enough of everything.

I spent two months in Lesnoi Zavod number 2. After that time, the Amnesty for Polish citizens was issued. My wife and I went to Novosibirsk together, and from there to Sverdlovsk. In Sverdlovsk I started to look for a job. I was an electrical technician by trade. I was engaged by the Soviet organization Stal-konstrukcja, which manufactured airplane parts in Kaminsk-Uralsk,[238] where Ukrainian and Belarussian [Belarusian] factories were concentrated, having been relocated there during the war. [It's] a real wilderness. The swamps come up to one's knees. We lived in tents, thirty people in each. The rain would not let [us] sleep, and it got even worse with the first snowfall. Out of ten thousand workers who worked in Kaminsk-Uralsk, nine thousand were exiles, most of them sentenced for *progul*, that is, for being late for work. I met a train driver there who had [once] turned up for work with a bottle of wine in his pocket, and for this was sentenced to a year's exile. A canteen was opened for those ten thousand, which dispensed meals for only two hundred people at a time, so that one had to wait for hours to get lunch. And that is why

236. The original uses the Polish name for Jelgava (Jelgawa): Mitawa.

237. Some women saved themselves by becoming mistresses not only of NKVD officials but also of the prisoners in charge of the camps/units.

238. Kamensk-Uralsky [original Polish correction: Kamieńsk Uralski].

people had to be late for work, unintentionally. Outside of the canteen it was impossible to get any food. The market was located in the neighboring town of Awas,[239] surrounded by the famous Ural aluminum factories. One went there for a few potatoes or a piece of bread; the route led through a river and the effort of [making] the journey was not always worth it.

A bucket of potatoes cost between twenty and thirty rubles. Everyone received bread but it was black bread, claylike, and we had to stand in line to get it. I earned seven hundred rubles per month and the work was not too taxing. It was only bad that we had no proper equipment and tools for work, and a lack of raw materials often prevented us from fulfilling our quotas. I was not to be envied. As the leader of the department, I was responsible for the results of the work—for fulfilling quotas—without tools, without the [necessary] raw materials, [and] with arrestees for workers. The factory had not been fulfilling orders for a long time. Instead of the two hundred tons set by the directors, we delivered only between seventy and eighty tons, and hopes had been placed on me for the production to pick up. I understood that if I did not bid goodbye to the job quickly, I would be accused of sabotage. Besides, the winter was extremely hard. The frosts were terrible and my wife, who was expecting a child soon, could no longer go to the canteen for a meal. The local doctor said that my wife could not deal with the harsh climate, but he did not want to provide this opinion in writing, and without a paper from a doctor there was no way for me to get released from work. In Sverdlovsk, our factory's chief of personnel was Sosnowski, a Pole. I was given an appointment with him and complained that I was not working in my trade. I was a specialist in electrical apparatus, yet I was working on electrical installations. I also showed him the prescriptions that the doctor had issued for my wife and asked for an exemption from work. The argument that finally worked was [the fact] that I declared my readiness to join the Polish army, as a Polish citizen. For a hundred rubles, the managers of the factory garage drove us to the station. I took five loaves of bread for the road and arrived safely in Chelyabinsk. It wasn't possible, however, to get a train ticket for the remainder of the journey. We waited patiently at the station. At the station I met a well-known lawyer from Łódź. I

239. No town with this name has been located. There is a town called Asbest in the Sverdlovsk Oblast.

was as happy as if I had received [personal] greetings from home. We invited him to have a meal with us, and if he so wished, to continue the journey with us. He agreed, spent the night at our place, and by morning, had disappeared. With him disappeared our bread and my winter coat. I was left without bread or a coat, and the line in front of the cash desk was not getting any shorter. In the first instance those who had special military permits got tickets, then the holders of *komandirovki* [business assignments], and [only then] were the empty spaces given to private passengers. This happened at every station where we had to change to a different train.

In Chelyabinsk, ten thousand private passengers were waiting and there were between four and five free spaces in each of the passing trains. Food was difficult [to obtain], particularly for those who were passing through. We paid thirty rubles for a kilo of bread. On the other hand, there was a lot of ice cream and we ate ice cream, one portion after another, in the deepest frost.

Finally, after ten days of waiting, I got a ticket and we dragged ourselves to the station of Chkalov [Orenburg]. There the same story began, waiting for long weeks for a ticket and living in the station. It was easier to get bread then, but only for those in possession of bread cards. We got bread in cafés where people waited for twenty hours in line for a loaf. I found out there that an *eszelon* with Polish citizens was leaving for Tashkent. I looked for the train at night, in the dark. I managed to put our belongings inside and get on the train in time, as it was setting off. My wife, who had all of our money on her, was left at the station. I couldn't jump out of the moving train. I got off at the first station. I was sure that [my] wife would follow me on the next train, and I waited for her at the station. An hour later the train arrived, without [my] wife. I returned to Chkalov. [My] wife had disappeared. I looked for her at the station; I looked in the city. I looked for her in the hospital. I roamed the city, hungry, devastated, without a penny to my name. For three days and nights I waited in the station and looked at all the arriving trains with the hope that my wife would get off one of them. On the fourth day this very miracle happened. As I was standing in the station, completely exhausted, a train from Tashkent arrived and an army man in a Polish uniform got off it. He asked me if my name was Zdrojowicz and gave me a letter from my wife. She wrote that she was waiting for me in the town of Ileck,[240] four stations beyond Chkalov. She had indeed gone after me, as I suspected, [and] saw me at the station with the suitcases, but the car [in] which she was traveling was locked; she could not get off during the train's short stopover. My wife would later tell me that the NKVD promised her they would send out a radio alert to try to locate me. We both went to Tashkent. For five days we stayed in the famous Tashkent "kindergarten" by the station, where thousands of refugees evacuated from all over Russia were sleeping. Hanka Ordonówna busied herself providing help to the Polish refugees there.

In Tashkent we received no bread. We ate apples, grapes, and other fruit. Typhus was widespread and claimed new victims every day. We did not find a [place to stay and] had to leave for Samarkand. After many days, we found a room in Samarkand. The apartment consisted of a room with a kitchen: in the kitchen lived a widow with a son and a daughter, a lawyer's widow from Siedlce with her daughter and son, and myself and my wife occupied the room. The widow of lawyer Tenenbaum and her son worked in Barnaul; they also had gold and silver on them. They were both, however, tremendously exhausted; the son was ill with pneumonia and she with typhus—they both died. We paid eighty rubles per month for a place to sleep. Since bread cost between fifty and a hundred rubles per kilo here, the rent for the apartment seemed low. We sold the remainder of [our] clothes so that we wouldn't die from hunger. Things were not worth [what they used to be] here. One pays as much as [the other] demands. We went hungry for entire days.

I got a job as a turner in Zawód Kołchoźnik. Agricultural machines were assembled there; I earned between forty and fifty rubles per week, while a kilo of potatoes cost twenty rubles. The meals were pitiful in the factory canteen. We got nothing to eat except *wodzianka* [watery soup]. I bought scraps of meat at the shochet's house. People stood in line for hours to get a kilo of meat scraps for two rubles. The baby's due date approached. [To get into] a state clinic was a pipe dream. My wife pushed her way into the hospital and gave birth to a girl there. The typhus epidemic ravaged Samarkand. Schools were

240. Likely refers to the town of Sol-Iletsk, south of Chkalov [original Polish correction: Sol-Ileck].

shut, and in the mornings one would see thousands dead in the streets who had been thrown out of homes. It was clean in the hospital, every corner was shiny, and we cried when [my] wife was leaving the clinic after the birth [to move] to our small kitchen. On 10 February, a Polish draft commission was formed, registering Polish citizens for the army. It was made up of five Russians and one Pole. The Russians did not want to accept Jews into the Polish army. In the factory, too, they frowned upon my desire to join the Polish army, and on the day I went in front of the commission, I was accused of *progul* and sentenced to one year in prison. I was put in police detention for the appeal. I received a piece of black bread once every twenty-four hours. Twice I was taken to prison and brought back because there was no space [there]. After two weeks the charge was dropped after an appeal. I understood that they would find another excuse at the factory to arrest me, and I escaped to Kermine, where the Polish army was forming. I traveled without a ticket in the restaurant car. In Kermine, they didn't want to accept me into the army, as I was a Jew. I did find there, however, many people I knew, refugees from Poland and Jews; we went together to hunt turtles, which we later cooked. The Poles evacuated us from Kermine. We were sent to kolkhozes. I got work in Maszynna Traktorna Stancja. There was a Polish agency in Kizeltef[241] that generously distributed money, supplies, and clothing to the refugees. We received sugar, tea, cheese, margarine, canned meat, and soups. I supposedly worked in a factory. But the electric motor was rarely in service there. Either the motor didn't work, or the fuel had run out. When I found out a week later that the Polish agency needed a clerk, I registered and got the job of a bookkeeper. People were starving—they cooked soup for themselves from poisonous goosefoot plants, and in the local children's institution, 40 out of 120 children died in one month. In the beginning of August, I found out that we would be leaving Russia. As an agency clerk, I was [being] evacuated along with my wife, and we prepared for the journey. The day before the transport's departure we were informed that we had been crossed off the list. A Polish major told me that the Soviet authorities were not letting either Jews or Ukrainians leave, and that we would be declared Russian citizens. I was left on my own in the delegation. The NKVD visited

241. An erroneous name for the town of Kzyl-Tu/Kzyltu, nowadays Kishkenekol [original Polish correction: Kzył-Tu].

us too often. They carried out searches constantly. I had to buy my way out with bribes so they wouldn't completely empty the storehouses of reserves. I saw that the storehouses would not remain in our hands for long. Meanwhile, twenty Poles arrived who had missed the transport. I didn't know what to do with them [so I] sent a telegram to the headquarters of the seventh division. I was told to put together a register quickly and come to the headquarters with it, as the last transport was leaving. I went to Kermine. The list was approved at night. In the morning, along with the twenty Poles, I left Russia. A few tens of Polish Jews were left behind in Kizeltef. They said goodbye to us with tears in their eyes and asked that we not forget about them.

Protocol 83

Testimony of **Szymon Turner**, age thirteen, from Osiany Dolne [?] in Eastern Galicia, son of Icchak and Leia. Came to Palestine with a transport of Tehran children in February 1943.

My father was a cattle tradesman. There were six of us children at home, we lived in [our] own small house and didn't fare badly. In addition to this, Father was the owner of an abattoir.

A few days before the outbreak of the war, [people] were already talking in town [about] the approaching danger. Father became very tense. He started to go around to the villages to collect on his accounts, as he was owed money from peasants for the cattle [he] had sold [them], but in the country, only a few debtors paid up. That's why when the war broke out Father was left with barely a penny to his name.

On Friday, 1 September [1939], panic broke out in town. There were trains standing in the station; Poles and Jews, anyone who was able, was fleeing in the direction of Lwów. Father had no intention of escaping, because how is one to set off into the world with six children and no money and leave all [his] wealth at God's mercy. But when they started saying that the Germans were already in Podhajce, a total of a few hours' journey from our town, and that the last train was leaving for Lwów and there would be no way to leave town later, Father—who still believed that the Polish army would successfully resist the Germans—changed his mind. We packed up [our] belongings, left Mama at home so she would look after [our] possessions—it was hoped at the time that we would soon return—and got ourselves into the car.

It was a horrific journey. It took two days and nights. The crowding was terrible. There was nowhere to sit or stand, children were trampled, people were stepped on. Cries, wails, and lamentations went up to the heavens. At every station, [new] passengers would join. Fights ensued between the newly arrived passengers and the old ones. From time to time, German airplanes would appear. The train would stop and the crowd of people, trampling one another, would jump out of the train to hide in ditches. When the air raid was over, [people] would push onto the train again. Families lost one another, belongings were also lost. [People's] calls to each other, children's cries, the curses of those who had been robbed went up to the heavens. Traveling like this, we arrived in Lwów.

Father found a small room. We settled there somehow, just like the thousands of other refugees who flooded the city. Thousands of soldiers were arriving in town. It was said that a huge battle would play out here and that Lwów would be defended. People dug trenches. Even old Jews with sidelocks and gaberdines were digging. German airplanes did not stop bombing the city. The Germans stayed in Lwów for a few days in total, but these few days cost the Jewish population a lot of casualties. Jews were captured in the streets and sent away to places unknown. I heard that they were taken outside of town and killed there. German soldiers burst into Jewish apartments, robbed and beat [the inhabitants]; they broke the locks off of shops and took away all of the merchandise.

Bolsheviks in Lwów

The Bolsheviks arrived a few days later. Jews began to leave their hiding places and come out into the streets. Father had already spent what was left of the money that he had brought with him from home. We had nothing to live on. Father took up trading. He traded everything: sugar, meat, saccharine; and his daughter, Sara, helped him in [it]. The lack of bread was noticeable in the city. People stood in lines for hours in front of bakeries, waiting for bread. We children learned to spend all [of our] days in line, and we would sell the bread we got. This way we helped Father. Our biggest worry was [our] fear for Mother. We didn't have any news from her. In vain did Father send "special people" to bring Mother here. They took the money but Mother did not arrive. In the city it was said that the Germans were killing off all Jews in the places they occupied. We cried days and nights, missing Mother.

Only after a few months did Mother arrive in Lwów. Sick and exhausted, she told us the story of her terrible journey. After arriving in town, the Germans rounded up all the remaining Jews and forced [them] to do heavy and demeaning work. During work they beat [and] mocked [them]; [they] ordered the Jews to cut off each other's beards, to spit on one another, etc. They did not respect women. They told them to wash the floors with their clothes and underwear and tormented them. Mother tried to get across the border a few times—she was captured, beaten, and tortured. When she tried to cross the border for the last time, she stood in the water all night long, in the San River, because they were shooting from both sides: German and Russian. Only in the morning did the shooting quiet down and Mother waded across the river [and ran] until she reached some village. She had to spend a whole day and night there to rest and to dry her clothes. When Mother arrived, a different life began for us. Not only did our worries leave us, but Mother began to run the household and our small room took on the look of a [real] home. During all of our stay in Lwów, Father would bring back more and more new, worrying news. He told [us] about arrests, about the elections to the Soviet, and about the passportization. It was said that refugees were being dispersed to small towns where it wasn't possible to earn [money]. When the time came that a decision had to be made about taking a Soviet passport, [my] parents decided not to do it, as it meant staying in Russia forever. We had our fortune [back] at home, after all. And when the registration of families who wanted to return to the German-occupied lands was announced, [my] parents decided to register, all the more because they did not believe that Germans would allow Jews to return to Poland, which they were occupying.

In Exile

It was on a Friday, at twelve o'clock at night, when there was an abrupt knock on our door, and Father, sensing something bad, did not want to open up. NKVD-ers armed with handguns entered the room, told us to get dressed quickly [and] pack our belongings, and loaded us onto a cart, which took us to the rail station in the suburbs. We were held at that station until the morning. In the morning we were loaded into freight cars, thirty-five people in each, and the cars were sealed. We waited at the station through all of Saturday. We weren't given anything to eat. Friends brought us food parcels but no one was allowed to come near us. After twenty-four hours of standing still we set off on the way. No one knew where we were going. Some thought that we were going back home. Only when we passed Kiev station did everyone understand that we were all condemned to exile. We traveled like this for four weeks. We weren't allowed to leave the cars throughout the whole journey. The crowding was awful. Only the old and the sick could fit on the one bunk [inside the car], the rest lay on the floor. But the worst was the toilet situation. People went in public, through a hole in the floor, and at first [they] were terribly embarrassed, especially women. Only later did everyone get used to it. We received bread once a day, and every night, when we'd finally fallen asleep, we were woken up to be given a bit of thin soup. After a month's journey we arrived in some place in the Sverdlovsk Oblast, Kamyshlovski Region. There we were allowed out of the car. We were taken to *posiołek* number 30.

In the *Posiołek*

In the *posiołek* we found barracks full of bedbugs, mice, and lice. There were no beds; we slept on the floor, and at night, mice jumped around on top of us. When we began to revolt, we were allowed to cut down [some] trees in the forest and make bunks out of wood planks. We all worked in the forest, even Mama; the men worked cutting down trees, the women loading up wagons. We worked from dawn until late evening. For the work we received a bit of bread and a few kopecks. We sold our old belongings and lived off that. We would be forced to work in the heaviest frost and didn't have warm clothing. Many people returned with their hands and feet frostbitten, and even though they could not move, they were forced to work again the next day. Adults were not allowed to communicate with other *posiołki*. Only children were permitted to leave the *posiołek*, and we would sell old belongings among the local people and Russian exiles. Many people in the *posiołek* died from hunger and disease. The most widespread disease was *cynga*. People's body parts were falling off. In our *posiołek* there lived a few thousand exiles, Poles and Jews. When new deportees arrived, we were sent to *posiołek* number 54. There was more room there but we weren't fed better.

Father Dies

My father was a healthy man. I don't remember him ever being sick before the war. At first, he felt quite well in the *posiołek* and worked like everyone else. Once, he felt weak during work. [Others] wanted to help him. But the supervisor said that he would be fine. In front of everyone's eyes, without help, he died in the forest. In the evening, as [people] were returning from work,

Father's body was brought in. All night we stood, Mama and the children, over Father's body, chasing away the mice. In the morning, a burial robe was sewn out of a few shirts and [he] was buried in the *posiołek*. On the boards we wrote down his name and surname as well as the date of his death.

War and Amnesty

A few weeks later the German-Soviet war broke out. Our situation in the *posiołek* worsened a great deal. We received smaller bread rations [and] it was demanded that we work twelve hours a day. After the announcement of the Amnesty, NKVD-ers arrived and demanded that we not leave the *posiołek*.

They all spread propaganda, explaining to us the benefits of staying put, and how insecure our future would be if we left. We were issued certificates [and] set off to Fiszmino [?], where there were already a lot of Poles. There was nothing to eat and everyone decided to set off for the south of Russia. There were no spaces in the freight car; a few families rented a freight car at a price of 150 rubles per person. Throughout the journey, we received bread based on the documents we held. We didn't get [any] other products. In Grzyduban[242] they did not want to let us off the car as there was a typhus epidemic there and thousands of people were sleeping on the street because of a lack of apartments. We went to Kogon. There, we were not allowed in for the same reasons and we went to Kizltube.[243] Finally, we got off the train car. We lived on the street in the city; there was no bread [and] we were literally starving. Seeing that death from starvation awaited us here, we got on a train and went to Kizduban.[244] We rented a clay hut, three families together. Mother and [my] older sister worked picking cotton. They received eight hundred grams of bread, and the children four hundred grams each. There was a Polish agency there and every week we received a bit of flour and canned foods. Mother tried to have us admitted to a children's center but each time they said that there were no places. Only when Mama cried a lot and [kept asking] was she given a slip for us to be taken into a reformatory. My sister Cyla, age eleven, my brother Jehoszua, age nine, and I were taken in there. There was enough food there, we even brought [some of

242. Grzyduban: likely an incorrect name for the town of G'ijduvon [original Polish correction: Giżduwan].

243. Probably refers to the town of Kzyl-Tu.

244. Kizduban: likely an incorrect name for the town of G'ijduvon.

it] home. We weren't allowed to speak Jewish. Only when the first transport had left, made up of ninety children, fifteen Jewish ones among them, did we start speaking in Jewish among ourselves. My brother Jehoszua fell ill with dysentery, he was taken to the hospital and was not discharged until I was leaving. I went with the second transport along with seven Jewish children. We went by car to Bukhara, Kogon, and Ashgabat, where we were washed, given new clothes, and sent to Tehran in cars. At first in Tehran I lived in camp number 3; later I was moved to a camp for Jewish children. I made it to Palestine, the only one out of the whole family.

Protocol 84

Testimony of **Małka Rozenblat**, age twenty-three, artist resident in Knyszyn near Białystok. Came to Palestine via Tehran.

I come from Šiauliai. My father was one of the richest citizens of the city of Šiauliai. For some time he held the position of president of the local borough. I lived in Knyszyn with my relatives, outside Białystok. I studied in Warsaw, finished a school for drawing and—it was said—had a talent for painting. I exhibited many paintings at public exhibitions. The war surprised me in Knyszyn—I was spending the holidays there with [my] relatives. Immediately after the Bolsheviks' entry into the city, some young man, who until then had had nothing to do with literature and art, proclaimed himself the commissar for cultural affairs. He turned up at my place and told me that he would send me to Moscow for further studies in painting. Since I complained that I didn't have any source of income, he gave me a recommendation letter for Białystok, to the local Cultural Commission led by the writer Bogusz and Rakowski.[245]

In Białystok I made my way to Sienkiewicza Street, to the former dance school, which the Bolsheviks had turned into a "Home for Writers." My situation did not improve. I was constantly starving and decided to go to Wilno. Through Lida, I crossed illegally to Wilno. Twice I was stopped at the border. After arriving in Wilno, I went to Šiauliai, where my father lived. Everyone was earning very well. Father was also doing very well.

Father's Deportation

My happiness did not last long, as a few months later, in June 1940, the Bolsheviks occupied Lithuania. After entering Šiauliai, the Russians arrested a whole rank of well-known citizens, among them my father, and sent [them] to Siberia.

Germans in Lithuania

I was in Šiauliai when the German-Russian war broke out. On 22 June [1941] I left for Kaunas. I thought it would be easier to hide from the Germans in a

245. Unknown whether "writer" refers to both individuals here or only Bogusz.

big city. Immediately after entering Kaunas, the Germans organized a pogrom. To create an appropriate atmosphere, the pogrom began with a concert by the army orchestra. Then the Gestapo burst into the Mapu library of Kaunas, demolished the premises, and chucked all of the books out into the street. When the pile was ready, the Nazis ordered all Kaunas Jews to gather in the square. The strongest and the healthiest were arrested and sent to Germany. Others were taken to the huge hall of the fire department. Storm troopers went around to the houses, dragged Jews outside, and took them to the square. They entered the apartment of Dr. Baruch at 16 Weiss Street. I was spending the night there. It was around morning time. They told everyone to get up. Dr. Baruch and his wife wanted to get dressed. They weren't allowed to. Half-naked, they were ordered to follow. They left me in peace because I showed them my American affidavit.[246] Street roundups and dragging people from their homes lasted for two days. Everyone was taken to the fire department building. They gathered together more than eight hundred Jews. The crowding was horrendous. The people weren't given anything to eat and drink. The Germans didn't allow food to be sent in. On the fifth day the Hitler thugs shot all the Jews present in the building with a machine gun.

The Gestapo reported the deaths of the eight hundred Jews and demanded from the local municipal office that they be buried. Many Kaunas Jews voluntarily reported for the grave-digging work. The head of the Gestapo, Kierman, issued a statement that the eight hundred Jews were killed because they had been shooting at the German army from [their] windows.

After that first slaughter, smaller massacres took place until there were [only] ten thousand Jews left in Kaunas. Then the order arrived for those still alive to move, within four days, to a ghetto that had been created in the smallest and dirtiest neighborhood, in Słobodka.

Pogrom in Šiauliai, Panevėžys, Tylża, and Kretinga

The Kaunas pogrom was a signal for a Lithuania-wide [pogrom] to begin. Physically and mentally broken, I escaped from Kaunas to Šiauliai after the pogrom. There too, however, the Germans ordered Jews to gather in

246. Affidavit: official confirmation of a surety issued by the person extending the invitation and living in the country to which the holder of the affidavit intends to go.

the market. Everyone was arrested, kept locked up for a few days, [and] then the healthiest and strongest were sent to Germany via Memel [Klaipėda], for work. The weaker ones, women, children [and] the sick, were taken to the community center and murdered. The same kind of pogroms took place in Tylża and Panevėžys. I still see in front of [my] eyes the image of mothers shielding children with their own bodies as the Germans fired machine guns. I also saw a mother who jumped out of a third-story window onto the pavement with two children in [her] hands.

The Germans used the same method in Ukraine and Belorussia [Belarus] as in Lithuania. I was told that in the town of Lelchytsy near Mazyr the whole Jewish population was exterminated this way. One hundred and fifty children were buried alive in a mass grave. The same was done to five hundred Jews in Yel'sk and many other towns of Belorussia [Belarus].

Situation in Vitebsk

At the time of the outbreak of the German-Soviet war, there lived fifty-two thousand Jews in Vitebsk, of whom 45,000 escaped into Russia. Seven thousand were left, elderly and sick for the most part, who could not bring themselves to leave.

After taking over Vitebsk, the Germans went around to the apartments and stabbed the surviving Jews with bayonets. In Ukraine and Belorussia [Belarus], the Germans strove to stoke hatred toward Jews among the local people. The German propaganda employed the argument that the Jews were responsible for everything that was bad. But when the war broke out, the Germans had to expand the propaganda [to include] the hatred of Russia.

How Poles Become *Volksdeutsche*

The Polish intelligentsia were being murdered systematically. But Poles got the "grand" privilege of becoming *Volksdeutsche*. Before leaving Wilno I saw a notice explaining exactly how a Pole could become a *Volksdeutsche* if he admitted that he had a drop of German blood. No documents are necessary. Poles of German origin are split into four groups depending on the amount of German blood they have in them. Naturally, the higher the amount of German blood in their veins, the better the privileges they get, but regardless, they have to prove their sympathies and positive attitude toward Germany over the preceding ten years. Above all, they have to carry out all duties imposed on Poles by Germans. After ten years' probation, the candidate receives the Volksdeutsche title, and alongside it, hundreds of privileges and compensation for the losses incurred during the probationary period.

The chief of Nazi Ukraine printed his credo pertaining to Ukraine's past in the *Estland* paper, and this article adorned tenement house walls in Kiev in the form of a notice. Ukraine had to be separated from Russia forever, which is why the German authorities ordered a mobilization in Ukraine to raise a strong Ukrainian army. Ukraine's destiny was to be the breadbasket of Europe, and particularly of Germany. The Germans had earned this well enough in liberating Ukraine from the Soviet and Polish yoke. The Germans informed the Belarussian [Belarusian] people about the soon-approaching mobilization and promised them the following privileges for [their cooperation]: the separation of the Orthodox church, a ban on speaking Russian, and the introduction of an official Belarussian language, alongside German.

In the declarations to the Lithuanian, Latvian, and Estonian people the same motifs were repeated. Before my departure from Kaunas the Nazi commissar informed people that eight thousand Germans were returning to Kaunas for whom a fittingly welcoming reception had to be organized. In the *Kownoer Zeitung* it was printed that all houses, apartments, rooms, [and] shops that had at any point belonged to Germans were to be immediately vacated and surrendered to the German authorities. All losses suffered by the German population during the Bolsheviks' stay were to be covered from Lithuanian funds. In another issue of the *Kownoer Zeitung* they announced that an organization had been created, with a German commissar at its helm, whose task it was to seize all real estate, tenement houses, [and] factories and return them to the previous rightful owners. Naturally, only to those who deserved it would have [their] wealth returned, that is, Nazi sympathizers and Germans. In the same paper I found a news item that some Lithuanian woman had been sentenced to death for providing assistance to Jews.

I Break through the Front and Go to Moscow

I dressed up as a peasant woman and traveled from Lithuania to Belorussia [Belarus] via Vitebsk, Mińsk, [and] Smolensk, and survived many dangers on the front line. I was even in a German prison, certain that I would never again see the world . . . I was helped by partisans working at the rear of the German army. One dark night I got through the Russian trenches and went to Moscow. After arriving in Moscow I went to the American consulate, exactly at the time when diplomatic agencies were being evacuated to Kuybyshev. The consulate secretary told me that no visas were being issued at that time.

Bitter, I went to the address I had been given at the station in Moscow, where for ten rubles I was to get a place for the night. I was welcomed warmly. I talked honestly about my adventures, certain that the landlords, who were Jews, would help me. At midnight I lay down to sleep. In the morning, two NKVD agents were standing by my bed. I was not frightened—I thought [I would] tell the NKVD [about] my adventures and add how I had been helping the partisans, but I realized that the more I said the worse [things got] for me. They replied that I should not have come to Russia, but should be fighting on the front [instead]. After an interrogation, I was arrested and sent to the harshest prison. A few months later I received a default judgment sentencing me to five years' prison. I knew I would not last five months. I learned about the Amnesty by chance. I was released, went to Tashkent, and made it to Persia from there after many adventures.

Protocol 85

Testimony of **Róża Hirsz**, age twenty-two, born and resident in Warsaw at 55 Żelazna Street. Graduated from a state gymnasium. Came to Palestine from Tehran.

I am the daughter of Szymon Hirsz. My father had, in his youth, taken a prominent part in the Polish revolutionary movement. He was one of the five members of the PPS Council, which fought tsarist Russia in 1905.[247] Twice he was exiled to Siberia and twice he escaped. In the year 1905 he was known as "comrade Samson." He took an active part in the attack on the train in Rogów, near Łódź.[248] Along with Boruch Szulman, he also took part in the attack on the governor-general and commissar of the 8th district, Konstantinov.[249] Piłsudski knew my father well.

After the rebirth[250] of Poland, my father was decorated with the Cross of Merit. He also received a lifetime annuity from the state for [his] contributions. Even though he was already of an advanced age, my father reported to the Polish army at the outbreak of the war. They did not want to accept him due to his age.

---

247. The opening paragraph of Róża Hirsz's testimonies contains a lot of inaccurate historical information, perhaps the fault of the protocol-writer. Her father was not a member of the PPS administration. He could, however, have been a member of the so-called "Jewish five" [Polish: *żydowska piątka*] of the Combat Organization of the Polish Socialist Party [Organizacja Bojowa Polskiej Partii Socjalistycznej; OB PPS] during the revolution period of 1905–7 (the entire structure of the OB, led by Józef Piłsudski, was based on a system of five-person groups). The makeup of this [particular] five has been identified by historians with the exception of a fighter under the alias "Kasztan" [lit. "chestnut"]. Perhaps Szymon Hirsz was disguised under this pseudonym.

248. Refers to an expropriative operation carried out on 8 November 1906 under the lead of Józef Montwiłł-Mirecki, a close associate of Józef Piłsudski, on a postal carriage outside Rogów. OB acquired thirty thousand rubles as a result of it.

249. Ignatiy Konstantinov [Polish: Ignatij Konstantinow] was not a governor-general but an assistant commissioner (captain) of the tsarist police in Warsaw, known for his cruelty in the repressive operations undertaken by the tsarist authorities during the revolution of 1905–7. The direct executor of the attack on Konstantinov was a fighter of the "Jewish five," Boruch Szulman, who died during the police pursuit. He was assisted by a few other fighters.

250. Translator's note: the source text employs the word *powstanie* whose potentially double meaning is probably unintentional. It is either "an uprising" or a process of coming into being (a beginning, creation of something)—the latter is relevant here as it refers to Poland's regaining of independence after 123 years of having been erased from the map of Europe following the third partition.

We—the children and [our] father—took part in the defense of Warsaw. Father was wounded [and] taken to the Piłsudski hospital.

I fought in a group of Polish academic youth. My task was to pass cartridges to the artillery who fired from the cemetery[251] toward Mokotów, where the Germans were.

I could not stand the sight of Germans, and as a Jewish girl, was afraid of them, [so] I decided to cross the border and go to Russia. Smuggling oneself was not easy; I was simply out of luck. I roamed the so-called buffer zone for a long time. Three times I was robbed by Germans. They even took a small packet of needles off me, removed my coat, took my undergarments, and said that they needed the underwear for their children and wives.

There were instances where the Germans took away Jewish women's clothes and gave them to Polish women. I saw how the Germans would take away all the clothing from Jews and tear it to shreds on the spot, just to hurt them.

The worst were the young Germans. You could manage with the older ones somehow and cross the border for a few grosze. I finally managed to bribe the patrol, and along with a few other young Jews, found myself on [the other] side of the border.

As soon as we had walked away a bit, the Germans started giving signals to the Bolsheviks and they started shooting at us from both sides.

We hid in ditches. Three of us, one young woman among them, were killed on the spot. The rest [of us] scarcely survived.

We spent two days in a ditch close to the Soviet border, without food or drink. As soon as we raised [our] heads and tried to get up, the shooting started. We could not stand it any longer, and risking [our] lives, started crawling on all fours toward the Soviet border. A Soviet patrol captured us. They treated us kindly. They gave us food and drink and "kindly" kicked us over to the German side. We often wanted to commit suicide. We were completely exhausted, mentally and physically. We were dead on our feet and saw no escape from the situation. A German patrol started hitting us with their gunstocks. They thought we had come from Russia. In our presence, unabashed

251. Refers to the Lutheran cemetery at Młynarska Street in Wola, where the fighting positions of the Polish artillery were located in September 1939. The protocol refers to the cemetery as "*sowancki*" cemetery, but the meaning of this adjective (or possibly a proper name) could not be found by the editor or translator.

by the [presence of a] crowd of people, the Germans raped two young Polish women, after which they beat them horribly. We spent another ten days in the buffer zone. We witnessed the most horrifying abuse of people. We saw [what happened] when a group of Jewish artists arrived, with Turkow[252] and Ida Kamińska[253] at the helm. They were well dressed [and] thought that if they announced that they were actors the Germans would leave them in peace. The Germans stripped Ida Kamińska naked. She had her valuable karakul [lambskin] coat taken away, all her underwear, all the gowns, and then, when she was completely naked, a young officer ordered her to act some role. My heart was breaking as I looked on at this barbaric scene. I admired the conduct of the artist. She gave it her all with a fake smile; her face was pale but she did not want to show the Germans that she was afraid of them. The same thing happened to a whole group of male and female artists who arrived at the border. They were released, naked, into the border zone. Luckily for us, the Gestapo strictly observed Hitler's directives around racial purity in the border zone. Even though some of the Germans in the military group were keen on Jewish girls whom they wanted to make happy[254] and whom they wanted to help, in exchange, to get across the border, they were afraid of the Gestapo.

Finally, our group managed to reach the Soviet side. It was at the end of the month, during a dark night, when having passed a Russian patrol, we made it to Białystok.

I felt excellent during the first days of my stay in Białystok. Although I had no roof over my head and was constantly hungry, the feeling of freedom and a return to human dignity after the weeks spent with the Germans gave me the strength to endure any hardships. Most importantly: one could walk freely in the streets. Soviet orchestras played happy marches. No one pulled out Jews' beards on the streets; there were no pale, trembling people. With nowhere to sleep, I decided to go to Łuck, where [some of] my relatives lived and where I had friends. I was welcomed there with open arms [and], even though hunger was widespread there, [they] tried to meet all of my needs. I began to look

252. Icchak Turkow (1906–1970): actor, director, historian of Jewish theater.

253. Ida Kamińska (1899–1980): prominent actress of the Jewish scene in Poland; after the war a long-standing director of the E. R. Kamińska State Jewish Theater.

254. Unclear whether this is a euphemism or not.

around for work, and on realizing that it would be difficult for me to get a job, lost my exuberance.

Meanwhile, a decree came out [stating] that all Polish refugees were to accept Soviet citizenship. I told myself that there was no way I would do it. I soon had to suffer the consequences of this. Despite the fact that I was ill and staying in the Łuck hospital, and the hospital doctor told the NKVD representative that to leave my bed would endanger my life, I was arrested. I was deported to a prison in [the Autonomous Soviet Socialist Republic of] Komi where, suffering terribly, I spent three months in a prison cell. After three months a default judgment arrived from Moscow [stating] that I had been sentenced for anti-revolutionary activity. The sentence amounted to three years in prison. Immediately after sentencing I was sent to a labor camp located in a primeval forest, where exiled refugees worked felling trees: Poles, Russians, Ukrainians, Belarussians [Belarusians].

Life in the forest was awful. We cut down trees ourselves, sawed the planks, and built barracks to live in from them. We received paltry meals, and mosquitos devoured us alive. I fell ill with *cynga*. Despite the illness I had to carry on working. They constantly repeated [to us] that we should forget about our homeland, Poland. The mortality rate was huge. I saw how much food was sent to us from the headquarters—it would [only] have sufficed to feed 10 percent of the exiles present in the labor camp decently. The entire Soviet administration stole completely flagrantly. If food transports are sent from Moscow to Komi and there are so many people in charge on the way, each one thinks it appropriate to take something for himself, and only a pitiful part of what had been sent makes it to its destination. Thus the central authorities are quite oblivious and know nothing about the fact that tens of thousands of people are dying from hunger in exile. None of the Soviet superiors receive sufficient pay for their work, and to stay alive, [they] have to steal from the state.

I have to admit that, like other refugees, I didn't always fare badly in Russia. There were [times] when we danced and sang, bursting with happiness. We were overcome with great joy on 22 June, the day of the outbreak of the German-Soviet war. We could not hide our happiness.

I was in a hospital when the Amnesty for Polish citizens was announced. I received the notice of the release of all Polish citizens in the hospital. Russia was open to refugees. It was only forbidden to settle in big cities and in the frontline zone. I also learned in the hospital about the formation of the Polish army. After leaving the hospital I went to Buzuluk. The situation in Buzuluk was awful. Hundreds of thousands of Jews, sick and desperate, who had arrived there from all over Russia with their last ounce of strength, wanting to save themselves somehow, learned that Jews were not being accepted into the army. The Poles did not dare say it openly after the suffering they had lived through together [with the Jews]. I myself suffered a horrible disappointment. I thought that as the daughter of a man who had fought so much for Poland's freedom, I would easily be accepted into the army. I had good qualifications: a higher education and full knowledge of a few European languages. From a physical perspective, there was no fault to be found in my constitution. Before my eyes, invalid Christian women were admitted to the army, while I was refused. I went to Bukhara. There, too, antisemitism was rife. I could not understand how the people who only yesterday had suffered so much and were humiliated alongside us could now torment and humiliate Jews. I understood, however, that to stay alive would mean to leave Russia. The Poles told me that the NKVD was not allowing Jews out of Russia. I checked this piece of information, [which] turned out to be a lie. I decided then to use illegal methods. I bought a passport from some Christian woman for two thousand rubles and went to Tehran as [Helena Zimińska.] With this passport, I got into the army with no difficulty. Many Jewish girls did the same and were saved as a result. It was considerably more difficult for men.

Protocol 88

Testimony of **Helena Ajzenberg**, age twenty-five, a soldier's wife. Came to Palestine via Tehran.

Until the war, I worked as a clerk in the Krysek[255] chocolate factory in Warsaw. During the bombardment the factory was open; all clerks remained in place and even spent the night in the factory to save [its] assets in case of a fire. The owners of the factory received a summons from the magistrate on the first day of the war to immediately deliver the entire load of goods [they] held in the depot to the city storehouses. We disapproved of this: we advised that half of the supplies [we] held be sent directly to the army and to hospitals.

We, the factory personnel, held direct talks on this matter with Mayor Starzyński.[256] He agreed that we would hand out a part of the supplies among the army ourselves. Risking [our] lives, we took the chocolate to the army positions and the frontline hospitals. Thanks to this, I visited not only all the hospitals but also the frontline hospitals and ambulatory points organized by the Red Cross during the bombardment.

One day, sharing out chocolate among soldiers near Wola, on the road [to] Błonie, I found myself in German captivity, along with a Polish patrol. One can imagine how terrified I was. To this day I can't understand how and when it happened. As I was standing with a group of Polish soldiers, offering them chocolate, I suddenly heard shots. I hid in the trenches along with the soldiers. [They] started fighting back. After half an hour, I was taken to Błonie with the group of soldiers. The Germans took away the Poles' weapons, ripped off [their] epaulets, and beat [them] for no reason.

I spent the day and the night in the courtyard of the German headquarters, which were located in a large garden in Błonie. At first it seemed to me that the stories of the German awfulness had been exaggerated, because they approached me politely and asked if I were hungry. I had not eaten in two days already [and] gladly took advantage of the supplies brought for me. And when I asked that they give coffee and rusks to the soldiers too, they replied

255. Likely refers to the factory S. Kierski i S-ka [S Kierski & Co], 64 Targowa Street, Warsaw.

256. Stefan Starzyński (1893–1943): Mayor of Warsaw in the years 1934–39. Murdered by the Germans.

that the army regime did not allow it. In the evening, the Germans ordered the captured prisoners to wash the floors, and slapped the Poles with wet rags. In the end, a group of prisoners refused [to do] further work until the officer arrived. The Germans started beating them with gunstocks. When the Poles responded to the blows with fists, the Germans [part of text missing]. On the third day, thirteen rescuees from the remaining group were sent off to Łowicz. I was left alone in Błonie. It was busy all day and night. Motorcycles came and went. I tried to hide in a corner so that the Germans would not see me, but it was in vain. I felt that the two German soldiers guarding me had bad intentions toward me. They were both too polite to me. They brought me a rubber cushion and two blankets. They asked me to come into the room to rest. I preferred to stay outside. I asked them why they were keeping me there [and] what awaited me. They replied that [they didn't] know yet what would be done with me: I could not be treated as a civilian, as I had been found in the trenches with soldiers, [nor sent off] to a prisoner of war camp since I was not, after all, in the army.

That same night, when I was taking a nap, I was woken by an argument between my two guards. I figured they were arguing about me. I didn't sleep anymore [and] waited, my heart pounding, for what would come next. Suddenly, I felt someone's hand on me. The German was lying next to me. His name was Hans.

Listen—he said—you know, surely, that according to the Führer's order a German cannot have relations with a Jewish woman. But I like you . . . Give yourself to me and I will arrange for you [to stay] safely in a small town at my friend's [place]. You won't lack for anything, you'll be my friend . . .

I felt how aroused the German was and weighed the words in my response, which would determine my fate. I did not refuse him, I only said that I was terribly tired and dirty and that I had to rest. Our conversation was interrupted by the arrival of the other German. I understood that they hated each other and that a battle was being fought over me. It was the only possibility for me to be saved—this very battle between the two Germans. At eight in the morning I was taken to the headquarters officer. He asked me, sternly, what I was doing in the trenches of the Polish soldiers. I said that I had been standing next to the trenches, looking for food in the countryside, and when I heard shooting, I took cover in the trenches. He said: You're lying, you had come to entertain the Polish pigs. He ordered for me to be arrested. I spent two days in jail. I was glad to have slipped away from the hands of the two German scoundrels this way, but had many worries because of my own hooligans. I trusted one of them, who helped me escape the Germans. There were a few arrestees in the cell. We all managed to escape to Warsaw in the evening. When I returned to the city, the capital was in flames. Walking down Elektoralna Street, I saw the hospital burning and the sick lying out in the streets, groaning loudly. Throughout the journey, from Karmelicka Street to Dolna [Street] where I lived, I didn't meet a soul. After many, many days the shooting ceased. After the holiday of Sukkot [28–29 September 1939], you would see individual Germans in Marszałkowska Street and in Nowy Świat, but it was known that the city would not be taken until the rubble had been cleared away. There was an announcement that Jews and Poles had to report for mandatory work cleaning up the city. After taking Warsaw, the Germans turned to Mr. Kaminer, the manager of the Jewish cemetery on Gęsia [Street] and representative of the local municipal office, with an order to bury all of those killed—five thousand of them—within one day. Should the order not be carried out, they would order all the dead to be burned.

With the help of Jews who lived nearby, the dead were put in collective graves in one day, 100 and 150 [bodies per grave], and by the evening, all were buried.

I Sell Sweets in the Street

Like thousands of women, men, and children [who] earned their living in the first days of the occupation by trading in anything they could on the street, I too took some sweets from our factory and went out with them into Karmelicka Street. During the first couple of days I sold a few sweets, gaining high prices for them. On the third day a group of Germans surrounded me; they began to make jokes [and] tease me, and took the box with the sweets away from me. As this was repeated a few times, I stopped trading.

Having sold all of the merchandise [and] collected a few hundred zloty, a companion and I set off toward Russia on 17 December. We smuggled ourselves across the Bug River[257] near Rembertów [and] walked via Miłosna,

257. Actually refers to the Wisła River rather than the Bug. Rembertów is located ca. six kilometers from the Wisła.

Mińsk, Kałuszyn, Siedlce, Mordy until [we got to] Siemiatycze. I breathed more easily when I found myself with my brother in Siemiatycze. I spent a few weeks there, ate my fill and slept peacefully, [resting] after months of torments in Warsaw. I had no occupation, however, and no possibility of finding work in this small town, so I went to Łuck. I got a job there as a cashier in a big restaurant. I began to be pressured to accept Soviet citizenship. I did not want to agree to it.

For this resistance I was arrested in the middle of the night and taken to the Łuck prison. I was not permitted to take anything with me. On 29 June 1940 I was loaded into a freight car, alongside criminals. I was deported to Malinowsko.[258] I was locked up in the notorious Malinowsko garrison and spent a few months there, not knowing what my crime was. The prison officials, like me, did not know what I had been put in prison for. I don't know either why I was released from the cell one day and ordered to work in the office. I worked there for two months. I was constantly hungry. The authorities rarely visited the prison. The kitchen, the administration—everything was run by the prisoners, most often bandits and thieves, dangerous criminals. No wonder things were running "perfectly" there. The local powers, that is, the prisoners in charge of the prison, ate everything there was to eat. They shared the supplies with women who sneaked into the prison or [with their] incarcerated [female] friends, and woe upon them who dared challenge that order.

Because of the hunger and vitamin deficiency I fell ill with a skin disease. I also went through typhus and dysentery in the prison. I often thought that my end was nigh, but I endured everything. After some time I was sent to Tomsk, in the Novosibirsk Oblast, with a group of four thousand people, Jews and Poles. We traveled on barges. I spent the entirety of the journey on the deck, because indoors you could suffocate from the stench. I was desperately freezing and starving but survived that journey too. In the *posiołek*, we settled in barracks. We slept in shifts because of a lack of space, and worked beyond [our] capacity and received a minimal amount of bread. There was no soap in the *posiołek*; we were all louse-ridden; there was nothing to wash underwear with. I sold everything I had on me so that I wouldn't die from hunger,

258. Likely refers to the town of Malinowka [Malinówka?].

and later sold a gold tooth for a piece of bread. This situation lasted until the announcement of the Amnesty.

The moment the Amnesty was announced we thought that we were saved. I went to Tashkent and made my way to the place where the Polish army was forming. But I had heard by then that the last stage of our [journey] would be the most difficult. I saw how Jews were persecuted during army recruitment and how awful the situation of a Jewish woman was. Polish women were readily accepted into women's divisions, but the Jewish ones had to go through a true ordeal. Most often they were not accepted. I felt that if I stay[ed] in Russia I [would] die from hunger and exhaustion. For the sum of four thousand rubles, I arranged a sham marriage to a soldier in the Polish army. On 7 August 1942, I went to Tehran alongside military families.

Protocol 101

Testimony of **Naftali Zylbersztejn**, age forty-two, from Łódź, 16 Piotrkowska Street. Arrived in Palestine from Russia in July 1943.

On the night of 5 September 1939, when the Polish army was leaving Łódź and the male civilian population had been ordered to leave the city alongside [it], I left [my] wife and four children and left home with the intention of going to Warsaw. It was two o'clock at night, Piotrkowska Street was dark, with people running on ahead. I intended to blend into the crowd and walk ahead. At the last moment, at the corner of Piotrkowska and Cegielniana, I met the owner of the café Astoria, Saul Bergheim, and his son Mietek, as well as his sons-in-law: Józef Weinberg, owner of the café Kaprys, and Jerzy Oppenheim. We decided to hire a droshky together and go toward Warsaw.

The merchant Chaim Winzigster joined our group. For 1,500 zloty we rented a droshky and set off on the way. From Łódź, we went toward Zgierz, and from there, toward Stryków and Głowno. The roads were full of people; I saw many women and children who had been killed in ditches; many injured people were moaning and begging for help. They were victims of German airplanes that flew down low, deliberately aiming at the refugees, children, and women. We were also bombed and shot at from machine guns a few times. From time to time, we got off the droshky and hid in woods or ditches. The droshky was riddled with holes from the bullets [and] our overcoats were full of holes too, but luckily none of us was killed. After a fifty-two-hour journey we found ourselves in the capital at eight in the morning.

Siege of Warsaw

I was a broker serving huge manufacture wholesalers[259] in Warsaw. I had a lot of friends in the capital. After arriving in the city, I made my way to Gęsia [Street] to [see] an acquaintance, Czarkowski, with whom I moved in. I lived in Warsaw through the three weeks of the siege of the capital, the bombings. Before my eyes, the entire Gęsia Street, the center of manufacture, burned down. The Jewish district, Nalewki—Gęsia all the way to Okopowa [Street]—[was]

259. Shops with textiles.

bombed particularly ruthlessly. The number of victims who were killed in the bombings was proportionally higher among the Jewish civilian population than the non-Jewish one. On 27 September the city surrendered, and during the few days before the Germans entered the capital, the recovery of the bodies of the dead and their burial was dealt with. I myself recovered from under the rubble the wife of Herman Grafman, a merchant, and Jehoszua Kestenberg and [his] whole family, made up of five people. They were buried in a collective grave. During the bombardment, a bomb fell into a house [at] 32 Nalewki and killed fifty-two people there, among them my cousin Motel Rubinsztejn, from Mińsk Mazowiecki. Immediately after arriving in the capital, the Germans began to round up Jews for [forced] labor, to clear away the rubble and the barricades, [and] to clean up the dead people and the horses that had been killed. Then they began the systematic theft of Jewish property—they would turn up in shops and order all the merchandise to be carried out [and] onto trucks waiting in front of the shop. Thus all of Gęsia Street was emptied of all manufacture. In mid-October, the arrests of social activists, distinguished Jews, and merchants began. From Gęsia, Mejer Czarkowski, Feldman, Furman, Kołodziński, Mendel Robinson, [and] Jehoszua Szafirman were arrested. They were all driven to the Supreme Court building in Krasińscy Square [Plac Krasińskich]. There they were imprisoned until 15 December. That day they were taken to the citadel and shot. A few days later, the following incident took place in Nalewki: in the house in question lived a tailor, Zilberding, who had a men's and children's clothing workshop. One night, burglars tried to get into the establishment. A Polish policeman, unarmed, tried to stop them. A fight broke out between the burglars and the policeman. He was wounded and died. As punishment, the Germans shot dead all the men living in that house, a total of fifty-three people. Among those sentenced to death was Rabbi Szapiro from Mińsk Mazowiecki. A few days later, after the execution of the innocent, the Gestapo demanded a contribution from the Jewish council. When the contribution was delivered, the Gestapo put up notices of the execution of fifty-three associates of a burglar gang.

I Escape from Warsaw

Seeing that the situation in the city was worsening by the day, I decided to flee the capital and get over to the Russian side. I went from Warsaw to Siedlce. On the Praga bridge, a German patrol stopped me, carried out a search, [and] took away everything I had on me. I was beaten up and set free.

A few searches were also carried out on the train. In Rembertów, two Germans entered the carriage, grabbed the Jews by their beards, and threw them out of the window as the train was moving. From Siedlce, I went to Mordy. This town is located on the Bug River. With no money, I spent the night at the home of a poor tailor, Chaim Silberman. In the middle of the night, Germans burst in, carried out a search, and then started flogging everyone with whips until we screamed to high heaven. The younger daughter of Silberman started to beg the Germans to leave us in peace. I got out of the house by a miracle and hid in the rubbish chest. When the Germans left, I ran off to the rabbi. The rabbi let me into his place, hid me, and on the following day, found a Jewish smuggler, haggled with him, and paid him out of his own pocket to take me across the border. I made it to the other side of the Bug and reached Białystok.

In Białystok

I arrived in Białystok without a penny in my pocket. I went straight to a merchant acquaintance, Papirmajster, at 7 Botaniczna [Street], and stayed there. Not wanting to be a burden to my host, I took up trading. I traded manufacture, leather, soap, [and] watches and earned well. But trading was becoming more and more difficult. Many merchants were already in jail. My attitude toward the elections[260] was negative. Even though my friends warned me about the disastrous consequences of boycotting the elections, I did not go to the polls. When the time of passportization came, I decided not to take a Soviet passport.

When the registration for a return home began, and many of my acquaintances registered to leave, I did not.

I Am Arrested

I believed that one should show oneself as seldom as possible in Soviet institutions. Despite the fact that I had not registered, I did not avoid the fate of the others, and on Friday 29 April [1940] at two o'clock at night, NKVD

260. The elections to the People's Assemblies of Western Ukraine and Western Belorussia [Belarus], October 1939.

agents appeared in my room. Understanding what the knocking on the door meant, I did not want to open up. With my roommates, Zeideman, a contributor to the *Kurier Warszawski* [Warsaw Courier] and Braud, from Warsaw, we hid under the beds. [The NKVD] broke down the door, burst into the room, pulled us out from under the beds, and beat us terribly. We were taken to the NKVD at 3 Mickiewicza [Street] in [our] underwear. There we were taken for an interrogation. We were beaten horribly during the investigation. Seidman [Zeideman?] wanted to go to the toilet—the agents thought he wanted to escape [and] threw him out of the third-floor window onto the footpath [below]. He died on the spot. We were accused of being Polish spies. [Our] explanations were in vain. They based their accusation on the fact that we had hidden when the NKVD agents arrived at our home. The interrogation lasted until ten in the morning. Then I was taken to prison, which was located in the Beker cured meat factory. I was shoved into a small cell where there were already sixty people, and during the six weeks I spent there, was called for questioning almost every night. During the questioning I was threatened with the death penalty. They tried to get the names of [other] Polish spies out of me. And when I insisted that I had nothing to say, they, stubbornly, beat me and insulted me with the worst obscenities. After a month in prison I was taken for a trial. It took place in one of the NKVD rooms, the judges were NKVD officials, and the lawyer was a certain Siemion Amczenko from Leningrad.

The judge read out the charges of my being a Polish spy and turned to me, [asking] that I confess [my] crime. I stubbornly repeated that this was a mistake, that there was no evidence against me. The prosecutor demanded the harshest punishment for me for being stubborn and for not pleading guilty. The defense [lawyer], whom I saw in the court for the first time, said a few words in my defense and fell silent. I received a sentence condemning me to eight years of hard labor in a camp.

In Exile

After hearing the sentence, I was escorted to prison. There I met well-known industrialists from Białystok, the brothers Cytron, the head of the Białystok postal service; and a few days later, I was taken to the station with the others. A bucket of water was placed inside a freight car, the car was sealed, and we were left [inside] for forty-eight hours. After forty-eight hours, the train started. We traveled for twenty-two days on that train. Throughout, we were not allowed off the train. Once a day, they threw a piece of bread for each of us into the carriage and placed one bucket of water to last the entire day. The filth was horrendous. When the cars were opened at the station of Sarajsk,[261] tens of dead [people] were pulled from them. We, the living, could barely stand up. We helped one another get off the freight car. Sarajsk is located in the Mordovian Oblast. We stayed in the station for two days, and since we had not washed throughout the whole journey, we looked like Negroes. [Our] clothes were rotting on us. After insistent pleading we were taken to the local bathhouse, where we were given [padded] jackets. We were overjoyed—we tore the lice-infested clothes from our [bodies]. Then we were taken further up, [for] ninety kilometers, to Archamlawaja,[262] where there was a camp in the middle of a huge forest.

We were accommodated in bedbug-infested barracks. The mosquitos would not leave us in peace. Mice and rats tormented us. We could not fall asleep despite being deathly exhausted; [we were] chasing after mice and rats at night.

At first, we worked building a road. We were given four hundred grams of bread per day to eat and a bit of *wodzianka* [watery soup] for lunch. We were rushed to work in a −55°C [−67°F] frost. However, it was better [to be] at work than in the barracks. The air in the barracks was stale and the mice would snatch the bread from our hands as we ate. We worked from seven-thirty until five in the afternoon. The day was short. During work, we were rushed and threatened with being sent to an even worse camp if we didn't fulfill the quotas. [People's] body parts crumbled off because of the frost and the lack of vitamins: noses, ears, fingers. There were no medicines, there was no doctor, [and] the entire camp looked as if it was made up of invalids. All of my teeth fell out, and since I could not chew my food well, I fell ill with a gut [problem], an illness that bothered me terribly.

---

261. An incorrect name of the municipality of Saransk in the Mordovia ASSR [original Polish correction: Sarańsk].

262. This place has not been located.

Women's Camp Rebellion

In the vicinity of our camp there was a labor camp for women, where the wives of [men] from our camp worked. The women were employed in tailoring workshops. One time the women rebelled and said that if they were not allowed to live with [their] husbands, they would not turn up for work. The *posiołek* commandant called for help [from] the NKVD. Agents turned up and began to pummel the women left, right, and center with their gunstocks. The screams of the beaten women went up to the heavens. We were at work and heard the screaming coming from afar. Since among the working [men] there were husbands of the women who were being beaten, they grabbed shovels and ran toward the women's barracks. As a sign of solidarity, even though we had no wives in the barracks, we followed them with [our] work tools. Our supervisors, seeing that nothing would stop us, began to shoot. A few of us collapsed, gravely injured. The NKVD-ers, seeing the exiles running in [their] direction and understanding that there would be no avoiding bloodshed, surrounded the women's barracks with their gun barrels pointed at us. If we didn't return to work, they threatened, they would shoot us like dogs.

We said that if it wasn't announced that women could live with their husbands, we would not move. There were more of us than there were of them—some men, driven to the brink by the women's screams, were ready to fall and would not budge. The NKVD understood that this business could cost them many casualties. They retreated. After a short while, high-ranking NKVD officers appeared and spoke to the exiles persuasively, promising that they would fix the issue. They also promised us that they would no longer beat us or rush us to work, and that they would increase the bread rations. Since evening had come, we put down our work tools and returned to the barracks. At night, sleeping deeply, we were surrounded on all sides—the [men] whose wives were in the barracks and a few women were dragged out. We never saw them again or heard what happened to them. Those remaining were threatened that should another rebellion take place, all would be shot. To the women they said: "What are you [doing] running like this to your husbands—if they kick the bucket there will be other men in Russia."

The mortality in the camp was huge. Out of the 360 men I arrived with, half had died after six months. Among the deceased were the owner of Warsaw cinemas—Lehman,[263] [and] Jakub Goldsztejn from Warsaw—owner of a fruit storehouse [at] 16 Muranowska [Street]. Out of the women, Mina Wollman died—daughter of the owner of a lottery shop from Warsaw [at] 29 Nalewki [Street].

War and Amnesty

Our situation only worsened when the [German-Soviet] war broke out. The bread portions were decreased [and] more work demanded. As allies, we had to work harder for the common good. We worked until 28 September 1941, when we were told that, on the basis of the Amnesty, we were free. We were paid for the work, given documents, and set off on our way. I traveled for three weeks to Gorky [Nizhny Novgorod]. On arriving in the city I didn't have any money. I started looking for [some of my] acquaintances. I met a factory owner from Zgierz there whom I knew, Noe Buez, with his wife and children, but their situation was no better than mine. We roamed the streets, starving. I started to beg. I looked for Jewish houses. One Jew allowed me in, let me get washed then fed me, [and] gifted me a coat and five hundred rubles. I thanked him, went out to the city, met Buez, shared the money with him, and told him to travel further with me. He was too weakened—and his wife was particularly weak—to leave. I went to Bukhara on my own. There, I met a factory owner from Łódź—Naftali Rozencwejg, [and] Mosze Ziegler with wife, children, and sons-in-law. They envied my new coat, saying I looked like a count in it. From Bukhara I went to Astrakhan[264] and from there to Tashkent. In Tashkent I fell ill with typhus. I roamed the streets with a fever, [and] knowing that I would not survive for long in this state, reported to a hospital. I stayed in the hospital for four weeks. I received no medicine in the hospital because there was no medicine [available]. The doctors were helpless—they could give me nothing beyond a cold compress. Anyway, even to get a compress I had to take off [my] shirt, which was [then] soaked in water. The beds were full of insects and there were no white sheets even on the pillows. I got a

263. Likely refers to one of the members of the Lejman family who owned a few cinemas in Warsaw.

264. It's unlikely the author traveled to Astrakhan, located two thousand kilometers by rail from Bukhara, in order to return to Tashkent. Likely refers to Ashgabat.

piece of black bread and hot water to eat. After leaving the hospital, I went to Kermine and reported to the Polish army. In Kermine I met: the theater director Celmejster, with his wife and son; artists Dzigan and Szumacher, who had been in the army but were arrested at the last minute by the NKVD;[265] a Łódź industrialist, Poznański; Rotman from the Łódź Chamber of Commerce; and Mowszenberg. They all stayed behind in Russia. On 26 January 1942, I went to Arpai, [and] from there to Krasnovodsk, Pahlevi, and Tehran. From Tehran, I was sent to Iraq, and on 20 July 1943, arrived in Palestine.

265. Szumacher and Dzigan were arrested as deserters from the Red Army and deported to Kazakhstan. They returned to Poland only in 1947.

Protocol 102

Testimony of **Dawid Auschibel**, son of Józef and Małka, born in Leżajsk. Arrived in Palestine via Russia and Tehran in February 1943.

My father was a carpenter. The family was made up of nine people. We lived in our own little house outside town. The first few days after the outbreak of war went by calmly in our town. Many refugees arrived from the area; they told horrible stories about how German airplanes were shooting at civilians. After a few days, however, our town too began to be bombed [and] there were many casualties. Near our apartment a girl was wounded, and a little Polish boy was killed in a ditch by a German pilot who flew very low, spotted him, and shot him.

When the Germans came close and fighting broke out between the Poles and the Germans, many people hid in their basements, thinking it would be safe [there]. Two days before Rosh Hashanah [14–15 September 1939], the Germans entered Leżajsk. The Jews did not go out into the streets. [They] were pulled from [their] homes and sent for [forced] labor. People were afraid to attend prayers. The Germans captured one older Jew on his way to pray, cut off his beard along with part of his face, and then photographed him. On the second day of Rosh Hashanah, the Germans set fire to the synagogue, the Talmud Torah,[266] and the slaughterhouse. The Germans stood watch next to the burning buildings so that no one would put out the fire. For a large sum of money, they allowed us to save the Torahs[267] from the burning synagogue. On Yom Kippur, prayers took place in our basement and the children stood outside watching so that no one would approach. Later it was said that since the Germans would persecute Jews, and the Russians were already on the other side of the San River, one should cross the San and settle under the Russian occupation. Shortly afterward, an order was issued for all Jews to leave town. Everyone was overcome with panic. Peasants didn't want to rent out [their] carts; a lot of money was paid for a cart—up to three thousand zlotys—and only the very rich could afford to bring a few belongings with them. Most

266. Talmud Torah: religious elementary school supported by the Jewish council.
267. Parchment scrolls of the Pentateuch (the five books of Moses).

people left town carrying bundles on their backs. We stopped in the village of Charlupka,[268] on that [same] side of the San. We spent eight days there. Mama and [my] older sister took turns sneaking into [our] house and brought back our belongings from there, bit by bit. From there, we went to Sieniawa, where we stayed for six weeks. We could not settle there, and [so] we moved to Lwów. As I said, Mama was traveling back and forth to collect our belongings. Once she could not make it across the border and was stuck on [the other] side of the San. Not until three months later, when we were living in Lwów, did Mama arrive. She told [us] how, after the expulsion of Jews from Leżajsk, Jews from other towns were brought there. They were tortured horribly, forced to [do] the hardest labor, and had money demanded from them at every occasion. One time a decree came out that the grave of the well-known Rabbi Ali Melech should be dug up [because] the Germans had received information that it contained famous treasures buried by Jews. The grave was dug up in the presence of the Jewish council. Naturally, no money was found, but the informers were arrested.

In Lwów

We lived in Lwów for nine months. We lived in a school with other refugees. There were lessons taking place there, but we only took up one part of the building. We fared all right in Lwów. We all [worked] trading. The children waited in lines and often brought back between ten and fifteen loaves of bread at a time. Father traded sugar, shoes, soap. An acquaintance of Father's prepared the soap himself. [It] looked like clay, but people would still tear the product from each other's hands. I delivered the soap to the merchants. Once, I was stopped by someone [who] dragged me to a gate and robbed me of soap worth 150 rubles, and took away my cash—fifty-five rubles. When the registration began, Father decided to register to return home.

In Exile

On 1 July 1940, we were all roused from our sleep. The NKVD surrounded the house where we lived, entered our apartment, told us to pack [our] belongings, and took us to the station. We were led to a train and placed thirty [people]

268. Likely refers to the village of Chałupki Dębniańskie.

in each car. We traveled for twenty-three days. During the journey we each received a piece of bread and a bit of soup once a day, but almost everyone had a bit of food from home on them because we'd been prepared for deportation. On 23 July the train stopped at the station of Tyumen, Omsk Oblast.[269] We stayed there for three days under the open sky, surrounded by guard[s] with guns. On the fourth day we were taken to the river [and] loaded onto barges, and we traveled on the Konda River for two weeks. After two weeks' journey, we got off in the woods near a place called Wierchnij Barak, where we found barracks formerly occupied by Russian exiles. The barracks were dirty and abandoned. Mice and other creatures walked on us during our sleep and were not afraid of humans. In the barracks there lived 360 people, mostly Jews. People worked in the forest felling trees, which were taken to the river and loaded onto rafts. For the work, one received a kilo of bread per day. The elderly and the children who did not work received half the bread ration, but those of the adults who did not want to work received nothing.

My brother Abraham Jakob did not want to work on Saturdays despite being constantly threatened with deportation and labor camps. Finally, he was sent to a penal camp for three months, where he received only half a kilo of bread per day and where he worked for free. He did not want to work Saturdays there either, and the Bolsheviks, seeing that they would not be able to manage him, stopped persecuting him. Father and Mother, being older, did not work anyway. They chopped wood for the peasants in the country. Apart from this they busied themselves catching fish, which they sold. This way, we did not go hungry.

In the summer, our situation improved. I picked berries and mushrooms in the woods. We would go—a whole group of children—and bring home bucketfuls of good berries. One day I got lost in the forest because I wandered away from my companions. I entered a muddy area and could not find the way home. Night fell, and afraid of staying in the forest, I climbed up a tree and planned to spend the night [there]. I was not worried about going hungry since I had the bucket of berries with me. Mother, seeing that I wasn't coming back, became very upset and hired [some] peasants to look for me. I wasn't found until the next day, asleep in the tree, and [I was] taken home.

269. Correctly: Sverdlovsk.

A month before the outbreak of [the German-Soviet] war, we were moved to another *posiołek* in the forest, 140 kilometers from the previous one. There, there weren't even [any] barracks. The deportees themselves had to cut down trees and build a barracks. It was a primeval forest, untouched by humans up until then. There were lots of bears and other wild animals there who howled at night. The children in particular were frightened and could not sleep. Once one of the guards killed a bear fifty steps away from our barracks.

War and Amnesty

After the outbreak of war between Germany and Russia, the release of Poles and [Polish] Jews[270] began. However, Ukrainians and Belarussians [Belarusians] who had come from Poland were not released. We received documents to go to southern Russia. However, we were not able to get there. We went on foot to places where one could get [on] a boat. Families lost one another on the way. We arrived at the place where the barges left but could not get onto any of them. We spent two weeks there, working for the NKVD, thanks to which we were able to get a spot some time later. The journey to Omsk took twenty-one days. After staying [there] for a few days, we set off [for the] south. We rented three carriages, which were [packed very] tightly. Everyone was sick and tired, and we reminisced, emotionally, about the times we had spent in the forest. At large stations, the train would stop and the passengers would run into town to get bread. In the town of Lamada [?] we binged on watermelons and most of us fell ill with dysentery. We traveled like this for three weeks, until the station on Andrzejak [?]. There we lay under the open sky, as there was no place to sleep to be found. The city was full of refugees. We eventually got a spot in a stable, where we settled, and began to trade. We spent a few weeks there. We earned well. My brother would bring in makhorka, for which one could get anything. One day, the NKVD-ers ordered all Polish citizens to report to the station, where they were to be sent to England. Armed guard[s] surrounded us and we were all sent to kolkhozes on carts. Our family was split [apart]: My mother, two sisters, and [one] brother were sent to one kolkhoz; myself, my father, and three brothers lived in another. Father and I were sent to the

270. As a result of the Amnesty for Polish citizens. See glossary: Amnesty.

kolkhoz Telman. We worked in the fields, picking peanuts and shelling them. We received five hundred grams of flour per day. We sewed large pockets into [our] trousers and stuffed them with nuts during work [and] got by thanks to that. We lived in a *czajhan* [Uzbek teahouse] with other refugees, most of whom were ill with typhus, dysentery, and other diseases. No one paid attention to them. Hospitals didn't want to admit them—most died lying [there] next to us, and the epidemics continued to spread.

After many efforts, we went to the kolkhoz where Mama was. Father could barely stand up. Mother sold the last shirt [she had] and bought a bit of rice and other foodstuffs to keep Father alive. But that didn't help. Father could no longer eat. He died in March 1942. That same day another Jew, Lejbowicz from Rozwadów, died in that kolkhoz, and both were buried in a local Russian cemetery since there was no other one.

My two sisters got jobs as seamstresses in Tashkent, in the Polish delegation, where they sewed undergarments for Polish refugees. I met an official there who had worked with my brother Abraham Jakob in the *posiołek*. Thanks to this official's protection I got into a children's center. On the way to Tashkent, we spent a night in a teahouse. There we were robbed of our belongings and documents. Luckily, the document [confirming my] admission to the center remained. I spent a month in the center, where there wasn't enough food [and] all the children were terribly famished. One time I binged on green apples and it made me ill. I was taken to the hospital. Lying in the hospital, I heard that our children were leaving for Persia. I was afraid they would leave me behind, and with a high fever, ran away from the hospital straight to the children's center. The children were to depart in three groups; I belonged to the middle one. The treatment of the Jewish children was becoming worse. The Polish children were fed better, given three or four plates of soup, and we only one—and [it was] watery, too. The Polish children were taken to the station on carts, and we, the seventy-two Jewish children, were told to go on foot. At the station, the Polish children were placed inside a carriage and the transport manager said that the Jewish children were staying behind. We thought it was a joke and that they would take us eventually. When the train started, we started to cry terribly. One priest was very moved by our tears, ordered that the train be stopped, and spoke for a long time with the transport manager. Finally we were loaded into the carriage and went to Krasnovodsk. We suffered terribly on the journey—we weren't given water to drink. I bought a bit of water with [my] last ruble. In Krasnovodsk, we spent the night by the port. First the army personnel were allowed on the ship, then children. In Pahlevi, we spent three weeks in a camp. I was very exhausted and weak [and] needed special care. When I returned to health, I went to Tehran, where I stayed for six months. In Tehran I fell ill with typhus and stayed in a hospital. During the six months in Tehran I received no messages about my family, and I think I am the only one who managed to survive.

Protocol 107

Testimony of **Jehoszua Frydman**, age sixteen, son of Rabbi Meir Abraham, from Tomaszów Lubelski. Arrived in Palestine via Tehran in Feburary 1943.

The Germans arrived in Tomaszów Lubelski on Rosh Hashanah [14–15 September 1939]. Straightaway they took to persecuting Jews—rounded them up for [forced] labor, ripped [their] beards out, beat [them]. On the first day, they killed one of the best-known local residents, Reb Nachum, [whose] surname I don't remember, a boy by the name of Lipa, Rafał Bernstein, and others. Many [Jews] were sent for labor [and] never returned home again. Among those who did not return there was the head of the yeshiva, Reb Isar. It was said in town that he had been killed. Before the Germans entered, the city was bombed. They dropped incendiary bombs and three-quarters of the town burned down. Forty-two people from among the Jews were killed and buried in a common grave. The Germans' first stay in our town lasted four days. In that short time, they managed to rob Jewish shops and apartments and called on the Poles to empty the Jewish apartments of what remained.

On the fifth day, the Germans left and the Russians arrived. As if famished, they threw themselves on the remnants of the merchandise hidden inside shops, and on clothes. They paid for the goods at first, and then they stole. They explained that they would not be staying in town, and that those who wanted to could leave with the army. Father decided to leave with the entire family and went to Horyszów, where my grandma and uncle lived. It was a few weeks before we reached the place. The road was covered with refugees escaping the Germans. Most dragged themselves on foot; the rich rented carts for which they paid a few thousand zlotys apiece. We left on a cart we had paid five hundred zlotys for. On the way, the cart driver kicked us off onto the road and hit Mother with a whip.

Finally we arrived. Mother took up trading and we settled in somehow. The Bolsheviks soon began to implement their regimen. They confiscated homes [and] shops, threw [people] out of [their] apartments without giving them work. During the elections, everyone was forced to take part and vote for the Ukrainian candidate. Despite the active propaganda campaign, very many Jews, particularly the observant people, did not take part in the elections.

The formerly rich were immediately deported to Siberia. The winter of 1940 began with the passportization. Father did not want to take a Soviet passport, as he saw no future for himself in Russia. He wanted to go to America or to Palestine, where he had relatives, and we went to Lwów to take care of the formalities. In Lwów we rented a small apartment. Father began to teach a few children; on Saturdays, prayers took place in our apartment, and this way, we made a living.

In Exile

One day, in the middle of the summer, on a Saturday at six in the morning, four NKVD-ers arrived [and] carried out a search. They looked over Father's books for a particularly long time. Father began to explain to them the meaning of those volumes, but they understood little of it since Father did not speak Russian well. They took the books, told us to pack [our] belongings, and drove us to the station. In the station, we came upon thousands of refugees. Everyone was placed inside freight cars, forty people in each one. There were only two bunks [in each car]; the rest [of the people] slept on the floor. We received a piece of bread and a bit of soup to eat once a day, which Father did not allow us to eat as he believed the soup was *treif*. But Father was allowed to leave at each large station, under the watch of the NKVD, to [fetch] hot water. We traveled for two weeks. In Kiev, the train waited for a few hours, but the guards did not let the local Jews who had brought us food approach us. After four weeks, we arrived at the station of Nowe Alale,[271] Sverdlovsk Oblast, and from there we went on foot to *posiołek* number 54, where we were accommodated in barracks alongside exiled Ukrainians. [The Ukrainians] treated us terribly—they took everything we owned from us, denounced us, and often beat [us]. We were 120 families in a crowd of a few hundred Ukrainians, and since we were a minority, our situation was unbearable.

We worked in the forest; even Father worked. The work quota was twelve hours a day. During that time, one had to saw three cubic meters of wood, and anyone who did not fulfill the quota had to starve. In that first period Father tried not to work on Saturdays and suffered terribly for it. He was [put] in a punishment cell a few times, until he had to give it up. Anyone who did

271. Novaya Lyalya (Polish: Nowaja Lala).

not fulfill the quota had to work longer than twelve hours. During work, falling trees often killed people. A falling tree broke my father's arm, and he scarcely survived the accident. During his recovery, which lasted six weeks, he only received half of the bread ration. The frosts were terrible—the snow reached people's necks. During a snowstorm I lay inside the barracks, afraid that the snow would bury me. We lived under a very strict regime. On Sundays [which were] free from work, it was even forbidden for a few people to gather together. Parcels that arrived from relatives went through a few searches, so that very little was left of them.

Yom Kippur in the *Posiołek*

The efforts of my father and Rabbi Hurwicz from Nowy Sącz to be exempt from work on Rosh Hashanah [3–4 October 1940] achieved nothing. It was only promised that older people would be released from work on Yom Kippur [12 October 1940], provided they did not gather together to pray. Naturally, that promise wasn't kept, and twenty people held services on Yom Kippur. In the middle of the day, our barracks was surrounded by the NKVD. As it turned out, the snitch was one Klein from Łódź. Everyone was released; only Father and Rabbi Hurwicz were arrested and sent to the city, to prison, where they stayed for six weeks until [their] trial. In prison they were beaten terribly and tortured, and given only bread and water. During the trial, a Jewish lawyer was designated as an interpreter since neither of the two accused knew Russian. The defense lawyer explained the significance of the religious holiday that is Yom Kippur, particularly for the clergy, and claimed that it would be difficult for the elderly to change many generations' traditions in a short period of time. The court released both [men]. Soon, the informant was punished by God. He was killed by a falling tree trunk during work.

War and Amnesty

We found out about the outbreak of the [German-Soviet] war two weeks [after the fact]. The *posiołek* was closed down, we were moved to the city, and after some time, received documents to go to Tashkent. We waited whole weeks for the train, selling off the remnants of our belongings. With the money we thus obtained, we rented a train car with other refugees, in which we set off for the south. The journey was long and difficult. Everyone was ill with dysentery.

We had no strength to stand up on our own two feet after two years of hard work and hunger in the *posiołek*. And when we finally arrived in Tashkent, they would not let us off the carriage. We were told that the city was full of refugees, that there was no more room even in the streets, and that an awful typhus epidemic had taken hold [there]. After four days' stay in the station, we sold the rest of [our] things, rented a train car, and went to Bukhara. In Bukhara we moved from place to place, unable to find a place to sleep. Father was taken in by a resident who was well known in the city [and] who had something resembling an apartment, and Mother slept in the synagogue. We were terribly hungry. Mother fell ill with dysentery from eating potato peels and died in a hospital, and a month later Father died of typhus. I was left alone, a full orphan, in the apartment of the Bukharan Jew, where I felt very unwell. I cried for days and constantly looked for Jew[ish] acquaintances who had known my father.

This time I was lucky. I found an acquaintance from our town, Mrs. Glancer, who took me in, put me down on her passport, and took money from the Polish delegation for me. Apart from the allowance from the delegation, she [also] earned a little. She would give me the money from the delegation, and I had to get food for it myself. In Bukhara there were lots of Jews from Poland who were simply decimated by epidemic diseases. Every day, tens of corpses lay in the street[s]. From time to time, raids were carried out on the refugees, and those who could not present permanent work certificates were sent to kolkhozes. The situation in the kolkhozes was worse than in the city, where one could trade a little. Those who received assistance from the delegation were not deported from the city. Mrs. Glancer found out that a Polish orphanage had opened in Kogon where only full orphans were admitted. She went to Kogon with me, where at first they refused to accept me; but then, when I presented documents [showing] that my father was a rabbi [and] that [my] parents had died, I was admitted to the orphanage. I was the only Jewish child in the whole orphanage, and during the five months I spent there, I suffered a lot at the hands of the Polish children—however, I was very polite to everyone. One of the teachers always defended me. I never complained, not wanting to antagonize the Polish children. In that period, a few children's transports were sent off to Persia, but I was always left behind because I was a Jew. Eventually I fell ill with typhus. I stayed in a hospital for two months and thought that the entire orphanage [would have been] sent away [in that time]. I learned that the last transport of children was leaving. I ran away from the hospital and turned to the teacher who always had affection for me. I managed to get on the transport, and along with the [other] children, left for Krasnovodsk, and from there to Pahlevi and Tehran. In Tehran I was placed in an English orphanage. When I returned to health, I was moved to a Jewish orphanage from where, in January 1943, I was sent to Palestine.

Protocol 108

Testimony of **Józef Barten**, age fourteen, son of Wolf and Rebeka. Born in Majdan Kolbuszowski,[272] Małopolska [Lesser Poland]. Came to Palestine via Tehran.

My father was a shochet. We had a slaughterhouse with kosher meat. The family was made up of four children: Hersz, age twenty-one; Rachela, age nineteen; Jeremiasz, age eighteen; [and] I was the youngest. We fared well so that the older children did not [have to] work, but studied [instead]. When the war broke out and the German airplanes appeared that dropped a few bombs, panic broke out in town. Luckily, the bombs fell onto fields and did not damage anything in town. Despite this, people left town in a panic, moving to other places. A few days later, the Germans arrived [in town]. The Jews went into hiding. They ran off into the neighboring villages, looking for hiding places with villagers they knew. Most Jews did indeed find shelter in the country, but many peasants refused [to help] even those Jews with whom they had had business relations for years. Father, too, hid with the family at the [house of a] peasant he knew, from whom he had bought cattle for slaughter. But the villager said that he was afraid of the Germans [and] did not want to have us for long. His wife, seeing our distress, said she would hide us after all, because she could not [bear to] see her old friends without a roof over their heads. We were hidden in the stables. We stayed there for a few days, afraid to go outside [for fear of being] spotted by the neighbors. Seeing that the situation was becoming prolonged, we decided to return home one night. At home, we found the door to the apartment open and the apartment burglarized. The Germans had taken the radio, the new wardrobe, and the best clothes, and turned the entire home upside down.

Germans in Majdan

During the few days we spent in the country, the Germans ran Majdan their way. They took a few of the most respected Jews and Poles out of the town, and tormented the remaining people, dragging [them] to [forced] labor and

272. Actually: Majdan Królewski (near Kolbuszowa), often referred to as Majdan Kolbuszowski. See Protocol 109.

beating [them] mercilessly. A few days after our arrival in town, the Germans surrounded the entire Jewish district, led all the men out into the main square, gave them bottles of kerosene, walked them to the synagogue, and ordered them to pour the kerosene over [it] and set it alight. They forced the Jews to dance in a line around the synagogue. The Germans stood, splitting their sides, watching this spectacle. Every day the Jewish suffering increased. Recognizing that we would not last long, Father decided to get [us] over to the Russian side. With the help of smugglers, the whole family went to Niemirów.

With the Bolsheviks

In Niemirów, we settled with an acquaintance of Father's, also a shochet, and planned to stay there. We didn't fare badly. Father worked in his trade. A few shochets started a company and traded together. [My] older brother, Hersz, was also involved in trading. He transported food products from Niemirów to the large cities. [My other] brother and sister helped him. They earned better than Father did in his slaughterhouse. However, Father was telling [us] every day about new restrictions against traders, particularly those trading in kosher meat. Should the Bolsheviks force him to trade *treif* meat, he would not do it under any circumstances. He told us about the elections and the registration. He decided not to go anywhere, neither for the registration nor the elections. Once, I heard Father telling Mother that everyone was being forced to take a Russian passport. He asked Mother's advice and they decided not to accept the passports, as they did not want to become Soviet citizens and lose the right to return home even after the war. My brother and sister encouraged Father to take a passport, saying that it would not matter after the war. One day Father told us that all the people who did not take passports would be sent home, to the Germans, so he asked [my] sister and brother to cease trading, as he wanted the whole family to leave together. He told Mother to pack up all [our] belongings, as he was sure that something would happen any day now.

In Exile

The thing that we were afraid of happened. One Friday night, in the middle of the summer, NKVD-ers arrived, carried out a search, and told [us] to pack [our] belongings. We were prepared for this and immediately went outside.

We were driven to the station [and] loaded into freight cars without windows, fifty people in each. We waited inside the sealed car at the station for forty-eight hours, without food or drink. When the train started, all the Jews in the carriage began to cry desperately. We, the children, seeing the adults cry, began to scream, but no one paid any attention. We traveled for three weeks, no one knew where to. Mother and the other women in the car fretted over [our] unknown future. All [that] time we were not allowed out of the train car. During the day we were given half a kilo of bread per person, at night—a bit of soup. A hole in [the floor of] the car was used for a toilet. After a week's travel we all fell ill with dysentery and [had to] wait in line to get to the opening in the floor. Children could not wait their turn and went in the car. The stench and filth were unbearable. Women fainted [and] there was no way [to escape]. No one heard when [we] called for help. The guards only watched the roof, [to make sure] there wasn't [any] opening through which one could escape. After three weeks' travel, we stopped at a station close to the city of Troitsk. We got out of the car. We were split into groups and taken on foot to Vostochna [Vostochny?]. We walked all day, despite being weakened from illnesses and the journey. We arrived at night [and] were accommodated in barracks, eighty people in each. We slept on the floor, dead to the world. We awoke in the middle of the night—panic broke out. Mice the size of cats were jumping over us. We shooed them away, but they were not afraid of us. We awaited dawn impatiently. When we complained about the mice to the commandant, he replied, "In Russia one gets used to anything." The next day we were split into groups. Some worked in the forest and some on rail embankments. Mother and I were exempt from work. When we arrived in the *posiołek* it was still warm, but then winter came, and the freezing temperatures reached −50°C [−58°F]. Even though no one had [any] warm clothing, we were rushed to work even in a −48°C [−54.4°F] frost. Workers received a kilo of bread per day and we, the nonworkers, only four hundred grams. You could get soup in the canteen. It was [nothing but] hot water and it cost two rubles. Throughout our stay in the *posiołek* we could not afford to buy soup even once. We went hungry for whole days, and envied the people who could afford the soup. I so dreamed of eating something cooked that I begged the people who bought soup for themselves to leave a little bit for me in the bottom [of their bowl]. After a few months we were moved to another *posiołek*, which was located in the forest. Russian exiles had lived there previously, but I did not see them. My brother, who worked as a *gruzownik*,[273] met with the exiles and told [us] that there were many well-known personages among them. In the new *posiołek* there was no kitchen. One had to travel a few kilometers to get soup. I would go to get the soup [for the people who bought it] and would receive two spoonfuls for each portion delivered. Because I would bring back five, six portions, I [got to eat a serving of] soup every day. One day, on the way to the kitchen, I almost froze to death. My hands got frostbitten and I could not move them for a few weeks. I wasn't allowed to deliver soup anymore. During the same time, my brother Hersz fell ill—we didn't know what with—and a few weeks later, without medical help, he died. We buried him in the middle of the forest.

War and Amnesty

When the [German-Soviet] war broke out we received no news about it. The guards told us about it one day, asking [us] to keep it a secret. Father said that he understood [now] why they had decreased our bread rations. After the Amnesty, we were all gathered together and asked to stay put, [and told] that things would improve for us. Naturally we did not want to stay. We received the [necessary] documents and left for Samarkand. We spent two weeks in Samarkand, sleeping in the streets like thousands of other refugees. Many died in the street, and there was no one to bury them. We would lie next to corpses, and we thought that we would die from starvation here. After many efforts, we managed to go to Turkestan. We were not allowed off the freight car [and] had to go on to Kuszata [?]. After spending the night [there], we were sent to the Burgen kolkhoz. We worked in the fields, receiving six hundred grams of bread, and Mother and I, as nonworkers, [received] three hundred grams each. The local residents lived as poorly as we did. There was no furniture inside the huts, only beds—knocked together from planks of wood. We refugees slept on the wet floor.

Parents' Death

Father and Mother fell ill with typhus. My brother and sister tried to have them admitted to a hospital. The officials wouldn't even give us a cart on which

---

273. *Gruzchik* (Russian; Polish: *gruzczik*): a carrier/loader. See glossary.

to take them there. After a few days of illness, without medical help, Father and Mother died on the same day. We mourned them all night long [and] buried them ourselves the next day. After [my] parents' death, [my] brother and sister tried to get me admitted to a Polish orphanage in Turkestan. After long efforts, I managed to get into the orphanage. I spent eight days there. The Polish children treated me badly, but the teacher defended me. One day we were taken to Tehran. I was there for a few months, until [my] departure for Palestine.

Protocol 109

Testimony of **Izrael Ferster**, age fifteen, son of Symcha and Gitla, from Majdan Kolbuszowski [Majdan Królewski]. Left Russia on 21 July 1943. Arrived in Palestine along with [his] two sisters on 28 August 1943.

The Germans entered Majdan on 12 September. Our town avoided destruction because the fighting took place tens of kilometers away from us. Despite this, before the Germans entered the town, hundreds of Jews escaped, among them the gray-haired rabbi, Bencion Hurwicz. The rabbi got hit by a German bullet near Kolbuszowa and was gravely wounded in the leg. A few Jewish companions took him into town; the news came later that he died from his injuries in Kraków.

My father was a raw wool trader. We had huge storehouses and were among the richest Jews in town. Immediately after the arrival of Germans, trucks arrived in front of our home and took away the entire contents of the storehouses. The same happened to other depots and market stalls. The more valuable things the Germans took for themselves, and the less [valuable] ones they gave away to the local Christian people, so that within a few hours, the Jewish population had been robbed of everything. The Germans tormented Jews in a cruel way: they ripped [their] beards out, captured them for [forced] labor [and] drove them out of town, from where [no one] returned anymore. After a week, we learned that Russians had entered Poland and that the Russian border was located by the San River. The Germans issued an order for the Jews from the neighboring towns to leave their apartments and cross the San. The expulsion took place in the town of Tarnobrzeg first, not far from us. The town had to be cleared of Jews within a few hours. The sick and the old, who could not escape quite so fast, were killed on the spot. One lame Jew who dragged himself through the streets with difficulty was killed by a German with a blow to the head with an iron bar. The horrific fate of our neighbors was talked about in our town, and when an order came out a few days later for Jews to leave Majdan, we left [our] home quickly, taking nothing with us and not [even trying to] look for a cart. On the way to the San the Germans teased us cruelly, as did the peasants, who not only would not let us spend the night in their huts but didn't want to sell us any food either. We slept in fields, and after crossing the San, reached the town of Niemirów. We lived in Niemirów for eight months. The crowding was awful because the escapees did not want to carry on ahead, but live close to home [instead]. From time to time, they would sneak over to the [other] side and pull out of hiding places the more valuable items hidden [there] before [their] escape. Father continued to trade in his industry. The trading wasn't easy, as the Bolsheviks confiscated private property. Trading was considered an illegal activity. Grandpa Eliahu Szefer, Grandma Miriam, and two uncles, Abraham and Menachem Szefer, with [their] families—altogether fifteen people—escaped town with us. We kept together and that's why it was easier for us to get by. In the winter of 1940, everyone was forced to accept a Russian passport. The passport holders were sent off to small towns. They were not allowed to be within a hundred kilometers of the border. Those who did not accept a passport had to register for a return home. Our family did not want to take Soviet passports; we had [our] fortune at home, which we did not want to give up. Later, Father learned that those who didn't have passports would be sent to Siberia. We wanted to leave Niemirów but [our] relatives insisted that we stay.

In Exile

On 31 [30?] June 1940 a few thousand people were sent to Siberia from Niemirów. [Their] houses were surrounded by the NKVD; the refugees were allowed to bring one hundred kilos of luggage per family. We were loaded into freight cars, sixty people in each, and after twenty-four hours, the train set off. From that journey I recall a song sung by the children:

I want to remember
Who I am and where I come from.
I don't know who my parents were.
I rebelled against Hitler and ran off to Russia.
Mama, I want to come back to you.
This country is not made for me.

We traveled for three weeks. We received a quarter of [a loaf of] bread and a bit of watery soup per day. Many people were ill with dysentery. Finally, we stopped in Altai Krai, in Troitsky area.

From the station we went on foot to the forest. The journey took all day [and] we finally reached a *posiołek* in the eastern district, barracks number 73. Forty people were accommodated in each barracks. It was terribly filthy in there; huge mice, bedbugs, and other insects tortured us day and night. We worked in the forest felling trees and loading wagons. The children peeled the bark [off of the trees]. Anyone who didn't work got no bread. During the work in the forest, many people were killed by falling trees. Others died of diseases, especially dysentery. Except for grave cases, refugees were not admitted to the hospital.

Death of My Parents

We lived in the *posiołek* for sixteen months. During that time we sold off all of our belongings to buy food, and were constantly hungry—[we even] envied those who died, ridding themselves of food worries. When the war broke out our situation did not improve: we worked two hours longer and received less bread. At the end of summer Father and Mother fell ill with a bad [case of] dysentery. We sold [our] last shirts and hired a cart, which took them both to the hospital. The hospital didn't want to take them in. Our pleading was in vain. Gravely ill, they were taken back to the barracks. They lay in the barracks for two weeks. Their condition worsened by the day until the warden himself took pity and drove them to the hospital, but it was too late then. Father died on Saturday, and Mama four days later. And so this way, we, the three children of whom I was the eldest, became full orphans. After [our] parents' death, I became the sole breadwinner and caregiver to my little sisters. I could not support them with my work, however—there was nothing to sell [and] we were all starving. I began to try to get us children moved to [be with] Grandpa and Grandma, who were in a *posiołek* in Novosibirsk. The *posiołek* commandant, who treated everyone unkindly, was unusually nice to us. He went to the city himself and obtained from the authorities a permit for us to be sent to [our] grandparents.

After eight days' stay at the grandparents', we received the news about the Amnesty. We received documents and planned to go to Bukhara. It took a few weeks before we got a space on the train. In Bukhara we met [our] uncles and the rest of their famil[ies]. They lived a few kilometers from the city and didn't fare badly. The uncles traded and earned [enough] for everyone. We, the children, received fifty rubles per month each from the Polish delegation, and a bit of food. But slowly, [our] uncles' trading ceased. We were threatened with being sent to kolkhozes, which we were afraid of the most. Epidemics like typhus and dysentery ravaged the population and the refugees. Out of our family, Grandpa, Grandma, my aunt, her husband, and [her] child died from these diseases within a short time. When I was admitted to the Polish children's center, I learned that the other child had died, too. Out of the fifteen people in our family who were deported to Russia, there were three people left—not including the three children who were in the Polish children's center. The same happened in other families. We too became ill with typhus and scarcely avoided death. After [Shavuot], we were sent off to a Polish children's center in Ashgabat. There were fourteen of us children [sent there] at first, later it came to eighty. Children's transports left for Poland[274] frequently, so that in the end, there were 320 children [who] left [on the last transport], including twenty Jewish ones. I and [my] little sisters stayed in the center until the last moment. I was there for ten months. I did not believe that we would make it out of Russia. The Russians treated us with hostility; they took our carts, food provisions, and clothes, and [it got to the point where] all children were to be sent to kolkhozes after the closure of the center.

But something changed at the last minute and we were allowed to leave for Persia. After the breakdown of Polish-Russian relations,[275] the situation of Polish citizens was very difficult. Everyone over the age of sixteen was forced to accept a Soviet passport. The stubborn ones were put in prison. From our center, twenty-five teachers were arrested and put in jail, where they were horribly tortured. Many of them died. The mobilization of Poles for the Wasilewska Army[276] began. No Jews or Ukrainians were accepted into this army, only Poles. Persecutions began of those who had not been mobilized, at which point 250 Polish Jews, my two uncles among them, reported to the

---

274. Children's transports were sent via Iran (Persia) to Palestine or India.

275. This happened on 25 April 1943, after the discovery of the crime against Polish officers in Katyn. The Soviet authorities began to again apply the memorandum of 29 November 1939 regarding Soviet citizenship and force Poles to accept Soviet passports.

276. Refers to the Polish First Tadeusz Kościuszko Infantry Division being formed in Seltsy on the Oka River.

Wasilewska Army. They were sent to an assembly point in Turkestan, and later the Jews were excluded from the ranks, sent back home, and told they would be called on should the need arise. They did not want to admit Jews to the Russian army either, as they had not voluntarily reported for it at the time [they were supposed to]. The situation of the refugees worsened by the day. There [are incredible levels of] hunger in Russia and one can only get bread on ration cards, forty dekagrams per day. To get these rations, one has to stand in line for twenty-four hours, and the bread often runs out. A loaf of bread on the black market costs a month's wages. The highest wage for a worker in a state factory is five rubles per day. People drop like flies. You hear cries and wailing in the streets: "Jews, help, I'm dying from hunger, give [me] a piece of bread." In the cemetery in Bukhara there are no spaces left anymore. Trading is strictly forbidden [and] those caught [doing it] are sentenced to harsh prison. The children in the children's center fared badly too—we received only 150 grams of bread per day [and] a bit of watery soup for lunch. The situation of the Jewish children in the center worsened too. It was said that Jews were responsible for everything, and the Polish children directed all of their anger at the twenty Jewish [ones]. Once, a bloody fight broke out for the following reason: the Polish children found a torn-up holy picture and accused two Jewish children, Jakub Reich and Rosenberg, of having ripped it up. The boys were beaten so badly that they had to lie [recovering] for a few days. We, innocent children, were also beaten, and it took a long time for the supervisor to manage to calm the children down.

Finally, on 21 July 1943, we were put into trucks and went to Meszchet,[277] on the Persian border. We spent two weeks in Tehran. On 15 August, all the Jewish children from Poland, whose number in Tehran was 107, set off on a journey through Iraq on army trucks, in the guise of Christian children. After eleven days' journey, we arrived in Palestine on 28 August.

277. Mashhad [original Polish correction: Meszhed].

Protocol 110

Testimony of **Dina Stahl**, age eleven, daughter of Józef and Estera, born in Rabka. Arrived in Palestine from Russia in February 1943.

A few days before the outbreak of the war, I saw, as I was playing with [other] children, that pieces of paper were being put up on house walls. I couldn't read yet and I ran to Mummy to ask that she read [for me] what was written there. When Mummy went out into the street there were already lots of people in front of the poster. It was explained to me that [people were being] called for the army and that there would be a war. Mama packed up [our] things. Soon after, Father returned, very upset, and said that everyone in town was already fleeing. A lot of money was being paid for a cart and it wasn't certain if we would be able to get one. We didn't get a cart. We stay[ed] in Rabka for a few days, until Saturday [2 September 1939], that is, the day after the outbreak of the war. On Saturday morning, Father returned home very upset and said that, apparently, the Germans were coming. Mother was reheating lunch at the time, she left everything in the kitchen and packed up one pillow, and gave my brother Meir, age twelve, a small suitcase [filled] with things. I was also given a small parcel with things and we set off on foot. Almost all the Jews escaped from Rabka. A few elders stayed behind who could not go on the journey.

We went toward Wiśniowa. We saw many tanks on the way. We could barely walk on the road; there were so many people with bundles on [their] backs, so many carts, so many cars that we [only] got to Wiśniowa by a miracle. We spent the night there, and the next day Father hired a cart to go to Jarosław, where Mama's family lived. We paid a lot of money for the cart. After a few hours on the road, the peasant told us to get off the cart and said he would go no further. Father started begging him to take pity on the children, Mother cried, but it was for nothing. He pushed us off the cart. We hoisted our belongings onto our backs and set off. Father had no strength to carry the bundle with the bedding, so he dropped it on the way, Mother dropped a suitcase also, and we reached Rzeszów this way. We spent the night in Rzeszów. The next day, we got to Jarosław by train. The train went very slowly [and] there was nothing to drink on the way. We got hot water from the steam boiler from the engine driver. The train stopped outside of Jarosław [and] we had to walk two kilometers to the city.

In Jarosław

When we entered the city, the bombardment was just happening. Father took such fright that he left us alone and ran off by himself. Mother shouted after him and only [after] hearing her voice did he return to us. We all hid inside a house. We were standing close to the station and I saw the station building burning. When things calmed down, we went to Grandpa's apartment, near the magistrate. We arrived in Jarosław in the second week of the war. The grandparents were overjoyed because they had suspected they would never see us again. We were so tired that we couldn't even eat. I slept all the way until Sunday morning, when the Germans knocked on the door of Grandpa's apartment. We took great fright; Grandpa jumped out of bed, as it was an early hour. The Germans didn't do anything to him, they said they only wanted to get washed and then they left. Next to our apartment there stood tanks, cars, and bicycles; new Germans came all the time and asked to be allowed to get washed. At first we hid from them, but [after a while] we understood that they would not harm us [so] we came out of [our] hiding place. Father said he was afraid to go out into the streets because the Germans were cutting off [people's] beards along with chunks of their face, capturing Jews for [forced] labor, and killing them. My father was an expert on women's purses [by trade]. Grandpa was a boot maker. They both got busy working. Father helped Grandpa to cut out boot shafts. The Germans brought in leather they took from Jewish merchants and ordered boots to be sewn from it, and were so happy with Father's and Grandpa's work that they gave them a permit to go out in the street.

Expulsion from Jarosław

After three weeks the Germans expelled all the Jews from town. It wasn't permitted to take any belongings except what one [could] carry. We walked out of town without [any] belongings, were chased toward the bridge over the San, and because the bridge was wobbly and the Jews were afraid of walking across it, the Germans threw the disobedient [ones] into the water. Afterward, the

Jews would swim up to the shore. We crossed the bridge and found ourselves in a village occupied by the Russians. We stayed in that village for two weeks with distant relatives and then went to Lwów. And because in Lwów, overflowing with refugees, we could not get a room, we went to Stryj. We lived there with Grandpa. Father and Grandpa worked together. The women and children stood in lines overnight waiting for bread, sugar, and other foodstuffs. Some shops would only sell to children, so we waited in line all day long.

In Exile

One day, Russians carrying shotguns came to our place. They told us to pack [our] things and said we were going home. We were driven to the station along with Grandma and Grandpa [and] loaded into a freight car. In the car there was no water. We were given a piece of bread and a bit of soup once a day. We traveled for a long time until we arrived in Assina.[278] In Assina we settled in a barracks that was full of bedbugs. [My] grandparents did not want to eat because the food was *treif.* There lived with us a rabbi who told Grandma that she was allowed to eat [*treif*] as she was sick. Then we were sent to a *posiołek*, and Grandma and Grandpa to another one. Father worked as a metalworker and earned three hundred rubles per month. Nothing could be bought with this, and if it weren't for the grandparents, who sent us parcels from the neighboring *posiołek*, we would have starved to death. Many people rebelled in our *posiołek* and went on strike, saying they would not go to work if they didn't get bigger bread rations.

War and Amnesty

When the [German-Soviet] war broke out, our situation got worse. We were given less bread and told to work more. After some time, we were registered, everyone received certificates, and we went to Fergana. We had nowhere [safe] to go there. Mama had a small child with her, my little sister Sabinka, who had been born in Siberia. After a few days, we went to an Uzbek kolkhoz. We lived there for a week, sleeping in kibitkas, on planks, and going hungry every day. They didn't want to keep us in the kolkhoz as they themselves had nothing to eat, and we were sent to a Russian kolkhoz. After eight days' stay in

278. An incorrect spelling of Asino.

that kolkhoz, Mother, myself, my brother Meir, and little Sabinka fell ill with typhus. We were taken to the hospital and placed in one room. [My] mother and brother stayed in the hospital for ten days; I stayed there two months. The doctor was very good to me and promised me all the time that I would soon get better. When [my] fever went down from 40°C [104°F] to 37°C [98.6°F], my brother came to visit. I asked him over and over for little Sabinka to be brought in because I missed her a lot. But the doctor forbade [it]. I came down with a fever again because of this and was moved to another hospital. There was no blanket there despite a heavy frost, so Father went to the first hospital for my blanket and contracted typhus. [He] stayed in the hospital for eight days, and when Mother arrived on the following day she found Father was no longer there. She asked to be let into the morgue and fainted there at the sight of Father's corpse. When I returned home, I understood from Mother's face that something had happened. She didn't want to tell us; only during work did she burst into tears and wailed dreadfully: "Children, you have no father anymore." Five months later, little Sabinka fell ill with dysentery. Mother was allowed to stay in the hospital with the child. I was left alone with [my] brother, and because we didn't work we weren't given anything to eat in the kolkhoz. We were starving. But no one as much glanced at us. Mama came one day and said that Sabinka would not hold out [much] longer. Brother and I went to the hospital. When we got [there], we saw Mother standing by the morgue and two men with shovels next to her. I was terribly afraid of those people with shovels [but] came up to Mama in spite of it, because I didn't want her to stand [there] alone. I was handed the child's dresses, and Mama left with the people. I cried terribly because I loved my little sister more than anything in the world. After returning home, Mother despaired greatly and couldn't work any longer. She began to try to have us admitted to an orphanage. In the orphanage we starved too. The worst thing was that the Christian children called us names [like] lousy Jews and teased us, [saying] they would go to Africa and we would be sent to Palestine. Once I retorted: "I'm not scared of Palestine at all because it's my homeland." Then, along with a larger group of children, I went to Krasnovodsk. Mama stood in the station as we were leaving. How hard it was to leave her, sick and lonely in a foreign land. From Krasnovodsk, through Pahlevi, we went to Tehran. After a few months' stay [there] I went to Palestine with [my] brother.

Protocol 111

Testimony of **Lonia Akierman** from Warsaw, age thirteen. Father was the owner of a clothing storehouse in Wałowa [Street]. Arrived [in Palestine] from Russia with [her] eight-year-old brother.

On the first day of the war we all left for Łuck, to [go see] my father's brother who lived there permanently. Mummy, [my] little brother, and I stayed in Warsaw at first and only Father settled in Łuck. Mama sold the clothes from the shop and sold out of almost all merchandise so that we could keep ourselves alive. Our home was bombed, and we scarcely survived. During the fire in our home, [my] little brother burned his hands. We only saved one pillow from the burning apartment. Before Rosh Hashanah [14–15 September 1939], when Mummy was making her way to the synagogue, the bombing started again. At the time we lived at [our] aunt's at Gęsia [Street], but her home burned down too. We were left out on the street. Around us, the fire raged. The next day, [some] kind people brought us food and we went to our cousin's in Pańska Street. We suffered terribly there. After a few weeks, [we] had to change apartments again, but the food [situation] was even worse. Mummy cried because she couldn't give us bread. One day, Father turned up. Everyone wondered how he'd made it to the city. He had looked for us for a long time until he found us. He brought us a lot of bread, sweets, and chocolate. Three whole days we ate the bread that Father brought. Then the bombings ended, and Father went to his shop. He said that a lot of his goods had been stolen.

On Sukkot [28–29 September 1939], the Germans entered [the city]. [They] captured Father as he was walking to the shop. They cut off half of Father's beard and left his face bloodied. Then they ordered [him] to take them to the shop [and] emptied [it] of all merchandise. [My] parents returned home late. Father looked awful. His whole face was bloody. The neighbors rushed in to look at [him]. Mother cried terribly [because the Germans] had taken everything from our shop. Some neighbors advised Father to cut off the other part of his beard; others said he should walk around like this with half of his face hairy. My father did not cut off the other half of [his] beard and went out in the street like that. On Wielka Street the Germans stopped him, grabbed his hands, photographed him, and beat him for not cutting off the other part of

[his] beard. After Father's return home, Mother burst into tears. [My] parents kept saying they could not take it any longer; Father shaved off [his] beard and went into town to borrow money to go to Łuck. He did not return for the night, and the next day, a few Poles we knew said that the Germans had captured Jews to clean up the parliament [building], and that among the Jews there was my father, who had asked [them] to let us know where he was. Father returned four days later, with swollen hands. He said that even if everyone was starving, he would not go out in the street anymore. He sent Mother to collect money that was owed him and they both decided to go to Russia. Things were really bad for us until we crossed the border. After eleven days of roaming around we found ourselves on the Russian side and went to Łuck, to our uncle's place. [Our] uncle clothed us, fed us, [and] we settled with him, where we fared well. Father worked and earned money, Mother also worked, and I was sent to school.

In August 1940, on a Friday night, we heard gunstocks knocking on the door. [My] brother and I took great fright; Father did not want to open the door, but the Russians started shooting. [My] uncle, white as a ghost, came to our room and told [us] to open the door. They dragged me and my brother out of bed and told us to get dressed. They didn't let us bring anything with us. The street was black with people; women were crying. We were rushed to the station on foot. We were loaded into filthy, cramped freight cars. The cars were locked, and we were kept inside for three days, without food or drink. In vain did we cry out to be given food and drink. After three days, the train started, [and it] went on forever. Finally, the car doors were opened, and Mama was passed a bit of water and groats. I got off the car [and went] into the station with Mama to help [her] cook that little bit of groats. At that moment, the train started, and my father and brother were [inside]. We started screaming like mad [and] the train was stopped. We took the undercooked groats with us. Afterward, we were afraid to leave the car, and [so] we ate raw groats. Later, we weren't even given [any] groats, and terribly famished, we arrived in Siberia.

We got off the freight car in Tomsk and were loaded onto barges there. Mother got pneumonia but later recovered. We were taken to a forest. Father worked in the forest and earned eighty [kopecks][279] per day. My six-year-old

279. The original uses an abbreviation *gr.*, possibly *grosze*.

little brother and I also worked. We were constantly hungry. Mama caught a cold again [and] was taken to the hospital, but her condition was not improving. In the hospital, Father said, the patients were not given [any] attention. Once Mother was feeling so unwell that she asked Father to bring the children to her because she wanted to say goodbye to them. Father did not find us at home because we were at work. We returned home from the forest [and] Father took us to the hospital, but Mama was already dead. Father begged the hospital manager to be allowed to see the deceased, but the doctor replied [saying] Mama's body was to be cut up [an autopsy performed] because young doctors had to learn. Father said that if they did that, he would commit suicide and kill both [his] children. All day long, Father ran from doctor to doctor and we children watched over the body. We cried desperately because we were scared they would cut Mummy up.[280] Before the evening, Father returned with a piece of paper, a permit to bury Mama. We guarded the body all night,[281] and in the morning, took Mama's body on a cart to the *posiołek*, where we planned to bury her. Father dug the grave with a shovel and we children with [our] hands. No one helped us because everyone was at work. We covered her up with sand and cried terribly. Father waited until evening, and when ten Jews had arrived after work, my little brother recited Kaddish. We went to Samarkand, where we were placed in an orphanage. We received forty dekagrams of bread per day. We worried that Father would die from hunger, so me and [my] brother only ate forty dekagrams of bread per day and gave the entire other ration to Father. Thanks to this our daddy didn't die. My brother and I fell ill with typhus but recovered. Along with other Jewish children from Poland, we were sent to Pahlevi; Father stayed behind in Samarkand. We received two letters from him during [our] stay in Palestine.

---

280. This is prohibited by the Jewish religion.
281. In accordance with a Jewish religious ritual known as *shemira*.

Protocol 112

Testimony of **Sima Siebcesser**, age thirteen, daughter of Mendel and Rajzla, from the village of Tarnówka outside Łańcut. Arrived in Palestine in February 1943.

Our family was made up of five children, three of whom died in Russia. Father was a sickly man, suffered from heart problems, and did nothing before the war except study all day long. We lived off the assistance from [our] relatives in America. The first days of the war went by calmly in our village—we only saw refugees running down the road. A week after the outbreak of the war, [our] aunt came running to us, screaming that the Germans were coming. We all took great fright because we had not suspected that the Germans were so close. Father, who wore a beard and was a very religious person, was afraid of staying in the village and ran off to town, to Łańcut, by himself. A few hours later, a few Germans knocked on our door. Uncle Lejb opened up. Five Germans entered and asked who the owner was. Uncle replied that the owner had fled to the city. "Why did you not run away?"—one of the Germans started shouting and flogging everyone with a whip. Then he asked where other Jews lived around here. My brother managed to sneak out through the side door and run to the neighbors, warning them to hide. When the Germans left our home, they saw Jews running across the field toward the town. They began shooting at them but did not hit anyone. Then the Germans issued an order that no Jew was to remain in the village by six in the evening, [and] if they came across any they would shoot them on the spot. We quickly packed up our belongings and set off for the town. In town, the Germans were rounding up Jews for [forced] labor [and] beating them; they robbed Jewish market stalls and homes. Some of the things they could not take with them they handed out among the local people, who readily helped [them] in [their] plundering.

One day, the Germans issued an order for [Jews] to leave town within two hours and cross over to the Russian side. All the Jews from the town and the [surrounding] areas who had escaped to Łańcut went toward the San River and tried to make it across to the other side of the river. The Russians closed the border and didn't allow anyone to get off the boats, forcing us to return to the Germans. All night, we went back and forth across the river and looked for a way to get to the riverbank. Finally, a few Jews gathered valuables from among the refugees and gave them to the Russian guard[s], who let us through. We went to the village of Stara Bircza where [some of] our relatives lived. We settled there in a peasant's hut; Father started trading, bringing in goods for the peasants from Przemyśl and taking food from the village to Przemyśl. We lived off this for half a year. All this time, Father was very worried about us. We had papers to go to America, where Father had been promised a position as a rabbi. Knowing that it was impossible to get out of Russia, he wanted to return to Germany,[282] to leave for America from there. That is why he registered for a return home.

In Exile

One Friday, NKVD-ers came to us, told us to pack [our] belongings, and said that we were going to Germany. We were taken to Przemyśl. [My] father and brother went on foot as it was a Saturday.[283] In Przemyśl, we were loaded into [train] cars, fifty people in each. The crush was awful. None of our friends were allowed to [come close] to us and we weren't given food. After twenty-four hours, we set off. In Lwów we waited another twenty-four hours. Individual people would sneak out into the city and bring back food. The next day the train started, and none of us knew in which direction—only a few hours later did we understand that we were going to Siberia. During the journey, we received a piece of bread and a bit of soup every day. Father only ate bread and water. In vain did we try to convince him to eat some more.

After three weeks' journey we arrived at the station of Tomsk Damosznika.[284] It was only three weeks later that we got to the labor camp from there. In the camp we didn't fare badly; Father worked in a sawmill and was free from work on Saturdays. At first he was threatened with further deportation, but when that didn't help, he was left alone. Workers received a kilo of bread per day, nonworkers—half a kilo per day. There was enough bread [to buy] in town at the price of one ruble per kilo, and because the town was only six kilometers away from the camp, and we had a bit of money [we had] taken from home,

282. Areas occupied by the Germans.

283. [Observant Jews do not drive or ride in any vehicles on the Sabbath.]

284. This place could not be located.

we never went hungry. The children were admitted to a Russian children's center. After six weeks' stay there, my two brothers, six-year-old Hersz and five-year-old Icchak, fell ill with measles. [Our] parents took them from the center [back] to the *posiołek*. The warden did not allow the children to be kept in the barracks and ordered them to be sent to the hospital. Mother begged for the children to be allowed to stay as they could catch a cold on the way to the hospital. But that did not help; the children were wrapped up in blankets and taken to the hospital on a sled. On the way they caught a cold and they died three days later. Father was worried that they would perform an autopsy on the children; he sat all day long in the hospital [and] was only given their bodies in the evening so that they could be buried. With [my] older brother's help, Father dug a grave and buried both children together in [it]. Then, Father fell ill [and] lay in bed for six weeks. During that time things were very bad for us. We didn't have any money and had to support the whole family by selling [our] belongings. The bread [supplies] had already run out in town. The former *posiołek* commandant left, and in his place there arrived a Ukrainian, who tormented us terribly. He moved us to the worst barracks, where even in broad daylight, mice jumped around the bed[s], not [allowing our] sick father to rest, so that I had to chase them away with a stick. Finally, Father recovered [and] started to work, and this lasted until the end.

War and Amnesty

Our situation got a lot worse when the [German-Soviet] war broke out. The bread rations were lowered to 600 grams for the workers, and the work hours were increased to fourteen per day. We could not go into town without a permit. Suddenly, we learned that an Amnesty for Polish citizens [had been] announced. We received certificates to leave, and rented a train car together to go to Uzbekistan. We suffered a lot on the way. There was neither bread nor water [and], when someone got off at a station to buy something, they would not find the train on their return; it took a few days for [people] to find one another. On the way, everyone fell ill with dysentery from [eating] watermelons, and when the train stopped at a station, everyone rushed out like mad into the fields to go to the toilet. Finally, we arrived in Samarkand. The city was full of refugees; we could not find a place for the night and we lived in the station. We covered a portion of the route, and when the train stopped in a field, we all got off the car with [our] belongings and returned to the city. We lived under the open sky for five months, like thousands of other refugees. People stole from one another and you couldn't even sleep at night because you could find yourself without a shirt on waking. Father decided to go to a kolkhoz with us, where we lived in a kibitka and worked in the fields [picking] cotton. We received four hundred grams of flour per day and suffered from hunger. Then Father fell ill with typhus and the leader ordered him to be taken to the hospital, against which Mother strongly protested, knowing the situation in hospitals. The hospital was located seven kilometers from the kolkhoz, and Mother walked there every day, bringing a bit of food that she had bought by selling what remained of [our] belongings. After six weeks, Father recovered.

Meanwhile, the situation in the kolkhoz got worse and worse. We were only given two kilos of flour per month, and in the end, were told to leave the kolkhoz altogether. We returned to the city, and [our] parents, on learning that there was a Polish children's center in Katargan,[285] tried to get me and my brother admitted there. We made it into the center, and Father and Mother settled in a nearby kolkhoz so that they could see us. In the center, the Polish children teased us a lot. After six weeks, my brother fell ill with dysentery, and Mama didn't find out about it until he was already in the hospital. Mother visited him every day, bringing him *lepyoshki* to the hospital, where they weren't giving him enough food. The course of the illness wasn't too hard, my brother was quickly improving, and Mother thought he would leave the hospital within a few days. Imagine her horror when one day, arriving at the hospital, she found [her] son's bed taken by another child. She was told that [her] boy had died suddenly and been buried. Mother fainted, and after being revived, began screaming that they had killed her child. They didn't even want to show her where the boy was buried.

After [my] brother's death, Father tried to take me out of the center but he did not manage it. There were four of us Jewish children in the center altogether, and when preparations were being made to go to Persia, [we] were told [we] would not be taken. We cried terribly and begged to be taken. One

285. An incorrect name for Kattakurgan [original Polish correction: Katta-Kurgan].

teacher took pity on us and told us to leave the city with her. Outside Katargan, at a tiny rail station, we waited all day until the train with the Polish children arrived. Our teacher ran from carriage to carriage and begged the supervisors to let us in. Finally, we made it onto a car, without any belongings [and] without having said goodbye to [our] parents. We went by train to Krasnovodsk, and from there to Pahlevi by ship. We spent a few months in Tehran [and] I came to Palestine with a group of Jewish children.

Protocol 113

Testimony of **Eliezer Hochmeister**, age fifteen, son of Dawid and Noemi from Warsaw, 41 Pawia [Street]. Arrived in Palestine on 28 August 1943.

My father owned a machine for the manufacture of hosiery in Warsaw and operated it himself. This machine was the source of our livelihood. There were three of us children in the house: Sara, age twenty-one; Chaim, age eighteen; and me. [My] sister and older brother helped Father [and] I went to school. We didn't fare badly.

During the bombing of Warsaw, one of the bombs hit our home, and at that point, on the fifth day of the war, we escaped to Ostrów Mazowiecka with Father. We traveled on foot. We went down paths and roads, carrying heavy bundles on our backs. We spent the nights at random huts whose owners had fled. We hid from the Germans [who were] coming in from all sides and were beating Jews on the way. Many captured Jewish escapees were taken to a camp. Father managed to avoid encountering the Germans a few times, but we did not [manage to] get away with it anymore outside Ostrów. They walked up to us and wanted to take Father and [my] brother Chaim with them. Mother and [my] sister started to beg for them to be set free, and seeing that there was little to be done, begged the Germans to release Father at least. And so it happened. The Germans took Chaim to Komorowo, where there were Polish [army] barracks. Mother, seeing [her] son being taken away, started crying, and I joined her. Father regretted not having gone with [Chaim]. Chaim spent three weeks in the camp in Komorowo. Mother and Sister brought him food every day. At first they wouldn't let [them] come close, then they allowed parcels to be brought in. Father's efforts to have Chaim released were in vain.

Only after a few weeks was Chaim let go, along with [some] others. When [he] returned to Ostrów we almost didn't recognize him. He could barely stand up, and he told [us] terrible things about what he had gone through. The Germans had brought in hundreds of people to the barracks, told them to kneel in the mud and left them in this position for three days and nights. At night [the prisoners] had reflector lights shining at them so that no one could escape. During that time, machine guns were aimed at them, so that it felt like they were about to start up at any minute. One day, they did indeed start to shoot, and the bullets hit two Polish soldiers who were on their knees close to Chaim. He survived only by a miracle. Many people died from exhaustion and not being able to last in the kneeling position. They were given neither water nor bread. When the people were ordered to stand up after three days, many could not straighten their legs, stiff from three days' worth of keeping them in water. Then, they were rushed to work. They worked for four days on a road, without food, and were only given a piece of bread and water on the fifth day, and [they] had parcels that had been brought in by relatives delivered.

In Ostrów, we lived with [our] uncle, Pesach Rase, a butcher who gave us a small room in his apartment. The Germans organized manhunts for Jews every day, grabbed them for [forced] labor and beat [them] during work. One Jew was beaten so much that the rifle buttstock split on his back, another one, wearing glasses, had the lenses broken [into his] eye.

Expulsion from Ostrów

My brother returned in the middle of October. A few days later, the Germans gathered everyone in one square and ordered them to leave town within an hour. We wanted to go home to [get our] things but the square was surrounded by machine guns, and we were rushed toward the Soviet border. At the border, our clothes were ripped up, and we were chased across to the other side. We arrived in the village of Simowa.[286] Father did not want to go on further as he planned to sneak [back] through the cordon and bring his belongings from town. After two days, Mother and Sister got back to town and took our things. Then we set off for Zambrów by cart.

In Białystok

A few days later, [my] father and brother went to Białystok by rail. I went out onto the road and asked Russian soldiers in an army car to take me [there]. Mother and Sister traveled in the same way. During the first days we looked for one another until [finally] we found each other at the Council.[287] Father rented an apartment in the house of Missionaries in Święty Roch [Saint Roch] Street; [my] brother got a job in a timber depot. We could support ourselves

286. Likely refers to the village of Szumowo.

287. In the office of the Jewish council.

modestly with the money brought over from Warsaw. When the prices shot up in Białystok as a result of the influx of refugees, and [my] brother lost [his] job, we set off for Kowel, where upkeep was a lot cheaper. In Kowel, [my] sister and brother worked, and we didn't fare badly.

In Exile

When the registration to go back began, Father, seeing that living in the Soviets was becoming more difficult by the day, decided to register to return. A few weeks later, on a Friday evening, NKVD-ers came to our place, allowed [us] to pack only small items, and took us to the station in a car. We waited at the station inside tightly packed freight wagons for twenty-four hours, until we set off. When we were sent away from Kowel, my sister Sara was in Białystok, where she had gone to find out if our family had arrived from Warsaw. Not finding us at home, she reported to the NKVD herself and asked to be sent away alongside us. She was indeed deported, but to the other end of Russia, and we knew nothing of her [fate] for a long time.

Only twenty-four people were traveling in our wagon, whereas in other carriages there were fifty. We received a quarter of a bread [loaf] and a bit of soup during the journey. We were allowed out of the wagon once a day. After a month's journey, we arrived in Assina.[288] There we were unloaded, taken to the river, and from there, went to Teguldet on barges. Thirty-five kilometers of trekking on foot [later] and we found ourselves in a place known as Sczet [Czet']. We arrived at night. Since the barracks were already full, we were ordered to spend the night outdoors. The next day, huts were put up. It rained—it was the rainy season. After one night, a windstorm carried off the tents[289] and we were left with no roof over our heads again. We were accommodated in the attic of a barracks, where we stayed for four weeks. Father and Brother worked in the forest; workers received a kilo of bread per day, nonworkers—five hundred grams. There was a canteen there, where one could get soup for thirty-five kopecks. Every day I would go to the forest for mushrooms and berries that Mother cooked, and that's what we lived on.

288. An incorrect spelling of Asino.

289. [May refer to canvas coverings on the huts.]

In the Penal *Posiołek*

The Jews from our *posiołek* did not want to work on Saturdays. The commandant threatened that if they did not work Saturdays, he would not give them bread for a whole week, and he also forbid the canteen to sell them soup. This, however, did not frighten anyone, and [people] did not work on Saturday. The commandant saw his threat through, and on Sunday, no one was given soup anymore, and they stopped giving out bread too. When people started to faint from hunger after a few days, the youth rebelled and beat up the commandant. The commandant called in the NKVD to help, and after looking into the issue, they decided that all the Jews would be moved to a penal *posiołek*. We were sent off to Assina, and from there, traveled by train for ten days until we arrived in the Sverdlovsk Oblast, where the penal *posiołek* was located. In the *posiołek*, there were copper and gold mines located eight kilometers from the settlement. Russian exiles worked in the mines. When we arrived in the *posiołek*, we were asked if we wanted to work in a mine voluntarily. The work was very hard but well paid. Most of the youth reported for work in the mines, but many were afraid to do it. Father worked with water pipes. He earned twelve rubles per month. [My] brother got into the builders' brigade, and as one of the most talented ones, earned three hundred rubles per month. Everything could be bought with money. The Polish refugees were watched carefully. They were not allowed to gather or to talk. During work in the mine, [the authorities] also made sure that the Poles did not talk with the Russians. We were allowed to sell things only through the *posiołek*'s commandant, so that we wouldn't make contact with the Russian population. The commandant would estimate the value of the items [and] the Russian exiles would come to him and buy our clothing off him. Until our arrival, the Russian exiles had worn rags, [and it was] only after we arrived that they [started to] look decent, after buying our belongings.

During our entire stay in the *posiołek*, Father was writing letters to various places and looking for [my] sister Sara. We thought we would never see her again. In our *posiołek* there lived a shochet from Kraków, whose son worked in a camp in the Novosibirsk Oblast. Thanks to him, we received news of [our] sister. After long efforts and pleading, my sister was able to make her way to us. Our joy had no end. [My] sister worked in a quarry [and] earned 110 rubles per month. We were constantly hungry despite these earnings, as the prices had gone up hugely. The commandant comforted us [by saying] we would never return to Poland, that we would be building Russian cities. The pious were not allowed to pray and [their] tallits were made into gowns for Russian women.[290] We had to work during the harshest frost because refusal was punishable by three months' prison.

War and Amnesty

When the war broke out between Germany and Russia and the Amnesty order came out, we went to Revda, and since we couldn't get an apartment in the city, we were sent to a kolkhoz. Brother worked in a brick factory day and night; he [supposedly] earned well but [in fact] was not paid at all. My father and sister were so weakened that they couldn't work. Father sold a fur [coat] and we went to Tashkent [with the money]. We suffered hunger during the journey. In Tashkent, we had nowhere to go. The city was full of refugees who were lying in the streets. It was impossible to get bread. Mother and I went to a kolkhoz to look for [my] sister and brother, whom we'd lost during the journey to Tashkent. We found them in Kogon. Two days later, we were taken out of the kolkhoz, where hunger was widespread, and sent to Turkestan, and from there to another kolkhoz.

We fared really badly in the new kolkhoz. We lived in a kibitka. There was no bread. My brother and sister worked in the fields; we received two hundred grams of flour per day but there were days when we got nothing. I found work in the stables, [and] later was made to harness the horses to the plow and to plow the earth. My last pair of shoes wore out during this work, and I only received one kilo of flour for ten days' work. I left the job and went to the city, where a Bukharan Jew hired me as help, [paying me in] food only. This Jew was a supervisor of army warehouses. After a few days, I suggested that he hire my brother for work, too. He agreed, and [my] brother and I worked for him together. But [there too] I went hungry, and having heard that there was a Polish orphanage in Bukhara, I reported there and said I was an orphan. I cried until they took me in. Three weeks later, a hundred children—forty-five Jewish ones among them—left for Ashgabat.

---

290. Tallit [Polish: *tales*]: Jewish prayer shawl.

In an Ashgabat Orphanage

On the way to Ashgabat, I caught a cold. I spent a few weeks in the hospital. During that time, a group of new children arrived [at the orphanage], and some were taken to Persia. When I recovered, there were 220 children in the orphanage. Three groups of children left in a few transports, but there were no Jewish children in any them. The new transport was made up of 320 children, only 20 Jewish ones among them. The Polish children bullied us cruelly, and even though the director, Ponikowski, tried to moderate the clashes, he could not control them. The Polish children knocked our mess tins out of our hands. At night, they put soap in our mouths, turned the lights off, and beat us in the dark. They poured water onto our beds, but we put up with this patiently, knowing our suffering would cease—we had no choice anyway, since things were worse in the kolkhoz. Our situation got a lot worse when relations between the Poles and Russians were severed. Ponikowski, the director, left along with the embassy, and we thought we'd be returning to the kolkhoz. NKVD-ers came around constantly, wanting to kick the children out of the orphanage and send [them] to kolkhozes. But the new director, Orłowski, constantly delayed the date of the move, and it was only thanks to him that we were saved. We were short of food all the time. We received only four hundred grams of bread per day, and soup. The director was afraid of letting us out into the streets, as they could arrest us and send us away, so we spent a few months in the courtyard of our home, surrounded by a fence.

We heard that all Polish citizens who did not renounce [their] Polish citizenship and take on a Soviet passport were being arrested. There were three types of passports: a two-month passport, a six-month passport, and a two-year passport. Refusal to accept a passport was punishable by two years' prison. Lots of people were arrested, among them many Jews.

I received a letter from [my] brother [saying] that Wanda Wasilewska[291] was mobilizing Polish citizens in Turkestan [but] that Jews were not being admitted. The Jews who reported [there] were given three months' leave. Jewish officers, however, were accepted.[292] Poles and Jews who refused to report to the

291. Wanda Wasilewska (1905–1964): writer, political activist in the USSR, co-organizer of the Union of Polish Patriots in the USSR and the Polish army in the USSR.

292. Refers to the draft to the Kościuszko Division of the Polish army. The First Tadeusz Kościuszko Infantry Division was formed on Soviet Union territory in May 1943. The Polish unit was

Wasilewska Army were deported somewhere far away. Where?—no one knew. The NKVD-ers carried out night searches in our orphanage many times. They were most interested in the grown boys. One day they turned up during the day and asked to be shown the grown-up boys. The director hid them in the basement and only presented small children [to the NKVD]. Seeing that they would not succeed through the director, [the NKVD] began an investigation among the children. They asked where our parents were and implored us to take Russian passports. We replied that we were full orphans, and those who had fathers said they were in the Polish army abroad and that they wanted to go to [be with] them. All the Jewish children claimed to be Christian, knowing that they would not be allowed out of Russia otherwise.

Death of General Sikorski

When we learned about the death of General Sikorski,[293] all the children wept terribly and cried that our father had died and that we would perish without him. The mourning lasted eight days; we wore black ribbons on [our] shoulder[s] and all the children lost [their] appetites and didn't want to eat. Our despair was so great that the director and the teacher had to comfort us, [saying] that the Polish government in London would not forget about us and would try to get us out of there. Three weeks later, a telegram arrived at the orphanage saying they were going to come for us at twelve at night and take us to a kolkhoz. The children cried and said they would not leave the orphanage voluntarily. The director comforted us, [saying] he would do everything to save us. When the people from the NKVD arrived, the children barricaded themselves in one of the rooms, even though the director said it was completely unnecessary. He did not let the NKVD-ers—who said that they would take us to kolkhozes by force—frighten him. The talks lasted all day long, and even though we were told to go to sleep in the evening, we decided to resist and fight the NKVD-ers if they tried to take us by force. The director went around in a car all day, intervened wherever he could, and when he returned at twelve at night, there was joy in the orphanage. The teachers were woken up

---

established as a result of the efforts of the Communist Union of Polish Patriots and was subordinate to the Soviet army.

293. Władysław Sikorski, General (1881–1943): in the years 1939–43 the prime minister of the Polish government in exile and commander-in-chief of the Polish army. Died on 4 July 1943.

[and] gathered in the office, typewriters started clicking, lists of children were put together. We didn't sleep all night. One child after another would run up to the teacher [and] kiss her hands so that she would tell us what the good news was. But she was quiet and only repeated from time to time: "It will be all right." Only in the morning were we told that we were leaving Russia. It's difficult to describe what happened to us. We started jumping, dancing, and singing. With [our] last few grosze we sent off telegrams to relatives and parents. [The staff] began to pack [our things]—everyone got three blankets, a few sheets, sweaters, shoes, and other things. We forgot about hunger. When night fell, the director told us to go to sleep wearing our clothes because the wake-up call was to be at six. None of us slept. The wake-up call rang out at four in the morning. It was 21 July 1943 when we got into Polish army cars[294] that took us away from the orphanage. The drivers were Russians. We were driven to the Persian border in two groups. At the border, the Russians wanted to take away all of our belongings. They particularly liked the blankets. We fought stubbornly for our possessions and did not let them be taken away from us. The search took all day [and] we arrived in Mashhad just before evening. The local Jews organized an enthusiastic welcome for us, gave us food and drink, and gave us gifts. On the fourth day, [some] cars arrived, and twenty Jewish children were taken to Tehran, while the Polish children stayed behind. The Jews in Tehran, where I spent two weeks, took great interest in us. After two weeks' stay, the group of Jewish children, made up of 108 [people], went to Palestine via Iraq in Polish army vehicles.

294. "Polish army cars" are not very likely since the Anders Army had left the USSR by then, and on 26 April 1943, the Polish government in London severed diplomatic relations with the USSR after the discovery in Katyn of the graves of Polish officers murdered by the NKVD.

Protocol 114

Testimony of **Eliezer Kretner**, age thirteen, son of Bencjon and Elka, from Małopolska [Lesser Poland]. Arrived in Palestine via Tehran in February 1943.

My father was a butcher. Mother died a few years before the war. There were four children left at home: Bajla, age eighteen; Brucha, age fifteen; Chana, age fourteen; and me. Father did not want to get married for the second time. [My] older sister ran the home, and Father worked in his trade until the outbreak of war. On the third day [after] the outbreak of war, shooting could be heard coming from the small forest close to our town. They were shooting in the neighboring town, and it was said that the front was located there. People said that lots of people had been killed in that town, many Jews among them. It was also said that one Jew had been hit by a bullet during prayer. When the Germans arrived in town, the Jews started to [try to] escape. The Germans shot at them. One deaf Jew, who did not hear the Germans when they called for him to stop, was hit in the stomach with a bullet. All of his guts fell out. He ran to his home with his guts hanging out and dropped dead on the doorstep. When the Germans arrived in our town, all Jews went into hiding, afraid of going out in the streets. Because the Germans were cutting off the beards of all Jews, my father did not go out into the street—even later on when we could move around town freely. At first, the Germans did not cause us any harm. Recognizing that nothing would happen to [them], [people] began to slowly leave their hiding places and busy themselves with normal things. The Germans stayed in our town a few days altogether; then they left, and the Russians came. When, a few days later, it was said on the radio that the Russians were leaving town, and those who wanted to could [leave] with the army—and hearing about what Jews had suffered in Lubaczów, where forty of [them] were burned alive—we escaped [from] town along with the Russian army and arrived in the village of Czitkow [?]. Father had nothing to do in the village and took up trading. He traded tobacco, matches, vodka. He transported food from the village into town and brought in from town items that had run out in the village. Sister worked in the first kolkhoz that the Russians opened up in the village. Nothing was lacking in that kolkhoz; the Russians brought everything there. As it was said in the village, they did it so that other villages would want to become kolkhozes. After some time, however, they stopped supporting that kolkhoz, and all of its members dropped out and spread out around [the neighboring] villages. Father's trading was going very badly. He was watched at every step. It was difficult to buy merchandise and difficult to sell it. [People] sold products reluctantly in the country. Constant searches took place on trains, and Father had parcels with goods taken off him a few times and was warned that if they caught him doing illegal trading he would be sentenced to prison. Father stopped trading and we lived off the pittance we had left over. We fared very badly. No wonder, then, that when the registration to return home was announced, Father was one of the first ones to register. A few weeks later, on Saturday evening, we were woken up by the knocking of gunstocks on the door—NKVD agents appeared and said that we were going home. We were driven to the station [and] loaded into freight cars. The doors were sealed, and a few hours later, we set off toward Lwów.

In Exile

In Lwów, still more people were packed into our freight car, other cars were attached [to it], and the whole train set off the next day in an unknown direction. The whole time, from when we left home until [we arrived at] the Russian border, we weren't given anything to eat or drink. It was extremely hot and cramped inside the wagon. [People] fainted one after another, and by the time we got over to the other side of the Russian border, a few people in our carriage had died. Only later did they start giving us a piece of bread and a bit of soup each. At every station, under strict convoy, we were let out for fifteen minutes to go to the toilet. My father did not want to eat the soup because it was *treif*. All month long, he didn't eat anything except bread and water. After a month, we arrived at a station whose name I don't remember. We were released from the freight car, and after spending two days in the station, loaded into cars that traveled through hills and forests, so that the car could barely make it through. In the middle of a huge forest there stood a barracks marked with the number 74. I was told later that it was [in] the Troitsky area. There was only one barracks in that place [and] there were no other deportees. We were the first Polish citizens in this place. Only a few weeks later was another barracks erected, and a hundred exiled Russians were brought in. We had no contact with those exiles. They were kept separate, and it was forbidden to communicate with them. Father worked in the forest sawing trees, for which he received two hundred grams of bread per day and watery soup, for which one paid thirty kopecks. When people began to complain to the commandant that they couldn't bear it, and asked for the bread rations to be increased, the commandant replied that if they didn't get used to it, then they would die. [My] older sister worked clearing the roads of snow. The quotas fulfilled by my sister and other women seemed too small to the commandant, who set high quotas, for which one would receive a larger portion of bread. [My] sister caught a cold from this piecework, returned to the barracks sick, and died of pneumonia two days later. She was buried in the forest. Our situation worsened to the point where a few people would die every day. One day, a tree broke both legs of an acquaintance of ours and he returned from the hospital on crutches a few weeks later. We were forced to work during the deepest frost. It was very cold inside the barracks. We children, wanting to warm up, kindled [some] wood and a fire broke out. Before we realized it, the barracks went up in flames. We tried to put it out with snow but it was in vain. The barracks burned down with all our belongings. We erected new barracks but had to sleep on bare planks, as the pillows had burned, and we had nothing to cover ourselves with. We had no undergarments either and suffered a lot because of it.

War and Amnesty

Our situation became a lot worse with the outbreak of the [German-Soviet] war. The bread rations were decreased, the work quotas increased. Father was so weakened from the hard work and not eating that he could barely stand. I went to work with Father every day to help him. To buy soup from the canteen was out of the question. Father earned [too] little, and we had nothing to sell. After a few weeks, the commandant gathered everyone and said that Polish citizens were free and could go to warmer districts. He gave us a few rubles each and [release] certificates,[295] [and] we set off toward Samarkand. In Samarkand, we had nowhere to go. We slept on the street. There was no bread.

After a few days, Father decided to go to a kolkhoz. The kolkhoz was called Dymitrow. We worked in a field [picking] cotton; even children worked. For

295. [See the glossary: Amnesty.]

this, we received two hundred grams of grain per day, which everyone had to survive on. One day [we] were given a bit of rye flour. It was a great celebration for us. We lived in kibitkas and slept on a clay floor. It was even worse here than in the *posiołek*. We went hungry for entire days and could barely work. After a few weeks, the Uzbeks told us that they could no longer keep us because they had no food for us. We [managed to] beg [them] to let us [stay] in the countryside for a bit. One day bandits attacked us and started shooting at us through the window. One of the women ran out with a bucket of water but thinking we would shoot, they ran away.

After that incident, we were afraid to stay in the countryside, and along with another Jewish family, the Fiszels from Łódź, we returned to Samarkand. There was nowhere to go [there and] we slept in the streets. We were constantly being forced out to the kolkhozes by the NKVD-ers. After a few weeks, Father found a stable where we settled. One day, I heard that a Polish children's center had opened in Samarkand. Father did not [give us permission to] go to that center, but I was so famished that I did not listen to [him] and went by myself. I said I was an orphan and was admitted. Afraid of Father, I returned home every day for the night so that he did not know I was in the children's center. I was very happy there. There was enough food, except the Polish children beat me often. I tolerated it because there [was] no bread at home, and not only was I full, but I brought home a piece of bread every evening, thanks to which both of [my] sisters [could] survive. Father would ask me where I spent all day and where I got bread from. I answered that I worked for some Jew in Samarkand who not only gave me food but also allowed me to take it home.

One day they were saying in the children's center that some number of children would be taken to Tehran in the evening, but since this was constantly being talked about, I did not believe it at all and went to sleep at home as always. When I returned in the morning, I found out that all of the children had left at night. I burst into tears. The director, who was a Jew, calmed me down and said that I too would go with the second group of children, but that I was not allowed to return home at night. This lasted a few weeks. The director was putting [a list of] children together, among them twenty-year-old boys written down as minors. We, the Jewish children, stopped speaking to each other in Jewish so that no one would suspect us of being Jews during the journey. One day, we set off on the way. When the train stopped at the station in Bukhara, we noticed all the Jewish children who had been taken in the first transport in the station. It turned out that they had been sent back to their places of residence. They cried and begged to be taken in our transport; some wanted to throw themselves under the wheels of the train. It was in vain, however—they were left behind, and we carried on. As it turned out, all the Jewish children from the first transport had been unloaded at the station and left at God's mercy. From Bukhara we went to Tehran via Krasnovodsk, where I lived in a communal camp at first, and was then moved to a Jewish orphanage and taken to Palestine.

Protocol 115

Testimony of **Luba Milgraum**, age twelve, from Kałuszyn by Mińsk Mazowiecki. Came to Palestine with a group of children from Tehran.

I was eight years old when the war broke out. I was attending an elementary school in Kałuszyn. My father was a chauffeur. Father escaped to Brześć right after the outbreak of war. Kałuszyn was bombed; many homes burned down, among them the house where we lived. We scarcely got out alive. During that fire my little four-year-old sister went missing. We looked for her for two days and thought that she had burned in the house. We found her in a village outside Kałuszyn, in a peasant's home. We settled in a peasant's hut outside Kałuszyn and Mother gave birth to a child there. The peasants brought us potatoes, milk, onions, and groats. Mama cried for days. Then the Germans came. They beat my mama with a whip and also beat us, small children. A few days later, Father returned. He stayed in the village for only two days [and] took us all [away] in a car. On the way, the Germans would stop us and beat us. We got to the Bug River and crossed [it] in a small boat. We came upon Russian soldiers, who arrested us but then set us free.

We went to Brześć. We fared very badly. We couldn't get bread. One had to stand in line for hours in freezing temperatures to get a loaf. One Friday night, NKVD-ers appeared and started to bang on the door to our apartment with gunstocks. We were living in an abandoned beth hamidrash. We took great fright and tried to hide in the darkest corner. The Russian soldiers came in [and] told us to get dressed quickly. Shooting could be heard out on the street. We got dressed and went out into the street where there were already crowds of people. We were taken to the main square. At dawn, all the people gathered in the square were taken to the train station and loaded into freight wagons, ninety people in each. The train waited at the station for three days. During those three days, they didn't give us anything to eat. They didn't let [our] friends bring us any parcels either; we were terribly hungry and suffered from thirst in particular, since they wouldn't allow water to reach us either. After three days, the train started. During the journey we received bread and hot water. From time to time, when the train stopped at a station, the children went out onto the platform and begged for food in the canteen. We were given guests' leftovers. We hid from the guards, who did not allow such begging. We soaked old pieces of bread in hot water.

After a few weeks' journey, we arrived in the Komi ASSR. We fared very badly in the *posiołek*. The warden appealed to us constantly and called for honesty. They wanted not only Father and Mother to work, but the children too. The Russians took [my] youngest sister, two-year-old Szajndele, to a Russian nursery. The tiny Chajsle had to walk six kilometers to school and back every day. And the four of us worked. Father and Mother worked building rail embankments, and my sister and I picked mushrooms in the forest. Even though the whole family worked, we had nothing to eat. Later, after Father and Mother had worked for many months, a commission arrived and said that the embankments were worthless. Fresh ones had to be dug up.

One day, Father returned home and said that the Poles and Russians had agreed [to] an alliance,[296] and that we would be able to leave Russia if we went to Samarkand. In Samarkand we met a lot of refugees. Father began efforts to get into the Polish army but they did not want to accept him because he was a Jew. We roamed the streets in Samarkand for three weeks without a roof over our heads, until Father and Mother fell ill with typhus. My little sister and I took care of them. Father's cousin, whose wife had died in Komi, arranged to get Father into a hospital. He said that after [his] wife's death, he had gone to Dżalabad,[297] and his children had been admitted to a Polish orphanage there. Now two of his children were leaving for Tehran with the Poles. Father asked [his] cousin to try and place us, the four children, in the orphanage, but the cousin said they only admitted children without parents. Hearing stories of how well children fared in the orphanage, I gathered my siblings and the four of us went to Dżalabad. We stopped on the street in front of the orphanage and cried for days. They didn't believe that we were orphans. They gave us sweets and toys so we would tell the truth about where our parents were, but we repeated that they had died and that we had neither a father nor a mother. Recognizing that we were stubborn and that they would not get anything out of us, the men from the orphanage finally admitted us. After a few months, we left for Tehran. We didn't say goodbye to either Father or Mother, and we never saw them again. In Palestine, we received a letter from Mother. Of Father, we've had no news.

---

296. See the glossary: agreement.

297. An erroneous name of the city of Jalal-Abad [original Polish correction: Działał-Abad].

Protocol 116

Testimony of **Mosze Lipowicz**, age eleven, son of Zelik and Rojza, born in Pułtusk. Arrived in Palestine from Russia via Persia in February 1943.

When the war broke out, the bombing of our town [Pułtusk] began. One bomb fell into a house next to us. Next to us there was also a Polish [public] office, where the Poles burned all the papers before leaving town. My father had a shop with tailoring accessories. We also had a shoe factory, where twenty [employees] worked. When the bombing grew heavier, we left our apartment and moved to [our] neighbor's [place] in another street. The Germans came to see that neighbor, a leatherworker,[298] and took away all his thick ropes. They ordered me to carry the package with the ropes all the way to the bridge, where they used the ropes to tie down the bridge planks that had come loose during the bombing. When I came up to the bridge[299] I saw files of Jews and Poles standing by the water. The Germans were shooting at them and their bodies were dropping into the water. I also saw how the Germans threw prams with babies into the water. Seeing all of this, frightened almost to death, I ran home and told Father about everything I had seen. Germans often came to our shoe factory and ordered shoes. One day, an officer came to us in the company of a few Germans and they forced Father to make them three pairs of shoes overnight. Father started explaining that it was impossible to finish this work in such a short time. To this they replied that if the shoes were not ready by the morning, they would kill him like a dog. All night long, the workers worked alongside Father to finish the shoes. The next day, the Germans came, put the shoes on, and walked away without paying a penny for them. From that moment, the Germans came all the time, ordered shoes, and didn't pay anything. After a few days, one very fat officer appeared. He took Father with him to some apartment, where they made Father take shoe measurements for many officers. When Father returned home, he told us how on the wall of the room there hung two portraits: [one] of Hitler and

298. Orig. *rymarz*: a craftsman working with leather, making mainly, though not exclusively, riding accessories.

299. Here and henceforth the reference is to the bridge on the Narew River.

[one] of Rydz-Śmigły.[300] The Germans had laughed as they pointed out to Father how Hitler defeated Śmigły.

Expulsion from Pułtusk

Before Sukkot [on] 27 September, when Mama went to the butcher's to slaughter a goose, Father came running to the house and said that the Germans had kicked him out of the shop and the factory, taken the keys from him, and simply told him to go away. Before Father had finished his story, Mother appeared and said that all Jews were being chased out of town. Father ran out into the street to see what was happening. He came back a moment later and told Mama to pack a few belongings. We, the four children, helped to pack whatever was at hand. Everyone took a bundle onto their back and set off. Tanks had been placed across the bridge. The Germans hurried the Jews along, and anyone who could not cross quickly was thrown in the water. We crossed safely to the other side of the river and hid in the village of Popławy, eight kilometers from Pułtusk.[301] In that village lived Mama's aunt. We spent the night with her, but the next day, the Germans came and started looking for Father. They said they would not harm him, that he should return to town. Father hid, and when the Germans walked away, we set off again.

On the way, fifteen kilometers from Pułtusk, we saw a mass of people who were on fire. It turned out that they were Jews from Wyszków, who having heard that we'd been kicked out of town, had run to help us. They fell into German hands, however, and were burned alive.

We walked day and night through abandoned villages, with basements full of supplies that we readily made use of. We stayed for two weeks in one such village. We were the only inhabitants in the village. After some time, the Poles arrived, civilians, [and] threw stones at us so that we barely escaped alive. A few Jews were killed by those stones. We journeyed on. During the day we walked; nights we spent in villages. The peasants treated us well, gave us a place to spend the night and food. Finally, we got to a train station, and from there, we set off for Białystok by train.

---

300. Edward Rydz-Śmigły (1886–1941): marshal of Poland, commander in chief. He left the country in September 1939, returned in 1941, and died soon after.

301. Likely refers to Brańsk.

In Białystok

The city was overflowing with refugees. We couldn't find a roof over our heads. We barely [managed to] get a corner in a school. It was very dirty, and many people were living there. Father went to a shoe factory and asked for a job there. Later, along with five friends, Father opened a shoemaking shop where he earned well, and we managed all right. One day Father told us that they were registering [people] to return to Poland, and anyone who didn't register would have to become a Russian citizen. [My] parents decided to register.

In Exile

After some time, at nighttime, NKVD-ers turned up at our place, told us to pack [our] things and said that we were going to Poland. We were taken to the station in cars [and] loaded into freight cars. The cars were sealed [and] we were left at the station for twenty-four hours without being given anything to eat or drink. Finally the train started. The journey lasted a very long time; we were hungry, because apart from a piece of bread and a bit of soup, we were given nothing. All this time [we] were not allowed out of the car. During the journey, many people fell ill with dysentery [and] fights broke out over access to the hole in the floor. We, the children, managed best, [as we had] a pocketknife with which we cut out another hole in the floor.

We arrived in Siberia. After getting off the wagon, we walked for a long time until we reached *posiołek* number 25. There were barracks there in the middle of the forest, and that's where we were put up. Father said that he was a shoemaker and immediately got work in his trade. Mother and we, the four children, worked picking moss. We had enough bread at first; the warden was happy with Father's work and brought him bread all the time. We shared it with our barracks neighbors. As a result, we were generally liked; children in particular treated us well and never beat us, knowing that they could always expect [to get] a piece of bread from us. By the summer the bread had run out in the *posiołek*, but we went to the forest [to pick] berries and mushrooms and did not go hungry thanks to that. One day, I got lost in the forest. I climbed a tree, looked around, and having spotted a small house from afar, went in that direction. I returned home late at night. Once, a few children got lost in the forest and didn't return for two days. [Their] parents were already mourning them, certain that they've been devoured by wolves. Only on the third day did the *posiołek*'s warden send people and dogs to look for the children. All day the dogs ran around the forest until they found [the children] in the evening, lying down, barely alive, under trees. They were so frightened that they lost their ability to speak for a few days.

In our *posiołek*, many people died from hunger. They were most often single people, who did not have the help that children provided by picking berries in the forest. We often took pity on them and gave them some of our berries, saving them from starving to death. It wasn't a lot, because the berries barely kept us alive too. Unable to work and exhausted from hunger, these people announced a hunger strike and refused food for a few days. The commandant paid them no attention. In vain did we try to convince them to eat our berries. Half of them died a few days later. Only then did the warden promise to increase the bread rations, and they returned to work.

No one in the *posiołek* knew about the outbreak of the war. We only found out about the Amnesty after some time. We received documents and went to the village of Medza [Madza?][302] in [the Autonomous Soviet Socialist Republic of] Komi. Only savages lived there. We were extremely scared of them because we'd been told they ate children. Father opened a workshop there and we got a lot of potatoes for it. Soon the potatoes ran out, starvation began, [and] we escaped in the middle of the night and went to Samarkand. We traveled for a long time, constantly hungry on the way. We had no bread. When the train stopped, children would run out of the train car [and] into a field, pull roots out of the ground, and eat [them]. Father would run into town [to get] bread but returned with nothing. A few times we almost missed the train. Mother despaired when Father wasn't coming back. Many people died during the journey; the dead were taken out at station[s]. They [were laid out] in the station and no one took notice of them. We children were so afraid of the sight of the dead that we would not get off at the station to find something to eat.

Exhausted from hunger, we arrived in Samarkand. The train station was overflowing with people. We had nowhere to go. We slept in the station building, and the NKVD-ers chased us from one place to another, [trying to] send us to a kolkhoz. Father wanted to go to a kolkhoz, but others convinced him not to, saying that there, too, people were starving to death and

302. There is a Mezen River in the Komi Republic. Otherwise, this village has not been located.

sleeping on bare ground. After a few weeks of wandering around, we went to Kurkurowsk.[303] After a few weeks of roaming around town, we finally got a stable to live in. Father looked for work in vain; we had absolutely nothing to eat and ate grass that Mama cooked. Hearing that there was a Polish orphanage in Kurkurowsk, I went there along with my sisters, Miriam and Cypora, and said I was an orphan. We cried until they admitted us to the orphanage. We had enough food in the Polish orphanage, but Jewish children were forced to pray with the Polish [ones]. From time to time, [our] parents came to see us and told us that they were starving. We would each put a piece of bread aside and give it to [our parents]. After a few months' stay in the orphanage, we were taken to Krasnovodsk and from there, via Pahlevi, to Tehran. I spent a few months in Tehran and then, with [my] two little sisters, I came to Palestine.

303. This place has not been located.

Protocol 117

Testimony of **Chaim Cymmerman**, age thirteen, son of Michał and Perla, from Hrubieszów. Arrived in Palestine with sister Małka via Russia and Tehran in February 1943.

My father was a shoemaker. We had two apprentices working for us. Father's clientele was made up exclusively of Christians, officials and rich landowners. There were always supplies in the apartment, out of which Father made shoes. Our family was made up of five people, of whom the youngest, Aron, stayed with [our] mother in Russia because Mama did not want to let him go on his own. The town [Hrubieszów] was bombed on the second day of the war. Twenty-two houses were destroyed, and many people killed. On [the] Saturday after Rosh Hashanah, 16 September 1939, the Germans entered the town and the Polish soldiers fled and hid in the mountains, where they shot toward the town. The fight lasted two days; the town changed hands [frequently]; there were dead [people] lying in the streets. Close to our home there was a bridge, which the Poles set on fire but which did not burn down. The Germans kept bombarding the town [and] we did not believe we would get out of the war alive.

All of a sudden, the Russians arrived, and things calmed down. The Germans ran away and the Polish soldiers were taken prisoner. The Bolsheviks descended on the market stalls like a pack of wolves. They bought out bread, shoes, clothing at high prices, and paid any amount for watches. We showed them where they could get leather. They ordered slippers from Father for their wives in Russia. After a week, we learned that the Russians were leaving town and that the Germans were coming. Panic broke out among the Jews; many escaped town. Father rented a cart, loaded it up with wares, work tools, [and] our belongings, and we set off. When we found ourselves deep in a forest after a few hours, our driver, a Pole, whistled. Two peasants ran up out of the woods, threw us off the cart, stole all of our possessions, and ran off. In vain did Father beg them to at least leave the lasts.[304] They took everything [and] we were

304. Last (Polish: *kopyto*, lit. hoof): a molded form shaped like a human foot used in the manufacture of shoes.

left on our own in the woods. Father was not so much worried about losing [our] belongings and leathers but rather about losing the lasts: "When I have [my] lasts, wherever I come I [can] sit down on a stool and I won't go hungry. Without the lasts I feel as if I had no hands." He left us in the forest [and] returned a few hours later carrying a bag on his back with lasts and a few pieces of leather that he had hidden in the basement. We went on foot the rest of the way until we reached the village of Korytnica. We got a small room there. Father began to work [and] received potatoes, flour, butter, [or] sometimes a hen for this work. We fared very well there, but Father did not want to stay in the countryside because the children could not be educated there. Mother encouraged him to stay because she was afraid of losing [our] livelihood. Not until five months later did we set off for Włodzimierz Wołyński, where our uncle lived, after the NKVD-ers announced that refugees were not allowed to live close to the border. The city was full of refugees and we had nowhere to go because [our] uncle, a shoemaker too, lived in a small shop with [his] six children. Father went out into town to look for an apartment. He saw an empty closed shop on the street. At night, he and [my] uncle broke the locks and we moved into that shop. The shop belonged to two business partners who had a falling-out, and that's why [it] was closed. One of them gave us permission to live there, the other one did not. The police said that we could stay. Father set to work immediately. Since there was no leather in town, everyone brought a piece of leather with them for the soles. The earnings weren't great, but we did not suffer hunger. The situation in town worsened by the day. The refugees were persecuted; cooperatives were formed that monopolized work, and Father was left jobless. As a result, all the refugees registered to return [home]. From our town, twenty-five thousand Jews registered to go back.

In Exile

A few months later, on a Friday night, NKVD-ers arrived at our [place] and we were told we were going to Germany. We were taken to the station, loaded into freight cars—forty people in each—and left inside the locked cars for forty-eight hours. The journey was horrific—on the way, we were given [only] a bit of sour soup and a piece of bread. The only good fortune was that we could buy food at small stations. In each car, a leader was picked who was responsible for all the passengers and who also distributed the soup and the bread. After a few days' journey, we understood that we were going to Siberia. One day Father left to get food at a station, and in the meantime, the train started. We despaired terribly, thinking we would never see Father again. It turned out, however, that Father, seeing the train set off, ran after it for so long that he [managed to] jump onto the last step of the last carriage. One day, the guard from our wagon would not let us look through the window because we were approaching Moscow. It was nighttime, and we saw the lights of the Russian capital from afar. After two months' journey, we arrived in Novosibirsk. In Novosibirsk, you could get anything you could dream of. Bread, sugar, and fruit were very cheap. But we were sent further on, to Tomsk.

In Tomsk, we were loaded onto a barge and continued on, bitten horribly by mosquitos, for three days, until we arrived at a *posiołek* deep in the taiga. We were accommodated in cramped barracks [and] worked in the forest, sawing and rafting timber. In the first few days, a few people were killed by falling trees. The work was so hard that we decided to strike. NKVD-ers came and listened to the reasons behind the strike. The *posiołek* commandant, a Pole, who spoke Polish and had been sentenced by the Russians to twenty years' exile, refused the NKVD-ers' decision to improve our situation. Eventually, it was decided that we would be sent back to Tomsk. Three thousand people stuffed themselves onto a small ship because everyone was afraid of staying there forever. The crowding was so terrible that one pregnant woman died, and her husband, seeing it, threw himself into the water. We were put in barracks outside the city, four [?] people to one. We worked in goods depots, for which we received fifty kopecks per day. Father, seeing that he could not live on a loader's job, turned to Warden Karczenko and offered to make him a pair of good shoes. As a reward, he was to receive permission to open a shoemaking shop. The warden agreed. Father sat down to work. Soon, his reputation as an excellent shoemaker was established. Father earned well—apart from money, he received bread cards for the cooperative. Everyone envied us. All the deportees worked very hard. Karczenko forced people to become Stakhanovites, [and] as a result, many died. For being late for work by one minute he would take away a month's wages. For being in the city without a permit he would order [people] to wash four floors.

War and Amnesty

The situation got a lot worse after the outbreak of the [German-Soviet] war. There was no bread. Father could not get leather for work. The only comfort was that Commandant Karczenko left for the army, and the new [warden] was much more lenient. When the Amnesty was announced, we were offered a piece of land to stay. They especially tried to convince Father [to stay], because he was a good craftsman. We thanked [them] for all the offers and went to Kazakhstan. The journey took a month. We suffered terribly during it because everyone was ill with dysentery. In Tashkent, we slept at the station, without a roof over our heads, for a few weeks. At night, we were scared to fall asleep lest we be robbed. Finally, we got a room at an Uzbek man's place; Father started to work and received once a bowl of sugar, once a bowl of flour for it. I waited in lines for whole days. The Uzbeks hated Jews and often attacked and robbed Jewish children. The Uzbek man threw us out of the apartment [and] we had to go to a kolkhoz. In the kolkhoz, called Intala, when Father said he was a shoemaker, there was great joy [at his arrival]. He immediately sat down to work and was given the necessary materials. But the manager treated us badly, even though Father made him a pair of shoes. The mortality in the kolkhoz was huge. We didn't fare that well; we received a handful of wheat each, which we ground with stones and used to make soup. Others were starving to death. One day, Father heard that a children's center had been opened in Turkestan. Along with [my] sister Małka, I went to Turkestan on foot. Mother did not want to let go of tiny Aron. After long efforts, we managed to get into the center. We stayed there for half a year. Groups of children left for Tehran a few times, but we did not want to go and leave [our] parents, because it was said that parents would be evacuated too. Only when we found out that the Bolsheviks were not allowing Jews out did we leave with the last transport to Tehran, and from there, after eight months' stay, we came to Palestine.

Protocol 118

Testimony of **Sara Mławer**, age twelve, daughter of Michał and Rywka, from Przasnysz. Arrived in Palestine with [her] brother via Russia and Tehran in February 1943.

My mother died eight years before the war. I didn't know [her] because I was a child then, at the time that she died. When I got a little older, my father's second wife ran our household. I had two siblings, [including] an older brother.

On Tuesday, a few days before the outbreak of war, we escaped with the whole family from Przasnysz because Father was expecting the outbreak of war any time now and [my] stepmother was about to give birth to a child. We went to Pułtusk. Hearing that the Germans were getting close, we decided to run further still, all the way to Wyszków, but we could not get into the town, which was in flames, [so] we carried on ahead. On the way, we were bombed by German airplanes. Walking in daytime was out of the question. We hid in the woods, looking for shelter from the German airplanes, and set off at night. This way we got to Węgrów. When we entered the town, it was still completely calm, and the residents learned about the horrors of the war from us for the first time. Father rented an apartment along with my uncle, Icchak Tabak from Przasnysz, who had escaped with us along with my aunt and [their] son. We lived off the money we had brought from home.

After two weeks' stay in Węgrów, my stepmother gave birth to a baby girl, [and] that same day, the Germans occupied the town. The Germans grabbed Jews for [forced] labor, beat them, cut off their beards with parts of their faces, and Father had to sit in hiding in the apartment. One day, the Germans came to our apartment and I, seeing that they were approaching, gave the signal to Father to hide. Father hid in the bed, which I covered with a duvet. The Germans were looking for the owner of the apartment but did not reach the bed because the puerpera[305] was lying in the bed next to it. They said they were certain we had hidden someone in the apartment. Mother took great fright. A doctor had to be called for her, [and he] said that had he come five minutes

305. A woman in childbirth or immediately after.

later he would not have found her alive. On Yom Kippur, Germans shot a rabbi from Węgrów. Father said that this happened because the observant Jews [who were] captured for [forced] labor did not want to work on Yom Kippur. They were asked who forbade them from working. They replied: "The rabbi." The Germans sent for the rabbi, who was reciting prayers at the time, and shot him on the spot. Everyone in town was in tears. After this incident, my uncle went to Przasnysz with his family, but was not allowed in the city, so he stayed in Maków [Mazowiecki]. He was afraid to return to Węgrów because he was a rich man, and such [people] were being taken hostage by the Germans. Later, he decided to come to [stay with] us.

In Węgrów, things worsened by the day. The Germans tormented Jews terribly. One heard more and more often how [the Germans] sent people away and they never returned. Father did not go out in the street. He wasn't earning anything. He complained that the money was running out and we'd have nothing to live on. When the baby turned a month old, [my] stepmother took the tiny baby in her arms, [my] brother, [my] father, and I threw bundles onto our backs, and we set off toward the Russian border. The border was still open. We went to Białystok. In the city there were already lots of refugees; we couldn't find an apartment. The baby cried all the time, [my] stepmother was exhausted from carrying it, and I could barely stand up. We went from apartment to apartment and asked to be let in. The apartments were full of refugees. Finally, some woman took pity on us and let us into her apartment. But she herself lived in a tiny room with four other people, and now there were eight of us. The little baby cried at night. [My] stepmother had no breast milk and the other roommates wanted to kick her out of the apartment at night. We barely managed to convince them to let us spend the night and promised to get out the next day. Father looked for an apartment all day and finally found a room. We paid two hundred rubles for it, for a year in advance, but the room was [in the outskirts].

Father started looking for work. He got a job with a leatherworker, and since [my] stepmother knew about tailoring, she also started earning [some money]. We did not fare well despite this. It was impossible to get bread, even though we, the children, waited in line all night. We would return in the morning after a night of not sleeping, often without bread. Father returned from work and told [us] about various restrictions and arrests and complained that wages were going down. We looked hunger in the eye. [My] stepmother had no fabric to sew dresses, or thread, or needles, so that she had to stop working. As our situation was unbearable at that point, Father decided to return home. Then he told [us] that he had registered himself and the family to go to America to [be with] our relatives. A few days later, Uncle Lejb was caught trading, arrested, and sentenced to seven years [in a] labor camp. He was immediately sent to Siberia.

In Exile

After a few weeks—it was on a Friday night—NKVD-ers woke us. They didn't let us bring any belongings with us and told us to go to the station. Only a Jewish policeman who was with them allowed us to pack up our things. At the station, we were loaded into freight cars, eighty people in each, and we lay on the floor, one on top of another. The car doors were locked. It was so stuffy that people were fainting. Children cried. Our little baby wouldn't settle, that's how hungry she was. Neighbors in the wagon were angry with us because the child would not let them sleep. I played with and comforted the little girl. The child was so hungry that she sucked my fingers. We traveled for two weeks until we got to Arkhangelsk. Throughout the journey, we were given a piece of dry bread and a little soup. Father was not allowed to get off the wagon at a station when he wanted [to go] get a bit of hot water for the child. In Arkhangelsk, we were let out of the wagon, loaded [onto vehicles], and taken to a forest. It was in the district of Kargafal [Kargopol], *posiołek* number 15. We were put up in barracks. At first, we slept on bare ground. There were no beds; everyone had to prepare bunks from the carved-out trunks for themselves. The barracks were full of bedbugs and mice. They wouldn't let us sleep at night, and we organized hunts. Father worked as a *gruzownik*[306] and was a Stakhanovite, [but] despite this, he was paid only seven rubles per month. [My] stepmother couldn't work, as she had a small child. [My] little brother and I were not fit for work either. If it weren't for the fact that Grandma and my aunt sent us parcels from Słonim, we would have starved to death. Also in exile with us was my uncle, Icchak

306. Should be *gruzczik/gruzchik*: a loader. See glossary.

Tabak, with [his] son. His wife had stayed in the German-occupied territories. [My] uncle and [his] son fell ill with typhus. They wouldn't admit them to a hospital [and] there was no doctor in the *posiołek*. They lay ill in our barracks, and my uncle died. I cried terribly at my uncle's funeral. I saw him buried in the forest, along with a few other Jews, because people died every day in the *posiołek*.

War and Amnesty

When the war[307] broke out, our situation in the *posiołek* worsened a great deal. There was less and less bread, and Father told [us] that they simply did not let him catch his breath during work. After the announcement of the Amnesty, we went to Turkestan. We could not find shelter in the city, which was overflowing with refugees. We slept in the streets, in the mud. People were dying from hunger; it was impossible to get bread for any price. Father got a job as a porter in a Russian orphanage. Since he transported bread from the bakery for the children, we no longer went hungry. We lived in a stable, next to the orphanage. At lunchtime, when the children were given soup, my brother and I would stand in line and also get a meal. Seeing that they would not be able to deal with us, the teachers [from] the Russian orphanage stopped giving us food. There was less and less bread. Along with my brother, I went to a Polish orphanage. There I said that I was alone in the world, that I had neither a father nor a mother, and I cried for so long that they took us in. We spent two months in the orphanage. We fared well there. We had enough food, though we were forced to pray with the Polish children and make the sign of the cross, which we didn't want to agree to. Only the tiny children agreed to [do] it. Father was very happy when he found out we had been taken into the orphanage. He only said that we [should] come back home if they decided to send us away. He didn't want to be separated from us. He said he would not survive separation. I felt sorry for [my] stepmother and the child. I didn't want to leave them behind, but when I remembered how badly we were starving at home, I decided not to run away from the orphanage. On the day of [our] departure, I confessed to Father that we were leaving him. Father and [my] stepmother

307. The Germans attacked the Soviet Union on 22 June 1941.

came to the assembly point. [My] stepmother carried my little four-year-old sister. She stretched her little arms toward us and asked us to take her with us. We cried terribly, and Father begged us not to forget about him. He gave [us] a piece of paper with the addresses of [our] relatives in Palestine, in which he begged [those] relatives to rescue him. When the car started, Father fainted and collapsed. What happened to [my family], I do not know to this day. From Turkestan, we went to Tehran via Ashgabat, and from there—after eight months—to Palestine.

Protocol 119

Testimony of **Estera Barasz**, born in 1926, an orphan. Arrived in Palestine in August 1943.

My parents lived in the town of Liski, the Sokal county, in the Lwów voivodeship. On the first day of Rosh Hashanah, on 13 September 1939, when Father and Mother returned from the synagogue, I learned that the Germans had occupied our town. Most of the residents were Ukrainians, only 150 Jewish families lived in town. At first, the Germans didn't beat Jews. A few days later, however, other Germans, worse ones, came and put a fine on the Jewish people, a contribution—a very high one. The local Jews were very poor [so] there was nothing left to do but flee. The town of Sokal, twenty-eight kilometers from us, was on the border of both occupations. The train station in Sokal belonged to the Germans and the town itself to the Russians. Local Jews rented carts and all reached the other side of the border within a few days. We left all of our possessions with a Ukrainian peasant we knew, and he took us to the river in a cart. The border was poorly guarded, and we made it to the other side of the San River without any difficulties.

In Sokal lived my uncle, Mosze Montag, and we found shelter with him. Those who had no relatives also were given a place to stay by the local Jews. It was after the holidays of Sukkot [28–29 September 1939] that dreadful shooting could be heard in town. We ran to the river that served as the border, and there, we saw the Germans chasing hundreds of Jews from Chełm and Hrubieszów across the river. It's difficult to imagine what was happening then. The Germans wouldn't stop shooting, the Jews ran on ahead with the cry of "Shema Yisrael," but the Russian soldiers were under an order not to let anyone through. We, small children, ran up to the Russian soldiers and begged them to let through the victims. The Jews cried out "Long live Stalin," but it was in vain. Only when a doctor, a Pole from Sokal who dealt specially with refugee matters, approached the Bolshevik commandant, did he [manage to] pressure him into letting the Jews from Hrubieszów and Chełm across the border. They reported horrible things about how the Germans had treated them, how they were chased down the road, and [how the Germans] shot at everyone who was weaker and could not keep up. Even after crossing the border, eight people were shot, just for fun. The Germans had counted that 400 Jews were supposed to cross the border, and since there were 408, they shot 8 [of them]. The ones shot were young boys. The execution took place in front of everyone's eyes, also in front of the parents. Those arriving had swollen legs—they said that the Germans had forced them to stand in water for [many] long hours. One child said how terribly the Germans had tortured him. The Russian soldiers grabbed him into [their] arms out of pity, and I ran up and put a piece of chocolate in the child's mouth. Later, many refugees arrived in Sokal, and the locals did everything in their power to help them. The sick were given help, those half-frozen to death were rescued.

As the crowding was unbearable in Sokal, my parents left for Radziejów, in the Tarnopol voivodeship, after the holidays. My grandfather lived there, and we were very happy there. Suddenly, on 29 June 1940—it was a Saturday—Father, Mother, and I were sent to Siberia in an *etap* [prisoner transport]. When we were arrested, we didn't know we would be deported. My father had not taken Soviet citizenship. [My] aunt, who had a Russian passport, stayed behind. NKVD agents carried out a search in our apartment, saying they were looking for weapons. We lived in a local authority house that had been given for use by refugees. We were told to pack some undergarments and bedsheets and put [them] on a cart. On [that] cart, we reached the train station, and there we understood what they were going to do with us. Around fifty train cars filled up with people were standing at the station. We were loaded into a car where there were fifty people. It was horribly hot and crowded. We were lying on the floor. Two days later, we arrived in Zdołbunów and had been given nothing to eat during that time. In Zdołbunów, we were moved to a smaller car in which we spent six weeks, until we arrived in Siberia. The station in Siberia was called Assina [Asino]. From that station, we were deported further. We traveled for two days and nights on the river, overgrown with a huge forest on both sides. The place of exile was called Nikaniejew.[308] Many Russian exiles lived there. When we arrived, they were moved to another place, and the empty barracks were given to us. The forest where Father worked was many kilometers away from the place we were staying. We were fed skimpily and couldn't sleep at night because of mosquitos. Since there were no strict controls around our

308. This place has not been located.

barracks, we escaped to the neighboring village, Semenovka, where there were a few wooden huts. There Father worked in the fields, and we lived off what he earned, that is, three hundred rubles per month, and off the remains of the cash we had brought from home. It was possible to get peas once a week in the cooperative. There was little bread [and] we all went hungry.

One time, the exiles revolted. It was at the funeral of a woman, a Jewess, who was killed by a lightning strike. All the exiles turned up for the funeral. Rabbi Frenkel from Kraków, also an exile, said that we should vow, over the grave of the deceased, that no one would turn up for work. The next day, indeed, no one went to work—people packed their belongings into bundles and intended to run away wherever their feet would take them. But in the afternoon, an NKVD unit arrived, called in from Novosibirsk. They shot into the air, arrested three leaders of the rebellion, and from that time on, the situation of the exiles became even worse. All of a sudden, an order came for some of the refugees to be moved to the Ural region. Again, we struggled along for three weeks in an *etap*, until we arrived at some station in the Sverdlovsk district. There were 360 Jews in our group. My father was hired to work as a carpenter in a big factory. The work was very difficult [and] they fed [us] little. Luckily for us, [my] grandfather in Tarnopol kept sending us products and food. On Yom Kippur the Jews asked to be excused from work, [but] the warden replied that anyone who rebelled would be sent back to Siberia. My father worked on Yom Kippur, along with other Jews. At night, after work, prayers were recited in our home. A few Jews had prayer books with them, and the service could be performed this way.

We spent a year and a half in the Ural, until the announcement of the Amnesty for Polish citizens. After the announcement of the Amnesty, we were taken to Bukhara and stayed in a field there, under the open sky, for two weeks, until Father found some hole [for us] to live in. All three of us fell ill with typhus. First Father and Mother [fell ill], then I lay in the apartment on my own for three days before the neighbors called for a doctor. We survived the typhus in one piece, but Father and Mother were very weak after the illness. Before leaving for the hospital, they left a gold watch and other valuables in our small room—someone stole everything while we were gone, and we were left in terrible destitution. I had nothing to feed [my] parents, weak after the illness. A Pole, an engineer, who lived next to us, helped us a lot. He waited in line, collected bread portions for us, sold a pair of shoes for Father so he could buy something to eat with it. Soon after this, my father, Szlome, died of dysentery at the age of forty-one; and a few weeks later, my mother, at the age of forty-two, died of the same illness. I sold their clothes so that I could bury them in the Jewish cemetery in Bukhara. I also put up a tombstone for them. I myself, as a full orphan, was taken into an orphanage. I stayed in Bukhara for four weeks. Then the children were taken to Ashgabat, on the Iranian border. There were three hundred Polish children and twenty Jewish ones. The Russians threatened to send all the children out to kolkhozes. Finally we were taken to Tehran. From there, the three hundred Polish children went to India, and the twenty Jewish ones to Palestine. When we were crossing the border, the Russians took away my gold [ring], a wedding ring—the only keepsake I had left from my parents.

Protocol 120

Testimony of **Meir Szpalter**, age fourteen, from Przeworsk. Came to Palestine via Russia and Tehran.

Germans Set Fire to the Przeworsk Synagogue

The Germans came in to Przeworsk exactly on the day of Rosh Hashanah [14 September 1939]. Before doing anything else, they set the grand synagogue on fire. The soldiers didn't want to do it alone. They rounded up a few old Jews, and threatening them with guns, ordered them to set fire to the synagogue. Three times they doused the building in gasoline and three times the fire went out. [The Germans] flew into a rage, took out the holy books and the Torah from the Ark of the Covenant and stamped on them with their feet. When the synagogue was set alight for the fourth time, a great flame engulfed the whole building. The German officers watched the burning synagogue, laughing, and took photos. The fire was so big that it spread to a few of the neighboring houses on Kazimierzowska Street. The beth hamidrash adjoining the synagogue was saved by a miracle. The Germans wanted very much to set the beth hamidrash on fire too, but the wind blew in the opposite direction and saved the building.

Expulsion of Jews from Przeworsk

On Monday, two days after Yom Kippur [25 September 1939], the Germans issued an order that the next day, Tuesday, at exactly ten o'clock, all Jews over the age of thirteen had to gather in the monastery courtyard. Not reporting to the assembly point was punishable by death. This order caused a huge panic among the Jews. [People] expected the worst. Rabbi Frenkel comforted the Jews, saying that the scriptures foretold the imminent coming of the Messiah. On Tuesday, the Jews gathered in the designated square. I was ten years old at the time, which is why I stayed home. My father and twenty-year-old brother, Efraim, went and had not returned by the evening. Mother was very worried. Women and children from town went in search of the men. But the Germans chased us away from the areas around the monastery and beat [us] mercilessly. Not until evening did Father and Brother return home, all bloodied. They told us about the horrendous things that had taken place in the courtyard.

Everyone was ordered to stand in a row. Then, the German chief called out: "Where is the rabbi?" The rabbi had hidden somewhere in a basement [and] the Germans threatened to kill a few Jews if the rabbi didn't turn up. Some shoemaker ran to look for the rabbi. The rabbi, crying on the way, arrived in the square. The Germans completely lost their mind at his sight. They tore hair out of his beard and beat [him] so long that he lost consciousness. They beat all the Jews with tree branches. Father said that he was ordered to walk on all fours, crawl on his stomach, etc. [They called it] exercising the Jews. The elderly who could not manage the exercises were beaten the worst. When everyone was beaten until bloody, the German soldiers walked through the rows, and holding out [their] iron helmets, ordered [the Jews] to throw in watches, purses, fountain pens, and cash that they had on them. Then everyone was placed into rows once again, and an officer read out an order in German and in Polish that the next day, 27 September, [by] nine in the morning, not a single Jew could remain in Przeworsk; they all had to cross to the Russian side. It's hard to describe what happened in the town that night. [People] packed in a hurry, everyone ran in search of a cart and a driver they knew. [People] gave the peasants the furnishings of [their] entire apartments in exchange for a cart ride. Our neighbor, a peasant, collected all the things from [our] home but did not turn up at the agreed-upon time and we had to go on foot. My mother was with child at the time and it was very difficult for her to walk. [People] left town in tears. The sick also had to be taken. On the way, we met many German soldiers who mocked us and unharnessed the horses from the carts. Everyone had to go on foot to the San River, fifteen kilometers away. No one had the strength to carry bundles with sheets with them [so] things were left behind on the way. We came upon a miracle. We spotted a peasant with an empty cart, and when Father started asking him to take pity on Mama, like an angel from heaven he took us with him. If it weren't for him, Mama would have dropped dead on the way. The peasant took Mama and a few sick Jews and drove them all the way. Near Jarosław, [the Germans] stopped the cart, took the whip from the peasant, and started beating the horse with it.

With the Bolsheviks

The huge bridge that led across the San River had been destroyed during a bombardment. The Germans had built a small wooden bridge. The San was the border between the occupations. We crossed the wooden bridge. A group of Russian soldiers walked with us. One of them, a Jew, called to Father in Jewish: "The Red Messiah has come." It was easier to get a cart on the other side of the river, and on Wednesday evening, we arrived in the town of Krakowiec, where a distant relative of ours lived. The whole town had burned down. From some small house, a light seeped out through a crack. Father knocked. A Jew opened the door and allowed us into the apartment. He said a holiday greeting to us, and Father remembered that it was the first day of the holidays. That Jew welcomed us exceptionally warmly. He took Father to the attic, told [him] to take as many potatoes as [he] wished, [and] also gave us other food products. We stayed in the small town a whole week. As we had many relatives in Przemyśl, Father decided to go there. Outside the city, Russian soldiers stopped us [and] said that refugees were living on the streets [in the city], which is why they couldn't let any more out-of-towners in. My sister Rachela smuggled herself into the city to let [our] cousin know that we were nearby. Thanks to her cunning, she managed to reach us and smuggle us into the city [too]. Father showed a platform ticket and told the authorities that our whole family, made up of six people, had to leave on a train departing from Przemyśl.

Through Przemyśl

In Przemyśl, we heard about the horrific fate that six hundred Jews had met before the Germans left the city. I went to the Przemyśl cemetery myself and saw the graves of the victims. The Germans had organized a manhunt in Franciszkańska Street in Przemyśl and shot dead six hundred Jews [they had] captured in a small forest outside the city. They used machine guns [and] everyone was buried [in that place]. When the Russians came, the Jewish council successfully implored the Bolsheviks to allow an exhumation of the bodies and their burial in the Jewish cemetery. Relatives and family identified the dead through clothes and items they found in their pockets. Everyone was buried separately—only the unidentified, the headless, were buried in a communal grave. The graves of the murdered were in the honorary part of the cemetery. From among the surnames on the tombstones I remember the surname of Doctor Tirkel, a well-known surgeon who had operated on my older brother. It was said that among those killed was the director of the Jewish hospital in Przemyśl. We lived in Przemyśl for a whole year. After three months,

Mama gave birth to a girl. We struggled a lot [living] in one room. All of a sudden, [people] in town started talking about searches and deportations. An NKVD agent, a Jew, came to us and asked about our passports. We had given our documents to the bureau because we were waiting to be issued Russian passports. Only Father didn't want to change [his] passport. A few days later, in the nighttime, NKVD-ers turned up at our [place] with that same Jewish official, who no longer wanted to speak to us in Jewish. Everyone was taken to the train station. There we found out that we had been sentenced to deportation. A Jew [named] Bromberg, a brush maker, was brought to the same train. He lost his mind in the station. We learned later that he had died.

In Exile

Our train got to Siberia particularly fast, in eighteen days. We found out during the journey that Father's brother, Meir Szpalter, and his son, fifteen-year-old Motel, were in the last car. They both lived in a village outside Przemyśl. We found each other at the station of Czermaszniki[309] in the Novosibirsk district. In exile Father worked hard in a railroad tie factory and earned [very] little. If it weren't for the parcels we received from Przemyśl, we would have starved to death. One day Father was late for work and was punished with four months of jail [time]. Mother fell ill during that time, and her little daughter caught diphtheria. However, we all survived Siberia. We fared a lot worse when we went from the deportation place to Samarkand on the basis of the Amnesty. We were all starving, while Father ran around markets all day looking for work. With no other choice, he took to trading sweets, and [when] caught once, he was punished with jail time for speculation. Since we were at risk of death from starvation, Mother, along with the five children, signed up to go to a kolkhoz. We stayed for some time in the Mołotow kolkhoz. There were nine of us Jewish families, one Polish one, and the rest of the camp members were Uzbeks. At first we received half a kilo of bread per day, and then came long days of fasting. The Uzbeks themselves were in a dire situation. We worked hard in the fields and even I, a twelve-year-old boy at the time, had my hands wounded and swollen from picking cotton. Later, we were moved to another kolkhoz, [called] Lenin. It was even worse there. Twenty-five people

309. Correct name: Cheremshanka [original Polish correction: Czeremszanka].

lived in a small room. We managed to get a separate wooden shack. It was a real good fortune because those twenty-five people were ill with typhus. Even though the epidemic was serious, there was no help [available]. Only 50 percent of people survived. From the Rotman family, made up of seven people, four died of typhus. The Polish family all died. When we were hungry, we were advised to eat grass that Mother cooked. There wasn't even [any] salt to go with it. Mother made cutlets from grass. We swelled up from this food. My legs were swollen. When the news arrived about the formation of the Polish army, my older brother, along with [our] uncle, went to Samarkand. They didn't want to admit them into the army. [Our] uncle was distraught and died from hunger. His son also died after him. Our situation in the kolkhoz was becoming worse and worse. Mama fell ill with dysentery, along with [my] older sister—they were taken to a hospital. I missed Mother and spent entire days in the hospital courtyard. At night, I would sneak into the hospital and sleep on the floor there. One [female] doctor found me there, took care of me, and started trying to get the Polish delegation to send me out of Russia. When I was leaving Russia, Father was in a hospital, sentenced to six years for speculation. The last time I saw him [was] in the street, under convoy, on the way to prison. He was unshaven and ragged. One day, he sent a message scratched out on a metal spoon: "Help me, I'm starving." He died of starvation. In March 1943, in Palestine, I received a letter from Mother [telling me] to say Kaddish for Father.

Protocol 121

Testimony of **Zeew Frenkel**, age fourteen, son of Rabbi Menasze and Miriam, from Leżajsk. Arrived in Palestine on 28 August 1943 from Russia, via Tehran.

My grandfather, Jecheskiel Landau, was the district rabbi in Leżajsk. As he was very old and could not perform the duties of his office, my father, his son-in-law, stood in for him, so that in fact, my father was the local rabbi. Our family was made up of five people, including three children, of whom I was the eldest. My siblings stayed with [our] parents in Russia. The Germans bombed the town before entering, there was a lot of damage [and] many casualties. Three days before Rosh Hashanah, on 11 September 1939, the Germans entered Leżajsk and immediately started [going about] their business of tormenting the Jews. [Jews] were rounded up for work, had their beards ripped out along with [parts of] their faces, and lived in constant fear. On the first day, the Germans set the synagogue [and] the beth hamidrash on fire. They also wanted to burn down the other synagogue, but it was located in between houses where Christians lived, so they were afraid that the fire would spread to the neighboring buildings. The work [done] by the Jews caught in the street consisted of cleaning the army barracks, washing floors, [and] cleaning apartments, and the German supervisors guarded [them], whips in hand, [and were] generous with the beatings. Jews also had to clean tanks covered with dust and mud. After two weeks, an order came out [stating] that all Jews had to leave town within one day and cross to the other side of the border, where the Russians were. My father placed us on a cart, for which he paid lots of money, and taking the essentials with us, we set off on our way. After a day's travel we stopped in the village of Charlupka. We met three Jewish families there. We settled with them because we were welcomed very well, and we stayed until after the holidays. On the last day of the holidays, we learned that the Russians were leaving town and anyone who wanted to could go with them. We went to Sieniawa. In Sieniawa we came upon thousands of Jewish refugees and couldn't find a place for the night. It was difficult to get bread and other products. Father decided to carry on ahead.

After two weeks' stay in Sieniawa, Father set off to look for a place where we could settle down. He stopped in the town of Sterwie,[310] near Brody, where some relatives and acquaintances of ours lived, [and they] took care of us. They found a furnished apartment for us; Father returned for us, and we moved to that town. Father organized religious services in our apartment. During the day, older children would come, and behind closed windows, Father taught them [from] the holy books. In the evening, older citizens came and studied the books with Father. The NKVD found out about these activities [and] they started persecuting Father. Every day at dawn he was called in for interrogations, warned to stop religious practices, which were forbidden in the Soviet territories, threatened with Siberia. After each interrogation, Mama cried and asked Father to stop the communal prayers and study. Father wouldn't hear of it and continued to carry out his calling, only being more careful. Small groups came every day, a guard stood outside, and Father did not give up teaching for a single moment. His situation was getting worse. He was being watched at every step. People were afraid of him and avoided him in the street. One day, the NKVD summoned Father and Mother and told them that because they thought Father's activities harmful, they were giving them a choice: a Russian passport and a move two hundred kilometers into Russia, or a return to the Germans.

In Exile

A week later, a group of NKVD-ers knocked on our door. We were told to pack [our] belongings, counting one hundred kilos per person. We were taken to the station on a cart, [and] there, loaded into a freight car, forty-five people to one. The cars were sealed so one could almost suffocate. After setting off, we received four hundred grams of bread per day, as well as soup, which we didn't eat because it was *treif*.

The first station, Równe, was besieged by thousands of people. Our train was connected up to another train, and the huge transport set off. In Kiev, we were allowed to get off at the station and take [some] hot water. We were watched so that we wouldn't communicate with the local Jews, who had brought food

310. This place has not been located.

for us to the station. We stopped in Assina [Asino]. We got off the freight car [and] were sent around to *posiołki* located in the taiga. In one of the *posiołki*, we were accommodated in a Russki[311] house and allowed to rest for two weeks there before we started work. The mosquitos and bedbugs would not leave us in peace. The next day, all of our faces were hurt and swollen, and we had to sleep in nets. The work in the forest consisted of sawing wood, loading up wagons, [and] digging up tree stumps. No one worked in our family. Father was considered an invalid, Mother looked after the three children. We lived off the parcels that our relatives sent us.

Rebellion in the Camp

After four months of work, everyone was so deathly exhausted that they could barely stand up. People would die from exhaustion and illnesses every day. After a day's hard work, the mosquitos would not let us sleep. The workers decided to abandon the work and demand to be moved to a different place. One day, everyone put down [their] work tools and went to the river to go to Assina. The NKVD-ers, alarmed, ordered the exiles to go to work. The exiles threatened the agents with saws and axes. The NKVD-ers threatened to shoot them, and indeed, they shot into the air. "We'd rather die than live like this," people shouted, continuing to walk toward the river. Suddenly, an airplane appeared and dropped leaflets imploring everyone to return to work, promising that in the coming days, the deportees would be moved to another *posiołek*, where work conditions would be much better. These leaflets made an impression, and the refugees went back to work. On the third day, an investigation took place and a few Jews were arrested [and] sent to Assina. That same day, a lightning [strike] killed a woman in the forest. During the funeral, all the deportees vowed over [her] grave not to return to work. No one worked in the *posiołek* for two days. The authorities didn't intervene. The days ahead loomed like a threat. On the third day, an order arrived moving us to another *posiołek*. We went back to Assina, and from there by train to Kamieńsk,[312] in the Sverdlovsk district. Life was indeed much better in the new *posiołek*. Workers received a kilo of bread per day, nonworkers—half a kilo. In the canteen, [you could] get

311. In the Polish transcript: *kacap*: a derogatory term for a Russian person (used as an adjective in the original).

312. Kamensk-Uralsky [original Polish correction: Kamieńsk Uralski].

nourishing soup for thirty kopecks. Mother went into town twice a week, sold our belongings and brought [back] products. The work in the sawmill in the forest was not as hard as in the old *posiołek*. After a few months, when an order arrived for us to leave the *posiołek*, no one wanted to move. [People] intervened with the NKVD but it was in vain. Russian exiles arrived, assigned for settlement here; [they] kicked us out of the barracks and beat up the stubborn ones. The third *posiołek* assigned for us to settle in was near Syktyvkar. They did not want to recognize Father's disability there and he had to go to work. But the work wasn't too difficult. I carried branches, and Father burned them. On Yom Kippur [12 October 1940], Father organized a communal prayer service in our barracks. Immediately NKVD-ers appeared and arrested Father. At the trial, Father was spared punishment, but had it written up that he was a religious criminal. Father's brother, Rabbi Joel Frenkel, lived with us in the *posiołek*. He too was proclaimed a religious criminal, and they both had to put up with persecutions from the NKVD all the time.

War and Amnesty

When the war broke out between Germany and Russia, and we found out that we could go where we wanted, it was in vain that the authorities tried to convince us to stay put. Unlike our uncle, we did not receive a permit to leave, because [my] father and uncle were considered religious criminals. The refugees went off [and] we were left on our own with a group of Russian exiles. Only four weeks later did the NKVD come to [see] us. An older official, [a] Jew, moved by Father's crying, promised that he would try and sort out the right documents for us, and indeed, a few days later our red papers, designed especially for criminals, and a permit to go to Revda, arrived. We waited for four days for the train in Assina,[313] and since the train only went 140 kilometers beyond Assina, we waited [another] two days at the next station before we set off. The journey was hard. There was no bread; our only meal[s] were potatoes bought in Assina, which we cooked at stations. In Revda, Father got a job in a brickyard. He cleaned the ashes out of kilns. He was often ill, but there was no choice—we didn't have a penny to our name. Later, Jews ran away from

313. From the flow of the testimony, it appears that, at the time of release, the author was in the region of Syktyvkar. He couldn't have been waiting for a train in Asino (in the region of Tomsk), located approximately 1,200 kilometers southeast [from there], on the way to Revda (close to Sverdlovsk).

Revda because an airplane factory was opened there, and [they were afraid of] German bombardment[s]. Father, weak and sick, decided to leave the city. From Revda we went to Sverdlovsk. We were not allowed into the city because refugees were forbidden to enter the big cities. A few days later, we went to Kermine. Until Father made the acquaintance of a few Bukharan Jews, who [managed to find] an apartment for him, we were roaming the streets. Finally, someone merciful gave us his room and settled in a stable himself.

Delegation at General Anders's

At that time, we found out that in addition to members of the military, distinguished rabbis could also leave Russia. A delegation of rabbis, with Rabbi Kaner from Kraków and [my] Father at its helm, went to Yangiyul, to General Anders. The general promised to grant the rabbis' request. After returning from Yangiyul, Father fell ill with typhus and couldn't take part in the preparation of the list of rabbis that was sent by Rabbi Kaner. The plan to send the rabbis [out of Russia] didn't work. Only some [of them] left Russia, individually. Among them was my uncle Rabbi Joel Frenkiel and the brothers Halberstadt. Others stayed in Russia. When a Polish children's center was opened in Kermine, Father made efforts to have the three of us admitted there. I stayed in the center for three months. When the list of children to be sent out of Russia was being prepared, an order came [stating] that only ten Jewish children would go. The Jewish director of the children's center intervened, in vain, to increase the number of children. At the last minute, lots were drawn [to decide] who would go. I drew one, [but] ninety Jewish children, among them my two brothers, stayed behind. I heard that the whole children's center was closed down. My brothers cried terribly when they heard that I was leaving and they were staying. I told the director that there was no way I would be separated from them. The director implored me to go; he eventually brought me an order from Father [telling me] to go. In that letter, Father wrote to me: "[Since] I had no luck going to Palestine, let my comfort be the fact that my son is there." I arrived from Kermine, via Ashgabat, the day after the transport left. I had to wait five months for another transport. We, ten children, were the only Jews in a big group of Christian children, who bullied us terribly. Finally we left for Persia, where I [was placed] in camp number 2, which was in the hands of the Jewish Agency.

Protocol 122

Testimony of **Frajda Celnikier**, age eleven, from Warsaw, 35 Niska, daughter of Mosze and Noemi. Arrived in Palestine from Russia via Tehran in February 1943.

My father was a hatter. There were three of us children, [all] girls: Marta, Tala, and me. Father didn't do too badly [and] we got by very well. During the bombing of Warsaw, we spent whole nights and days in the basement. We ate through all of the supplies that Father had bought earlier. The bread ran out, and just like our neighbors, we were all hungry. Father, unable to see us starving, went out into town to look for [work]. Mother would not let him go out, saying that it was better for the children to go hungry than to lose [their] father. But Father paid her no attention and always brought something to eat back from town. The worst was when the water ran out. One had to go to the Wisła to get [it]. Many of our neighbors who went out for water never returned again because they were killed by bombs. When a bomb fell into the sprat and cucumber cannery on our street, we all ran out, and ignoring the fire, dashed into the cannery, taking away cans of cucumbers, tomatoes, [and] sprats; and thanks to this, we survived the siege of Warsaw without hunger. The sauce from the preserves quenched our thirst. One day a bomb fell onto our house [and] ripped off a part of a wall. Luckily, the basement where we were staying was not destroyed. The Germans, straight after entering the capital, started rounding up Jews for [forced] work, to clean the city; [and people] were beaten, spat on, and had their beards ripped out during [this] work. German soldiers went around to Jewish apartments and stole what they could. The soldiers visited us too, [and] took the felt intended for hats, saying they would send it to their wives. Our situation worsened. Father didn't go out in the street because it was said that those captured for work were sent off to places unknown. We decided to leave the capital. This was in the middle of December.

When we had packed some [of our] belongings, we set off for Małkinia by train. At the station, the Germans separated the men from the women. Women and children were allowed into the carriage and the men were stopped. Mama and the other women didn't want to move. Children started crying terribly. The Germans threatened that, if we didn't calm down, they would shoot at us. We moved to the side, [staying] close by. I saw Father and the other Jewish men being led into some house. Immediately, screaming was heard, [which meant] our fathers were being beaten there, and we started crying terribly. Soon, Father returned, like the rest of the Jews, all bloodied. We went toward the border. We spent two days in the border zone. We waited for them to open the border. One day, some Jew ran up [to us] and said that the border was open. We started running, racing ahead like mad people until we made it across the border. The Russians were shooting into the air but that didn't frighten us. We made it to a train station and went to Białystok from there. In Białystok, we couldn't find a place to spend the night. We lived on the street for a few days. Father, seeing that he would not manage, went to Grodno. In Grodno there were many refugees, and until Father [managed to] find a room, we roamed the streets for a few days. Father took up trading; he traveled from town to town and we fared all right. Later the Bolsheviks threatened [people with] arrest, and it was no longer possible to trade. The lack of bread was noticeable in the city. Father took a Soviet passport for the whole family for three months. After three months, when it wasn't possible to earn anything anymore and the whole family was starving, Father registered to return to Warsaw.

In Exile

A few weeks later, on a Friday evening, armed NKVD-ers arrived at our apartment, told us to pack [our] belongings and said that we were going to Warsaw. At the station, we were loaded into freight cars, eighty people in each, and the doors were sealed. After twenty-four hours, during which we weren't given anything to eat and drink, the train started. Everyone rejoiced, convinced that they were going home. Mother said that although things were bad with the Germans, they were even worse with the Russians. Only after a few days did we understand that they were sending us to Siberia. Crying broke out; we children banged our fists on the door but it was in vain. We traveled for a whole month. Every day, they gave [everyone] a piece of bread, and at night we got soup. We were not allowed out of the car. We literally lay on top of another. The stuffiness was horrible, people fainted and only regained consciousness a few hours later as there was no water.

After a month, we arrived in Arkhangelsk. There, we were split into groups and taken to Kubasza,[314] where there was a *posiołek* called Berezovsk. At first Father and Mother worked sawing wood. Then Mother became weak and they let her chop the wood. We got four hundred grams of bread each per day, and the workers six hundred grams. Soup in the canteen cost sixty kopecks, but none of us could afford it. Constantly hungry, we went to the forest to [pick] berries with other children. The forest was wild and thick. We held each other's hands so we wouldn't get lost. Thanks to these berries, we weren't hungry like before. One time a tree fell on top of Father, who was only saved from death by a miracle. Many exiled Russians died in such accidents. The Russian exiles teased us, [saying] that we would never return to our homes and that we would all die here. Father's legs swelled and [his] fingers got frostbitten from working in the forest. But the warden didn't want to release him from work and threatened to send him to jail. Many people were sent to jail for being late for work, and we never heard from them again. In our *posiołek* there lived a pious Jew who prayed every day and didn't want to work on Saturday. He had a wife and seven children. The warden arrested him on a Saturday and a search was carried out in his barracks. All of [his] belongings and a gold ring were taken. The wife and the seven children who stayed behind were starving, because the warden didn't give them bread. One child died from hunger. If it weren't for the fact that we brought them a few glassfuls of berries and some mushrooms, the whole family would have perished from starvation.

War and Amnesty

After a year's stay in the *posiołek*, Father returned from work and told [us] about the outbreak of the [German-Soviet] war, and about an assembly where the warden had called on the exiles to work more energetically, threatening harsh punishment for not fulfilling quotas. Even we children were no longer allowed to go to the forest but were forced to work instead. Suddenly, we heard the news about the Amnesty and set off for Velsk. We lived outside the city, close to the river. One day, Father left the house and never returned again. Mama started to look for him and found out that Father had fallen into the

314. Likely refers to the town of Kanash [original Polish correction: Kanosza].

river, was caught by a current and drowned. In vain did the people standing by the water try to save him. Mother couldn't manage on her own; she cried for entire days. We cried with her. We didn't leave the house; we were afraid of getting close to the river that had taken our father away. We were starving terribly until Mother, seeing no other choice, went to Samarkand with us. In Samarkand, you [had to] step over people [lying] in the streets. It was impossible to get bread, [and] many refugees died in the street. We decided to go to a kolkhoz. We were starving in the Uzbek kolkhoz, too. For hard work in the fields, we received a bit of grain mixed with watermelon seeds. [We] would grind it between two stones. Mother baked cakes from that flour. They didn't want to keep us longer than one week. The Uzbeks kicked us out, saying that they had nothing to eat themselves. We went back to Samarkand, where Mother fell ill with heart [problems] and couldn't move. We ran from house to house, begging for Mother to be taken in. We got to an seniors' home and cried for so long that one of the managers took pity and took Mother in. We were left alone in a strange city and wandered the streets. We went to a Polish orphanage and begged until they took us in. We lived there for half a year. The children teased us terribly, but the teacher was very good and wouldn't let us be harmed. I didn't see Mama [even] once. We couldn't leave the home when they told us that we were leaving Russia. After six months, we set off for Krasnovodsk and from there, via Pahlevi, to Tehran. I lived in Tehran for eight months and then, along with [my] two sisters, went to Palestine.

Protocol 123

Testimony of fourteen-year-old **Józef Wajdenfeld** from Bielsko. Arrived in Palestine via Tehran in the year of 1943.

Before the war, we lived in Bielsko in Górny Śląsk [Upper Silesia]. My father, Jakob Wajdenfeld, was the owner of a large textile factory. Two days before the outbreak of the war, all the Jews left Bielsko [which was] located by the German border. Father, Mother, myself, and [my] older sister went to Grzymałów, [in the] Skałat district [county] where my grandfather lived, [my] father's father [and] a well-known rabbi. The Germans did not come there. We spent a few difficult days in that town. The Polish army had left, and the Russians hadn't arrived yet. A gang of Ukrainians took advantage of these two days without anyone in charge [and] started stealing the possessions of the Jewish inhabitants of the town. They beat Jews, attacked [them] in the street, and [people] were afraid to leave [their] apartments. There was a fear that the Ukrainian peasants from the neighboring villages might organize a huge raid on the town. Luckily, two Polish policemen were found who kept order. When the Ukrainians started stealing at night, the policemen shot dead two of the thieves. This scared off the rest, and [things] calmed down a little in town. We lived like this in this town, calmly, until deportation.

On Saturday, 29 June 1940, our family was arrested and sent off, like criminals, to Siberia. We traveled by rail for 14,000 kilometers. We didn't leave the carriage for six weeks, as we had been sent to one of the wildest and emptiest places in Siberia. Our labor camp was called Posiołek Internacjonalny [International Posiołek], because many Ukrainians, Jews, and Poles lived there. Our *posiołek* was located two thousand kilometers from Vladivostok: in Russia, [that's pretty much] the same as going from the center of Białystok to just outside it. It is difficult to imagine what we, innocent exiled Poles and Jews, had to suffer through. In that district, the winter lasts ten months and the freezing temperatures reach −40°C [−40°F]. Two months, July and August, are considered summer months. It is only possible to get to our camp during those two months, as there is no train nearby. We traveled for five hundred kilometers on a truck. The camp warden, an exiled Russian, said to my father as soon as [we] arrived: "If you get used to life here then that's good; if not—you won't last long." The warden said that no one gets released from his camp, that there was no way of returning to the world from there. Father worked sawing wood in the forest. The route to work was six to eight kilometers. The day was very short—one worked from nine in the morning until four in the afternoon because after that it was dark. People returned from work in the dark, and that walk was the worst. During a frost, the workers had their hands, feet, ears, and noses frostbitten. There were instances where frozen body parts had to be amputated. A young Russian doctor worked in that district and she performed operations.

My father was very pious. There was a canteen in the labor camp, but Father did not want to use it because the food was *treif*. We had to eat only the dry bread we received, half a kilo per person. Mama bought potatoes with the money she earned by working in the fields. I also worked. I got two rubles for a day's work. Despite this, we were always hungry, and it was only thanks to parcels that Grandpa sent us that we survived the harsh days of our ordeal. One time Grandpa sent us grease and Mama cried with joy [because] she had something to enrich soup with. Father organized communal Saturday prayers in one barracks. It lasted for [only] a short time, however, because everyone had to go to work. One time, on Rosh Hashanah [3–4 October 1940], everyone turned up for the communal prayer. Among the deportees there was a cantor [synagogue singer], who sang so beautifully that the goys [non-Jews] from other barracks came running. The warden found out about this. He burst into the barracks exactly when the most solemn part of the service was taking place. Furious, he stopped the prayers and chased the Jews away. He was angry [to see] small children taking part in the prayers. He grabbed me by the arm and shouted [at me] not to dare pray anymore. "None of you will get out of here alive anyway," he screamed, "don't waste time on prayers." Despite this, the Jews were not frightened, and on Yom Kippur [12 October 1940] no one went to work. The warden flew into a rage and threatened punishment but did not see the threat through. Only four Jews, two women and two youths, chose not to stay home on Yom Kippur. It was said later that great misfortune befell those four. One of the youths was killed during work; one of the women had her hand frostbitten and it had to be amputated. And [the other] two who had worked on Yom Kippur were punished as saboteurs and deported to a place in Siberia [even] further out.

Father fell ill as a result of the freezing temperatures and couldn't work. He was often released from work. My sister developed a heart problem and was very weak. To this day I can't understand how I was able to stand the frost. We slept in big wooden barracks, and all night long, a designated person added wood to the huge furnace. Mother wrapped me up [any] way she could; I slept in [my] clothes, wrapped up in rags. When I woke up, I had to break piece[s] of ice off my ears. Finally, the news about the Amnesty arrived, [and] it seemed to us as if God himself had sent that message. The warden walked around, embarrassed. It seemed to us that we were coming back to life. We were taken away in a transport, and after five weeks, arrived in Samarkand. It turned out that our situation [there] was worse than in the camp. We lay in a field, in the snow, outside the train station [because] we had no place to stay the night. Eventually Father found a clay hut for which we paid an Uzbek man a hundred rubles per month. There were rush mats on the floor—they were our beds.

It was even worse with food. People stood in line [to get] four hundred grams of bread. The lines were long; we waited whole days and nights for that awful, claylike bread. The Uzbeks kicked us out of the lines, insulting Jews. After a few months, Father died from hunger. Mama demanded that I be admitted to an orphanage, with which I came to Tehran. Father's brother was a famous gaon[315] in Poland, his name is Berisz Wajdenfeld. He was deported to the Ural, and from there moved to Bukhara, where he is to this day. Father's second brother was a rabbi in Biała; he escaped to the Bolsheviks and died from exhaustion.

---

315. [Eminent rabbi.] See the glossary.

Protocol 124

Testimony of fifteen-year-old **Saul Gliksberg**, from Różan. Arrived in Palestine from Russia via Tehran in September 1943.

Our town, Różan, on the Narew River close to the Prussian border, suffered through a lot during the German-Polish war. This was because the Poles had prepared a powerful defense outpost in our town, and on the first day of the war, an order arrived for the civilian population to leave town. My parents, along with other Jews, moved to the neighboring town, Długosiodło, where a few thousand Jews from other border towns had already gathered. We left all of our property in Różan. My father was a very rich man; he worked for many years as a representative for the whole district for the Galicja oil company. We asked around about what was happening in our town and found out that the battle with the Germans had lasted for three days and nights. The Germans began the attack on 30 August[316] and only managed to take over the town on 4 [September]. The whole town lay in ruins. Homes were bombed or burned down. Going back home was out of the question. Immediately after entering Długosiodło, the Germans shot dead a Jew they came upon in the street. I don't remember his surname; I only know that he was the brother-in-law of our friend from Różan, Paskowicz. We immediately understood what fate awaited Jews, as thousands of Jews who had been expelled from Wyszków started to flow into Długosiodło. This was the first expulsion of Jews committed by the Germans in the Polish territory. The Jews came running into town almost naked. German soldiers had rushed the Jews across the river, and [the Jews] barely avoided death. In Długosiodło, that tiny and poor town, there was no room for refugees, although the local residents did everything to fit in the unfortunate exiles. A people's kitchen was set up, but there wasn't enough money for anything. On the Day of Atonement [Yom Kippur; 23 September 1939] there were so few German soldiers in our town [that] no one prevented Jews from holding communal prayers. People rarely went out into the street. All of a sudden, at twelve at night, a truck carrying storm troops[317] arrived in the main square, [and] their officer

316. The military operations began on 1 September 1939.

317. The witness most likely means SS units.

gave an order for all Jews to leave town by two o'clock at night. "Let the Jews make their way to their friends on the [other] side of the river," said the officer. He pointed at the Russian side as he [said it]. [Everyone] knew that there was no other choice, and [people] started packing belongings into bundles to bring what they could with them. Meanwhile, the storm troops went around to the apartments, looking for what they could steal. A great panic broke out. Mother had been preparing treats for the end of Yom Kippur, and left saucepans [on the stove] in the kitchen. At two o'clock at night, whistles and shots could be heard. All the Jews ran out into the street. Refugees from other towns were mixing with the people of Długosiodło. The storm troopers chased people into the forest, onto the road leading to the town of Zambrów, which belonged to the Russians. In the forest, people breathed a sigh of relief and checked that all the children were there. Father checked—there were seven of us, including him. Meanwhile, people remembered that it was the night of Yom Kippur. I will never forget how Father, along with other observant [Jews], started reciting a prayer in the middle of the forest, and then dancing and singing to the rhythm of religious melodies.

We stayed in Zambrów for a short time [and] then went to Białystok. Father had some money with him that was enough to live on. It was impossible to find an apartment; we lived in a wooden barracks [belonging to] a summer camp outside town. Many Jews lived in those [summer] camps, and when the winter came, we almost froze [to death]. In the summer, when the situation got a bit better, the Bolsheviks issued an order for all refugees to move one hundred kilometers away from the border zone. Father remembered that we had a relative in Iwie, a town near Lida, and we went there. We came upon masses of refugees in town, [but] despite this, we didn't fare badly. The local Jews helped the refugees however they could. We would stand in line for bread and then the local Jews would allow the refugees through before them. We were given clothing, food, and work. If someone was sick, they received medical help. We stayed in Iwie for a few months, until the deportation.

In Iwie, as in other places, all refugees were arrested on 29 June 1940. Our family was deported to Arkhangelsk; there were six of us children because [my] sister was in a town outside Pińsk. She was lucky not to be deported and was able to help us [when we were] in exile. We found ourselves in Arkhangelsk after a three-week-long journey. When we arrived there, everyone had to work. I was twelve years old then and my work was peeling the bark off trees and packing it together into bundles. Old Russkis make winter shoes out of the bark. A pair of shoes and slippers like that cost three rubles. They were worn over foot wraps, otherwise they would hurt your feet, but there were no other shoes, and a pair of shoes like that stopped your feet from getting frostbitten in freezing temperatures. My father worked sawing wood. Each worker had to saw at least five cubic meters of wood per day, but there were Stakhanovites, working themselves to death, who could saw ten cubic meters. Every Stakhanovite received as a bonus from the warden a pair of padded trousers or a sweater, which was a valuable item. Even though there were six of us children working, we almost starved to death. [Our] sister helped us [by] sending food in parcels, and apart from that, my three brothers, after tilling a piece of land, harvested some potatoes for the wintertime. My brother[s] and I, fifteen-year-old Mosze and ten-year-old Josele, decided to cultivate a garden too. We dug up a piece of cleared forest and planted potatoes. It was not easy work. We had to pull out stumps and clear the earth of roots, and our hands bled during this work. We had barely finished [it when] we were given cucumber seedlings and potatoes from the cooperative to plant. Luckily, there were three of us to [do the] work, and soon we had our own potatoes. But they didn't last us long, only two weeks. After the announcement of the Amnesty, we went to Bukhara. To pay the rent for a small room, we sold the last rags off our backs. Father could not [stand to] watch us starve, and managed to get a permit from a Russian doctor acquaintance for the three weaker children to be admitted to a sanatorium. My two younger brothers and I were indeed sick.

We spent two months in the sanatorium. Then the Polish government started providing help to refugees and a Russian doctor managed to have us moved to a Polish orphanage. There were two hundred children in the orphanage, 160 Polish ones and 40 Jewish ones. Our care was poor. We were given little to eat, and those who wanted to would run into town to find some extra food for themselves. The Polish children went out into town in groups. They got into orchards and picked unripe fruit. Many children were sick. Awful epidemics spread around the orphanage. Around eighty children died within a few weeks—between four and five children would perish every day. Both of my brothers left for Tehran a year before I did. I was sick and had to stay in Russia, in an orphanage located close to the Persian border. Only in July 1943 did we arrive in Tehran, and I made it to Palestine in September. How great my joy was when I found my two brothers [there].

Protocol 126

Testimony of **Józef Bojmowicz**, age thirty-one, son of Benjamin and Jochwet, from Pomiechówek by Modlin. Arrived in Palestine via Tehran in June [July?] 1942.

Modlin was bombed in the first hours after the outbreak of war. The sound of bombs bursting reached our town, located near the Modlin Fortress. Pomiechówek itself was not bombed; only one bomb fell on the station by chance—others exploded in the neighboring fields. This lasted until lunchtime on 6 September [1939]. Suddenly, a rumor spread that the Germans were approaching. Almost all the residents readied themselves to escape.

Since we had a bakery, I had to stay in town to continue delivering bread to the few [people] who remained, also to the remaining policemen and officials.

On Friday 8 September, it was said that the Germans were already in Nasielsk, fourteen kilometers from us. The police started to run away. I was baking bread at the time—I left it in the oven, and without looking back, ran toward Warsaw. As it later turned out, all [these] messages had been spread by saboteurs to create confusion among the local people. The Germans were, at that time, sixty-five kilometers from our town. The road from Pomiechówek to Warsaw was full of refugees and civilians. Broken bridges, roads destroyed by bombs; on the way were tipped-over carts, cars, dead horses. Injured people were lying in ditches, moaning aloud. No one paid them any attention. Everyone was pushing one another and rushing to get to shelter in the capital, as still more airplane squadrons flew in, bombing the refugees on the roads. They descended very low and shot at civilians from machine guns. I dragged myself onward for two days. I finally made it to the capital on Sunday, at twelve o'clock. I made my way to 30 Świętokrzyska Street, where my parents were; they had left Pomiechówek before me. When I was approaching the house, an emergency siren sounded. A bomb had hit the very house my parents lived in. The house went up in flames. The residents attempted to save it. I helped in trying to put out the fire [and we] managed to extinguish it after two hours. My parents were afraid to stay in the destroyed house [so] we went to 2 Grzybowska [Street], where my uncle lived. A few hours later, another air raid took place. I ran to the shelter, [while my] parents stayed at home, in the first-floor apartment. A bomb fell into the house, destroyed the left side of it, killed a few people. After the raid I returned home—I did not recognize my relatives, they were black and red from the soot and the bricks, and completely out of it with fear. We wanted to go back to Świętokrzyska but could not make it across the street, since Królewska and Graniczna [Streets] were in flames. We continued walking in between the ruins and the flames until we found ourselves in the old apartment of the bombed-out house, where we lived throughout the siege of Warsaw.

After entering Warsaw, the Germans set up field kitchens and gave out soup to the famished people. Since I didn't look like a Jew, I joined the line, waiting for [my] soup ration. At first, they didn't differentiate between Jews and Poles. Later, German officers came, pulled all the Jews out of the lines and started beating them. I wasn't beaten. After that, Jews no longer benefited from German generosity. At home, the situation was worsening. Luckily I owned a bicycle, and I made trips on it outside the city to [get] food products, which I sold in the city [and] with which I supported our family of eight.

The situation in Warsaw deteriorated. Jews were captured for [forced] labor, beaten, harassed, mocked; they had merchandise taken from [their] shops [and] weren't allowed to stand in line for bread. The Germans took away my bicycle and I had to give up trading. With nothing to live on, I went to Siedlce by train on 8 October, from there to Drohiczyn, and at night, made it across the Bug River to the Soviet side. From Siemiatycze, where I found myself, I made my way to Białystok.

In Białystok

At first, I fared very badly in Białystok. I couldn't find a place to sleep and spent nights in a school building full of refugees. It was dirty and crowded there; lice were crawling over everyone [and it was so bad] that I preferred to sleep outside, and I left that refuge. I came upon two acquaintances in the street, Blakman and Fajnsztajn, who loaned me a few grosze. I took up trading. I found a box, placed a few pieces of soap, some thread, soda, [and] Lux[318] inside it, and earned a few rubles a day selling those. One day, I was arrested and taken to the police station, along with my tiny stall. My merchandise was

318. Laundry powder.

taken away and I was set free after being held for a few days. Seeing that I would not [be able to] live on trading, I decided to open a confectionery with a few friends, since I was a baker by trade and knew about making cookies. The business went well. We thought we would wait out the war here. I took part in the elections, voting for a candidate I knew nothing about. Later, when the passportization began, I didn't take a [Soviet] passport, but I didn't want to register to leave, either. I was generally of the mind that one should avoid any contact with the authorities.

In Exile

On Friday, 29 June 1940, at one o'clock at night, there was a knock on my door. Two NKVD-ers appeared [and] told me to get dressed, and since I was told that they were taking me for questioning at the [police] station, I didn't even bring a hat with me and left my apartment half-dressed. But instead of the police station, I was taken to the Beker preserve factory, which had been turned into a concentration camp.

There were a few thousand people in that camp. It was said that families would be released immediately but that turned out to be a lie. Food was not provided, and people were starved from Friday to Sunday. We were only allowed to drink the water from the taps located in the courtyard, and even that only twice a day.

At twelve on Sunday, we were given a bit of watery soup. Frantically, we threw ourselves at that small amount of warm food. Then we were asked who wanted to go home for [their] belongings. I reported with a few others, but instead of [being taken] home, we were driven to the NKVD, where we were taken for interrogation. They asked where I was from, how I had crossed the border, whether I was a party member, which [party], and whether I had taken active part in the war in the year 1920. I replied that I was seven at the time, to which the embarrassed official said nothing, and I was made to sign the [interrogation] protocol. I did not want to sign. They threatened me with grave consequences [so] I signed it.

I thought that they would let me go to [get my] things after the interrogation, but I was taken to an assembly point outside the city. I was questioned about everything once again, a body search was carried out, and I was placed in a group [of people]. We were taken to the rail station under convoy, loaded into freight cars, seventy people in each; the doors were sealed, and we were left without food again for twenty-four hours.

Through the cracks in the freight car, I saw new transports of people being brought in every hour. I spotted many of my friends and neighbors among them. No sooner would one group be placed in a carriage than another one would arrive. This lasted forty-eight hours. People fainted from thirst and lack of air; cries, screams, and wailing went up to the sky, but our guards were not moved [by the cries].

Only when the train had started, after a few hours' journey, was a bucket of water brought into each car. We threw ourselves at the water—there was only a little—like mad people. It was only enough to moisten [our] lips. The journey took two weeks. During the journey, we received a piece of bread in the day and a bowl of soup at night. If we demanded water, we were taken to a special penal carriage as punishment. We were stripped naked there—it was a punishment cell of sorts. It was cold at night; we moved closer to each other to warm ourselves up. This way, we got to Kotlas. We were taken to a hub where there were more than ten thousand deportees, among them Russians. The deportees bullied and robbed us, and beat us up if anyone wanted to tell on them. Eng. Szereszewski from Łódź, who wouldn't let [them] take his watch away, was beaten so badly that he had to be taken to the hospital.

After ten days' stay in that camp, we were taken to Istwum[319] on barges. The camp was located in the woods. We were put up in empty barracks and slept on the ground. We spent two days there. The bedbugs wouldn't leave us in peace. Then we were taken on trucks to a different hub, two hundred kilometers from the first one. It was located in a primeval forest. The group, made up of six hundred people—[all] Jews, with the exception of ten Poles—was accommodated in overcrowded barracks. Additional barracks had to [be] built. When the barracks were ready, sixty Russians arrived who had been sentenced to exile for counterrevolution. They were our brigade leaders.

We worked in the forest. The quota was seven cubic meters of wood to be cut down daily. We received half a kilo of bread per day and soup from a kettle—depending on the work we had done. Those who fulfilled 50 percent

319. Correct name: Ust-Vym [original Polish correction: Ustwym].

of the quota got soup from kettle number 1, which was the thinnest and least nutritious. Number 2 contained thicker soup; number 3—the best, and it was intended for those who fulfilled [their] quotas. Despite incredible effort, I could never fulfill the quota, or even achieve 50 percent of it. My bread rations were lowered to three hundred grams, and I received soup from the penal kettle—this was normally [just] hot water. During work, tragic accidents would happen. A falling tree killed a man named Nusbaum, from Łódź, and his companion and friend, Brajtman, had a heart attack as a result and died the following day. They were both buried together in a grave out in the field. Another time, a young man from Zgierz died; I don't remember his name. Another one from Zgierz, Telma, got dysentery [by] eating leaves from the forest and died. Out of the 600 Jews who arrived in the camp, 150 died from hunger, and 50 from other diseases. After some time, I fell ill with *cynga* [and] pieces of my body were coming off. I asked to be taken to the hospital, but it was in vain. Only when I made a scene in the administrative office did I manage to be sent to the hospital.

After a few weeks I was sent to the part [of the camp] for convalescents, who did lighter work. I cleared the roads of snow [and] gathered brushwood. For this work, I received three hundred grams of bread and the watery soup, [kettle] number 1.

War and Amnesty

The outbreak of the German-Russian war did not bring [any] respite for us. On the contrary, bread rations were decreased considerably, and the quota expectations increased. We worked fourteen hours a day. Only when the Amnesty was announced did the *posiołek* commandant change his attitude toward us. He asked us to stay and promised to improve our conditions. Naturally, no one listened to him. We made preparations for the journey. I was paid 220 rubles [owed for my work] and given train tickets for Tack.[320] On the way, we learned that Tack was overcrowded and went to Tashkent [instead]. We came upon a lot of refugees there. It was impossible to find a place for the night. I decided to go to a kolkhoz. I worked picking cotton. The quota was thirty

320. An incorrect name for the town of Totskoye [original Polish correction: Tockoje]. Appears as Tack or Tock in the testimonies.

kilos of cotton per day. For this, one received four hundred grams of flour daily. Since I couldn't feed myself with that, I would steal potatoes that the kolkhoz members had hidden from the authorities. When I was caught in this crime, I threatened the kolkhoz member that I would inform on him. He got [very] quiet. The peasants complained about hunger and the ruthlessness of the state that took everything away from them.

They didn't want to believe me when I told them how people lived in Poland, in the country and in cities.

Eventually I was kicked out of the kolkhoz. I returned to the city. I went to another kolkhoz, Kaganowicz, but was told that I wasn't needed. I went to Kermine. They didn't want to admit me to the army. I said I was a Christian. I said, in front of the commission, that my father's name was Stanisław and Mother's Agata [and] that I was of the Roman Catholic faith. But the doctor attested that I was a Jew. As a myopic, I was classified as category D. I was sent off to a hub to [get] clothes. I stayed there until March 1942 as a Christian, until everyone was sent to Persia. In Tehran I went through typhus, after which I was sent to Palestine, where I arrived on 18 July 1942.

Protocol 127

Testimony of **Arie-Lejb Klajncaler**, age fifteen, from Czarny Dunajec, Kraków voivodeship.

My father was the owner of a dairy in Czarny Dunajec. There were about one hundred Jewish families living in that town [and] they all made a good living. On Friday, 1 September 1939, at five in the morning, an acquaintance of ours burst into [the apartment], woke us up, and said that war had broken out and that he had seen German airplanes. A few hours later, shooting could be heard. We packed our belongings and hid them in the shelter. The Polish authorities issued an order to leave town and go to Nowy Targ. The train station was bombed so we had to go on foot to the town, fourteen kilometers away. There were evacuation trains in Nowy Targ, and we went to Lwów. The journey took three days; our train was bombed, but no one was killed. Our family, made up of seven people, decided to go to Podhorce, where we had relatives and where it was easier to get food. We stayed there for two weeks, until Rosh Hashanah [14 September 1939].

Then the Bolsheviks came. We spent ten months with [them]. At first, the Bolsheviks behaved decently but then the trouble began with the registration, and [there were] arrests. The whole family worked, trading. The other children and I helped [our] parents. We traded everything: manufactured goods, sugar, wine, [ethyl] alcohol, and we earned enough. The Bolsheviks asked us a few times if we wanted to return home or become Soviet citizens. We didn't want to stay in Russia. We wanted to wait out the war in a small town where things were relatively quiet. We avoided the registration because we didn't want to go back to the Germans.

Then one night—it was at one o'clock at night on a Friday—NKVD-ers knocked on our [door] and said that they were sending us to the Germans. We cried, [saying] that we wanted to stay there, but [it] was in vain. We were told to get dressed and bring one hundred kilos of belongings with us. The Russians didn't let Father bring [any] manufactures, only clothes. In the morning, we were taken to the train station and locked in a freight car. A policeman with a gun was watching us the whole time. Our journey took twelve days. We were given only enough food so we wouldn't die of hunger. Throughout the journey, we were not let out of the car; there was no toilet. We went to the toilet through a hole in the floor.

After twelve days' journey, we found ourselves in a thick forest. The train stopped in the Sverdlovsk district, at the Oszczepkowo[321] station, district 240. There were one thousand people in our transport, all Jews. On the first day, we were given unlimited food. [Our] surroundings were completely wild. Exiled Russians lived in the barracks, and they treated us well. We were allowed to rest for three days. On the third day, we were taken out to work, sawing wood and loading wagons. According to the law, [people between the ages of] sixteen [and] fifty-five had to work. I was twelve at the time but reported for work [anyway] because the earnings of the rest of the family and Father were not enough. We were paid very little [and] sold [our] belongings to make a living. We worked for eight hours. Only the "*gruzowszczycy*"[322] worked without a set time. The warden forced them to work mercilessly because he had to pay for empty wagons, for the waiting time. My father was a *gruzowszczyk* [and] things were very hard for him. A school was opened in the camp, and children were forced to attend a Soviet school. I wouldn't give up the Saturday rest [Sabbath observance] for anything. When I didn't go to school on Saturday, I was arrested. They said they wouldn't arrest Father because it would be a waste of a worker. Many others were also arrested for this offense. At school, only the Russian language was taught. The children received extra food. The Bolsheviks didn't allow communal prayers; everyone was supposed to pray on their own. The NKVD-ers issued a new order: they forbade the selling of old [personal] belongings. They said that we had to work more to earn more. Thus we had [say goodbye to] the eight-hour working day. We spent fourteen months in the labor camp.

After the announcement of the Amnesty, we were released and went to Tawica [Tavda], in the Sverdlovsk district. Father worked as a *gruzowszczyk*. On Yom Kippur [1 October 1941], he fasted and didn't work. I became a cart driver. I had a cart and two horses and drove the wardens [around]. My brother worked in a carpenter's workshop. The winter was hard [and] a few families decided to go to warmer places, to Tashkent. Father sold a gold watch to cover

321. Oshchepkovo. A town in the Sverdlovsk district.

322. From the Russian word *gruzchik*. See glossary.

the cost of the journey. We went toward the Bukhara area; the journey took five weeks. We almost froze to death in the train car. We paid huge amounts for food. Barely alive, we made it to Bukhara and found out there that the evacuation train for Iran had already left and that we had to carry on ahead. We came to Kyzyl-Tepe, which means Red Steppe in the Kyrgyz language. The whole family found jobs. Father became a *gruzowszczyk* again. We had a nice surprise there—we ran into Uncle Szymon, the brother of Mother's father. He was twenty-eight years old but looked like an old man.[323] His hands had been frostbitten. He had been sent to [the Autonomous Soviet Socialist Republic of] Komi for illegal border crossing. He was tortured terribly there, kept for hours in a punishment cell and watched by dogs and a soldier with a gun. He lived in a camp in the middle of the wild tundra. My uncle was a Stakhanovite in order to support himself but [now he] could barely stand up. He ate oil cakes all the time and had a bad stomach from it. We didn't get to enjoy [our] uncle for long. He fell ill with dysentery and died.

Father got typhus. He stayed in the hospital for three weeks. Then [my] mother, brother, sister, and I fell ill with typhus. One [of us] would leave the hospital and another would enter. Mother got dysentery after the typhus, lost weight, and died. Father also fell ill with dysentery. He didn't suffer long; [he] died a few days later. We became full orphans. We had sold all that we had to save [our] parents.

We went to a Polish children's center located twenty kilometers from where we lost [our] parents. Out of forty children, eight were chosen to be sent to Persia. Only full orphans were picked. All four of us were taken [together] so that we wouldn't lose one another. We were taken to Kazan,[324] twelve kilometers from Bukhara. We waited for a transport of fifty children in order to be sent to Ashgabat. Finally, we found ourselves in Tehran, in Persia. We spent six months there—the older children in tents, the younger ones in barracks. The children who came from Russia told us how they had seen small children throw themselves under the wheels of the train when they lost [their] last hope of being taken. In Tehran, many children were ill with typhoid fever. At

---

323. [There is a likely error here in either Szymon's age (twenty-eight) or his relationship to the witness (his great-uncle).]

324. Error on the part of the testimony's author: refers to Kagan, not Kazan in the European part of Russia.

first the Poles looked after us, and then we were sent teachers from the Jewish Agency[325] who prepared us for life in Palestine.

I want to add, too, that we learned about the Amnesty by chance. The warden of our camp in Oszczepkowo was a bad man, a Russian exile, [only] interested in having us work as much as possible so that he would be rewarded for it. He forbade us to listen to the radio, so we were cut off from the world. But we managed [to get around it]. We received parcels from Podhorce with flour, lard, and other things. Those items were wrapped in newspapers. From these newspapers we found out about the Sikorski pact. We showed it to the warden and asked to be released. Seven of us left Poland, [while] three died of hunger and diseases.

325. Jewish Agency: nongovernmental institution with a mandate from the League of Nations to represent Jews to the mandated powers in Palestine, the Great Britain government and the League of Nations. Currently active, working primarily organizing the aliyah to Israel.

Protocol 128

Testimony of **Icchak Rochman**, age twenty-two, from Warsaw, 15 Nalewki, son of Jakub. Arrived in Palestine via Russia in April 1942.

I was an activist for many years in a Zionist youth group, the workers' left wing. My father, a weaver, had for many years belonged to the Poale Zion party, and I had been raised in the spirit of my father's beliefs. I was in the capital during the bombing of Warsaw. When, at the time of the holiday of Rosh Hashanah [14–15 September 1939], the Nalewki district was bombed particularly violently, we moved to 52 Złota Street, where an acquaintance of Father's lived. After some time, [we] had to escape from Złota to Śliska Street, where we lived with an acquaintance, Perelman, until the arrival of the Germans in Warsaw. I hid in the house and tried to go out into the street as little as possible. The Jews were terribly disheartened—every day they had to contend with new restrictions.

We began to go hungry at home. My father had no job. We, the children, couldn't find any source of income. My little brother, Szulem, no longer able to stand our destitution, took a few zlotys from Father and took up street trading. He sold sweets and chocolates that he bought from our acquaintances. One day, when he was standing on Złota Street with his small sweets box hanging around his neck, he noticed that the streets had been closed and that the Germans were starting to lead all of the Jewish residents out of the houses. The SS were shooting the people coming out. One of the [bullets] flew toward my brother. Some Christian man grabbed [my] brother by the hand and dragged him into a stairwell, hid the box with the merchandise, and he himself told the boy to take cover on the fourth floor. When the boy heard the Germans climbing up the stairwell, he pretended to be walking out into the courtyard. However, one of the Germans recognized him as a street trader, and another one ran up and started pummeling the boy with a whip and his buttstock. The boy collapsed, bloodied. Then the Germans dragged the child under a tap, laughing, and released a stream of water onto him. They dragged him out into the street and put [him] in a line along with other Jews. [They] pulled the oldest Jews first from the line. They were bearded Jews, who were to walk at the front of the procession. When the procession paused at the corner of Złota and

Żelazna [Streets], all the Jews were ordered to stop, take their hats off, and sing "Hatikvah."[326] Then they were forced to sing the Polish national anthem. The officers stood at a distance and laughed at the desperate [people], and anyone who didn't sing loud [enough] was beaten mercilessly. Then they were rushed further on, and the same scene was repeated on each [street] corner, until they arrived at the corner of Twarda [Street]. The pavement of Twarda had been completely destroyed by bombs, and since it was during a rainy period, the Jews were ordered to run down the street. They ran at a fast pace, fell on the way, got up smeared with mud. The Germans wouldn't let them catch their breath, and watched the display as they walked. When everyone was smeared with mud, they were put into rows and taken to Grójecka Street, to a student residence. There they were told to wash the floors and the windows but weren't given [any] rags to clean with. They had to use their own clothes to do that. My brother, as the youngest of the group, was taken by some officer to his room. [The officer] ordered him to clean his boots and didn't give him a brush. My brother cleaned the boots with his jacket. He got a lunch for it from the officer. He couldn't finish the whole [meal] and wanted to give it to other Jews. The officer beat him for that and set him free. At the gate, a soldier on guard duty added a few more blows, and like this, the battered boy returned home. On 6 October, I was caught [and taken] to work in the sewers. I was taken to 37 Twarda. We carried out this dirty work under a barrage of blows and insults. In the middle of the work, we had to raise our hands and undergo a search. They were looking for weapons. Bearded Jews suffered particularly badly.

I Escape from Warsaw

I couldn't stand these persecutions anymore, and on 20 October, I escaped from Warsaw, going toward Małkinia. I stayed a few days in Małkinia and waited for the border to be opened. I crossed over to the Soviet side, to the village of Zaręby Kościelne. I arrived when they were preparing for the Belarussian [Belarusian] elections.[327] There was a public meeting taking place in the middle of the main square. A Belarussian man was speaking, heavily criticizing the former Polish authorities, accusing them of using terror in Bereza Kartuska

---

326. Hatikvah [Polish: Hatikwa]: the anthem of the Zionist movement. See glossary.

327. See the glossary: elections.

and so on. I had nowhere to sleep [so] I stayed the night in the synagogue and made my way to Białystok the next day.

In Białystok I slept in the train station, so overcrowded with refugees that one simply [had to] walk over those who were lying [on the floor]. I came up with a great idea and slept in empty freight cars. Usually when I woke up in the morning I would find myself at some strange station, from which I would return to Białystok. I took part in the elections. One day I prepared a place for myself in an empty carriage to spend the night, as always, and woke up in Brześć. I went into the city, where I saw a long line of young people registering to go to Russia. As I was exhausted by [my] roaming by then, I joined the line. I waited until four in the afternoon. When I had already given up on registering, an official appeared and asked if there was a trained leather tanner [in the line]. I said it was something I knew how to do. I was registered and told to wait for departure. I went to a club where there was a kitchen for refugees. Luckily I ran into an acquaintance [there] who worked in that kitchen. He hired me. I peeled potatoes [and] in return got a place to stay and food. I spent a few days there until, one day, someone came running and said that all those who were registered were to report to the station, where fifty train cars were waiting for them. The first cars were intended for families, the further ones for single people. We were given food, bread with kielbasa. At nine in the evening, we left Brześć in a good mood. We traveled through Pińsk, and at the border we saw a sign welcoming us with the words: "Greetings to the workers of Western Belorussia [Belarus]." We were moved to different cars, to a train traveling on wide tracks. A few Komsomol members appeared and took us from the station for a celebration. Music was played, a speech was made in our honor [and], after the party had finished, we returned to the train. Half of the transport was sent off, the half with me went to Homel. I saw many trains with Polish exiles on the way. They were in an awful situation: they were begging for bread, which they wanted to pay for, but no one would accept Polish money, so they were literally starving. I overheard a conversation between a Russian soldier and a Polish prisoner of war at one of the stations. The Russian soldier teased: "You had watches, but we had tanks."

In Homel, we were greeted with music, and when we disembarked from the train cars we were taken to a bathhouse, disinfected, and taken to a huge restaurant, where we were served a good lunch. The lunch consisted of several courses and everyone was still asked if they wanted to eat more. Then we were taken to the opera. The opera was decorated with posters printed especially in our honor, and before the performance, a Party commissar greeted us in Russian and Jewish. After the performance, readings took place—an excerpt from a novel by Wanda Wasilewska was read, among others. We were divided according to our skills. We were told that everyone would work in their trade, but we were all sent together for grunt work, to build railroad tracks, and lived in a village called the Sixth District. We lived in a large barracks, girls along with boys, and slept on bunks. After four days' rest, we were split into brigades and taken for work. The work was hard: we worked from morning until sundown, received a kilo of bread [per day], and twice a day, a bowl of watery soup. After a few days, people began to rebel. We had been deceived, as we had been assured that everyone would work in their trade. We weren't allowed to rest after work, and we were fed Communist propaganda. We weren't given warm clothing, so our hands and feet got frostbitten in the freezing temperatures. We demanded warm clothing, but everything ended with promises. We got fifty rubles for the first week. We were told that we had only fulfilled half of the quota. Then we earned 2.60 [rubles] daily.

We grew more dejected by the day; we stopped singing and started protesting—quietly, of course, as there were informants working among us. A few of those more seriously suspected of rebellion were led out of the barracks one night and taken away. We were told that they'd been moved to a different place of work. Unfortunately, it was prison. After a few weeks, the temperatures fell further, and we were still wearing light clothing. This time we started to rebel openly. Realizing that no promises would be fulfilled, I decided one day to go to the city. I got a job at an *artel* where buttons and dominoes were manufactured. In Russia, those who can't prove they are employed are not allowed [to rent] apartment[s] and can't receive a food ration card. Since I had a job at that point, I made my way to the Party bureau and asked the secretary to point me to a place [for me] to stay. The secretary started asking me if I had permission to leave my place of work, because in Russia you are not allowed to change jobs of your own accord. I said that I couldn't get used to the Russian habit of sleeping in the same barracks with girls. Those girls had lost all decency. As I was still too young to taste adulthood, I had decided to leave [my] place of work in the country. The Party secretary was a woman. She started asking me what relations between men and women were like in Poland, and told me that those relations led to the development of prostitution, which did not exist in Russia. There were no brothels in Russia—if a woman took a liking to a boy, he would live with her. The state looked after the products of such relations. I thought that after this conversation, she would give me a place to stay, but she told me to find a room myself, and only then come to her for the appropriate papers. I couldn't find a place to stay for two weeks [and slept] in a different spot every night. I could barely stand up [when] an older Jew who worked with me took pity on me and gave me a corner in his room to sleep. I thought he did it out of pure mercy, but it turned out he was after something else. In Homel there were many Jewish girls who couldn't bring themselves to marry Christian men. Generally, Jewish boys married Russian girls, and so the Jewish girls were at risk of spinsterhood. When Jewish workers arrived from Poland, the [local] Jewish families would basically stalk them. The Jew who gave me a place to stay in his apartment wanted, in all haste, to make me his son-in-law. I pretended not to be indifferent to the young lady's allure, but I was looking for ways to get out of there.

I earned five hundred rubles per month, which was barely enough to live on. I made the acquaintance of [some] young women whose husbands had been deported for Trotskyism,[328] and got permission from a few of them to live with them. I was ready to accept the offer of one of the friendly women when [they] started sending all of the Poles signed up for work to Chelyabinsk, to a coal mine. I escaped from the [threat of] Chelyabinsk to Kiev. My cousin ran a buffet at the train station in Równe, and invited me to come stay with him. With nothing to do in Kiev, I went to [my cousin's place]. It so happened that the day before, my cousin's license to run the buffet had been taken away, and he was left with no livelihood. We both took up trading. We were persecuted a lot, so to deflect suspicion, I signed up to work on construction of a road from Lwów to Kiev, which passed through Równe. I got eight rubles per day building the road, and earned extra through trading so I wouldn't starve to death.

At that time the registration began for a return to Poland. Anyone who wanted could get a Soviet passport with paragraph 11, according to which

---

328. In practice, members of the Communist Party accused of Trotskyism, which rarely meant subscribing to the beliefs of Leon Trotsky.

[they] were prohibited from living in a big city or living close to the border. From 20 June [1940] onward, the police were going around to apartments looking for people without passports. Apartment owners risked deportation for harboring illegal tenants. The manager of the roadworks was a French engineer, a Communist Jew. He persuaded me to take a passport and promised me a raise. I was planning to do so.

On 1 July, as I was walking in the street in the company of a girl, I was stopped and asked for [my] passport. I was taken to the police station. The chief swore at me and said that parasites like me should be shot like dogs. Since I didn't want to sign the protocol, he handed me over to the NKVD. Because I was working in road construction, I was given two days' time to sort out the formalities. When I turned up [in the agreed place] at the set time, instead of releasing me, [they] took me to the NKVD. I stood for two hours with my back to the wall and was then interrogated. Finally, I was led out into the courtyard. [After] being put in an ambulance, I was driven to prison along with a few Poles. I was in cell number 30 with thirty-eight fellow companions in misery. It's difficult to describe the crowding and the filth inside the cell. With me there were: Berliner from Mława; lawyer Sznitterman, the head of the Teachers' Association; a Poale Zionist[329] Het from Równe, who, in a Poale Zion meeting, had advocated taxing [the members] for the benefit of the party; Steinberg from Brześć; Captain Hajek from Równe; a few Communists accused of counterrevolution; a few peasants accused of anti-kolkhoz operations; a member of Petlura's[330] government; Lisiecki from Zdołbunów. I spent two months in prison. Once, at night, I was called for an interrogation. I was accused of illegal border crossing, escaping from Homel, and working for the German secret service. I replied that I was as much of an enemy to Germans as my judges, and that I escaped from Homel because I wasn't able to settle there, and my relatives were calling me to Równe. I was promised a judgment within three days. Three months later, I was called in to sign the protocol [and] sent to Dubno, to prison, [where] I spent a month. In the cell with me there were: a dentist,

329. See glossary: Poale Zion.

330. Szymon Petlura [Ukrainian: Symon Petliura] (1879–1926): Ukrainian political activist. After the February Revolution in 1917 in Russia [and] until 1919, he was the leader of the Ukrainian national army movement. In 1920 his units took part in the Polish-Soviet war, on the Polish side. He was an émigré in Poland in the years 1920–23. He was murdered by a Soviet agent in 1926.

Rina, from Ostrowie; a priest, Kalecki; and a Russian doctor, Panczena, who had escaped from Russia during the revolution and lived in Równe.

After a month, an official from Moscow read me the verdict that sentenced me to three years of penal camp. I didn't want to sign the judgment because it had been issued without any legal proceedings. An NKVD-er told me that trials took place in Moscow, and if I didn't sign the judgment, things would get much worse. I was taken to Lwów, to the prison in Brygidki. We slept on bare ground, and it's difficult to describe the filth there. The arrestees looked deranged. After three days, I was taken to Kiev [and] from there to Kharkiv, where I stayed a month. The regime in Soviet prisons is incredibly harsh. Cells are overcrowded, [and] people lie on top of each other at night. In Kharkiv and Kiev, people are not allowed out for the mandated walk. Books and newspapers are out of the question. People live there without [any] contact with the outside world, because even parcels from outside are not allowed—one has to live on what one gets to eat in prison. Twenty-year-old youths look like old people. Everyone is sick, dejected, demoralized, distraught; there are plenty of sexual diseases. I think these are the worst prisons in the world. In the Kharkiv prison, I met the owner of an electric light factory in Warsaw, from Okopowa Street, Neumann.

After a month, I was taken to the station along with other prisoners, and from there, via Kursk, Orel, Tula, Moscow, Yaroslavl [and] Vologda, we reached Yezhovo, where the penal camp was located. I traveled for eleven days in the sealed freight car. We received a piece of bread and a bit of cold water once a day. When we arrived in Yezhovo, the thermometer indicated −50°C [−58°F]. Many of us had no shoes. Various parts of our bodies got frostbitten. In the camp, a doctors' committee split us into groups. There were a thousand people in the camp who had been deported for counterrevolution. The people in charge were political exiles. The doctor was a famous surgeon who had operated on Maxim Gorky. Initially sentenced to death and then to exile, he was accused of hastening the death of the great writer.

I was sent to the shoemakers' section; others worked in the forest. Only old Jews worked in that section, [those] sentenced for counterrevolution, for contact[s] abroad, for writing letters asking for help. I wasn't a trained shoemaker, but my companions in misery helped me when they could. Soon it became clear that I wasn't a shoemaker and I was sent to a sawmill. Many Jews worked in the sawmill, [and they] helped me. The bread ration for specialists was higher than that for black workers.[331] I met the following people in the camp: Pomeraniec, an activist from Białystok; Bukier from Zwolik [Zwoleń?]; there was also a former member of the Moscow City Council there; and Mrs. Bannerowska, a member of the Communist Party in Poland. I also met a Jewish Communist from Palestine, from Tel Aviv. His name was Dorfsmann. He had gone to Russia in 1931 and was then sentenced to labor camp. The lightest sentence amounted to eight years. Most didn't [further text missing].

War and Amnesty

Our situation worsened when the [German-Soviet] war broke out. The bread rations were decreased, the number of working hours was increased, and those who did not fulfill their quotas were sent to punishment cells. Russian exiles who had hoped to be released lost [their] last chance of freedom. When we found out about the Amnesty, they began releasing Polish deportees, [and the Russians] couldn't hide their envy. I got a rail ticket to Arzamsk [Arzamas] and worked in a suitcase factory there, earning two hundred rubles per month. I lived in the workers' club and stayed there until 15 February 1942, at which point I received a summons to report to the army. I replied that I wanted to serve in the Polish army and was sent to Gorky, where Polish army divisions were forming. We went to Turkestan, where those who came from the areas occupied by Russia were segregated out. The Jews were sent into Russia, like the Ukrainians and Belarussians [Belarusians]. As a Warsaw resident, I was not kicked out of the army, and I was sent to Terczlak [Chok-Pak], where I went in front of a commission for the second time. Ninety percent of Jews were classified as category D. After a few months' wandering around Russia I made it to Persia, and from there, to Palestine.

331. Unskilled workers. From Russian *chernorobochiy* [original Polish spelling: *czernoroboczyj*].

Protocol 129

Testimony of **Meir Bogdański**, age twenty-eight, born in Piotrków, tailor by trade, socialist activist in the Łódź area.

I was mobilized on 24 August 1939 in the first mobilization phase for the Polish army. On 27 August, our division left Łódź and began a series of marches that lasted a whole week. During that week, the marches tired out the army terribly. On Saturday, 2 September [1939], we found ourselves in Tomaszów [Mazowiecki] and felt the consequences of the war firsthand for the first time there. We heard an artillery cannonade and were told that the Germans had entered Poland. Up until then, the leader of our division had hidden from us the fact that war had broken out. On Saturday evening, we received an order to march out on the road toward Opoczno. The shots were getting closer. We had been assigned to defend the forest. On the way, we came across refugees from Piotrków and Wieluń. They were rushing headlong like crazy people and obstructing the progress of the army. The refugees told us that Wieluń had been taken by the Germans. At this point, we were ordered to turn toward Piotrków and take up positions there. We marched on ahead, passing burned-down towns. Sulejów lay in ruins [and] only the bridge on Pilica River remained intact. Our column did not reach our destination because Piotrków had already been occupied by the German motorized divisions. We were on foot and it's no surprise that we lost out to the Germans—the German cars had arrived earlier. We received an order to go east, and from that moment on, we ceased to be a fighting force. Command told us that we were going east to form new divisions there. The march was hard; we were constantly bombarded. We entered Radom county and reached the Wisła River. By the second week of the war, we were surrounded by the German army. In addition to us, some of the artillery regiments were surrounded, among them the Third Regiment from Wilno. We were distraught, as we felt that there was no way out. Out of despair, we decided to give [it one] last try. We aimed the cannons toward the road [and] started shooting, to [try to] break through the line of the army surrounding us. The barrage was overwhelming, and the goal was achieved. We broke out of the trap and made it to the town of Głowaczów, where a battle was taking place. In the evening, the Germans regrouped and began bombarding the town. We set off toward the Wisła. In that location its width was four hundred meters. We started to build a floating bridge but ran out of materials. We received an order to unharness the horses from the lager [cart?] and set them free. In the order, we were [also] told to take the breech-blocks out of the cannons and throw some of the most important parts in the river. There was no way to take the cannons across the Wisła. The [local] peasants had no boats. The commandant told us not to wait on the bank or we would be shot dead. My companion found a raft somewhere and suggested that we [try to] make it across the river. The raft was 2 meters long and 1.5 meters wide. The major advised that we go with the current since there was no other possibility. We battled the water for an hour, and eventually made it to the other bank. A few small groups crossed the river this way. No new divisions were formed; only random groups of soldiers gathered together. The peasants wouldn't let anyone into [their] huts because soldiers were known to steal various items. This way, unaided, we got to Łaskarzew, where an assembly point had been set up for soldiers who had lost their divisions. We learned that a lot of Polish soldiers had been killed by bombs when they tried to cross the river. We stayed for a few days at the assembly point, without food and without assignment[s], and we didn't know what to do with ourselves. I decided to go toward Warsaw. A military policeman stopped us outside the city and told us to go back to the assembly point. Meanwhile, a company of soldiers had been formed who had guns and a bit of ammunition. I made my way to Dęblin with this company, but most of them ran off in various directions during the journey, and we entered the Dęblin fortress as a small group. There were no troops there anymore, only a guard division watching the ammunition.[332] We didn't know what we were supposed to do. The lieutenant, already dressed in civilian clothes, advised us not to stay—he told us to go to Lublin. On the way, the peasants wouldn't let us into [their] huts. We [had to] use threats to force them to give us a place to stay and provide a little food. We stayed overnight in [one of the] village[s], as there were partisans roaming the forests [and] shooting at soldiers. The village was hit by artillery fire at night, and the peasants shouted that the shooting was our fault. At dawn, we set out on the road

332. [The village of Stawy, near Dęblin, held one of the largest ammunition depots of the Polish army.]

[connecting] Lublin and Warsaw. The bridge had been destroyed on both sides, but the middle was intact. We had to jump onto the middle part to get to the other bank. We arrived in Lublin on Saturday [and] found the city in ruins. No one would have recognized the beautiful street of Krakowskie Przedmieście. We made our way to the assembly point to register and were assigned to the appropriate division there. On Sunday morning, Lublin was bombed anew and the houses in our assembly point were destroyed. The army dispersed and had nowhere to return to. Out of [its] remains, a company was formed, and we set off toward Chełm on Sunday night. On the way, I met [my] companion from Łódź. He had been walking [around] for two days by that time—they wouldn't let him into Chełm as the town was overflowing with the military. On the way, the company decided to change direction [and go] to Hrubieszów, and we arrived there two days later. We came across the lagers [carts?] of the 14th and 16th divisions during the journey, going in an unknown direction. They asked that we go with them [and told us] they were going to Romania. There were no officers to be seen. The soldiers wandered around like an abandoned herd. We were told that all the officers had run away. General Sawicki[333] was shot by a court-martial for deserting the division.[334] It was said that the war has ended. We came upon a huge concentration of many units in Hrubieszów, but they were all leaderless. The nearby forests were full of weapons, ammunition, [and] military equipment. We spent Yom Kippur in Hrubieszów. Specialist divisions were being formed. At night, an assembly of [all the] divisions took place and some soldiers had their weapons and military equipment taken away in order to outfit others. I had a gun taken from me because I had no ammunition. I had had to drop the ammunition on the way, as it had gotten wet while I was crossing the Wisła. A national guard was formed from the [fully] equipped soldiers. The task of these divisions was to defend against the Ukrainians, who were attacking soldiers and taking their weapons away. Meanwhile, the shooting of the town began. We were certain

333. Kazimierz Jędrzej Sawicki (1888–1971): general of the Polish army; in September 1939, he led the operational group "Włodzimierz." After the entry of the Soviet army, he dissolved the group and crossed the Hungarian border. He returned to the country in 1941 and was active in conspiratorial activities.

334. [This report is incorrect. Sawicki was still active in the Polish army until at least 1941, and he died in England 2 March 1971.]

that the Germans were already there. We were lined up into rows and told to march to Chełm, fifty kilometers away. We hadn't eaten anything for many days; the kitchen and the cook had gotten lost somewhere. Along the way, the soldiers would go into the local villages to look for food. The division was dwindling. Gangs had formed along the route who attacked soldiers and ripped off their uniforms. Outside Chełm, we lodged in a village. We continued on in the morning, and as we advanced, we noticed that a column of Soviet tanks had surrounded us. We were taken prisoner. Fighting began in the city. A group of Ukrainians with red bands [on their left arms] appeared, and as it turned out, it was they who had given us up to the Soviet soldiers. They led us from one commandant to another. We learned about the Russian occupation from them. In one Ukrainian village, a Ukrainian peasant woman told the Soviet soldiers not to talk to us, since we were their enemies. We felt the hatred toward us grow. We weren't fed. We were led to Hrubieszów. We came across freed soldiers who comforted us, [saying that we would be freed] in Hrubieszów. There was a revolutionary committee in the Hrubieszów county office. Prisoners of war were registered here, but we weren't registered; instead we were added to a group of officers, policemen, and officials. This seemed suspicious to me. We weren't kept in the city but led further. I decided to escape. I told a policeman that I couldn't walk so that he would let me ride on the cart. When night fell, I jumped off the cart and hid in the forest. I returned to the city, walked to a Jewish home, and asked for water. I was allowed to stay the night. The following day I worked for [the Jewish man]. He was a young tailor, who gave me food and one zloty for a day's work. I stayed in the city and started to look for a job. An acquaintance of mine took me to his sister, who asked me to make a coat for [her] child. Unfortunately for me, there was an assembly point for prisoners of war in that same courtyard. I made plans to go to Wilno, but the bridge on the Bug River had not been repaired yet. I took to sewing the aforementioned coat. Sitting by the window, I looked on as they brought in new groups of Polish prisoners, one after another. They brought in German prisoners too, who had been captured by the Poles, who freed them and took them to the German border.[335] In Hrubieszów, I met the leader of the

335. [Probably refers to the border of the occupied territory, since Hrubieszów is in eastern Poland, not near the border of Germany.]

youth Bund movement, from the town of Dolinów. His name was Boruch. We planned an escape together. Meanwhile a raid on Polish soldiers was organized in town, and I never saw him again. As I was working, a policeman came into the apartment and said that I had evaded him twice, and that now he would arrest me. My employer's statement that I had been working for her since five in the morning was fruitless. All the prisoners were gathered in the local beth hamidrash. I met [my] aforementioned companion, Boruch, there, who had reported voluntarily since the raid was very harsh; incredibly rigorous searches took place. The Soviet soldiers advised us to sell [our] watches and razors, as they would be confiscated anyway. The prisoners were taken to Włodzimierz Wołyński and put up in [army] barracks. Then everyone was given a portion of bread and they were taken into freight cars in groups. We were told that we would be released from captivity in Kowel. In Kowel we were led out once more, underwent searches, and were loaded into the same cars again. The transport was made up of three thousand people. A rumor spread that they would take us to the Germans. Panic broke out. Many jumped out of the cars as the train started. It turned out that we were taken to Shepetivka. Thirty thousand prisoners had been gathered there, [and] soldiers were separated from officers, the police, and civil servants. There wasn't room for everyone. One couldn't even stretch out on the floor. Shepetivka could not provide [enough] bread for thirty thousand people. The kitchens didn't have enough soup. That is why each prisoner received no more than an eighth of a small loaf of bread and a small tin of fish and soup every other day. The kitchens worked twenty-four hours, and soup was served from four in the morning until twelve at night. Within a few days, the entire army was famished and lice ridden. The barracks were stuffy; there was no water for washing—the taps were only open for two hours a day. We were told over a loudspeaker that England was reportedly ready to take over the care of Polish prisoners of war, to which the Soviets replied that the prisoners were being fed three times a day and weren't lacking anything. Indeed, the following day we each received a packet of makhorka and [enough] silk rolling paper for three cigarettes. This aroused envy among our guards, who were rolling cigarettes out of newspapers. We spent twenty-four days in Shepetivka. Sometimes we were taken out to work, but [it was] not hard [work]. [People] were paid for their work. They bought various products on the way and sold them in the camp at a large profit. I knew some who earned ten thousand rubles in a few days. Those who stayed in the camp, meanwhile, were deathly exhausted. Later the prisoners started being registered according to their place of origin. I gave Wilno as my hometown. The address went: 6 Zawalna [Street].[336] I ran into many acquaintances and companions in the camp. One [man named] Perkal told me that he had met Wiktor Alter in Kowel. The Bund members in Kowel were organized; they looked after each other. Meetings took place all the time, but arrests put an end to these assemblies. An investigation took place in the camp. Among the questions asked, the most important one was: what political organization do you belong to? I didn't say that I belonged to the Bund—I only said that I was a member of a trade organization. I learned that Wilno had been given to Lithuania [by the Soviets]. I didn't know what changes would take place there. It was said that the Lithuanian border was carefully guarded. I said to the *politruk* in the camp that I wanted to stay in Shepetivka for now. Those who wanted to stay in the city were locked in a separate room and fed well. It seemed like we had found ourselves in a guesthouse. The group was made up of 150 people, Jews and Poles. Two days later, we were taken to the NKVD and underwent an interrogation. Again, the same questions were asked. Everyone said, naturally, that they had nothing to do with politics. Finally, we were taken to a sugar factory and told that we would work there and receive ten rubles per day for two hours' work. We were no longer guarded. We were advised not to show ourselves in the streets; we weren't given any papers. We received excellent meals in the factory canteen. It seemed to us that we were in paradise. After being thoroughly disinfected, we got new clothes and were assigned to appropriate divisions. My work consisted of burning lime. After six days' work, I was paid out only eight rubles, and the rest was kept for the food. I should have received fifty-four rubles. Every one of us was cheated this way because we hadn't fulfilled the quota, which, I believe, was impossible for a man to fulfill. In the end, we got between two and three rubles for the hard, eight-hour-long workday. I resisted and demanded to be given a job in my trade. After long bargaining, I was taken to a tailoring cooperative, where I worked for eight hours [a day]. Here, for the first time, I learned about the awful slavery of a Soviet citizen. When I told stories about labor strikes in Poland, which aimed

336. [As a member of the Bund, he did not want to disclose his actual identity and address.]

to improve the workers' lot, they thought I was lying and [that] I was an agent of Polish overlords. They didn't believe that there were any workers other than slaves in Poland. One day when I returned from work I was arrested. I came upon many prisoners at the NKVD. We were kept in jail for five days [and] brought food from a local restaurant. When we protested against the arrest, the warden told us that we hadn't been arrested, but were rather under observation. After five days, we were taken to the station and loaded into freight cars. The journey took ten days. We passed through Kiev, Kharkiv, made it to Donbas [the Donets Coal Basin], where we were taken to the village of Nowotroick,[337] located seventy kilometers from Mariupol, Stalin district. In that village there was a camp for Polish prisoners, made up of a few wards. I stayed in a ward with five hundred prisoners. The camp was surrounded with barbed wire. We lived in barracks. The camps were situated near quarries, where the prisoners worked. We met Germans there. The stones were used as an additive in steel manufacture. There was a German expert commission there who inspected the stone, and huge transports of it were taken to Germany. We were fed splendidly so that our work would be more productive. We worked seven hours a day. We received meat, a lot of bread, and even butter. A lot of money was paid for fulfilling one's quotas. We benefited greatly from the fact that Germans were in charge there. The command made sure we had clean underwear, baths, and that the barracks were cleaned and well heated. Those who had money could buy many nice things on top of the basics we received. A liter of milk cost only fifty kopecks, and a kilo of white bread 2.80. In the canteen, one could buy eggs, butter, Swiss cheese, soup—items you would later not [be able to] find in Russia—for pennies. We slept in beds with mattresses and our sheets were changed every week. The work was hard. The transports to Germany increased, but we were strong and did the work. For now, we stuffed ourselves as much as we could. These ideal relations did not last long. On 22 May 1940, we were loaded into freight cars and told we were going home. After eight days of a truly hellish journey, we arrived not at home but rather in Kotlas. Kotlas is a city that sends a shudder of fear [through anyone] in Russia. There are *etap* prisons there, through which millions of people pass. In the prison, one ends up lice infested within two days. There are mixed

337. Novotroitskoye [original Polish correction: Nowotroickoje].

prisoners of all statuses and classes there, from all corners of Russia: career criminals and professors, and starting recently, important Soviet figures. Transport to various camps—labor camps and penal camps—takes place here, as well as [transports of] those given indefinite sentences. On 14 June, we arrived at an assembly point located three hundred kilometers from Kotlas. The camp [complex] was called Północny Obóz Narodowego Komitetu Spraw Wewnętrznych.[338] Among the responsibilities of each camp was the construction of a rail network. We sawed trees to begin with, which we took to a sawmill, and there railroad ties were made. The prisoners of war were locked in a separate camp. Next to us there was a camp of the *bytoviki*, that is, bandits and armed robbers. Both there and at our camp prisoners were fed equally badly. We were deathly exhausted. We worked alongside criminals. One day, the criminals rebelled and pillaged the storehouses. All of the food supplies were eaten. The guard[s] ran away in fear. The warden had his bones broken. All of the armed forces in the district were mobilized, but the supplies had been eaten, and the culprit[s] weren't found. That rebellion taught us how one must behave when food is not provided. A few days later, [the people in] our camp did not go to work. We demanded more, and better, food. But the command mobilized forces before a rebellion [could] take place in our camps. A punishment kettle was brought in, and we were called for a meeting. The warden threatened us were we to continue the strike. A strike is considered sabotage in Russia. It didn't help us at all, and our rations were determined according to the quotas of work carried out. For 100 percent of the quota—nine hundred grams of bread and a bowl of soup. We were told that the lack of food was due to transport difficulties. There was no rail connection from Kotlas. Food was brought in on barges and it got stolen on the way. The strike was broken because eight hundred prisoners from one barracks went out to work. On 8 July, we were lined up and told to march. We asked for food for the road. The warden replied that we would get food on the other side of the gate. He lied to us. We started to revolt. Meanwhile, we left seven thousand prisoners in the first hub. A hundred of us, I among them, were put up separately. We were told to build shacks as the rainy season neared. We slept on bare ground, in mud.

338. Northern Camp of the National Committee for Internal Affairs.

We were told that we were near the town of Kniaź Hagaz.[339] In the morning, our group was given bread, tea, and sugar, and told to continue marching. We walked all day long. We slept in the rain again. We walked along a river. There was no food [left] by the second day. The guards had rucksacks filled with food. They would get together during rest [stops] and eat. They didn't give us even a piece of bread. They buried the leftover food in the ground, as they were forbidden to share food with exiles. Food was a reward for work, and after all, we were doing nothing. We took the oat sacks off the horses and ate that for two days. The hunger forced us into rebellion. We decided to go back. The guards promised that we would finally get food. We agreed to wait until the food arrived. Indeed, food arrived on a barge, enough for two days. The task of our group of one hundred people was to study the area and mark where the rail line was to go. But how could we do anything if we were hungry. We were sent [either] moldy or raw bread that had to be baked again. We worked like this—under inhuman conditions, tormented by hunger—from 18 July until 1 October. Many of us fell ill; many died. Everyone suffered from dysentery. We were fed without [any] salt; we had to put salted fish into the soup. We never [even] saw any lard. We longed for the time when, thanks to the German commission, we had received clean underwear. We didn't know what was happening in the world. On 1 October, cars arrived and took us to the town of Kozwia,[340] and from there, we traveled to Central Russia, to Wiazoluka.[341] We heard about the Amnesty for the first time. We were told that we were free soldiers of Allied Poland again, and a Polish division was formed that included us.

---

339. Knyazhpogost [original Polish correction: Kniażpogost].

340. Correctly: Kozhva [original Polish correction: Kożwa].

341. Likely refers to the town of Buzuluk [original Polish correction: Buzułuk].

Protocol 131

Testimony of **Jakub Rabinowicz**, age sixteen, son of Rabbi Jechiel from Siedlce. Arrived [in Palestine] from Russia via Tehran on 28 August 1942 [1943?].[342]

Siedlce [was] already being bombarded in the first days of the war. The bombardment lasted a few days, and the whole town was burned down. My father, known as the Rabbi from Biała, had many supporters in our town, who had bought him a house. Our house was burned down together with all our belongings, precious books, and items inherited from [our] grandparents, which were of great value. We left the apartment wearing what we had on our backs and made for the village of Gagulec [likely Golice]. There we hid in a haystack and waited out the bombardment, and when the Germans occupied Siedlce before Rosh Hashanah [14–15 September 1939], we returned to town. The Germans stayed in Siedlce until Yom Kippur [23 September 1939], and then the Bolsheviks came. Only then did the Jews leave their hiding places and begin to assess their losses. Men and women raked through the rubble with iron rods, but no one found anything, and everyone became poor. The destitution was universal in town. Formerly rich people were left without a penny to their name. The atmosphere was getting worse, all the more so since an imminent withdrawal of the Bolsheviks from town was predicted. And when the Russians began to retreat one day, most people went with them, including my father, who knew that [even though], as a rabbi, he would suffer with the Bolsheviks, he [still] would prefer to go to Siemiatycze rather than stay with the Germans. On the way out of Siedlce, I came upon Jewish refugees from the neighboring towns who were almost naked. A few women gave birth to children in our train, but no one paid any attention to them. The town of Siemiatycze was full of refugees; it was impossible to find a place for the night. We went to Baranowicze, to [stay with our] uncle, Rabbi Alter Perlow.

We settled at [our] uncle's somehow. His situation wasn't great. The Bolsheviks did not allow religious practice. The NKVD accused him of espionage and threatened that if he did not cease [his] rabbinic duties, they would

342. [Jakub Rabinowicz appears to be the brother of Gitla Rabinowicz, whose testimony is recorded in Protocol 77.]

send him to Siberia. [My] uncle was not frightened [and] he remained at the helm of the synagogue. He taught children who had no religious school [to go to]. And when, one day, the NKVD-ers arrived to close down the school, [my] uncle resisted firmly. Unable to deal with him, the authorities severely punished the parents who sent their children to the yeshiva. Seeing that the situation was difficult, the pupils from the yeshiva escaped to Wilno, which belonged to the Lithuanians, where people weren't persecuted for taking part in religious practices. Poverty was making itself felt at [our] uncle's by then, and at that point Mother, with the help of [my] older brother Hersz, took to trading. Goods were brought in from Białystok and sold in Baranowicze. Both families lived off the proceeds. Searches often took place at [my] uncle's. Holy books were taken, which were later returned. When the registration began of people wanting to leave for home, for Lithuania, Palestine, and America, my uncle registered to go to Wilno.

In Exile

A few weeks passed between the registration and the deportation. Various pieces of information made their way around the city. Some said that we would be sent to Siberia [and] others said that everyone would be taken to the place he registered for.

It was a Friday, 28 June 1940, when armed NKVD-ers knocked on our door. The apartment was lit up with spotlights, we were rushed to get dressed more quickly, and when [my] uncle asked where we were going, some [of the agents] replied that they were sending us to the Germans. We didn't manage to pack all of our belongings in time. We were loaded into cars and driven to the station. We traveled in sealed freight cars, and [our] friends who brought us food to the station were not allowed to [come to] the train. We received [our] first drop of water only after twenty-four hours. We were terribly exhausted; children were crying and calling for food. Distraught parents tore down the doors and got out of the car at a station, but the soldiers, their guns drawn, pushed them [back] inside the car. It was only then that we received, for the first time, soup and half a kilo of bread each. Even though we were famished, Father did not let us eat the *treif* soup, and we lived off bread and water throughout the entire journey. Forty people traveled in our car—it was cramped, dirty, [and] it stank. After two days' journey, a few people fell ill with typhus. The sick were taken to a hospital at a station, and I didn't see them again. [We weren't allowed] to get out to use the toilet, and small children did their business through the barred windows, while adults suffered and waited for the closest station where, under strict guard, they would be taken to a toilet. We traveled for eight days, until we arrived in Tavda. We got out of the car, were taken to a river, [and] were loaded onto a small barge, where there was little room for passengers next to the cargo. We were pushed on like cattle and not allowed to buy any supplies beforehand. People fainted from exhaustion. We traveled for five days on the water. We were given hardly any food. Mosquitos bit us constantly. Swollen [with bites], the children cried. The guards taunted us, saying: "You will grow old [without] laying eyes on Warsaw again. Your children will learn Russian [here] and forget the Polish and Jewish languages." Yet they would never give a piece of bread to the children who were crying with hunger. When we reached a riverbank five days later, we were rushed off the barge. We were so tired that we couldn't disembark on our own. Men carried women in [their] arms. They were themselves so weakened that many fell into the water. [People] rushed to their rescue. The NKVD-ers stood, unmoved, saying it was the first bath the Polish overlords had received in Russia. Our belongings were transported on carts, and we went on foot. The journey was difficult. The carts traveled over [a pavement of] logs so that they wouldn't get stuck in the mud, mud that we could barely lift our feet from. We were plagued by thirst [and] there was no water. On the way, a few carts tipped over. We barely [managed to] lift them [back up], and it took all day before we arrived in Trzacz [?] in the Sverdlovsk Oblast. There was a long speech made to us. The warden repeated that anyone who wouldn't work had no right to live. Then we were put up in barracks without windows. The mosquitos wouldn't let us sleep, just like the bedbugs, so that we had to burn wood at night and the smoke would drive away the mosquitos. In the morning, we were split into brigades and sent to work in the forest. We worked eight hours a day [and] even the Stakhanovites couldn't fulfill more than half of [their] quotas. We wore nets on our faces, which we had to make ourselves. It didn't help much—people would return with their faces swollen. My father did not work at first. The warden himself turned up [and] took Father into a brick factory, where he was told to carry clay. Since this work was too hard for Father, he was moved to the job of cart driver in that factory. But Father could not manage a horse. He was shown how to beat it. Because Father did not want to beat the horse with the rod that they gave him for that purpose, he was sent home and told that he would not receive any bread. A few weeks later, Father was given lighter work, twisting ropes. I carried sacks. Father did not want to work on Saturdays, at which point the warden wrote up an official statement of the charges [saying] Father was sabotaging work, and told him to sign [it]. When Father didn't want to sign the statement, he was threatened with jail. The jail was a dark room, damp and full of mice. Father was there for two days without food, and they didn't allow food to be brought to him. Father returned to work after two days but still did not work on Saturdays, and the warden pretended not to see it. On Rosh Hashanah [3–4 October 1940], everyone prayed between six and eight. There was no Torah, but we found a shofar.[343] During the prayers, the commandant and a few policemen entered and used knouts to disperse those praying. Father and a shochet were taken to the administrative office. He was accused [of] getting people together to pray during work [and told] that he was sabotaging work, an offense punishable by a few years in prison. Father's explanations were in vain—the warden sent the protocol off to Tawrig [?]. Soon a response arrived [saying] that Father would have 25 percent of his earnings docked for six months, and that the leniency of the punishment was due to the fact that this was his first offense. Nevertheless, when Yom Kippur [12 October 1940] arrived, Father managed to persuade the warden to let Jews be released from work. On Sukkot [17–18 October 1940], the warden would not allow a sukkah[344] to be erected because he was worried about a fire. But Father ignored the ban and put up a sukkah. We worked in −50°C [−58°F] frost. People were only released from work when they had a fever of 39°C [102.2°F]. Many prisoners had frostbite on various parts of their bodies—there was no cure for it and people's fingers, ears, [and] noses would fall off. The warden demanded constant work. We earned three rubles per day, for which one could get two kilos of bread.

There were horrendous windstorms. They would topple hundred-year-old trees, which often fell on the people working in the forest and killed them. Many people died of starvation, particularly small children, who could not

343. Shofar: A wind instrument made from a ram's horn, used in synagogue services on Rosh Hashanah and Yom Kippur. See glossary.

344. Sukkah [Polish: *kuczka*]: a hut built from branches for the holiday of Sukkot. See glossary.

withstand the hunger and the freezing temperatures. In the middle of winter, Father had his books taken from him. [He] was accused not only of spending too much time over them, but also of teaching children. The warden wanted to burn the books. Father wrote a request to the NKVD and received a response that the books would be removed [but] not burned. Father got them back in one piece before leaving the *posiołek*.

A few children were sickened by the frost and lost their speech. They didn't want to admit them to a hospital because only the gravely ill were admitted. As soon as anyone fell ill, they immediately lost the right to [their] portion of bread. Next to our barracks were the barracks of Russian exiles, older people who had been sentenced to ten to fifteen years in labor camps for counter-revolution. They didn't know where their families were and were themselves so numb by then that they took no interest in what was happening in the world. These people assured us that we would never leave Siberia.

War and Amnesty

When the [German-Soviet] war broke out, the situation in the *posiołek* got a lot worse. The warden said that we were spies, and we were watched at every step. We worked for twelve hours. The bread portions were decreased to six hundred grams for adults and four hundred grams for children. Two days a week, we worked for free to defend the country. When the news of the Amnesty arrived, the warden told us that this applied to Poles, not Jews. However, the Sverdlovsk authorities issued our documents. We received a permit to go to Czerniowsk.[345] People waited by the river for weeks for a ship. Many were ill. The NKVD-ers wouldn't give us barges, and advised that we go by car or cart along the riverbank, which we couldn't dream of, naturally. A delegation with a man from Warsaw named Kornblit at its helm went to Tavda and demanded that we be given a barge [to carry] our belongings. We ourselves went on foot. The journey to Tabarina [Tabory] took two days. Along the way, kolkhoz members didn't allow us into the village[s] because they had received an order not to. In Tabarina they gave us a barge [to go] to Tavda. We traveled for four days without bread. We ate potatoes that we dug up on the way. In Tavda, we roamed the streets for a few days until we got train

345. There is no such town. Possibly refers to the town of Chernikovsk near Ufa.

tickets to Chelyabinsk. After spending four days in the station in Chelyabinsk, we were sent to Chkalovo, and from there, to Turkestan. We spent two days at the station in Turkestan, without bread. We ran toward the city, eight kilometers away, to find something to eat. NKVD-ers kept sending refugees off to kolkhozes. With no other option, we went to Ittaku[346] in the Turkestan region. The kolkhoz was big, made up of a thousand Uzbeks. They ate well, but wore rags. They lived in kibitkas, without windows, and slept on the ground. They didn't know what furniture was. [My] brother and I worked digging up potatoes; Father—picking cotton. We each received four hundred grams of flour per day. We sold our belongings to the Uzbeks and [were able to] eat more as a result. Five hundred refugees from Poland lived in the kolkhoz. After a few months' stay in the kolkhoz, many refugees fell ill with typhus. Everyone in our family was ill except Mother. After six weeks' stay in the hospital, we all recovered and were released. Weakened by the typhus, we couldn't work and were unable to earn money. Hungry, we went to Turkestan. [My] brother worked at the station and received three rubles and three hundred grams of bread, as well as three hundred grams for the family, for ten hours of work. We were starving and slept in the streets. My mother and sister started trading. They would bring things in from Tashkent and sell them in Turkestan. Despite this, we could barely afford food, and trading was a dangerous business. When Mother and my sister could no longer go [back and forth] because there were constant arrests and searches on the trains, my younger brother Dawid, age fourteen, and seven-year-old Bencjon and I got into a Polish children's center. Only children up to sixteen years old were admitted there. My sixteen-year-old brother, Hersz, was admitted too. The Polish children treated us badly, but we dealt with all of the hurt with a smile because we knew we would save [our] parents from prison this way. After a month's stay in the center, we were taken to Ashgabat. It was the third transport—only Polish children went with the first and second ones. When we got to Ashgabat, the Polish children greeted us with a cry: "The kikes have arrived." A doctors' commission examined all the children and established that five [of them] were over the age of sixteen. It was decided that they would be sent back to Russia. Polish children over the regulation age were not sent back. My brother Herszel was one of the five

346. Perhaps Itatka? There are no records of a camp there, however.

boys who were. We threw ourselves at the doctors' feet, but it was all in vain. I spent three months in Ashgabat. The Polish children beat us, spat in our faces, filled our mouths with soap at night, teased and mocked us. We left for Persia three months later. The Persian Jews gave us a warm welcome. They took us out of the children's center and fed us very generously. They gave us gifts, and the Jewish children left for Tehran separately. In Tehran, Polish children threw stones at us and shouted: "The Yids have come." The same thing happened inside the barracks. We lodged a complaint with Dusza, the county prefect, who punished a few children, and that was the end of the fun. I spent seven months in Tehran, and together with a group of 108 children, arrived in Palestine on 23 August 1943.

Protocol 132

Testimony of **Szoszana Elkes**, age twelve, daughter of Józef and Chana from Pułtusk. Arrived in Palestine with three sisters and a brother in February 1943.

My father was a merchant. We had two large warehouses. Father would buy hay from the peasants and take it to Warsaw and other big cities. We had our own house and fared well. All the Jews escaped from Pułtusk before the arrival of the Germans. But we stayed behind because Mama was weak, and Father was afraid of running away with small children by himself. We spent a few weeks with the Germans there. [They] took away the entire contents of our warehouses, paying for [only] a part of it, so that we had nothing to live on. Some of those who had escaped returned to town and took up [their] old jobs. On Sukkot [28–29 September 1939], a neighbor we knew, [a] Pole, came [to our apartment] and told us that something was brewing for the Jews. The Germans planned to force all [of them] out of Pułtusk. That same day, the Germans got into my grandfather's warehouse, where my father happened to be, and took him away with them. The neighbors said that they had seen the Germans lead Father to the main square. We started to cry terribly. Mama ran out into town and forbade the children to leave the house. Father was not in the main square anymore. It was said that the Germans had taken him to some garden, searched him, taken away [his] money [and] documents, and had beaten him awfully. They ripped up his papers and took him somewhere. That same day, the Germans issued an order for all Jews to leave town. A Christian acquaintance [of ours] gave us a cart. We loaded it up with [our] belongings and set out from Pułtusk. The Germans stopped the cart on the bridge and told all the adults to get down from it, our mama among them. The children were allowed to ride across the bridge, and we made it to the village of Popławy. We cried terribly, certain that we've been left without a father [or] mother. We heard that a dreadful massacre had taken place on the bridge. The Germans had thrown many Jews in the water, where they were drowned. Some they had killed, and we were sure that our mama had met this fate. However, Mama came to us the next day, telling [us] that she had managed to escape from hell. She had run along the side paths because all the Jews were being killed on the main road. She knew that we were in the village of Popławy and she had made her way to us somehow. Mama did not stay with us for long. She decided to go back to Pułtusk to find out what had happened to Father. She came back a few days later and said that Father had been released together with our grandfather, and that they both had successfully [managed to leave] Pułtusk. However, she didn't know where they were. Since we had relatives in Węgrów, Mama thought that Father and Grandpa were there, and we decided to go find them. Mama didn't have money to hire a cart, so we went on foot. Each of us carried some of [our] belongings on their back. In the villages, the peasants didn't want to allow us in to spend the night. We sometimes managed to sleep inside barns. Mama paid with pieces of underwear for a piece of bread. This way, after four days, we arrived in Węgrów. How great was our joy when we came upon Father and Grandfather. Father had wanted to look for us a few times but was not permitted to. One time he set off and returned very upset. As he told us, he met some Germans on the way who wanted to shoot him. He barely escaped from them and went back toward Węgrów. Despite this, the Germans did not shoot at him. Father hid in the forest and escaped death by a miracle. All this time the Russians were in Węgrów. We found out that they were leaving town. Father and Grandfather decided to go with them. We went to Białystok. We fared very badly there. We didn't get an apartment and slept in a beth hamidrash. Other refugees lived there [too]. People stole from each other. They were always arguing, buzzing like a beehive day and night. The beth hamidrash wasn't heated and we almost froze. Father took up trading and earned all right. After some time, we didn't [have to] go without bread anymore; then we got a room and started leading a normal life. [My] older sister and mother helped Father. The situation got worse by the day. Father complained that they were preventing him from trading and taking away his merchandise. Once my sister was caught carrying soap [to sell]. She was taken to a police station, had the soap taken from her, and [they wanted] to find out where we lived so they could confiscate the rest of our merchandise. [My] sister wouldn't reveal our address for anything, even though they beat her at the station and kept her in jail all night. She returned home the next day. From that moment on Father was afraid of trading and once again there was no more bread at home; and because the registration to return to

Warsaw began at that time, Father registered, thinking that he would get by somehow in a big city.

In Exile

One day, on Saturday morning, NKVD-ers came to us, told us to pack [our] belongings, and told us that we were going to Warsaw. We were taken to the [rail] station [and] loaded into freight cars, forty-five people in each. The cars were sealed. We waited in the station for forty-eight hours, after which the train started, and we traveled for a very long time. We were given bread and a bit of watery soup once a day. It was forbidden to leave the car; it was very dirty [and] many people were ill. My six-year-old little sister, Lea, fell ill with scarlet fever during the journey. Everyone started making a fuss, afraid that other children would be infected. The NKVD-ers wanted to take the child away but Mother didn't allow it, saying she wanted to get out of the train car with [her]. After much arguing and crying, Mother was allowed to get out of the car with [her] child, and we traveled on alone. We arrived in Assina [Asino]. We were led out of the car and taken to a *posiołek*. In the *posiołek*, Father turned to the commandant and told him the story of [my] mother and the sick child, and said that he didn't know where they were. The commandant told him to send in a request to the NKVD headquarters, but there was no response. Only after five applications [for information] did we find out that Mama was in a *posiołek* in the Arkhangelsk district, and that Father would receive further news when it was available. For ten months we lived without Mother, who was making a vain effort to get to us. Meanwhile, Father worked in the forest and earned ten kopecks per day. We couldn't afford to buy soup in the canteen. Father's hands and feet were frostbitten. We sold [our] old possessions and lived off that.

Mama Is Found

As I mentioned, our grandfather had lived with us in Białystok. During the registration, Grandpa took a Russian passport, which is why he was sent to Stolin, by Pińsk. We knew Grandfather's address—we would write to him and would receive *posyłki* from him.[347] Mama, however, did not know Grandpa's

347. *Posyłka* (from Russian): a mail parcel.

address. One day, an acquaintance from Pułtusk who knew Grandfather's address arrived in the *posiołek* where Mama was. Mama wrote [Grandpa] a letter, reporting that her efforts to reunite with the family had been unsuccessful. Grandfather sent our address to Mama, and hers to us, by telegram. We were given the choice of staying in the *posiołek* or going to Mother. Because our *posiołek* was considered one of the worst, we decided to go to be with Mama. Under the eye of two NKVD-ers, we traveled for twelve days until we arrived in Mama's *posiołek*. [Our] situation improved there. Father, very much weakened, got a job in the kitchen. Later he worked in a sawmill with Mama and [my] older sister, which, together with the *posyłki* we received from Grandpa, allowed us to survive the hardest times.

War and Amnesty

Our situation got worse when the [German-Soviet] war broke out. The food parcels stopped coming [and] bread rations were decreased to a third. Adults received two hundred and children one hundred grams of bread. We worked for twelve hours. Father said that he would not survive [this] work and hunger. Then the news arrived about the release of Polish citizens, and since we didn't have warm clothing, we decided to go to warmer regions. The train journey to Tashkent took a few weeks. However, we could not stay [in Tashkent], because people were piled on top of each other in the streets, [and were] stealing from one another. We, too, had a bag of belongings stolen from us. Father was very upset because his tallit was in that bag. From Tashkent we went to Samarkand, but there, too, we lived in the streets, sleeping in the mud, and we often wished to die. We went to the kolkhoz Utra, where Father worked in the fields and we children worked picking cotton. Father received one kilo of rye per day, and we received half a kilo each. Mother would grind the rye and bake *lepyoshki* with the flour. Later the rye portions decreased. First Father, and then all the rest of us, fell ill with typhus. Mother didn't want to send us to the hospital, saying that they poisoned [people there]. We stayed in the kibitka, without medical care, and there wasn't even anyone to get us a glass of water since Mama was working in the fields. We [the sick] weren't given anything to eat. But God helped us [and] we all recovered. They didn't want to keep convalescents in the kolkhoz anymore, and we went to Turkestan. There we got into a Polish children's center. Only three children were accepted at first, and then, when the evacuations to Persia started, two more managed to get in, so that we were all together. The Polish children teased us badly, but we didn't care, because a piece of bread and a little soup were the most important thing[s] to us. We would save [some of] the bread and give it to [our] parents when they came to visit us. Finally [and] luckily, we left Russia. [Our] parents stayed there. We left for Krasnovodsk, from there to Pahlevi and to Tehran. After eight months' stay in Tehran, all five [of us] came to Palestine.

Protocol 134

Testimony of **Judel Dembowicz**, age thirteen, from Suwałki. Deported to Russia. Came to Palestine via Tehran.

Our town, Suwałki, was first occupied by Russians, and only afterward by Germans. I remember that the Russians entered [the town] a week after Yom Kippur.[348] The Russian occupation lasted a week altogether, and a neighbor came to us one day saying [they] were retreating. The town was evacuated in a single night. Polish hooligans ran around the streets and beat up Jews. We were all terribly scared. The Germans entered town after Sukkot.[349] At first they behaved calmly, and then they began to torment Jews. They burst into the synagogue, pulled the Torah out into the street, and stomped on it with their feet. A friend of ours, Lubliński, whose son lived in Palestine, in Ramat Gan, was shot in the street by the Germans. They grabbed all Jews, older and younger, for [forced] labor. My father, who traded in fruit, stopped earning money because he constantly had to work for the Germans. One day they arrested Father and put him in jail under the "Clock," located behind the magistrate building. Luckily, it turned out that the caretaker of the house where the jail was located was a Polish acquaintance, and he released Father from jail in exchange for some amount of money that Mother had given him. My father was beaten up by the Germans for no reason a few times. One day when I was walking in the street with Father, a German military policeman ran up to us and started hitting Father for failing to greet him. An older German officer happened to be walking down the street, and he swore at the policeman for beating us. The Germans plundered all the Jewish stalls and shops, down to the very last piece of merchandise. Some Polish policemen, dressed as civilians, went from house to house and sniffed around [to find out] where things were hidden. The Russians took many Jews with them when they left town. The town was half-empty. Many apartments were locked up, and the Jews from Suwałki moved to Augustów, not far from our town, which belonged to Russians.

---

348. In reality, it was the day after Yom Kippur, which was 24 September 1939.
349. The Germans occupied Suwałki on 9 October 1939.

Many went to Białystok. When the German persecutions worsened, Mother said that she would no longer stay in Suwałki, and she smuggled herself to Białystok, where Grandfather lived. Father didn't want to leave the apartment in God's hands and he stayed in Suwałki. Suddenly, in October 1939, a rumor spread that the Germans were planning to force all Jews out of Suwałki. Father hired a cart and we all went toward the Russian border. We heard stories later about how the expulsion took place. The Germans closed down the Jewish streets one day and rushed all the Jews, old and young, to the synagogue. Even the eldest were not spared. They were kept locked up all night. The Germans ordered the Jews to pray [and] sing and beat them bloody. The next day, the Jews were loaded into a special train and sent to Lublin. The crowding was so bad that many weak [people] and small children didn't make it. From Lublin, some were sent to Biała Podlaska, and the rest to Łuków. We received desperate letters from our relatives who were expelled. My uncle, Mosze Saradkobel, was deported to Biała Podlaska with his family. He wrote to us [to say] that everyone was dying from hunger and cold. We received a message from Łuków that the daughter of [our] uncle Abraham Orlański had died from hunger. When we were trying to get across the Russian border, we had a bit of luck. Father had hidden tea, sugar, and chocolate under the straw on a peasant's cart. We stayed the night with a villager, and that villager stole everything from us. He left the boxes [but] took away all the goods. I felt hungry in the middle of the forest. Father wanted to get to the boxes and found one last box of chocolate that the peasant missed. We didn't know how to get out of the forest. On one side there were Russians, on the other Germans, and we didn't know which way to go. We spotted a hut in the middle of the forest. An old, compassionate Christian woman lived in it. She gave us water to drink and allowed us to stay the night. We couldn't stay with her longer because she said that her husband, a forester, hated Jews, and if he found us there, he would give us up to the German guard. The next morning, she got us ready for the journey and gave us a guide, who led us out of the forest to the Russian side. The boy kept shouting watchwords on the way. Not far from the border, we saw Germans drive a whole truck loaded with Jews, women and children, who were being beaten so badly that their screams could be heard from afar. Because the Germans were busy with those Jews, our guide gave us a sign that the border was open, and we crossed over to the other side. I saw a pole with a red star, and I thought that we were saved. However, we had to go through a very strict Russian checkpoint at the entrance to the town of Augustów. We encountered Soviet guards at every step. The only way to get to the Russian area was to cross the Wigry Lake, located next to Augustów Canal.[350] The lake was dangerous, and Father began to look for a way to get across it. A peasant took pity on me and said he would help me. The local villagers were allowed to go to church in Augustów on Sunday without going through checks. The peasant gave me a *maciejówka*[351] and told me to go with his son. The boy told the Russian guard that we were going to pray. This was how I got to Augustów. The peasant took me to a restaurant where I had arranged to meet with Father. It took two days before Father made it across the border. Father was very miserable because he had seen with his own eyes how a Jewish family drowned while attempting to cross the border in a boat. Father had not let go of [his] tallit and *twilin*[352] throughout the entire crossing and said that he was only saved by a miracle, because there was a storm over the lake. In Białystok, we met up with Mother, and you can imagine how great our joy was. We lived for some time at Grandpa's place, at 11 Piłsudski [Street], and fared all right. Then the deportation of Polish citizens took place. With the exception of my twenty-year-old brother, Chaim, who happened to be in Grodno on the day of the deportation, our whole family was sent to Arkhangelsk.

Our *posiołek* was located two hundred kilometers from the White Sea. Father stated that he was a cook, and it was a very good trade [to work in]. He immediately became the kitchen supervisor, and we had enough food. Everyone who had anything to do with the kitchen would take home as many [food] products as they could. Father worked in the kitchen for a week, and the warden was very happy with him. But when the first Saturday came, Father gave up the job, because they required people to work on Saturday[s] there. Only then did [our] real destitution begin, and we owe our survival through the[se] days of hunger solely to the berries in the forest. Mother and I picked berries and raspberries for whole days. It was dangerous in the forest. There were lots of wild animals and birds. One day we came upon a dead old woman from our *posiołek*, her eyes picked out by birds of prey. Not far from us, a Russian

350. Polish: Kanał Augustowski.

351. A soft cap with a hardened peak.

352. Tefillin [original Polish correction: *tfilin*]. See glossary.

kolkhoz member shot and killed a bear. He received a bonus of five hundred rubles, and the bear meat was cooked for a meal for everyone who worked in the forest. Many children fell ill with dysentery from eating berries. I myself got eczema on [my] left leg and spent many weeks in a hospital, suffering terribly. [My] body was covered in sores, but the medicines that were used only did me harm. A young German doctor deportee lived close to our *posiołek*, and she cured me. Later [our] brother would send me food parcels from Grodno, and our situation improved. We got matzo for the holidays.

After the Amnesty, we were moved to Turkestan in Kazakhstan. The journey took three weeks. During the journey I lost Father and Mother, because Father sent me off to [get] water from a well at one of the stations. The train left and I was left alone. All week long I roamed around different stations looking for [my] parents, as none of us knew where we were going. At the Chkalovo station [part of text missing] on the Siberian border there was a Polish agency, and I learned there that the train my parents were on had gone to Turkestan. A week later I found [my] parents living inside a freight car at the station in Turkestan. It wasn't possible for a refugee to find an apartment in Turkestan, and that is why no one wanted to leave the carriage, [and stayed] until NKVD-ers came [and] took all of the refugees to kolkhozes. We were taken to the International kolkhoz, located [part of text missing] from Turkestan, on a cart pulled by two camels. Father fell ill with pneumonia, and there was no one to save him. Mother begged for a doctor in vain. Father's life flickered out like a candle. Two Jewish youths who were in the kolkhoz buried Father. I saw Mama wash his body and wrap him in a sheet. Father's grave was located in the kolkhoz. No prayers were said for him as there was no one to do it.[353] After Father's death, Mother fell ill with typhus and was taken to the hospital. I was left on my own. I received four hundred grams of black flour every day and learned how to bake cakes from it on hot bricks. I lived in the kolkhoz for a long time until I was taken to a Polish orphanage, from which they took me to Tehran, and from there to Palestine.

353. There was not a minyan, consisting of ten adult Jewish men, as required to recite the prayer.

Protocol 135

Testimony of **Motel Gejer**, age fifteen, from Łaszczów, Lublin district. Came to Palestine via Tehran in September 1943.

In our town, a real war took place. Three times the Germans entered and three times the advancing Polish army pushed them out. [This] fierce struggle lasted almost two weeks in our town, and naturally, nothing was left of it but ruins. On 14 September 1939, I saw the Germans for the first time. They came in tanks and brought a group of Polish prisoners of war with them. My father leaned his head out of the window to see where they were being taken. A German soldier aimed a gun in his direction. Luckily, Father took cover, and the German soldier, busy with the prisoners, couldn't go after him. Later a few German soldiers burst into our grocery store and started stealing everything they could while shouting that they would shoot everyone. Mama took such fright that she left the house and ran away. The German plundering didn't last long this time because the next day, 15 September [1939], the Germans retreated from our town. Not far from us, in the forests of Tomaszów, a battle between the Poles and the Germans was taking place, and this time the Poles managed to win. A few German tanks had been left in town, their crews all dead. German soldiers lay dead in the streets. An acquaintance of ours, Icchak, said that he had stabbed a German soldier to death with a knife at night. The retreating Polish army set fire to the storehouses, and then the Germans burned everything they could as well. The whole town was burned down, including our home. Despite this, our joy at the Germans' defeat was great. The Polish army held out for another week. Fighting took place every day, and the airplanes called in to help did not help the Germans at all. [On 21 September 1939], two days before Yom Kippur, the Germans entered our town. This time, too, they suffered a defeat and were all killed by the Polish soldiers, who came from the Tomaszów forest. Again, we were overjoyed. On Yom Kippur [Saturday 23 September 1939], the Germans [again] occupied the town, this time with a great force of tanks and cannons. On Sunday, we saw large groups of Polish prisoners and understood that the Poles were not resisting anymore. But this time, too, the Germans didn't stay long. On Monday the Russians came, [and they] occupied the town for a whole month. Only after a month was our town given over to the Germans again. When they were leaving town, the Russians took the Jews with them. At first Father hesitated to cross over to the Russian side, but the next day he made up his mind, and having hired a cart, we set off toward Kubnow,[354] by Rawa Ruska, where the border point was. The Russian guard let us across the border, saying only that they would not allow the peasant with the cart to come back. The peasant didn't want to drive us further, and only after Father's imploring, aided by a packet of matches, did the Russian soldier allow the peasant to go back. We lived in the town of Kubnow for nine months. The Jewish population's main occupation was smuggling. Sugar and foodstuffs were brought over from the German side, kerosene and salt from the Russian side. Many people crossed the border illegally in that place. There were many casualties. Once a German soldier shot dead a man named Zelatyner who tried to cross the border. I remember how the whole town was agitated because of it. The soldier tied a stone to the dead man's neck and lowered him into a hole in the ice. The local authority tried to recover the body and bury it. The chief of the border outpost allowed them to. The whole town took part in the funeral. I often met groups of Jews who had managed to cross the border. Their clothes were torn and they were covered in blood. Their hats and caps had holes in them, and they said this was how the German soldiers allowed each Jew across the border, taking away their valuables and robbing [them of] everything. In the summer of 1940, Father was summoned to the police station and asked if he wanted to become a Soviet citizen. Father said no and was told they would send him to the Germans. Other refugee families were called in too and asked if they wanted to go abroad. Some said they wanted to go to be with their relatives in America, others to Palestine. One night, all were arrested and deported to Russia.

Our group was sent to Altai Krai, in the Troitsky area. Our family was made up of Father, Mother, [my] older brother Mosze, age sixteen, a nine-year-old little sister, and me. Father worked in the forest as a logger but didn't complain about the work. He was happy to be able to spend Saturdays resting. On Saturday[s], he would bring a tallit and a prayer book to the forest with him. The guards turned a blind eye to the Jews' prayers. Mother also went to work in the forest. She received seventy kopecks a day for cutting off branches. It

354. Likely refers to the town of Uchnów, near Rawa Ruska.

was difficult to live on that [but], luckily, Father had brought a bit of manufacture, haberdashery, buttons, and ribbons with him. In Siberia these items are worth their weight in gold, and we got potatoes, bread, etc. in exchange for that merchandise. After the outbreak of the [German-Soviet] war, the situation got a lot worse, and we received only sixty dekagrams of bread per day; children—twenty dekagrams. We were on the brink of death from starvation. Many people received a piece of land to work then. It was hard work and it took a long time before anything grew [on that land]. We got a better piece of land from a Siberian man in exchange for some haberdashery. [My] brother and I worked [the land], but we were so hungry that as soon as the first cucumber appeared, we ate it straightaway in the field, not waiting for it to grow [bigger]. We sustained ourselves with berries. We ate them in the forest, too. This lasted a year, until the news of the Amnesty arrived. We went to Samarkand. The journey was hard. On arriving, we didn't find a place for the night, and we lived in the station for two weeks. Father went to Dzhambul to look for an apartment. Meanwhile, we children and Mother were taken to a kolkhoz outside Turkestan. Mama ran away from the kolkhoz to look for Father, and only by a miracle, came across a loader she knew in the station in Tashkent, who told her that Father was in Tashkent. Father came to be with us in the kolkhoz. We worked in the cotton fields. I myself picked a thousand meters of cotton plants per day and received half a kilo of rye flour. [My] brother Mosze and I fell ill with dysentery. The delegation took us from the hospital to a children's center in Turkestan. After three months, we were taken to Ashgabat, and from there, to Iran. We were in the last group of children who were allowed to leave Russia.

Protocol 136

Testimony of **Miriam Lipowicz**, age thirteen, daughter of Zelik and Rojza, from Pułtusk. Arrived in Palestine in February 1943.

Two weeks after the war broke out, the Germans entered Pułtusk.[355] They immediately began persecuting the Jews and took many [of them] to camps. It was said in town that fifty Jews were burned alive on the bridge. They were ordered to pour gasoline over one another and then were set alight. Among those burned to death was my uncle, Icchak Gołobroda, with [his] wife and five children. Jews were rounded up for work every day. During the work, the Jews were beaten and told to perform horrible jobs. [People] said in town that this was only the beginning of the persecutions, and Father was pondering how to escape. After two weeks in town, the Germans issued an order for all the Jews to gather in the city park within fifteen minutes. When everyone gathered, they were all photographed [and] told to hand over [their] money and jewelry; body searches were carried out. Then everyone was taken to the bridge. The bridge was surrounded by tanks. They started to rush people onward, and those who couldn't squeeze between the tanks were pushed into the water. That terrifying image from the bridge lives on in my memory as if it were [today]. The screams of small children and the laments of the adults went up to the heavens. Mothers clutched their small children close to squeeze in between the tanks. My father and mother and my two older sisters held me and my little brother Mosze tight. I thought I was going to suffocate then. I screamed loudly: "Mama, you will suffocate me," and Mama replied: "Quiet, my child, I want to save you." Beyond the bridge, we found ourselves in a field. Father showed us that this was the place where the Germans had burned the fifty Jews alive. Even though the Germans were shooting at us, my father and a few other Jews stopped and said a prayer for the dead in the place where my uncle and his family had been killed.

We went to Długosiodło. We spent one night there. Before we awoke, at six in the morning, the Germans arrived and chased us on, threatening to kill us if we didn't keep running. We walked through fields, villages. The countryfolk

355. In reality, Germans occupied Pułtusk on 7 September 1939, the seventh day of the war.

took pity on us; they gave us bread and water. This way we reached Ostrów [Mazowiecka] and made it across to Zambrów, to the Soviet side, in good shape. We went into a house where there were already many refugees. There wasn't even room to lie down on the floor. After one day's stay, we went to Białystok. The city was overflowing with refugees. Father started looking for an apartment. We lodged in the premises of a certain organization, where we spent a whole week. There were many people there. Father told us ahead to watch [our] stuff, because people were stealing from one another. Father looked for an apartment all day. Finally, he found a room in Internacjonalna Street, formerly Jewish Street. Father took up trading. [My] older sister, Ester, helped him. We went around to the neighboring towns, brought in goods, and sold them at a large profit. We lived all right off this. However, Father complained that traders were being persecuted. Mother prohibited him from trading, but when the bread ran out at home, he had to take up his old job again. Father didn't want to accept a Soviet passport, and when he came home and told [us] that they were registering [people] to go back, Mother convinced him to register, because here he was at risk of starvation.

In Exile

A few weeks after the registration, on Friday night, NKVD-ers knocked [on our door]. Father knew what they had come for and didn't want to open the door. Only when they started banging [on the door] with their gunstocks was [it] opened. They told us to get dressed [and] pack [our] belongings and took us to the station. We were loaded into a freight car, fifty people in [each], and after forty-eight hours—during which we weren't given anything to eat or to drink—the train set off. We traveled for a whole month. We were given a piece of bread once a day and a bit of soup at night. We weren't allowed out. Many people were ill, but the guards didn't want to hear about them, saying that if they died, there would be fewer Polish overlords in the world. We arrived in [the Autonomous Soviet Socialist Republic of] Komi, in the town of Selamadza [?] in the Kargierowski district.[356] There were exiled Russians living in our *posiołek*. They tormented us horribly and said that we would never taste freedom again. The warden rushed us to work, and laziness was punishable by prison. Five

356. Likely refers to the area of the city of Kargi in the Sverdlovsk Oblast.

people were sentenced to a few months' prison for being five minutes late for work, among them our friend Gurman, from Pułtusk. In our *posiołek* there was also a pious Jew, and people prayed in his barracks like in a synagogue. One day NKVD-ers appeared, and he was sentenced to four months' prison for organizing [prayers]. His wife, having four small children under her care, couldn't go to work and was refused a job and [her] bread ration. If it wasn't for the food parcels she received from relatives, she would have starved to death. The warden, furious that she was being fed somehow despite not receiving the bread [ration], accused her of speculating in food products. The woman was arrested, and the children were left alone in the *posiołek*. My mama took pity on the children, took them to her barracks and said to Father: "Let me think that I have three more children." Another [female] acquaintance in the *posiołek* who had brought along a few furs was accused of having stolen [them]. She had everything taken away and was sentenced to a few months' prison. Because Father developed heart problems and a doctor said he was not allowed to work in the forest, we were sent to the village of Salamadza [?]. We lived in a clay house, in among half-feral people who ate raw meat and bark off the trees. They ate the animals they caught in the forest raw. When we went to the forest for berries, we found human bones. It was said that cannibals lived in that forest. [Our] parents were afraid to have us go into the forest, but we were hungry [and] would sneak out of the house and run to the forest [to get] mushrooms and berries. One day a wolf appeared and grabbed a little girl, the daughter of our neighbor. The little girl's name was Jagoda. We ran away and watched from afar how the wolf tore the child into pieces and ate her. We were no longer allowed to go to the forest; we had to make do with the piece of bread we got. Father worked manufacturing jam from the berries the villagers picked in the forest. Everyone earned very little, fifty rubles per month at most, and one had to live on that. Our family received a kilo of bread per day, and we bought soup, at eighty kopecks per portion, with the money that Father earned. Very often we didn't have enough for soup and ate only bread and water. Terribly famished, we would run to the feral Komi [people] and beg them for meat, eating it raw, like our neighbors. They told us in their language to eat bark off the trees, but that we could not get used to. However, we would dry out the bark, grind it with a stone, and Mama would make dumplings from it, as if from dough. After four months in the village, Father fell ill with pneumonia. There was no hospital [and] Father lay for two months in a wet clay room. He didn't have medicine, but God helped us, and [he] recovered.

War and Amnesty

We didn't know anything about the outbreak of the [German-Soviet] war. Father didn't understand why the bread rations were decreased and so much was demanded [of the workers] at work. Only after some time did two NKVD-ers come and tell [us] about the Amnesty for Poles. We went to Syktyvkar. We lived outside the city. There was no bread. Father didn't get a job, and we decided to go to Samarkand. Things were no better there. We didn't even have a roof over our heads. They didn't want to sell us bread [and] we were told to go to a kolkhoz. We resisted at first [but] eventually went to the kolkhoz Piatiletka, outside Samarkand. Father, Mother, and [my] two older sisters worked with cotton. For this [work] the whole family received a kilo of flour and we all had to survive on it. Father went to the city in an attempt to have us admitted to an orphanage. He succeeded, and [my] sister, brother, and I were placed in a Polish orphanage, where there were only Jewish children. When the time for [our] evacuation came, [our] parents came to say goodbye and proposed that we stay. But we didn't want to stay. We arrived in Tehran via Krasnovodsk and Pahlevi. After a few months, in February 1943, we all came to Palestine.

Protocol 137

Testimony of **Hersz Szulman**, age thirty-four, resident of Łódź, head of the Łódź Tailors' Association, tailor by trade, member of the Central [Commission] of Polish Trade Unions.

On 25 and 26 August 1939, a mobilization took place in Łódź, which brought on a mood of disquiet in the city. The outbreak of war wasn't a surprise to anyone. Until 5 September, Łódź hadn't experienced the effects of air raids, even though German bomber planes were constantly circling above the city. On the night of 5 [September], an order was issued on the radio for all men capable of carrying weapons to leave the city. Thousands of people spilled into the streets, heading toward the suburban roads. I too found myself on the road to Brzeziny, in among the crowd of people fleeing. I left the city at five in the morning and Brzeziny [was] bombed at eight. We followed the Polish army. The roads were overflowing with civilians and blocked with carts and cars, to the point where the army could not move. German airplanes flew low above the roads and bombed the refugees. I found Brzeziny in ruins. This sight caused a great panic among the refugees. There were corpses of soldiers and policemen lying in the streets. We were literally stepping on corpses. The residents of Brzeziny, half-mad, were looking for their relatives among the ruins. I went down the road toward Rawa Mazowiecka, but [it] too turned out to be hell. It was constantly under fire. Rawa stood in flames. People were running around the streets with what remained of their possessions. One couldn't walk on the roads during the day. It was dangerous to stay in Rawa. People slept in the fields during the day and marched on at night. From Rawa, I went to Grójec via Nowe Miasto. From the incomplete messages that reached us, we gathered that we were surrounded by the Germans and that we could come face-to-face with them at any moment. On 9 September, the Germans cut us off in Góra Kalwaria. So our journey came to an end. On 12 September I returned to Łódź. The city looked dead. During the first four days we didn't go out into the street, because from the very first day the Germans had started grabbing Jews for work. They pulled them out of houses and beat them terribly. Of those who were taken to work, 10 percent didn't return home. Those who returned were barely alive, [suffering] from beating[s] and exhaustion. I too was caught a few times. Once I was taken outside of the city in a large group, to a square where there were horses standing. We had to clean the manure from the square with [our] bare hands, even though there were shovels nearby. The Germans placed the shovels next to us deliberately but didn't let us touch them. When we took the horses to the watering place, they had to be left a hundred meters from the water, and we had to carry the water [to them] in buckets ourselves. We were watched by German soldiers, [who] beat us bloody with knouts. In Łódź, we were only allowed to be out in the streets until six in the evening, and we were released from work at half past five. We would run the whole way home in a panic, and the Germans shot at the laggards without mercy. Slowly, people began to grow used to these horrors [and began] to go out into the streets. On the sixth day they were in Łódź, the Germans organized a raid on the Astoria café. Jews from different walks of life would gather at that café—merchants, craftsmen, factory owners. The Germans took eighteen innocent people away with them and shot them dead. When the senior [member] of the Council[357] tried to intervene with the Gestapo, he was beaten bloody and thrown out on the street. From that time on, life ended at six in the morning—after eight, manhunts would begin in the streets. Shoemakers and tailors had a lot of work. They fulfilled army orders. Apart from this, people were buying clothes for themselves, because orders had been issued about cash limits. One got up for work at six to avoid being caught. The Germans forced the Jews to open [their] shops, which soldiers and German civilians robbed in broad daylight. The response to complaints was that stealing was forbidden, but that no one could intervene in Jewish matters. I learned in the ghetto that [arm]bands for Jews would be introduced after some time. All associations[358] were closed down. The young people escaped to the Soviet side, across the Bug [River], en masse. On 5 October I left Łódź with [my] wife. [We] went to Warsaw by bus, and from there to Małkinia by taxi. A German patrol stopped us in a border zone village. A rigorous search was carried out on us under the guise of looking for weapons; our best possessions were taken from us. We

357. The witness is likely referring to the Judenräte, or the Jewish Councils of Elders, mandated by the Nazis to carry out designated tasks, including policing of fellow Jews, the disposal of Jewish corpses, and the selection of Jewish community members for labor and deportation.

358. [Probably refers to organizations such as Zionist groups, philanthropic organizations, and sports and theater associations.]

were set free and shown which direction we should go. But they didn't want to let us cross the border. We spent two days in no-man's-land. Then the border was opened, and we crossed over to Zaręby Kościelne, a small town on the Soviet side. It was said there that the town was going to be given over to the Germans, so we set off for Białystok. I found myself in Białystok on 9 October and came upon thousands of homeless refugees there. They didn't know what to do with themselves. [People] were sleeping on the streets. The lucky ones set up camp in the station. Food ran out in the city. The Bolsheviks began [their] propaganda [campaign to get people] to sign up for work in Russia. People were being registered to go to Magnitogorsk, Vitebsk, and the Northern regions. The first transports were sent off with music. Nevertheless, this registration wasn't popular, as it wasn't guaranteed that everyone would get work in their trade. Meanwhile, the first ones were returning to Białystok, escaping from Russia. They told stories about horrendous working conditions, about hunger and chaos in Russia. The registrations ceased completely. Life became impossible in Białystok as there was no work. I decided to go to Lwów, where life was supposedly easier. I left for Lwów on 24 November. I got accepted into a trade union as an activist and representative of a tailors' association. My task was to organize the tailors' cooperatives. The cooperative I created reported to the artisans' central office. At first, the working conditions were very difficult. We were receiving no orders. Then orders were coming in, and we thought that life would become normal. On 29 July, a meeting took place between the central office and the representatives of all the cooperatives. During the meeting, the Russian chairwoman of our cooperative came up to me and asked me to stand in for her on telephone duty that night. The telephones in all the cooperatives had to be manned twenty-four hours a day and be at the NKVD's disposal. I was the vice-chairman of the cooperative. I was very confused by this proposition, but as it turned out, this Russian woman knew that all the refugees were being sent to Siberia that night and wanted to save me. That night screaming and crying came from the street[s]. Vehicles were speeding down the streets all night long. I saw thousands of people being sent off in trucks. There was crying coming from inside [them]. That night, a companion of mine from Łódź turned up by chance and told me that the NKVD had deported my wife. I closed the cooperative and returned the keys to the chairwoman. She told me it was no news to her that refugees were being deported and that if I began to intervene in my wife's case, I myself would be sent away. I replied: "I dedicated my efforts to starting the cooperative—I didn't have much to show for it, though I expected a better future. But I won't allow my wife to be torn away from me." The chairwoman got very angry with me. I saw [my] wife at home. She was delaying the packing of [her] belongings, waiting for me to arrive. The NKVD-er who was watching her told me he was taking [my] wife, and that I was to stay in Lwów. He started to curse, [claiming] she had tricked him by saying she would go voluntarily, that she only wanted to say goodbye to me. I replied that nothing in the world would separate me from her. Eventually an NKVD officer was found who said: "people like this will come in handy over there, too." They transported us like cattle, on trucks and then in freight cars. We traveled for thirteen days, and even though cars with food were attached to the transport, we weren't given anything to eat for the first few days. After a few days, they announced that food could be obtained for a bribe. We bribed the NKVD-ers [and they] brought [us] food. When we ran out of money, we turned to the train manager, who was angry with us for reporting [to him] so late, and cursed the guards for taking bribes. They were reprimanded and that was it. We still didn't get food, only excuses that all the chaos was the doing of Trotsky saboteurs. At our destination, in Sozwa,[359] we were welcomed very warmly. We received food at state prices. After some time, we were again loaded up—[this time] onto rafts covered with paraffin and oil, so that we were completely blackened. The crowding was so awful that we couldn't even stand up comfortably. People fainted; there was no medical help. In this atmosphere, some of the Poles started to mock the Jews, and the NKVD-ers got involved in the game. We complained to the higher authorities, even listing the surnames of the culprits. In the town of Gari, two NKVD antisemites disappeared, and we were told that they had been sent to prison. After four days' travel on the water, in these same inhuman conditions, we arrived in the *posiołek* Zimnij. It turned out that the *posiołek* was not ready to receive us. There were no barracks, [only] a few huts—without windows or doors, or even stoves. [There were,] however, swarms of mosquitos that attacked us and bit us terribly. We slept in a field at night [and] were placed in small, half-destroyed huts in the morning. A small family received a room with

359. Correctly: Sosva [original Polish correction: Sośwa].

a kitchen, a bigger one—two [rooms]. Luckily, there was a half–burned-down sawmill not far from the *posiołek*, where we found a few rusty tools. We made nails out of rusty wire, and within two weeks, [we had] furniture in our huts. On the twentieth day after our arrival, some of the deportees were taken out for haying, to a place ninety kilometers from the *posiołek*. They didn't [even] know how to hold a scythe. It turned out that the working conditions were deadly. The hay was growing in swamps; there were no instructors; the grass was being cut down in a primitive way, and quotas weren't fulfilled. [People] returning from work were lice ridden [and] famished and were punished for not fulfilling the quotas. Those who remained in the *posiołek* became artisans, carpenters, and cart drivers, who busied themselves with cleaning [and] the transportation of products and building materials. When there was no more work in the *posiołek*, the young people, [who made up] 99 percent of the deportees, were hired out like slaves by the regional NKVD-ers, to carry out black work[360] in the forest and on the roads. We were only hired for work in the 11th division [of the NKVD], and in reality, still belonged to the NKVD district—in Gari. The NKVD treated us mercilessly. Families were torn apart and it was only through chance that I was not separated from [my] wife. But how pleasantly surprised we were when we found good conditions at the work[place] in Likino.[361] New barracks, nice surroundings. Our joy did not last long. Our warden was a man called Czerbakow, a common degenerate without [even] the most basic qualifications. During one of the assemblies, in which the secretary of the Bolshevik Party Raikom[362] took part, I spoke up and said that we didn't have appropriate qualifications to do the work, that we needed to be trained, that we didn't have the proper tools, and that we rarely fulfilled [our] quotas because of this. I also said that we had sold everything we had with us and that we were starving. The secretary said that our requests would be fulfilled and that we were not to work until we had received tools and clothing. The next day, 99 percent of the exiles did not turn up for work because of the lack of tools. Czerbakow accused everyone of *progul*.

---

360. Unskilled labor.

361. No place called Likino in the Sverdlovsk Oblast could be located.

362. Raikom (Polish: Rajkom): a district committee of the Soviet Communist Party, All-Union Communist Party (Bolsheviks); Polish: Wszechzwiązkowa Komunistyczna Partia (bolszewików), WKP(b).

Twenty-five percent [of the workers] were punished with lowered wages. Another assembly was called, where the chief the 11th division was present. He told us to stop dreaming about returning home because we would never get out of there, and to get used to the conditions instead. Anyone who didn't get used to them would die like a dog. That speech made a grave impression [on us]. I spoke up and said that only opponents of the Soviets could speak this way and that I could not imagine that people would be condemned to moral suffering in the USSR. I turned to the secretary with [my] accusation against the chief. [There was] no response—instead, the assembly was dismissed, with the promise that a new one would be called. We were released from work that day. The next day our owner, who had hired us out to the 11th division, arrived. The warden of the Gari division wouldn't listen to any of us; he only said that he knew of destructive elements among us. Everyone would get clothing and tools and would prove themselves with [their] work results. Within fourteen days, the results proved remarkable. Thirty percent [of the workers] qualified as *udarniki*,[363] 50 percent were fulfilling the quotas, and only 20 percent were fulfilling [only] 80 percent of the quota. The warden thanked us, and as a reward, decided to withdraw the *progul* complaints from the court. This situation was unbearable to Czerbakow. He started to stir up intrigues between the Poles and the Jews. It got to a point where, during an assembly dedicated to Parisian Communism,[364] the speaker wasn't allowed to speak until the issue of the relations between Jews and Poles was resolved. As a result, Warden Czerbakow was sent off somewhere else, and two Poles were also sent away to the neighboring *posiołek*. On the anniversary of the October Revolution, the Party secretary promised to assign work to people according to their prewar jobs. He fulfilled the promise in part. Shoemakers, ironworkers, and tailors got jobs, the administration was entrusted to the deportees, and the end result proved to be surprisingly good. This way we won more-or-less good working conditions for ourselves—we built a hospital with our own hands; trained people in the carpentry trade. All this caused the mortality in our *posiołek* to decrease, [and] it was minimal compared to the mortality in other *posiołki*. [Our] *posiołek* gained renown; [other] exiles tried to get into it. In one of the

363. *Udarnik* (Russian): a leading worker.

364. The anniversary of an uprising in Paris (18 March–28 May 1871) that broke out during the Franco-Prussian war. It was suppressed by the right-wing government of Adolphe Thiers.

places of exile, a Siberian district where our companions' relatives lived, three hundred people went on strike. A well-known Polish activist, [Bolesław] Drobner,[365] led the strike. The conditions in that place [were] horrific. [People] feared the approaching frosts. The mortality rate was terrifying. They heard about our *posiołek* and demanded to be sent somewhere different. The three hundred strikers loaded their belongings onto sleighs and drove out into a field. They didn't want to work. They spent two weeks in the field, unrelenting. As a result, they were all deported to Sawna [?], and the strike organizer, Drobner, [was deported] to an unknown place.

In January 1941 I was called in to the NKVD by telephone and offered [the job of] sewing uniforms exclusively for the NKVD. I accepted the offer and began to work. Six weeks later, I was offered [the opportunity] to open a sewing workshop. They agreed to let us live in the town of Gari, a truly unusual privilege for exiles. I put together such a workshop using the local [work]force. In the meantime, the following took place: the leadership set a goal of having the exiles employed to pick berries in the forest. The Russian women from the neighboring villages didn't want to help [with it]. In response, the NKVD announced that it would teach the peasant women tailoring as a reward for diligent berry picking. The tailoring course began with forty women in attendance. After a few days, 15 percent of the women gave up studying. They were illiterate [and] couldn't understand the complicated lectures or handle scissors and a pencil. Six weeks later, the remaining women finished the course with distinction and were able to apply for jobs in sewing workshops and tailoring cooperatives. This way the NKVD fulfilled the berry-picking plan.

With the outbreak of the [German-Soviet] war, the workshop in Gari was closed down, and [my] wife and I were sent to the *posiołek*. Soon we learned about the Amnesty and started preparing for the journey. I was approached and asked to stay as a *volnonayemny*. I agreed at first and worked another whole month. But when everyone left, a great anxiety overtook me. I had a nagging thought that I wasn't actively fighting against Fascism and Hitler. I told the warden I was resigning from work and went south with the next transport.

---

365. Bolesław Drobner (1883–1968): distinguished activist of the PPS [Polska Partia Socjalistyczna; English: Polish Socialist Party; PSP], post-1948 a PZPR [Polska Zjednoczona Partia Robotnicza] or PUWP [Polish United Workers' Party] activist.

Tashkent looked like Białystok in the fall months of 1939. A lot of Polish exiles had come there from the north. There was no organized care for them, it turned out that no one had any resources, and there was no work to be found. The locals claimed [this was the case] because of fear of competition, because Polish deportees had significantly better work qualifications than the Russians. We decided to go to Kogon. At the station past Samarkand, the NKVD issued an order for all refugees to be taken off the train and directed to Turkestan. We didn't want to leave the train. We said that as free citizens we had the right to choose our place of residence ourselves. We were dragged out by force and loaded onto a train going to Turkestan. We were sent to a kolkhoz. I don't remember its name. The nearby kolkhozes were named after Marx and Thälman,[366] which I considered sacrilegious. I despaired at the sight of our exiles who had been staying for some time [fragment of text missing] kibitka without a door or windows. A simple hole in the wall served as both a window and a door, and smoke escaped through another hole in the ceiling. The prospect of such a life seemed horrendous to me. I decided to get away at the first available opportunity. I would rather live in a field, under the open sky, than in a dirty stinking hole of a kibitka. Everyone wanted to escape to Turkestan at any cost. We gave our last few grosze to the kolkhoz residents to help us in [our] escape. In Turkestan, we looked for work in vain. We couldn't find [any] because of competition. Kazakhs are generally bad workers. The cooperatives didn't want to take us in, and when [we] managed to earn something privately we had to work below our level. We knew we would be judged harshly for work that was too good. We were left with no livelihood. I wanted to take on work [to do] at home—I rented a manual sewing machine and worked with it. I didn't even earn [enough] for bread. I sold everything I had with me but that wasn't enough either. I decided to join the Polish army. I informed the war commandant about this, said goodbye to [my] wife, and went to Czerpak,[367] where the eighth division was being put together. I was desperate to arrange for me and my wife to leave for Persia together. However, the following event took place. At a station between Arys and Czerpak, in Tyulkibas, we were stopped by two Polish officers. We were traveling in a group of 330 Jews. The

366. Ernst Thälmann (1886–1944): leader of the German Communists, murdered in the Buchenwald concentration camp.

367. An incorrect name for the town of Chok-Pak [original Polish correction: Czok-Pak].

officers told the Jews that, even though they had been mobilized, they could not come into Czerpak because typhus had taken hold there. We thought that the reason was true and appropriate. We asked to be given documents [certifying] that we were Polish soldiers who couldn't be assigned to a division because of the typhus. They didn't want to give us the document[s], which seemed suspicious to us, especially when [the officers] started whispering something to the Polish soldiers who had arrived with us in Turkestan. There were three soldiers late to the first mobilization. We noticed that the officers bought those soldiers train tickets from the cashier. We turned to the station manager, who ordered that no one be sold a ticket. He informed the appropriate institutions by telephone, [and] we were told to wait patiently because a Soviet officer would provide an explanation on this matter. At ten o'clock in the evening, a Soviet colonel arrived on a freight train from Alma-Ata. He ordered a list of the mobilized [soldiers] to be put together and told us the following: "Tomorrow a train carrying the Eighth Polish Division for evacuation will pass through this station. We will attach your cars to the transport, and this way you will automatically become a part of the Eighth Division since you are Polish soldiers." The next day, the train arrived under the command of a Polish general whose surname I do not remember. The general simply said: "I'm not taking Jews, they're not Polish soldiers." At that point, the Soviet authorities said that if the general didn't change his decision, the whole transport would be halted. After conferring with [his] officers, the general agreed to have the cars with the Jews attached to the end of the train. The Soviet authorities did not agree to this, saying the Poles would detach the cars during the journey. They demanded that our cars be joined in in the middle of the transport. The general acquiesced. But the NKVD still did not believe [him], and sent a convoy with the transport. Our train traveled through Krasnovodsk, and from there it was supposed to go to Persia over the Caspian Sea. During the journey, our Jewish division was formed into platoons [and] had officers and seconds-in-commands assigned to it. We were under military discipline during the journey. We were told that we would receive uniforms in Persia. We suffered a lot at the hands of the officers, who led the soldiers by bad example. In Pahlevi, when the army was split according to positions, our officer appeared and asked what we were waiting for. We replied that we were waiting for [our] uniforms. [In response], he ordered us to disperse, saying, brusquely, that we had no business with the army. The representatives of our group asked that we be given documents, be allowed to wash and given blankets. The officer replied: "I have nothing for [this] pack of civilian Jews. Let those who sent you here give you blankets and uniforms." We spent two days outdoors, in the pouring rain, naked and hungry. We had no papers or clothes. We fell into despair. An English commission took an interest in us and intervened with the Polish army authorities. The Poles replied that they had nothing to do with us. The English demanded a thorough report from us. There was an English Jew in the commission, a captain who spoke Jewish. He took all the testimonies from us and promised he would send us to Tehran the following day. In the meantime, he ordered that we be given blankets and tents. He also promised us he would do everything [he could] to have us recognized as a division of the Polish army. The next day, the captain arrived and took us to get washed. The Polish authorities said that the baths were currently occupied. Three times we were taken to get washed and three times we not allowed to bathe. The English commission lost patience [and] removed the Polish personnel from the bathing establishment and installed Englishmen in charge. After we washed, we were given uniforms and sent to Tehran as an army division. We were taken to camp number 4 and brought up in front of an army commission. The commission deemed everyone unfit for army duty and classified us as category D. Then we were taken to tailoring workshops and given bands with the letter *C* [to be worn on our] left arms. We were forbidden to take these bands off. They were specifically for Jews. We were moved to a civilian camp where we were given the hardest jobs. Here no one considered us sick and unfit for duty, as the commission had ascertained. One day an English commission visited the camp [and] found plenty of young, healthy men in the civilian camps. [The commission] asked why these young people weren't in the army. The warden replied that they were sick, unfit for duty. At that moment, a large Jewish youth came out of a storehouse with three huge sacks on his arm, and the letter *C* [on his arm]. An English officer stopped the youth and asked him: "What is wrong with you?" To this, the boy replied: "I'm missing one more sack." Meanwhile, I fell ill with typhus and when I returned to the camp, it was still a group of sick Jews with the letter *C* on [their] arms serving in the camp instead of black workers. I was given a band with the letter *C* as soon as I left the hospital. In May 1942, the bands with the letter *C* were taken off and we all went in front of a commission, which deemed those gravely ill and crippled fit for army duty. In the meantime, I organized a tailoring and sewing course in the camp, and even though I was offered a similar job in Tehran, outside the camp, with a salary of 350 tomans per month, I agreed, at the delegation's request, to teach Polish refugee women [instead] for 35 tomans a month. Seven hundred women finished the course with excellent results, and the delegation increased my salary to ninety tomans a month. I set up the tailoring courses in such a way that they continued running even after my departure.

[(A pencil-written note): There was no such course in the camps at that time. The managers of tailoring workshops were exclusively women.

(signature) Glass.]

Protocol 138

Testimony of **Szymon Rosenblum**, age forty-two, born in Łódź, housepainter by trade. Came to Palestine via Tehran in August 1943.

On Friday, 8 September [1939], Germans entered Łódź, and since I lived at 87 Brzezińska Street, and the first German outposts appeared at the side of Brzeziny, all the [local] Jews locked their gates and windows, afraid to go out in the streets. The streets were empty. We watched the approaching Germans through a crack in the gate. First motorcycle riders arrived in full armor, each holding a gun in his hand aimed straight ahead. Then the trucks came. The streets were, as I said, deserted. No one slept on Friday night. All the Jews gathered in one apartment; we sat without a word, huddled together, afraid of our own voices. Opposite us there was a Christian bakery. The next day after the arrival of the Germans, a long line formed in front of the bakery of [people] expecting to get bread. The women stood in the line because the men were afraid to go out into the street. The German soldiers kicked all the Jewish women out of the line, and those who resisted were beaten mercilessly. I didn't allow my wife to [join] the line, even though after a few days I did start to feel the lack of food supplies in the house. I am a housepainter by trade. I had no work, naturally, nor did I have [any] money set aside, [so] disregarding the danger that faced me, I started trading in sugar, flour, and wood. Every time I left home, the family made a scene, protesting. [My] wife and children said they would rather die from hunger than have me take the risk. Every hour, the Germans would surround Jewish homes [and] drag all the residents out, so I preferred to be picked up in the street rather than suffer all the humiliations that could await me at home. Besides, it was easier to hide from the raids in the streets. A few weeks went by like this. I went out into the streets every day and bought what I could. My brother, Mordechaj, was the owner of a shop at 61 Łagiewnicka [Street]. He also sold iron and haberdashery in that shop. I stopped at [my] brother's every day. The Germans would come into his shop and take whatever they liked. Slowly, the shop emptied. My brother came to the conclusion that it was dangerous to live in a non-Jewish neighborhood, so he moved in with his brother-in-law, the owner of a bakery at 57 Piłsudski [Street]. This way I received a loaf of bread every day through my little niece.

My brother told her not to give the bread to anyone but me, [so] he would find out this way whether I was home or whether I had fallen victim to a German raid. Recognizing that I would not survive this situation for long, I decided to stock up on some products and set off from home. I didn't know where to go, but felt that the time was near when I would have to leave home and leave [my] wife and four children in God's hands.

What Happened in the Main Square in Bałuty

On 9 October [1939], a Friday, at six in the morning, my wife returned home from a line where she had been [waiting] for bread. She was white as death. She started kissing me, [begging] me not to go out into the street. She was so shaken that I could not get a word out of her. Finally, she told me that the Germans had hanged three men in the main square in Bałuty. When [my] wife left home, I could not contain my curiosity and I made my way to the Bałuty square to find out what in fact had happened. My brother-in-law, Abraham Bankier, lived in the main square in Bałuty. When I arrived at the square, I saw the following scene: in the middle of the square stood three tall gallows, and on those gallows hung three corpses, two Poles and one Jew. The victims were wearing their [own] clothes, and the Jew had a Jewish cap on his head. On their chests, signs had been attached: "This is how our Führer punishes those who oppose him." Further down stood one more set of gallows with the writing: "For the offenders." Next to the gallows stood German soldiers with shotguns, and people walked past and glanced at the gallows out of the corners of their eyes. Upset and distraught, I went into the house where my brother-in-law lived. Both of us went to my brother's place, to 38 Zgierska [Street]. We didn't know what to do; we were afraid to run away because we'd heard that the Germans at the border shot at every Jew trying to cross [it]. We decided to gather at my brother's after dinner, together with the whole family, to decide what to do next. My brother was a scrooge. He didn't help anyone in the family before the war, even though he was wealthy. This time, however, he gave us all the money he had, saying: "Take as much as you want and let's all save ourselves." He himself, however, decided not to leave Łódź, and to take care of our wives and children [instead]. On Saturday, 17 October, my brother and his son and I went to the bus station. We waited all night, and in the morning got onto a bus going toward Warsaw. Before I left, all [our] relatives turned up at the station, and the children called out [asking] that I not forget about them. In Łowicz, we took off [our] yellow badge[s], and we arrived in Warsaw before evening. We spent the night with an acquaintance of my brother's, Weisfeld. At five in the morning, the Germans surrounded the house and dragged the Jews out for [forced] labor. I hid in the toilet, and since there were three pretty girls in our apartment whom the Germans took an interest in, they gave up the search and we were saved. At seven in the morning I went to Małkinia by train—there the Germans were capturing all the Jews getting off the train. A few of us escaped. All the way to the border, every few steps, there were soldiers with dogs that attacked people, bit [them], and ripped their clothes. I managed to hide. I saw that the Germans were only capturing people on foot, and letting through those riding on carts. I wanted to get onto a cart, but before that I found my brother and his son, and together with them, walked toward the border zone. We were searched and had everything taken off us. [The Germans] ogled every woman and the prettier ones were stripped naked, searched, and beaten. A small boy climbed a tree out of fright; they started shaking the tree, and when he fell, beat him up horribly. [Some] people had already been waiting in the border zone for eight days. The border was closed. It was opened two hours later, and we made it to Zaręby Kościelne. It was late at night, but I knew the town from 1920, when I had served in the army. I found an apartment I knew, went to [look for my] brother but did not find him. I did, however, meet other people from Łódź, and fifteen [of us] settled in a small room. We whisked off our wet clothes. Terribly famished, people started to sniff around in the corners, and we found a pot of food in the dark. We practically inhaled its contents. In the morning it turned out that it had been prepared for the cattle. We were cold, so we lit a fire, which aroused the suspicion of the NKVD. They surrounded us, arrested us, and sent us to Czyżew. The town had been burned down. We spent the night on top of the ruins, and in the morning, I made my way to the station and went to Białystok.

In Białystok

I could not find a place to stay in Białystok, [which was] full of refugees. I slept in a different place every night—in organizational facilities, in a beth hamidrash—and only a few weeks later found a free attic at the house of a Polish woman, Mrs. Szymanowska. I took up trading. I traded in bread rolls.

I paid ten kopecks apiece and sold [them] for twelve kopecks. Then I went to Sokółka, outside Białystok, and bought everything I could there. As I often didn't get anything in town, I bought a kilo of pumpkin seeds and buckets of herring. Then I traded in cigarette papers and made a living somehow. [My] biggest worry was the fate of [my] wife and children, from whom I hadn't received any messages. With family in Poland, I naturally didn't want to apply for a Soviet passport, and I was summoned to the NKVD one day and asked why I didn't have [one]. I replied that if they brought in my wife and children, I would immediately become a Soviet citizen. They said there were enough other women in Białystok and told me to decide: whether I was going home or taking the passport. Naturally, I replied that I wanted to go home. A short time later, on 27 June 1940, at two o'clock at night, there was a knock on our door. I was living with Maniek Apelbojm from Łódź and two cousins whose husbands were staying out of town. We were told to get dressed and go to Pieracki Street. [My] cousins were left in the house. After a few hours, we were taken to Bekier's cured meat factory, which had been turned into a camp. I found my brother and his son there. There were two thousand people there. The windows were closed, the doors were closed, they almost suffocated us. Our screams were in vain, until the people who were out in the courtyard started breaking the windows with stones. A stone hit a man named Cymmerman, from Łódź. After eight days in that camp, we were taken to a camp outside of town, in Sosnówka. There were doctors, engineers, officers, professors, political activists, and others in that camp. There were three large barracks [there], two intended as accommodation, the third one—for interrogation[s]. For eight days, we were let out for fresh air only once a day and given [only] a piece of bread and a bit of water to eat. Later we were permitted a half-hour hygiene walk [since] we were all completely lice infested. Before long you would see high-ranking individuals on the grass in front of the barracks, stripping naked and killing the lice. People would then lie naked on the grass, cooling their lice-bitten bodies. This pleasure was banned after three days because the grass itself, it was said, had started to crawl. We were given three hundred grams of bread per day and herring soup. One would get so thirsty after this soup that there wasn't enough water in the wells. One day I was called in for an interrogation and told to sign a protocol. On 28 July we were all photographed, a detailed search took place, then we were put into rows and taken to the station. The transport was made up of fifty freight cars, which were sealed after being filled with people. I traveled for nine days. We were given bread to eat, and chlorinated water. This way we arrived in Kotlas. In Kotlas we were sent to a camp where there were also Russian exiles. We waited for a barge that was to take us to Ustin.[368] We were packed in like sardines and traveled for five days on the river. Many people went blind during the journey. In Ustin, we were put up in barracks, a few people in each, split into brigades, and sent off for work. I was sent to the camp Knaiz Fagas[369] with [my] brother. There we were washed [and] given clean underwear, and I was sent off again to Czybluchta,[370] and [my] brother to Witelsjan.[371] There were oil fields twelve kilometers away, where I was supposed to work. We were refining the oil, and like the Poles, we were forbidden from doing the same work every day so that we wouldn't become qualified workers. We worked somewhere different every day. We were woken up at four in the morning, [and] at four-thirty there was a roll call. We walked twenty-four kilometers to work every day. We weren't given food all day long, and we ate berries and roots we pulled up on the way. At six in the evening we received a bowl of watery sour cabbage soup made from the so-called wild cabbage. For fulfilling one's quota one got nine hundred grams of bread, others received seven hundred grams. We slept on bare boards, and mice ran around over our heads. There were Russian exiles living with us, a few thousand men and a few tens of women. At night the Russians would steal anything they could from us. They were so skilled that we couldn't hide anything, and anyone who complained risked a beating. After a few months' stay in that camp, many of us fell ill with lung problems. Only sick people who had a high temperature were exempt from work. Many people died from hunger and lung diseases. There were neither doctors nor medicines, and people were rarely admitted to a hospital. Cases of *cynga* were common. Everyone almost lost their teeth, and even those who were seriously ill were told they were faking their illness. It got to a point where even the most gravely ill stopped complaining about [their] disease[s] and simply died during work. The death of a friend no longer had

---

368. Ust-Vym [original Polish correction: Ustwym].

369. Knyazhpogost [original Polish correction: Kniażpogost].

370. Perhaps: Ukhta (formerly Chibyu, renamed in 1939). It's possible that the two names were combined.

371. Vetlosyan [original Polish correction: Wietłosian].

an impact on anyone: you would stop working for a few minutes, and using the very same shovel you worked with, dig a grave for a friend who had worked alongside you only yesterday. Among the brigade leaders, I met a man named Fiszhaut from Warsaw, a Communist, who had escaped from Poland ten years before the war and was sentenced to four years of camp in Russia. On Yom Kippur [12 October 1940], we gathered for prayer. We had no prayer book and recited the service from memory. Fiszhaut saw us as we were praying and said that he would tell on us to the warden. We dispersed. I cried so hard that night that I fell asleep in tears. The next day, I reported to the doctor. After an examination the doctor said: "You're faking it; you don't want to work because today is a holiday." I had to work on Yom Kippur.

War and Amnesty

We didn't know whether the outbreak of the [German-Soviet] war would worsen or improve our situation. They started reducing the bread rations, and as if sensing we would be freed, we saved the bread and dried it for rusks. We decided to leave the camp all together, [because we were] afraid of being robbed during the journey. The Russians envied our freedom. When we hadn't been issued [our] documents after a month, we abandoned [our] work and decided to walk out of the camp. The brigade leader told us to turn back, but we were no longer allowed to live with the Russians. At night, the Poles sang national songs, and Jews prayed openly. The warden did not react. They tried to convince us to stay, [saying] they would improve our working conditions, that we would get land and a goat. Some stayed. Most, however, set off on their way. I went to Tatsko.[372] I signed up for the Polish army. Six weeks later, I was sent to Koltupanki,[373] and from there to Guzar. From Guzar I went to Tehran. On 1 August 1943 I arrived in Palestine.

---

372. Refers to the town of Totskoye [original Polish correction: Tockoje].
373. Koltubanky [original Polish correction: Kołtubanki].

Protocol 140

Testimony of **Jakub Piwko**, age twelve, son of Berisz and Hinda, from Brok on the Bug [River]. Came to Palestine via Russia and Tehran in August 1943.

There were four of us siblings at home, and only I alone came to Palestine. One brother stayed in Russia, another went to Japan and is in Shanghai. My father had a small shop; we lived in our own little house and got by all right. On the day the war broke out, a notice was put up in the streets that the Germans had attacked Poland. Panic took over the town. People started running away, but Father didn't want to leave home. In the evening, when we went to pray in the synagogue, a Polish peasant we knew told us that the Germans were already close. People were running away wherever their feet took them. The Germans started bombing the town. Fires broke out and all the houses burned down. Before the Germans entered our town, the Poles destroyed the bridge on the Bug [River]. A battle was taking place outside town [and] bullets wounded many people in the streets. The battle stopped by evening, and the Germans arrived in town. Straightaway, they issued an order for all Jews to gather in the church. [Both] the young and the old went. The old people had Torahs in their hands. The Germans locked the church and told us they would burn all the Jews together with [it]. We lived through a horrible night. The screams of those locked up went up to the heavens. The next day, a German officer released everyone from the church. The young people were taken for [forced] work. The old ones and the children were set free. Father was set free, and since our home hadn't burned down, many Jews gathered at our place, with the rabbi at the helm, because everyone was afraid to go out in the streets where the Germans were ripping out people's beards and beating them. German soldiers came to our place all the time, took away various objects and destroyed the rest. One day, they came for a few kilos of flour and spilled the whole sack. Our house remained unburned, the only one on the entire street. The Germans set fire to it one night, and we barely escaped in one piece. We went to a Polish acquaintance's place and spent the night in his storage room. After our home was burned, there was only [one] Jewish home remaining in town, which belonged to Szmul the shochet. The Jews gathered at his house. One night, the Germans knocked [on his door]. [The door] wasn't opened immediately because there were many people sleeping on the floor and it was difficult to get to the entrance. The Germans threatened to shoot everyone if [the door] wasn't opened immediately. When the door was opened, they fired a shot straightaway and one Jew, by the name of Kapranski, was killed on the spot. The Germans carried out a search of the apartment and took away everything of any value. Then they separated the women from the men. They led the men to the main square and killed [them]. Among those killed was my father. The rabbi and his two children and the shochet hid and slipped out of town at night, going toward Ostrów [Mazowiecka]. On the way, they came upon a German car. Two Germans got out of it and started shooting at them. The shochet dropped dead, and the rabbi was wounded. Then the Germans drove away, leaving the dead shochet and the injured rabbi on the road. The rabbi made it to Ostrów with his last bit of strength, crossed over to the Russian side, made it to Wilno, and today he is in America. After Father's death, I was left alone with Mother. My brothers had gotten away earlier. A peasant we knew took us over to the other side of the river. We made it to [the place of] a Jewish landowner, Czecziner, who was a friend of [my] father's. He welcomed us warmly. We stayed with him for a few days. We wanted to go to Kosów [Kosów Lacki], because my brother was there. Meanwhile, the Bolsheviks had entered Brok, so we returned home and began to look for our belongings, since we had run away from town almost naked.

The Bolsheviks only stayed in Brok for four days. Before they left, they said that anyone who wanted to could go with them. We went to Kosów, where my married oldest brother lived. Then [my] brother came from the yeshiva and tried to convince us to go to Wilno, as even the war would end [eventually].

Both brothers worked in a sawmill and made good money. But the younger one didn't want to stay with us and went to Wilno. We were left on our own and struggled a great deal. My older brother had to support Mama and me [as well as] his family. Mama tried her hand at trading, but it was difficult; they threatened to lock her up in prison. We fared so badly that when the registration was announced, my mama registered to return home. One night [my] brother came running to us from the sawmill and said that all refugees were going to be moved to Białystok that night, and that he wanted to help us pack [our] belongings. Indeed, the NKVD-ers came that night [and] took us to the sawmill, where the refugees had gathered. Fifty people were loaded into

[each] freight car, and we set off. We all thought that we were going home, but we realized after some time that we had been deported to Russia. For food, we received a piece of bread and a bit of watery soup once a day. The crowding in the car was horrendous; there was no water to revive those who fainted. There was no toilet either. Children did it through the window, and adults were let out at the stations under convoy. The journey took three weeks [and then] we arrived in Arkhangelsk. We were supposed to be sent straight to a *posiołek* from there. We spent a few days under the open sky, eating fish we cooked over fire. There was cheap sugar there, which we bought. One day at dawn, we were loaded onto a ship. We traveled for a few days and then disembarked onto a bank. We got to the *posiołek* on foot. We lived in a barracks full of bedbugs. Mosquitos bit us terribly. Mother worked in a brickyard and received eight hundred grams of bread, and we, the children, four hundred each. Mama felt unwell—we ran the household, making sure she had a bit of warm soup when she returned from work. All day long we sang a song that started with the words "Hungry, cold, and a long way from home." One day a commandant arrived in the *posiołek*, and Mama complained to him that she was weak and could not work. An order arrived a few days later moving us to another *posiołek*. There were small brick houses there, and we got a room with a kitchen. There was also a canteen there. We got soup for free in the first [few] days; then we [would have to] pay 2.50 rubles for [it]. We couldn't afford such luxury. We lived off dry bread and hot water. Mama worked in the forest with [my] brother, and I took care of the household. We spent a whole year in that *posiołek*, until the outbreak of the [German-Soviet] war. The administrators and all the young men went to the front. Another warden arrived, an old Russian with a long beard, who was good to us. [The work consisted of] digging trenches. The bread rations were decreased. One day we were told that we were free. We went to Samarkand. The journey took two months. On the way we got cheap fruit in various towns and we were so famished that each of us would eat ten kilos of fruit per day. We fell ill with dysentery. A few people from our group died on the way, but we arrived in Samarkand healthy. We couldn't find a place to stay [and] spent a month on the street. We went to the kolkhoz Woroszyłow. It was an Uzbek kolkhoz. Mama was so weak that she couldn't work. [My] brother and I worked picking cotton. We received four hundred grams of bread each per day, which was later decreased to two

hundred grams. We were terribly famished and ate wild herbs that made us ill. We decided to run away from the kolkhoz. We heard that a group of Polish citizens was being put together in Dzhambul to go to Persia. We sold some belongings and went to Dzhambul. It turned out to be untrue. We roamed the streets and had to go to a kolkhoz again, [this time] kolkhoz Uzbek. We worked hard and would have died from starvation had I not learned how to steal and stolen handfuls of rye for Mama every day. I knew it was forbidden to steal, but I couldn't help myself when I saw the flour. After a year, when we again heard that Poles were leaving for Persia, we went to Samarkand. We arrived on a rainy day and spent the night [sleeping] in the mud. [People] ripped things from one another['s] hands. They robbed us of our last shirt, and Mother despaired terribly as a result. She managed to place me in a Polish children's center, and she herself left for a kolkhoz with [my] brother. I spent a year in the center. The Polish children teased us a lot. We were forced to say Christian prayers, and anyone who didn't want to would be beaten. I fell ill with typhus and pneumonia during that time. I spent a few months in the hospital. In the meantime, Mama left the kolkhoz and lived in a stable in Samarkand so that she would be able to visit me. I left Russia with the last transport of children and went to Tehran. I was in Tehran for six months and came to Palestine alongside 108 [other] children.

Protocol 142

Testimony of **Cipora (Fela) Enoch**, age thirteen, from Bielsko-Biała, daughter of an officer in the Polish army.

We lived in the town of Bielsko-Biała, on Kościuszko Street. My father, Wolf (Wilhelm), turned thirty-five in the year of the war. He was a secretary to a lawyer and was called the lawyer's deputy in town. My father was a Polish officer. Every year he was called in for exercises; he was a lieutenant. Two weeks before the war broke out, Father went to work, to the office, and didn't return. It turned out that an order to mobilize immediately had been delivered to Father at the office, so that he didn't even have time to come home and say goodbye to the family. Where Father went, we didn't know.

Mother Is Left with Four Children

Our town was located just by the German border. Many Germans lived among us and they were constantly making threats at the Jews. Mother packed [our] belongings and ran away from our home with [her] four children. My oldest brother, Abraham, was fifteen at the time. The two younger sisters [were]: Marta—ten years old, and Roza—eight years old. Mama wanted to hire a cart to put our things on—some sheets, undergarments, and clothes—but it was impossible to get horses since they had all been requisitioned for the army. On the road, we came upon many other mothers with children as well as "Silesians"—the runaways.[374] There were a lot of military people on the roads. The soldiers were good and put children onto carts or [into] cars. One cart, loaded up with products, could only take children. Mother ran after [it] so that she wouldn't lose the children. I got onto another cart. It was in the middle of the night [that] our cart turned off onto a side road and I realized in the morning that Mother wasn't there and that I'd been left on my own.

374. [May refer to the Silesians who fled East Upper Silesia when it was annexed by the Germans in 1939. From 1920 to 1939 the area was an autonomous province (the Silesian voivodeship) in the Second Polish Republic.]

Looking for Mama

I cried terribly, and the soldiers let me get off the cart, as they were in a big hurry. The Germans bombed the roads. In the morning, the airplanes flew so low that I saw the people sitting in [them]. The soldiers hid in the woods. I was left alone on the cart, covered with a tarp and thinking to myself that it would be good if they killed me since I had lost Mother. Then I [left the cart and] ran, down different roads, and looked for Mama. I had taken a box of clothes and other things with me on the cart. I left all of that behind on the way. I was really unhappy and burst into tears again. Polish soldiers were passing by and stopped to ask why I was crying. They calmed me down, took me with them on a cart and said that they would take me to Kraków, because my mama was surely there. I did not find Mama in Kraków, but I met a neighbor from Bielsko, named Rachel, who had also run away from the Germans. She had six children. There was a father in the family too, who hadn't been called up for the army. That man had been killed by the Germans. It happened in Wisznica. Kraków was under a storm of bullets. Mrs. Rachel decided it would be better to move to a small town with the children. We went with her. We arrived in the town of Wisznica late at night. Our cart was not allowed to go further. All the roads had been taken over by the army. It was said that the front would be passing through town, and everyone hid in basements. A Polish medical attendant went around to the cellars and checked to see if there was good ventilation so that the children wouldn't suffocate. All night long there was shooting, and in the morning the Germans arrived. A German soldier ran down the street and shouted: "Come out, Jews, or I'll shoot." Our Bielsko neighbor, Wolf, the father of the six children, came out of the cellar. The German rushed him off to work. The brother of our neighbor Rachel, Abraham, was also captured for labor. In the evening the men returned from work. Our neighbor Rachel ran to look for [her] husband and brother, to bring them a bit of food. She heard that the Germans had shot many Jews in the square in front of the church. She ran there, and I followed her. We saw both young men, Wolf and Abraham, dead. I saw it with my own eyes. The square was full of blood. Other Jews were lying there too, and also soldiers. It was said that they were Jewish soldiers, captured by the Germans. It is hard to describe what was happening in that square. People were tearing out their own hair. The Germans stood at a distance and laughed. It was even worse in the cemetery. At first the Germans wouldn't allow those killed to be moved. But a few prominent Jews went to the general. The general gave permission for the Jews to be buried and ordered this [decision] to be passed on to the soldiers. The soldiers didn't want to believe it when the order came, and said that if this thing turned out to be a lie, they would shoot a hundred more Jews [from those] they had rounded up for labor. The general confirmed the order and the dead bodies were taken to the cemetery. I was at that funeral. Never before in my life had I cried like this. Something pierced my heart. Together with the six children, I watched as my neighbor Rachel helped to dig her husband's grave. Many graves had to be dug and there weren't enough men to do this work. Many children cried. They were children from Wisznica whose fathers had been shot dead. I noticed that many children came to the cemetery with chocolate in their hands. [They] said that German soldiers were giving out chocolate to kids. They were soldiers from Austria. They were immediately recognized because they never beat Jews. They just took away merchandise from the Jewish shops and often shared it with the poor. The Austrian soldiers would give out chocolate to Jewish and Polish children, with no difference. They would call to Jewish boys, speaking Jewish to them. They talked with them and laughed. In the cemetery, the children dropped the chocolate and the older ones cried, watching their fathers and relatives be buried.

A Good Boy

We were afraid to stay in Wisznica any longer. Three women and ten children set off from there. The two women were [our former] neighbor Rachel [and] her sister-in-law Frajda, the wife of Abraham, who had been killed; and [there was also] Masza, a lady from Bielsko whom we had met in Wisznica, with [her] four children. She too cried constantly, telling [us] how the Germans had shot her husband Icchak while he was at work. On the way we saw lots of soldiers going back and forth. We would have starved to death if we hadn't met a particular Jewish boy. I don't remember what he was called or where he came from. He was running away with us. He spoke good German and didn't look like a Jew. He stopped German cars a few times and got food from the soldiers. The Germans thought he was a German boy and gave him bread, cheese, and tinned foods. The boy shared with us every bite he received. Masza blessed him, saying God had sent us an angel. Once a German patrol was passing by and asked who we were and where we were going. The boy said that [we] were orphans whose fathers had been killed. "Who killed them?" asked the Germans. We lied, saying bandits had attacked innocent passersby. The Germans took pity [on us] and said they would drive us home to Bielsko. This they did. At twelve at night, we found ourselves in Bielsko with the German car.

I Found Mama

Many Jews still lived in Bielsko. We knocked on [the door of] one of our relatives and spent the night there. In the morning, I ran looking for Mother and almost lost my mind in joy when I opened the door to our home and saw [my] mother, brother, and [my] two sisters in there. Mama said that she hadn't run far away, and knowing that there were Germans everywhere, had returned to Bielsko. She was, however, distraught by my disappearance. She asked me how I had gotten back home. I told Mama about our neighbor who had been killed and about other Jews. Th[is] news spoiled [her] joy at finding me. She started crying loudly because she remembered the square behind the church and the dead Jews. A German Christian woman, [our] neighbor, came to our house. When Mama told her about these atrocities, [the woman] started to laugh. Before the war, we had thought she was a decent woman—now her children spat in Mama's face, shouting, "Jew!" and she looked on calmly. Meanwhile, horrible scenes were playing out in Bielsko too. The Germans set fire to all the synagogues in Bielsko and in Biała. They joined the two cities together and abolished the bridge guard. They announced that Bielsko was a German city and that the Jews had to leave it. That's what our neighbors said. They took all the men—Jews—for work. Every day German soldiers came to our apartment to look for Father. They turned everything upside down, searched under beds and in wardrobes. The Jews were driven to a forest outside the city called Cygański Las.[375] It was said that Jews were tortured horribly there, burned alive and killed. In the city the situation kept getting worse, until an order was issued [saying] all Jews would be sent to Kielce and Warsaw. My mother was lucky because she got a train ticket for herself and the children all the way to Kielce. Mama looked for Father. We had nowhere to live. Mama was

375. "Gypsy Forest."

from Łódź, where her family [still] lived, two sisters and a brother. We went to Łódź and spent a week there. Mama traded in bread. A relative of ours was a baker; Mama got bread from him and sold it on the street. In Łódź, Jews were being rounded up in the streets and beaten. Mama was afraid to stay there, and we went to Warsaw by train. We arrived at night. The station was completely burned down; we weren't allowed into the city [and we] didn't know what to do with ourselves. A German soldier stopped us and he showed us mercy and took us to an empty apartment in a half–burned-down house. A doctor must have lived there, because there were lots of small white beds in the apartment. The German gave us water to drink and we went to sleep. We didn't see that German again. Mama said that she wanted to go to the other side of the border as she might find Father there.

We Find Father in Białystok

Crossing the border was very difficult. Mama gave all the money she had for a place in a car that was to take us to the border. We got out not far from the border and were supposed to cross on foot. Horrible things were happening there. The Germans stripped women and children naked in the harshest of frosts. They shot at many [of them]. We crossed the border [safely]. When Mama saw the first Soviet soldier, she asked him to take pity on the little children and give us a corner to warm up in. The soldier took us to a peasant's hut and told the peasant to light a fire there. We got something to eat in exchange for a piece of underwear. Then we went to Białystok by train. We had no friends in Białystok and had to stay in a beth hamidrash, where there were other refugees living and where it was very dirty. Mama couldn't manage and registered to go to Russia voluntarily. The refugees who registered to go to Russia were given a number and were no longer tormented. We were supposed to go to Ukraine, to the Kherson district [obłast], but every time we planned to leave, something stood in the way of our journey. Mama was very sad. One day my brother, Abraham, came running to us with the news that Father had been found. We didn't want to believe him until Father himself turned up at home. Mama was waiting in line for bread at the time. Father burst into the apartment and started to kiss us. [My] brother had been standing on the street in front of a shop display, looking at shoes. All of a sudden, he spotted an acquaintance of Father's who used to visit us. [My] brother told him that we had been looking for Father in vain. He had heard that Father was in Białystok and was looking for us. Father had been wounded in battle: a bullet had pierced through his arm.[376] He had spent a few weeks in a Russian hospital and wanted to go to Hungary with the regiment. Even though he was wounded, since he was an officer, he was taken. The Russians had put him in a prisoner of war camp. He had escaped from there. Father had a lot of money and [still] earned a lot. We went to Lwów with him. It was even worse there than in Białystok, and Father and Mother decided to voluntarily go to Russia.

Departure to Russia

We were assigned to the Kherson district. We were put up in a forest factory and fared very well to begin with. Father didn't work for a month. He was told to rest. The factory was led by Jews. Father was a specialist in the forestry trade because he used to work in it. A few officials wanted to have Father carry out a very important project in the factory. But the manager didn't allow it. Father was sent to become a simple [forest] ranger. One day he caught a chill and fell gravely ill. In the hospital they didn't know what it was at first, then it turned out it was tuberculosis. Father was very weak still from the front, where he had been eating very badly. After leaving the hospital, he was deemed unfit for work, and we were sent to Lwów. A few days later, before we had managed to rest, the arrests began, and we were all sent to Ural.

In a Sovkhoz in Ural

Our camp was located in Krasnouralsk, in the Sverdlovsk district. Father was ordered to work in a coal mine, and we were put in a sovkhoz. The difference between a sovkhoz[377] and a kolkhoz is that, in a kolkhoz, everyone has their own piece of land and works for himself,[378] whereas in a sovkhoz everyone works for the state. Father would faint every day during work. He was taken to the hospital. The Russian [nurses] were very good. When we children came to visit Father, we were taken to the kitchen and given food. We brought home

376. Or: hand.

377. Sovkhoz: a state agricultural holding in the USSR.

378. Not fully accurate. Kolkhozes were sometimes considered an intermediate stage of nationalization and were made up of individual workers put together into a cooperative; sovkhozes were state-run entities.

gifts from the hospital. Despite this, we were faring badly [and] it was fortunate that [my] brother started working for the peasants in the field[s]. The doctors at the hospital said that the only thing that would save Father was going south, to Kazakhstan, [where there were] oranges. We went to a kolkhoz [in] Kazakhstan with [our] sick father. Father stayed in bed all the time. The kolkhoz was poor [and] we had nothing to feed Father with. He was taken to the hospital, and I never saw him again. He died and I don't know where he was buried. We, the four children, were put in a Polish children's center. When [my] mother found out that we were being evacuated, she followed us. She was stopped a few times but managed to sneak across the Russian-Persian border. Now Mama lives in Jerusalem, supported by the Polish delegation, and we, the four children, live in Jewish children's homes.

Protocol 143

Testimony of **Chawa Wawerman**, age ten, from Biała Podlaska. Arrived [in Palestine] from Russia, alone. Parents' [graves] in Siberia.

My father escaped to Kobryń, to his sister's place, before the Germans occupied our town. Father wanted to bring Mother with him, but Grandma did not allow it. At the last moment, when the Germans were just outside town, Mother grabbed me by the hand and we crossed the Russian border. I'm an only child, and today I am alone. I have neither a father nor a mother. Mother saw the Germans from afar after crossing the border. But [I] have never seen a German to this day. Despite this, I have seen many horrible things. I saw my mama die, and then Father. They both died from hunger.

After crossing the Russian border, we wanted to go to Kobryń straightaway, but on the way, when we got out of the carriage to change to a different train, we ran into Father. He didn't know we were on our way to [find] him. He had been coming to [see] us, to Biała Podlaska, and had to change on the way too. We [all] met this way. We fared well in Kobryń. [My] uncle worked in a mill and we had enough flour. We had other nice things too, but one day Father and Mama were arrested, and they wanted to deport them. I was not arrested. [My] parents wanted me to stay with [my] uncle in Kobryń. I didn't want to stay; I cried terribly [and] eventually I got into the car where Papi and Mami were. The train was [taking people] into exile. The Russians were mean and stern. They locked the cars and didn't let anyone leave. There was no bench in the cars and only small windows, like in prison. Through these windows, we smiled at the Russians. We didn't know the Russian language but the Russians, taken by our smiles, allowed the adults to get out at the stations to buy something to eat. We were constantly hungry. We were given a piece of black bread so hard that even water wouldn't soften it. We waited at stations for a very long time. We would run out into the fields, pick flowers, and decorate our dirty cars with them. The adults would look for something to eat. They would trade clothes and other knickknacks in exchange for bread or something [else] to eat. At one station, someone from our car cheated a little Russian girl out of a tin of sprats. He gave the child some old bread, inedible, and convinced her that it was good. The people traveling in our car were very happy with that tin of sprats. Everyone got one to try. We were taken to Ural. When we arrived, it was extremely hot, there was enough food, and one could even buy herring, two for a ruble. Father worked in an iron ore mine. In the mine, Stakhanovites earned between four and five hundred rubles, but the earnings of the others, my father for example, amounted to sixty rubles per month. Father worked very hard. One day a piece of ore fell on top of him. Luckily, he was only injured. I went to a Russian school. We were taught to write there. I wrote mostly circles and lines. Weeks went by, but the Russian children [still] could not do a straight line or a nice circle, which I had learned on the first day. The teacher praised me a lot. There was nothing for me to learn at school and I ended [my] education at that. But [our] relatively easy life came to an end. We were moved from Ural to a kolkhoz located outside the town of Krasnogvardeysk. We lived with two refugee families there who had also come from Ural. There were bad people there out in the country. One day the kolkhoz chief, an Uzbek, went to the city and drank away a lot of money. When he returned to the village on horseback, two of our neighbors met him and tricked the drunk out of the last few grosze he had on him. Immediately afterward, a group of Uzbeks turned up at our home and beat the two men horribly. My father would have surely been beaten up too but he hid in the attic at the last moment, and the Uzbeks didn't find him. Both families had to leave the kolkhoz immediately. We were left in peace because it was known that Father had had nothing to do with that business. Despite this, the Uzbeks treated us with hostility, and we fared very badly. Mama went out into the fields to pick radish[es] and in return received soup twice a day. I couldn't stand the taste of that soup so Mama cooked radish[es] for me in hot ash, which the Uzbeks left in the fields. The Uzbeks did not complain of a lack of food. They cooked some weeds in huge kettles, which they then ate with their hands. There wasn't a [single] spoon in the whole kolkhoz. We struggled a lot until we received sheet metal spoons from the city. Then we left the kolkhoz and moved to Krasnogvardeysk. Most of Father's earnings we paid out for rent. We didn't have anything to eat. Twice a day Mama cooked little dumplings out of flour mixed with chaff, which prickled [our] tongue[s] when we ate them. One day Mama met a friend who gave [her] a piece of bread for me. Father fell ill from hunger. He swelled up all over, then wounds appeared on his body that oozed pus, and each drop of pus created a new blister. He suffered terribly; his shirt was wet with blood and matter [pus]. Mother contracted [the disease] from him. I had to squeeze Father's ulcers myself then. Mama didn't cry or moan, but once she fell on the bed and could not move [again]. Father couldn't go out into town as he was covered in open sores. He sent me into town to bring something to help Mother. I sold Father's clothes and brought back a bottle of milk and some marmalade. I wanted to push [it] into Mama's mouth instead of medicine. Mama clenched her teeth and didn't want to eat anything. She shook her head so strongly that she spilled the milk. I saw Mama fall asleep in some strange way and she became stiff like a rock. Father didn't want to tell me that Mama had died. He said that she had fallen asleep and would get up soon. Father had no money to bury Mother. In the end, he received fifty rubles from the Polish delegation. Mama lay dead at home for four days, and I wouldn't leave her; I watched her until [some] strangers came, took [her], drove her somewhere, and buried her. Some Russian woman took pity on me and wanted to take me to [live with] her. But I didn't want to leave Father alone. A few days after Mother's death, Father died. I noticed that Father had slipped off the bed onto the floor. It wasn't actually a bed, only a pile of straw we slept on, covered in rags. I tried to lift Father off the floor but I couldn't manage it. He was very heavy and swollen all over. Each arm was fat and weighed a pood. I tried to wake Father up, I cried, I called, but he didn't answer. His eyes were just rolled back. Father always had blue eyes but this time they were a different color, completely rolled back. From those rolled-back eyes, tears flowed. I started to cry terribly. I had cried when Mama died, too, but then Father had calmed me down. [Now] I was alone. After a moment a neighbor came in and started to comfort me, [saying] that Father was asleep. I wouldn't let myself be tricked; I understood that he had died. I cried and cried out that he had to be buried. But there was nothing to pay for the funeral with. My neighbor's husband dug a hole, and I helped him, and we buried Father this way.

When I was left alone in the world, I was admitted to a Polish children's center and then taken to Palestine via Tehran.

Protocol 144

Testimony of **Miriam Krambajn**, age thirteen, daughter of Natan and Dwojra, from Łańcut. Came to Palestine with younger sister Hawa, age eleven, in February 1943, via Tehran.

The Germans occupied our town eight days after the outbreak of war but stayed there for only two weeks. Despite this, I will never forget what I experienced during those two weeks. The Jews were afraid to go into town, but Germans went from house to house and dragged [them] out for [forced] labor. The Jews were beaten during the work, had their beards ripped out, and many of them never returned home again. [No one] knew what had happened to them. The Germans burst into Jewish shops and apartments [and] stole the most valuable things, and the local people followed them at every step and waited until the Germans gave them some of the stolen items, which happened often indeed. My father worked in the manufacture of brushes; we were never too rich, which is why many [other] Jews kept their belongings in our apartment, hoping that there would be no searches at our place. Many of those things were left behind in the attic or the cellar as we had to leave town with [only a few] hours' [notice]. It was before the holiday of Sukkot [28–29 September 1939] and we were getting ready for the holidays. There was already a sukkah in the courtyard when, all of a sudden, at two o'clock at night, an order was issued for all Jews to gather in the main square within one hour. The Germans ran from house to house and rushed [people] toward the square, beating them with knouts [and] hitting anyone who didn't run to the square fast enough with gunstocks. When all the Jews had gathered in the square, the oldest German read out the order: "By the hour of four o'clock not a single Jew is to be found in the square, and whoever remains in town beyond that time will be killed on the spot." A panic broke out; people ran like mad, falling on top of each other. [Everyone wanted to] get home as fast as possible and pack [their] belongings. The rich hired carts, which they paid huge sums for. My father, together with two neighbors, tried to hire a cart too, but they didn't have as much money as the peasant demanded. We tossed our bundles onto our backs at the last moment, ran toward the San River, got onto a boat, and crossed over to the other bank, where the Russians were. We went on foot to the village of Zalin [?], where a few Jews lived, and where Father had friends. We found ourselves in Zalin [?] late at night and got to a house where many refugees were already staying the night, and since they wouldn't let us go the next day, we stayed there for a few days. Father couldn't find work in the village [so] we went to Sieniawa. We stayed there for a month. We stayed with many [other] refugees in a huge house, [which] was dirty and crowded. Even though Father earned a little [by] trading, he didn't want to stay in the town, and we went to Kałuszyce[379] from there. At first, we lived in a beth hamidrash. Winter was coming, [and] we didn't have a roof over our heads. Father ran around searching for an apartment for days on end, but to no avail. Finally, we got a corner of a big room in a house intended for refugees. The living conditions weren't any better here than in Sieniawa. Father, a pious man, suffered because of [our] neighbors, who did not observe holidays and didn't respect the Sabbath [rest]. But since the winter was harsh and we had no warm clothing and couldn't travel farther, Father decided to spend the winter in Kałuszyce and go to Lwów in the spring. Traders were persecuted in Kałuszyce, and Father had to give up trading. He got a job in a sawmill but earned very little money. We had to sell what remained of our belongings to be able to eat. Before Easter we went to Lwów, where we lived for two months in one room at a relative's [house]. Father traded anything he could. One time he'd sell apples, another time sugar [and] soap, and he made a living this way. The apartment situation was the worst. It was very crowded; there were ten people living in one tiny room. You couldn't breathe at night. Our relative demanded, firmly, that Father leave the apartment. There were constant rows in the house [and] the neighbors would come running and make fun of us. There was no other solution—we had to move to a village located thirty kilometers from Lwów, where we rented an apartment from a peasant along with an acquaintance of ours. Father transported food products from the village to the city and didn't do too badly. One day when he came home, Father told [us] that the Bolsheviks were demanding that refugees either register to return home or choose Soviet passports. As we had no roof over our heads and had left a small inherited tenement house back at home, Father decided to register to go home. Two months later, on a Friday evening, NKVD-ers knocked on

379. Likely refers to the town of Oleszyce.

[the door of] our hut, told us to bring our things, and said that we were going home. Together with other refugees, we were taken to the train station in Lwów on trucks and loaded into freight cars there that were guarded by soldiers. We were kept locked up all of Saturday, in cramped and stuffy conditions, without water or food. We almost lost our minds, but our screams were in vain. On Sunday the train set off. No one knew where [we were going], but the longer we traveled, the more convinced we became that they were taking us into Russia. We traveled for two months and received a piece of bread to eat once a day and a bit of watery soup at night. Almost everyone in the car was ill with dysentery. Instead of a toilet, we used a hole in the floor. The place was very dirty, and the air in the car—deadly. We begged to be let out at stations but our pleading was in vain. Finally, the train stopped in Novosibirsk. We got out of the car. It was the middle of the summer but it was already chilly there. Everyone was so weakened from the journey, the undereating, and the diseases [that they] could barely stand up. We were allowed to lie down for a few hours and were then told to march on for a few kilometers. Even though many people were collapsing from exhaustion, the guards threatened to beat [them if they didn't carry on]. We arrived in a thick forest where our *posiołek* was located. We were put up in barracks and split into groups for work. Father worked sawing trees, Mother cut down branches, and I ran the household. We received four hundred grams of bread per day each, and children two hundred grams. The bread was like clay and impossible to eat until it had been dried out. In the canteen, soup was sold for 1.20 rubles a serving, but Father and Mama didn't earn enough for us to afford [it]. Recognizing that death from starvation awaited us, we started to sell off the last of our belongings. After two months' stay in the *posiołek*, Mama caught a chill. She lay [in bed] with a high temperature for eight days before a doctor turned up, said it was pneumonia, and gave [her] a [referral] card for the hospital. Father tried to get a cart, but the warden said that no horses would be available for three days, that right now they were busy with work. In vain did Father cry and repeat [over and over] that Mama would not last until Sunday. The warden said that in Russia, work was the most important thing, and they couldn't allow it to be interrupted because of one person. Meanwhile, her fever was increasing, and Mama [grew] sicker and weaker, and she died on Saturday morning. She was buried in the forest, in the place where other deportees were buried too. Some time later, the warden gathered everyone and said that those who wanted to improve their lot could go to Ural, to a coal mine. Since we didn't have anything to eat, and there was nothing to sell anymore either, Father decided to go to Ural. We traveled for eight days, all the way to Rudnik,[380] by Lopiel [?]. Father was assigned to a brigade loading the coal onto a wagon. He earned three hundred rubles per month and received a kilo of bread per day, and half a kilo for each of us [children]. We got a room in a workers' house. After half a year's stay in the barracks, we felt like [we were] in paradise here. But Father was working very hard and could barely stand up. He kept moaning at night. I gave him food when he was already in bed; he often fell asleep while we were eating. Nevertheless he was happy that we weren't starving like [we had been] in the *posiołek*. This lasted until the outbreak of the [German-Soviet] war—then work [hours] were increased by two hours and the bread rations decreased. After the announcement of the Amnesty, the warden [tried to] convince Father to stay in the mine, offering him better working conditions and explaining that he would be able to leave Russia with a Polish passport at any point. Father wouldn't hear of this; he got the [necessary] papers and we went to Uzbekistan. We traveled for two months until we arrived in Tashkent. There we lived in a teahouse, and Father started earning money by trading in old items. We had to leave our apartment because a typhus epidemic broke out. We roamed around for a few weeks without a roof over our heads. Father couldn't earn any money because he was constantly busy looking for an apartment. My youngest brother, five-year-old Zysel, fell ill. Father managed to have the child admitted to the hospital. I went in every day to find out how [my] little brother was feeling. One day, I found the bed empty. I understood that he had died. I brought Father in. We were told that the child had died and been buried. They wouldn't show us his grave. We still didn't have an apartment, but Father managed to place me and [my] sister in a Russian orphanage, where many Polish children lived. Father himself went to Samarkand, where he is to this day. After half a year, all the Polish children, and we along with them, were sent to Persia. We traveled through Krasnovodsk [and] Pahlevi to Tehran. We lived in a Jewish camp in Tehran until we were taken to Palestine.

---

380. Likely refers to the town of Rudnichnyi in central Ural.

Protocol 147

Testimony of **Jakub Rosenblum**, age thirty-one, from Kraków. Came to Palestine via Tehran.

I left Kraków on 3 September 1939. On the first day of the war, Kraków was bombed. The first air raid was thought to be a test raid, but the numerous casualties showed what a tragic mistake that had been. A mass exodus from the city began, and the streets were full of carts and cars and pedestrians heading toward the local roads. Despite this, there were enough people to continue building defense trenches. Planty [city park] was completely dug up.[381] I was the leader of a brigade digging the defense trenches and I saw older women and corpulent men, unused to physical work, apply themselves with their last bits of strength. On Tuesday the first refugees from Bielsko arrived in Kraków and told [us] about the entry of the Germans into Poland from the Czech side. Panic took over the city; [people] started looking for carts to leave [on]. [People] paid fortunes for carts, and cars were completely out of the question by then. Panic was growing by the minute. The roads were full of refugees. We went toward Lublin. I got to Ożarów during the bombardment of the city. The tar paper factory was in flames. The black smoke was suffocating, [and] everyone thought that the Germans were dropping gas bombs. Panic took hold of everyone. People pulled out masks, ran full speed ahead. [People] started looking for anti-gas liquids.[382] On the last bridge on the Wisła, military policemen were checking documents. Tragic scenes were playing out because many people had lost their passports in the rush. A priest was crossing the bridge with us. He was wrapped in white cloth and claimed that [he had] relics hidden underneath it. It turned out that he was a German spy who was marking places for the Germans to drop bombs with white spots. From Lublin we ran away toward Pińsk, where we came upon fighting between the Polish and Soviet armies. Bullets flew over our heads, and we barely managed to take cover in a cellar. In that cellar, we met two sons of a shoe factory owner from Warsaw, Abramski—Aleksander and Tadeusz. We were certain that, hidden in

381. [Planty Park encircles the Old Town in Krakow.]

382. For improvised gas masks made from gauze or cotton wool wadding, most often soaked in vinegar.

the cellar, we had escaped the danger, but nevertheless we trembled with fear. A few hours later the Red Army occupied the town and arrested all the refugees. Everyone was asked [to show their] documents and then released. Even though there were many local Communists in Pińsk, the Polish nationalist sentiments were respected. The Jews were persecuted, though. A Jewish informant who had told the Polish authorities about the existence of Communist cells was lynched in the street. I met a married couple on a Soviet train going from Pińsk to Lwów who had escaped from the Polish concentration camp in Bereza Kartuska.[383] The young woman had gone gray within one night in Bereza. They looked like skeletons. They told [me] how they had to walk a three-hundred-meter-long lane, shackled, and how they were beaten from both sides. Immediately after the outbreak of the war, the Bereza authorities fled, fearing the revenge of the arrestees. The remaining officials, however, tried to keep up the regime. They did, however, stop tormenting [people]. One night the arrestees noticed that there was no guard. They walked out of the camp, and no one stopped them. I arrived in Lwów on 16 October [1939]. The city was so crowded that it was impossible to find a place to spend the night. People were sleeping in cafés and empty cinemas. There was enough food, and the prices were quite high. But starting in December, the peasants stopped bringing in foodstuffs to the city, and there was no fuel. There were long lines in front of cooperatives. It was more and more difficult to get something to eat. The Polish underground movement was engaged in active work—nationalist leaflets were handed out on 11 November, encouraging people to persevere, and foretelling the return of an Independent Poland. I got a job in a Soviet construction office in Lwów. I earned three hundred rubles a month, but the prices were so high that we had to organize our own workers' cooperative, thanks to which we were able to get by. We didn't work too hard. The preparations for the plebiscite in Lwów were extremely grandiose. At our office, the clerks were simply told to go to vote, and the reluctant ones were threatened with dismissal. Trucks took people to electoral bureaus; some people voted a few times, and even though the elections were supposed to be secret, [voters were] watched very closely [to see] what kind of card they

383. Bereza Kartuska: Polish camp intended for active political opponents of the government, active in the years 1934–39.

returned. In March 1940, a German commission started to operate in Lwów, accepting registration[s] for a return to [people's] former places of residence. I didn't register with the Germans. I did, however, go to Germany[384] as a clerk from the construction office. We wanted to obtain a permit to receive bricks from a brickyard operating on the German side. A German officer asked if I was a Jew. I replied that I had come there as a Soviet official. "Are you a Jew?" the officer asked me, red with rage. I said yes. He said, "[Tell them] not to send us any more Jews." At the beginning of June [1940], there was growing unease in Lwów. The Germans had established the borders near Przemyśl. [People] understood that [the Germans] had no intention of allowing Jews into the lands they were occupying. The Bolsheviks were insisting that [people] show Soviet passports. People felt nervous; they awaited the approaching night with worry. Every morning, you would run to relatives and friends to ask if [their] night had passed peacefully. As a Soviet clerk, I felt calm about my fate, but I feared for my fiancée, who was at risk of deportation. First single people were sent away—they were simply dragged from their beds and locked in prison. On the night of 26 June [1940], entire refugee families who didn't have Soviet passports were dragged out of their homes. I was in a completely different situation. I wasn't allowed to [even] think about leaving, since I was a clerk and my departure would have been treated as sabotage. But my fiancée and her parents had already been arrested and found themselves inside a freight car going to Siberia. I had to beg, running from one bureau to another, to be sent away too. I knew that otherwise I would never see my fiancée again. After many efforts, I managed to get on the transport. The transport was big; more than a hundred cars were going to Siberia under NKVD supervision, and cries and heartbreaking screams of children came from inside the cars. In our car [people] were singing, [and] we had our wedding [there]. People were joyful, and I was worried about where I could get a bouquet of flowers for my fiancée. We spent fourteen days and nights in that freight car. We had enough food. Besides, the NKVD-ers brought us food every night. We were sent to Sverdlovsk first, and then to *posiołek* number 45. I worked in various different divisions in the *posiołek*: first as a tile-stove setter, building stoves. Then I was sent five hundred kilometers from the *posiołek* for haying [and] logging, work for which I

384. Areas occupied by Germans.

received nothing but a portion of bread and a bit of groats. We had enough to eat [only] thanks to parcels we received from Lwów and from the sale of clothes. We would sneak into a kolkhoz in the dark of night and swap our clothes for bread and meat. We often returned with nothing, as the NKVD would lie in wait on the way and take everything away. On Pesach [12–19 April 1941] we received flour for matzo. A rabbi from Trzebinia, who didn't work, certified that the baking was kosher. Our work in the *posiołek* was not enough for the NKVD-ers. We were sold to a sawmill and sent there. At first I worked as a carpenter there, then as a structural technician, and I earned six hundred rubles a month. I stayed there until the announcement of the Amnesty. After the Amnesty, we planned to go to the south of Russia, as it was warmer there and closer to the border. We knew nothing about what the south of Russia looked like. When we were asked where we wanted to go, I said at random, Urgut.[385] It was a lucky guess. However, it was too far from the refugee center, so my wife and her family decided to go to Samarkand. Huge masses of Polish and Russian refugees were flowing toward two cities by the Caspian Sea: Tashkent and Samarkand.[386] It was impossible to find a place to stay. Under the influence of the Poles, antisemitism had increased among the Uzbeks, who [now] didn't want to rent apartments to Jews. People slept in the streets. Samarkand looked like a huge refugee camp. The financial situation of the Uzbeks wasn't bad. There were many rich kolkhozes around the city. There was enough food. Excellent fruit. But the refugees brought terrible chaos to the city. Masses of starving, sick, and broken people were arriving. Before help arrived from the Polish government, the refugees had to content themselves with a cup of tea from a teahouse, and the famished crowd turned the city upside down. The residents themselves could not recognize [their] beautiful Samarkand. In the winter, a typhus epidemic broke out; hospital beds ran out, the sick were lying out in the street[s], and the epidemic spread so rapidly that in one month thirty thousand typhus cases were counted in Samarkand. People were buried en masse, and those surviving felt like candidates to become [the next] corpses. Polish delegates advised the refugees to go to kolkhozes, where the hunger was as bad as in the city. The only thing [different] was that

---

385. Urgut: a city in Uzbekistan, close to Samarkand.

386. [This statement is not accurate geographically. Tashkent and Samarkand are not near the Caspian Sea.]

there people died in droves and no one knew about it. The refugees took up trading, which increased the Uzbeks' antisemitism. In the streets there were already shouts of "Jew-Yevrey,"[387] and one [had to pay] over thirty rubles for a kilo of bread. In this situation, the announcement of the formation of the Polish army was joyous news, and when a mixed Russian-Polish commission started to operate in February, all the Jews reported for the army. The commission took no notice of the health of the applicants, and only Polish citizens of the Roman Catholic faith were admitted. Jews were only admitted if they had connections in high places [and if they] claimed to be Catholics. I didn't want to register as a Catholic. I didn't have [any] connections, either, and I went to Kermine as a civilian, thinking I would have a better chance to be evacuated to Tehran there. Only military families were receiving permission to go to Kermine. Many people paid bribes to receive certificates [stating] that they belonged to a military family. Without a *komandirovka* and without a train ticket, for which one had to wait for weeks, I went with [my] wife and in-laws to Kermine, [and] from there to Krasnovodsk and to Pahlevi. I gave out bribes left, right, and center. There was no antisemitism in Krasnovodsk, with small exceptions. All Jews were evacuated to Pahlevi. In one city, 260 Jews reported for the army. The Poles did not want to accept [them, but] on the orders of the NKVD, they went with the Polish army to Pahlevi. Since NKVD orders [meant] little, in Pahlevi [the Jews] were kicked out of the army, and they went to Tehran with the help of an English officer. In Tehran, they wore the letter *C*, meaning *civilian*, on their military uniforms. This situation lasted a few months, until they were accepted into the Polish army after an intervention by the English. There were Jews living in Persia who had come there ages ago, [as well as] escapees from Soviet Russia from the time of the revolution and emigrants from Hitler's Germany. Overall, they all fared well. There were many rich people. A committee of Sephardic and European Jews was formed in Tehran after our arrival, which helped us a lot. There were 562 of us Jewish civilian evacuees, [and we] were given a large sum of money thanks to the help of Rabbi Bromberg. We were also given medicines. The Jewish Agency provided assistance as well. Those among the refugees who were specialists got jobs straightaway. They moved out of the camps, as it was easy to get an

387. Yevrey (Russian): Jew.

apartment in the city. Women worked as waitresses in Tehran restaurants. Because of this, the moral standards of the refugee women went down considerably. The European women were given jobs as household managers. [Even] the ugliest European woman was [still] hugely popular in Tehran.

The Persian youth are very sympathetic to Hitler. Naturally this is related to antisemitism, even though officially [no one] knows anything about antisemitism [there]. But on the streets antisemitism was not evident, and the refugees fared well. It was clean in the Polish camps, [there was] a lot of food—a real paradise after the Soviet hell. In August 1942, two thousand civilians arrived in Tehran with the second evacuation, among them a thousand children.[388] The second lot of refugees found a Polish connection already organized, a special commission that admitted Jews to the army. Many Jews tried to get to Palestine, others settled in Tehran. They received full maintenance from the Polish government, as well as clothing and 1.50 for small expenses.[389] My wife's parents died in Tehran. And the two of us came to Palestine, via Iraq, as managers of a transport of 160 children.

388. See the glossary: evacuation of the Polish army.

389. The currency is not indicated. Refugees sometimes received small amounts of money from the administration, but this amount of 1.50 is likely incorrect.

Protocol 148

Testimony of **Chaim Hades**, age forty, resident of Łódź. Arrived in Palestine via Tehran on 20 October 1943.

On Tuesday night, 6 September 1939, after an announcement on the radio that all men capable of bearing arms should leave Łódź, I packed a small suitcase, said goodbye to [my] wife and child and set off on my way. The streets of Łódź were dark with people: the army and the civilians rushed headlong, women walked with prams, older babies were carried in arms—but no one knew where they were going. Everyone was heading for the Brzeziny road [going] toward Warsaw. We didn't travel in peace for long. The residents of the village of Nowosolna welcomed us with shooting and stones. We didn't know where the shots were [coming] from. Only when the first victims fell [did we] understand that it was the Germans, who lived on Polish land and made themselves rich on Polish land, who were shooting at Polish citizens. Tens of victims collapsed [dead]. We were only able to continue the journey in peace after we got to Brzeziny. At dawn, airplanes appeared. They descended over us and shot at the defenseless refugees with machine guns. [One] squadron replaced [another]; we had to hide in a forest and only set off at sunset. Many people fainted from exhaustion; many families lost each other in the crowd; some collapsed from [their] injuries and lay there in among the dead horses and broken carts—and no one looked back at them. This was how I dragged myself to Garwolin. The city was already in ruins, and even though I was very tired, I could not rest, because I didn't find even one room intact, and the airplanes were still bombing the city. From Garwolin I made my way to Warsaw. On the way I learned about the horrific bombardment of the capital, and I decided to go back to [my] family. I spent the night in some village, where the Germans arrived the following day. At first the Germans didn't do anything bad; on the contrary, they even handed out bread to people. I went toward Rawa Mazowiecka. German soldiers stopped me near the city and took me to a place where there were already a few thousand people, Jews and Poles. We stood for hours in an empty field, not allowed to sit down. People fainted because we were not allowed to get to the water. Two people, unable to stand it any longer, tried to escape, but were shot on the spot. When night fell, we were rushed on ahead. Suddenly shooting rang out. Straightaway, [people] from our group who had been shot started to fall, one after another. The crowd drew in tighter and [people started] running over the corpses and the injured. I too ran on in the dark, trampling over bodies. This way we were herded into the main square in Rawa Mazowiecka. The shooting started again in the square; everyone ran off [wherever] they could. I hid in a church in the square that was already full of people. The Germans started to shoot at the church. This lasted all night, and in the morning, the Germans said that it was the Poles who were shooting at us, and we were ordered to come out of the church. We were placed in the square and [they] started sorting us. The *Volksdeutsche* were set free. The Poles, on seeing this, started shouting that they didn't want to stand together with the Jews. They were separated from the Jews and taken in separate groups. A few thousand people were taken to Tomaszów Mazowiecki. [They] were split into groups, and I and [some] others were taken to the barracks of the former police reserves. All this time, we weren't given anything to eat. I wanted to go out to relieve myself. A German military policeman took me and a few others out into a courtyard, lit up by floodlights so that no one would escape. The policeman rushed us to go to the toilet, but when we were there, they started to shoot at us. The military policemen ran up to the toilet, one jabbed my companion in the exposed body part with [his] bayonet. Another one beat [us] with gunstocks. When I saw another policeman approaching me with similar intent, I asked him, in good German, why he wanted to kill me. He seemed to get embarrassed, and he shouted, "Get dressed and come with me." [He asked] "Where are you from," then took me to the barracks, and when the military policeman on guard duty there took aim to hit me in the head with his buttstock, he stopped him and said, "Let's leave it." This way I avoided certain death. In the morning, we were all led out into the courtyard, where an order sounded: "Hands up." We were taken out into a field. We were ordered to undress and empty [our] pockets, and [they] threatened us with death should anything be found hidden in [any] pocket. Then, a body search was carried out on everyone and [we] were told to get dressed, leaving [our] shoes, and were taken onto the road, barefoot. We were herded toward Piotrków. The Germans rode motorcycles, and we walked barefoot. Outside the city they started to shoot at us again. Panic broke out. Everyone ran full speed ahead. The Germans stabbed those who were fleeing with bayonets. I was hit with a bayonet in [my] injured side. As I was falling, I felt two Jews who were running next to me take me under [my] arms and run with me. The Germans stopped us. One of them asked my companion his profession. He replied that he was a teacher. He was beaten so horrifically that a stream of blood spurted out of his mouth and ears. The other one was beaten up for saying that he was a merchant. I don't know what happened then. When I came to, I was lying on a truck on top of a bunch of people. I lost consciousness again, and when I regained it for the second time, I was lying on a road and someone was shouting over me: "Get up, you damned dog." "I can't," I whimpered. "Then I'll shoot you!" replied the German, and he approached me with a shotgun. I didn't feel afraid. I continued to lie peacefully because it didn't matter to me whether I lived. The German, however, didn't shoot. He only kicked me in the side with his military boot so that I spun around a few times, and I was left in the middle of the road. I heard the throbbing of the engine of an approaching car. Closer and closer. I [could] already see the lights of the car but I wasn't able to move. I thought, "Let this be the end; I have no more strength." When the car was very close, it stopped [and] someone pulled me aside by the leg so as not to run me over. I regained consciousness in the Piotrków prison. After many days of total fasting, I was insanely happy to get a piece of moldy bread. A few days later they started to sort us again. Poles separate and Jews separate. A few Poles asked the Germans for the clothes that the Jews were wearing. The Jews were ordered to undress, and their clothes were given to the Poles. Then [we] were led out onto the road. Outside of every town and village stood a gauntlet of German soldiers with sticks and gunstocks, and we had to walk through that gauntlet while they beat us horribly. This was how we got to Częstochowa. They started shooting at us outside the city. People dropped like flies; I thought that my time had come. Suddenly I heard shouting: "What is going on here? I will not allow it; I am the commandant here."—and the shooting stopped. The Germans lined up into a gauntlet leading underground and beat us along the way as we walked into an underground vault. We were kept for three days without food or drink. And when rain came down and someone stuck out a tin they had found in the vault to get some water, he was stabbed with a bayonet. We were released from the vault three days later and given a piece of moldy bread and water. I will never forget the sight of people throwing themselves on moldy bread like animals. They began sorting us. The older ones, over twenty-five, were set free, the young ones were kept. Tragic scenes played out. Fathers didn't want to be separated from [their] sons, and they begged to be kept too. Half-naked, barefoot, and ill, I barely [managed to] drag myself to a Jewish home. The Jews of Częstochowa helped us a lot. Women and girls pulled the freed people into [their] homes. We were clothed and fed, and they didn't want to let us go until we recovered. I spent a few days in such a home, where I was treated like [their own] son, and [then I] went to Łódź at the end of November.

In Łódź

The situation in Łódź was very difficult. Every day the Germans carried out searches in homes, dragged Jews out, and sent them for work. There were constant raids in the streets; Jews were beaten during work, humiliated, told to walk on all fours, ordered to sing, etc. Women were kicked out of the breadlines, and the intervention of the [Jewish] Council elder, Rumkowski,[390] did not achieve much. After such an intervention, the president of the local borough would often come back beaten up. On 16 September the borough secretary—Pinchas Nadel, the manager of the press department—Szefer, and the manager of the social work [department]—Bunin, escaped from the borough together with the president, Rabbi Lejb Mincberg. All of them, with the exception of Rabbi Mincberg, had returned to Łódź after the fall of Warsaw and started working for the borough. Under threat, however, they ran away for the second time, and no one knew where they had gone. Lejzer Libacki's daughter, a lawyer by trade, was beginning to be active in the Jewish council. As a woman, she could intervene more easily, and she helped the Jews a lot. In Łódź the Gestapo competed with the SS in tormenting the Jews. They would overstep their authority—for example, when the Gestapo wanted to go easy [and] an order was issued, the SSers would decide [to do things] differently. Naturally this competition took a disastrous toll on the Jews. Before the war, I had been a reporter for the Polpress Agency. After returning to Łódź, unable to work in my trade, I started working for the Jewish council. My work consisted of supplying Jews for labor. We wanted to avoid the home searches this

390. Chaim Mordechaj Rumkowski (1877–1944): head of the Jewish council in the Łódź ghetto, died in Oświęcim (Auschwitz).

way. For a while this system yielded good results. The manhunts stopped. But then they started again, so Jews couldn't go out into the street. It took [only] ten or fifteen steps for a military policeman to appear and grab [his] victim. I decided to escape from Łódź and left the city on 31 December 1939. As I could no longer travel by train then, we took our Christian servant with us and she bought two tickets, and I went to Warsaw as her husband. After a few days' stay in Warsaw, I went to Siedlce, smuggled myself across the Bug, got to Siemiatycze, and from there to Brześć, where my aunt lived. [My] aunt was faring badly; the Bolsheviks had taken everything away from her. Unable to stay with her, I set off for Śniatyn in order to get across to Romania. The Russians captured me at the border and put me in jail. I escaped from jail on the first night and went to Brześć. I registered as a bookkeeper and got a job in the town of Wołkowysk, in an *artel* for tailors and shoemakers. Getting the *artel* set up was very difficult, because the shoemakers and tailors were resistant to such [a setup]. However, the high taxes made it impossible to run [one's] own workshop, and the lack of materials, too, finally forced the artisans to work together. I worked for two months as a bookkeeper, but when I didn't want to accept Soviet citizenship, I had to leave the job and return to Brześć. During the registration, [after] standing in line for a few hours, I finally got a departure card [to the German-occupied zone], which was considered lucky at the time. A German officer spoke to the crowd of Jews and asked, "Where are you going, Jews? We won't kill you." By evening, the trains were full of people going home. I was at the station, standing on the steps of a train car going back to Łódź, but I changed my mind and stayed. Another registration took place then of those who had wanted to return [but] had stayed in Brześć. We thought we would be given passports. It turned out that they were deporting us to Siberia. When NKVD-ers started to bang on [the door of] the apartment on the night of 2 July [1940], my sister, who lived with me, hid. I was arrested. When I asked if I should bring anything with me, they said they were taking me for de-registration at the police station, and that I would return home straightaway. I went with them as I was. When I walked out into the street, I saw whole families being led out of their houses. I was taken to the prison in Brześć. There I was told that I had no permanent residence, and as such, I was a counterrevolutionary, and I was put in a three-person cell where there were forty-three people. Everyone was naked because of the stuffiness and the heat.

Of my companions in my misery I remember Rosner, a wood merchant from Lublin, and a Jewish journalist from the *Moment*[391] whose surname I've forgotten. I spent two and a half months in prison and then was taken to the station. After three weeks' journey in inhuman conditions I arrived in Kotlas, and from there, after five days' journey by water, we arrived in Ostwim.[392] We were kept outdoors. We were swollen up from mosquito bites. After a few days we were taken to Kniaź Pagaz[393] on foot, and again a few days later, to Achta Trziba,[394] in [the Autonomous Soviet Socialist Republic of] Komi. There we were put up in barracks and sent to work in the forest. Despite [my] efforts, I was never able to fulfill the quota and I received only five hundred grams of bread per day. Seventy-five percent [of the people in the camp] were Jews. There were Russian exiles among us from 1937. Some had been sentenced to fifteen years of labor camp for speaking to a foreigner or for receiving a parcel or a letter from abroad. The Russians claimed that we had come to a paradise in the *posiołek* with ready-made barracks and kitchens, whereas they had spent whole years under the open sky. The wardens were all exiles. Among them [part of text missing] professors, doctors, and other [members of the] intelligentsia. Most of the intelligentsia were in labor camps, according to the Russians. There isn't a family in Russia without some member missing who's been sent to Siberia. To the Russian exiles my sentence of five years in the camp seemed incredibly lenient. One of the wardens, a university-educated man, told me: "I will be good to you, but if you care about being treated well, don't tell me you're a Jew." Later, when I was free, I encountered evidence of antisemitism at every step. I was sent to work in an oil well, but Poles weren't allowed [to do] any skilled work. We found out about the outbreak of the [German-Soviet] war right away, but even though we were happy, we were treated [the same] as before. Only after the announcement of the Amnesty did conditions change, and a propaganda campaign was begun [to make us] stay. We were given papers. I went to Tacko [Totskoye], to the Polish army, where I served until 1942. Along with the Polish army, I went to Pahlevi and to Iraq, and from there, to Palestine.

391. *Der Moment*: a Yiddish-language daily published in Warsaw in the years 1910–39 [by Noach Pryłucki (1882–1941), the leader of the Jewish People's Party].

392. Likely refers to the Ust-Vym labor camp.

393. Knyazhpogost.

394. Could be Izhma, by Ukhta [Polish: Iżma].

Protocol 151

Testimony of **Jaffa Iras**, age thirteen, daughter of Józef and Bracha, from Zagórz in Galicja. Came to Palestine in February 1943 via Russia and Tehran.

My father was the owner of a pub. There were three of us children. The eldest, [my] brother Mosze—age fifteen, me, and Szoszana—age twelve. [Our] parents never complained about not getting by well, and we, the children, didn't lack for anything. When the war broke out, panic broke out in town. We hid in the cellar during the bombardments. This lasted until 9 September [1939], when the Germans occupied our town. Straight after their arrival, the Germans started grabbing Jews for work. They ripped their beards out, beat them, and ordered them to dance in the middle of the main square. Father didn't want to open the pub because he was afraid to go out in the street, lest the Germans capture him and cut his beard off. Because our pub was among the best in town and was full of good wines and liqueurs, a few officers came to our house and gave Father a guarantee that they wouldn't do anything to him if only he would open the pub. Elsewhere, the Germans stole everything. They chased the owners out of Jewish shops and didn't let them take anything with them, but they didn't do anything bad to Father because they knew him from the pub. Some paid him for the vodka, others did not. Father was happy that they didn't torment him and never demanded [any] money from the Germans. Every night the Germans would surround a few houses, drag out a few Jewish families, and not allowing them to take anything with them, would expel them from town. I heard cries and laments during those raids, as well as the Germans' shouting. We children were very afraid and begged [our] parents to leave town. After a month, all the Jews were sent away from the town. The Germans gathered everyone in the main square, allowed them to take [only] small bundles [of their belongings], and forced [the Jews] out of town. A few Jews remained, in hiding. My father, too, stayed behind in town. He didn't hide, and he wanted to leave town with all the others. But the Germans stopped him, along with a few tailors and shoemakers, and said that they would be allowed to leave later. However, Father couldn't get permission for his family to stay. We left town with the other Jews and went to

Linsko,[395] where [some members of] our family lived. Father wrote us letters at first, then the letters stopped coming, and what happened to Father—we don't know. A few weeks later, the Germans expelled all the Jews from Linsko too. We went with Mama to the San River. The Germans were searching everyone on the bridge, taking away their belongings and not letting all the carts through. Mama went on one cart and we on another. The Germans let our cart through [but] stopped the one that Mama was riding on, and she only made it across to us the next day. She told us horrible things about what the Germans were doing to the Jews. I remember that we cried terribly listening to these stories. We lived in a small town close to the Russian-German border. Mama didn't want to leave there because she thought she might receive a message from Father. Despite her efforts, she never found out anything about Father's fate. My grandfather—Father's [father]—Hersz Iras, an elderly man, lived with us. Grandfather cried over the fate of our father, his son, for entire days. We lived in that town all year. Mama traded, my brother Mosze helped her, and we didn't lack for anything. Then [people] started talking about the registration [to return] to former places of residence, and Mama wouldn't change her citizenship for the world, [to be sure] she would be able to return to Father. It was said in town that everyone who registered to go [back] to the Germans would be deported to Russia. Some, however, believed that they would return home. One day, on a Friday night, we were woken by the knocking of gunstocks on the door. NKVD-ers told us to pack. Our old grandpa and the children burst into tears. The NKVD-ers wouldn't tell us what they were going to do to us. We were given carts and sent to the train station. We were loaded into a freight car, sixty people in each. We waited at the station for a whole twenty-four hours. We weren't given anything to drink or to eat. At night, the train started. No one knew where we were going. Only after a few days' journey did we understand that we had been deported to Russia. It was crowded in the car; people lay on top of each other. The doors were sealed. We received a piece of bread each during the day, and watery soup at night. We weren't allowed out of the car, [and] went to the toilet through a hole in the floor. The stuffiness was awful; many people

395. Here and henceforth likely refers to Lesko.

fainted and there was nothing to revive them with. Many people were ill, [and] a few died. We demanded that the dead be taken away, but the guards pretended not to hear our request, and only when we tried to break the door open at one of the stations did [some] NKVD-ers appear and take away the bodies. My grandfather could barely stand up; he didn't want to eat the soup because it was nonkosher and he ate only dry bread with cold water. After three weeks' journey, when we thought that we were going to the ends of the earth and the journey would never end, the cars were opened, and we were told to get off. We were taken to a *posiołek* located in the Novosibirsk Oblast, Serovsky district,[396] on trucks. The *posiołek* was located in a forest. We lived in barracks. It was dirty and crowded there. Lice, bedbugs, and mosquitos bit and tortured us. At night, we would chase away mice, which weren't afraid of us in the slightest and jumped all over us like cats. Grandpa, Mother, Szoszana, and I didn't work in the forest. Only Mosze worked, and he received a kilogram of bread for it, whereas we got half a kilo each. It was possible to get soup in the canteen, but we didn't have money for it. Mother complained that she couldn't watch us go hungry. She sold all [our] possessions [but], despite this, we weren't able to buy the soup. When the heavy frosts came, Mosze couldn't work, because his hands, legs, and ears got frostbitten and he was covered in sores, [and] there was nothing to treat them with. After a year, Grandpa fell ill with dysentery, but they didn't want to admit him to a hospital as he was too old. He died a few days later. He was buried in the forest, where the *posiołek* cemetery was located. Mosze carved Grandfather's name on a tree [part of text missing] visit his grave. We missed him terribly because, when hunger was troubling us, Grandpa would tell us many stories about himself and Father, and then we would forget about [our] hunger. When the [German-Soviet] war broke out, our bread rations were decreased. Everyone had to go to work, even [our] sick mother and I, even though I was eleven. Nine-year-old Szoszana ran the household. When the warden told us that we were free and started trying to convince us to stay in the *posiołek*, no one wanted to hear of it. Like the other Jews, Mama sold [our] last shirt, and we rented a freight car together. We traveled for a few weeks, starving all the time, until we arrived in Kurgan [in the Tashkent Region]. The city was full

396. There is a Serovsky district in the Sverdlovsk Oblast, not Novosibirsk Oblast.

of refugees; we had no roof over our heads and slept on the street. Many people were dying from hunger. There was no other choice—we had to go to a kolkhoz. We worked with Mama picking cotton and received *lepyoshki* for it, and sometimes ten dekagrams of flour. We were starving horribly. The Uzbeks tormented us terribly and called us "Jewish overlords." They constantly threatened to kick us out of the kolkhoz. Mama had to beg them to let us stay. Only when Mama heard that there was a Polish children's center in Karassul[397] did she go there with us and place us there. Mosze didn't want to leave Mama and didn't go to the center. Mama and Mosze returned to the kolkhoz, and I never saw them again. I spent two months in the center. Although the Polish children tormented us a lot, the teachers were good. After two months I left for Krasnovodsk, together with Szoszana, with the first group [and], from there, to Pahlevi and to Tehran, where I lived for a few months until January of the year 1943. I came to Palestine in February.

397. Most likely refers to Karasu.

Protocol 152

Testimony of **Abraham Elkan**, age eleven, son of Józef and Chana, from Pułtusk. Came to Palestine in February 1943 via Russia and Tehran.

I spent two weeks with the Germans. The Jews were afraid to leave their apartments, but the Germans went from house to house, dragged [them] out, beat them, took away [their] money, and dragged them off to work. Many Jewish apartments and shops were completely looted. One day, the Germans issued an order [saying] everyone had to report to the main square in fifteen minutes. All those who didn't report there would be shot. All the Jews gathered in that square. We children were very scared and clung to [our] parents. The Germans walked around the Jews, whips in hand. They separated the women from the men and then searched everyone, even small children. They took away everything they could get their hands on. Then they photographed us all and told us to march. We marched toward the bridge. Many people had gathered there—men, women, and children—and the road was so blocked that [we] couldn't get through. Suddenly the Germans started to shoot at us. A great panic broke out, and screams rang out. A few people [who had been shot] collapsed. Many people started jumping off the bridge into the river. Mothers lost [their] children, children lost [their] parents. Somehow we pushed through [part of text missing] and got to the village of Popłowiec [Popławy]. The Germans were chasing us all the way. When we got to the village, the local peasants were afraid to let us in, fearful of the Germans. Night fell [and] we continued on down the road. Suddenly, a car appeared with Germans [in it] who started shooting at us. We jumped into a ditch, hid there, and this way avoided death. When things calmed down, we got out of the ditch and went on ahead until we reached a village where we managed to spend the night. The next day we set off [again] and got to Długosiodło. We spent two days in Długosiodło. The town was full of refugees and we couldn't find any place to stay. We spent the night in a stable. On the third day, the Germans kicked us out of Długosiodło. We left town but the Germans started shooting at us again on the way. Panic broke out and we started to run back. The Germans ran after us, grabbed Jews and cut off their beards. We turned to a German officer, explaining to him that we had been kicked out of Długosiodło and couldn't return there. He told us to go to Ostrołęka. We walked for four hours. We had no strength anymore, so we stopped in a village to spend the night. We arrived in Ostrołęka the next day. We found many acquaintances from our town there. Among them was my aunt, who had been the last to leave Pułtusk, and she told [us] about the horrors that the Germans had carried out in Pułtusk. She listed the surnames of Jews who had been shot. We cried terribly, because many of our relatives were among the victims. We didn't stay long in Ostrołęka, because Father heard that the Germans planned to expel all Jews from there, and he decided to cross over to the Soviet side. He hired a cart and we went to Dąbrowa. Dąbrowa was located close to the border, and Jews would gather there to get to the Bolsheviks. The border was open, and the Russians were letting everyone in. We were searched at the border [and] had [our] money and valuables taken away. After the search, we crossed over to the Soviet side and got to Białystok by train. In Białystok, we came upon masses of refugees. We lived in the station for the time being, [while] Father looked for an apartment for us. We lay on [our] boxes and fell asleep from exhaustion. But we were waking up every other minute because people were bumping into us. Father returned in the evening and said that he hadn't found an apartment, and that we would have to spend the night in the synagogue. We went to the city and found a small corner to spend the night in the synagogue, which was filled with people, dirty, and crowded. At night, screaming woke us. Someone was shouting that he'd been robbed. A guard was installed at the door, [and] then everyone was searched and [we] had to [spend all night] repacking our things, until the morning. The next day we left the synagogue, found a space in another one, and spent two weeks there. In Białystok, Father took up trading in leather and shoes. He rented a shop and started selling things there. Meanwhile, the situation in Białystok was getting worse. Father was arrested for illegal trading and threatened that, if he were caught trading leather again, he would be sent to Siberia. Mother sold flour [and] sugar herself, and we children were starving because [she] earned very little. When the registration began, Father registered to return home, because he had heard that [some] Jews had returned to Pułtusk and started to make a living there. A few weeks later, all those who had registered got deported. They didn't come to our apartment during the first arrest[s], and we were certain they'd forgotten about us, but three days later, the NKVD-ers did come and say they'd been looking for us for three days and that we had given a fake address. We were sent to the station and had to travel with strangers, because all [of our] friends had left earlier. We waited all day in the station, without food or drink, and set off in the evening. Mama was in good spirits because she thought we were going home. Father believed that we were going to Siberia, and he was right. Mother suffered a lot watching the children starve and greedily eat the dry slice of bread they received during the day. She fell ill, and a doctor who was in the same car said that [she] had pneumonia. [Other] passengers started demanding that Mother be taken to the hospital. They promised that they would take her to the hospital at the first station. And so it happened. Mother was taken away on a stretcher, unconscious. We begged to be allowed to stay with Mother, but it was in vain; we continued on our own. After four weeks' journey, we arrived in the Arkhangelsk district. We got out of the car and went to a *posiołek* in the forest on foot. Father tried to find out what was happening with Mama. The warden showed us a lot of sympathy and said he had sent a letter to the NKVD about Mama's case. A response came three months later [saying] Mama was healthy and in the Novosibirsk Oblast, but there was no exact address. Her address was discovered by our uncle, who had a Soviet passport and lived in Białystok. He sent us parcels all the time and wrote once that he had received a letter from Mother. A few weeks later, a letter from Mother came, in which she informed us that she was a cook in a *posiołek*, and [that we should] come to [be with] her. At first the warden didn't want to hear about us moving, but we, the children, went [and stood] outside his window every day and cried, [saying] we wanted [to go] to Mama. The warden told Father that the children would get cold on the journey. Finally, the permission to go to Mother came through. We got onto a sledge, Father received fifteen rubles per day for two weeks and we children, five rubles each. It was −50°C [−58°F], we thought we wouldn't survive. It was very far from one town to the next one and it wasn't always possible to stay the night. After three weeks' journey, we arrived at Mama's [*posiołek*]. Everyone in the *posiołek* was very happy that we had arrived. We had brought a few things with us, which Mama sold to feed us, as we were completely exhausted. Father earned five rubles per day working in a sawmill. There were many deportees [in the *posiołek*]. Many died. This lasted until the outbreak of the [German-Soviet] war, when the situation got worse because the canteen was closed and the bread rations were decreased. We had [already] given up on life when, one day, we were told that a Polish officer had visited, and that we could go wherever we wanted. We chose the south of Russia. We went to the closest rail station, located two days' journey from the *posiołek* on foot. At the station, we came upon thousands of Polish citizens already waiting for a train. We rented a freight car with a few [other] Jews and went to Samarkand. The journey took a long time. There was nothing to eat; we ate weeds that Father had brought, and many people were ill with dysentery. In Samarkand we lived in the station, [as] we had nothing left to sell. We went to a kolkhoz and lived in a clay hut. Everyone worked in the field[s], harvesting grain. During the harvest, we received a kilo of rye per person per day. After the harvest, that ration was reduced to a half, and in the end, it was decreased to three hundred grams. We all went through typhus in the kolkhoz and [had to] stay in a hospital. We didn't want to go back to the country after recovering. Mama began trying to have us admitted to a Polish orphanage. My sister and I were taken in, and the remaining three children stayed with [our] parents. We lived in a village sixteen kilometers outside town, and visited [our] parents often. After half a year, we were told we were going to Tehran. We went to say goodbye to [our] parents, and on returning to the orphanage, found there were no children there, [as they] had gone to the station. Mama ran with us. The train was standing in the station, and the manager didn't want to let us in. But the teacher [managed to] convince him to allow us in. After eight months' stay in Tehran, we came to Palestine.

Protocol 154

Testimony of **Halina Landfisz**, age twenty-eight, resident of Bochnia before the war, currently in Tel Aviv. Master of Science in Pharmacy by trade.

On 3 September 1939, together with [my] parents and brother, I left Bochnia on a simple cart on which another ten people were traveling. Rail transport was already irregular then. We went toward Lwów, hoping we could stay in some small town outside Lwów. Things were moving fast, and even though we tried to settle in various villages, we had to keep running away from the German bombs. Along the way, we often traveled under a rain of bombs and bullets from German airplanes. Throughout the whole journey, we enjoyed the hospitality of villagers, who treated us very warmly. When we found ourselves in the Ukrainian regions, people's attitudes changed completely. The Ukrainians, peasants and city dwellers alike, treated us in a very hostile manner. We traveled together, Poles and Jews, and suffered a lot from this Ukrainian hostility. Not far from Radziejów,[398] a group of Ukrainian partisans shot at our cart and killed a woman. We later witnessed a Ukrainian division attacking some Polish soldiers and killing them. I was in Radziejów when the Soviet army arrived. It didn't make a great impression on me: the soldiers were poorly dressed and poorly armed. [The army's] motorized support amounted to a few small tanks. The next day the Soviet authorities called an assembly, during which they promised [everyone] freedom and a happy life. Immediately afterward, the Soviet army started buying everything that was in the shops, and I had to stand in line for a few hours to obtain food products. We left for Tarnopol. It was complete chaos there. Soon the shops and houses started to be sovietized. High taxes were introduced. The sovietization led to [a situation where] one had to wait in line for bread for entire days. After a month, [they] started throwing residents out of their apartments to free up the apartments for Russian officials. These actions were carried out by a criminal. Later, all the posts were filled by Russians brought

398. Possibly refers to Radziwiłłów (now Radyvyliv, Rivne Oblast in western Ukraine), a town with a big Jewish community in the interwar period.

in from the interior of Russia. A Russian metalworker took over the leadership of the city. I have to say that everyone was able to get a job then. But the wages were set very low. I also saw with my own eyes how the Ukrainians immediately made friends with the Soviet authorities and soon received important positions in the city administration. In March 1940, a planned operation of deportations to Siberia began. First of all, the colonists[399] were sent, and Ukrainian peasants were installed in their place. A month later, former soldiers started being deported. In May we were faced with a dilemma: either to accept Soviet citizenship or to register to return to our original place of residence. Ninety percent of the refugees didn't want to accept Russian passports. A few days later, the authorities ordered an air-raid drill. This was justified by the possibility of an attack on Romania. Everyone was ordered to stay at home. At night, patrols arrested people, going from house to house [and] promising them that they would be sent to their [previous] places of residence. They were gathered in the station, put into freight cars, and kept locked up for two and a half days. On that crucial night, many families were split up. There were cases where the husband was put in one car and the wife in another. The journey to Siberia, inside locked freight cars where the sick lay on the floors, was absolutely horrifying. The dead were thrown out of the window. We gathered from talks with the guards that we were being taken to our deaths. On the way, [some] cars were left behind. The car from Tarnopol stayed in Turgulińsk [?]. After a long journey, we got to a *posiołek* by a sawmill. Everyone was ordered to go to work. Work lasted from sunrise to sunset. We worked in percentages of a set quota. Since we weren't used to working, most of us went hungry. The selling of old clothes wasn't allowed, and it's no surprise that, one day, after the Russians sent a gravely ill [man] to work, an open uprising ensued. We all lunged at the warden, who came in with a gun. Nine of us were arrested, and the rest sent to another *posiołek*, where the conditions were no better than in the first one. People worked beyond their strength, in terror. Three women were sentenced to prison for being three minutes late. The worst, however, was when someone fell ill. Avitaminosis,[400]

399. Poles who had settled in those regions during the interwar period.
400. Illness caused by a lack or a deficiency of a particular vitamin in the body.

night blindness, and *cynga* were widespread. There were no medical treatments, and home remedies led to disaster[s]. There were Jews and Poles living in the *posiołek*. Generally [their] relations were good. We organized among ourselves and put up a united front. When the Amnesty was announced, no one wanted to stay in the *posiołek*, even though we were promised the moon. Everyone registered to leave, and pointed to a completely random place on the map to show where they wanted to go. We picked Dzhambul as [our] destination. A special delegation of refugees went to Sverdlovsk and simply bought a train there. It is evidence of how spiteful the Russian authorities were toward refugees that one family received papers for Costa Rica a few days before the Amnesty [but] they weren't allowed to go with us, and they remain in Russia to this day. The same was true for the English. We traveled for long weeks. On the way, cars were attached to our train carrying component parts from evacuated factories as well as the personnel from those factories. At almost every station, cars were attached carrying Russian refugees escaping the Germans. Those refugees were in terrible shape and their situation was pitiful. They were all starving. There was another category of escapees: rich Russians. I saw with my own eyes an express train with sleeper carriages full of well-to-do Russians. As in all of [the rest of] the world, the difference between the rich and the poor was conspicuous. Whenever we tried to make contact with the local Russian people, we encountered mistrust and silence. The administration[401] was completely chaotic. In Tashkent, we forced ourselves onto a train carrying people to Dzhambul. After a real battle between us and the army and the NKVD, we won and traveled on. Dzhambul was a dead city. We found ourselves in an awful situation. We received no help from the Russians. They didn't give us work and didn't want to rent us apartments. The Polish assistance [organizations] had not yet been set up. [We] lived by selling [our] last rags and last pair[s] of shoes, just so we wouldn't die from hunger. The Russian people, generally apathetic and completely resigned, exploited us shamefully. Many Kazakhs had large estates, because the kolkhozation hadn't reached those areas yet. Our situation

401. The chaos described by the witness concerns the many operational factions involved with assisting the newly released refugees.

improved in October [when] the Polish government organized help. We were given money and clothing. Nevertheless, a typhus epidemic broke out, claiming thousands of victims. Children died en masse from measles. There were still no medicines. The delegation could not fix this shortage. In January, the Polish army went through Dzhambul and was stationed in the village of Lugovaya. We started making efforts [to be] evacuated. My family and I received permits to leave easily because my brother, a doctor, was an officer in the Polish army. Three months later, we left for Iran via Krasnovodsk, and from there, to Palestine.

Protocol 155

Testimony of **Alter Zajdmann**, age thirteen, from Kałuszyn. Came to Palestine from Russia via Tehran.

I remember the beginning of the war with the Germans well. The closest rail station to Kałuszyn, Mrozy, was bombed by German airplanes in the first days of the war. Panic broke out in our town: people were afraid to go out into the streets and hid in cellars. I saw the planes come down really low and destroy the whole rail line. In our town, a bomb fell near the church and killed thirty-two people. The victims were Jews who had been waiting in line for bread. I recognized our friends, six-year-old Mendele and eighteen-year-old Icchak, among the dead. [By] the next day, the whole rail line had been destroyed, and airplanes were bombing our town. Fires broke out and people abandoned their homes. The fire spread further, and the airplanes descended over the town and shot at it constantly. Father took me by the hand and ran with me to the ice cream factory in the suburbs. The [building] was [made of] brick and there was enough water there. There were many people there already, but [we] had to get away from there too, because the fire was getting closer. There was nowhere to run to. The town was a sea of flames. I lost my father, and my brother Abraham took me out into a field outside town. We spent a day and a night there, watching the burning city. It was so light at night that the whole field was lit up. Children were hiding in ditches, crying from hunger. One of the Jews ran to a nearby village and brought us something to eat. In his arms he was holding a tiny, months-old baby, whose mother had died. On the third day, there was more smoke than fire coming from the city. I went with [my] brother to see what was left of our home. We could barely recognize it. All streets looked the same: ruins, collapsed houses, blackened chimneys. The smell was horrible. Many horses and cows had been burned alive in [their] stables. Many people had burned [to death] too, because the fire broke out so suddenly that the sick and old couldn't leave their homes in time. [My] brother and I went to our street. There was a stream there that allowed us to find the spot where the ruins of our home were. We were cleaning up bricks and rubble when, all of a sudden, [my] brother gave a cry of joy: he had found Father's sewing machine among the ruins. My father was a tailor and that machine constituted his entire fortune. Apart from the machine, we also found a few pots for cooking, and that was all that remained of our possessions. The same fate befell the whole town. Only a few people had managed to take out some items before the fire. Many people paid with their lives for trying to save their possessions. Lencki the milkman got so badly burned [trying to] save his possessions that he died from his injuries a short time later.

As we were picking through the ruins of our home like this, Father came up to us, his eyes filled with tears because he had learned that our grandpa had died in the flames. My grandpa, eighty years old, was blind and lived on the second floor. He hadn't managed to get out of [his] room in time before the fire, and his burned remains were later found in the ruins. There were many more such horrific cases, because the fire had spread very fast, due to the gasoline that the Germans poured on the burning houses. A few brick houses on Warszawska Street and the synagogue remained. All of the homeless [people] took shelter in the synagogue. It was awfully crowded there. Small children were crying; older ones roamed around the city through the ashes, looking for various items. Soon the Germans arrived in town. As soon as they entered the town they started running around the streets, shouting: "Jews, Jews." A German officer gave an order for all Poles and Jews to gather in the church that had been spared. We saw one German grab the oldest rabbi, Naftali, by [his] beard and push him into the church too. Dead people were being carried in the streets, covered in blood. They were the first Jewish victims. Inside the church, we were told to stand with our arms up. The Germans searched everyone, took away everything they found, and after the search was finished—beat [us]. We thought that the Germans would blow up the church to kill all of us inside it. One of the officers ordered twenty Jews to strip naked and stand by a half-destroyed wall. A German tank drove up and started to fire at that wall. The wall fell down, but a miracle occurred and none of the Jews were killed. That wall fell down [toward] the other side, and so the Jews avoided death. The mayor of our town, a Pole, arrived at the church. He negotiated with the Germans and received permission for the women and children to go home. After some time, the men were released too, but the Jews were taken straight for work. My father worked burying the dead. [They] were loaded onto carts, and Jews had to pull those carts. The Germans beat them with crops and pushed them to run faster, and laughed a lot while doing it.

There was awful hunger in the city. It was said that there were cars filled with foodstuffs on the rail line by Mrozy, left behind by the retreating Polish army. We went to the station, sneaked into those cars at night, and took everything we could. There were cigarettes, sacks of rice, tins of conserves, etc. People said that inside each car there were small boxes filled with banknotes. I sneaked into a car once and found a Polish pilot's uniform there. I took it home, and later escaped to Russia in that very outfit. There was great destitution in our town—besides, masses of refugees from other towns had come there. The Germans beat everyone and ripped out Jews' beards. Once, an older German who was good came to our neighbor, a shoemaker, and paid him to fix [his] boots. My father was present [there] and got a few cigarettes from that German. Father saw that there was nothing to do in Kałuszyn and decided to go to the Soviet side [of the border]. My mama had been out of Kałuszyn all [this] time because she had gone to Warsaw before the war and had stayed there. Father smuggled himself into Russia and we, the two brothers, stayed at the shoemaker Mendel's place in Kałuszyn. Father made it to Wołkowysk, where he got a job. Soon he sent a smuggler to bring us over to the Russian side. We were crossing the border in wintertime. We were supposed to go across a lake. We got into a boat, and when we were halfway [there], the boatman stopped and said he would not go further unless he was paid more. We had to give him all [our] money. When we made it to the other side of the lake, we entered a deep forest. The Russians lit up the whole area with flares, but luckily, they didn't spot us, and we made it to Wołkowysk. We stayed there until [our] arrest and deportation to Siberia.

Our *posiołek* was located in Siberia, in the Vologda Oblast. Father worked as a logger, and we helped him. We sawed the wood into small pieces. For six cubic meters, we received 1.20 rubles per day, and that was [supposed] to be enough to live on. You could just about survive in the summer—when hunger bothered us, we picked berries, raspberries, and mushrooms in the forests. But summer in Siberia does not last long, and after three months, the harsh winter came.

After the Amnesty, we were taken to the Bukhara Oblast. Everything was very cheap there, plenty of fruit almost for free. We received a kilogram of bread per day, and if you stood in line twice, it was possible to get bread twice. But that didn't last long; hunger spread [in the city], and the bread rations were lowered to four hundred grams per day. Father got a job in a kolkhoz, but there too, there was nothing to eat. Father also tried to join the Polish army, but they didn't want to accept him. Father went to Tashkent and handed me over to a Soviet orphanage. There were lots of Russian hoodlums there and they called me "Yevrey"[402] and beat me. We were fed well, but I couldn't stand it there any longer. I cried to be released from there, but the teacher would not allow it. One night I dug a tunnel under the fence and escaped. A bad dog attacked me and bit me severely. I was barely saved. I was afraid I would be sent back to the orphanage and quickly [made up] a story for [the people who saved me]. I [ended up] in a Polish orphanage and was taken to Tehran with all the children.

402. See footnote in Protocol 147.

Protocol 156

Testimony of **Gedali Niewiadomski**, age thirteen, from Siedlce. Came to Palestine with the Tehran children.

There were nine of us children, six brothers and three sisters. At first, five of the siblings escaped to the Bolsheviks and four stayed with the Germans, then three returned to the Germans and two were deported to Russia: me and my oldest brother, Izrael. I lost my brother on the way back, and this was how, despite [having] numerous siblings, I was left on my own.

In our town, Siedlce, where many Jews lived, there was no war,[403] but the Germans constantly bombarded us. On Saturday, the second day of the war, the bombing and the fires started. Piękna Street, where the rich Jews lived and where the nicest shops were, was completely burned down. Kozia Street, too, the street of the artisans, was unrecognizable. The same thing happened to the nicest streets. I remember when the Germans entered the town. We hid in the garden among the trees. The next day, the Germans opened Jewish shops with [their] bayonets and took away the merchandise. A German with a bayonet came into our courtyard, walked up to [our] neighbor, and asked, "Jewess?" She replied, "No." To this, the German [replied], "If [you] were, I would have killed [you]." The Germans couldn't tell at first who was a Jew and who wasn't. But the Polish peasants, and Polish women in particular, ran after the Germans and pointed out the Jewish shops to them. For identifying a Jewish shop this way, they would get as much merchandise as they wanted. The Germans watched the plundering and took only chocolate themselves. I saw a German soldier burst into a shop, drag out a whole box of chocolate, and start sharing it among his companions. But those who ran after the Germans were looking for other goods and took away manufacture, shoes, and haberdashery. The Poles would take away whole cartfuls of merchandise from the shops opened by the Germans. The Germans captured Jews for forced labor. [My] father, who had a food storehouse, was ordered to wash cars. Even eighty-year-olds were forced to work. [The Germans] didn't have [any] work for them and told them to stand in the street with their hands raised for hours. They didn't let

403. Probably means that there was no military activity on the streets.

them move, photographed them, and laughed. [People] from our town were sent to work far away, seventy kilometers from town. They were forced to run [there], and those who didn't have the strength to run were shot at. My father was sent to Węgrów. My sister Rachel and I found out that the German supervisor there took bribes. We went to Węgrów and bought Father out of the work camp for ten zlotys. We didn't recognize Father when he came back. He'd spent eight days in the work camp. His beard had been ripped out and he looked like death. He told [us] how they starved and tortured him there. The Jews would sneak out into the neighboring fields at night and eat raw potatoes and tomatoes there. Without that, they would have starved to death. Many were killed in the camp. One day Mother sent me to the beth hamidrash with a bowl of food, to give to the town fool. Mama always took pity on him. When I walked into the beth hamidrash, I saw the Germans throwing away the holy books and stomping on the Torah with their feet. I ran home quickly. Later Jews from various towns who had been brought to [ours] by train by the Germans were put up in the beth hamidrash. People from Kalisz were the biggest group. Small children slept on the floor. Some of the homeless walked around the streets and begged or made money singing songs in courtyards. They ate at a soup kitchen opened by the local authority. One day we heard that the Germans were leaving, and that the Bolsheviks would be coming to [our town]. It was said that the Bolsheviks placed special importance on our town. One morning I saw the Russians approaching in big tanks. The town was overtaken with great joy. The Jews opened up the shops, and those who had a little merchandise started trading. There wasn't a lot of it, since the Germans had taken everything. The only things left were cigarettes and a few barrels of herring. The Russian soldiers descended on the shops and bought everything. My father knew the Russian language and heard the soldiers' stories about the awful famine in Russia and how nothing could be [bought] there. The soldiers had a lot of Polish money and didn't haggle. The town was completely emptied of goods. Meanwhile, a rumor spread that the Russians were leaving Siedlce. On the last day before [their] departure, the Russian leader issued a decree that anyone who wanted to could follow the Russian army. There were freight cars standing in the station, and anyone who wanted to could get in. [My] eldest brother demanded that Father leave town with all the children. Father would not agree [to go]. The eldest brother took the four younger children—the three older ones stayed with Father. The three freight cars were filled with a few hundred civilians and attached to the army train. We traveled like this on that train to Brześć. There we got off, and my brother took us to Biała Podlaska, located twenty kilometers from Białystok. We spent three days in the station, until my brother got an apartment. He started to work as a shoemaker but struggled to support his family and the four of us as well. We went hungry. Meanwhile, messages were arriving from Father [saying] that things were calm in Siedlce and that [he] was earning money. One of my brothers was involved in smuggling and was transporting manufacture [and] leather across the border, and was earning good money. He came to see us and said that Father wanted the children to come back to Siedlce. First, he took [my] twelve-year-old brother, Noe, and seven-year-old sister, Sara; the second time—[my] ten-year-old brother, Szlomo. He wanted to take me across the border too, but was too late. NKVD-ers caught him, took away his merchandise, and put him in jail for a few days. I was left alone in Biała Podlaska with my oldest brother, the shoemaker, until that awful Saturday came in the middle of summer, when we were deported to Siberia. We were told to pack our belongings in fifteen minutes and didn't manage to take everything. At the train station, we were loaded into a freight car. Russian soldiers with guns watched us throughout the whole journey. The car doors were locked; there was no toilet. The air was horrible. We traveled for a long time, a few weeks. We passed through Moscow and other big cities. We weren't allowed to get out at the station[s]. The train would wait for hours, but only in the fields. We received a piece of bread and a bit of watery soup each. We arrived in Siberia in the middle of summer. [My] brother had brought some leather with him and started to work as a shoemaker, earning good money. The leather soon ran out, and he had to start working in the forest. He earned one ruble per day, which wasn't enough to live on, especially since [my] sister-in-law had had a baby. Being nine, I had to start working in the forest [myself], and I earned a few kopecks transporting the wood. I had brought a pair of warm trousers from home, which soon ripped. I had nothing to wear. My hands and feet got frostbitten in the freezing temperatures. Once I got lost in the forest and heard the horrible howling of the wolves. In that forest there were also bears, and people walked around armed. Luckily an armed ranger saw me and took me back to the *posiołek*. After the announcement of the

Amnesty, another awful journey began. We were told to go God-knows-where. There were only Poles on the train. They had been working in Siberia, in the fields, and had taken whole baskets of potatoes with them. This saved them from hunger. But my brother hadn't taken anything, and it was heartbreaking to watch his small child starve. I got off at one of the stations when I saw Russian soldiers eating bread. I asked for a piece of bread and they gave it to me. I wanted to give that bread to my little nephew, [but] in the meantime the train had started, and I was left on my own. I cried terribly, until the station manager asked the soldiers to take me with them and leave me at a station somewhere where there were Polish transports. I found [my] brother there, who shouted at me for leaving the car. Hunger bothered me so much, however, that I continued to get off at each station and beg soldiers for bread. Once I got a packet of rusks, and the baby had something to eat for a few days. But once again, I couldn't find my train. Three times [I managed to] find [my] brother, but the fourth time I didn't. The manager sent me to a kolkhoz, [and] from there I was sent to a Polish orphanage not far from Samarkand. I walked barefoot in the snow. The manager of the orphanage took pity on me and accepted me. For a hundred Polish children there were twenty Jewish ones. We were very happy; the older boys were allowed to pray. The director, Mr. Franciszek, wouldn't let anyone harm us. Then, we were taken to Tehran. I went to Samarkand a few times and tried to find my brother but didn't succeed. I was the only one remaining from the whole family.

Protocol 157

Testimony of **Ida Bauminger**, age fifteen, born in Kraków, resident in Tel Aviv.

I left Kraków two weeks before the outbreak of the war. My parents sent me off to Przemyśl, as they were expecting the arrival of Germans. When the war broke out and the bombardment of the city began, we noticed that the Germans were trying to bomb churches and public buildings. The houses next to our apartment were completely destroyed. The Germans occupied Przemyśl on Friday, and the next day the owner of my apartment was arrested. He was called Herszfeld. He returned home a few days later, badly beaten. He suffered for two weeks and soon died. There was a doctor living in the same house who was gone from home for a long time. [People] started to look for him. [His] family found his body in a field, among other dead bodies. They recognized him by his clothes. There was a thermometer in his pocket. One day a soldier came into our apartment, demanded kerosene, and threatened to kill everyone if he wasn't given what he had asked for in five minutes. I remember one search. A whole family who lived on the second floor was shot then—for no reason. The Germans stayed in Przemyśl for two or three weeks and then left the city. As they were leaving, they demolished houses and blew up the beth hamidrash. I saw Jews and Poles putting out the fire. Generally speaking, the Jews and Poles helped each other. After the Russians' entry, my father was one of the many refugees who made it over to the Soviet side. We were sent to Lwów. When we had started to get used to the conditions [there], mutterings began about deportation[s] to Siberia. Father, like many other Jews, didn't want to give up [his] Polish citizenship. The deportation of Polish citizens took place within twenty-four hours. Our turn came at one o'clock at night. We took some things [with us, but] I wasn't allowed to bring books. We were taken to the station and loaded onto freight cars there, eighty people in each. We waited in the station for two nights, then we set off on the journey. We received water at stations. During a thunderstorm, lightning struck our car and ripped off the roof. None of the people in charge took any notice of this. After three weeks' journey that [can only] be called [what it was: pure hell], we were let out at the station of Teszma,[404] in the Sverdlovsk district. Some people were assigned to a brickyard, some to logging. We received five hundred grams of bread per day, but [sometimes] it turned out that the bread didn't come [and] then we would go hungry. Month after month went by with hard work, broken up by bad illnesses. We had become completely dejected [by the time] the news of the Amnesty reached us. The *posiołek*'s warden suggested that we stay, but we did not take him up on that offer. A short time later, [we] began a horrendous journey to Samarkand that lasted three weeks. Fifty kilometers outside the city we were stopped, and we had to live under the open sky until we got accommodation in the city. It soon became clear that it would have been better to have stayed outside the city. The destitution in Samarkand was difficult to imagine. It was impossible to [find either] bread or work. [People] sold everything to get a piece of bread, which they had to stand in line for. I spent whole nights in line[s]. In the *posiołek* I had gone to school, but in the city, school was out of the question. The scariest thing, however, was the typhus epidemic. Thousands of people were dying in the hospital, and hundreds collapsing on the streets because they couldn't [get] a place in the hospital. My father fell victim to that awful epidemic. After some time, a Polish delegation began operations. Clothing and food were given out. I was accepted to a Polish orphanage. Finally the coveted day of leaving Russia arrived. Not all the children survived the journey to Krasnovodsk. In Krasnovodsk, the Polish military authorities took good care of us, and from there we went to Pahlevi, where the Polish and English authorities looked after us. We got new clothes and were sent to Tehran. In Tehran, Mrs. Czertok looked after us. We lived in a camp outside Tehran. Many children died in that camp despite the attentive care. Straight from Tehran, I came to Palestine.

404. Tesma [original Polish correction: Tieśma].

Protocol 158

Testimony of **Pola Kukiełka**, age twenty-two, from Kielce, elementary school teacher. Came to Palestine with the children from Tehran.

Before the outbreak of the war, I was a teacher in a Jewish elementary school in Kielce. Immediately after entering the town, the Germans started persecuting Jews. They forced Rabbi Rapaport to carry out the most humiliating work. They ordered the establishment of a Jewish council that had no real voice. The Germans used sadistic methods on Jews. Once they called in all the Orthodox Jews and ordered them to dress in festive clothes and bring prayer books with them. The Jews awaited this gathering with despair. They were told to wear ritual clothes, and one of them had to blow a horn. It turned out later that all of that was being filmed. Throughout all of the Germans' stay, we tried not to go out into the streets, to avoid seeing them torture Jews. One day a Jew who was being chased by the Germans came running to our apartment. We hid him in a wardrobe. The Germans found him, however, and beat him terribly. They took him away with them. Since I had intervened in the case of the beaten man, my neighbors advised me to leave the apartment. That same night, the Germans arrived at our apartment to arrest me. I had to get away from Kielce. As I had relatives in Ożarów, I decided to go there. At the station, the Germans recognized that I was Jewish [and] beat me terribly, and I got to Ożarów barely alive. [My cousin], a fifteen-year-old boy, was the only one left of the family. He looked at me like [I was] a madwoman for having come to their place. "The Germans have been tormenting us here for six days," he said. "They locked 350 Jews in the synagogue and are not giving them anything to eat." I learned that the Ożarów Jews were being tortured because a Jewish girl had slapped a German officer in the face when he tried to rape her. The interventions of the Jewish council to provide food to those sentenced to death from starvation were in vain. The Jews who remained in town fasted as a sign of solidarity. On [part of text missing] I heard horrible screams coming from the synagogue. I jumped out of bed and ran to the window. The whole building was in flames. My cousin and I started to cry terribly because we knew that all the Jews locked in the synagogue would be burned alive, among them my aunt, my uncle, and their children too. The next day the president of the local borough went to the German commandant and asked for permission to bury the bodies of those who had been burned to death. The commandant replied: "We'll let you bury them if you sign a protocol saying the 350 Jews deserved their fate fair and square." The protocol was signed. The commandant told the borough representatives to come at one o'clock at night. He allowed them to prepare a few graves during the day and wash them with lime. At one o'clock at night, we made our way to the commandant with the president. We were led to the synagogue under a Gestapo convoy. Before our eyes was a horrifying sight. The books on shelves and walls were still smoldering. All the Jews were burned beyond recognition. We didn't know what to take out first. We couldn't tell the corpses apart. It turned out that the Germans had poured gasoline on the people and things [in the synagogue]. Taking out the half-charred bodies was a horrific task for us. We took them all to the cemetery and buried them in communal graves. Before we knew it, it was already dawn. We went home, and taking essentials with us, [my] cousin and I escaped to Jędrzejów. We found the situation much better in Jędrzejów. It turned out that the local commandant wasn't depraved. The town was regularly supplied with food, and people weren't being captured for work. Poles and Jews went to work voluntarily. Even though the schools were closed, I got a job straightaway as a teacher for eleven children. I thought I would stay there for a while. Three weeks later, an order arrived that we did not expect. All women between the ages of fourteen and thirty-two, Poles and Jewesses, were called in to [see] a district doctor for an examination. The mere fact of having the women called for an examination seemed suspicious. Many women reported at the set time. All were stripped naked. Eighty-five percent were qualified as "fit for service" and sent to brothels for the army. Those who had hidden were met with an awful fate. The Gestapo searched homes, and the women who were found were beaten and forcefully put in front of the commission. The same applied to people in the country. I avoided the horrible fate of a prostitute only by a miracle. When the goal of the medical exam became clear to everyone, the altering of passports began. Fourteen-year-old children became younger, twenty-year-old girls older. Changing the age in a passport cost eight hundred zlotys; the money went into the pocket of the German commandant. I decided to run to the Bolsheviks but didn't manage to cross the border that easily. I wandered around cities and towns in the Kielce voivodeship for entire months. What didn't I do to keep myself alive[!] The border was closely guarded, [and] smuggling was punished severely. However, I did manage to achieve my goal. It cost me a lot of money. I was persecuted on both the Russian and the German sides. One has to remember that both the German and the Russian soldiers were equally demoralized. For crossing the border, they demanded not only rings and money, but also gifts in kind . . . I suffered a great deal. Finally, I made it safely to Białystok on 12 May 1941, that is, a month before the German offensive. I suffered a lot in Białystok. Passports with paragraphs were no longer being issued; I bought myself a paragraph-free passport for four hundred rubles, and having that passport, immediately got a teaching job in a Jewish school. I earned decent money and received meals. I felt happy, [but] my happiness did not last long. Even though I didn't meddle in politics, I was affected by the purge carried out among refugees. On 22 [June 1941], after the outbreak of the [German-Soviet] war, tens of thousands of people were leaving Białystok and going into Russia. I had no intention of staying in Białystok, as I wanted to avoid falling into the hands of Germans. But I happened to be sick at the time and was in the local hospital. The less-seriously ill were evacuated, but I stayed in the hospital for a while and didn't know what the Germans were doing in Białystok. They didn't come to the hospital. I only knew that the food rations were decreased. I heard about the mass burning of Jews in the synagogue[405] but didn't see it with my own eyes. After the establishment of the ghetto in Białystok, there was less than two square meters of living space for each Jew. Forty thousand Jews were squeezed into one neighborhood, and beyond that, more refugees continued to arrive. Dysentery and typhus epidemics spread because of the crowding, and the diseases caused particular devastation among children. All the Jews had to pay rent, even homeowners. In addition, one paid twenty pfennigs for each occupied meter of an apartment and a 20 percent residence tax. The Jewish police force was made up of three hundred people. Its task was to ensure cleanliness and order and to guard the gates of the ghetto. The Gestapo didn't trust that police [force], and instead of weapons, they were given only batons. The fire service was especially important. The Jewish Fire Service was called to put out fires outside the ghetto. The Germans closed all philanthropic, professional, and cultural Jewish institutions. The huge Jewish hospital moved

405. This took place on 27 June 1941. That day about two hundred Białystok Jews were burned inside the synagogue, shot, or killed by other means by a division of Einsatzgruppen, special police units for murdering Jews.

to the TOZ[406] building. The orphanage, the old people's home, and the refuge for the mentally ill were closed down. The buildings [left] by these institutions were given to the local authority, whose bureaucratic apparatus amounted to six thousand persons. The old people were moved to a private apartment. Two Jewish schools were operating, where the teaching was exclusively in Jewish and Hebrew. The teaching of German was strictly forbidden. The teaching took place in three shifts, like shifts in factories: from eight to twelve, from twelve to two in the afternoon, and from two to six. Jewish libraries were burned down, gymnasia destroyed. The German newspaper was banned in the ghetto. Cinemas were closed down, youth club activities paused—like the activities of trade unions—so on the outside, the cultural and social life of Jewish Białystok stopped. But the Jews were managing somehow. Risking their lives, [they] brought newspapers to the ghetto. People would listen to the radio in basements, particularly [broadcasts] from London. To listen to the radio, one paid a ten-mark entry fee and risked one's life. Despite this, the business flourished—until the Gestapo discovered it. The radio was confiscated and the Jew [who was responsible] bought himself out of a death sentence with half a million marks. I was a teacher at a Jewish elementary school. It was impossible to get books [so] the teachers put together textbooks from memory. Despite the fact that the Germans had burned all prayer books [and] closed all synagogues, the Jews gathered to pray in cellars and in attics. People studied, prayed, [and] gathered, employing the highest degree of caution. In September, rumors began about the liquidation of the ghetto. But the military authorities said that, for now, the army required Jewish labor. I set off on my way [out of there]. I walked for hundreds of kilometers along both fronts. I made it to the interior of Russia through Kharkiv. People didn't believe me when I told them about my experiences. The NKVD imprisoned me and sent me to a penal camp in the Mari El district. When I arrived there, the Poles had already left the camp. I tried to get into the army too. It took a long time before I was released from prison, and then they didn't want to accept me into the Polish army because I was Jewish. I found a way to get a passport and a baptismal certificate for myself. This way I made it out of Russia. I arrived safely in Tehran, and then in Palestine.

---

406. Towarzystwo Ochrony Zdrowia (Society for the Protection of the Health of the Jewish Population): Jewish social organization founded in 1912.

Protocol 160

Testimony of **Noemi Dobrin**, age twenty-five, resident in Bugdacz [?].[407]

I left our hometown, where I lived with [my] parents, on the third day of the war. The town was constantly bombarded. The station and the bridges were bombed. In the first days of the war, attacks on the Polish army units by groups of Germans diversionists took place. We went toward Kutno, under a shower of bombs throughout. The army helped us a lot along the way. The country-people, too, were generous with their help, giving us food products, until we got to Kutno. A battle was taking place not far from us. The Germans started their rule with requisitions. Everything possible was requisitioned. A levy was imposed, [to be paid] in goods and in money. Then the anti-Jewish regulations began. Thousands of people were shot dead. I worked in a hospital. After three months the hospital was closed down, the soldiers sent home, [and] the officers and doctors interned in camps. My father went to Łódź to obtain papers to leave. When he was at the Astoria Hotel, a search took place there. Everyone was taken out into the courtyard. Out of the two hundred arrestees, every tenth was shot dead. My father saved himself by giving a German [soldier] a gold watch and the money that he had on him. After that incident, we decided to cross the Russian border. [My] parents stayed behind in town. Three times I tried to cross the border, and finally managed it. I made it to Lwów through Białystok. In Lwów, I wanted to get into a medical school, because the lecturers were still Polish professors. But the situation was becoming more difficult; I couldn't stand the atmosphere and I gave up [my] studies. I signed up for a nursing course. I couldn't find work after finishing [it] because I didn't want to accept Russian citizenship. [Things in] Lwów were completely disorganized. The first Bolshevik orders were good for the people, but we soon learned what Russian administration meant. The Russian army bought out the entire contents of shops, officials requisitioned all the apartments, thousands of people were arrested. Then it was time for [more] persecutions. One night NKVD-ers turned up at [my apartment] and told me to pack [my] belongings. The same happened with other refugees. The patrols acted brutally, not

407. Most likely: Bydgoszcz.

sparing the ill and the elderly. Families were split up, parents separated from children. I approached the deportation calmly. It was admittedly a painful resolution to our situation as it was, [but] better than the fear and uncertainty that we had lived in for the past few months. The peasant who took us to the station on a cart wanted to hide us at his [place]. We gave up on that [plan]. We traveled in cattle cars. We were locked up for two days without food and drink. Only when the train started were we given a bit of water. After two weeks we arrived in the Tatar Republic, and from there, via the Volga, went to the Mari El Republic. We weren't allowed to buy food; we were terribly famished. At [our] destination we were assigned three small barracks that were to fit 370 people. Most [people] lived outdoors. Many people got blood poisoning from mosquito bites. Only after some time were there new barracks erected. Twenty-five families lived in each; we slept on the ground, one next to another, in filth and dust.

The day after [our] arrival, the men were sent to work in the forest and the women in the fields. People were paid according to the quotas they achieved, and we were all starving there. Selling clothes saved us. For whole weeks, forest berries were our [only] meals. The Russian population was made up of exiles and former kulaks. They treated us well as long as we still had something to sell; then they grew hateful toward us for our memories of the good times. They hated the Soviet regime also. I worked in a primitive health station with a young [female] feldsher and a teacher who belonged to the Komsomol. I often told them about Poland, but they didn't want to believe me. The teacher was hostile toward Poland, and she spread propaganda in the school around that belief. [Our] fairly hard work was increased to sixteen hours per day, which became unbearable. Being late for work was punishable by six months' prison. Ten-year-old children were sent to work; talking was forbidden during work; [we lived in] horrible terror. When one of [the Jews] went to the city, he brought us back news of the Polish-Soviet agreement.[408] We called a meeting, but the warden broke [it] up and arrested many of us. Only after some time did he come to us with the news about the Amnesty. The Russians wanted to keep me with them at all costs. I managed to get to Kuybyshev. I worked as a nurse in a Polish hospital. Things were completely chaotic there.

408. From 30 July 1941. See glossary: agreement.

The city was overwhelmed by refugees who were sleeping in the streets, and it was impossible to get bread. Help from the embassy amounted to a drop in the ocean. The Russian refugees fared better—we were chased from one place to another and were only allowed to do [our] shopping in street markets, where things were very expensive. During the journey from the Mari El Republic to Kuybyshev, I met a group of Georgian students who made my journey possible. They were Russian patriots but had a positive view of Poland and supported Polish independence. From Kuybyshev, I went to Frunze via Alma-Ata. Throughout the whole journey, I observed people's hostile attitudes toward not only Polish but also Russian refugees. Government assistance was only in the first stages of organization. The [Polish] delegation in Frunze was already working well, thanks to the delegate, who spared no energy. We noticed with surprise that the attitude of the Russian people toward Poles was warm and kind. We put on performances together and sang national songs. In Frunze, an army doctor encouraged me to go to a nursing course in Vrevskoye. After long efforts, I managed to get there. Traveling through the Kyrgyz region, I stopped by chance at a *posiołek* where German colonists lived. They spoke German, were German patriots, and believed in Hitler's victory. They treated Poles in a friendly manner, claiming that Poland would only flourish under German occupation. When I arrived [in Vrevskoye], I was told, without any tests [or] an examination, that I was not fit for [army] duty. I was very disappointed. Pleading and protests didn't help—I was left with no money and no roof over my head. I fell ill with pneumonia, and if not for the help of a Russian family who took care of me like their own child, I would not have survived. After I recovered, I tried to get into the army again. I was being helped from all directions, and this way I made it to Pahlevi with a transport. In Pahlevi, however, I was assigned to a camp for civilians. The Persians welcomed us more than hospitably [but] despite this, thousands of people died from exhaustion. This situation lasted for quite a long time before things settled. I received a certificate in Tehran, and this way, came to Palestine.

Protocol 161

Testimony of **Aszer Merzec**, age twenty-six, from Kraków, student of a yeshiva in Lublin. Came to Palestine from Shanghai and Tanganyika in August 1943.

When the war broke out, I was at my parents' in Kraków, where I was spending the summer holidays. By the first day of the war, plenty of refugees had already arrived in Kraków from the neighboring towns [and were] looking for shelter in the city.

On Sunday evening, 3 September, when it became clear that the Polish army wouldn't defend the city, a great panic broke out. People ran headlong, not knowing which direction to go. The panic increased when it was announced on Sunday that young people should leave the city and go east. I left Kraków that morning. Together with me were my brother, my brother-in-law, and my sister's fiancé. We went on foot, covering a distance of seven hundred kilometers from Kraków to Łuck in two weeks. We experienced many things on the way [and] stared death in the eye. At times we stopped believing that we would survive. An incident in the town of Brzesko has imprinted itself in my memory particularly strongly. As we were nearing the station, expecting to carry on east by train, we found a group of people there—women, men, and children—mostly Poles. We couldn't get into the carriage. All of a sudden, an airplane squadron flew in, descended just above the carriage, and started to shoot at the train so that it went up in flames within minutes. Human legs and arms flew in the air, and only few people were saved. In Niepołomice we met a large army unit that had been joined by many civilians. Suddenly, German airplanes came down low, just above the heads of the marching columns. We took cover in a ditch and survived this way. On 13 September, we arrived in Horodenka by Kowel. Completely exhausted, we decided to stay there for a few days. In the evening, we went to pray in the synagogue. Suddenly panic broke out, and people called out that the Germans were coming. We didn't even go back for our belongings; we ran on ahead with such haste that we covered sixty kilometers in one night and found ourselves, at ten in the morning the next day, in Maciejów. My brother fell ill there [and] developed a fever. We couldn't leave him. During that time, the Bolsheviks entered Maciejów. There was no reason to rush. We stayed in town and then made our way to

Łuck. Since we'd been left without clothes and without money, we decided to go to Lwów and make contact with Kraków from there. The journey from Łuck to Lwów took a few weeks. The railway line was broken up in many places. We often [had to] change from one train to another and had to walk across a damaged bridge. On the way we would light a fire and bake potatoes [we] had dug up in a field. We often bought food products from the peasants, too, and sold them on the train, earning money to live on this way. We couldn't find a place to spend the night in Lwów. Our uncle lived outside Lwów, in the town of Niżankowice. We got in touch with [our] parents in Kraków and went to [our uncle's place]. Two weeks later, my sister arrived from Kraków. She had brought a few things and some money. We went with her to Przemyśl, where her fiancé's parents lived. Half of Przemyśl belonged to the Germans, half to the Russians. After murdering five hundred Jews in Przemyśl in the first days of [their] occupation, the Germans kicked those remaining over to the Russian side. My sister got married and stayed in Przemyśl. [My] brother-in-law took up trading, while my brother and I, wanting to continue [our] yeshiva studies, decided to go to Romania or Lithuania. I went to the Romanian border, and realizing that I wouldn't be able to cross it, returned to Lwów. From there, I left for Lida in the middle of November. The journey was hard, the train overcrowded. In Lida, we were told that getting across the border was very difficult. The city was full of refugees, and it was only after long efforts that we got a counter in some shop that served us as a bed. After eight days' stay in Lida we went to Oszmiana, where we spent three months. We attempted to cross the border five times, with no success: three times we were caught, held for a few days and released. The fourth time, we took a peasant as a guide, who promised to drive us across the border for three thousand rubles. We left at one o'clock at night, and after traveling for a few kilometers, we were told to get off the cart. When we got off, supposedly because the horse was struggling, the peasant ran off with our money and [our] belongings. We returned to town at three o'clock and went to the beth hamidrash for the night. Those experiences shook my brother so badly that he almost gave up further [attempts to] sneak across. But a few days later, my companions from the Lublin yeshiva arrived—Sznejerson from Podgórze and Jecheskiel Rubin, son of the rabbi from Tomaszów—and told me that they were prepared to take us with them. There was only room for one. I sent [my] brother. They were caught at the border, and in the morning I got the news that they were in jail. I attempted some interventions but didn't get far, and they were deported to Siberia after spending a month in prison in Oszmiana. I decided to cross over to Lithuania at all costs. It was in February 1940. Snow had covered all roads. I made the acquaintance of a guide who said he would take me across the border if I learned how to ski. I bought myself skis and after ten days of practicing, set off on the way. At night, the guide told me that we had to abandon [the rest of] the journey as it was a moonlit night. We spent the night at a peasant's place and only set off [again] after a few days. There was a small bridge at the border that we had to cross. My skis came off, and at that same moment, I heard a suspicious murmur. My guide disappeared and I never saw him again. I tied [my] skis on and went on ahead. I had traveled a few hundred meters when I heard the tapping of army boots on the bridge. I didn't look back until I awoke in Lithuanian territory, where I found my companion, who told me I had [only] survived by a miracle. We set off for the town of Turgiele. I changed into peasant clothes in a villager's hut and marched on to Wilno with a basket of vegetables. In Wilno I met [my] companions from the Lublin yeshiva, who were continuing their studies. When the Bolsheviks occupied Lithuania, I was able to get a Japanese visa and received a Russian departure visa for Japan. Intourist[409] demanded two hundred actual-value dollars each from all the yeshiva members for the journey, a sum none of us could dream of. The yeshiva director decided to go around to the small towns and collect the sum we needed. Five times he went to take up a collection, and five times we had our visas extended. In Latvia the situation of the Jews was much worse. There Orthodox Jews were persecuted particularly cruelly. The local authority chief in Riga—the former MP Dubin—intervened in Moscow despite the danger that he faced, and many Orthodox [Jews] and Bund members were released as a result of this intervention. Dubin was threatened with arrest, but nevertheless continued [his] efforts to intervene. I went to Riga and made contact with Dubin and the Riga rabbi, Zak, who was later burned to death by the Germans during the Riga massacre.[410] Thanks to their help, I managed to put together a large sum of money, which I later exchanged for dollars. As I was afraid of

409. Intourist: the Soviet state travel agency.

410. Likely refers to the massacre of approximately 2,700 Jews by Latvian fascists during the first days of the German occupation (the Wehrmacht entered Riga on 1 July 1941).

traveling with such a large amount of money on me, I went [back and forth between] Riga and Kaunas a few times and transported all of the money. When I was in Riga for the final time, MP Dubin was arrested by the Bolsheviks, and that arrest had a big impact. Arrests were taking place more and more frequently in Wilno and Kaunas. In March 1941 I went to Moscow, and from there to Vladivostok. I found out that the Japanese were not allowing [people] into the country with visas issued in Kaunas. Their explanation for the ban was that the refugees didn't have visas [for further travel], so they [might] stay in Japan. Our group was made up of sixty people and we were threatened with being sent [back] to Lithuania. We sent emergency telegrams to America, Switzerland, Sweden, England, [and] Japan, but to no avail. We spent six weeks in Vladivostok. Tens of times we were taken to the station. Fortunately for us the director of the hotel we were staying in was a Jew, reputedly a Zionist, who helped us any way he could. He intervened in consulates, particularly in the Japanese consulate, looking for a way for us to be able to leave. The Japanese consul sent telegrams directly to Tokyo, but the responses came back negative. Money was running out. When we could no longer stay in the hotel, and they wanted to send us to Siberia, the hotel director invited the captain of a Japanese ship that went between Vladivostok and Tsuruga to come over, and having gotten him drunk, got permission [from him] for us to cross in exchange for a large sum of money. It was agreed that if they didn't let us into Japan, we would return to Vladivostok. Immediately after the captain's departure, we were taken, at twelve o'clock at night, to the port. The port authority office was opened up and we left Vladivostok. In Tsuruga, representatives of the Jewish committee were waiting for us, having been notified of our arrival earlier, and after long negotiations, those with residence visas were allowed off the ship. Eighteen people with only transit visas remained on the ship. We were locked in a cabin and threatened with being sent back to Russia. I managed to send a telegram to a rabbinic association in America. A few hours later, the Dutch consul arrived on the ship accompanied by a representative of the Jewish commission, issued everyone visas to Curaçao, and we were allowed off the ship. I spent six months in Japan. I obtained an American visa, but before I received [the document], a ban went into effect [stating that] people who had relatives in German-occupied countries would not be allowed into America. As I had said that my parents were in Kraków, the ban applied to me. In September 1941, I was sent to Shanghai with all the [other] refugees. As a war had broken out with the Allied states, we were treated like citizens of a hostile country. The Japanese interned [blocked] the international concessions.[411] Panic broke out among the refugees. We moved to the French territory, which the Japanese were not occupying. There was unrest in the city. Barricades stood on the streets. Our situation was unbearable. We lived twenty to a room. A Shanghai rabbi, Aszkenazy, helped us. We were sent money from America, via Sweden. Later we rented a town house, where 150 yeshiva members lived. A group of journalists and writers from Poland also lived in that house, with Lazar Kahan at its helm. I was the administrative manager of the house. The yeshiva from Mirów,[412] made up of 250 students, also moved to Shanghai and rented a house there. We opened a soup kitchen and cooked meals twice a day. There were other refugees living in the city. Some were traders. Altogether there were 950 Jewish refugees from Poland in Shanghai. In January 1942, the Polish ambassador and current foreign minister, Count Romer,[413] came to Shanghai. He created a refugee assistance committee made up of nineteen people, which I belonged to as well. I worked with him for a year. Count Romer intended to take all the Jewish refugees to Palestine via Russia. Negotiations with Moscow were taking place on the matter. Eventually, a negative reply arrived. In January 1943, news arrived of a diplomatic exchange [of diplomatic staff] between Japan and the Allies. Because the number of Japanese diplomats was larger than that of the Allies, it turned out that there were four hundred free places for civilians on the list. Forty-two spots were assigned to Polish citizens. Count Romer called a meeting of the refugee representatives and asked that a list be put together including representatives of all political creeds. We couldn't come to an agreement [and], in the end, Count Romer himself set out the number of spots. As arguments broke out even after this, Count Romer put the list together himself. I was on this list. There were five Orthodox [Jews], five Bund members, three Zionists,

411. Autonomous districts in the modern part of Shanghai, in effect ruled by the colonial powers of the time.

412. Should be: Mir (currently in Belarus). A well-known yeshiva established in the second decade of the nineteenth century in the town of Mir, Nowogródek area, on the Radziwiłł estate.

413. Tadeusz Ludwik Romer (1894–1978): Moscow ambassador of the Polish Government-in-Exile; from 14 July 1943 to 24 November 1944 the foreign minister of the Polish Government-in-Exile.

three Poale Zionists, eight baptized [Jews], and the rest Poles. We traveled on a luxury ship, on which there were a thousand [other] people, all diplomats. We traveled for twenty-six days, all the way to Lorenzo-Marco.[414] The forty-two civilians were told that they were being sent to Africa. We called a strike and would not get off the ship. I was told that if I wanted to go to Palestine, I had to disembark. Others set off for England. I stayed a few weeks in Lorenzo-Marco. I said goodbye to Count Romer, who returned to Moscow as a Polish ambassador. From Lorenzo-Marco, I traveled to Palestine via Tanganyika. Because there were no [transport] connection[s], I was sent to a Polish camp in Tanger, in central Tanganyika, where there [were] three thousand refugees, including forty Jews who had been brought there from Tehran. The conditions [were] very primitive. People lived in huts [belonging to] the natives. The intelligentsia worked in offices, the specialists in their trades. I got a job in an office too. The administration in the camp was Polish. After three months, I went to Ambassa,[415] the outskirts [?] of Kenya, and spent two months there in an apartment of a Jew named Fris, who cared for us like a parent. At the end of July, I went to Aden on an English ship, and from there, to Port Said. I arrived in Palestine at the end of August.

414. This place has not been located.

415. Likely refers to the town of Mombasa.

Protocol 162

Testimony of **Abram Klok**, age twenty-five, born in Warsaw, leader of a Printers' Union. Came to Palestine via Russia and Tehran.

I was mobilized on 24 August 1939, and that same day, went to Dęblin and registered at the 15th Infantry regiment, which was stationed in Dęblin permanently. I was assigned to the Ninth Battalion of the Ninth Company. Within two days, the regiment was ready to march out. We marched out of Dęblin before the outbreak of war toward Wieluń, where the division to which the regiment belonged was to take up appropriate positions. I don't remember whether we reached our destination, or whether the battles started before that and we took up provisional positions. One day at sunrise, the Germans opened artillery fire in our direction. The war began. Despite many casualties on our side, we remained at [our] posts. The artillery opened fire and the fighting was very fierce. The Germans sent a lot of tanks toward us, which tore through our poorly defended positions. I did not see a single German in the section where I was. As [our] line[s] had collapsed, our troops had to retreat, and we were attacked by a staggered formation of tanks on the road. There was no space or time to assume new positions. The tanks advanced on our infantry columns, and a great panic broke out. The regiment was broken up; the soldiers dispersed, running, abandoning their weapons. It was difficult to hold out against the kind of assault that the Germans opened from [their] tanks. There were fifteen of us soldiers left in one spot, with a master corporal at our helm. The master corporal wanted to form a defense line. Suddenly, an officer in a Polish uniform approached. I don't know for sure if he was a Polish officer or a saboteur. When the master corporal reported to him that he was planning to put up a defense, the officer took out a gun and shot [him] dead on the spot. We were standing close to a bridge, and two Polish pioneers had planned to blow [it] up, but at that moment, someone wearing a Polish soldier's uniform appeared and shot the two pioneers from behind, killing them on the spot. After these experiences, our group no longer walked on the road, but walked in the fields instead. We walked toward Łódź, all the while remaining in the zone of German bombardments and shooting. We crossed small rivers and our uniforms were completely soaked. There was no way for us to spend the night anywhere and dry out our uniforms. After a few days we found ourselves in Łódź, and we learned that the Germans were just outside the city. We ran up the road toward Warsaw. Hundreds of thousands of people were walking and running with the army in the same direction. German airplanes bombed the roads. On both sides of the road, in the ditches, there lay dead people and horses. Many people fainted from hunger and thirst. It was difficult to rest [even] for a moment. There wasn't a single minute when the road wasn't being bombed by the planes, which flew so low above people's heads that many were injured just from the air pressure caused by the machines flying by. After each raid, the road was full of dead people. Meanwhile, wounds appeared on our feet and we couldn't carry on walking. Every day, my boots were full of blood. We arrived in Warsaw through Wola. Even though I was barely [managing to] drag myself forward, I went to my home to see my parents and other people in the house. I only [had to] march across Warsaw. The streets of the capital were barricaded and there were ditches [dug] in front of the barricades, intended to protect the city from tanks. The barricades had been built out of overturned trams, sandbags, planks, furniture, and apartment doors. The city looked dead. Hardly anyone showed themselves on the street. A militia force with yellow armbands was keeping the order. I found out from the passersby that Warsaw had been bombed several times. This was on 12 September. We went toward Otwock over the Poniatowski Bridge. My feet were bleeding. I asked an officer traveling by car to take me with him. I was taken to an army hospital in Lublin. At five in the morning, I remember, there was a horrible air raid on Lublin, during which Germans deliberately bombed the hospital. The nurses ran off and left the patients behind. We saw them out of the window getting into cars and driving off. Panic broke out among the patients. The bombing continued. A hospital wing caught on fire. At that point, all the patients left the hospital; even the most gravely ill dragged themselves down the stairs [using] crutches. By the time the last patient had left the hospital, the building was already on fire. I didn't feel the injury to my leg; I ran [along] with everyone and wasn't even tired. On the way, I met a Jew from Kraków riding on a cart loaded up with things. He allowed me to sit on top of [them], and this way, I made it to Kowel. The roads were full of injured and dead [people]. Soldiers and civilians were running in various directions. Many were returning [after] hearing about the terrible bombardment of Lublin. In

Kowel, I got into a military hospital again. Soon afterward, I heard the droning of tank engines through the window. I ran to the window and saw Soviet tanks. It was a complete surprise to everyone, because it had been said in the hospital that the Polish army was gathering in the borderlands to resist the Germans. The arrival of the Soviets meant the end of the Polish army. Panic arose in the hospital; the nurses ran away, the doctors changed into civilian clothes in fear. Polish soldiers and officers were arrested in the streets. I often left the hospital to go into town. I met Wiktor Alter, who was living in the building of People's Bank with a group of Bund members. Some of them were members of a tailors' union, others of the Jutrznia sports organization. The tailors made a padded jacket for Alter, since frosts had already began, and [he] didn't have a coat. It was said at the time among the Bund members that the GPU was looking for Alter. What happened to him later I don't know, because the whole hospital was moved from Kowel to Brody. We were being starved in the hospital. I spent eight weeks [there] until my wounds had healed, and then ran away, because all the patients were told they would be treated as prisoners of war and sent to Russian camps. I escaped with a whole group of gunners, and armed guards shot at us. I spent six months in Lwów. I was horrendously short of food [and] couldn't get work despite being a good Linotype printer. I tried to do some trading at the Lwów market so I wouldn't starve to death. There I met a man named Pulwer who traded sweaters, and who gave me merchandise to sell. I started to earn decent money and I lived with Pulwer himself. One day the police carried out a search in our apartment and confiscated all the sweaters. Pulwer was arrested and accused of speculation. I was a witness in his case. Out of gratitude, Pulwer gave me ten thousand rubles. At that time people were talking a lot about going back home. Living with no future seemed horrible to everyone and I, like many others, decided to return [home] to [my] parents in Warsaw. I went to Brześć. I ran into my cousins there, who advised me against going, telling [me] about how Jews were being rounded up for work and how they never came back. At that point, the Bolsheviks had put up notices about the passportization, and since few people were taking Soviet passports, numerous arrests began. I got a job with a Russian newspaper, *Zorza*. I met a printer from the *Moment*[416] there named Mates. A

416. See footnote in Protocol 148.

few Communists from Warsaw who were working there made me the head of the printing house. A man named Kagan took me under his wing and [tried to] convince me to become a Soviet citizen. I didn't want to hear of it. My apartment was located close to the prison. Once, NKVD-ers turned up at my place, and acting very politely, asked me about [my] passport. They told me not to worry too much, that I would get the passport and that they would take me to register. I never came back home from that registration, even though they hadn't allowed me to bring any [of my] belongings. There were sixty of us in a cell intended for ten people. This was in June 1940. The heat was so horrendous that we could barely stand it. We weren't even let out to go to the toilet. Washing was forbidden. I spent six weeks in these conditions. Food consisted of salted fish and salted water, and drinking water wasn't provided. After a few weeks' stay in prison, I no longer looked like a human being. I was carried out of the cell, as I couldn't walk, was shaved and given a sign with [my] surname on it. Then the search began: all of my clothes were ripped to check whether I had anything hidden there. I was told to bend over and two soldiers with an electric light looked in [my] private areas. Then, I was called for interrogation and found out that the Communists from the *Zorza* printing house had denounced me for being a former Polish soldier. The investigating judge threatened me with a gun. I was told I was a prisoner of war, and that after the fracas I had caused in prison, I was being sentenced to a punishment cell. The fracas consisted of me not wanting to eat salted fish without water. When I was led to the punishment cell, I decided to tease the guard and pretend I was a madman. I talked to myself, but the guard didn't fall for it. I spent one day in the punishment cell, after which all the arrestees were taken to the station, having been called up by their surnames. We were driven in trucks and told to cover our faces so that we wouldn't see the city. Empty cars stood on the siding, and tens of trucks brought in people from all directions; [they were] loaded into the cars, forty people in each. The loaded cars were sealed. The train waited for two days, until the city had been cleared of refugees. We weren't given even a drop of water for twenty-four hours. We knocked on the doors—the whole transport joined this demonstration. In the end, the NKVD-ers paid us back for this. They brought in hot bread, just out of the oven, and cold water. The famished people ate the food quickly, and the whole transport fell ill with stomach problems. Because we weren't allowed out of the cars, they became [our] toilets. Some people couldn't move. The NKVD didn't allow parcels from the city to reach us. The journey took three weeks. Throughout that time, we were fed bread and water. We arrived in Kotlas weak and lice ridden. Those who had clothes and underwear with them looked better. I didn't even have a shirt with me, and the only one I was wearing I couldn't wash. A disinfection was carried out in Kotlas and we were sent out to *posiołki*. I met a Jewish writer, Abram Zak,[417] and the son of Szereszewski there. The latter had brought plenty of things with him, and big suitcases. Immediately after he entered the camp, his suitcases were confiscated. After a search, I was sent along with 126 [other] people, to Czibiw [?],[418] where the camp was located. We walked for sixteen kilometers. We slept for a long time in the camp, and then an NKVD chief arrived on horseback from the headquarters and made a speech to us. He painted our future in stark colors [and] told us not to think about Poland anymore, that that country of overlords had been eliminated once and for all, and anyone who wanted to think about that cursed land, and anyone who wouldn't work, would starve to death [like a dog]. We fell into deep apathy. I met people in the labor camp who had come there before me. Among them there was Kapliński, son of a typesetter at *Moment*, who was seriously ill with heart problems and couldn't work. He was starving, and the camp authorities persecuted [part of text missing]. Later he was sent [away] and I never heard anything about him again. I also met a man named Kamień from Warsaw, 15 Dzielna [Street], who belonged to a youth organization Przyszłość.[419] He was killed by a falling tree during work. For a year and a half, I was moved around to different camps in the area. I continued to be terrified by the chief's original speech, that if we didn't work, we'd die. I decided to work no matter what and thus became a Stakhanovite. I got up before the others and was already in the forest at sunrise. I worked so quickly that my quotas were done by twelve o'clock [in the afternoon]. Thanks to this, I was the warden's favorite; I got a pair of *valenki*,[420] a shirt, and a padded jacket. I also received better food. Many refugees were angry with me for my diligence, but I explained to them that I wanted to survive and return to

---

417. Abraham Zak: poet who wrote in Yiddish. He survived a labor camp and left Poland in 1948.
418. Possibly the same as the town referred to as Dzibiwa in Protocol 164.
419. The correct name: Cukunft: the youth wing of the Bund [From German: *Zukunft* (future)].
420. Felt boots.

Warsaw. This work had its bad aspects. As a Stakhanovite, I was put with the *bytoviki*, former thieves and criminals, who were all Stakhanovites. In reality, I was the only one who worked—the *bytoviki* had received the title and the privileges of a Stakhanovite from the warden by terror[izing him]. They didn't work at all; they forged [their] quotas and forced the guards to write in more for them than they had worked. Among these thugs, I gave up [my] diligence, since I no longer needed it. The thugs weren't afraid of the regime, and the regime was very strict in that camp. The guards would kill an exile for any slight misdemeanor. Both the *bytoviki* and the authorities had a good attitude toward me. [Once] a guard shot a *bytovik* dead when the *bytovik* bent down to pick something up along the way. The *bytoviki* called a strike. They demanded that the guard be kicked out of the camp. The warden came running with a gun and threatened to shoot everyone. Some got up, opened up their shirts to bare their chests and said: "Shoot, [you] scumbag,[421] as much as you like." Life meant little to a *bytovik*. I spent half a year among these demoralizing element[s]. I didn't catch [their degeneration] from them. I looked at them like actors in a theater. When the Amnesty was announced, I wasn't released because I was among the *bytoviki* and considered a Stakhanovite. I was sent to Kiermany [?] with a gang of two hundred *bytoviki*. I worked for three weeks and was only released on 15 September. I went to Tacko[422] and reported to the army as a prisoner of war. After eight months, we were sent to Guzar. I fell ill with typhus there, twice. I was very weak, and when we were sent off to Kermine, I got jaundice and sunstroke. In Persia, where I came as a member of the army, I could still not believe I was alive and that I had survived those awful events in one piece.

---

421. Original: *swołocz*. From Russian *svoloch*, meaning bastard, scumbag.

422. Totskoye.

Protocol 163

Testimony of **Rebeka Frenkel**, age twenty-five, from Limanowa. Came to Palestine from Tehran via Russia.

My parents had a clothing shop in our town, located by Nowy Sącz. We were well situated, and Father was the president of the local borough. On Saturday, 2 September, the town was bombed, and in the evening, the Germans arrived. My brother and father left town with [their] families alongside other Jews. We followed them. The roads were bombed; many people dropped dead. We reached Biłgoraj in the Lublin voivodeship. There was a battle taking place in Biłgoraj. The town kept changing hands [and] was eventually occupied by the Germans. The Jewish population suffered terribly at [their] hands. It started off with theft and ended with murder. Because [my] mother and sister had stayed in Limanowa, and the Germans were following our trail, we decided to return home. We went to Tarnów. I left my father and brother there, as I was afraid for them to come home, and I went [home] to Mother by myself. In Limanowa, all the richest Jews had been arrested as hostages, and the Germans had been looking for [my] father for many days. A few times the Germans took the seventeen hostages out into a field [and] told them to dig graves, and then to go back to jail. One day, the Germans ordered all Jewish people, including women and children, to gather in the market. Failing to follow the order was punishable by death. Everyone turned up in the square. The Gestapo arrived, and the seventeen hostages were brought in. Drunk Napol, the Gestapo chief, said that the seventeen hostages had been sentenced to death. He forced all Jews to go to the cemetery and watch [the Germans] bury the seventeen hostages alive. [People] burst into tears. The Germans watched the Jewish suffering with joy. [The chief] chased everyone into the cemetery. Some comforted themselves, [saying] that [although] such displays did happen, they were only intended to frighten people. People trusted in a miracle. [But] this time there was no miracle. The hostages were ordered to dig graves. The Germans wouldn't allow anyone to help them, and before the graves were ready, machine-gun fire rang out, and the seventeen Jews were killed. They fell into the open graves. The Germans buried them with their shoes on. Then, all the Jews were ordered to stay home for twenty-four hours. After those exhausting ordeals, I left Mother, who was unwell, and went on my own to Tarnów, to [be with] Father. The Germans were cutting Jews' beards off. They came to Father's apartment, took him to a barber and ordered his beard cut off. I was pleased. I thought that they wouldn't harm Father this way. It turned out that my joy was premature. The Germans tied Father's hands, and one of them cut Father's beard off using a blunt bayonet, wounding his entire face. I fell to the German's feet, kissed his hands so he wouldn't kill Father, but the more I begged, the more they tortured the poor man. Finally I took him home, unconscious, where he stayed in bed for a few weeks. I witnessed many such scenes involving beards. I saw, too, how the Germans chased Jews to the new synagogue in Tarnów and locked them inside. Then they shot at the synagogue from cannons. A few Jews were killed. They died calling: "Listen, Israel."[423] I felt I would not survive for long [here] and encouraged [my] father and brother to smuggle themselves across the border with me. Father acquiesced. We set off toward the San, and when [our] boat was in the middle of the river, the Germans opened fire in our direction. We thought our final hour had come. However, we made it to the other bank. A rabbi from Dąbrowa, Wajdenfeld, was traveling with us. The Germans were on the other side of the San as well. They tormented us horribly. The old rabbi had a heart attack. We did everything to save him, but it was in vain. He died in my arms. We carried his body on our backs for ten kilometers until we arrived in Sieniawa, where we buried the rabbi in a cemetery. During the border crossing, the Germans and Ukrainians took away everything from us. We were happy that they let us go free and that we were in Soviet territory. In Lwów, we couldn't find a place to sleep; thousands of Jews were roaming the streets, and since we had nothing to live on, we went to Bolechów where [some of] our relatives lived. We lived all right from trading for six months. We didn't want to accept Soviet citizenship. One night, when we weren't expecting anything, NKVD-ers arrived at our place, and it turned out that our previous relations with the Soviet authorities weren't much help to us. We saw the real face of Russia. They wanted to separate me from [my] brother and father. We eventually managed to convince them not to do it. We were sent to Siberia. After many weeks of a horrendous journey, we arrived in a *posiołek* in

423. [The Shema prayer, central to Jewish prayer services. Traditionally the Shema is the last thing a Jew is supposed say before death.]

the Novosibirsk Oblast, and were then moved to the Sverdlovsk Oblast, where we worked in a forest. We built barracks for ourselves [and] didn't get paid for [our] work. Father, exhausted by [these] ordeals, could barely stand up. The warden accused him of sabotage. Older people were dropping like flies. After many months of suffering, we received news of the Amnesty, but while everyone was celebrating, for us that date was [one] of mourning. On hearing the news about the Amnesty, Father had a heart attack from the excitement and passed away. We encountered many difficulties with the funeral. [My] brother lost his mind out of despair. He was locked up in a home for lunatics, [and] I had to deal with Father's funeral on my own. I carried him to the cemetery myself and buried him myself. Everyone had gone away—I wanted to leave too but felt bad leaving [my] brother. I sold everything to save him, but it was all in vain because he died a few weeks later. I was certain he had been poisoned. I asked for [my] brother's body to be released, but to no avail. I went to Bukhara and Tashkent. I arranged a sham marriage to a Polish soldier to obtain papers and made it to Persia this way. Thanks to this, I found myself in Palestine.

Protocol 164

Testimony of **Natan Birman**, age thirty-seven, from Warsaw, hairdresser by trade.

The outbreak of the war found me in Warsaw, where I lived through the siege of the city. I was a member of the civilian guard and was out in the streets almost all the time, tending to the wounded. The civilian guard was employed in set districts from the beginning. The Jewish [guard worked] in the Jewish [district], but later, when the calamity spread farther and farther, things got disorganized, district boundaries no longer applied, [and] we would run to help wherever there was a need. Overall, there was a serious lack of doctors. Many of the injured died because they did not immediately receive appropriate help. As a feldsher, I helped two hundred people during the bombardment. There were no bandages either—I used torn-up shirts and sheets. Iodine and all [the other] antiseptics ran out. All we could do to save the patients was to wrap [their] wounds and stop the bleeding. Despite this, I didn't have a single case of blood poisoning. I worked in the Holy Spirit Hospital on Elektoralna [Street]. I often ran out to the pharmacy on the corner of Solna and Elektoralna and helped the wounded there. The German airplanes flew so low that they almost touched the hospital roof. They dropped bombs and immediately soared up high. They were aiming at the front building; there were ten airplanes bombing the hospital. The first ones dropped explosive bombs; the others incendiary [ones]. Few of the wounded could be saved because the front building collapsed and buried the exit into the street. Polish scouts [and] Jews from the neighboring areas helped to treat the injured. No one knew where to take them. They were placed in nearby courtyards where they died immediately. Not [even] a hundredth of the patients from the hospital were saved, and it must be remembered that there were a few thousand people [there]. All the corridors and rooms and administrative offices were full of injured military personnel and civilians. With [few] exception[s], they all perished in the fire that broke out. For a full twenty-four hours, moaning was heard from under the ruins, but it was impossible to get to those buried under the rubble. The corpses were laid out in the nearby gardens and squares. When the Germans occupied the city, they ordered that the bodies be exhumed and moved to the cemetery. Many had been buried under the rubble, so you could smell the stench of decomposing bodies in the streets of Warsaw for weeks.

At first the Germans treated Jews and Poles the same. They filmed the distribution of food among the local people. A few days later, everything changed. The soup kitchens operated in set places, [and] Poles standing in the lines pointed out the Jews to the SS, and [the Jews] were removed from the lines. The anti-Jewish atmosphere increased by the hour, until a blue notice appeared regarding [offering] assistance to people, and Jews were stripped of [the right to] any assistance. There was even a notice about the regulation of grave prices in the cemeteries of Warsaw, but it did not apply to the Jewish cemetery. These were the first signs of the special treatment of the Jews. Only Jews were mentioned in the notice about combatting speculation. The Germans captured Jews for [forced] labor while hiring Poles legally for paid work. The plundering of Jewish shops, storehouses, and private homes began. The confiscation applied only to the Jewish people and had a corrupting effect on a particular segment of the Polish youth, who robbed the shops and threatened [their owners] with denunciation. A Jewish life was not worth much. Young people started leaving town and crossing over to the Soviet side; trading ceased; Jews were prohibited from trading leather or manufacture. It was forbidden to have more than two hundred zlotys, and a bank deposit could not be greater than twelve hundred zlotys.

I decided to leave town and went to Małkinia with a group of people. There the Germans took away everything we had with us and gave it to the Polish people who were standing nearby at the station, with baskets and sacks, ready to receive the bounty. They even took off our coats and ordered us to clean latrines with our bare hands, then beat us bloody and told us to run over to the Bolsheviks. There was a strip of no-man's-land close to Małkinia. We spent two days outside there, in a group of a few hundred people, because the Bolsheviks weren't allowing people in. I managed to get through to Zaręby Kościelne through a forest, and from there to Białystok by train. I arrived in Białystok on 2 October 1939, at a time when the city was so full of refugees that there were thousands of people staying in the station. I was left with no money because the Germans in Małkinia had taken away my two hundred zlotys. I suffered from hunger [and] couldn't find work. I didn't have a place to stay either. I was advised in a hairdressers' union to register to work in Russia. I didn't want to go far from [my] family, who were in Warsaw, and I asked them to find me work in my trade. I was advised to change to a different line of work. Then the commissar of the union accused me of being an enemy of the people. I didn't go to see him again, and I started trading in the market square. [My] trading began with the sale of my own jacket. I bought towels with the money I got for it and made a thousand rubles within a week. With that amount, I bought sacks and earned six thousand rubles on them. Within a short time, I had a fortune worth twenty thousand rubles. I stopped trading and started to look for a job in my trade.

Meanwhile, the time had come to decide [whether] to take Russian citizenship. Few people could bring themselves to do it—most wanted to return to their [former] places of residence. The German commissions were beleaguered by people asking to be allowed to go back.[424] The border was closely guarded, [but] I decided to cross it nonetheless. I paid 1,500 rubles to a smuggler, but he got arrested at the border and I had to escape from Siemiatycze, as all refugees who did not have Soviet passports were being arrested there, and go back to Białystok. When I arrived in Białystok, a raid was just taking place in the station; I was arrested and taken to prison. The prison was full of refugees caught during the raid. One Jew had been brought in in his long johns because he had been caught at night when he was walking out of his house to go to the toilet. There were fifty of us in a cell intended for five. We stood all day long, and at night, it was possible to sit down and sleep, crouching. Twice a day we were each given a piece of bread and soup. We weren't allowed out for walks [or] even let out to go to the toilet, and the bucket was only emptied four times a day, which wasn't enough for fifty people. We didn't wash for two weeks; we were lice ridden and covered in dirt. People didn't [even] look like themselves. Many fainted but couldn't be helped as they couldn't even lie down. When we were led out of the cell, no one was able to walk. People were crawling on the ground because [their] legs were stiff from standing on the stone floor. We were loaded onto a truck, sitting one on top of another. There were forty people in the truck. We were covered with a tarp and driven through the city. There was a train in the station, we were loaded onto [it], and the NKVD-ers guarded the platform and didn't allow the family and friends of the refugees

424. Mixed Russian-German commissions dealing with resettlement affairs.

to approach. Someone was waiting for a Jew from Kraków, to deliver clothes to him, but he wasn't allowed to, and [the Jew] was chased down the platform in [his] underpants. People looking at us through the windows of the car were laughing bitterly and crying. We traveled for three weeks [and] were fed clay-like bread and salted fish. Water was provided only once a day, and only for drinking. I hadn't washed in many weeks. My underwear was full of lice, I had to throw it away and bought myself a shirt from one youth in that same car.

We arrived in Kotlas. It was a central assembly point from which arrestees and refugees were sent out across all of Russia. An infamous ten-thousand-person prison is located there. A doctor deported from Odessa told me that there were fifty thousand arrestees in the prison at times. We were washed and our clothes were disinfected. For the first time in five weeks I felt the pleasure of a bath. The man who disinfected [our] clothes spoke Russian badly. He told me he was an English doctor who had come to Russia as a specialist in 1937, [then] was arrested and sentenced to fifteen years in exile. In the camp you'd come across people of various races, even Chinese. Our hairdresser came from Vienna. He had come to Russia after the fighting in Vienna.[425] He, too, had been sentenced to fifteen years in exile.

After two days, we were rushed to Kierman [?][426] in a group of two hundred people. We walked for two days without food and arrived in the city at night. We slept outdoors. Two days later, we were rushed to Dzibiw [?],[427] searched, and sent to a forest. We found two wooden barracks there [and] were ordered to build new ones. In four days, we built two more barracks [and] made bunks and tables. Then, we were gathered together and told to pick a type of work. Anyone who didn't want to work risked dying from hunger. I was told that I'd been given a sentence of five years in prison, and when I asked why, the warden replied that twenty years wouldn't be enough for a spy like me. We were told to cut down trees [but] no one knew how to start. At that point, the warden gathered us together and cursed us [for] not fulfilling even 10 percent

425. Refers to the uprising of the Schutzbund, a paramilitary self-defense organization formed by the Austrian Social Democratic [Party], which was bloodily quashed by the Austrofascist government of Engelbert Dollfuss. The fighting took place in February 1934 in Vienna and other Austrian cities.

426. This place has not been located.

427. It's possible that this is the same town as the one referred to as Czibiw in Protocol 162.

of the quota. He said he would knock Poland out of our heads with the axes intended for work, and that there was no place in Russia for saboteurs. Later we were given watery soup and bread, but none of us could eat and everyone had tears in their eyes. Our work was more productive the next day, but we didn't get more food. Within a few weeks, we were fulfilling 100 percent of [our] quotas, 50 percent of which was being stolen. Fifteen people were picked from our group and sent for haying. We found a makeshift camp for women and men there, mostly *bytoviki*.[428] I slept in [my] clothes and shoes because the *bytoviki* would steal everything. One day during work, a Russian man fainted. I said I was a feldsher and would try to revive him. However, it turned out he was already dead. The Russian was taken away, and two doctors from central came to the camp. I was present at the autopsy of the body. The doctors determined that the cause of death was exhaustion. Under the skin of [his] face not even a millimeter of fat could be found, which is present even in people who die from starvation. The organs were the size of a child's.

After that incident, I stayed in the camp as the manager of the medical center. I witnessed horrible things. Most of the women had venereal diseases; some had arrived there at the age of twelve. They were prostitutes or the children of arrested parents. Lesbian love was very popular among the women. Relations in the men's camps were similar. There were instances when the *bytoviki* would sell their male lovers during games, which normally ended in tragedy. The warden, afraid of revenge, never punished the *bytoviki*. As a result, they had no respect for the authorities. They never fulfilled their quotas [but] nevertheless they received food from the [same] kettle as the Stakhanovites and, like those, got the best clothing. They cursed in a truly unbelievable manner. Many refugees from the neighboring camps reported to our center, ill with *cynga*. They were covered in horrendous sores, had no teeth, and the arms of some were covered in blotches. There was a typhus epidemic in the last few months. [People's] weakened bodies could not withstand the fever and they died on the seventh day of the illness, even without complications. In a neighboring camp, five children died in one day. Children were dropping like flies. I registered 150 deaths in three camps in three months. The number of people there was around a thousand. Most cases were refugees from Poland. Mortality

428. People convicted primarily of petty crimes.

among Russians was minimal because their bodies are stronger. The Russians had gotten used to horrendous living conditions over many years. I noticed that Russian children survived hunger well, whereas Polish children died from malnutrition.

I learned about the Amnesty of 17 October, and from that day on, refugees were no longer sent to work. The warden told us we were free. However, they advised us to stay in the camp, saying that a journey through Russia would mean death from hunger and cold. No one wanted to stay. It turned out that the Amnesty did not apply to everyone. A number of people stayed behind, and we later envied them for not coming with us. We walked for three days to get to Kotlas. We came upon many refugees there and couldn't get into a train. Six weeks later, I got to Tashkent, which looked like Białystok in 1939. It wasn't possible to find work; people slept in the streets [and] many went to Turkestan and [joined] kolkhozes on the way. I found myself in Kermine and reported to the Polish army. I found out that Jews weren't being accepted. Two NKVD-ers who sat on the commission asked me if I was a Jew [and] I replied that I was a Pole and that I wanted to fight the Germans. A Polish doctor, a captain, discovered that I had a congenital heart disease. I started [protesting] that I had never been ill with heart problems, [but] the NKVD-ers said I was unfit for army duty. I was given category C, which was later changed to category A in Tehran. It was said that Jews would not be taken to Persia—I heard about such cases—however, I went with the first transport after all and was saved this way.

Protocol 165

Testimony of **Gita Wagszal**, age fourteen, from Nowy Sącz, deported to Siberia. Came to Palestine via Tehran.

My father was a bookkeeper in the Jewish cooperative. He was well versed in politics and had always predicted that a war with Germany would break out, and that [we] would have to get away. Our town wasn't far from the border, and Father [tried to] convince Mother to leave Poland. A week before the outbreak of war, Mother, along with us small children, left [to go] stay with [our] grandfather, Szmul Wagszal, who lived in Rozwadów, a town located by a railway connection hub.

But things were even worse at Grandpa's after the outbreak of war, because there were huge arms factories close to Rozwadów, and people were afraid of German bombardment. We suspected that in aiming at Stalowa Wola, the Germans might well hit our town, too. It turned out that [the] Germans didn't bomb the factories, only [bombed] the station a few times. The Poles said the Germans didn't know where the factory was. Then the Germans came. They immediately gave an order for all workers to report for work; the factories were operating within a few days, and Grandfather said that the Germans had been saving the arms factories because they wanted to use them [themselves]. Not a single Jew lived in Stalowa Wola, and Jews weren't allowed to work in that factory. I heard from Grandpa that the Poles had prohibited Jews from living in Stalowa Wola. The Germans organized manhunts in the streets and rounded up Jews for the hardest work. [The Jews] were beaten and tortured during the work. My Grandpa was the president of the local borough in Rozwadów. Despite this, and despite the fact that he was sixty-six years old, he was picked up for forced labor [and] ordered to dance and sing. One day, on a Saturday, Grandpa was called in to the magistrate. He was taken in front of the highest-ranking officer of the Gestapo, who told [him] that the Jews had to leave town immediately and cross over to the Russian [territory] on the other side of the river. When Grandpa returned home, panic broke out. Women were shouting that they wouldn't run away because [their] small children wouldn't survive the freezing temperatures. To this, Grandpa responded that there was no choice; let the women go to the Gestapo with a delegation themselves. Their crying counted for nothing, because the Gestapo officer said that the order was irrevocable—but he moved the expulsion to Sunday morning. At seven in the morning, everyone gathered in the main square. Apartments and shops were left without supervision. Christian neighbors took everything that the Jews had left behind, because one could [only] bring as much as one could carry. This was limited to clothes. The Germans were beating everyone in the square. Older Jews and the sick, dragged out of their beds, could barely stand up. Prodded with bayonets, the Jews set off [to the sound of] German shouting: "Off you march to your Red brothers." Mothers abandoned [their] boxes so they could carry [their] little children in their arms.

We left town this way. The Germans were beating us and rushing us ahead. Our neighbor had a cart, with a skinny horse harnessed to it. Small children and sick people were loaded onto that cart. Since the horse wasn't able to pull the weight, the Jews pushed the cart. I went on foot, holding the hand of my four-year-old little sister, Sarele. During the expulsion, our father was with us, as well as two more [of the] children. Father had come there from Nowy Sącz, where things were even worse. He had thought he would stay in Rozwadów, but found the expulsion [happening] there. On the riverbank, the Germans searched everyone. Anyone who had a watch had to give it away. There was a boat waiting by the bank that took the Jews over to the other [side]. Suddenly the boat tipped over, and Grandpa fell into the water along with [some] other Jews. He was pulled out barely alive. He was revived, and ill, taken to the other side of the border. We got to the village of Wisznica, which was held by the Russians. Father asked that we stay in the village because rumors were going around that Rozwadów, too, would belong to the Russians, and that we [would be able to] go back home. We were at risk of arrest [in German-held territory]. Because of this, with his last bit of money [my] father went together with our neighbor Elbogen and bought a cart and horse. We all got on the cart and went to the town of Biłgoraj, and then to Zylków,[429] located thirty kilometers from Lwów.

We fared very well in Zylków. Father found a job as a bookkeeper, and Mama worked, too, but one night, there was a knock on our door. NKVD-ers appeared and told us there was a car waiting and that they were sending

429. Likely refers to Żółkiew.

us home. The car took us to the nearest train station. We were loaded into freight cars, and after twenty days' journey, found ourselves in Siberia. Our train stopped in Krasnoyarsk Krai. Our barracks were on a hill, and it was freezing cold and dismal in winter. Mama fell ill and died. She was so young. She was [only] thirty-one years old. There were four of us left, orphans. Father was deathly exhausted. We were given little to eat. Father worked as a logger and earned twenty rubles per month. We would have died from hunger if we hadn't sold [our] dead mother's belongings. We didn't go to school because it was four kilometers away and we had no shoes. We sat in the barracks and warmed one another. From Siberia, we were sent to Samarkand. Father got off in Dzydzak,[430] 120 kilometers from Samarkand. There was an awful famine there. We had nothing left to sell. We all fell ill with typhus. We were taken to a hospital. Father was the only [one] who wasn't ill. When I recovered, I found out that Father and [my] youngest little brother were in the next hospital, ill with dysentery. [My] little brother died. From the hospital we were taken to the orphanage of the Polish delegation. There were three of us there. There was no order in the orphanage; everyone was dirty and hungry. For the hundred Polish children there were twelve Jewish ones. Everyone wanted to get away from there. Then a transport was organized to India and everyone wanted to go. Thirty-five children were picked, including three Jewish ones. Later all the children were taken to Tehran. My brother got malaria and was left behind in Russia. [My] little sister Sara and I arrived in Palestine. We get letters from Father, who complains about hunger. I've sent him a parcel.

---

430. Most likely refers to Jizzakh, northeast of Samarkand.

Protocol 167

Testimony of **Icchak Rosenberg**, age twenty-five, son of Lejb and Sara from Warsaw. Arrived in Palestine in August 1942.

Following the radio call of Colonel Umiastowski,[431] I left Warsaw on the night of 6 September with my brother-in-law, Jakub Appel, and went toward Grochów. Outside Grochów, German airplanes had prepared a "warm welcome" for us. We took cover in a ditch and saw bullets flying over our heads. When we left [our] hiding place, we saw lots of dead and injured people lying on the road, but we didn't so much as look back at them, but [instead], hurried toward the road [to] Lublin. Such air raids were repeated all the time, so we decided to hide in villages with the peasants during the day and march on at night. Traveling this way, we got to Mińsk Mazowiecki. The city was full of refugees. There were many freight cars in the station, and dead and injured people were being carried out of them. The town looked like hell. I decided not to stay there but to carry on ahead. After spending the night, we went toward Siedlce. We found the city in flames. We left it behind and went on. We walked behind an army lager going toward Brześć. All of a sudden, shooting broke out. People collapsed right next to me. I found my wits, ran from the road into a field, and waited to see what would happen. I was certain that we were surrounded by the Germans, because every now and again the darkness was broken by searchlights. When things got quiet, we set off toward the Bug [River]. I arrived in Łuków on 13 September. I was extremely exhausted and wanted to rest, but seeing everyone running away, I followed them. On 15 September I found myself in Włodawa. The city was almost empty; everyone had fled. I went to the outskirts of Włodawa, [took lodging in the house of a Jew], and collapsed on the bed from exhaustion. I woke up in the evening and set off on my way.

By 17 [September] I was in Kowel. I heard that the Russians had crossed the border and occupied the Eastern parts of Poland. Apparently the Polish army was fighting the Bolsheviks. The Ukrainians became emboldened as a result of

431. [A message urging all the able-bodied men in Warsaw to go to the front, to defend against the German invasion.]

these events. The Red Army entered Kowel the next day. Huge tanks, cars, and cannons arrived. There were many [soldiers from] the Polish army in the city, whom the Russians had allowed to return—without weapons. I spent ten days in Kowel. The city shops were emptied of all their goods in the first [few] days. Soup kitchens were opened, and thousands of refugees waited in line for soup. I met a number of rich people from Warsaw and Łódź in [one] such line, doctors and professors. The city lived off trading with the soldiers, who bought literally everything they were offered. The Russian army was heading west, and since it was said that it would reach Warsaw, I decided to go to the capital on the first train. They were Polish cars requisitioned by the Russians. The trains were out in a field, damaged by bombardments. It took me three days to get to Zamość. The train wouldn't go farther. During the journey, I saw the awful devastation that the war had caused. I arrived in Zamość to a terrible panic. It was said that the Germans were coming. The next day, a notice was put up at the magistrate's office saying that the Russians were leaving town and that those who wanted could follow them. I went to Lwów.

In Lwów

Lwów suffered relatively little in the war, only the station was destroyed.[432] The city was full of refugees. Long lines formed in front of shops. I lodged with my representative,[433] and my brother-in-law decided to go to Brześć, to his relative's place. I didn't see him again because he set off for Warsaw from there. I also started trading. I had twenty zlotys on me and sold cigarettes on the street. Later I traded clothes, shoes, [and] watches. The trading was concentrated in the Miklasz passage. At first the Bolsheviks turned a blind eye to the traders, [but] then raids and confiscation of merchandise began. I changed to a different activity and transported vodka, wine, and watches to Brześć. Life was getting harder by the day.

At the end of January I received a letter from my friend in Tarnopol, who worked in a restaurant cooperative, asking me to come there because [they

432. Compared to Warsaw, Gdynia, or Wrocław, Lwów lost fewer buildings and structures during the initial part of the German invasion. The city was not captured in battle; Lwów surrendered when it became clear that the Germans had won. However, the station—which was one of the first buildings bombed—was not the only structure that was destroyed.

433. It is unclear who the author is referring to here.

had] a waiter vacancy. Without much thought I went to Tarnopol and took up the post. The wages were low, but the tips generous and the food free. After a few months, a Russian from Moscow took over the business and introduced a new order. We worked between twelve and fifteen hours per day, [and] he threatened us with prison for any kind of misdemeanor. During that time, I received letters from [my] parents in Warsaw—they were asking me to come stay with them. The registration to return home began. I went to Lwów, because the registration committee sat there. There were masses of people in front of the office, shouting: "We want to go home; we can't stand it here." I couldn't get into the office and gave up on the trip. I got a place to stay with some Christian man on the outskirts of town.

One night, raids began, and people were being sent to Siberia. There was a cellar in my host's apartment, where we decided to hide in the event of a search by the NKVD. Hearing a disturbance in the nearby homes one night, we hid in the cellar. Soon the Russians arrived in our apartment, and finding no refugees, went away. We spent five days in hiding. Our host['s wife] feared for her life. We left [our] hiding place. There were no refugees left in the city. I went to the student residence where my friends lived. I had [my] *matura*[434] [results] with me and tried to get into the university, which was impossible because I wasn't a Soviet citizen. I spent three days in the bathroom of the residence, but we could not continue to hide there. The Soviet passport market was flourishing. You could get a document for thirty thousand rubles, but I didn't have that kind of money. I decided to go toward Bessarabia and Bukovina, which the Russians aimed to occupy. I went to Kołomyja. After eight days, I got a Soviet passport there. With [that] passport, I went to Horodenka on the Romanian border.

Our group was made up of three people. We stayed at a Jewish hotel, and one of [my] companions went to the border to investigate the crossing options. The other one went to a hairdresser. The arrival of a stranger aroused the hairdresser's suspicion. He started a conversation in Jewish, and [my] companion told him the story of our arrival [in the city]. The hairdresser expressed willingness to help and pointed us to a peasant who would take us across the border. An hour later we were all sitting at the hairdresser's, negotiating with the

434. *Matura*: a Polish secondary school–leaving exam and certificate.

Ukrainian villager. We agreed on the price of three hundred rubles per person. We agreed that a droshky would wait for us outside the church. I was anxious. The whole thing seemed suspicious to me. The droshky driver seemed [like a setup] to me. Outside the city, we came across a policeman who greeted the driver and showed him the way with his hand. This relaxed me. A few hundred meters from the border, in the dark, we noticed two Soviet soldiers, seemingly waiting for us. The driver advised us to go on on foot. We obeyed him and walked straight toward the two people, who turned out to be NKVD-ers. It turned out that the driver was in cahoots with them.

We were taken to a police station. The investigating judge asked why I wanted to go to Palestine. He grilled me about [various] organization[s] and didn't want to believe that I didn't belong to any of them. The interrogation lasted three hours [and] was accompanied by beatings. I was forced to make a confession that I belonged to a secret organization. In the prison cell, I found fifteen beaten-up Ukrainians. It was horribly dirty in there. On the second day the interrogation began again, and we were beaten even worse than on the first day—with a whip and an iron [bar]—and our hands were tied. I was taken to a different cell. I found my companion there and it became clear that the hairdresser had denounced us. The hairdresser turned out to be a provocateur, [and had been one] for many years. We were sent to Stanisławów and had our belongings confiscated. We were kept separate in Stanisławów. That prison was a real hell. Seventy people were kept in a small room. After three weeks, I was called in for an interrogation. In the prison I met Dr. Anzelm Halperin, the president of the Stanisławów borough, who had returned to Poland from a Zionist convention on 3 September. The lawyer Baron was imprisoned with him. They were accused of establishing a committee for refugees without permission.

After four weeks' stay in prison, a thousand people were loaded into freight cars, everyone was given a loaf of bread and two herrings, and [the train] set off. We went to Kiev and [then to] Romny. There we were unloaded from the car and put in prison. After four months in prison, I was called for an interrogation again and was sentenced a few days later. I was sentenced to five years in a camp. We went to Homel. [From] there, after spending ten days in prison, we set off again, to Orsha, where the prison was located in an old convent. After eight days we were moved to a cell full of Polish criminals. The ringleader of the cell was a well-known thief, who actually treated me well. I was treated better thanks to his outbursts. I fell ill at that time and asked to be taken to the hospital, but my request was denied. Only after the intervention of the ringleader of our cell, who caused a scene, was I taken to the hospital. I fared all right there. Later, after I recovered, I was sent back to the same cell. There was no longer anyone I knew; the crowding was even worse, and even though it was winter, we walked around the cell naked.

Eventually we were sent to Siberia, to Kotlas. From Kotlas we went to Trzbi [?],[435] to an oil refinery. We lived in barracks in the camp and received seven hundred grams of bread per day. My work consisted of carrying barrels of oil, and since there were few trolleys, I would wander around for days without work. Ostensibly, this counted as me fulfilling my quota, and I got food from kettle number 1. I stayed in that *posiołek* until March 1941. Jealous friends tried to denounce me to the [camp] authorities. Eventually I was sent to another camp, Tasznia,[436] which was intended for Russians, many of whom had been there for fifteen years already. Our work consisted of sawing wood, and since the *bytoviki* weaseled their way out of work, I didn't work either. I received three hundred grams of bread per day and soup from the first kettle. I was so weak that I lay for days on top of the bunk, waiting for death to come and release me from [my] suffering. In the end, I was taken to a different labor camp, which was not guarded. It was a camp for invalids. Our work consisted of picking berries, and I stayed there until the outbreak of the [German-Soviet] war.

When I found out about the Amnesty in August 1941, I went to Buzyluk [Buzuluk] to sign up for the Polish army. I received seventy-five rubles in cash and [the trip took] twenty days instead of [the usual] two. I was admitted to the army in Buzyluk and sent to Tacko [Totskoye], where a Jewish battalion was to be formed. I didn't want to serve in a Jewish battalion [so] I escaped to Koltubanka, from where I snuck over to Persia, and from there to Palestine.

---

435. Could refer to Chibyu, now Ukhta.

436. Likely: the camp of Tesma [original Polish correction: Tieśma].

Protocol 170

Testimony of **Ludwik Ferster**, age sixteen, from Warsaw, 39 Koszykowa [Street], son of Józef and Pola. Came to Palestine via Russia and Tehran in February 1943.

I was the youngest at home. I have two brothers and a sister. They are all already married. My father was the owner of a huge estate with an area of eighteen thousand hectares, a sawmill, [and] a carpenter's workshop. The estate was outside Łuniniec. We were living in Warsaw when the war broke out. Between Wednesday and Thursday, that is, 6 and 7 September, when the order came out for all men to leave Warsaw, Father rented [part of text missing] and we set off on the way to go to our estate. We traveled through Mińsk Mazowiecki to Brześć. We were constantly bombarded on the way. Father doubted that we would get to our destination. After a few days of wandering around, we got to Brześć, [then] to Łuniniec by train [and], from there, to our estate on horseback. As soon as we arrived, the station in Łuniniec was bombed by German airplanes. There were two army trains and one medical train in the station. Seventeen people were killed, and a few tens injured. Then it got quiet and we rested on our estate.

The day before the Russians occupied Łuniniec, the local Poles informed us that they were planning to blow up the ammunition-carrying trains standing in the station so they wouldn't fall into Russian hands, and advised us to leave our estate. A panic broke out. The trains didn't know which way to go. [Some] officers who came to us, confused and demoralized, didn't know where to run, and neither did Father. It was decided that we would hide in a wood-tar factory nine kilometers from Sarny, which was closer to the town. We left our home and escaped to the factory without any belongings. We didn't stay long there. We set off for the town on a cart and stayed in a local hotel. Before we managed to get [any] rest, the first Russian tanks appeared. A few days later, my brother-in-law, Mieczysław Aronson, went to the estate to check on our things. He found there was nothing there. The safe was broken open and empty. Father tried to enlist the help of the local authorities and managed to secure a two-militiaman escort for [my] brother-in-law, to conduct searches among the local peasants, who were suspected of having committed the theft. Indeed, half of the items were found in the homes of Ukrainian villagers, but the other half—and, importantly, the money and the jewelry—they had carefully hidden.

After a few days, the Russians started introducing their laws. My brothers, Bernard and Samuel, aware of the fact that as former capitalists they would be denounced in the small town where everyone knew them, decided to go to Lwów. They thought they would make it to Romania from there. My brother-in-law returned to Warsaw with [my] sister. We later found out [that] [my] brother-in-law had stayed in Warsaw, and [my] sister in Łódź. I stayed in Sarny with [my] parents. My brothers were earning good money in Lwów. One was the manager of a restaurant; the other a waiter. They came [to visit] us and brought various products with them. At first Father looked after the estate, [but] then he had to flee to Sarny on foot because they threatened him with arrest. We spent the winter in Sarny, at 10 Kupiecka [Street]. The winter was hard. We had to buy wood from our former workers, who brought it in from our estate. In the meantime, our sisters-in-law traveled from Lwów to Warsaw and brought back some of the things that had been left there. We lived off [the proceeds of] selling these things. At the end of April, all former capitalists, social activists, and [members of] the intelligentsia were arrested in Sarny—including the administrator of our estate, a Pole—Kuczyński. He was deported with his family and we never heard anything more about him.

My father was afraid to stay in Sarny and left for Lwów a few days later. We lived in a room at [my] brother's place. Then we moved to 12 Piłsudski [Street]. The same day that we moved to the new apartment, NKVD-ers turned up and registered us. A registration of the residents was taking place at the time. Father rarely went out in the street and wasn't earning anything. [My] brothers, too, lost their jobs and took up trading. They told [us] that the main buyers were soldiers, who bought everything they could get their hands on and paid whatever prices were asked. After a few weeks, Father said that there was a German commission in town registering [people] to return to the German-occupied lands. He also told [us] that, even though the Germans were causing difficulties for Jews around the return, many thousands of Jews had registered. Father and [my] brothers registered to go back to Warsaw too and didn't want to report [to get] Soviet passports, thinking it would be easier to get across the border from Warsaw.

On Friday night, 29 June [1940], NKVD-ers came into [our] room, told [us] to pack [our] belongings, after carrying out a search, and told us to get ready to leave in half an hour. My things were at [my] brother's. Father begged that I be allowed to go and get them. They wouldn't agree to it. We were forced into a car and taken to the station. There were forty people sitting inside the freight car. While waiting in the station, inside the car, I saw my brother being led to a different [one]. We begged the guards to allow us to make contact with him. They laughed at us. We didn't know until the last moment what our brother's fate would be. After twenty-four hours, we set off. It was cramped and dirty inside the car. Lice crawled over us. We went to the toilet inside the car. During the whole journey, we were only allowed out twice, for fifteen minutes. We suffered from thirst. Only one Catholic was traveling in our car. The rest of the passengers were Jewish craftsmen. Among them were many who had escaped from Russia after voluntarily reporting for work [there]. They "entertained" us with stories about the horrendous [conditions] and hunger in Russia.

Passing through Shepetivka, Homel, [and] Kazan, we got to Sverdlovsk. The journey had taken two weeks. From there we set off for Berezniki on ships. We slept under the open sky. The mosquitos welcomed us "warmly." They bit us so badly that we didn't recognize one another in the morning. At dawn, another ship took us to Czerdina [?], and from there, [we went] to a *posiołek* in Jadosz [?] on trucks. We found our brother in the *posiołek* and were very happy [to see] him. We knew nothing about where [my] other brother had been exiled. The *posiołek* was in a deep forest, nine kilometers from the closest settlement of Ural peasants. Nearby there was a *posiołek* for exiled Ukrainians, and [also] close by, a labor camp for exiled Russians. We kept in contact with the village. Those in the labor camps had no communication with the outside world. The *posiołek* was made up of two-room huts. Each family got a room with a stove. At first, we weren't rushed off to work, and it wasn't mentioned.

Then, all men between eighteen and fifty-five were ordered to gather and were told that they were being sent to work in the city of Krasnovishersk for four weeks. They were [actually] deported for twelve months. Among those deported were my brother and sister-in-law. Their camp was located twelve kilometers from ours. They lived in big barracks, forty people to [one]. Women and men separately. They worked ten hours a day there. The Stakhanovites earned 150 rubles per day, others 50 kopecks. Those wages weren't even enough for bread, and if I hadn't brought [my] brother something out of our supplies twice a week, he would have starved to death. They didn't have warm clothes. Only after their hands and feet got frostbitten did they get padded trousers and lice-ridden padded jackets.

In our *posiołek*, one didn't have to work. We didn't get bread [rations] either. Everything was bought with one's own money. We lived off parcels we received from [my] sister in Warsaw. I was the courier between our *posiołek* and the neighboring villages. I would get two bucketfuls of potatoes for a shirt. For a pair of trousers, I would get twenty buckets of potatoes, which was a real fortune in those times. The Ural village was better off than the Ukrainian [one]. The Ural peasants had a few cows each in assets [and] ran dairy farms. Butter was very expensive, and throughout all of [our] exile, I only brought back a piece of butter for Mother once. The Ukrainian peasants were [former] kulaks, sentenced to five years [in the camp]. They had lived there for fifteen years already, overcome by total apathy. They laughed at us, we who believed [we would] leave Russia. Their children were being raised in the Soviet spirit. In our *posiołek*, I remember, there were: Landau from Kraków, Lichtblum, and Flajszer. And Poles: Cegielski and Hartman from Warsaw. Generally the Poles coexisted well with the Jews, and only some were teaching Ukrainians antisemitism.

My parents worried about my brother Samuel, not knowing where he was. One day we received a letter [saying] he was living in a *posiołek* in the Yakutsk district. My sister Regina was in Lwów at the time, and her husband, Mieczysław Aronson, in Warsaw. What happened to them we don't know. I studied in a Soviet school, which exempted me from work. Once some boy said: "In our home, in Russia." To this I said: "Not our home." The teacher took me for questioning, and I tried to get out of it any way I could. The next day the commandant summoned and interrogated me too. Another time, a Christian girl, thirteen years old, blackened the eyes of a portrait of Stalin with a pencil. There was a scandal. They threatened to send the children to a reformatory. The district commandant came, and God knows what would have happened if it weren't for the parents' pleading.

After twelve months, we were sent to a different *posiołek*, Tieplowska, three kilometers from the city.[437] The city of Krasnovishersk was ten years old and had ten thousand inhabitants. It was a hub of paper production. The workers' homes were small, one story high. Only the school and the hospital were in large brick buildings. The workers lived in poverty; [they] often didn't have enough clothes and food. A week later, the German-Soviet war broke out. The regime in the *posiołek* became stricter. Parcels stopped coming. I got a job sawing small pieces of wood for heating the tractors. I earned five rubles per day. It was impossible to get anything with that money. There was nothing to buy in the local shops.

After the announcement of the Amnesty, we set off for Samarkand at our own expense. We went by ship on the Volga to Astrakhan. In Astrakhan, we lived on the street for a week. The city was full of [people who had been] evacuated from Ukraine. We went to Krasnovodsk over the Caspian Sea, where there were no refugees yet [part of text missing]. Even though we could have settled in Krasnovodsk, we left for Samarkand out of fear of the Germans. [In Samarkand] we came upon masses of refugees already there, and after a week of wandering around, got a little stable as a place to stay. During our stay in the stable, my father sent a letter to President Roosevelt asking him for help for the refugees.[438] He was arrested that same night. The next day a judge came to carry out a search. Friends advised my brother to try to bribe the judge. [My] brother offered him a few hundred rubles. He was summoned to the NKVD the next day and accused of trying to bribe the judge. He didn't confess his sin. Left alone with the judge, he begged him for mercy. The judge advised him to confess and promised to release him. [My] brother did so. He was released and told to report [back] the following day. At that point, [he] ran away. Father was in prison in Samarkand. At that time, my brother from the Yakutsk Oblast arrived as well. He tried to have Father released. He got in touch with the same judge [my other] brother had tried to bribe. Neither the intervention of the Polish delegation nor that of Jan Kwapiński helped.[439] While Father was

437. Tiepłowka (Teplovka).

438. Franklin Delano Roosevelt (1882–1945): president of the United States of America in the years 1933–45.

439. Jan Kwapiński (1885–1964): PPS [Polska Partia Socjalistyczna; English: Polish Socialist Party; PSP] and union activist. See also note in Protocol 27.

in prison, Mother fell ill with typhus and died. Meanwhile, the judge and the prosecutor who had accused my brother of attempted bribery were arrested. We informed [my] brother [that he could] come back. Our situation was getting worse by the day. [My] older brother reported to the Polish army, but the younger one had to stay to [try to] save Father. However, as a Jew, my brother was not accepted into the army.

After long efforts, I got into a Polish orphanage, where out of two hundred children there were fifty Jewish ones. I was treated kindly. After two months' stay, I was sent to Krasnovodsk, and to Tehran via Pahlevi. In Tehran I got a telegram [saying] my father had been freed. Four months later, I left for Palestine with a group of Jewish children.

Protocol 171

Testimony of **Abraham Frenkel**, age sixteen, son of Rabbi Efraim from Mielec, Małopolska. Came to Palestine via Tehran in 1943.

There was an airplane factory and an ammunition factory in our town, employing a few thousand workers—not a single Jew among them. Those workers were horrible antisemites and spoiled the atmosphere in town. Our town was bombarded on the first day of the war; there were forty-two casualties. The bombardments were repeated for a few days, and then a concentrated attack on the ammunition factory took place. Seventy people were killed. The next day more than twenty people were shot dead for espionage and passing on information to the enemy—from the factory: the director and the foremen, among others. The factory management had been taken over by spies. On Saturday night, one of them had been found sitting in a tree giving signals to the airplanes. We decided to leave town. We hired a truck with a few other Jews and left Mielec on Tuesday, at twelve o'clock at night. The Germans bombed us on the way. The roads were crammed full of carts, cars, and pedestrians, and when the planes flew in, people would push each other to [go] hide in a ditch. This way we got to Radomna.[440] We had our truck taken away and had to stay for two days to buy a cart and a horse and carry on, and then we reached Niemirów. It was calm and empty in Niemirów. I will never forget what we went through during our escape. I saw thousands of corpses and injured [people], and no one was helping them. There were times we barely managed to get through the barricade[s] of smashed carts, carriages, dead people, and horses.

What Was Happening in Mielec

We learned of the fate of the Mielec Jews from people who had come to Niemirów from [there]. The Germans occupied the town on 12 September. On the first day [they] didn't bother anyone. On the local authority's orders, both shochets, Chaim and Jasza, went to the slaughterhouse to kill a few cattle for the Jewish people for the holidays. Jasza, the butcher, walked there accompanied by his son-in-law. During the slaughter, the Germans burst into the

440. Likely: Radymno.

slaughterhouse shouting: "Here are the Jewish murderers" [and] shot both shochets and the one's son-in-law dead. Then the Germans made their way to the mikvah, which was full of people since it was the eve of the holiday. They chased everyone, naked, out and into the slaughterhouse and shot them dead there. Sixty-four Jews perished this way. A two-year-old boy and a fifteen-year-old [one] managed to survive, and [the latter] was the one who told us those stories. A few days later, the Germans gathered all the Jews in town, lined them up outside the rabbi's home and stripped them naked. They wanted to shoot them. A German general happened to be driving by, asked what was going on, and after a short conversation with the officers, gave the order for everyone to be released. Most Jews ran away from town without even going back home. The next day the Germans burned down the synagogue, the beth hamidrash, and the rabbi's home. Living in the rabbi's home at the time were the rabbi, Menachem Mendel Hurwicz, and a twelve-year-old boy, an orphan, who was being raised by [him]. The rabbi jumped out of the window and thus saved himself, but the child got caught on the fence [trying to] jump out. A German saw it and killed the boy on the spot.

In Niemirów, things were peaceful. We knew that the Germans were coming, but not knowing what to do with ourselves, we didn't run away. The health resort where we were staying was three kilometers from town. On 12 September the Germans occupied Niemirów. They didn't come to the health resort. The next day a crowd of Ukrainian peasants, men and women, arrived with sacks and carts and started stealing Jewish property. A delegation [from the Jewish council] went to Niemirów, to the Germans, asking the German commandant for protection. The commandant turned out to be an Austrian. He received the delegation well and sent [some] soldiers to pacify the thieves. The soldiers stayed in the resort; they were all Austrians, but they told us that the SS would be coming after them and things would get bad for us then. For now, the Jews prayed in the synagogue as always. Patrols chased away the Ukrainians trying to steal again.

On Sunday, 17 September, the real Germans arrived, and the situation changed immediately. Jews were expelled from all villas and put into one house. They started rounding up Jews for work, beating and persecuting them. It was no longer permitted to pray on Yom Kippur [23 September 1939]. A group of Jews, including my father, gathered in an attic and prayed quietly. We stood guard. The day went by calmly. It was said that the SS would arrive any day now. The next day an older German from Vienna, whom we had befriended, came to us and said he was bringing good news: the Bolsheviks were coming. The Germans left Niemirów. First the medical units left, then the military headquarters. No one paid attention to the Jews.

On 22 September the Russians took over the town. We left the health resort then and moved into town. The first days went by peacefully. The Russians bought up everything, and the Jews busied themselves with trading. But every day new orders would come out, and the traders started being persecuted. We left Niemirów after seven weeks and went to Lwów. Sixty thousand refugees reportedly lived there at that time. Our family was made up of thirteen people. [My] uncles and old grandma—everyone wanted to live together—and it was impossible to get an apartment. As a result, we went to a small town, Brzuchowice, located seven kilometers from Lwów.

In Lwów

In Brzuchowice there were a few thousand people living, unable to find a place in Lwów, who would travel to the city at dawn and trade there. Father and [my] sisters also went to Lwów every day and didn't do [too] badly. This lasted a few months. Then the arrests of former capitalists began, and it was said in the city that everyone would be sent to Siberia. Some rich people were thrown out on the street simply because they had a roof over their heads. Then they weren't given [any] work. My sister pointed out a waitress to me in the restaurant where we got soup every day, and said she was the daughter of Professor Schorr[441] from Warsaw and the wife of Maks Kon, son of a millionaire from Łódź, Oskar Kon. My father met an eminent rabbi, Halberstadt, who had a plane in his hand, as he was working in a carpenter's workshop. The rabbi from Bełżec, Aron Doka, had a work card too, but had been exempted from work due to poor health.

Many young people registered to go to work in Russia. They were sent off with a fanfare but would return after a few months, reporting awful things

441. Mojżesz Schorr (1874–1941): historian, orientalist, professor at Warsaw University, senator of the Republic of Poland, rabbi of the Great Synagogue of Tłomackie [Street]. He was arrested on 10 October 1939 and died 8 July 1941 in a camp in Uzbekistan.

about the living conditions in Russia. Then the registration began, and one had to decide between taking Soviet citizenship or returning to Poland. Most turned down the [offer of] citizenship as they were afraid of severing contact with the [rest of the] world, and also because a Soviet passport for refugees condemned [them] to staying in small town[s], where it was difficult to earn money. We decided to register to go back home.

At the beginning of May, arrests began [that] lasted until mid-July. I remember how NKVD-ers turned up at our home one Friday night, gave us two hours to pack our things, and took us to the station, where there was already a long train waiting, with freight cars, intended for the refugees. We set off and traveled for a long time without getting either a drink or bread. Only after some time did they start giving out bread and soup, but Father didn't allow us to eat the soup. We weren't allowed to get off at station[s] to buy anything. We crossed the river Volga and the Yenisei [River], and after twenty-three days' journey, found ourselves in Krasnoyarsk Krai. We got off and spent a whole day in a field. In the evening, [some] carts arrived [and] took our belongings, [while] we were told to walk to the village, thirty kilometers. It was the most difficult part of the journey: the carts would tip over; we were trudging through a thick forest [and] people lost each other; shoes were torn, feet were bleeding. There was no water throughout the journey.

After a day and a half's journey, we found ourselves in the *posiołek*. It was called Wierch Bazajra [?] and was surrounded by a primeval forest where there were many wild animals. Wolves often came to visit us. Forty people lived in one barracks. The mosquitos, bedbugs, and mice wouldn't let us sleep. We worked in the forest, cutting down trees. For being late for work, you would be docked 25 percent of your wages for three months. After three times being late, you'd get three months in jail. With the exception of Father, who was exempt from work due to exhaustion, everyone in our family worked. No one, however, could fulfill their quota, and our earnings amounted to thirty kopecks per day. Workers got a kilo of bread per day—this was later lowered to six hundred grams. Nearby there were villages of exiled Russians and Ukrainians, who we sold our things to in exchange for potatoes. We [had extra food] thanks to the products sent to us from Lwów. On the first day of Rosh Hashanah [3 October 1940], no one went to work. NKVD-ers came, made a racket, and started to look for the organizers of this sabotage. They threatened such horrendous punishments that everyone worked the next day. They even worked on Yom Kippur [12 October 1940], fasting, and recited prayers during work.

We spent fourteen months in the *posiołek*, until the outbreak of the [German-Soviet] war. Then our life turned into hell. We were told to work for twelve hours and weren't given anything to eat. Many people fell ill, and no one had [any] faith that we would survive [to see] a better future—and then the Amnesty was announced. The warden started a propaganda campaign to encourage us to stay, but everyone wanted to leave. It took a month before we got [our] documents and during that time we worked and didn't receive [any] bread. A delegation went to the NKVD, [and] we were finally given the papers, as well as a tractor and a sledge, which took us to the station. We waited for a train for two days and then, finally, we got to Novosibirsk, and from there we set off for Tashkent. The journey took a few weeks. We were constantly hungry, had no bread, [and] lived off melons. Everyone was ill with dysentery and could barely stand up. In Tashkent, we lived outdoors, and one refugee would steal from another. Unable to settle in Tashkent, we went to Samarkand, where the situation was no better. We stayed out in the street all week before we got a barracks, for which we paid a buyer's fee[442] with a gold watch. At first there were enough food products, then hunger began, and a typhus epidemic broke out. Out of thirteen people in our household, eleven fell ill. Father died after a few days of illness, then Grandma. We lived off the sale of old things, jewelry, and gold that we had on us.

At that time orphanages were opened in Samarkand and I got into one of them with [my] sister and two cousins. Later they started sending children away. There were only ten children left, my sister among them. We were sent to Krasnovodsk from Samarkand, where we were dying of thirst and [where] I bought myself a bit of water with [my] last few rubles. The water situation wasn't better on board the ship. In Pahlevi, we spent [part of text missing] days under the open sky before we were taken to Tehran. After six months' stay in Tehran, I came to Palestine.

442. [A bribe.]

Protocol 172

Testimony of **Ruth Lofler**, age eighteen, from Bielsko, daughter of Salomon and Waleria. Came to Palestine via Tehran in February 1943.

My father was a clerk in the company Sztok. There were two of us children: me and [my] older sister, Gerda. We fared well. Both [my] sister and I went to a gymnasium. Ten days before the outbreak of the war, after mobilization orders had been put up on the city streets, all the people of Bielsko were evacuated.[443] Father didn't know where to go: to Warsaw or to Lwów. Since no large quantities of belongings were allowed on the evacuation train, we left everything and decided to go to Lwów, to be close to home and to retrieve a few things from the house at the first opportunity. After arriving in Lwów, we got an apartment on May Day Street and settled there. The situation in Lwów was very tense; people said that Poland wouldn't be able [to defeat] the Germans. Others, however, laughed at the pessimists and said there would be no war and it was just a scare. My father wandered around, confused, and didn't know what to do. [We had only a] small amount of savings. On top of that, we didn't have our belongings [with us]. Immediately after the outbreak of the war, Lwów was bombed. [People] thought that it was a test alarm at first. A few thousand people died due to [this] mistake, and it wasn't until the next alarms that people did take cover in the shelter. The fighting between the Polish and German armies lasted until 20 September. Lwów was surrounded by the German army on three sides; only the northern side was open. There were Slovak and Carpatho-Russian soldiers among the German [ones]. One day a German tank column burst into the city, and many of [the tanks] were destroyed by Polish soldiers, who threw gasoline-filled bottles at them. The Germans retreated.

The fighting lasted until the 20-something of September, until the moment when Russian tanks appeared on the east side.[444] Immediately after the tanks, Russian airplanes appeared over the city, dropping leaflets for soldiers [and]

443. The opening part of the testimony contains some inaccuracies.

444. The Red Army entered Lwów on 22 September 1939.

for workers calling [on them] to give assistance to the Russian army. There were also leaflets for Ukrainians and Jews, announcing that the Red Army was coming to save [them] from the persecutions of the Polish overlords. When the streets were white with leaflets, the army started to flow into the city from all sides. There was no fighting between the Russian and the Polish armies. Things were limited to [a few] specific incidents. The Bolsheviks, seeing how the people were behaving, ordered windows and gates to be shut [and] emptied the streets of civilians. All day long no one was allowed to go out into the streets, and normal traffic was only reintroduced the following day, when the army had completed its advance. During the first days of the Russian occupation, a people's militia kept the order on the streets of Lwów. It was abolished after a few days and replaced with a Red militia, picked by the Bolsheviks. In the first days, people were grabbed for [forced] labor in the streets, which consisted of filling in ditches and removing barricades from the streets. Only the better-dressed people were picked up, that is, the bourgeoisie. Nothing changed in the city during the first weeks, except that there was a curfew from sunrise until nighttime.

Only after the Russian administration arrived did the new order begin. Apart from Russians, there were Ukrainians and Jews, mostly youths, who were members of the administration. The Jews held lower positions, and the Russians and the Ukrainians, higher. Registration of the residents began, and before it was finished, registration of the refugees started, particularly of Polish officers. Political activists [and] industrialists started being arrested, among them Dr. Sommerstein.[445] Then came the nationalization of homes. Former [home]owners were kicked out on the streets and weren't given [any] work. Huge apartments were requisitioned, and at least three people had to live in each room. Lines formed outside bakeries and grocery stores, and one waited for hours to get bread. Father went to the country and brought foodstuffs from there. All refugees were traders. The buyers were Russian soldiers who would pay any price for the items offered. The streets were dark with buyers and it was difficult to get through them. Then the police started arresting the sellers.

445. Dr. Emil Sommerstein (1883–1957): lawyer, Zionist activist, MP of the Republic of Poland in the years 1922–27. See also note in Protocol 232.

Elections were organized with great pomp.[446] The streets were split into blocks. A commandant was in charge of each block [and] his task was to [ensure] that no one shirked the elections. Ballot boxes were delivered to the chronically ill. There were neither Jews nor Poles on the candidate list. People voted for a predetermined list that everyone was given.

My father, who had been a clerk in the Sztok company and knew a bit about manufacture, talked to his friend from Bielsko, and together they started a cooperative making marmalade and juices. The business was going well. [My] sister and I worked too, so that we didn't lack for anything. We didn't have to wait in line for bread, because other cooperatives that bought our marmalade sent us everything [we needed] in return. The situation got worse, however, because the raw materials ran out. The food trust that was supposed to supply fruit was selling it at much higher prices on the black market. Arrests of the trust's directors didn't help, [and] we had to close down the cooperative [as we had] nothing to work with. Things weren't any better with the lack of other products. All [producers] closed down.

In 1940, the passportization took place. Ostensibly, everyone was to get a passport, [but] it turned out that refugees got special [ones]. Men from eighteen to [part of text missing] years of age had to go in front of an army commission, but they were not called up for army [duty]. In February, mass arrests began. Officers' wives, social activists, Zionists, [and] Bund members were deported to Siberia. Twenty-five thousand people were arrested in the city. After closing down the cooperative, Father took up trading. [My] sister and I couldn't find work. Since Father was a clerk, we were considered bourgeois children and [no one] wanted to hire us. Because Father had no passport, on 29 July 1940, at night, we were arrested and sent to Siberia with everyone else. We thought we would die from hunger on the way. We were only given soup and bread after some time. After two weeks' journey in horrendous conditions, during which two people died in our carriage, we arrived in the Sverdlovsk Oblast. We were taken in cars to a *posiołek* located deep in the forest and put up in barracks. Father and [my] sister worked in the forest. Father worked as a *gruzowik*,[447] and [my] sister and I earned so [little] cutting down branches

---

446. Elections to the Western Ukrainian National Assembly. See glossary: elections.

447. *Gruzchik* (Russian): loader.

that we had to buy soup with our own money. Naturally, we could never afford this soup. Many people in the *posiołek* fell ill, and many more died. When the [German-Soviet] war broke out, our situation got worse because the working hours were increased, and there were days when we got no bread at all.

It's difficult to describe our joy when we learned about the Amnesty. How the Russian exiles envied us. We went to Samarkand, where it was difficult to find an apartment. There was an awful epidemic there. My father worked in a brickyard but earned very little. [When] a Polish children's center opened up, Father [managed] to have me admitted there. I spent two months in the center and was then sent to Pahlevi via Krasnovodsk, and later to Tehran. I came to Palestine from Tehran with a group of Polish children.

Protocol 173

Testimony of **Wilhelm Lichtblau**, age fifty-nine, resident of Tarnów.

I lived in Tarnów for seven weeks alongside the German [occupiers]. As the owner of a cinema where anti-German films were shown, I risked the death penalty. The union of cinema owners, located in Kraków, informed me that a few cinema owners had already been shot under these circumstances in Gdynia and Poznań. I was advised to hide and told that they would let me know when there was an opportunity to escape. During my stay in the city, the attitude of the Germans toward the people was not particularly cruel. Although they did carry out searches, during which people were often humiliated, generally speaking no horrific events were taking place. We explained this by the fact that Tarnów was occupied by the Austrian military,[448] and its leader was an Austrian commandant. During a search at my apartment, the search leader stressed a few times that he wasn't a German but [rather] an Austrian.

The day before my departure, power shifted into the hands of the Gestapo, and that same night, a synagogue was burned down, leaving the large synagogue, which was later blown up with dynamite. After seven weeks I managed to get onto a special train going in the direction of Sanok. On that train there were Jews who were being evacuated to Russia. At the station in Sanok we were stopped by the Gestapo, gathered in a room, and told to stand facing the wall. We stood like this all night long. The next day there was a search, during which people were beaten terribly, had everything taken from them, and were then released. The Germans said that they hadn't come to an agreement with the Bolsheviks as regards our deportation. We roamed around Sanok, and the local people treated us extremely kindly. [They] made it possible for us to cross the border. A peasant woman, for a hefty price, herself guaranteed to get us across the border. When we arrived at the San River by night, where the guide was waiting for us, we instead found a member of the Gestapo. A whole unit was hiding there, and they launched themselves at us with knouts in hand, beating us horribly. It turned out it was a frame-up by the peasant woman. The

448. That is, by Wehrmacht divisions stationed in the city, made up of Austrians to a large extent.

Gestapo ordered that all our belongings be given to her as a reward, and we were rushed to the river by force.

It must have been by a miracle that I made it to the other side, where I came upon a Russian patrol. They carried out a search and took me to a prison in Lesko. There were already eighty people in the prison cell. When I was released, after eight days, I went to Lwów. There I lived off what I had managed to hide on my person and waited for further developments. As things were getting steadily worse for me and I didn't want to accept Soviet citizenship, I decided to go back to Tarnów. The Ukrainians were helping the Germans on one hand, and the Bolsheviks on the other. Without fail, however, they were against the Polish.

One night I was transported out of Lwów. We traveled for fourteen days, living off only bread and water. We stopped in a deep forest [and] stayed in tents, where mosquitos bit us so badly that our arms and legs were swollen. The following day, we were ordered to go to work. We received a dry piece of bread for the work, and no one could fulfill their quota. It's difficult to describe the tragedy of the people in the camps. Many lived outdoors, and often when somebody couldn't fulfill their quota they weren't allowed in the barracks at night. Seventy percent of the people perished. We got our first spoonful of hot soup after three months in the labor camp. The people who lived in the vicinity of the camp had a decidedly negative attitude toward the Bolshevik government. They told us that [while] we had been suffering for months, they had been [suffering] for years.

After two years of horrific suffering came the salvation of the Amnesty. I got to Samarkand. It was even worse there than in the *posiołek*. There was nowhere to live and nothing to eat. People were dropping like flies from starvation. The Polish delegation was only starting its activities and had neither the power nor the means to help us. When a load of matzo arrived for the Jews one day, it was all sent to the army and we didn't see a single matzo from the American donation. In Samarkand I learned that I had a certificate obtained by my children, who had a lot of influence in London. The delegation's intervention didn't help much because the NKVD didn't want to approve the list of civilian refugees.

I left for Jang-Iul,[449] where the Polish army was. In Jang-Iul, I reported to General Szyszko-Bohusz, who treated me extremely kindly and promised to

449. An incorrect name of the town of Yangiyul [original Polish correction: Jangi-Jul].

help me. On his orders I went to Ashgabat, where Polish divisions had gathered that were supposed to cross the Russian-Persian border. The general came a few days later and gave his personal order for me to be taken with them. Not everyone was this lucky. Thousands of my acquaintances left [their] *posiołki* to join the army and weren't accepted. It wasn't possible to go back to the *posiołek*. I personally had nothing to complain about and was treated very well during the journey to Tehran. I want to point out that as I was leaving Samarkand the local people were organizing committees to greet the advancing German army. The NKVD suppressed these committees and hundreds of Russians disappeared without a trace that night. In Samarkand, I was present at the opening of a new Jewish cemetery, and when I was leaving a few months later, there was no more space in that cemetery.

Protocol 174

Testimony of **Józef Tajchtala**, age forty-three, resident of Kraków, [currently] resident in Tel Aviv.

The outbreak of war caught me in Lublin, where I had gone on business. I wanted to get back to Kraków, but it was impossible. There were lots of people and carts on the roads, and I only made it via roundabout roads to Bochnia, where I fought for a space on a train going toward Tarnów. The train was bombed on the way. I barely survived, and the remaining [part of the] journey took place on foot. I was in Tarnów for a short period of time—by 5 [September] I had already headed east. I faced the dangers of air raids throughout the journey. The German airplanes came down low and fired machine guns right above the heads of the refugees. On the way, the cart I was traveling on was hit by a bomb. The horse fell down dead, and I barely managed to avoid disaster. From Przeworsk, where I saw the mansion of Count Henzlich burned down,[450] I went to Sokal, and from there, to Równe. Throughout the whole journey, I encountered incredible kindness from the local people, contrasting with the Ukrainian people's hostile attitude toward refugees. The Ukrainians were preparing for a ceremonious welcome of Hitler's army divisions.

After the entry of the Bolsheviks there was total confusion in Równe at first, and many Polish officers greeted the advancing army, thinking they were dealing with friendly forces. From Równe I went to Lwów. In Lwów, the requisitions of shops and apartments, the buying up of all products, the arrests and searches had already begun. It was complete chaos. Every day it became more and more difficult to obtain food products. I registered to go to Kraków, where my family lived. I didn't want to lose [my] Polish citizenship.

On 24 June [1940], deportations to Siberia began. The first victims were single people. At one o'clock at night, after a thorough search in my apartment, I was transported to a camp. I was put in a cell where there were a few hundred people, and [where] even the sick received no mercy from the guards. The next day, a Russian officer told us that we had been arrested. Among us

450. Likely a mistake on the part of the author. The only mansion in Przeworsk is the residence of the Lubomirscy, which was not destroyed. The identity of Count Henzlich could not be established.

were the editor Szewczyk, from Łódź, a few priests, university professors, and officers. The Bolsheviks tried to get us to reveal who was an officer, promising they would release [them]. We acted in solidarity and didn't give anyone up. I want to point out that those same officers later paid us back in a rather ugly way. We sat, or rather stood, like this for three weeks. We were let outside for five minutes every now and again. Body searches would take place every few days. Our documents were burned. We were called up for interrogation[s], where we went through real torture. One of the judges asked me if I would sell him my watch. It was an unambiguous question.

After a month we were transported to the station and loaded into freight cars. It was horribly hot; people were simply dying from thirst, but they wouldn't give us even a drop of water. Even the window latches were closed. You can't imagine how we suffered. Only after a week's journey were two water buckets put inside, which were supposed to be enough for all the passengers. People were ill and lay there with no assistance. [A] dysentery [epidemic] broke out. We only got [our] first spoonful of warm soup after eight days. I couldn't drink anything.

After eleven days' journey, the train stopped in the middle of a forest. The station was called Suchowodna, Garkawska Oblast.[451] When the car doors were opened, we threw ourselves into the ditches on both sides of the tracks, and even though we were being beaten with bayonets, lapped up the water greedily. We were dying of thirst and weren't thinking about what was to come. We slept under the open sky; mosquitos bit us so badly that we were completely swollen up. I have to point out that, during our journey, the Russian guards treated us kindly and would throw what they could into the cars. We often saw women crying at the sight of us, and that gave us faith. At sunrise we were split into groups and the brigade leaders were chosen. People were sent to get bread. They left at six in the morning and returned at sunset. Our work consisted of digging ditches alongside the railway [tracks]. The work site was located six kilometers from the barracks. We had to work from six in the morning until eight in the evening. We returned home at nine, and supper went on until twelve. At four, we were woken up for work. Anyone who didn't

451. Correctly: Sukhobezvodnoe, Gorkovskaya Oblast [original Polish correction: Suchobiezwodnoje].

get up was beaten. And it went on like this, day after day. People died en masse. Even the sick were forced to work. Our legs were swollen, and our complaints were in vain. Death was the best salvation. The rainy season began, worse than the frosts. By the time we got to the work site, we would be covered in mud. Fifty people a week died in our camp. If someone couldn't go to work, they had their shoes taken away. The doctors were powerless: people were exempted from work [only] with a temperature of 39°C [102.2°F], and the number of exempt people could not exceed one hundred. Otherwise the doctor would be sent away and not return. Night alarms were a common occurrence. We'd barely get to undress after returning home, [when we would be made to] run to the assembly point, in rain and in frost.

When the camp authorities realized that we wouldn't manage to fulfill our quotas despite the terror, a specialist was sent to us, a certain Kowalski from Warsaw. That one [commissar] treated us inhumanely, beat us and called us Polish pigs. It was worse than death. One night, when we were loading wood into wagons, our tormentor showed up among us and started to beat us, ordering us to work at double time. I collapsed, unconscious. We were all taken to the hospital after returning from work. As I had a fever of only 37.8°C [100.04°F], I was sent to work. I returned the next day with a fever of 41 degrees [105.8°F]. I stayed in the hospital. It was a well-heated barracks, where thousands of people were dying. At that point the doctors complained to the higher authorities, and the specially dispatched commissar let up a little. As a convalescent, I was sent to a different camp. I had to go there on foot, in freezing temperatures. In that camp there were Ukrainians who had been exiled eight years prior. People worked very little or not at all. But they were starved horribly there. As nonworkers, we invalids didn't receive normal food [rations]. Anyone who couldn't survive on five hundred grams of bread died. We kept ourselves alive with foul-smelling leftovers thrown out from the kitchen. Eventually, the sick and the invalids were made to work again. We were taught how to make slippers. Since the very first day, the Ukrainians had wanted to kill me, and I avoided death only by a miracle. I learned the trade. I received food then, even from the first kettle—that is soup with rice and with bread.

Generally there was peaceful coexistence among the residents in [the] labor camps. In the camp with me was Professor Grabski, to whom the Jews showed a lot of kindness.[452] Dr. Sachs did what he could to improve the professor's situation. Finally, the moment of the Amnesty came. We thought we would have [our] freedom immediately. The Russians, however, explained that we had to increase our war efforts as allies. The [amount of] inhuman work was increased; the food rations decreased.

After a long journey, I set off for Buzyluk [Buzuluk], where they'd started to assemble the Polish army. From there I was sent to Tashkent and Samarkand. The delegation couldn't help all the refugees. I moved to Turkestan, where I lived through a lot of difficult times. A military commission deemed me fit for service, assigned me to a unit, and sent [me] off to [see] a colonel in Czerpak.[453] There, however, the army authorities wanted to get rid of me. My situation was untenable [and] I only managed to get to Pahlevi after an intervention by General Rakowski. I'd prefer to forget about the behavior of my travel companions. In Pahlevi we were at the disposal of the English authorities. We came to Tehran as a special Jewish group, where we went in front of an army commission for the second time, which discharged us. I received a certificate and came to Palestine.

452. Stanisław Grabski (1871–1949): economist and politician, twice a minister in the [19]20s. He was arrested by the NKVD in Lwów and deported to Siberia. Released as a result of the 1941 Amnesty, he went to London [and] became the chairman of the National Council. He returned to Poland in June 1945 and became a vice-chairman of the State National Council.

453. Likely refers to Chok-Pak.

Protocol 175

Testimony of **Estera Barasz**, age sixteen, from Liski by Lwów. Came to Palestine via Tehran.

Liski was occupied in the first days after the outbreak of war. The town lived through a lot, because the fighting between the Germans and the Russians was taking place in our area. Both armies met there and shot at each other. Then the town fell into Bolshevik hands and a Russian notice appeared [saying] the mutual shooting [by both] armies had happened by mistake. The Russians created a militia [force]. Things were quiet at first. Hasids from Bełz sent my father [there] to bring the great rabbi to Liski. Father, risking his life, brought the rabbi in and put him up in our home. Ten days later, we found out that the Bolsheviks were leaving and the Germans returning. Father went to the rabbi to ask for advice. The rabbi ordered all the Jews to leave town, and he himself went to the town of Sokal by night with [his] whole family. They took only the Torah with them. Mother and I stayed at home in order to hire a cart after the holidays and take [our] belongings and the manufacture we had in our shop out of town.

After entering the town, the Germans accused the Jews of shooting at them and pouring hot water over the soldiers. A contribution of one million zlotys was levied on the town, and the Germans arrested [and held] twenty-four Jewish hostages until the contribution was paid. During that time, Jews were rounded up for forced labor, even though the local authority had taken it upon itself to provide workers. I saw the Germans rip out Jews' beards. The local authority put together one million zlotys [only] with difficulty, and among those who gave money there were a few older Poles. The money was paid, but the Germans didn't release the hostages. Many shops with merchandise, as well as goods from factories, were confiscated. The Germans said that they would keep the hostages until the Jews handed over all of the merchandise they were hiding. Shops were robbed every day. We had all our merchandise taken and decided to go with Mama from Liski to Sokal, where the Bolsheviks were and where my father was.

Our departure was moved forward due to the fact that the Germans attacked a number of Jewish apartments one night and raped many women and young girls. Getting across the border was very difficult. The Germans stripped us naked and ripped [our] clothes, looking for diamonds. They kept us in the station for twenty-four hours, hungry, and then gave us castor oil to get the diamonds out of us. Eventually they let us go free. Before that we were terribly beaten. Half-conscious and battered, we crossed the border. The Russians searched us for weapons. They too tore open [our] barely-stitched-together clothes and took everything we had on us. Half-naked, we arrived in Sokal. The rabbi from Bełz helped us.

On 29 June 1940, NKVD-ers came in and told us to get dressed, saying we were going back to the German side. We traveled for six weeks, dirty and lice ridden, hungry and ragged, until we arrived in the Novosibirsk Oblast, in a *posiołek* in a forest, where there was not a single house. We slept under the open sky, and later constructed a barracks and bunks to sleep on for ourselves. A few weeks later, we got lodging with a Russian man and his three children. A tragedy happened in the *posiołek*. A lightning strike killed a woman from Zamość. Typhus and dysentery were common visitors to the *posiołek*. Hardly anyone made it to the hospital. No one believed they would get out of this prison alive. Realizing that we wouldn't last long, we decided to get away. We set off down the river during a heavy frost, in small boats we had built with our own hands. In the end, a group of NKVD-ers stopped us and chased us off to a different *posiołek*, located in a desert, where we were often visited by white bears. Once a bear grabbed a Jewish child from Ostrów Mazowiecka from a barracks. We begged to have [our] work assignment changed and were sent to Ural for haying. There we swelled up from hunger and mosquito bites. We earned twenty kopecks a day, but not even that laughable sum was paid out to us. We were then sent to the Sverdlovsk Oblast, to the Saszla [?] *posiołek*. We weren't excused from work even in a –60°C [–76°F] frost.

Seeing that we wouldn't last long, we decided to run away again. This time [we] succeeded. We went to Uzbekistan. After five weeks' journey, we arrived in Kogon [and] from there went to Bukhara, where we rented an apartment. We slept on the bare floor. We suffered like this for eight months, until the order to release all Polish citizens arrived,[454] and we were told to go to Dżambauł.[455] We set off for Samarkand, got to Katapurgan[456] by train, and

454. The author is referring to the Amnesty, which took the form of an agreement that the camp administration was informed of—but not necessarily ordered to act on.

455. Refers to Dzhambul [original Polish correction: Dżambuł].

456. Refers to Kattakurgan [original Polish correction: Katta-Kurgan].

traveled the rest of the way by cart, by water, on a donkey, and on foot. The Russians persecuted the Polish refugees. We were advised to go to a kolkhoz, where things would be good for us, and where we wouldn't have to work a lot. Because we didn't want to hear about it, we were sent to Bukhara. The Uzbeks didn't want to let us [back] into our home. We slept outdoors for eight days, and [my] parents caught a chill. Even though I knew that Father was dangerously ill, I couldn't [convince] the hospital manager to admit him, [despite] my pleading. I managed to place [my] parents at an Uzbek man's [place] but had nothing to feed them. They had a high temperature for three weeks. I ran to the doctor every day, until he finally took pity on me and said that [my] parents had the flu. I knew it was typhus. I hired a droshky and dragged Father and Mother out myself—no one helped me because they were [all too] busy with themselves. I went to the hospital with them. I left them in front of the hospital because they didn't want to admit them. I simply abandoned them [there] because I thought they would surely not leave them in the corridor. They were taken into the hospital during the night. I went home. I felt unwell [and] figured I had typhus. I lay for two days without a drop of water. I begged my neighbor to take me to the hospital. I stayed in the same hospital as [my] parents but we weren't aware of each other. I was unconscious. I learned later that [my] parents had already gone home. I returned home and found out that we'd been robbed of everything. The thief turned out to be the Uzbek [man]. I sold a pair of Father's shoes for 180 rubles. We lived [off this] for a few days, then Father got a job in the delegation in Bukhara, but soon fell ill with dysentery and died. Mother died of the same illness.

When I got back from Mother's funeral, the Uzbek didn't want to let me into the apartment. I slept on the street. I sold a few rags [and] rented a corner for myself, but when the young Uzbek I was renting from saw that I was alone, he tried to break in[to my room] at night. I managed to defend myself but knew that this would not last. I went to an orphanage. The Jewish children envied me for being a full orphan.[457] I was sent to Ashgabat, where there were twenty Jewish orphans in a group of three hundred Polish [ones]. We traveled through the mountains in huge trucks, to Tehran, from where I came to Palestine.

457. [A full orphan qualified for admission to an orphanage, where it was safe.]

Protocol 176

Testimony of **Jakob Płoński**, age sixteen, from Wilno, son of Tauba and Manes. Came to Palestine via Russia and Tehran in February 1943.

Wilno suffered relatively little at the outbreak of the war. German airplanes dropped a few bombs in the first days of September but there was no serious damage. Most bombs fell in the district of Zarzecze, a few onto a forest, uprooting some trees. It resulted only in fright. Many refugees came to Wilno. It was said that the Lithuanians would take over Wilno after the fall of Poland. The relations between the Lithuanians and the Poles were very tense. As news about the bombardment of Polish cities reached us, the Lithuanians in Wilno grew emboldened and readied themselves to settle their business with the Poles. It didn't come to that, however. On 18 September Soviet tanks drove into Wilno, and it was said that the Bolsheviks would occupy Wilno, just as they had occupied the Eastern parts of Poland. We breathed easy in [those] first days. The German threat had gone away. The Bolshevik soldiers threw themselves on the shops, buying everything they could. The whole city turned into a huge market. Everyone traded, starting with rabbis and ending with high-ranking Polish officials, judges, and lawyers. People hung around the streets, holding old clothes, and bought bread with the money they got, [because bread] was starting to run out.

When the news had spread that Wilno would be given over to the Lithuanians, a mass emigration of refugees began, particularly Jews, who were headed for Russia, fearing Lithuanian antisemitism. On the other hand, masses of refugees were arriving in Wilno in the hope that it would be easier to cross the border from there. Wilno became a refugee hub. All the apartments were full. Bread ran out in the city. All the shops were ordered to open, and everything was to be sold. Lines of people formed in front of the shops and bought out the goods. News of the Bolsheviks' departure from Wilno turned out to be premature, and we didn't want to believe it when the Bolsheviks [were granted] army bases in the Baltic countries, thinking that now, not only Wilno but also Kaunas and Riga would belong to the Soviets. People were moving to Białystok, Brześć, and Lwów then, so that it would be easier [for them] to communicate with home. The exceptions were the yeshiva students [part of text missing] and HeHalutz members, who were afraid of the Bolsheviks because of political persecution.[458] On 27 October 1939, the Lithuanians occupied Wilno.[459] The first day of Lithuanian rule was the day of the Jewish pogrom. That day shops were plundered and Jews were beaten in the streets. Depraved Polish elements joined the Lithuanians. Tens of thousands of Jews were hurt. The Jewish population lived in fear for three days, afraid to go out into the street. But slowly things started to calm down. Lithuanian policemen introduced order. Shops were opened; food products appeared that had disappeared during the Bolshevik times. White rolls and cakes sat in the bakery windows, like [they had] before the war. But at the same time, the circulation of the Polish zloty and the Russian ruble were abolished. Lithuanian litas were the only currency in circulation. People with wallets full of zlotys and rubles ended up paupers. At that time, a few thousand Jewish and Polish refugees lived in Wilno. A refugee assistance committee and a special committee for helping Jews were formed. At first the money came in from Lithuanian Jews, who sent in wagons full of food and clothing. Hundreds of soup kitchens were opened; everyone had a roof over their head. This was the result of [the] Joint [Distribution Committee]'s activities. The situation of Jews during Lithuanian rule was not good. There was a lot of unemployment, merchants weren't trading, the social center moved to Kaunas. The Wilno Jews lived by subletting [their] apartments and providing food for the refugees.

In July 1941,[460] the Bolsheviks occupied the Baltic countries and three new [Soviet] republics were formed: Lithuanian, Latvian, and Estonian. It seemed that they might be autonomous, but the Sovietization of these states began shortly. Homes, shops, and factories were nationalized. Their owners were thrown out on the street and not given work. Religious and political life died out. Lines formed in front of the shops, and there wasn't enough food. During the elections to the Lithuanian Soviet, carried out with real brutality, people were forced to vote. The refugee committees were closed down, and the situation of the refugees became desperate. The only ones [managing to] survive

---

458. HeHalutz [Polish: He-Chaluc]: Zionist movement whose aim was the practical implementation of Jewish settlement, primarily agricultural, in Palestine. See also the glossary.

459. The Lithuanian army entered Wilno on 28 October 1939.

460. Error on the author's part: it was in June 1940.

were the yeshiva students, who were still received money from America, and the HeHalutz members, who formed work divisions.

In the early days of Soviet rule, foreign consulates were still operating in Kaunas and Wilno. The few lucky people [who] had received certificates for Palestine and visas to America tried to obtain departure and transit permits for Russia. Others beleaguered the foreign consulates. The Dutch consulate started issuing visas to Curaçao, which was a great help to the desperate people. Based on that visa, the Japanese consul issued transit documents. One received a visa on producing a Nansen passport,[461] which was issued by the Lithuanian government as a temporary ID. The Japanese consul issued a few hundred visas per day.[462] Three thousand Jews received travel documents this way. Weeks went by before the other formalities were sorted out. The fate of the refugees hung by a thread.

Finally an order arrived from Moscow [confirming] that the visa holders could leave Soviet Russia. Special bureaus were opened in Wilno and Kaunas. NKVD-ers brought everyone in for questioning. Now it was about finding 125 dollars at the exchange rate to pay the travel costs to Vladivostok. Many social activists from Poland, however, didn't receive departure visas—among them, the president of the local borough from Łódź, Mincberg, and senator Jakub Prokenheim from Warsaw.[463] A few Bund activists were arrested.[464] Later on, visas were checked very carefully. After the nationalization of shops, my father, owner of a haberdashery shop, was left with no livelihood. I studied in a yeshiva and didn't know the first thing about trading or any other work. We went hungry and lived off the things we sold. But there were plenty [of other people] like us, and no one wanted to buy [those] items. A relative of mine, an actor in the Jewish theater, found a job for Father as a ticket seller in the theater, thanks to which Father was deemed a useful element and was

---

461. A stateless person's passport.

462. Sempo Sugihara (1900–1986): consul general of Japan in Kaunas; issued transit visas to Jewish escapees so that they could get out of the danger zone. He did this of his own accord due to [his] humanitarian [beliefs], contrary to the instructions of the Japanese authorities. He was removed from diplomatic duty as a punishment for [these actions].

463. Refers to Jakub Jankiel Trockenheim, senator in 1935–38, MP in 1938–39, member of the Agudas Yisroel Party. Likely perished in the USSR.

464. [The original Polish group noun is *buntowszczycy*, an unusual form that nonetheless suggests Bund. This is suggested by the original Polish footnote.]

evacuated with the family after the outbreak of the Russian-German war, on a train intended for officials. My father had managed to go to Grodno before that [and] bring Grandma and [my] aunt from there, and we went to Russia with them. We were welcomed very kindly and fed generously at the Russian stations. We couldn't stop, however, because the Germans bombed the train and there were many accidents. Everyone wanted to run as far away from the front as possible, to somewhere the Germans couldn't reach.

We traveled south through Mińsk, Homel, Smolensk, Moscow, Kazan, and Gorky, as ordered by the authorities. We traveled for four weeks and things were getting worse. We received neither bread nor soup. The train would stand for hours in fields, where we would eat melons and [then] fall ill with dysentery. Some people didn't manage to make it back to the train in time. There were masses of refugees in Samarkand. We were sent to kolkhozes, and the young men were taken for the army. We were sent to the kolkhoz Mołotow. We lived in a kibitka, worked picking cotton, and received four hundred grams of bread per day. Later the bread rations were decreased so much that we had to go back to Samarkand, where there was a typhus epidemic. We found shelter in a dirty teahouse. We all fell ill with typhus. First Mother and Grandma. They were only taken to the hospital after eight days. Grandma died, [and then] Father fell ill with typhus and died.

We were without livelihood [and] I couldn't manage to get into a Polish children's center. I did get into a Russian [one], which was later turned into an orphanage. I spent three months there, bullied by the Polish children. They wouldn't let me pray and called me names like "Jew." From time to time I ran away from the orphanage to [see my] Mother, to bring her bread I had not eaten. One day I found Mother in such bad condition that I didn't want to go back to the orphanage anymore. She wouldn't let me stay with her [and] went to Bukhara instead, where my aunt was. I returned to the orphanage and was evacuated to Persia from there. I came to Palestine with a group of Jewish children.

Protocol 178

Testimony of **Ida Kowen**, age seventeen, born in Jarosław. Arrived in Palestine via Russia and Tehran on 17 August 1943.

There were four of us children at home. Father was one of the most respected residents in Jarosław. He was a pious man, a Hasid, and the owner of a candy factory. As soon as the war broke out, the rabbi from Bełżec[465] issued an appeal for all the Jews to go fight against the Germans. This appeal was printed in Jarosław and was later discovered by the Germans. The discovery of that document was the reason behind the massacre carried out by the Germans in Jarosław and [behind] the expulsion of Jews from town. The local Gestapo chief treated Jews without cruelty at first. This doesn't mean there was no stealing of Jewish property, grabbing [people] for labor, and ripping out Jews' beards, but we were spared the [kind of] atrocities that were happening in other towns. Because of this, many Jews from Galicia came to Jarosław. A few Jews even made the acquaintance of the Gestapo agents and it seemed that the relations would work out somehow. The Jewish council had a lot of influence. It sent Jews out to work. Through its mediation, Jewish goods that were needed for army use were appropriated. The Germans allowed Jews to pray.

After a month, a new Gestapo team was sent to us [and] after taking over, they organized a mass slaughter of Jews in Jarosław. As I mentioned, the reason behind this was the discovery of that ill-fated appeal, undated, [which] seemed suspicious to the Germans. They believed it had been printed at the time of the German [occupation] of Jarosław, and after the massacre, they forced the survivors out of town. The expulsion of the Jews took place at dawn, after the fateful night of the massacre. That night, my father and us four children were hiding at a Polish man's home, a friend of Father's, who was risking his life by hiding us, because the Germans threatened anyone who harbored Jews with the death penalty. Never in my life will I forget that night. We were hiding in a closed wardrobe. We huddled up to one another. Our teeth were chattering with fear. It seemed to us that the Germans were already in the apartment and

465. Refers not to Bełżec but Bełz, residence of the renowned rabbi, Aron from Bełz (1880–1957), fourth Rebbe of the dynasty. The rabbi managed to get to Palestine via Slovakia and Hungary.

that they would pull us out of the wardrobe. At sunrise, the Pole, Kowalczuk, [at whose house] we were hiding, told Father quietly that the pogrom had evidently ended, because all Jews had left town and were going toward the San [River]. Kowalczuk said he was prepared to continue to hide Father; however, since the Germans had issued an order for all Jews to leave Jarosław, it would be better if Father left town. We got out of the wardrobe and found ourselves on the street. We saw an awful scene in front of us. The Germans were rushing hundreds of Jews along. They weren't allowed to bring anything with them. Taking nothing from home, we went with everyone toward Sokal. On the way, the Germans searched the Jews a few times, lest anyone had hidden some of his riches on him. If they found anything, they shot the person being searched.

Finally, tired and exhausted, we reached Sokal. One can imagine what happened in Sokal when, all of a sudden, the entire Jewish population of Jarosław turned up. Father repeated that we had to continue on because the same thing that had happened in Jarosław could be repeated in Sokal. We hadn't [even] managed to rest when we were told that around a thousand Jews from Hrubieszów had arrived there at night. The Germans had arrested them for allegedly pouring hot water over [the German army] and had chased them from Hrubieszów to Sokal on foot. The border guard[s] by the San drew [their] machine guns at the Jews. At one moment, when the Hrubieszów Jews found themselves on the bank of the San near Sokal, [the guards] had opened fire on them with machine guns and killed them all. We were certain that no other fate [could] await us. The next day the Germans came to the council and ordered the bodies of those killed and washed up on the riverbank to be buried. A few hundred dead were buried in the cemetery in Sokal in a communal grave.

Meanwhile, our life was becoming harder and harder. We decided to cross the border. The rabbi from Bełżec, Aron Rokach [Rokeach], and his relatives smuggled themselves with us. German agents took us across the border, charging 1,200 zlotys per head. We made it safely to Lwów. Father immediately got a job in a candy factory in Tarnów. [My] brother also got a job there. We moved to Tarnów and fared very well. Father went [to see] the rabbi on Saturdays. The Bolsheviks left the rabbi in peace at first, and we thought this would last until the end of the war. However, the registration began a few months later, and people were being forced to take Russian citizenship. Father resisted. The rabbi from Bełżec didn't want to become a Soviet citizen either.

Ten days later, NKVD-ers turned up at our apartment, drove the whole family to the station and loaded [us] into freight cars. We traveled for six weeks in a terrible state, hungry and lice ridden, without changing our underwear, and arrived in the Sverdlovsk Oblast, Agaarymski district,[466] *posiołek* number 67, after six weeks. We were sent to a forest. There wasn't even a hut there. We spent a few nights under the open sky, sleeping in the snow. Saws were brought in [and] we were told to cut down trees and build barracks out of them. We suffered with hunger and cold. My youngest little brother fell ill with measles. There was neither a doctor nor medicine, and the little one died. We spent a year and a half in that forest, until the news arrived that an agreement had been made between Poland and Russia. We left for Tashkent, and went from there to Kazakhstan. We all fell ill with typhus. Mama passed away eleven days later. [My] oldest brother, who was nineteen years old, died too. I went to the Frunze district with [my] sick father and one remaining little brother. It was said that one could get more food there. Father fell ill with dysentery and died in a hospital eight days later. He was buried in a forest. Out of the whole family, I alone was left with [my] little brother. I went to Turkestan with him, where we were taken into an orphanage, and four months later, we were sent to Tehran, and from there to Palestine.

466. Likely refers to the Garinsky district.

Protocol 179

Testimony of **Mosze Weinberg**, age twenty-seven, student and HeHalutz member from Grodno. Came to Palestine via Russia and Tehran.

In the year 1937, that is, two years before the outbreak of war, I finished a *hakhsharah*[467] in Białystok and was ready to leave for Palestine, but I was called for the army that same year, and in March 1939, sent off to Mława with [my] regiment, where I served in the artillery. After the outbreak of the war, we were immediately sent to the front. On the first [of September 1939], we found ourselves in East Prussia, but we had to move back two days later. I didn't rest for a moment until we arrived in Warsaw. I was assigned to the division whose assignment was to defend Warsaw. The cannons wouldn't let us rest, day or night. I was at my post in the Jewish cemetery on Gęsia [Street]. Our positions were hidden between the trees. At the time of the cease-fire agreement after the siege of Warsaw, it was decided that our division would not be taken prisoner but set free [instead]. Despite this, it took a few weeks before we were released from the makeshift prisoner of war camp. Everyone was sent back to their birthplace, but since my hometown was occupied by the Bolsheviks, I had to go to Warsaw. I suffered [at the hands of] the Germans twice over. First of all, as a Jew, I suffered alongside [other] Jews. I was picked up for forced labor a few times. Once I was sent to Wawer, another time to Radzymin. The Germans tormented Jews terribly during [the forced] work and humiliated us, forcing us to sing and dance and to hit each other.

During my work between Radzymin and Wyszków, I developed friendly relations with a group of German soldiers who hated their superior. The *Oberst*[468] forced them to rob the Poles and Jews who wanted to get over to Małkinia. He would [then] take away all the stolen treasures from the soldiers and send them to his family in Germany. He himself beat Jews and Poles, raped young women, and was equally savage with his soldiers. His name was Hoffman and he treated his own soldiers brutally too. They had to watch as he conducted [his] dubious smuggling business and help him with it. They didn't

467. *Hakhsharah*: training [program] for future Jewish pioneers. See glossary.
468. *Oberst* (German): colonel.

hide their hatred [for him], even from the Jews. I'd been working for seventeen days there when, one evening, they told me they would gladly get rid of their commandant. That evening, a large group of Jews arrived from Warsaw, among them artists of the Jewish theater [Izaak] Turkow and Ida Kamińska. The *Oberst* robbed them blind, stripped them naked, and ordered [them] to kiss his hands. When the group of Jewish actors, still naked, set off toward Małkinia, I got into a conversation with the Germans. I saw them burning with hate, because the commandant had gotten all of the loot again. The Germans told me they would help me kill the savage *Oberst*, and that same night, they smuggled me over to the Soviet side. Having made a plan with the soldiers, I entered the commandant's room quietly; he was out cold after a daylong drinking binge. I lunged at him and grabbed him by the throat. The Germans standing guard ran up and confirmed that the *Oberst* was dead. They then gave me one of the stolen furs, 1.0 [part of text missing] zlotys [and] a bottle of cognac, took me to Małkinia, and got me over to the Soviet side.

When I arrived in Grodno, at my parents' place, I found them in a pitiful state. Even though [my] sister was working in a government job, she couldn't support them all. I quickly grew disillusioned with the joys of the Soviet regime. I heard that Zionist activists and HeHalutz members were gathering in Wilno and preparing to go to Palestine. Three times I tried to get from Lida to Wilno and three times I got caught. I had to return home and [continue to] struggle, working hard for a piece of bread. Every day was more difficult still for the refugees living in Grodno. I fared better as I was not a refugee. And when the refugees were sent from Poland to Siberia, I was left in peace, even though I had arrived in Grodno quite late. The day before the outbreak of the German-Russian war, a German airplane appeared over Grodno. The next day large numbers of troops marched through the city, and the evacuation of [state] offices began. Panic broke out; there was no bread. Thousands of homeless people from the area appeared in our city. All the young people were told to leave town. The police were terror-stricken and were the first ones to leave the city. Grodno was left with no protection, not even a citizens' militia. I was insanely afraid of falling into German hands.

Even though I felt sorry for [my] parents, I left the city, and my sister left the day before. We set off on foot toward Mińsk. We got to the Stołpce station. We crossed the former Russian-Polish border on foot and found ourselves in

Russia. The German airplanes were coming behind us. The Germans moved with unprecedented speed, so that the refugees who left Grodno with us didn't manage to escape in time, and on their way they were surprised by the Germans—only I and a few of my athletic companions [managed to get] ahead. We stopped in Kojdanów for one day.[469] We got [our] first piece of bread there after a few days' fasting, and *kipyatok*.[470] We slept on the street and set off again the following day. The kolkhozes, which were [in the process of] being evacuated, couldn't feed us, and we were constantly hungry. Before entering Mińsk, we found out that the city had been bombed and that it was terribly crowded there. We were advised to go toward Mogilev. There we were fed and we rested for a day. The city was full of refugees. It was terribly chaotic. We hired a cart and set off on our way. We traveled on the cart for two weeks. On the way, we were constantly bombarded.

Finally we got to Tambov, outside Saratov in Central Russia, and there I had to join the Soviet army. I served in the army until the Polish-Soviet agreement. Then all Polish citizens were released, from the military as well. We didn't know what we should do. A group of Zionists decided to go in the direction of the Caucasus, where [they would be] closer to Palestine. But we soon learned that it was impossible to leave Russia for Palestine of one's own accord. After a few unsuccessful attempts to cross over to Turkey, we went back to Tashkent. The journey took two weeks, in inhuman conditions. Unable to reach [our] destination, we turned toward Sverdlovsk, looking for [better] luck there. There were times when I wanted to commit suicide. We managed to make it to Tashkent eventually, and from there, planned to set off for the Afghanistan border. We set off for Buzyluk [Buzuluk] in −45°C [−49°F] weather, to where [the] Polish army was being assembled. They didn't want to accept us into the army as Jews, even though I had served in the Polish army during the war. [We] were sent from commission to commission until we arrived in Kermine. We were deemed sick and unfit for military duty [by] the commission.

Not being allowed in the Polish army was a real tragedy for us. We did not give up, however, on leaving for Palestine. One day, as we were saying goodbye to a companion who was leaving for Tehran with the Polish army, it occurred

469. Likely refers to Kėdainiai [original Polish correction: Kiejdany].

470. *Kipyatok* [Russian; *kipiatok* in the Polish original]: boiling water, normally available at rail stations. Kipyatok often saved the lives of people in transit.

to us that we should get onto [that] train illegally. As soon as the train started, we ran after the last carriage and smuggled ourselves out of Russia this way. Our surnames were not on the list of people traveling on the train, but knowing the Russian system, we thought [we would be] successful. The worst thing was that we had no food [ration] cards and nothing to eat. We were used to going hungry and so were not afraid of the journey. A Jewish woman, the wife of a Polish officer, took care of us. We confided in her about our misfortune[s] and she promised to [add] us to the list of people being evacuated from Russia. She also brought food to our car. In Krasnovodsk, we became illegals again, because the train list did not match the army list. By a miracle, we managed to sneak onto the ship and get to Pahlevi. Representatives of the Red Cross and the English government welcomed us warmly there. We were fed, clothed, [our] old clothing was burned, and we were sent to a Polish camp in Tehran. I fell ill with typhus in Tehran. I was sent to an Indian military hospital. After recovering, I received a certificate, and thus made it to Palestine.

Protocol 181

Testimony of **Józef Geller**, age thirteen, son of Mordechaj and Miriam from Oświęcim. Came to Palestine via Russia in February 1943.

My father was a baker. We had our own bakery and employed ten workers. We also had a huge granary with flour, and a shop with baked goods in the market. We didn't lack for anything and lived peacefully until the outbreak of the war. On Friday [1 September 1939] at nine in the morning, the town was bombed by the Germans. A bomb fell close to our home and killed three people. Panic broke out in town because our town was close to the border. Jews and Christians [were trying to] escape town. Officials and military people would stop cars, tell the civilians to get out, and escape in the cars themselves. My father thought about running away. A harnessed cart, ready to go, stood in front of [our] home. But since bread had to be baked for the army, Father couldn't afford to run away. The soldiers said that [defensive] positions were being prepared around the town, that we could relax, that they wouldn't give up the town. Father told Mother, Grandma, and me to leave town, but [we] didn't want to hear about it. Mama didn't want to be separated from him. On Saturday, the station went up in flames and many factories were on fire. Not until Saturday evening, when the army requisitioned our bakery and removed Father [as manager], did we get on the cart, take [my] uncle, [my] aunt, and the children, and set off on our way, eleven people altogether.

It was difficult to drive through the crowded road, which was constantly being bombed and shot at by German airplanes. We hid in ditches and it took a long time for us to find one another. We lost Grandma and didn't find her until a few hours later, injured in the forest. A doctor in a town tended to her wounds. Our horses were killed by the bombs, and we had to go on foot and carry Grandma on [our] backs until Father bought new ones. Grandma moaned in pain and asked us to leave her behind. After three weeks of such journeying, we arrived in a small town and found the Bolsheviks there. We breathed easy and wanted to rest for a bit, but the town was full of refugees and Polish soldiers, escapees from German camps. There was nowhere to sleep, even in the middle of the street[s]. We went on ahead and arrived in Jagielnica, where my uncle lived. Grandma fell ill on the way and stayed in a peasant's barn for two weeks. We didn't think she would pull through. But God helped her, and we carried on.

One day, NKVD-ers came to my uncle's apartment, told us to pack [our] belongings, and said that we were going back home. We were driven to the station, where we came upon many refugees. We were loaded into freight cars, the cars were sealed, and we waited like this until morning. It was very dirty inside the cars; there was only enough room for fifteen people, while [the number of passengers was] forty-five. We traveled like this for three weeks until we got to Tavda. There we got out of the car, were taken to a forest in cars, and Father and Mother got jobs in a sawmill. We lived in a huge barracks, a few tens of people in one building. Grandpa and Grandma were exempt from work because they were too old. Grandma ran the household and Grandpa helped. I went to school, and when I returned home, Grandpa would teach me the Talmud. Father worked as a *gruzownik*[471] and earned seventy rubles per month. Mother—thirty rubles. We couldn't support ourselves with this money and [had to] sell [our] belongings to get bread. Grandpa gathered the children from the barracks and taught them, told them about Jewish history. On Friday evening, prayer services were held with Grandpa.

The commandant hassled Grandpa and called him a religious propagandist. Despite the commandant's threats, Grandpa carried on with his work. Before the holiday of Rosh Hashanah [3–4 October 1940], the commandant summoned Grandpa and told him he would punish him severely if he organized prayers at his place. Indeed, there were no prayers at our place on Rosh Hashanah; however, on Yom Kippur [12 October 1940], no one went to work, and communal prayers were organized at Grandpa's place in the barracks. The commandant walked in during the prayer service and forbade [it]. No one moved. One of the people praying tried to explain to the commandant what the holiday meant. The commandant threatened arrest[s]. No one was afraid. People prayed, and went to work the following day. The commandant didn't charge anyone, afraid that the authorities would laugh at him [for] not being able to deal with the Jews. We spent a whole year in that *posiołek*, until the

471. Equivalent to *gruzchik* (Russian): loader.

outbreak of the [German-Soviet] war, when our bread rations were lowered and the food parcels from [my] uncle stopped coming. One worked for two hours longer [per day, and] children had to work too.

We were [already] certain we would die from hunger and exhaustion when we learned about the Amnesty. A few days later, an NKVD representative came to us and encouraged us to stay, promising us freedom, land, wood for a hut, and a cow for each family. But we didn't want to stay. We went to Bukhara. The journey took four weeks. The train would stand in a field for hours on end, and we suffered terribly from starvation until we reached our destination. In Bukhara we had no place to stay—we slept in the mud, resting our heads on our boxes. The Uzbeks stole from the refugees; there were people lying in the streets ill with fever, and sometimes corpses, which no one paid any attention to. The Bukharan Jews tried to help us but they were very poor themselves. After spending five days in a field, we finally got a stable but [still] had no income. We would wait in line for entire days, waiting for a piece of bread that we would sell at a higher price. In the end, we went to a kolkhoz where we spent three months living in a kibitka and receiving a bit of inedible flour for [our] hard work. My little cousin died from hunger in that kolkhoz, and seeing that our future looked bleak, we went to the city.

The whole family fell ill with typhus and everyone recovered. We got back from the hospital completely famished and ate wild herbs, after which we fell ill with dysentery. My grandma, Róża Szpajchler, age sixty, and my grandpa, Pesach Szpajchler, died at that time. On Saturday, my father passed away too, then Mother, then [my] uncle Mosze Weicenblum and his wife, who was only twenty-three. Of our family of eleven, there were four left. Two aunts, myself, and [my] three-year-old cousin. After many efforts, my cousin and I were taken into a Polish orphanage, from which, after three weeks' stay, we went to Persia and then to Palestine.

Protocol 182

Testimony of **Helena Wojtowska**, age twenty-five, primary school teacher in Płock. Came to Palestine via Russia and Tehran.

After the outbreak of the war, I went to Warsaw with a group of friends and took an active part in the defense of the capital. A friend of mine, Jan Wojtowski, a Christian, encouraged me to cross over to the Soviet side with him. We set off for Małkinia to cross the Bug [River] from there. What we went through there shook me to the core. There were approximately one thousand people in the so-called no-man's-land, 90 percent of whom [were] Jews. German soldiers and Gestapo agents would come there every day before evening, take away everything people had on them, so that they were left basically naked, [and] rape women and girls in the presence of the men and parents. We were witnesses to an awful tragedy. In our presence, the Germans shot dead four men and one woman. The reason for the shooting was that those five people were suspected of planning to complain to the higher authorities about the stealing. They didn't allow the dead to be buried. They lay [there] for four days and their bodies were decomposing. [Still], however, the Germans wouldn't let them be buried. Eventually, they threw the murdered people into the river outside the town of Brok.

After two days, we made it over to the Russian side at night, in a group of two hundred people, and found ourselves in Swisłowice.[472] I got a job straightaway. I drew posters and drafted maps. My friend Wojtowski and I supported ourselves with that money. A few times I sent money and letters to my parents in Płock through [some] Poles. In response, they asked me to come for them and bring them to Russia. When I received the letter from Mother [saying that my] parents wanted to see me, I set off [toward Płock]. I went the same way and suffered a lot at the hands of [both] Russians and Germans. I arrived in the border zone on 18 December [1939]. My friend Jan Wojtowski took me to the border. A hunt for Jews was taking place there. My friend identified himself as a Christian. I didn't have paper[s, so I] was beaten terribly and chased into the woods with a thousand [other] Jews. In my presence a Mr. Fleischer, a Jew,

472. Likely refers to Svislach [original Polish correction: Swisłocz].

unable to watch how the Germans were tormenting the women, hit a German in the face. He was shot dead on the spot.

I roamed around the so-called neutral zone for ten days [and] finally got into a train carriage. I jumped out of the train in Rembertów because the Germans were checking to see if there were any Jews [on the train]. I broke my leg then and was laid up for a few weeks. Then I set off to go see my parents. I planned to go to Płock by ship. Since the Germans weren't allowing Jews to use transport by then, I decided to get married and change [my] passport to an Aryan one. I tore up [my] old Jewish documents and married my friend Wojtowski. I immediately felt different. Nevertheless, we decided to go by cart so that we could stop by [my] husband's sister's place in Pułtusk on the way. In Pułtusk we found a desperate situation. The day before, a German officer had been killed there. Immediately German witnesses were found who claimed that the shots had come from a Jewish window. Three hundred people were dragged from their houses, women and children among them, and buried alive. My brother-in-law, Stefan Kowalski, was one of the Poles who had been rounded up for [forced] labor and forced to dig a grave for the three hundred Jews. He said he saw how the earth over the graves moved for a few moments as those buried alive fought against death.

I felt I would not last in Pułtusk any longer and I set off for Płock. The city looked like a graveyard. Jews wouldn't go out into the streets. I experienced a huge disappointment in Płock. My parents' Christian neighbors told me that [my] parents could no longer stand the German persecutions and had left for Warsaw. I went to Warsaw straightaway and found out where my parents were living. I found Father badly ill with typhus. After my arrival at Mother's place, [my] sisters told me that the Germans had been tormenting my parents, arguing that they had too much wealth. After many searches, they demanded half a million zlotys, threatening that if they were not paid, they would send [my mother and sisters] to the house where [my] sick father was, the so-called typhus house. I didn't want to believe my sisters, but after forty-eight hours, when the deadline given by the Germans had passed, three agents turned up at my mother's house and demanded that the whole family go with them to the typhus house. Fearful for the lives of the four people, I collected 20 percent of the aforementioned sum from the rest of the family and this way saved everyone. [My] sisters told me that the incident was commonplace, that the

Germans were extorting all the jewelry and all the money from Warsaw's Jews this way. My parents, sick, physically and mentally broken, couldn't go with me. Two sisters came with me; the third one stayed to look after [our] sick parents. We crossed the border again the same way as before, [and] I finally got to Swisłowice on 2 May 1940. I got my [old] job [back] straightaway, but could not [even] recognize my bosses. They weren't the same people. All of a sudden, they had become enemies to refugees. I saw that they didn't trust me.

After some time, all the Jewish refugees were moved from the big cities to small towns, away from the border zone. In July 1940, German commissions registering Polish citizens who wanted to return to Poland[473] arrived in Białystok, Równe, Kowel, Łuck, Brześć [and] Lwów. Many Jews registered to leave, myself included. [But] the Jews were the only ones who weren't allowed to go. I was ready to go back to Warsaw but backed out at the last minute. At the end of July, the demands began for us to accept Soviet citizenship, to which my husband and I and my sisters did not want to agree. The relations between the refugees and the Bolsheviks worsened by the day. We went to Brześć, thinking things would be better there. The Bolsheviks issued a ban on renting apartments to refugees from Poland. Harboring a refugee was punishable by six months' prison.

After spending a few nights in the station, we were arrested and sentenced to deportation. During the arrest, my sisters were put in one group, and [my] husband and I in another. We were sent to the Waligodzka Oblast.[474] The journey was horrendous; we were starving all of the way. It's difficult to describe the misery we suffered, working twelve hours a day in the forest, hungry and cold. We were all sick. Few people pulled through. I myself went through typhus [and] dysentery. I don't know how I survived that period of going around hospitals. The news of the Amnesty brought me back to health. [My] husband went to Guzarow [Guzar] and joined the army at the rank of lieutenant. I didn't go to Tashkent until a year later, but received food parcels from [my] husband throughout all that time. As an officer's wife, I got to Persia and Palestine easily.

---

473. That is, areas occupied by the Germans.

474. Likely refers to the Vologda Oblast.

Protocol 185

Testimony of **Guzel [Gutsel?] Zaf**, age sixteen, son of Rachela and Lejb from Wyszków. Came to Palestine via Russia and Tehran in August 1943.

The Germans bombarded our town the day after the war broke out. There were many wounded; houses collapsed; men, women, and children jumped out of windows, running away from fires. Panic broke out in town. It lasted a few days, until 9 September, when the Germans occupied Wyszków. [When they] heard about the Germans' approach, the Jews went into hiding and didn't go out into the street. My father, a shoemaker by trade, wasn't afraid of anything; he continued to sit in his workshop and work. The Germans rounded up Jews for [forced] labor [and] ordered them to clean the streets of rubble. During the work, they tormented the Jews and beat [them], told them to sing and dance, and insulted them. Every day they went around to Jewish homes, stole whatever they could, took away whatever they saw, and dragged [away] the men for work. They came to our apartment a few times as well, and seeing that Father was working, allowed him [to continue] and didn't take his work away from him. This lasted a whole week.

On Saturday, the Germans carried out a search of all Jewish apartments and led all the men, women, and children out of them, into a field. When they entered our apartment, I hid in the cellar, the entrance to which was in the kitchen, and lying down in the basement, heard the crying of [my] mother and the laments of my brothers, Szymon and Heniek. Mama begged the Germans to leave us in peace, [saying that] we were poor people [and] they had nothing to gain from us, but it was in vain. Father, Mother, and [my] two brothers were taken outside. I stayed in the cellar. I was shaking with fear and crying, not knowing what was happening with my family or whether I would see them again. I was afraid to leave [my] hiding place, however, and decided to stay in the cellar until I died. I stayed like this until Monday morning. I didn't move from my spot. I was even afraid to go into the kitchen for some water. I felt my strength leaving me, and begged God to call me to him, as I understood that no one from my family would come back again. Meanwhile, the Germans had come to our apartment. They searched everything [to see] if anyone was hiding [there]. They found the entrance to the cellar. Two of them walked down the steps and found me, half-dead. They started to hit me with their gunstocks. They dragged me out of the cellar like a sack of potatoes and threw me into the kitchen. I lay on the floor as if dead from the blows, exhaustion, and fear. They started kicking me with [their] heavy boots and told me to get up. I couldn't move. Seeing that I wasn't able to move, one of them grabbed me by the legs and stood me up on my head. I didn't scream, didn't moan, not because it didn't hurt but because I had no strength to make [any] sound. They grabbed me by the hands and dragged me out into the street. Thirty people who had been found hiding had already been gathered there, among them a few old Jews. I was taken under the arms and led out into a field. We were kept there for a few hours. We weren't allowed to sit down or move, we had to stand upright. A few Jews were holding me up because the Germans threatened to shoot me if I sat down. A few hours later, a car arrived with a machine gun on top. Before we had noticed, the gun started firing. Everyone fell to the ground as if cut down, and I among them. I didn't know if I was alive or dead as I lay among the thirty dead Jews. When it got dark, I felt a blow to my side. I took great fright, thinking the dead were coming back to life. When I felt a second blow I turned around and saw in front of me Father's acquaintance Mr. Stański, who had been among the thirty victims. Seeing that I was alive, he helped me up and dragged me to the forest with his last bit of strength. On the way he told me that he had fallen to the ground and played dead on hearing the first gunshot, and when it got dark, he came up to everyone, poked at them, and spoke, thinking that perhaps some of the Jews might be found alive. Thus my turn had come. We were the only ones out of the whole group who weren't killed.

The night was so dark that we couldn't see each other, and advancing in the forest, I lost my guardian in the dark. I started to call for him [but] was afraid of calling out loudly lest the Germans hear me. I was left alone in the forest in the dark. I had no more strength to drag myself on. I lay down under the trees and fell asleep. I woke up when it was light. I gathered the last of my strength and dragged myself on. I didn't know where I was going. I walked for a long time until I saw a village. The first people I met were German soldiers leading a huge dog. They sicced him on me. The dog bit my leg and the Germans, seeing blood streaming out from my leg, laughed and carried on walking. I was afraid to show myself in the village, bleeding. I stopped the bleeding with mud and dragged myself on until I reached the village of Wilka [?]. Ten Jewish families lived there. One Jew took me into his apartment. My wound was dressed, I was fed and forbidden to carry on. My host advised me to stay with him. He let me graze [his] cows. I agreed readily. I looked after my host's cows for three days, but my heart was restless. I wanted to find out what had happened to my family and whether they'd met a fate like the one that had [stared me in the face]. I set off toward Pułtusk. It wasn't possible to get to Pułtusk over the bridge, as it had been blown up. Some woman came up to me [and] took me across the water in a boat, and I reached the city this way. I stayed the night and set off toward Wyszków the next day, looking for traces of my family. Imagine my luck when, suddenly, I met Mama and my two brothers on the way. We cried with joy and told each other about our experiences up until our meeting.

The Germans—Mama said—took all the Jews out into a field. Everyone was ordered to kneel. They were kept in this position all day and all night. No one was allowed to move. [People's] legs stiffened and swelled. Children cried in pain, older Jews fainted, women went mad seeing the suffering of their families. But the Germans didn't let anyone move and [people] even went to the toilet on the spot, in the same position. The Germans talked among themselves as they walked around the victims, saying that the car of death would soon arrive and kill everyone like dogs. The next day, an order arrived for everyone to line up standing up. [People's] legs were swollen after twenty-four hours of kneeling. No one could move. The Germans hit [people] on the head with gunstocks; blood poured out like water. Screaming went up to the heavens, but it was all in vain. The Jews had to stand up. After a few hours of standing, everyone was rushed on ahead. People were told to run, and those who couldn't run fast were killed on the spot. After a few hours, [Mama and my brothers] arrived in a village. [They] were chased into a field. Since night had fallen, [they] were ordered to kneel again, and knelt like that until morning. In the morning, [they] were driven on again, all day long, and at night [they] knelt again. This lasted four days. The number of people went down: children, women, and elders whom the Germans killed dropped off on the way. On the fifth day, the Germans separated the men from the women and children. The men were loaded onto a truck and driven away, and the women were told to go back home. Mama and [my] two brothers returned to Wyszków, crying bitterly. The house was empty; everything had been stolen. They left Wyszków and set off toward Pułtusk to get over to the Russian side. Mother thought the Germans had shot me dead.

After they had been in Pułtusk for two days, the Germans started kicking everyone out of town. Because not everyone could cross over the broken bridge, the Germans threw many people into the river, and those people drowned. We crossed the bridge, and from the village of Madar [Maków Mazowiecki?] went to Białystok. In Białystok we roamed the streets until we got a place to stay in the synagogue on Jerozolimska Street. Although the synagogue was already full, a corner was given up for us. Mama took up trading, and I washed dishes in a soup kitchen and helped [her] this way. When the passportization order came out, Mama didn't want to take on Russian citizenship, because it was said that it wouldn't be possible to leave Russia then and see Father. One night NKVD-ers arrived at the synagogue and told everyone to go to the station. There we were loaded into freight cars, and we set off after twenty-four hours. It was cramped and dirty inside the car. People were lying on top of each other. We traveled for a month, receiving a piece of bread in the day and a bit of soup at night, until we arrived in the Arkhangelsk Oblast. We were assigned to the Kaldinsz *posiołek* in the Plesetsky district. We lived deep in the forest, in barracks. Everyone had to work, even my youngest brother. The work was difficult [and] I could never fulfill the quotas. We each received four hundred grams of bread per day, and soup had to be bought with one's own earnings. The wages weren't enough; many people died of hunger. We felt our strength leaving us and didn't think we would ever get out into the free world. There was a glimmer of hope when the news of the Amnesty reached us. We went to Turkestan, which was also full of refugees from the German-occupied cities. It was impossible to get bread; we had to go to a kolkhoz. Things weren't any better in the kolkhoz. We all worked with cotton and received 250 grams of grain for [our work], which we had to grind ourselves as there was no mill. We ground it with stones and Mama made soups from the flour, and we lived off that. Realizing that we would starve to death there, we returned to Turkestan. We all fell ill with typhus and all recovered after a stay in the hospital. Mama got malaria and stayed in the hospital, and we children roamed around, eating weeds that we picked in a field. After leaving the hospital, Mama went to the delegation and begged for [my] two younger brothers to be taken into an orphanage. Mama's and my situation was so awful that she decided to put me in an orphanage. I didn't want to leave her but there was no other choice. I spent one day in the orphanage, and the next day, all the children left for Ashgabat, on the Persian border. From there, I went to Tehran and to Palestine. Where my brothers are, where my Mama is—I do not know.

Protocol 186

Testimony of **Tauba Tuchschneider**, age thirteen, daughter of Fryda and Zajnwil from Chełm Lubelski. Came to Palestine with [her] siblings, three sisters and a brother.

My father was a craftsman in the hat-making trade. There were four of us children at home. We had a stall in the market and a workshop at home, where Father made caps and hats. The Germans bombed our town in a horrible way. They demolished a few houses; there were lots of fires and casualties. A few days before the war, my uncle, Warzagier, went to Warsaw to buy merchandise. He was on his way back home on the day the war broke out. The train was bombed, and a bomb hit the locomotive outside Garwolin and [it] could go no farther. [My] uncle, seeing that he wouldn't be able to go on, returned to Warsaw on foot. When the order was issued for all men to leave Warsaw, [my] uncle left the capital on foot but was wounded in his arm on the way. A doctor tended to his wound in a neighboring town, [and (my) uncle] carried on with a bandaged arm because it was said that the Germans were already getting close. After a six-day walk, [my] uncle arrived in Chełm. We were happy when he arrived, because people in town had said that Warsaw was in flames and people were dying like flies. [My] uncle told us about all the atrocities and advised that we immediately leave town, which was constantly being bombarded because of the large number of munitions factories in it.

We hired a cart and with [my] uncle and a few acquaintances, went to the town of Dubienka, where my grandfather, Mama's father, lived. We arrived there after three days' travel. On the way we met many people who were escaping the city. Cars, farm wagons, [and] carts were blocking the passage of the army. New cars stood unattended because their owners had no more gasoline. We arrived in town two days before the holiday of Rosh Hashanah [14–15 September 1939], exhausted by the journey and by our experiences. It was calm there, although many refugees had come—but no one thought the Germans would come this far. When we were on the way to the holiday prayer service, a rumor spread that the Germans were already approaching. Father harnessed a horse to a cart and we set off, even though Grandpa begged us to stay. If I left my home, said Father, to escape the Germans, I don't want to fall into their hands now, in a strange town. We traveled all night. We recited the holiday prayers in a barn we found, and since there was a rabbi among us carrying a shofar with him, the service was conducted in the proper way.

We spent a whole day in the barn. At night, we set off and traveled [throughout it]. We spent the next day in a similar manner, until we reached the town of Kamień Kaszyrski. Throughout the whole journey, Father urged on the tired horse, afraid that the Germans were coming after us. Only after we arrived in the small town, where everything looked like it had before the war, and where the county prefect said that the Germans were a few hundred kilometers away, did Father calm down and decide to stay. We couldn't get an apartment because of the influx of refugees and we lodged in a beth hamidrash. On the fifth day after our arrival in Kamień Kaszyrski, the first Russian tanks came into town. The Poles and Russians were shooting at each other outside town. A few soldiers fell. Then the Poles left, and the Bolsheviks took over the town. The Jews breathed easy; shops were opened and filled up with Russian soldiers. The Russian army marched [through] all day long, singing songs. Children ran after them, and the Jews thought the war had ended.

When we heard that Chełm [now] belonged to the Russians, we decided to go back home. We had to postpone our departure because [my] uncle became seriously ill when the wound he had suffered during his escape from Warsaw opened up. We planned to set off three weeks later, [but then] the news reached us that Chełm was occupied by the Germans again. Since Father wanted to live as close to home as possible, to perhaps save some of [our] possessions, and he had no work in Kamień Kaszyrski, we decided to go to Kowel. We went by train. The journey took a few days because the train tracks had been destroyed by bombings. We would get out of the carriages during the journey, light a fire, and bake potatoes [we'd] dug up in a field. Father came upon many of his acquaintances in Kowel. They told us how the Germans had tortured Jews in Chełm, and warned Father not to dare cross the Soviet border. After a few weeks, Father got some work; Mama traded, and we got by somehow. The people who had come from Chełm told [us] about the slaughter that the Germans had carried out [there]. They had gathered a few hundred Jews, taken them outside of town, told them to dig graves, and shot the five hundred Jews dead. Many were buried alive and only a few managed to survive and were smuggled to the Soviet side. Among those killed were the best-known Jews in town, our good friends. We cried terribly on hearing [this] news, and Mama almost lost her mind from despair.

Father worked in an association of hatmakers in Kowel but earned so little that we could [only] afford dry bread. Mother helped him with [her] trading at first, but antitrader regulations were becoming more and more strict, and Mama gave [it] up. [My] parents didn't want to take Soviet citizenship, afraid that they would never be able to leave Russia, and as a result Father had his job taken away and our situation became desperate. Heedless of the danger, Mother went to Równe [and] brought back merchandise. We bought bread by selling it.

One Friday night, in the middle of summer, NKVD-ers knocked on our [door], told us to get dressed, and took us to the station. Forty-five people were loaded into [each] freight car, and we waited like this for a whole day and night, without food and without drink. The next day the train started. We traveled for three weeks. The journey in the filth, and with the crowding, was horrendous. We cried from hunger, but it was in vain. Thus we arrived in Vologda, where carts were waiting to carry our belongings. The people [had to go] on foot. We walked through a thick forest, the undergrowth hurting our feet. In the middle of the forest, seven kilometers from the *posiołek*, there were barracks. We were put up there. We had to walk to the *posiołek* for bread and cross a river on the way. Father almost drowned once on the way to get bread.

Father worked as a *gruzownik*,[475] Mama chopped branches, and together they earned so little that we couldn't afford to buy soup. We didn't starve to death thanks to the berries and mushrooms we picked in the forest. After a few months, we learned that Grandpa and Grandma from Dubienka were in a neighboring *posiołek*, located ten kilometers from ours. Father attempted to have us moved there. After a few weeks, his efforts were rewarded. We went under the guard of NKVD-ers, on a cart that the commandant had loaned us. The road was difficult—it led through a forest dotted with ponds. The horse caught a chill from walking in the water and died. We had to walk many kilometers before we reached the *posiołek*. We stayed there until the outbreak of the German-Soviet war, when the situation got worse [and] the bread ran out. We had to work more, and even children were taken for work.

475. *Gruzchik* (Russian): loader.

Suddenly, the news of the Amnesty came. We set off from there, first by ship, and then by train. There was nothing to eat; we ate rutabagas and melons. Everyone was ill with dysentery, and we were so weak that we didn't think we would survive. After arriving in Tashkent, we roamed around for a few days, without even a roof over our heads, until Father got a job and an apartment. Grandpa and Grandma went to Turkestan, as that's where our uncles lived who were faring well. Father worked, but Mother was so weakened that she couldn't look after the household. We were placed in a Russian orphanage, where we spent a few months. One day [my] uncle came, took us out of the orphanage, and we went to Turkestan with Mama, [while] Father stayed in Tashkent. When the uncles' earnings stopped and times became difficult for us, Mama found work in an olive oil factory. She got sunstroke during work and died. After Mama's death, Father sent us to a Polish orphanage, which we left for Ashgabat after a few weeks, [and] from there we went to Tehran. After four months in Tehran, all four of us set off for Palestine.

Protocol 186.A[476]

Testimony of **Hala Kirszbraun**, age twelve. Arrived in Palestine in February 1943 from Tehran.

My father, Dawid Kirszbraun, was the son of a member of Parliament, Eli Kirszbraun.[477] He worked as a clerk in a canned goods factory, the firm Krajowa Fabryka Konserw, in Warsaw. The owner of the firm, L. Bluman, a friend of my father's, had a private car that wasn't requisitioned during the war. We escaped from Warsaw in this car in the first days of the war. Mr. Bluman got gasoline somewhere, took his relatives with him and the three of us—Father, Mother, and me. We drove all night to Lublin, on a road full of refugees. In Lublin we stopped at an acquaintance's [place] and spent a few days with him, but the Germans were bombing Lublin brutally due to the presence of the government in the city. We hid in a field outside the city. It was terribly hot; we had nothing to eat or drink. We saw the airplanes descend just above the city. We would return home at night, but one night our house caught fire during an air raid. Luckily, the car wasn't burned, and we set off [out of the city]. We drove toward the Romanian border alongside the army. We were moving so slowly that it was better to go on foot. We got to Czortków but didn't manage to cross the border in time as it was already closed. The Bolsheviks arrived in town in the middle of the night and immediately took our car away. Father got lost somewhere in the panic, [and] I was left alone with Mama. Then news came that Father was in the town of Pilatkowce,[478] and we went to [be with] him. The factory owner, Bluman, continued to look for a way to Romania; he apparently succeeded in crossing the border, and when we found ourselves in the middle of Russia two years later, we got a telegram from him [saying] he was in [part of text missing]. Father was a good bookkeeper and got a job in the local bakery straightaway. We didn't fare too badly because Father would bring home flour. Father's younger brother, eighteen-year-old Kuba, came to Czortków and told [us] that

476. For reasons unknown, there is one protocol numbered 186 and another numbered 186.A.

477. Eliasz Kirszbraun: MP of the Republic of Poland in 1922, representative of the Parliamentary Group of Jewish Orthodox Organizations [Polish: Klub Posłów Organizacji Żydów Ortodoksyjnych].

478. Likely refers to Pilaszkowice.

there wasn't a single brick left from [my] grandfather's house on Grzybowska Street. Father's brother got a job too, and we didn't lack for anything.

One night NKVD-ers arrived at our place, told us to get dressed, and took us to the station. We traveled for two weeks in awful conditions, until we arrived at the Tavda station, in the Sverdlovsk Oblast, on the Ural-Siberia border. It was cold there already, in July. The area was full of Russian exiles who were [then] moved to a different place, [while] the Polish deportees stayed. Father worked in the forest. Once there was an accident that almost led to his death. [Some] heavy beams that he was working with at the sawmill slipped out of his hand[s], and one of them almost pinned him down. For this work, he received fifty rubles per month. Mama sold clothes. She got a bucket of potatoes and some milk from a Russian peasant woman in exchange for one gown. We almost froze to death, until Mama bought cotton [padding] in the cooperative and sewed coats for us. There were many Poles living in our *posiołek*. Russian doctors took some of the Poles to the city, to hospitals, [while] engineers and lawyers worked in the forest. If you took off a glove during work, [your] fingers would get frostbitten straightaway. One person had to have theirs cut off.

After a year, we got a piece of land to work. I helped Mother plant potatoes, and when they grew, we were no longer starving. We then went to Samarkand, and there it seemed to us that our time had come. We roamed around for two months, without even a roof over our heads, and Father, jobless, had to take up trading. I helped [him]. I risked two days in jail if I was caught trading [and, if I got] caught again, [my] parents would be arrested. I knew how to weasel my way out of police hands. Father sold *lepyoshki*. We waited in line in front of the cooperative all night, bought *lepyoshki* at thirty kopecks apiece, and sold them at five rubles apiece. Later, when the *lepyoshki* ran out, Father started to sell soap that his friend made in a tiny secret factory. I would deliver the soap to the buyers. Still, we had nothing to eat. When a Polish agency came to help refugees, Mama got a job as a cook in an orphanage through their connections. Being a cook in Russia is a real career. The orphanage where Mother worked was set up for four hundred Jewish children. That home was treated worse than the others; it was only ever given black flour, and potatoes were rare. Mama could only cook dumplings in water. But to us this was good fortune, because the whole house had something to eat. After the children were evacuated from Russia, my parents decided I would go along too. They themselves stayed behind in Russia.

Protocol 187

Testimony of **Rosze [?] Sznal**, age fourteen, son of Matias and Gitla from Tarnów. Came to Palestine via Persia in February 1943.

We were rich people. My father ran a brewery with my uncle, and next to the brewery was our house. Both the house and the factory were in the factory district of the city, next to an ammunition factory that employed a few thousand workers. On Friday, the first day of the war, our city was heavily bombed. Because the ammunition factory became a target, bombs were falling onto our house. A fire broke out and we barely survived, hiding in cellars. We didn't take anything [with us] from the house. We ran to [the home of one of our] relatives, who lived in the Jewish district. The bombardment didn't stop, and we left town a few days later with a few friends, thinking we would be less exposed to the bombs in the country. We never saw [our] hometown again. Rich people only a few days earlier, we suddenly found ourselves destitute, owning only what we carried with us. The journey was hard. We couldn't walk on the road because we were constantly being bombed and shot at by German airplanes. When we hid in a ditch or in a forest and then returned to the road, we would find lots of dead horses and people and overturned cars. We decided to spend the days resting in peasant barns, eating baked potatoes, and set off [again] at night.

We reached Radomyśl this way and lodged at our relative's place. On hearing that the Germans had occupied Tarnów, [and] even though our relative didn't want to let us go, we set off [from Radomyśl] one day and went to Zylków [Żółkiew], where we found the Russians already there. The first days of the Bolshevik occupation were very nice. People went out into the streets, looked at the tanks; children followed the soldiers around. The soldiers bought up everything from the shops, and within a few days, the products had run out and long lines formed in front of the bakeries. The city was full of refugees, who were living in all public buildings. Many people were sleeping in the streets. We got a small room, and everyone envied us for it, but Father had no job. He decided to go to Lwów, alone at first, and then returned to Zylków [Żółkiew] a few days later. From that time on, he would go all the time, and trade. He got start-up money by selling a gold watch. He would bring in the goods from Lwów—usually leather, butter, sugar, and flour—and make a living selling these products.

But the conditions for traders were getting worse. Searches were being carried out on trains. Father was arrested once, threatened with deportation to Siberia. [He] bought a cart and a horse with a few friends, and from then on, they would travel to Lwów on side roads. One day an army car drove into the cart, killing the horse and injuring Father. Wounded, he was taken to Lwów, to a hospital. [He] spent three months in the hospital and none of us did [any] trading during that whole time. Mama sat with Father in the hospital, and we were starving. When Father left the hospital, he was lame in one leg and couldn't trade. Then Mama, who couldn't make her peace with being a smuggler, would go to Lwów. We were faring so badly that when the registration was announced, Father registered to go back home. We had heard that our brewery was open and operating, and that [my] uncle had stayed there as the foreman. Father thought he would manage to get a job in his brewery.

We were living in the hope of going home when one night, on a Friday, NKVD-ers came into our apartment and told us to pack [our] belongings. Mother rejoiced, thinking they were sending us home. We were taken to the station [and], from there, in a freight car, to Lwów, where after waiting for twenty-four hours, we set off on a horrific journey in a sealed freight car, without food or drink. Our family was made up of four children. The eldest brother, Gecel, was sixteen, I was second, Herszel was eight years old, and [our] little sister, Fajga, was five. I fell ill. Father had been feeling unwell since the cart accident. Mother became apathetic and wouldn't speak a word all day. That is the state in which we set off for Siberia. The journey took five weeks, until we got to Krasnoyarsk Krai; from there we were sent through thick woods in cars to Novosibirsk. We were sent farther on, to quarries up in the mountains. The stone was broken up with dynamite and the refugees' work consisted of breaking huge stones into small ones. Father worked with [my] brother [while] Mama stayed at home. We received eight hundred grams of bread for the workers and five hundred grams for the nonworkers, as well as twenty kopecks a day [each]. Soup could be [bought] in the canteen but it cost a ruble and a half. Only Mama and [my] little sister ate soup. The rest of us lived on bread and hot water. After two months, Father could no longer work, and [my] brother became the sole supporter of the family.

Father started to try to have us moved to a different *posiołek*, for lighter work. We were moved to a brickyard. The journey to the new *posiołek*, located in a deep forest, took three days. Life was much better there. [People] lived in small barracks, three families in each; workers received bread and soup from the first kettle, and nonworkers from the third kettle. Each family got a patch of land to work. We got land too, where we planted potatoes. Mama, my younger brother, and I worked in the field, and Father and my older brother were assigned work in the forest. When the potatoes ripened a few months later, our hunger was over. We sold some of the potatoes and with the proceeds bought butter and lard that people had received in parcels from Poland. Mama felt better after work, and better times began for us. When the [German-Soviet] war broke out, the situation in the *posiołek* got a lot worse. We were told to work twelve hours a day, and the bread rations were decreased. I had to go to work too, since I was twelve, but [our] potato supplies were enough for all and we did not go hungry. One day NKVD-ers came, gathered the deportees, and told us we were free. It's difficult to describe our joy, and the envy of the Russian exiles. The commandant asked us to stay, promised us more land [and] wood for houses, but we didn't listen to him.

Since all [the major] cities were full, we were told to go to Szachrijzabs.[479] We set off straightaway after renting a freight car with a few other families. The journey took a few weeks. It wasn't possible to get bread; there was nothing except hot water at the big stations, and at the small [ones], we would stand for hours. In Uzbekistan, we realized what a bad decision we had made in leaving the *posiołek*. Hundreds of people were lying in the gutters, the sick alongside corpses, the living with the dead, and no one paid any attention. Children got so used to seeing dead people that we stopped being afraid of them. People stole from one another, and the Uzbeks stole from everyone and were impossible to get rid of. We went to a kolkhoz. We all worked hard in the fields and got a handful of grain each for it. We were so weak that we couldn't move. Father was first to get sick. He got bloody dysentery. They didn't want to admit him to a hospital, and he died the next day. Two weeks later, when Mama and my eldest brother were at work, my little sister, Fajga, died in my arms. Afraid that it might affect Mama very badly, we carried her out into a

479. Shahrisabz [original Polish correction: Szachrisjabz].

field in our arms and buried her there. When I remember Mother's despair when she found out about [Fajga's] death, I go weak in the knees to this day. A few weeks later, Mother fell ill with typhus and we barely [managed to convince] the kolkhoz warden to give us a cart so we could take her to the hospital. She died on the way. We brought Mama [back] to the kolkhoz and buried her next to Father and [my] little sister. A few days later, [my] youngest brother fell ill with typhus. I didn't want to take him to the station anymore, and after a few days, we dug yet a fourth grave—for our brother. We were left alone; we sold what things there were remaining and left the kolkhoz. At Kitab station, where we spent the night waiting for the train, we had all our money and belongings stolen from us. On our arrival in Szachrijzabad, we went straight to the Polish agency. There we were immediately given blankets and were taken into an orphanage the next day. I spent a few weeks in the orphanage and was very happy in the care of the Jewish teacher. After a few weeks, we were sent to Ashgabat, and from there, to Mashhad, where the Persian Jews welcomed us warmly and gave us gifts. Then we set off for Tehran, and from there we were sent to Palestine three months later.

Protocol 188

Testimony of **Abraham Rozenband**, age fourteen, from Warsaw, 100 Wolska [Street], son of Hipolit and Estera. Came to Palestine in August 1943 via Russia and Tehran.

My father was a bill collector in a factory whose name I don't remember. There were five of us children at home, three sisters and two brothers: Helena, age sixteen; Irka, age fifteen; Rena, age seven; me; and three-year-old Heniek. The elder siblings were studying and preparing to take up jobs to help Father, whose earnings weren't enough [for us]. During the bombardment of Warsaw, we all hid in the cellar. Mother was so scared of the bombs that she wouldn't leave the shelter even after Warsaw surrendered. [My] sister Helena ran the household. She made meals and brought them to us in the cellar. Our home suffered a lot in the bombardment, and in the next [one], many people were buried [under the rubble] in the cellar. Despite this, Mother wouldn't let anyone go out into the streets. We stayed in the cellar until the city was taken over by the Germans. When the news reached us that the Germans were sharing out soup and bread among the civilians, Mother, who didn't look Jewish, went out and brought us a bit of food. After a few days, the Germans noticed that Jews were making use of the kettles, too. They followed every Jew, and on learning that Mother was Jewish, threw her out of the line and beat her. Mama came home all bloodied.

[After] seeing Mother beaten up [like this], Father said he wouldn't stay with the Germans for another moment; we packed [our] belongings into bundles and set off for Małkinia by train. The Germans beat all the Jews during searches, took away their belongings, ordered them to dance and sing, and only allowed them to approach the border after they'd been tormented like that. A Pole who was traveling with us told the Germans that we were his family, and thus we avoided a beating. There was a strip of "no-man's-land" at the border. Jews—men, women, and children—whom the Russians didn't want to let in, were waiting there. They were all standing with [their] boxes, ready to cross the border, which was opened for [only] a few minutes [at a time]. At night, special lookouts were posted who waited to see if the right time had come. This went on for a few days. We were hungry; there was no bread. One had to walk very far to get water. It was raining, the ground was soaked, [and] we struggled to light a fire. Some thought they would meet their end in this strip of "no-man's-land." Finally the border was opened, and the crowd surged forward, trampling one another. Parents lost their children; they couldn't find each other in the dark. Mother tied me, Heniek, and [my] younger sister to herself with a rope and held the older [children] by the hand. We couldn't see each other in the dark; we only called out to each other. Others were doing the same, and such a clamor ensued that people thought the world was coming to an end. We arrived in a small village, went from there to a small town, and made our way to Białystok by train.

In Białystok we began the hopeless search for an apartment. We were all exhausted [and] dirty, lice were biting us because we hadn't been changing our underwear. Father found shelter for us in one of the synagogues set aside for refugees. It wasn't easy to get into a synagogue full of refugees who didn't want to let new arrivals in. Luckily we found a few of our friends there. The next day Father took up trading. The children helped him. I traded cigarettes, needles for Primus stoves, sweets. Father sold flour, [while] Mother traveled to small towns by train to get food supplies and merchandise. The police caught me a few times when I was selling cigarettes. The policemen said they wouldn't harm me if I gave them the address of the merchant who had supplied me with the goods. I said that I was there alone and didn't have a fixed abode, and that I bought cigarettes at random, on the street, from people whose names I didn't know. I was threatened with arrest and deportation to Siberia. I was released a few hours later, but they didn't give the merchandise back.

When the order came out about taking Soviet citizenship, Father registered to go home. A few weeks went by. One Friday night, NKVD-ers knocked on the door, told everyone who was staying in the synagogue to pack [their] belongings, and drove us out to the station. There we were loaded into freight cars, and twenty-four hours later, set off on our way. We cried and screamed to be given food, but to no avail. We were only brought bread and soup [after we set off]. Our journey took a month. The conditions inside the carriage got worse by the day. No one was allowed out at the stations, only the car commandant went out to get soup and bread.

After a month we stopped in an empty field, and from there we were taken to a river on foot. We were loaded onto a small ship and taken to a place in [the

Autonomous Soviet Socialist Republic of] Komi called Syktyvkar. There were barracks there, in a huge and beautiful forest. Eighty people lived in each barracks; there was nothing to sleep on. We made [some] bunks ourselves after a few days. In the morning everyone went to work, to cut wood. Workers received four hundred grams of bread every day, nonworkers—two hundred grams. Soup was sold in the canteen for fifty kopecks per portion, but wages were so low that no one could afford [it], and we lived on dry bread. Nearby there were the barracks of Russian exiles, with whom we were not allowed to communicate, but children would often sneak out to those barracks. The Russians fared no better than we did. They were starving, they worked in the forest, wore rags, and they laughed at us when we said we would leave Russia someday. They said that no one left exile alive. Father fell ill. The doctor said that he was unfit for physical work, and Father got a job in town as he was a bookkeeper. We weren't allowed to go with him. He would come to see us on Sundays, and would bring bread and nice things with him. Later, Father only came once a month. In the meantime, the [German-Soviet] war broke out, and Mama begged Father not to go into town anymore as it was said that we would all be released. But the commandant didn't allow [him to stay], and Father had to return to the city. In the meantime, we received [our] documents and set off with everyone else. I never saw Father again [and] we don't know what happened to him.

The journey to Tashkent was very difficult; we went hungry for entire weeks and couldn't find anything to eat at any of the stations. We pulled out weeds in the fields and ate them. Meanwhile, Heniek fell ill with typhus. [Our] travel companions didn't want to let a sick child travel in the car with us because they were scared of [getting infected]. Mother had to get off at one of the stations with the boy, and we four children went on to Tashkent on our own. We roamed the city streets, hungry, and couldn't find anything to eat. After a few days, I and my two sisters, Helenka and Irka, fell ill with typhus. We lay in the street, unconscious with fever, until we were taken to the hospital, [which] we left after a month, recovered. I have horrible memories of the hospital. There were no medicines, we ate black bread, but we recovered regardless. After leaving the hospital, we met up with Mother, but without Heniek. The child had died in the hospital after a few days. Mama sold the last of [our] belongings, and we lived off that. After a few months, we met our aunt from Warsaw, Fela Berkowicz, in Tashkent. Since she lived in Turkestan and her husband was earning money, we moved [there]. We fared better there; Mother and [my] sisters were earning money, but even so we still went hungry. One day I went to the Polish agency and asked to be taken into an orphanage. After a week's stay, we were sent to Ashgabat with the other children, where we stayed for a whole year. We were happy; we were studying and there was enough food, but later, when the Polish army left and relations between Poland and Russia were severed, the Russians were forcing the older children to take Russian citizenship. The orphanage director and all the teachers were arrested. The Russians wanted to close down the orphanage, but the central director delayed the closing date day after day, until the moment when a telegram arrived [saying] we were going to Persia. The Persian Jews welcomed us warmly; the Jewish children were sent to Tehran and the Polish ones to Africa. After two weeks' stay in Tehran, I went to Palestine.

Protocol 191

Testimony of **Dawid Lewin**, age twenty-four, from Warsaw, son of Abraham and Estera. Came to Palestine via Russia and Persia in February 1943.

I'm a carpenter by trade. Before the war, I worked at a construction site. There were fewer and fewer workers [after] the war broke out, and when I turned up for work on 7 [September 1939], there was no one left anymore. I saw strange scenes on the street as I was leaving home. The shops were closed, the trams were running off schedule, and people were running around the streets with rucksacks full of stuff. No one, however, knew where to run to. In spite of the panic, I went to work. I went to see a companion of mine, where I found a few friends who were ready to go on a journey. They managed to convince me [to go] and I went off with everyone. Our group was made up of twenty people. It was Thursday, the seventh [of September 1939], when we set off from Warsaw, going toward Brześć. We only got as far as Siedlce. It was difficult to get through on the crowded road, which was constantly being bombed. We hid in forests; there were a lot of dead and injured. We found Siedlce burned down. The streets were on fire. We struggled to push through the rubble and the flames.

We set off [again] the next day. After two hours, we saw German airplanes that descended over the road and shot at us from machine guns. A great panic broke out [and] people dispersed. The bombardment lasted a few hours, and when we returned to the road, an awful scene stretched out in front of us. It looked like a battlefield. There were lots of wounded and dead people, particularly women and children. Before we knew it, airplane squadrons flew in again and began shooting at the escapees. Things only calmed down at night. We spent that night in the woods. The cries of the wounded reached us, [but] we couldn't move from our spot to help them. Many died on the road leading from Siedlce to Brześć then. We set off [again] but only some said they were continuing on—the rest went back to Warsaw. I was with those who returned. All the towns up until Kałuszyn were in flames. We were bombed again on the way. Finally we got to Kałuszyn. We spent three days there. It was said that Warsaw had been occupied by the Germans and that there wasn't a brick left of it. There was nothing to go back for then. We only traveled at night, and the roads continued to be mobbed by civilians and by the army going east. Everyone was going in the same direction, so it was difficult for us to walk back. We were caught in artillery fire in one of the forests and dropped to the ground. We avoided death by a miracle. We found ourselves in Warsaw on 17 [September]. The house hadn't suffered much in the bombardments, but the neighboring [ones] were damaged, and the number of casualties grew by the day. There was awful hunger [and] no water. This lasted until the surrender.

After entering Warsaw, the Germans distributed bread and soup generously among the hungry people, kicking Jews out of line. These scenes were filmed. After a few days, raids began in the streets, as well as manhunts. I couldn't stand the constant fear any longer and decided to leave Warsaw, even though Mother asked me to stay. I went from Warsaw to Siedlce by train, and from there to Drohiczyn, on the Bug [River]. I traveled to Brzešć by train. In Brzešć, I registered to go to work in Russia voluntarily. One had to stand in line for twenty-four hours to get on the list, and I was told two days later to report to the train station. A few hundred people had gathered in the station. We were loaded into a freight car. We were convinced that we were going into Russia, as promised. A few hours later, we were let out in a village outside Pińsk. We were taken to an estate, to a mansion that had been plundered so completely that not only the door handles but even the electrical sockets had been taken out. The peasants had completely cleared out the mansion. We were given straw to sleep on. We thought we would go to work the next day, but two weeks went by and no one paid any attention to us. We weren't being fed and we decided to flee to Drohiczyn Podlaski. I got a job in my trade there in a local department, where [part of text missing] local [...], but the prices were so high that my wages weren't enough to support one person. The shop and the houses in town were nationalized, [and] settlers, Zionist activists, and social activists were arrested. During that period, various registration bureaus were opened, but none of the registrations were finalized and no one could explain [their] objective. A month before the elections, propaganda rallies took place, and people were being encouraged to pick the Communist Party candidate. At one of the meetings, people were called on to vote for a former Communist who had fought as a partisan during Russia's occupation of Poland. It turned out a week later that the partisan was nothing more than a criminal, who had stolen Polish and Jewish property during the transitional time in September 1939.

People were gathered again, and some Belarussian [Belarusian] Communist [woman] was put forward as a candidate. The elections took place in a club, with music playing. Each voter was allowed to buy a white bread roll, sweets, [and] kielbasa in the club. They would pass through a room where an orchestra was playing and you could dance, carrying a parcel with these treats. It was in this joyous mood that the elections took place.

Three months before the elections, everyone had been summoned to the NKVD and told to accept Soviet citizenship. Many people didn't want to take the citizenship because their families were still in the German-occupied areas. Ninety percent of refugees asked to be taken home. I too was among them. After some time, those who were registered to leave were told to go to Brześć, where a German commission was operating. It was difficult to get an appointment. The first transport [going toward] the German-occupied region left in April. No more people left [after that]. And when the German commission was leaving Brześć, Jews ran after the car they were traveling in, begging to be taken away [with them]. The Germans said they would come back. They didn't come back—[instead], on 17 June, the Bolsheviks arrested everyone who had registered.

I was living with my sister, Rywka, and [my] brother-in-law, Jehoszua Frydrych, when the NKVD-ers arrived at my apartment. They sent away [my] sister and brother-in-law and took me, a single person, to prison. I stayed in prison for six weeks, in a small room intended for fifteen people, where seventy people were confined at that time. It's difficult to describe the filth, the crowding, and the hunger [there]. I was summoned for interrogation six times, mostly at nighttime, and was constantly asked the same questions: where I was from, who my parents were, and why I wanted to go back. The protocols [that were issued], however, did not match our statements. They said that we wanted to go back because we didn't like the Soviet regime. [The following people] were in the cell with me: Jechiel Feldstein from Łódź, the brothers Iwentarz from Warsaw, Goldwasser from Warsaw, Wajchman from Dęblin, and Władysław Pienczak, a metalworker from Warsaw. There were many women in the prison. The regime was strict. We were allowed to go to the toilet twice a day. It was forbidden to talk among ourselves or play any games. It was also forbidden to sleep during the day. The cell was so small that one person would sit on top of another, not saying a word, as that was punishable by [time in] a punishment cell. People left the punishment cell half-deranged. We believed they would eventually send us home.

However, we were sent away in freight cars and began our journey. At Stolin station, [additional] carriages were attached to our train, and [continuing] this way, our transport was made up of fifty cars. A search and a [roll call] would take place at each of the larger stations. When we asked for bread, we were told we wouldn't get any because we weren't working. After four weeks' journey, we arrived at the station of Karela, not far from the Finnish border.[480] I was sent to a forest, to the Pialma *posiołek*. Our group was made up of a thousand men and thirty-seven women. Of these, 75 percent were Jews. We slept on bare bunks in barracks. The women lived separately. We worked cutting down trees. My work consisted of sharpening the saws. I worked at night. No one fulfilled more than 30 percent of [their] quota. For hitting the quota, you would get nine hundred grams of bread and soup with groats twice a day. Those who fulfilled less than 70 percent received four hundred grams of bread. The camp quotas applied not just to the deportees, but also to the warden. And since we didn't complete the required work, our wardens would change every month. We were threatened with jail, with hanging, but even so, we could not fulfill more [of the requirements]. Three months later, some Russian exiles arrived [in the camp]. The NKVD thought they could improve the quality of our work this way, but they were wrong. There were foreign nationals among the Russian exiles, Communists who had come to Russia [and] had been arrested in 1937 as Russian citizens. Among the foreign nationals was a man named Aron Bernstein, a Jew who had come to Russia in the year 1918. I also made the acquaintance of an engineer from Kiev, a Jew who, according to him, used to earn six hundred rubles per month, while his wife made four hundred rubles working in an airplane factory. They had two children and had never been involved in politics. One night, she and he were arrested, deported separately, and what had happened to the[ir] children he didn't know. No one knew why they had been arrested. They waited patiently for the miracle that would set them free. They told us we had it better because we had come to ready-made camps, whereas they had built those camps [themselves]. Terrible theft began with the arrival of the Russian exiles. There were fights every day between the

480. Most likely refers to Kirillovskoye [original Polish correction: Kirillowskoje].

owners of the items and those suspected of stealing. We were faring worse and worse. We were completely exhausted, and within four weeks we had come to understand that we would all die from hunger and cold there. I could barely stand up and was assigned lighter work. After six months, a judgment was read out to us, sentencing everyone to five years in the camp. We were called up to sign the judgment. Fifty percent of the convicts were gone by then. There was a Palestinian citizen among us, Margolit from Tel Aviv, who had come to [see] his family in Pińsk just before the war.

Faced with the increasing mortality, the NKVD decided to hire us out in our trades, and we were sent to the city, where only arrestees lived. There were huge sewing rooms there, where undergarments for the army were made. It turned out that it was the new warden, a Jew, who had sent us to the city, [and who] was later arrested for showing us this generosity. After the outbreak of the [German-Soviet] war, it was decided that we would be evacuated. We were taken across the lake on wooden barges, fed only herring. We drank water from the lake and many of us fell ill. After a horrendous three-day journey, we arrived at an assembly point, where we found three thousand people. It turned out that they were citizens of the Baltic countries who had been arrested before the outbreak of the war. In that group was Rabbi Wasserman, one of the greatest authorities on Talmud in Poland, a seventy-year-old elderly man who could barely stand up.[481] We were sorted into groups according to where we came from, and we set off on foot. We walked for five weeks, covering forty-five kilometers per day. We slept outdoors. It was July [and] we were thirsty. We weren't given [much] food during the march—only around evening a piece of bread and watery soup were provided. We would wake at sunrise, wet from the dew. People collapsed from exhaustion—they were left behind as fodder for the wild animals, and we carried on. Our legs swelled [and] we didn't believe we would reach [our] destination. We reached [Yertsevo?] in the Arkhangelsk Oblast, where the penal camps were located. We were sent to work in the forest.

After three weeks of work, we found out that an amnesty for Polish citizens had [been announced]. We set off to the south to reach the Polish army. We

---

481. This is likely Elchonon Wasserman, a prominent rabbi from Lithuania who gave Torah lectures in Baranowicze in Poland.

found no Poles when we arrived in Arzamas. I got a job as a carpenter in a factory and made skis for the army. I earned around a thousand rubles per month but had to go hungry despite that. I was able to get lunch in the local canteen, where you had to wait in line for two hours for a meal. For six months I didn't eat hot food and I slept in my clothes, since I didn't have a duvet. I washed my shirt [only] once because of a lack of soap. There was nothing [one could] buy with money. I decided to leave, but it was difficult. I wrote to the authorities with a request to join the army and didn't go to work for three days. My supervisor said my request had been sent to the central office and promised he would improve my situation. I worked for another three weeks, and since things weren't improving, I went to the court myself, where I was told I was risking seven years in prison for skipping work. I told [them] about my situation. I was asked whom I would be fighting for. "Against Germans," I replied. I was let go; I went to Gorky and my journey to Wierewskaje[482] took six weeks from there. Thousands of people died on the way. I would have died from hunger too if I hadn't broken into a freight car. I got to Gorchakovo, where the major who received me said I would soon come before an army commission. In the meantime, the last Polish army transport was leaving. I got into a freight car and smuggled myself to Krasnovodsk, and from there to Pahlevi. From Pahlevi I went to Tehran, where I received [my] certificate.

482. Presumably: Vrevskoye [original Polish correction: Wriewskoje].

Protocol 192

Testimony of **Sara Zylberfaden**, age thirteen, from Warsaw, daughter of Mordechaj and Rywka, who came to Palestine via Tehran in August 1943.

My father was a carpenter. We had a workshop with a few workers. Mother died when I was three years old. Father married for the second time, and [my] stepmother was good to me, like my own mother. There weren't any other children in the house. When the war broke out, I was living in a summer resort in Falenica. During the first days of the war the Germans bombed an orphanage in Otwock and killed many children. Mother left everything behind and went to Warsaw with me. There were horrible things happening at the station. People were pushing, German planes were flying past every other minute. After a few hours of waiting, realizing that we wouldn't get onto a train, we went to the light rail line, which arrived in Warsaw many hours later. The dark city made a terrifying impression on me; I was afraid of getting lost from Mama. I didn't find Father at home. The neighbors said that he had gone to get us. He didn't come back in the evening or the next day; he didn't come back until Sunday with [our] belongings.

I lived through the siege and the bombardment of Warsaw. I spent whole days in the shelter, and one day, our house caught fire. We escaped to Grandma's place, to Smocza Street. That journey took a few hours. When we got to Grandma's, we saw that her house had been destroyed and we returned home. This [siege] lasted four weeks. There was no water or bread. A neighbor who went out to get bread was killed by a bomb. When the Germans occupied Warsaw, they started by giving out bread to the people, but Jews were kicked out of the lines. Father had a lot of work. People were getting [their] doors and windows fixed, and we probably would have gotten a lot of money if it wasn't for the Germans [forcing] Father to work [for them], from which he would return beaten. He said he wouldn't stay in Poland. We planned to go to Pińsk, where some of our relatives lived, but Mama wouldn't allow it, saying that [Father] was earning good money there [in Warsaw]. Father returned from the German forced labor beaten up one time and said he wouldn't spend another moment in Warsaw.

The next day we set off in a droshky for the station, where we came upon thousands of people who wanted to escape from Warsaw, like we did. We found ourselves in Małkinia a few hours later. We lost Father. I went to stand with Mama in the spot where the Christians were standing, and we crossed the border this way. We looked for Father all night long. Despairing, we took the advice of people who told us to look for Father at the border outpost. We roamed the neutral zone for two days. It was raining [and] we were standing in the mud. Finally the border was opened, and we found ourselves on the Soviet side with a crowd [of people]. We went to the Zaręby [Kościelne] station on foot, [and] from there to Białystok by train, where we found Father at the station. He told us he had crossed the border on the first evening and was sure we had gone back to Warsaw. We slept in a basement in Białystok, and seeing that we wouldn't be able to get an apartment, went to Pińsk.

In Pińsk we stayed with relatives and later rented a room. Father started working, I went to school, and we fared very well, but the situation was changing slowly. [Father's] wages weren't enough to live on, and Mama had to take up trading. Father wrote to his brother in America, asking him to get visas [for us]. After sending [one of these] letter[s], he was called in to the NKVD. He returned very agitated and said to Mama: "They are worse than the Germans." When the decree came out about passportization, Father didn't want to hear about Soviet citizenship, worried that [as a Soviet citizen] he wouldn't be able to go to America. One Friday a few weeks later, NKVD-ers knocked on our [door], told us to pack [our] belongings, and sent us to the station. We were loaded into freight cars, and they were sealed. We weren't given water or bread. The journey took four weeks. We would get a thin slice of bread and watery soup at night during the journey. People were ill, [but] there was no doctor. We weren't allowed out of the car. Thus we arrived in Arkhangelsk. We were fed; the children were given groats. Eight days later, we were taken to a *posiołek* on trucks. The *posiołek* was located in the Krasnoyarsk district. It was in a deep forest, where there were a few huge barracks, dirty and cramped.

Father was employed in the construction of a barracks, [and] Mother worked [too], but even both of their wages weren't enough for us to be adequately fed. I went to school at first but couldn't study because I was constantly hungry. In the summer, I would run off from school into the forest to [pick] berries and mushrooms, and we got by much better then. One day Mother got pneumonia and Father tried to get a permit to take her to the hospital, which was located eighty kilometers from the *posiołek*. She returned from the hospital six weeks later but couldn't work. Father couldn't work either, from exhaustion. We were sent to a *posiołek* for invalids. We spent three months there; Father worked in a sawmill and Mother in the kitchen.

After the outbreak of the [German-Soviet] war, the situation in the labor camp got worse—more work and less bread. One day Father returned home and told us with great joy that we were free and could go wherever we wanted. Our journey to Arkhangelsk took two weeks. After a few days' stay in the station, we left for warm[er] places in a shared freight car. Our journey took six weeks; we were constantly hungry and dirty. We got bread once every four days. Many people became ill with dysentery from eating weeds they picked in the field[s] and died. They were buried out in a field. We got to Szachchazad this way.[483] We had no roof over our heads [and] roamed the streets, which were overflowing with refugees, lying in rows. Father got a job but couldn't get an apartment, so we moved to a kolkhoz. We lived in the kolkhoz and all three of us worked in a field and got two hundred grams of grain per day for it. Mother fell ill with malaria and [had to] lie on the wet floor. She was taken to the hospital a few days later. Father returned home very sad and didn't want to tell me how Mama was doing. It turned out that Mother had died on the way, and instead of the hospital, Father had taken her to the cemetery.

After Mother's death, I looked after the household. We ate weeds from the field until Father got sick. I begged in vain to have him taken to the hospital. Father passed away eight days later. I became a full orphan [and] turned to the Polish agency, going to Szachnozad on foot. I was given a coat, shoes, and two blankets, and was told to come back in a few days. As [some] things left over from [my] parents were back in the kolkhoz, a woman I knew sold them [for me] and I arrived in the city with a large sum of money. I found out at the delegation that the orphanage wouldn't be opened for a few more days. A delegation clerk, a Jewish woman, took an interest in me; she asked how much money I had with me and whether I had [any] relatives. She suggested that I live with her, [and said] that she would look after me like her own child. I

483. Szachchazad, Szachnozad: most likely refers to Shahrisabz [original Polish correction: Szachrisjabz].

lived with her for six weeks. The whole time that I had money she treated me well, kissed me and cuddled me, and coaxed a bit of money out of me every day. And when the money ran out, she started to beat me, torment me, and she forced me to leave. Various men came to visit this woman. I had to leave the room whenever the men came to see her. Realizing that she couldn't [just] get rid of me, she concocted a story that I had stolen from her and threw me out into the street, forbidding me to take the coat and blanket I had gotten from the delegation. I went to the director, crying, and told him everything. [He] gave me another coat and blankets, and sent me to Kogon straightaway, and from there, to Ashgabat, [and] from there we were sent to Tehran after four months. I was in Tehran for two months and went to Palestine from there.

Protocol 193

Testimony of **Amalia Finkler** from Kraków, resident of Tel Aviv, age fifty-two.

On 29 August 1939 I left Kraków for Lwów, which is where the outbreak of the war caught me. I survived the bombardment of the city there [and] witnessed the tragic scene of the burial of those killed in the bombardment in a common grave. I spent ten months under Russian occupation. On 29 June[484] [1940], the Bolsheviks ordered a registration of everyone who wanted to go back to the German-occupied area. One night, adults' screams and children's crying rang out—it was the NKVD gathering refugees for deportation. Two officials entered my room; they told me to pack [my] belongings and come with them. I tried in vain to explain that my son wasn't home. I was taken to the station [and] loaded into a freight car with a group of people.

It's difficult to describe what life in Lwów was like after the arrival of the Bolsheviks. The Soviet authorities closed down private shops and opened a chain of cooperatives. As a result, one had to stand in line for food all night long. The winter was hard; there was no [fire]wood. I lived by selling things I had brought with me. One day a Russian actress who performed in a Lwów troupe invited me round. The women at the event were wearing nightgowns. At one point the Bolsheviks were registering the unemployed, who could sign up voluntarily to work in Russia. Soon, however, the news arrived about the awful fate of those workers.

We arrived in Ural after a few weeks' journey. There were 380 people in our labor camp. We were told to build barracks and slept outdoors until they were ready. The place was called Altynay, in the Sucholoczynski district.[485] We stood in mud that came up to our knees and worked. The sick were not exempt from work. As a result, within a short time we buried one of our people, and the Russians warned us that we would all end up like this. We worked constructing a rail line. Luckily, the climate in that area was very healthy. I

---

484. The author is mistaken: the registration took place in March 1940. By June, the NKVD had already started the deportations of families who registered to return to their former places of residence. See also glossary: registration.

485. Most likely refers to the area around Sukhoy Log, Sukholozhsky district [original Polish correction: Suchoj Łog].

looked after the children. When they got sick, it was due to frostbite on parts of their bodies, because they had to help the adults during work even in −35°C [−31°F]. After the Amnesty, we were released from the camp. The officials told us that the older people could stay in seniors' home [in] Tavda. Things were very good there, apparently. From Altynay, I went to Sucholcza by train.[486] I sold a few things there to buy myself a train ticket. Through Chelyabinsk I got to Orsk, where we slept in the station. I was robbed during the night. We set off [again] and went to Samarkand via Tashkent. Our situation was desperate. We slept on the street, didn't receive [any] bread, and [our] friends [had to] help us. I lived with Mrs. Skoczyl [part of text missing]. She got into a hospital in Samarkand as a nurse and [then] left. I fell ill with typhus but recovered thanks to the doctors' help. After [my] recovery, I received assistance from the Polish delegation. I worked in the hospital kitchen, then in an orphanage set up by Kwapiński.[487] Thanks to Delegate Milstein, I got a passport and left for Kermine. Three times I was crossed off the list. I got a job in an army kitchen. Kermine was called the valley of death. Thousands of people died there. I eventually got a job in a casino for officers. I managed to get on the list and went to Krasnovodsk. The journey on the ship to Pahlevi was awful. People died like flies from disease. We had no water. From Pahlevi we were sent to Tehran, and from there to Palestine.

486. Likely: Sukhoy Log.

487. Jan Kwapiński (1885–[1964]): PPS [Polska Partia Socjalistyczna; English: Polish Socialist Party; PSP] and union activist. See also note in Protocol 27.

Protocol 194

Testimony of **Roman Weiss**, age twenty-eight, resident of Rzeszów.

On the day the war broke out, I was with the 17th infantry regiment, taking part in maneuvers. We were given an order to march on Tarnów. We came upon the enemy outside Tarnów and, surrounded by the Germans after heavy fighting, attempted to pull away toward Tuchów. A new army consolidation took place there. A few hours later [we came upon] another German army column, equipped with heavy tanks. Under artillery fire, we retreated step-by-step from Wielopole, by Pilzno, as our commander had been hit by a grenade and some of the unit had been killed. I received a bad shotgun wound in my arm. Fellow [soldiers], passing by, laid me on an anti-tank cart [?] and drove me to the [field hospital]. We stopped in a field, one kilometer away from the German artillery. We were retreating in the direction of Krasne. The Germans bombed the [field hospital] in Zawistowo. Lieutenant Skalski, from Kraków, lost his mind right in front of me. We arrived in Przemyśl like this, being shot at from all sides. Soon afterward, the Germans took over the city. The hospital fell into German hands, and I didn't want to stay with [them]. I left the hospital despite my injury.

In the city, German terror reigned. The Gestapo picked up people in the streets, dragged them out of [their] homes, loaded them onto platforms, and took them out of town, supposedly for work. Six hundred Jews were killed outside the city one day. I decided to go back to Rzeszów. Going back on foot, I found signs of German savagery in every small town and every village. In Dynów, I passed by a village where the Gestapo had just murdered thirty people and were not allowing the women to approach the bodies. I heard a shot behind me and thought the bullet was intended for me, but [it was] a Gestapo officer shooting at a crowd of women, not letting them get to the bodies of their murdered husbands, fathers, and brothers. I neared my hometown with a pounding heart. My wounded arm had turned completely black [and] I turned to a Ukrainian doctor for help, [but he] refused.

The situation in our town was getting worse. I decided to go to Romania, where the Polish army was being formed. I hid in Przemyśl for some time and made it over to the other side one night. I made contact with smugglers. I found myself in Kuty, but was arrested when crossing the border. It turned out the smuggler was a police agent. I was put in a small cell with others [and] beaten terribly [as] they tried to force me to sign a protocol accusing me of preposterous things. I was then moved to Stanisławów, where sixty people were locked up in a tiny cell. We were sent to Żytomierz, via Lwów. It's difficult to describe how we were treated during the journey. We were sent to Kharkiv without a trial. During the journey, the cars were inspected all the time, and [we] were beaten during [these] inspection[s]. We got two buckets of water for sixty people. We traveled for a long time, all the way to Murmansk, to a prison camp where the worst criminals were. We were told to build barracks because four hundred [new] people had arrived. The next day, surrounded by guards and dogs, we were sent to work.

Those deported from Poland lived in complete harmony with each other—the Russians, on the other hand, treated us with hostility. Former Russian actors [?] watched us, taking their savage tendencies out on us. Diseases spread in a terrifying way. Thirty percent [of people] had dysentery and *cynga*. We couldn't complain to the NKVD about our criminal guards, as [the consequences could be] even death. When the Russian-German war broke out, we were sent to [the Autonomous Soviet Socialist Republic of] Komi. We met Eskimos [?] there.[488] We lived in tents. Our clothes were rotting on us.

We received the news about the Amnesty at that time. We were set free and given three options to choose from. We chose one—to go to Buzyluk,[489] to [join] the Polish army that was forming. During the journey, we could see the incredibly poor quality and destitution of Russian life, as well as the strong patriotism of [the country's] inhabitants. In a beautiful restaurant in Sverdlovsk, one could only get soup to eat. I fell ill with typhus in Buzyluk. When I recovered ten weeks later, I was told there was no more room in Buzyluk, that I had to go to Uzbekistan. In Tashkent, army registration was being postponed, and I was assigned to work in a kolkhoz. I worked for five months with the Uzbeks in a huge and prosperous kolkhoz, where nonetheless

---

488. The so-called peoples of the North consist of forty-one ethnic groups. Eskimo peoples (Yupik) occupied Chukchi Autonomous Region, which is located on the eastern coast of Siberia. The Komi are a Permian ethnic group, residing along the edges of European Russia. The author may have meant other indigenous people of Komi.

489. An incorrect name for Buzuluk [original Polish correction: Buzułuk].

it was difficult to get a piece of bread because of the poor administration and corruption of [its] officials. The Uzbeks hated the Russians and were awaiting [the arrival of] the Germans.

Hearing that new army divisions were forming, I reported to the commission and was classified as category E, unfit for duty, even though I referred to my injury and the September battles. My friends, young and strong Jews, were assigned to the same category. We were sent to kolkhozes. After some time I went in front of the commission [again] and received the E category again. They wanted to send me to Omsk. I decided to take things into my own hands [and] went to Wadewsk,[490] where groups leaving for Iran were being put together. We had to provide evidence that we had been under German occupation in September 1939. With difficulty, I got into a train going to Krasnovodsk. I was denounced at the Ashgabat station, and a Polish military policeman wanted to hand me over to the NKVD, but I managed to get away. In Krasnovodsk I barely managed to get onto a ship. I was caught during an inspection [and] went into hiding again. I thought I was safe. On the last day of the journey, when you could already see Pahlevi from afar, eleven of [my] traveling companions and I were handed over to the NKVD, who wanted to send us to Baku. We were set down onto a bank and sent to a Polish camp. We appealed again. We went in front of a commission. Out of thirty-two people, twenty-eight were deemed fit for army duty. Two months earlier, that same commission had assigned them to category E. I got a certificate in Persia, on the basis of which I came to Palestine.

490. Likely refers to Vadinsk [original Polish correction: Wadinsk].

Protocol 195

Testimony of **Izrael Wajner**, age thirteen, son of Józef and Chaia from Włodawa. Came to Palestine via Tehran in August 1943.

I don't remember the moment the war began. I only remember that there was a bombardment. Houses were on fire; we ran from one house to another, and it was said that many people died. Many people escaped from town but returned straightaway, saying it was even worse outside of town and even more dangerous. I remember when the Germans entered Włodawa. The Jews were very scared and hid in attics and in cellars and we children trembled with fear, holding onto our mother's skirt. When we cried, Mother told us to quiet down because the Germans might hear. Out on the street, the Germans were rounding up Jews for [forced] labor. [They] were beaten horribly during the work, had their beards ripped out, and some were beaten to death. One day an order was given [that] all Jews, men and women, had to gather in the cinema room. It was so crowded that many people fainted. The doors leading into the cinema were secured by German guard[s]. Everyone thought they would set the cinema on fire, but before evening, everyone was allowed to leave. People said that high-ranking officials were passing through town and that's why the Jews had been locked in the room, because the Germans were afraid of an assassination attempt.

After a few days, they started rounding up Jews again. This time it was only the men. They were all locked in the synagogue. Panic broke out in town. Mama was crying, and we children were too, because our father was among those captured, and it was said in town that the synagogue would be set on fire that night. Armed Germans surrounded the synagogue building. They wouldn't let the women come close; they shot into the air every now and again to scare off the crowd. The women waited until the evening and then went away, because Jews weren't allowed to be out in the streets [at night]. We didn't sleep a wink that night. Mama stood by the window and watched [to see] if the synagogue had already been set on fire. At dawn, Mama left with a basket of food and walked toward the synagogue. She was allowed to take the food over. All the women did the same. At noon, all the men were released. The Germans didn't stop tormenting Jews. Father was caught one day and taken to the bridge on the Bug [River]. The Jews were given gasoline and tar and told to set the bridge on fire.

The next day the Germans left, and the town was occupied by Russians. They stayed for eight days. The town was full of Russian military personnel [and] the soldiers bought out everything in the shops. Many Jews returned, and people expected that things would be peaceful now. All of a sudden, people learned that the Bolsheviks were leaving town, and were taking along those who wanted to come with them. People hurriedly packed [their] belongings into bundles and crossed the river, which was supposed to be the border. It was horribly crowded on the bridge. Some people were on foot, others rode on carts, and all the Jews crossed to the other side of the Bug [River] by the suburb of Włodawka, four kilometers from town. We decided to stay there to be close to home. Mama went [back and forth] into town and brought our things out little by little. All the Jews dealt in smuggling and earned good money. Day and night, without pause, people were going in both directions. The suburb was already so full of people that [they had to] sleep in the streets. A few months went by. Father worked, Mama traded, [and] we fared all right.

One day an order came out [saying that] everyone who lived within twenty-five kilometers of the city border had to move [farther inland]. At the same time, a registration bureau was opened for those who wanted to go to Russia. Since we had no relatives in Russia and the neighboring towns were full, Father registered to work in Russia. We went to Homel. Our family was made up of six people, [my] parents and four children. We were greeted with music and a feast and speeches at the station. Father got a job in a brickyard, but his earnings weren't enough to live on and we had to sell our things. We settled into a small room in a workers' house, where a thousand people were living. The taps were constantly broken, and Mama had to go a long way to get water. It was dirty [and] cramped. Father worked hard, and when he returned home he said he would not last long. Father had to work on Saturdays, and it bothered him a lot. They didn't want to excuse him from work. Father found a synagogue in Homel where old Jews prayed [and] went there for prayers from time to time. After four months of working in the brickyard Father decided to run away. The family was too big for us to be able to leave town together. Father was [supposed] to go to Ukraine and then write to us, and we were to go to [join] him. He went to Równe, where some of his friends lived, neighbors from town. He got a job as a painter and earned decent money. He rented a room and wanted to bring us there. Mother went to the NKVD, said that Father had abandoned us, that she couldn't manage with four children, and that she was asking for a permit to go to Ukraine where our relatives lived. She was told to submit an application. There was no answer. Mother went to the NKVD again, where she was told to submit an application for the second time. The response came a few months later: it had been decided that the children would be put in an orphanage, and that Mother was to go to work.

Without waiting, Mother escaped from town and went to Równe. We arrived there on Easter in the year 1940. It was a huge surprise for Father. We cried with joy. Father worked [and] Mama traded. It was like paradise compared to Homel. Already familiar with "Russian prosperity," Father didn't want to accept Soviet citizenship, but he didn't register to leave either. One Friday night, NKVD-ers arrived at our [place], told us to get dressed, and said we were going to German[-occupied] territory. We were taken to the station, loaded into freight cars, and the cars were sealed. Twenty-four hours later, we set off. The journey was long and horrible. It was cramped and dirty inside the car. We received a piece of bread each [and] weren't allowed out of the car. Many people were ill [and] we had no medical help. After three weeks' journey, we arrived in Chad.[491] From there we were taken to a forest, where there were five barracks intended for two thousand people. Filth, crowding, bedbugs, [and] mice made our life impossible. People worked in the forest, cutting down trees and burning branches. The forest was muddy, mosquitos bit people [so they] returned from work with swollen faces. We got six hundred grams of bread per day, [but] no one had money to buy soup in the canteen. Father, Mother, and [my] older sister worked in the forest, and I ran the household.

Everyone was unhappy and protested. One day the warden appeared and said that families with school-age children would be sent to a different *posiołek*. After a few days' journey, we reached the Sverdlovsk Oblast, where we worked digging a canal. In addition to six hundred grams of bread per day, we got twelve rubles per month. A pood of potatoes cost a hundred rubles. Anyone who didn't get to work on time had 25 percent of their wages taken away, and after three times, would be sentenced to jail. Everyone worked; only

491. Chad: town in central Ural [could not be located].

[my] brother and I went to school, where we were given watery soup. We spent ten months in this *posiołek*. Many people died. Father fell ill with rheumatism [but] had to work in spite of it.

After the outbreak of the German-Russian war, our situation got worse. We thought we wouldn't get out of there alive, [but then] the news of the Amnesty came. We went to Turkestan. There was nothing to eat on the way. We looked for food at the stations. We lost [my] brother one day, but he was found four days later. In Turkestan people slept in the streets and stole from one another. We were robbed too, so, realizing that we wouldn't get anywhere there, we went to a kolkhoz. We all worked in the field[s] and received four hundred grams of grain per day, until everyone fell ill. [My] brother and I were taken to the hospital. When we left the hospital, Father managed to place us in a Polish orphanage, where later on, my two sisters were [also] accepted. After four months, a group of children left, but we were left behind. We were sent to Ashgabat. They didn't want to bring my eighteen-year-old sister. They threatened to leave us behind in Russia for any small infraction. In the end, there were twenty [Jewish] children left to three hundred Polish ones. They suffered a lot. We were beaten, insulted, and humiliated at every step. After eight months, we were sent to Mashhad [and], from there, to Tehran and to Palestine. Three of us have arrived [there]; I've had no news of [my] older sister and [my] parents.

Protocol 196

Testimony of **Mosze Szrajber**, age thirteen, from Rozwadów, son of Pinchas and Leia. Came to Palestine via Russia and Tehran in February 1943.

Our town is located in the very middle of the COP. When the war broke out, there was panic in our town because people were afraid the Germans would bomb the COP as a priority, and that the town would suffer for it. On Friday morning, the Germans bombarded Stalowa Wola, the "central" point of the COP. Because Stalowa Wola is close to Rozwadów, two bombs fell on the town. Many houses were destroyed, and there were casualties. The residents left town and took cover in the woods. We, too, a family of four, escaped to the forest. We roamed the forest for a few weeks, moving from place to place. We bought food in the neighboring villages, but the villagers wouldn't let us stay in the countryside. They said that every time the Germans saw refugees gather in a village, they would bomb all homes mercilessly. When the Germans occupied the whole area, we returned home. We didn't recognize [our] town; many homes had been destroyed. The streets were covered in rubble. Some homes were still smoldering. Our home had burned down, along with all [our] possessions. We lodged in the apartment of a relative and his family. My father had been a bookkeeper in a watch shop before the war but was now without any income.

The persecution of Jews began. They were dragged out of homes and taken for hard labor, cleaning up the rubble and blowing up the remaining walls. Many Jews perished during this work. Outside of work, they were tormented, mocked, told to clean toilets with their bare hands, to clean the windows of German apartments with their own shirts and then put the wet shirt[s] on. During work, no difference was made between the old and the young. Once they caught a rabbi, cut his beard off, and told him to clean a latrine with his bare hands. Poles and Germans watched this work [being done] and they were all laughing out loud. The same was done to other members of the council.

After three weeks in town, the Germans issued an order that all the Jews had to leave town and get to the other side of the river within an hour. Terrible panic broke out. Those who were away from their homes had no time to go back for [their] belongings. Parents lost their children; the elderly and the sick were carried. And [this] crowd, made up of a few thousand people, young and old, women and children, set off toward the San [River]. Two boats were waiting there, each intended for twenty people. A hundred people got into [each]. Because the Germans standing on the bank were beating [people] with their gunstocks, everyone was pushing, and the Germans were laughing at the spectacle. But it was impossible to transport such a large number of people in one hour. The Germans threatened to shoot those who were left behind. A large boat was found somewhere for a huge sum of money, and everyone got across the river. When they were already on the other bank, the Germans opened fire. We started running away toward a village, but the peasants wouldn't let us in. We ran on ahead, careened around fields, our legs giving out under us. We bought a cart and a horse with another family and started off again.

One night some Ukrainians attacked us, beat us, took away the horse, the cart, and [our] belongings, and when Father started to chase the bandits driving away on the cart, we lost [him too]. We were left alone in the dark forest without Father, without [our] belongings, without money, and without food. All of the next day and night, we looked for Father in vain, and afraid of the Ukrainians, we carried on until we reached the town of Chołoszyce,[492] where we hoped to find Father. He was not there. [Some] good people gave [us] a place for the night, fed and comforted us, [saying] Father would come. The town was full of refugees. They were living in the beth hamidrash and the Talmud Torah.[493] Many slept in the streets. We decided to go to Lubaczów since we had relatives there. Our neighbors from Rozwadów said that Father had been killed by Ukrainians, but we didn't want to believe that. In Lubaczów, our relatives were very happy [to see] us but gave evasive answers regarding our Father's whereabouts. They said he had gone to Kowel or to Lwów. Mama didn't want to stay and went looking for Father. She went to Lwów by train. In Lwów, she got on a tram going to [her] friends' [place]. On the way, Father got on that same tram. Mama fainted. Father told [her] that he had come to Kowel looking for us, and having learned that we were in Lubaczów, planned to travel [there] via Lwów.

492. Likely refers to the town of Oleszyce by Lubaczów.

493. Jewish [elementary] school (see glossary).

The whole family set off for Lwów. Father started working but earned little; we lived mainly by standing for hours in line, buying things cheaply, and selling them on the black market. Since we had none of [our] belongings, Mama decided to go [back] home to get some of the things that were hidden with our Christian neighbors. She left but never returned. In vain did Father pay smugglers to bring her to Lwów. Unable to take care of [my] tiny two-year-old sister, when we had abandoned hope of seeing Mama [again], Father took [our] little sister to Sieniawa, where our grandma lived, and returned to Lwów himself. At that time, a commission began operating in Lwów to register those who wanted to go back to the German-occupied territories. Father was the first to register. One group of people indeed left, but the rest were left behind. It was said that the Bolsheviks would send those who registered to Siberia. One day in June, NKVD-ers came to us and told Father he could go home. Father asked the NKVD-ers to allow him to go into town so he could buy some [things] for the journey. He swore he would report to the station voluntarily. We got ourselves into a freight car in which there were fifty people. We were in good spirits, expecting that we would see Mama soon. But instead of a four-hour journey from Lwów to Rozwadów, we traveled for long days in a dirty, stuffy car, and understood [then] that we were going to Siberia. In Kiev, we were allowed to buy food. Then we traveled for eighteen days, until we reached Yoshkar-Ola, eight hundred kilometers from Moscow.

We were taken on carts into a forest, muddy and deep, where you could hear the howling of wild animals at night. The journey through the forest took three days. After arriving in the *posiołek*, we were offered two types of work: either cutting wood in the forest or digging a canal. Father chose the second. Anyone who fulfilled the quota received six hundred grams of bread and a hundred grams of sugar. At first only Father worked, but later I too was forced to chop branches, threatened with having [my] portion of bread taken away. We received letters from Mama and parcels and managed to survive the hard times somehow. The death of a Jewish officer in the Polish army, Flemin, who was killed by a falling tree during work, had a terrible effect on us. His son cut his wrists with a shaving knife after learning of [his] father's death but was saved. Our situation got worse with the outbreak of the [Russian-German] war. We lost contact with Mama [and our] relatives were no longer sending parcels. Our bread rations were decreased; we were rushed to work and had no time for a moment's rest.

We abandoned work on finding out about the Amnesty, even though the warden was very angry. We were supposed to go to Astrakhan. On the way, we were told that things were very bad in Astrakhan and we changed direction to go to Syzran, near Kazan. We traveled toward Kuybyshev and reached Samarkand. We lived by selling our belongings. Father fell ill with typhus, and when he got out of the hospital, we went to a kolkhoz. I got malaria and tuberculosis from working. Seeing that I would not last long, Father returned to town with me. He took up trading and earned decent money, but spent everything on the doctor and medicines for me. My illness cost us two thousand rubles. I had such an appetite after returning to health that I could eat three kilos of bread a day. I noticed that Father wouldn't allow himself a bite of bread and gave everything to me [instead]. Later Father fell ill with dysentery and we fared very badly. Eventually, Father managed to place me in an orphanage. I didn't want to leave him, but I understood that I was a burden to him. I was in the orphanage for only a month. When I found out about the transport out of Russia, I took clothes and blankets to him and left everything [else] at home. We cried a lot when saying goodbye. Father told me to be a good Jew and not to forget about him. From Samarkand, via Krasnovodsk and Pahlevi, I got to Tehran, and from there to Palestine.

Protocol 197

Testimony of **Danuta Warszawska**, age eighteen, a schoolgirl born in Warsaw.

The outbreak of the war caught me in Śląsk [Silesia], in Katowice. My parents, who lived in Warsaw, telephoned and asked me to come home. The train was full of refugees. They were all in good spirits; [people] had faith in a Polish victory and particularly in the defense of Warsaw. Soon waves of refugees began to come into the capital, and were directed to public buildings by the magistrate and charitable organizations. The capital only learned about the gravity of the situation from the statement by General Umiastowski on the radio and the order for men fit for army duty to leave the city.[494] Meanwhile, the bombardment[s] were getting heavier. The street[s] looked different. You [could] see wounded soldiers and troops returning from the front. One day the bombardment became unbearable and we learned about the siege of the capital. [Mayor] Starzyński appealed to the people to provide defenders to the city. Immediately the whole population reported to defend the city. [There were] small boys and seventy-year-old elders, Jews with beards and in gaberdines, as well as many workers.

For ten days the city was bombarded in the cruelest way, and blasted by cannon fire. On the street where I lived, only two houses were left intact. The Germans [planes] raked the streets with machine guns, flying very low. One day they started a particularly methodical destruction of the hospital where there were sick and wounded children. When the capital surrendered, we and our friends took flowers to decorate the graves of those who had fallen defending the city. Most of the graves were in garden squares. A German unit lodged in our home because the owner of [the house], as well as the bar located [there], was, as it turned out, a *Volksdeutsche*. We learned that the German soldiers were giving out bread. Hundreds of people who had not set eyes on bread for a long time threw themselves at the trucks. It wasn't more than tiny and scarce portions, but we did notice the Germans making

494. Roman Umiastowski (1893–1982): Colonel, [in] 1939 the director of propaganda in the staff of the Commander-in-Chief of the Polish army. On 6 September 1939, he put out a call over the radio for men capable of bearing arms to leave Warsaw.

a film about [how they were] giving out bread to the people of the capital. Soon, the reign of the Gestapo began. Men were picked up in the streets and many never returned home again. A yellow badge for Jews was introduced. German pilots were lodged in our apartments, blindly obedient to all Nazi orders. The introduction of a ghetto was ordered, but for now, people could move freely around the city. The ghetto was only closed off completely some time later. Policemen were posted at the ghetto's gates: a Jewish one, a Polish one, and a German one. Leaving the ghetto was punishable by death. The Jewish police were responsible for everything and suffered a lot of unpleasantness from the Germans. Two hundred grams of bread were given out [to last] two weeks. One kilo of smuggled bread cost five zlotys. Special German patrols drove around the ghetto every day, beating, and sometimes killing, Jews.

We escaped to Lwów in March 1941. I got into a carriage, into the part [reserved] for Germans. An older gentleman, a German, threw me out of the carriage. None of the passengers reacted. I got to Lwów after the period of deportations. You could get food in the city; my time in Lwów seemed to me like paradise after Warsaw's ghetto. However, the situation was worsening because of the Ukrainians' hostile attitude toward Poles. Just like the German-Polish war, soon the Russian-German [war] broke out, and the bombardment of the city began. The Ukrainians were carrying out a diversionary action in the city, shooting at the passersby from windows and roofs. The rail station, the Opera, Akademicka Street [and] the Mikolasz passage were bombed. We decided to run away farther. After many difficulties, we managed to get into a carriage where there were a hundred people. We traveled toward Kiev, and from there to Poltava. On the way we often saw German paratroopers dropping from airplanes. The local people would find and kill them. We spent eight days in Poltava. Life was going on completely normally there. We headed out toward Kuybyshev. The deeper [we went] into the country, the worse the situation became. The food ran out. In Kuybyshev, we came upon thousands of refugees. We lived in the station for two days, without food. We decided to carry on toward Tashkent. We spent six days on a train with Russian evacuees, who treated us very politely and shared everything. We fared all right in Tashkent—the wave of refugees had not yet arrived there. Despite this, we had no apartment and had to sleep in the station. It was difficult to get work and food. The local people treated us kindly at first, but then everything changed. We were met with resistance and hostility from the locals, there wasn't enough food, diseases decimated the refugees. The Polish army was being formed at the time, and my father was accepted into [it]. With no [further] adventures on the way, we were taken, Mama and I, with a transport to Tehran, and from there in Palestine.

Protocol 198

Testimony of **Sar [?] Cadok**, age thirty-two, resident of Lublin, son of Naftali and Bajla. Came to Palestine via Russia and Tehran in February 1943.

Lublin was already being bombarded on Saturday, the day after the outbreak of the war. The Germans focused the main attack on the ammunition factory, LWS, located close to the main square. Many people died as a result of that bombardment. When the factory caught fire, the workers left the industrial building in a rush. It was then that the German airplanes descended, and the escaping workers were fired on by machine guns. Few survived. The area looked like a cemetery.

Air raids happened every day. [It was] mainly the rail station that was bombed; the air raids lasted a whole week. People lived in shelters during that time. One squadron would leave the city, and another would arrive. There was no way of leaving the shelters; food products ran out in town, and we were starving. On Friday, 8 September [1939], the bombardment stopped. People went out into the streets [and] we thought this was the end [of it], but at eight in the morning on Saturday, eighteen airplanes flew in and dropped a huge number of bombs onto Lublin within fifteen minutes. The ground shook beneath [our] feet, houses collapsed one by one, fires broke out. We thought it would be better to go out into the streets because we were afraid the house would collapse and bury us inside the shelter. I too went out into the street. I could still hear the hum of the airplanes flying away. On Narutowicza [Street] where I lived, houses were in flames, the pavements were covered in a thick layer of broken glass, and even though the sun was shining, the streets were dark with smoke and soot. I ran to my sister and brother-in-law's apartment to see what they were doing. I found them in the shelter. [My] sister was holding her little child and didn't want to be separated from him. I thought she had lost her mind. My brother-in-law and I tried in vain [to get her] to leave the shelter. She didn't want to hear about moving. I left town on foot. I saw thousands of injured [people], overturned cars, [and] ripped-out telegraph poles on the way. Only then did I understand directly how enormous the destruction caused by the air raids had been. I considered which direction I should go. I was caught in a mass of people and all of a sudden found myself in a field. I was going toward Chełm. I returned to the road, which was jammed full with the army. We were often bombed on the way. During an alarm, people would disperse into the fields, looking for shelter in forests and ditches, and families would lose one another. Later people would be looking for one another, calling out, children getting underfoot, lost and crying. This lasted all day. By evening I found myself in the town of Piaski. I spent the night [there] and carried on toward Chełm, thinking that things would be better there. However Chełm had been bombed too. I found only men [there], as the women and children had been evacuated. I stayed in Chełm until 14 September. I survived a few bombardments in the first few days. Realizing that the situation was no better there than in Lublin, I made my way to Kowel. Normally this was a journey that took two hours. This time, interrupted by air raids, it took twenty-four hours. Airplanes came down low, bombing each car individually. There were many injured and dead, and the roofs of the cars looked like sieves.

Kowel. The city was overcome with gloom. The Polish army tried to get set up and resist the Germans. Meanwhile people learned about the Bolsheviks' entry into Poland, and on the twelfth,[495] the Polish army was disarmed by the Russians. The Russians behaved like guests at first. Jews weren't interrupted when praying on Yom Kippur, but people soon learned that the owner of a shoe warehouse had been arrested for not allowing shoes to be sold to soldiers on Yom Kippur. Soon arrests of factory owners, political activists, [and] landlords began, and interventions by the families of those arrested were in vain. I was living with the secretary of the Tarbut gymnasium and the city councilor, Jakob Kupsztyk. I rarely showed myself on the street. I could find out about everything [outside even while] staying at home. The Russians requisitioned the Tarbut school building [and] turned it into a hospital for soldiers but let Kupsztyk remain free for now. As I didn't want to be a burden on Kupsztyk's finances, I started to look for work. I'm a tailor by trade [and] I got a job with Beniamin Krell. We fared progressively worse. We were forced to join cooperatives. My supervisor delayed closing the workshop from one day to the next but had large taxes levied on him. They didn't want to sell him needles and thread [and] he was forced to close down the workshop, and he joined a cooperative with [his] son. Only people who owned their own machines were accepted there.

495. The Red Army entered the territory of the Republic of Poland on 17 September 1939.

Meanwhile, soldiers and officers bought everything they could. By chance, a Russian officer was billeted in my apartment. I read the officer's wife's letters to her friend in Russia. She wrote: "Get here quick, [it's a land of] milk [and honey], and the streets are paved with gold." Meanwhile, unemployment was growing, and the new masters opened up recruitment bureaus, registering volunteers for work. People were promised that they would work in their trade, but they were sent for unskilled labor into the depths of Russia. Horrifying letters arrived from those people, begging [their] friends not to make the same mistake. One day I met a well-known Lublin Communist in the street, Szlomo Stokfisz, who had been sentenced to five years in prison by the Polish authorities and escaped to Russia after serving the sentence. He confided in me that he had come there illegally and wanted to return to Lublin. At that time, the first groups of peasants coming in from Russia arrived in Kowel. They had been brought in to form kolkhozes there. They would run away back to Russia, and they organized demonstrations in Mińsk demanding to be sent back home. Many were arrested; they roamed the streets.

All of this took place after Easter. Then a German commission arrived that was registering those who wished to return home. Thousands of Jews waited in line. Only one transport left for Poland. On 16 June [1940], news spread that the NKVD was arresting those who had registered. My friends were among them: Eng. Kuterman and Weisman from Warsaw, Selin from Lublin, and others. I expected to be arrested any day. I didn't sleep at home [but] roamed the streets [instead]. One day I heard that they were arresting [people in the streets]. I tried to get out of town. We hid in a barn, but a few moments later, we noticed a Ukrainian peasant leading a few NKVD-ers [over]. We were arrested and taken to the building of an elementary school that had been turned into a prison. I spent [part of text missing] days in prison without food. I received parcels from friends on the outside. Then we were photographed, taken to the station, and sent off. We traveled toward Kiev. The police guarded us at first, then, after a thorough search, the NKVD took custody of us. The NKVD-ers wanted to take away the old newspapers we were using to roll cigarettes. They didn't want to leave me [any]. I resisted when they tried to take away my watch, but had to give it up at another station. It was dirty and stuffy inside the car; they didn't want to open the doors for us. People fainted. After eight days' journey we arrived at the Kotlas station. We were taken to a river and went to Ukhta. The barge was crowded [and] we lay on top of each other. Everyone was hungry; we received three hundred grams of rusks and three herrings per day. There wasn't enough water to drink.

From the barge, we were taken to an assembly point where there were two thousand people, Poles and Jews. We were split into groups and sent off in different directions. I was taken toward Barkutta Kazwa, close to the White Sea.[496] We walked all day—the swamps were waist-deep—until we reached our destination. At a certain point the men were ordered to say goodbye to their families. The women were in hysterics, the men threw themselves on the NKVD-ers. It was all in vain. The men were taken seventy-eight kilometers from Ukhta. There they were left in a primeval forest where no man had been before. We were told: "Here you'll live and here you'll die." [Our] living hell began. We slept outdoors, on top of branches, without anything to cover [ourselves with]. Mosquitos ate us alive, as did lice, and mice jumped over our tired bodies at night. Things got worse when the rainy season came. We slept in the mud and had to go to work in the morning. There were no set quotas; we were [simply] rushed around all the time. After five months, it was announced that each of us was sentenced to five years in a labor camp; those who had stated that their parents were workers got only three years. In our group, 160 people weren't given a sentence, and we didn't know if this was a reward or a punishment.

I suffered in that forest until April 1941. Through all that time, we never knew what a barracks was. We dug pits in the ground and lived in [them]. We lived on small portion[s] of bread [and never] saw a cooked meal. In the evenings, we lit a fire and heated water. Haircutting and shaving were out of the question; we looked like animals. At the beginning of April, the 160 people who had never received a sentence were sent to Kazba, where there were still heavy frosts in April.[497] But we lived in barracks, there were stoves, and I washed myself for the first time in many months. I spent three months there, then we were sent to Kniaź Pagaz, to the central camp administration.[498] There I met another two hundred people from our transport who hadn't been given a sentence. The regime was lighter there. People were building a

496. Route Kozhva–Vorkuta.

497. Likely refers to Kozhva [original Polish correction: Koźwa].

498. Likely: Knyazhpogost [original Polish correction: Kniażpogost].

road and working in the forest. We got hot soup and slept on bunks. Later a few of us, only Poles, were released from the camp and sent to the capital of [the Autonomous Soviet Socialist Republic of] Komi. After some time I was moved again, from the camp to a sovkhoz, where I worked in a field. Things were much better there than in the camp.

I stayed in the sovkhoz until the announcement of the Amnesty. We were all sent from the sovkhoz to Kotlas. We were put in a camp for Polish prisoners of war. We thought we were free then, but the commandant forced us to work, for which we received only 270 grams of bread per day. We called a hunger strike; NKVD-ers came, and we were promised an improvement to our food provision. On 1 September, the first snow fell, and we received the coveted documents then and set off for Tacko.[499] We passed by a village inhabited entirely by [people] evacuated from Lithuania. I met a few [old] companions who told me that out of the five hundred camp residents, only two hundred were still alive. From Tacko, via Krasnodar[500] and Pahlevi, I was sent to Tehran, and from there to Palestine.

499. Should be: Totskoye [original Polish correction: Tockoje].
500. Most likely refers to Krasnovodsk.

Protocol 199

Testimony of **Julian Abramowicz**, age forty-six, from Łódź. Came to Palestine via Russia and Tehran along with [his] wife, Maria, and son, Ignacy, in September 1943.

Łódź was bombed on the second day of the war. The alarm lasted one hour, from ten until eleven o'clock. The Germans wanted to set the city on fire [and] particularly focused on areas where there were gasworks, waterworks, the new army hospital, and barracks. One bomb fell on 4 Bandurskiego Street, onto a house that belonged to Jehoszua Landad [Landau?]. In that house lived Mosze Wojdysławski, the director of a trade loan bank—a bank where I was a manager. Luckily he was at a holiday resort with his family and thus avoided certain death, because the bomb destroyed the apartment. A house next door caught fire too, at 6 Bandurskiego [Street]. I lived nearby, and when things calmed down a bit, I went to see what damage the bombardment had caused. My family was staying in Śródborów, at a summer resort. On Monday 4 September [1939], I got into my car with a small suitcase and went to see my family, to bring them to Łódź. The apartment was left in the care of my seventy-five-year-old mother. On the way to Warsaw, I came across a lot of army troops; the roads were being bombarded, but I hurried on to make it to Śródborów as quickly as possible. I got to Śródborów on Tuesday morning. There was panic [in town]. Everyone was shaken by the terrible bombardment the Germans had carried out on the TOZ building.[501] I planned to return to Łódź, but my brother-in-law, Mieczysław Pinczewski, advised me against going back home. The everyday situation was getting worse. Explosions were heard [coming] from Warsaw [and] everyone was called up to defend the capital. My car was requisitioned, and I set off for Lublin in [my] brother-in-law's car. It was difficult to get through [with] the road full of pedestrians and carts. At times, the sky darkened with airplanes flying down low and shooting at people. We looked for shelter in ditches, in fields, and in forests. It was dangerous in the field[s]—the Germans would shoot at peasants harvesting grain. On the way,

501. TOZ: [Polish: Towarzystwo Ochrony Zdrowia Ludności Żydowskiej; Society for the Protection of the Health of the Jewish Population]. Active in Poland from 1921 to 1942, and after the war until 1950.

we came upon a cart on which the president of the Jewish council of Łódź, an MP, Lejb Mincberg, was riding.[502] He was terribly distraught. We couldn't help him as our car was full [but] took his wife [with us] and dropped her off in Lublin. We ran out of gasoline on the way. It was on the road to Pińsk, where my sister and other relatives lived. We continued toward Pińsk on foot. We managed to get a cart after some time and got to Pińsk this way. We came upon many refugees there. The town had been bombed many times. One bomb had fallen onto an Orthodox church, another one onto a restaurant filled with patrons.

In Pińsk I met the factory owner Frajberg, from Łódź, the architect Landau, co-owner of Grand-Hotel, [and] the industrialist Mandeltort. They were all roaming around, homeless, and envied me for having a place to sleep with [my] relatives. People didn't know what to do with themselves—some said that Russia would rush in to help Poland, others talked about a new partition of Poland. On 12 September [1939], an order was issued that all refugees must leave town, and men must report to a draft committee. But the draft committee was no longer operating. We decided to get farther away, toward Northern Galicia. I had a kidney attack during the journey in the town of Płotnica, and after two days' stay in a clinic, we set off toward Dawidgródek. There I met the banker Rafał Szereszewski, Wolf Heller, Sztilerman, and others. In Dawidgródek, I lived with the brothers Rymarz, owners of a huge sawmill.

The town was taken over by the Russian army a few days later. [People] didn't know what was going to happen next. The Polish zloty stopped being accepted, and all the refugees were left without money to survive. I remember when the local chemist gave my brother cotton for free [but] wouldn't accept zlotys. The Soviet soldiers were friendly toward the people, and took children [for rides] on the trucks. They told stories about the prosperity of Soviet Russia, but no one believed them. A sixteen-year-old boy, Pilczyk, became the town's chief [mayor]; his father, a wealthy man, had a heart attack from grief.[503] We prepared to journey on. We looked for a cart, and in the meantime, learned that our friends from Warsaw had already left the city. I got a cart after many attempts and planned to go to Łódź to take my elderly mother out of

---

502. Lejb Mincberg: MP in December 1922, from the Parliamentary Club of the Organization of Orthodox Jews.

503. [Likely the father was ashamed of his son, who was cooperating with the Russian occupiers.]

there. Realizing that I would not make it to Łódź, I decided to go to Białystok, where many of my friends had gone.

Białystok was, at the time, a hub for the escapees from the German occupation. More than a hundred thousand refugees roamed the streets, left without even a roof over their heads. [And] this wasn't even the final total. I got a room in [the apartment of] the wife of a major, the former director of the Agricultural Bank, Szwejkowski. I had left Łódź without [any] belongings or money, thinking I would manage to return home. I was living off what my brother-in-law gave me. Not wanting to become a burden to him, I started to look for work, but couldn't get [any] since I didn't want to work in a registered organization. During my stay, a branch of the Bank of Poland operated in Białystok with eight Polish clerks, who ran the bank's affairs. Clerk Guszec had signature authority, but he had a commissar above him. Having no other work, I signed up as an honorary associate for the dissolution of the bank, which took place in the following way. All the assets and liabilities were transferred to the Russian Gosbank, a branch of which was opened in Białystok.[504] The same was done with other banks. In the Russian Gosbank there were people working who had no qualifications, but who were loyal to the Party. When the compulsory passportization began, the eight clerks from the Bank of Poland ran away to Warsaw. I didn't show my face at the bank again. At that time, the registration to return to Poland began. I registered to return to Łódź to bring back [my] elderly mother, [since] I was her only son. When I returned home and told my wife that I had registered to go back to Łódź, she burst into tears, because she knew it meant deportation to Siberia. I registered for a second time despite this. The last date for issuing Russian passports fell on 10 April 1940. I decided to leave Białystok and go to Lwów before [then]. In order to leave one needed a permit, which cost a few hundred rubles. [My] wife sold [her] only ring for ten thousand rubles, of which we spent 1,500 on the journey to Lwów. It was difficult to get an apartment in Lwów; moreover, there was a panic [in the city] because of the mass deportations to Siberia of people without their families. The passport issue wasn't as pressing there as it had been in Białystok. In Lwów, I ran into an acquaintance of mine, industrialist Marcel Kochański, [as well as] Dr. Maiblum, a Pole, and Gutman from

504. Gosbank: National bank of the USSR.

Będzin. We lived off the money left over from the sale of the ring. I didn't look for work. There, too, registration began [and] I rushed to register.

On 24 June 1940, at four in the morning, NKVD-ers knocked on our [door], told us to pack [our] belongings, took us to the station, loaded us into freight cars, and after thirty-six hours, during which we were given neither water nor bread, we set off. It was cramped inside the car; the children [took up] the only [available] bunk. The sanitary conditions were atrocious. The toilet [situation] was the worst, [but] we soon got used to [these] animallike living conditions. Also traveling in our car were Godlewski and his wife, and the elderly mother of a Warsaw rabbi, and Mrs. Zamaniewska—apart from that, only [ordinary] Jews. The journey took two weeks. It was three days before we received [our] first meal. At the station of Pastavy, the train cars were opened, [and] we were taken to a canteen under convoy and given tea with bread. I will never forget the sight of the famished people, practically the social elite of Poland, throwing themselves frantically on the food. We were taken back to the wagon later and sealed in.

We arrived at the station of Saszwa,[505] in the Sverdlovsk district in the Ural. We were driven on carts through a virgin forest, where no human had set foot before. Mosquitos bit us terribly. We arrived at the *posiołek* Teszma,[506] located twenty-two kilometers from Saszwa. We were accommodated in small houses surrounding the camp, where Russian exiles [lived]. We went to work together. Apart from the Russian exiles, there were [some] completely demoralized individuals there, sentenced to indefinite exile—there were members of the intelligentsia among them, too. One of them asked me for a handkerchief. He was an archaeology professor, who, incidentally, told me his story: "I was never involved in politics; I was only interested in my profession and my family. I don't know what I was sentenced and deported for. The troika[507] deported me; they did not listen to the defense of [either] the accused or the lawyer. They only listen to the sentence [being read out]. I was sentenced to fifteen years in exile without the right of [correspondence?] for more than twenty-five years. [*sic*] A war will break out [and] Russia will follow the Germans [afterward]."

505. An erroneous name for Sosva [original Polish correction: Sośwa].

506. Correct name: Tesma [Teśma].

507. Normally, the sentences of prisoners of the NKVD were passed summarily and signed by three NKVD officers.

Other deportees envied us our fortunate past; they were full of hatred toward the regime [but] undecided about which was better: Hitlerism or Bolshevism. I worked in the forest cutting down trees. Once a tree fell and a man named Better, from Katowice, met his end under it. I got a job as a postman because I knew the Russian language. I walked twenty-five kilometers, to Saszwa and back, carrying letters, money, and parcels from relatives. There was an outbreak of glanders[508] in the area and horses from Saszwa weren't allowed to come to the *posiołek*. There was a neutral zone between the town and the *posiołek*, two kilometers wide. I had to carry the parcels to the other side of the strip. This work was life-threatening, because the local people often attacked the postman, and after robbing him, would kill him. I had an entire sled full of parcels taken away from me once, but I knew that the recipients would confirm [their] delivery for fear of reprisals. I was sure that the commandant would hold me responsible, and this was punishable by fifteen years in prison. Luckily the sled was found the next day. After four months of work, my job was changed. I was assigned to burn the corpses of dead horses. It was a lousy job. The stench was unbearable. Luckily I was moved to the construction of a railway line. I had to walk seventeen kilometers on foot to [get to] work, cut down trees for the rail ties, build embankments, lay down the ties and the rails on top of them. Later I became a waste collector. I fertilized the potato fields. The road from the stables to the field was very difficult. The worst thing was that we had to push the wagon ourselves. I then worked burning branches [and] clearing tree stumps, which was very hard as the ground was frozen. The assembly began at seven in the morning [and] the work went on until seven-thirty [in the evening]. We didn't actually know what our quotas were. One day, in a −45°C [−49°F] frost, we quit work at six in the evening. We came across a controller from the NKVD on the way, who told us that this wasn't Jewish Palestine or imperial Poland, where one worked by the hour.

There was a doctor in the *posiołek* who wasn't allowed to treat patients. He didn't have tools or medicines anyway. He sent me to a doctors' commission, but it didn't achieve much. Generally speaking, we were treated badly. Bread often ran out. We were given a kilo each per day at first, then the rations were lowered to four hundred grams. Even pregnant women worked. There

508. [An infectious disease that occurs primarily in horses.]

was no solidarity among the deportees, one would denounce the other. I was working in the forest as a fire lookout at that time. The shift was twenty-four hours long [and] I would be held responsible [if a fire broke out]. With me were the director of the Universal Bank of Warsaw, Władysław Błoński, Eng. Litowicz, Jakub Katz, from Tarnów, Maurycy Beryl, from Kraków, Marysia Norymberska, from Będzin, and Nirenberg from Łódź. After receiving the appropriate documents, and a fourteen-month-long stay in the *posiołek,* I set off for Kokand in Uzbekistan with [my] family. We had to have a lot of money for the journey. Fortunately, on the eve of [our] departure, I received two parcels that my cousin, Philip Hau, had sent over from America. They arrived via Lwów. We rented a wagon together with the [money made from] selling the items and set off. We wandered around the streets of Kokand for two weeks until we found a place for the night. After some time, the NKVD-ers sent us to a kolkhoz, [but] they didn't want to take us in there. We traveled back through the same town to a different kolkhoz, and on the way, slipped away from the NKVD-ers. My boy fell ill with smallpox and pneumonia but soon recovered. In September 1941 a Polish delegation was opened, with Mr. Dobosz at its helm. I became a member of a citizens' committee and worked until March. In March, we were ordered to report to a Polish-Soviet military committee in Margilan. Before I got there, the committee moved to Tashlak. I was accepted into the army, and since our transport was to go to Kokand, I sent a telegram to [my] wife and son [asking them] to wait for me at the station. Together we went to Krasnovodsk, and via Pahlevi, to Tehran. In Tehran, [my] wife fell ill with typhus and was in a hospital for three months. We had to remove the gold crowns from our teeth and sell them to save her life. Later on, I got a job at the Imperial Bank, where I worked until December 1943.

Protocol 200

Testimony of **Mosze Sznajder**, age thirteen, son of Jakub and Perla from Tomaszów Lubelski. Came to Palestine via Russia in February 1943.

My father was a shochet. We had our own little house. There were five of us children. We were all studying [at school] and didn't lack for anything. I went to a cheder until the outbreak of the war. On the day the war broke out, chaos took over the town. People were running to and fro, not knowing what to do. The rabbi was so upset that he sent us home from the cheder. On Sunday, as always, I went to the cheder. Only a few of [my] friends were [there]. In spite of this, teaching was taking place [as usual]. Suddenly, horrible crashing sounds rang out. We couldn't tell what it was, but after a moment, we noticed that the ceiling over our heads was on fire. The teacher opened the window and told us to jump out, one after another. We wanted to run home, but the rabbi wouldn't let us because the sky was already black with German airplanes dropping bombs. He gathered us and took us to a brick house, where the shelter was.

That day our home, along with all [our] possessions, burned. The fire was burning as I returned home. Mother was standing there and crying; Father didn't say anything, he just gathered us together, and happy to have all the children with him, put us on a cart and drove to a village outside the town. Father said: since we have no home anyway, why risk our lives living in a town under bombardment. It's better if we hide in the country where it is less dangerous. We settled in a peasant's barn. He set up a little fire pit for Mama out of a few bricks, where she cooked potatoes. Later, we moved to another home and were living decently, not [hearing] anything about German airplanes. Since there were still many Jews left in town without a shochet, they sent for Father. The holiday of Rosh Hashanah [14–15 September 1939] was approaching. Mama wouldn't allow Father to go into town alone. We went back as a family on the eve of the holidays and lodged with [our] relatives. The Germans arrived the next day. We received the news of this [while] at the synagogue. Everyone took great fright. But the prayer [service] had finished, and everyone ran home as quickly as possible. The next day, the Germans set fire to the beth hamidrash and the synagogue, [and] Jews were afraid to go out into the streets.

During the Germans' two-week-long stay in our town, there were manhunts on [the] streets every day. Jews had their beards cut off, they were tormented and forced to do the dirtiest work. Some didn't return from [this] work and [no one knows] what happened to them. Father hid in the attic and wouldn't leave his hiding place. The Germans robbed all the market stalls, taking the more valuable things for themselves and giving the cheaper ones away to the gang of hoodlums who always accompanied them. All of a sudden, we heard that the Germans were leaving town, and this did indeed happen, but for two days there was no one in charge.

On the first day of Sukkot [28 September 1939] the Russian tanks [finally] pulled into town. The Jews breathed a sigh a relief. They left their hiding places [and] returned to their homes. The Russians bought everything that hadn't been stolen from the market stalls. We thought they would stay there until the end of the war, but we learned after eight days that the Russians were leaving town and the Germans were coming back for good. People didn't want to believe it until a notice was put up in front of the magistrate's office [saying] that any civilians who wished to leave town could accompany the Russians. Many Jews left town. Our family too left Tomaszów. We traveled on a truck for a few hours, then got on a train, and after a day's journey arrived in Rawa Ruska. The city was full of refugees. We slept in a dirty and crowded beth hamidrash at first, but then moved in with a shochet we knew, who rented us a tiny room. Mama took up trading, and Father went from village to village and slaughtered cattle according to kosher law for the local Jews. That meat was then brought into town. Father was warned a few times that if he was found performing ritual slaughter he would be sent to Siberia. Mama asked Father to give up his work, but since Mama's earnings weren't enough to live on, Father continued to work as a shochet. One day, Father was caught in a slaughterhouse [and] arrested; the calves were confiscated, but Father managed to bribe the guard on the way to the police station. Father gave his word that he wouldn't risk his life anymore.

Even though he stopped being a butcher he was still under police surveillance. This hindered Mother's trading, as there were constant searches of our home. We were faring very badly, and Mama [had to sell our] belongings. During the registration, Father still [part of text missing]. A few weeks later, on a Friday, NKVD-ers knocked on [our door], told us to pack [our] belongings, and took us to the station. We came upon thousands of refugees there. We were loaded into freight cars, forty-five people in each, and the cars were sealed. We waited in the station all day and night, without bread or water, before setting off. At first we thought they were taking us home, and Father calculated that we would be there in five to six hours. But when the night went by and [the next] day and we still hadn't gotten off, we realized that we were going to Siberia. We traveled for a few weeks. We were fed bread and watery soup, which Father wouldn't touch. It was cramped inside the car; people were lying on top of one another. Many people were sick. We thought the journey would never end.

Finally the train stopped in a thick forest. It was the Altai Krai, Troitsky area. We got off the car [and] were loaded onto carts. We traveled through a thick forest where there was no road. This journey took all night and all day, until we got to forest station number [part of text missing]. We were put in barracks, two hundred people in [each]. We all had to go to work. At first the workers received a kilo of bread each per day, and the nonworkers half a kilo. In our family, Father, Mother, and my eldest brother worked. We got five kilos of bread. Later these portions were decreased, [and] besides, Father could never fulfill [his] quota. It was easier in the summer because the children picked berries and mushrooms. But in the winter, you couldn't leave the barracks. Father and Mother got up at sunrise [and] returned at sunset, working at a site a few kilometers from the barracks. Many people died. After work, Father carried out the duties of undertaker and rabbi, along with a few [other] Jews. Thus a small cemetery came to be, which we surrounded with a wooden fence. The *posiołek*'s commandant bullied us, particularly Father, because he didn't want to work on Saturdays. Father wasn't afraid of the commandant's threat[s], even though he constantly heard that he would never get out of the *posiołek*.

When the [German-Soviet] war broke out, the NKVD leader came and delivered a speech to us, [saying] we should work together [against] the common enemy. [Our] situation got a lot worse immediately. [My] parents worked for fourteen hours a day, the supply of parcels from Poland stopped, and we were staring starvation in the face. We thought we would all perish; then the news of the Amnesty came. We bought tickets with the money from selling [our] last shirt and went to Samarkand. The journey was long and hard. People were ill with dysentery. The train would often stop on the way. [My] brother would get off the train, run to the village [and] bring back rutabagas and cabbage, and this is what we ate. In Samarkand we found thousands of refugees roaming the streets. We spent eight days in the station, unable to find a place for the night. We waited in lines and sold the products we obtained [this way] on the black market. Then we all fell ill with typhus and all recovered in a hospital. However, Father got pneumonia, didn't recover from it, and died. Mama put us, the four [younger] children, in an orphanage [while our] eldest brother stayed with [her]. We spent a few weeks in the orphanage, and from there we went to Krasnovodsk and Pahlevi. From Pahlevi, after a few months' stay in Tehran, I came to Palestine.

Protocol 201

Testimony of **Aron Glikman** from Warsaw, age thirty-three, son of Abraham and Fajga. Came to Palestine via Russia and Tehran in October 1943.

I was mobilized on 29 August 1939. I was assigned to the First Regiment, stationed in Warsaw, to the anti-aircraft division. Our division was stationed in Rembertów. In the early hours of 1 September, the first air raid on Warsaw took place, and we were engaged [to operate] the anti-aircraft cannons. The soldiers were in good spirits; we all thought that we could cope with the enemy. Our mood was soured by the fact that the officers were completely lost when it came to their tasks. They were reservist officers, mobilized a few hours earlier, who didn't know what to do with themselves. Our division held out until 10 September, until the moment when the order came to retreat to Mińsk Mazowiecki, where the Seventh Cavalry Regiment was. We abandoned our positions at night, quietly. A few hours later, we found ourselves in Mińsk Mazowiecki but found no lancers regiment there. Many of our [men] fell during air raids, which came one after another, and we were ordered to retreat toward Warsaw the following day. From Mińsk we went to Latowic [Latowicz] and Garwolin. On the way, we engaged in a few regular battles. The Germans were approaching from the direction of Kałuszyn, destroying all the small towns on the way and burning down villages. A group of soldiers joined us from the Seventh Regiment of lancers, which had been broken up after the defense of Kałuszyn. They told [us] it was difficult to hold back the Germans' advance. Everyone panicked. We had no contact with headquarters. We dragged ourselves toward Stoczek Łukowski, and after four hours, an officer gathered us together near Siedlce, where we attempted to fight the Germans. It wasn't a regular army, but reinforced front-line units. Warsaw was besieged from all sides by then. We couldn't storm into the city as a group, so we ran in disarray, leaving the initiative to each individual man. I made it across the Wisła [River] by myself and ran to see what was going on with my family. It was on 22 [September 1939], before the holiday of Yom Kippur. I didn't find anyone at home. The neighborhood of Nalewki was completely destroyed. Air raid followed air raid. The Jewish district was in flames. On Yom Kippur [23 September 1939], the sky over Warsaw was on fire. Houses collapsed and hundreds of unfortunates perished under the rubble. I ran around the streets like a madman, looking in vain for my mama, wife, and child. In the morning, I found my family in an unfamiliar apartment at 14 Twarda [Street], but before I [even] said hello to my child, an air raid began. The airplanes flew down very low over the neighborhood where I was. One bomb hit the right wing [of the house] and all the residents were buried in the rubble. Fortunately we were in the left-hand annex. I threw my child onto my back, grabbed [my] mother with one hand and [my] wife with the other, and ran out into the street. When I found myself on the street, another bomb hit our apartment and killed all those who were there.

I roamed the devastated streets with [my] family by my side, hoping to reach Mokotów. This journey took [us] three days. Air raids were repeated every moment, and what the bombs didn't manage to destroy, the shrapnel finished. We spent two horrific days in Mokotów, until the surrender of the capital. A few days later, with a few Zionist comrades from the party of Grynbaum,[509] I—like everyone else—started digging out the bodies from under the rubble and burying them. You had to have a permit to do it. I turned to the temporary commissar for the neighborhood of Mokotów at the time, Hans Krigherz, who refused to issue this certificate to me, a Jew. We carried out our sad work despite this, illegally. I got a certificate from the local police commissioner. I pulled thousands of dead Jews from under the rubble and buried them in the fields of Mokotów, since moving [them] to the cemetery was impossible. From one basement we pulled out a whole family who had been killed. Later, we drove the dead to the Warsaw cemetery, where there were five thousand bodies waiting to be buried in common graves, three or four hundred in each. The Germans threatened to burn the bodies if the work wasn't completed in time. After a few days, manhunts began on the streets, beards were ripped out, [people were] ordered to clean latrines with their bare hands, to beat each other, [and] to sing religious songs. It was impossible to get bread. Jews were kicked out of line and beaten. I went to the countryside with a Christian neighbor and brought food products to Warsaw. The prices were very high. The villagers were reluctant to sell. I pretended I wasn't a Jew. For two weeks I was involved

509. Icchak (Izaak) Grünbaum (1879–1970): Zionist activist, MP of the Republic of Poland in the years 1919–33, leader of the Al ha-Miszmar [Mishmar] faction, member of the World Zionist Organization Executive.

in smuggling foodstuffs into Warsaw. Then, I got a job in Węgloblok [coal depot]. I had been in contact with that company before the war, and thanks to this, got a permit to trade in coal, as I had before the war. I was the only Jew among the six hundred Polish deliverymen. One day my Christian cart driver got into a fight with another driver, also a Christian. The man who had been beaten came to me with a German military policeman and said I had beaten him for being a *Volksdeutsche*. I hid, and when the policemen left, decided to leave Warsaw immediately.

I went to Siedlce by train, from there to Mordy, crossed the Bug [River] to the Russian side and went to Białystok by train from Siemiatycze. Białystok was full of refugees. I couldn't find a place for the night. One would stand for hours in front of soup kitchens to get soup. I arrived in the city without a penny to my name and started to look for work. I found it a few days later in the local slaughterhouse. I couldn't stay long in that establishment because they demanded a detailed résumé from each worker. As I was afraid to tell the truth about my Zionist beliefs and I could not lie—because there were a few Bund members working in the slaughterhouse who knew me from Warsaw—I had to leave the position. I went to Wilno. The Bolsheviks stopped me at the border. Along with me they also stopped the lawyer Trepman, [his] wife, and a group of HeHalutz members.[510] During the interrogation, I stated that I came from Wilno, the HeHalutz members said the same, and after eight days in jail, we were set free. Trepman and his wife were taken to a prison in Lida. On the Lithuanian side, the Lithuanians stopped us—they were easily bribed.

After five days in Wilno, it was decided during a meeting of our party group that I would be sent to Lida to bring back [some people who had been] freed, the lawyer, Trepman, and [his] wife, as well as Mrs. Rakowicka. I prepared for the journey and crossed the border on 5 January. Six kilometers into Soviet territory, the Bolsheviks captured me and I was taken to prison along with two Polish officers, Glaszewicki and Pilecek. We were accused of being partisans and of carrying out espionage. A map of the border area was found on one of the officers. I didn't confess to anything, even though the investigating magistrate, Szerman, badgered me with questions. Seeing that I wasn't confessing

510. HeHalutz: Zionist movement whose aim was the practical implementation of Jewish settlement, primarily agricultural, in Palestine. See also the glossary.

to anything, they called in two Russian soldiers, who beat me terribly. [After I was beaten up,] they started asking me [questions] again. Having no more strength, and afraid that they would beat me to death, I confessed to belonging to the Zionist organization and firmly denied all the other accusations. This was enough for the judge. Zionism was considered counterrevolution, and I was taken to a cell. On the way, I got frostbite on my right leg, and have suffered from it ever since. At the other branch they started examining me again, and I wasn't spared [another] beating. I got kidney damage from the beating. On 11 January, I was deposited in a prison in Oszmiany, in a cell intended for eighteen people; ninety-seven were in it at the time. You could neither stand nor sit. [People] would lie on top of each other. The regime was cruel. We got six hundred grams of bread to eat, and three times a day, ten liters of water for the entire cell. I was exhausted [and] plagued by a fever. The kidney attacks recurred, my frostbitten leg was causing me pain. I couldn't stand up. It was only thanks to a [man by the name of] Szapiro, from Oszmiany, who had various medicines with him, that I survived those awful days. I was howling in pain like a wounded animal, but they wouldn't admit me to a hospital. When I lost consciousness, I was taken to a cell for people who had been sentenced to death. There were five Poles there and I was the only Jew. The Poles' names were as follows: Piotr and Jan Wysocki, landowners from the area; Waryfaj, a National Democracy leader, also a landed citizen; and the former chief of the tax office, Sznajder. Half an hour [after] I was brought to the cell and regained consciousness, the young[er] Wysocki came in. He was returning from the punishment cell, where he had spent three weeks. He was so exhausted and hungry that he ate a piece of soap that was in the cell. The [tax office] chief, Sznajder, was accused of having burned a hundred thousand zlotys from the office safe.

The Poles treated me well. They had their own medicines that they loaned to me, they bandaged my leg, and thus I came to feel all right again. The Poles were taken out of the cell a few days later, and I didn't see them again. I spent nine months in that prison, moving from one cell to another. In one cell I was with sixteen [other] Jews. With me there was the shochet Gurewicz, who had crossed the border to slaughter a calf in a neighboring village, was arrested for it, and was accused of counterrevolution. He lived off only bread and water, as the food was nonkosher; and throughout all of the holiday of

Pesach [23–30 April 1940] would eat only three spoonfuls of sugar a day that he got from the Poles, giving them bread in exchange. Before Easter a new victim was brought into our cell. He was the head of the yeshiva in Oszmiany, Szalom Kiewer. It was said that this was his assumed surname. He had been arrested for teaching illegally. We gathered for prayer on the eve of Pesach, but the Poles started to harass us, shouting that they didn't want to have a synagogue there. A brawl broke out. Sergiusz Kościałkowski, son of minister Kościałkowski, intervened [and] took our side.[511] They informed the prison warden, a Jew, who said that if the prayers were repeated, he would send the Jews to the punishment cell. When the warden left the cell, the Poles moved off into a corner and asked us to pray. Then we conducted the Seder. We didn't have a Haggadah but our shochet knew it by heart.[512] We cried that evening. There were also assimilated Jews in our group, like the owner of the Tricot company from Marszałkowska Street in Warsaw, Fryderyk Rosenberg. They cried too. The Poles were very moved, even more so [after] we translated the words of the prayers for them. They asked us for forgiveness. We concluded the evening with the Hatikvah anthem.

The prison's [cell's] headman was a Lithuanian man who, on the second day of the holidays, forced us to wash the floors, and even though the Poles were prepared to do the work for us, it didn't help. The shochet resisted particularly strongly, [and] the headman started to hit him. I grabbed the bucket of water and threw it at the headman. Blood was drawn, an alarm was sounded, the warden came running and threatened me with a gun. He lunged at me, the Poles took my side, [but] I was dragged out of the cell and sentenced to ten days in the punishment cell for this. I will never forget what I went through in the punishment cell. It was a rathole in the ground where you could neither stand nor sit, only lie down, as if in a coffin, [and] where there was no air supply. I thought I was going to suffocate. Every day, a small slice of bread and half a liter of water were thrown in for me. [I] wasn't allowed to leave to go to the toilet, the stench in the hole was unbearable. When I was taken out of the cell, another of my companions in misery who

511. Marian Zyndram-Kościałkowski (1892–1946): prime minister of the Republic of Poland (1935–36), minister of the interior (1934–35), minister for welfare (1936–39). Émigré from 1939 on.

512. Haggadah (Haggadah shel Pesach; Polish: Hagada szel Pesach): text read during the Seder, the ceremonial meal that begins the holiday of Pesach. See glossary.

had taken part in the fight was led there. A young man from Wilno lost his mind in the punishment cell.

After some time, I was sent to Slutsk in an *etap*, where the prison regime was a bit milder, [and] where, [after] they led me out for execution three times, I confessed to everything they accused me of. I was only left in peace after confessing to the crimes I hadn't committed. I was in a cell with prisoners of war, soldiers, and officers. An eminent Polish doctor, Major Karpiński, was among them. Weeks went by [and] I thought nothing would change, but in June 1940, I was read a judgment stating that I'd been sentenced to eight years in a labor camp. Along with many others—forty-five people to a car—I was sent off. I reached Kotlas two weeks later. We were loaded onto barges, 1,500 people on each, and there were eight of those barges. On one there were only Jewish women. Many had to be carried, as they couldn't walk. After two weeks' journey, we arrived in Wajkinia.[513] During the journey there was an outbreak of dysentery. Every day the dead were thrown in the water. Two doctors, Dr. Bromberg from Pińsk and Dr. Sirota, turned to the people in charge [and asked] to be allowed to save the sick. The response they received was that there was enough room for graves in Russia. Out of 1,500 people, only 550 arrived at the destination, and the percentage who died on the women's ship was considerably higher. [Once] on the riverbank we were rushed on ahead, in a downpour, walking in mud that reached our knees. Every few meters another person would collapse, and no one [even] glanced back at them. The road was littered with people who had died or fainted.

Thus we got to Wajkinia [?]. Everyone was ill with dysentery. We were told to sleep under the open sky [and] weren't given either bread or water. We'd pay with a pair of trousers or a shirt for a glass of water brought by the Russian exiles. [In Wajkinia] I met Aron Cincinatus,[514] the editor of a Zionist newspaper from Wilno, the *Zeit*[515]—he was unkempt and ragged and burst into tears when he saw me. He told [me] he had been in the Kharkiv prison and [was sentenced to] eight years of labor camp. I never saw him again. I

513. Likely refers to the town of Aykino [Polish: Ajkino], near Syktyvkar.

514. Correctly: Cyncynatus. After the war, in 1947, editor of the organ of the Zionist-Socialist Workers Party "Hitahdut," "Bafrajung," published in Łódź until 1949.

515. *Die Zeit*: daily paper published in Wilno until the outbreak of World War II. [Possibly refers to *Di Tsayt*, a weekly Yiddish newspaper published in Częstochowa in the late 1920s and early 1930s.]

spent three days in Wajkinia [?]. Then we were loaded onto trucks and sent to Ukhta, where we were taken into a virgin forest. There wasn't even a barracks there. We were told to stay there. On the second day, I and two others, including a Polish sailor, Służewski, decided to run away. We sneaked up to the wire fence at dusk, cut the wire, and got out of the camp. We crawled on all fours, and twelve kilometers from the camp, [some] dogs attacked [and] bit us. Guards followed the dogs, beat us up, and drove us to [part of text missing]. We weren't punished, it was just noted in our papers [that we were] suspicious element[s]. We put up shacks ourselves [and] covered the roofs with moss, but the rain was so heavy that we would wake up in the morning soaked through. One day one of the shacks collapsed and buried thirty people underneath it. We worked in the forest, building a railway. For fulfilling the quota we got nine hundred grams of bread and soup with groats three times per day. No one fulfilled the quota. There was a new outbreak of dysentery. A few tens of people died, and were it not for the help of Dr. Węgrzynowski, who treated us with herbs, we would all have lost our lives. We worked in two shifts—one during the day, another one at night. Soon I lost the ability to work and received only three hundred grams of bread per day, plus water. I begged the brigade leaders, Pawłow and Zdołbunów, to give me a bit more bread. "You'll kick the bucket here, [you] dirty Jew"—one of them responded, for which I threw an ax at him. I got thirty days in a punishment cell. The cell was [dug into] the ground. I was stripped to my underwear and put in [there] as if into a grave. I only survived this punishment thanks to the help of a Polish companion, the sailor Służewski from Rzeszów, who ripped out a board and threw in something to eat every day. Służewski was the [camp] authorities' pet because he could sing beautifully and would perform when asked. That didn't save him from the punishment cell when his offenses related to me were discovered.

In January 1941, a group of 250 of us was put together and sent to the tundra close to the White Sea, to a station [called] Pieczara.[516] I was in that group. When I found myself in front of a commission to examine me [to determine] whether I would survive this journey, a doctor dismissed me, stating that I had *cynga*. Later she said to me in Jewish: "Brother, you suffer in innocence, [but] all of this will change." This way I avoided certain death, because we soon

---

516. Perhaps refers to the town of Pechora [original Polish correction: Pieczora].

learned that the six hundred people who were sent there froze to death. I was assigned to a group of weaker [workers] and sent to a *posiołek*. The *posiołek*'s warden was a Pole from Wilno, Nowicki, a former brigadier in the Soviet army, who was arrested in the year 1937 and sentenced to twenty-five years of prison. He gave me lighter work and treated me well—until a fight broke out between a Pole and a Jew. I interrupted the fight and for that was sent to a penal colony, where the regime was very strict and where I found myself among criminals. Not fulfilling [one's] quota was punishable by [time in] a punishment cell. The quota amounted to 11.5 square meters of dirt, which one had to load into a wheelbarrow, [push] for 160 meters, and load into a wagon. No one fulfilled the quota, and every evening, everyone dragged themselves to the punishment cell. Fortunately, I had a good brigade leader who turned a blind eye to [our] failure to achieve the standard. The situation worsened considerably when the war broke out and the bread rations were lowered, and the quotas increased.

I heard about the Amnesty but didn't believe I would [live to see it]. We almost went mad with exhilaration on learning about the Amnesty. We set off [from the camp]. We traveled on the Volga to Kuybyshev, and from there, to Buzuluk. On the way I met Cincinatus, with whom I traveled to Gorky, [and] that's [when] we split up. In Buzuluk, I went hungry for a few weeks and didn't have a place to sleep. I became unbearably exhausted, and one [day], got on a train with Polish military families going to Krasnovodsk. I got on a ship this way and went to Tehran, via Pahlevi, where I stayed for over a year.

Protocol 202

Testimony of **Helena Ribbel** from Nowy Sącz, age thirty.

The outbreak of the war found me in Kraków, where I had been living for a long time. I returned to Nowy Sącz to my parents. The city folk were running away in a panic. I [too] was seized by the general terror. I found myself in Józefów, where a hospital for wounded soldiers had been set up. As I had finished an Air Defense[517] course, I reported [there] as a nurse. One day, the Germans bombed the hospital in a horrific manner. They flew just above the building and must have seen the red cross. The following day, they occupied the city. The first order commanded the people, Jews and Poles, to gather in the building of the beth hamidrash. [The Germans] started shooting at those who gathered [there]. I stepped forward bravely and started shouting that there were wounded Germans in the hospital who were being treated humanely, according to international law. The Germans were brought in from the hospital [and] confirmed my words. This saved us all, Jews and non-Jews. I received a travel certificate and set off for home.

When I had gotten to Przeworsk, on Yom Kippur [23 September 1939] the Germans lined up those who were praying and killed them. I was saved by the [travel] pass. During the rest of the journey, I often looked death in the eye. I arrived in Nowy Sącz during the pogrom. Father had his beard cut off along with [his] lip. I couldn't bear it there for long. I decided to go to Russia, and after many difficulties, managed to get to Lwów. My brother came there too, beaten within an inch of his life, and told me that Father had been arrested and was at risk of a death sentence. I decided to go back to save Father's life. The Gestapo caught me on the other side of the river along with [some] others. They chased us to the river and said that [those] who could swim would survive, and the others would perish. I managed to swim across the river and arrived in Nowy Sącz using the old pass. I was witness to an [event] where the Germans gathered all the Jews in a square, ordered them to put on ceremonial clothes, to sing and dance, and filmed those scenes. Then they set fire to the Jews' beards and lit [their] cigarettes from [them]. The attitude toward Jews was better from the Austrians. Fifty of

517. [OPL, that is, Obrona Przeciwlotnicza, Air Defense, in the original.]

them were shot dead for helping Jews.[518] The relations between the Jewish and the German populace [part of text missing] shot dead for patriotic sermons. After many tribulations, I managed to leave [my] hometown and cross over to the Russian side again. I was stopped at the border. I had a photograph from [a] mountain excursion on me and was suspected of espionage because of it. I managed to slip out of the guard's hands and escape to Lwów. I worked as a nurse.

The fact that I had a [skilled] job did not save me from deportation. Like others, I found myself inside a freight train taking us north. There were many cases of typhus during the hellish journey. I looked after the sick the entire time. We arrived at the intended destination, in Assina.[519] I worked in a camp hospital the entire time, except for a period of illness. I contracted typhus. The work in the hospital did not bring me satisfaction as there weren't enough medicines. We did what we could. Relations between the Poles and Jews were good.

When the Amnesty was announced, me and my friend, a relative of General [Władysław] Anders, decided to head south. We arrived in Kokand, where I worked as a health assistant in an evacuation point. Because I had heard that a transport to Persia was being organized in the south, I set off there. It was the hardest experience I have ever been through. I traveled without a ticket, moving from train to train, not sleeping, not eating, chased like a dog. We arrived in Sarii.[520] I got a job in a hospital. The job did not last long. The neighbors, envious of my well-paid position, denounced me as a spy. At that point I was newly married, and I ran away to Kermine with [my] husband. The memories of the *posiołek* seemed like a paradise to me. [In Kermine], one slept in the street. We were starving. [We] began the burdensome process of running around trying to [get permission] to leave. I made it onto a list thanks to [my] husband's connections, but was thrown out of the carriage. The following day I was sent off to the garrison hospital instead of the station, [and told that] I would be leaving with the next transport. It turned out that my husband was not on the list for the last transport. I decided to go on my own and arrange for him to leave through an intervention. I went to Pahlevi and to Tehran. All that time I lived in a Mother's Home with [my] child, who had been born in the meantime. I came to Palestine, then, in October 1943.

---

518. No corroboration of this piece of information [exists] in other sources.

519. Correctly: Asino.

520. Could be Shirin in Uzbekistan [Polish: Szyrin]. Original Polish correction: Szarii.

Protocol 203

Testimony of **Herminia Neid**, from Kraków, dressmaker by trade, age thirty-two.

We left town on 3 September with no great difficulties and arrived in Czortków without [any] adventures. We witnessed the entry of the Bolshevik army there. We stayed in Czortków until March. I then moved to Lwów. I had a permanent job in my trade. Relations with the Polish citizens were very harmonious. One night NKVD-ers came to my apartment and told me to come with them, which I resisted because my husband wasn't home. They gave me two hours to find my husband, who was in hiding, and threatened to take me with them after this time had passed. I found [my] husband after a long search, and we were taken to the station. We were loaded into freight cars, the cars were sealed, and [we] were taken into Russia. We traveled for eleven days, to the station of Pomieziorowo,[521] and from there, twenty-five kilometers by cart to the *posiołek* Panina.[522] The men were on foot, the women rode [on the carts]. The first days of [our] stay in the *posiołek* were awful. There were no barracks, the food provision hadn't been organized yet, and the mosquitos were eating us alive. After a few days, everyone was sent to work. I didn't work because I had a small child. My husband worked chopping down trees. We both worked hard and were constantly hungry. Anyone who had money could even buy cake or chocolate. Relations between Jews and Poles, particularly among the intelligentsia, were exemplary. Assemblies were organized to the extent approved by the warden. The Bolsheviks treated us like slaves, like people who would never leave there, but we weren't being particularly tormented. The chief of the NKVD, an old Russian, had some human decency. The work conditions were hard; being late was punishable by jail. After the Amnesty, we were set free and set off south. We found ourselves in Tashkent after a three-week journey. There the worst times came. I begged to be allowed into an apartment with [my] child at night [but] was refused. We wanted to commit suicide. We eventually got a hole [to stay in], [but] we were soon kicked out of there. Polish assistance had not yet been organized. We learned that the Poles were preparing an evacuation of

521. Likely refers to the town of Ponazyrevo [original Polish correction: Ponazyriewo].

522. Most probably Pavino, north of Ponazyrevo.

[their] citizens. We registered and went to the designated station, [but] got off when we found out they were taking us to a country [from which] no one returned alive [?]. We jumped out of the car as it was moving and were left out in the middle of nowhere. It wasn't easy to get on a train going in the opposite direction. We managed this for the price of [our] last watch. We decided to go to Bukhara, where we had heard there was bread. The conditions in Bukhara had worsened, and one had to wait in line for twenty-four hours to get bread. The Uzbeks, who were very kind to us to begin with, started showing their hostility after a few months. After some time, transports of the Polish military started being organized. My husband was not accepted into [the army]. By chance, thanks to an influential friend, we got on the list of people who were to leave [from] Kermine. The journey from Bukhara to Kermine, which was to determine our future, was horrific. We jumped out of and onto speeding trains, and once my husband scarcely avoided disaster. We were thrown out of one of the trains. There was still time before the departure. We got on the list and left for Tehran. My husband reported to the Polish army and was accepted, [and] I worked as a dressmaker until [our] arrival in Palestine.

Protocol 204

Testimony of fourteen-year-old **Abram Reif**, from the town of Krasnobród, Lublin district. Came to Palestine via Siberia and Tehran.

Our small town was located near Zamość, in the Lublin district. My father was a cattle trader; he had a lot of money. His customers were peasants and landowners. There were four of us children at home, three boys and one girl. A few days [after the outbreak] of the war, you could already hear shooting in our town. The Germans were advancing quickly. Clouds of dust were seen on the road, black tanks were speeding ahead. Father was afraid to stay in town, [and] we ran away to the neighboring village where many Jews lived, Father's friends. It was quiet in the country. You had to go into town to find out what was new in the world. The town was in a valley. On one side of the hill were the Germans, on the other one the Poles, and they shot at each other. It started on Saturday evening when suddenly German tanks with swastikas arrived.[523] The Germans didn't bother anyone in town; on the contrary, they handed out chocolate [and] white bread among children, talked with the Jews and didn't beat anyone, and after some time they continued on. Only the next day, on Sunday, did the real Germans arrive from the Gestapo and take to beating the Jews straightaway. They kicked the praying Jews out of the beth hamidrash and told them to [stay] in their ceremonial clothes and bury dead horses, whose corpses lay out in a field because there had been a battle there. They made a show out of this too, because they ordered the horse corpses to be wrapped in Jewish tallits. One of them was the cruelest—he ordered the Jews to undress and chased them down the street naked. The son of Aron Debora, the town baker, was stripped naked. He was told to bury his clothes and returned home naked. A German chief who spotted this ordered the Jew to dig his clothes back up again and get dressed. He was angry with the soldiers, but they did not stop [their] cruelties. Many Jews they killed, and many they burned alive. The Germans left town a few times because the Polish soldiers chased them away. This situation lasted all week. You couldn't see the airplanes, only the shrapnel, which flew from one end of town to the other. Civilians took part in the

523. German tanks were marked with black-and-white crosses.

defense of the town too. In our town there were many refugees from Kraków, Tarnów, and other cities that had been taken over by the Germans back at the beginning of the war. Two youths who helped to pour gasoline onto German tanks had come from Tarnów. The German tanks were afraid of no one, and they drove three abreast. Once the civilians, peasants and Jews, armed themselves with bottles of kerosene and threw them at the tanks. The Jewish soldiers fought very bravely. One soldier, a Jew from Włodzimierz Wołyński, was shot at the doorstep of our home. He took a bullet to the head and dropped dead in the hallway. Father ran to help him. A prayer book and his papers were found inside his rucksack. Later, when we all moved to Ludmir,[524] the mother of the dead soldier tracked us down and asked after her son. Father didn't want to tell her the truth.

When the Germans settled in town, they started stealing Jewish property. The Poles helped them in this, partly [by] pointing out which shops were Jewish. The Jews did not resist. Yom Kippur came [23 September 1939]. People were afraid to organize communal prayers in town. The Jews sneaked out to the country and prayed there. In the country there was only a patrol stationed that operated from time to time. Things were worst in our town when the Germans were planning to give it [over] to the Bolsheviks. It was on Thursday, the first day of Sukkot [28 September 1939], when the Germans started setting fire to all the Jewish homes, with the people [inside]. They poured gasoline and kerosene on the houses and then set them alight. They would lock the doors before that, and there were children, elders, [and] women in the apartments, and [the Germans] would then stand outside the house with loaded guns so that no one could escape. Almost all of the town was burned down this way, and to this day it isn't known how many Jews met their fate in the flames. I don't remember all the names. I only know that the town cantor, Szmul Elizer, and his son were burned. I remember that on Friday, when the Bolsheviks entered town, and things calmed down, the rabbi ordered the ashes and bones of those burned to be collected, and Jews walked around the houses with white sheets, looking for charred body parts. The remains of the victims were buried according to Jewish ritual. The Germans also set fire to the synagogue. It was a beautiful new synagogue, built not long before the war. An old

524. Ludmir: the name for Włodzimierz Wołyński used by Polish Jews.

Jew from town ran up to it and begged to be allowed to save the Torah. The Germans laughed at him, but the oldest one said that he would agree to it on the condition that after saving the books, [the Jew] would lay them out on the ground and dance on them. The old man said nothing to this. The Germans shot him dead. Then the synagogue was set alight and the body of the old Jew was thrown inside.

The Russians stayed in town for only two days. Their leader announced that the Russian border would be moved seventy kilometers away from us, to the Bug River, and anyone who wanted to go with the Russian army could do so. We all went. They gave us a lift to Ludmir in cars. Father earned good money [there]; he supplied cattle for the Russian army. He received a monthly salary and food products. He wanted to take a Soviet passport, but Mama didn't let him. When the arrests came, we too were deported to Siberia. But Father got by in Siberia. He was accepted to [work on] railway vehicles as a rail station worker, close to our *posiołek*. He supplied water to the locomotives. He made the acquaintance of the railway staff too, which became very useful to him. There was an exiled Pole in our *posiołek*, a neighbor from [our] town. Father took him on as a partner and they delivered kosher meat to the entire neighborhood. Father would buy cattle from the peasants and bring it to the rail station. The shochet would slaughter it and then it would be offered for sale. A kilo of kosher meat cost between thirteen and sixteen rubles. There were many observant Jews who would starve themselves [rather than] eat *treif*. *Treif* meat cost four rubles a kilo. Father paid a great deal for live cattle. Many observant Jews ate only potatoes and fish on Pesach. Some Jews received a bit of matzo and [special kosher] flour in parcels [sent by relatives] and shared it with others. Later, when we were released and traveling south, Father traded in kosher meat again. It wasn't an easy thing in Turkestan. A kilo of kosher meat cost fifty rubles. There were, however, pious Jews who would pay any price for kosher meat. My parents stayed in Turkestan. Because of the insanely high prices there, Father decided to send me and my brother Jakob to Tehran. Mama resisted, but Father was not able to feed the whole family and in the end she had to agree. [My] younger siblings stayed [part of text missing].

Protocol 205

Testimony of **Henryk Zylbiger**, resident of Kraków, director of a printing shop by trade.

I left Kraków on 2 September [1939]. On the way to Kolbuszowa, I met an army division, and continued along with them. In Kolbuszowa we came upon a German tank division and began to fight with them. The Germans were murdering all civilians. I managed to get to a prisoner of war camp with the soldiers, and from there I sneaked out and returned to Kraków. I found [my] apartment untouched and the shop open. At the time, I was printing, among other things, a German-Polish dictionary, on the instruction of a man named Rembowski. The Germans closed down my printing shop in December. I got a job with the Jewish council. At that time the president of the council was Bilerstein, whom the Germans [later] shot dead.[525] The chief of the Gestapo, Zybert,[526] treated us in a humiliating manner. He beat and tormented the members of the council. Immediately after entering the city, the Germans carried out a search in the homes surrounding the Wawel [River]. Many people were taken from [their] apartments and they never returned. I left Kraków at the end of October. I had been denounced and was at risk of being arrested. I crossed the Russian-German border near Przemyśl. The Germans took everything away [from me] at the border crossing and beat [me] terribly. Barely alive, I dragged myself to a Soviet guard booth. There I was arrested. We were taken to the Przemyśl prison on foot, through swamps. There were twenty-nine of us in a cell [intended] for eight [people]. We weren't allowed outside for a breath of fresh air, weren't allowed to wash. When I asked for some water, the custodian spat in my face. We were only allowed to walk around for five minutes after ten days. After twenty-three days, the examination[s] began. I was released from that responsibility as [I was] gravely ill. I went to Lwów and spent six months there. Even though they kept sending people to Siberia, I managed to hide from the NKVD during that period. We were caught eventually and deported

525. [Refers to] Prof. Marek Bieberstein, arrested by the Gestapo in 1941; killed by the Germans with a phenol injection in the Płaszów camp in 1944.

526. [Refers to] SS-Oberscharführer Paul Siebers was the chief of the Jewish department in the office of the Head of Political Security for the Kraków district.

in a freight car. We traveled for fourteen days inside a freight car and were only let out of [it] in Tyumen. From there, we were sent on boats toward a *posiołek* called Wierchnij Barak. We built our barracks ourselves. On the third day after [our] arrival, we were sent to work. We cut down trees [and] picked moss, and for that [work] received soup twice a day, as well as three hundred grams of bread. We were not allowed to pray on Yom Kippur [12 October 1940], but did not stop the prayer service [on the eve of the holiday] in spite of the punishment we risked. The next day we didn't go to work, and the Poles stood in solidarity with us. We were punished by having our bread rations taken away for two days. In mid-February we were sent to a completely wild area where [we] had to build another *posiołek*. Mosquitos bit us mercilessly [and] we weren't expecting to get out of that place alive. The Amnesty saved us. We set off southward, toward Tashkent, [and] reached [our] destination via Omsk. On the way, the NKVD took everything away from us. In Tashkent, we could barely stand up from exhaustion. Unable to continue to sleep on the streets, we moved to Kokand, and then to Leninabad. I went to Guzar to report to the army, which I succeeded in doing after many difficulties. I was assigned to a technical division and went to Iran with a transport. Outside Baghdad, in an army camp, I was discharged from duty. I returned to Tehran and got a job in the English administration. I came to Palestine in October.

Protocol 206

Testimony of **Emanuel Rotkopf**, resident of Kraków, mechanic by trade.

I left Kraków with my family, that is [my] wife and child, at the time the bombardment was starting. In Bochnia, we had our cart and horse taken away. We got a truck and carried on in a group of twenty-eight people. We traveled on side roads, avoiding the [main] roads where the travelers were being bombed. After a few days we arrived in the area of Tarnów, in the town of Karszyn.[527] We did not stay there for long. The police commandant advised us to carry on. We turned back toward Lwów, often stopping on the way, blocked by the moving military troops. We were often stopped by [other] obstacles in the form of bridges that had been blown up. Thirty kilometers from Lwów, we fell victim to a horrific air raid. The Germans shot at civilians mercilessly with machine guns and there were many killed. We escaped from the assault by a miracle and set off for Mikuliczyn [Mikulińce], outside Tarnopol. We rested and were planning to carry on when the Russians took over the town. There was shooting in the area for another few days. It was the Polish soldiers fighting the Bolsheviks and the Ukrainian divisions.
We spent four months in that place. We saw the Russians begin their rule with arrests, confiscation of property, etc. One day they deported the rich Ukrainian peasants en masse. Our turn came later on. One night NKVD-ers turned up at our apartment and told us they were sending us back to our former places of residence. We were loaded into freight cars [and] waited at the rail station for two days. After a six-week journey, the horrors of which [are] difficult to describe, we arrived at the camp of Tavda. We were told to build makeshift barracks and report for work the next day. We sawed wood in a sawmill, transported it, worked in the forest. Life was hard; we were treated like criminals. Four months later we were placed in a *posiołek*. [Things] weren't [any] easier there; we were working in a swamp. Women and children worked too. We received only four hundred grams of bread per person. Relations between us and the Poles were very good the entire time. The attitude of the local people was also marked by a lot of sympathy.

527. Likely refers to the town of Nowy Korczyn.

When the news of the Amnesty came, they didn't want to release us, [and] forced us to continue working [instead]. We only had our documents issued after many interventions. We decided to go south, toward Tashkent. After many difficulties (the journey took seven weeks), we found ourselves in Tashkent. Our car was sealed and [we were] sent away to Uzbekistan. We lived in clay kibitkas there. Life was difficult, hunger was widespread, one waited in line for twenty-four hours [to get] a piece of bread. After some time a Polish agency was opened, which, however, could not provide help to all who required it. The assistance came in the form of coupons. I reported for the Polish army a few times, without success. I then found out that there would be an evacuation of civilian citizens as well. I found myself among thousands of people who had registered to leave there. On the way, I learned that those transports were being sent into Turkestan, to *posiołki* located three hundred kilometers from the station. By a miracle I got out of this *posiołek* with my family and went to Fergana. After some time, I managed to get into the army as a specialist. I didn't want to hear about leaving, however, since my family was not with me. I was assigned to an army camp in Guzar, and [my] family came there. Guzar is the most horrifying place in the world. We were all starving, and soldiers shared their small rations with the civilians. Families lived under the open sky and slept on sand. Hundreds of people simply died of thirst as there was no water. Within two weeks, my two children had passed away. [My] wife carried them both and buried them with her own hands in a common grave, where another four children were [buried]. I came home two days after the first child's death and my other child said to me: "Papa, you brought me bread but I won't be eating it anymore." [The child] passed away. I carried [the child] to the cemetery myself. The people in the street, overtaken by apathy, paid no attention.

Finally the time came for [our] departure. Some soldiers had been stripped of their uniforms and had to abandon any further journey. I arrived in Persia safely. In Persia I fell seriously ill and stayed [for a while] in a hospital. [After] being brought in front of a commission, I was discharged. We lived outside Tehran, sixty people to one barracks. The delegation tried as best it could to help us; however, it wasn't always possible to distribute the help fairly. I came to Palestine from Tehran with [my] wife, in October [1942].

Protocol 207

Testimony of **Rachel Abramowicz**, age twenty, from Łódź. Came to Palestine with [her] mother and sister in October 1943, via Russia and Tehran.

My father had left Łódź for Palestine many years before the war. In Łódź he had been a building contractor and specialized in the construction of small workers' homes. And since he could not find the [right] type of work for himself in Poland, he went to Palestine to look for work there. I did not see Father for three long years. We lived with Grandpa Krajcer, my mother's father, the owner of a tannery. After the outbreak of the war, we completely lost contact with Father.

After entering Łódź, the Germans began to run things their way immediately. The first casualties were Jews who lived in the main streets of Łódź. Since we lived in a workers' district, inhabited mainly by the Polish proletariat, we suffered relatively less [at the hands of] the Germans. German soldiers rarely came to our neighborhood to steal because they knew they wouldn't find beautifully furnished apartments there. The situation in Łódź grew worse by the day. The Germans robbed neighborhoods inhabited by Jews. They would order [people] to leave [their] apartments within an hour, and didn't allow anything to be taken except a small bundle. Jews were prohibited from riding trams, and a curfew was in force starting at five in the afternoon. Soon a decree about the yellow badge came out. Then the yellow badge was moved from the arm to the back and the heart. The badge bore the [Star] of David and a large "J" in the middle. In our neighborhood—as I mentioned—we didn't feel the German persecutions, and would definitely have not left Łódź were it not for the decree forbidding Jews to stay in the city, under penalty of death. Panic broke out. Everyone was thinking about where they should go, which wasn't an easy thing since Jews were prohibited from traveling by train, and bus journeys were also very dangerous. The decree was withdrawn a few days later as a result of the intervention by the Jewish council. Even though it was withdrawn, the decree had such an effect on us that we decided to leave Łódź. Other Jews did the same. With no other transport [available], we set off on foot. Only young men and young women escaped at that time, since others were not able to get away on foot.

We went from Łódź to Stryków, and from there to Głowno. The road was full of people running away. We were searched a few times, because the border separating the General Government[528] and the Reich ran between Stryków and Głowno. We were not spared humiliation from the Germans during the searches. Men were beaten bloody, women debased. We took all of this calmly, waiting for the moment we would find ourselves in the General Government. In Głowno, we took off the yellow badge[s], got on a train, and set off for Warsaw. We spent [only] a few days in Warsaw, even though the situation was much better there than in Łódź. Knowing the Germans, however, we decided not to stay under their occupation but to cross to the Russian side [instead]. We set off for Siemiatycze via Siedlce and the Bug [River], [and] from there to Brześć and Mikaszewicze, a town on the Russian side where [some of] our relatives lived. We arrived there at the end of January 1940. The Bolsheviks had nationalized private property by then and kicked the rich people out of their apartments. Everything in the market stalls was being bought out and food products ran out. Then a [ration] card system was implemented, six hundred grams of bread per person. Unable to rely on [our] relatives [to support us], we started to look for work. My sister Estera, a dressmaker by trade, got a job in her trade. I was employed in a butter factory. I worked around ten hours a week[529] and earned 120 rubles per month. You could buy hardly anything with this [kind of] money because the market prices were incredibly high. We wanted to move to a bigger city with more earning possibilities. However it was impossible to find an apartment in a different city, which is why we stayed put, and [we] had to comply with all the orders of the authorities, such as accepting Russian citizenship, since we were being closely watched. We starved for days, looked like shadows [of our former selves], [and] could not expect [any] help.

We lived in Mikaszewicze until the outbreak of the Russian-German war, which caught us by surprise. Panic broke out in town. We learned that the Germans were already in Pińsk. Then German airplanes flew in and bombed

528. [The central zone of the Second Polish Republic under German administration. It was formed following Hitler's Annexation Decree on the Administration of the Occupied Polish Territories on 8 October 1939.]

529. Likely a mistake and means ten hours of work per day.

the town. Mikaszewicze was located on the Belarussian [Belarusian] border.[530] We were evacuated in the direction of Kiev. We traveled in transports, but the trains would stop every three minutes and wait for hours, of out fear of bombardments. We experienced a terrible bombardment at the Ovruch station. It was at night; the airplanes descended to just above the roofs [and] shot directly at the cars with machine guns. People ran out of the cars, trampling one another in the dark. Screams went up to the heavens. Everyone was looking for shelter. Searchlights broke up the darkness and the moaning of the wounded came from all around. I was left alone inside a car. I decided not to move and to wait for death there, since I'd lost Mama and [my] sister. Suddenly, I felt a horrific pain in my leg. I didn't know where it had come from, but all of a sudden, I saw blood and understood that I had been wounded in the leg. I don't know how long I lay in the car. I remember people returning, the lights were turned on, and [my] mother and sister, seeing me lying in a pool of blood, tore up a shirt, tied it around [my] leg and stopped the flow of blood. A lot of people were killed during that bombardment. The train started off on the rest of the journey to Kiev. We were soon taken to a zoo, where we spent three days outdoors. The town was constantly being bombarded and the nights were lit up with fires. Entire streets were burning. We huddled together and each explosion shook us to the core. We asked to be let out, and three days later, we were taken into Russia in freight cars. We traveled for two months, until we arrived in Kazakhstan via Ural. The journey was long and horrible. We were given refuse to eat. We suffered from the rain, got soaked through; every day someone else would get sick. We were dirty and lice ridden. Many people died on the way. [The corpses] were thrown out of the cars onto the rail embankments. Family members lost each other during the journey, because [people would take turns] running into village[s] to look for food. Everyone prayed for a quick death.

This was how we arrived in Chkalovo. We got off and were sent to kolkhozes. [Our family] was sent to a kolkhoz not far from Chkalovo, where we lived in tents. There were many Poles and Romanian peasants from Bessarabia among us. The men worked building a railway line to Tashkent.

530. That is, the former border between Poland and the Belarussian Soviet Republic.

I worked as a cleaner. I earned 110 rubles, which could buy you nothing, and everyone suffered from hunger. Kyrgyz and Kazakhs lived in this area. Their living standard was very low; they lived in clay huts. They envied us our clothes. We stayed in the kolkhozes until December 194[1]. An awful winter began, and realizing that we would not survive the frost in tents, we ran away to Tashkent. On the way, we got off at the station of Fergana. This was already after the Amnesty, when all of the Polish deportees were coming to the south of Russia. The whole area was full of Polish refugees; one couldn't get a place for the night, or bread. Thousands of haggard people roamed the streets, and no one paid them any attention. The lucky ones lived in kibitkas without heating. The snow came up to your knees; people didn't have adequate clothing. A typhus epidemic broke out. I got infected and my sister started trying to get me admitted to a hospital. The nurses in the Russian hospital paid no attention to the patients; they shouted at them, sometimes [even] beat them—we were treated like dogs. I was on the verge of unconsciousness when a nurse ordered me to leave the bed to have a bath. She pushed me into the bathroom [and] into a bathtub [filled] with cold water. Then without even drying me off, she led me through the cold corridor and took me to the sauna. I thought I would suffocate. Many of those who were forced in there lost their lives. I started to scream but it was in vain. I had a hemorrhage and lost consciousness. I don't know how long I lay [there] unconscious. When I woke up, two nurses were standing by me and they told me to come with them. They finally carried me to the third floor [?] and put me in an ambulance. There were already a lot of people in that ambulance, lying on top of each other. In this state, we were driven to a hospital called the Evacuated Hospital of Moscow. When I regained consciousness, I was lying in a clean bed. I was much happier in the new hospital, although they still didn't give [us] food, and the doctors didn't have any medicines. It was only by a miracle, thanks to the help of a Jewish doctor, that I was saved.

At first we lived by selling [our] belongings; then I got a job washing rags that paper was made from. I got a ruble for a kilo of washed rags. However, I was given a food card for six hundred grams of bread per day. I worked like a dog in order to earn more. I [could] see, however, that I would not be able to manage this [kind of] work for long, and I decided to set off for Jag-Iul,[531] where the Polish army was, which—it was said—was going to be evacuated. We fared very badly there to begin with, but tried to get on the evacuee list. We eventually managed to get on that list and went to Tehran via Krasnovodsk and Pahlevi. In Tehran I lived in a camp for a whole year and didn't fare [too] badly. We made contact with Father, who sent us certificates, and thus we made it to Palestine.

531. Correctly: Yangiyul [original Polish correction: Jangi-Jul].

Protocol 208

Testimony of **Chaim Janower**, age thirty-four, son of Berył and Pesi[532] from Otwock. Came to Palestine via Russia.

I'm a metalworker mechanic by trade. I had my own workshop in Otwock, where I lived with [my] wife and child. I got by, not [too] badly. I was mobilized a few days after the outbreak of the war. I was sent to the 36th regiment, stationed [in Warsaw] in Praga. There I found that things were disorganized. It took a few days for me to get [my] number and assignment. I normally was part of the sappers [but], on the day the war broke out, was assigned to the infantry. My attempts to convince [my] supervisor that I knew nothing about this [kind of] service were in vain. They replied that this wasn't the time [to worry about such] trifles. Our regiment set off for the front that same day. We traveled toward Częstochowa but didn't make it farther than Łódź. Our train was bombed a few times on the way, some cars were destroyed, and a few hundred soldiers were wounded. The airplanes flew down just above the cars and dropped hand grenades on us and shot at us with machine guns. We lay on the floor under the rain of bullets since we weren't allowed to leave the train—later, an order came [saying] we had to get away from the car and move off into a field during each air raid. That order was issued because some soldiers had shot at the planes with [their] guns, exposing where the army was located. Once, after a horrific bombing that lasted three hours, I found only a pile of rubble when I returned to the train. The cries of the wounded whom no one was helping came from under the wreckage. Only I and a few companions still left from the broken-up regiment managed to help the injured as much as we could.

Since we didn't know where our regiment was, we decided to set off toward Łódź. We started down the road, which was cluttered with cars, carts, and pedestrians. One could hardly move. The situation on the road was no better than on the train. There, too, airplanes flew down low and bombed the refugees. Everyone had to take cover in ditches. We soon gathered that there was no point in going to Łódź. Some said that the Germans were already there.

532. The nominative form of the name is unclear: there is also a Hebrew name Pesa.

We decided to go to Łowicz, where there was an *etap* station. I was sent off to Rembertów [from] the *etap* station, where everyone [from broken regiments] had gathered. The journey from Łowicz to Warsaw took two days. I wanted to get to Otwock to find out what had happened to my family, but the Germans had already surrounded the whole area. I decided to find [my] relatives who had lived in Praga before, but in the part of the city that had been bombed particularly heavily. The Germans targeted water cisterns, ammunition stores, ammunition factories, [and] grain stores in the [Warsaw] East railway station. I went to the Citadel the next day. I found out that my division was in Lublin and that I should join it. I decided to leave the capital, as it was said that it would surrender any day now. Through Wiązowna I went to Garwolin and Ryki. I reached Lublin three days later. However, I didn't find my division there, either. They were in Chełm. On the way to Chełm, I received a minor gunshot [wound] from a German airplane. My leg was bandaged up and I got onto a passing cart going toward Chełm. [And] indeed, I did meet a few tens of [my] companions from the regiment there. The regiment itself did not exist [anymore]. We asked for [another] assignment, roaming around Chełm.

Two days later the Russians arrived in town. We hid our weapons so they wouldn't fall into Russian hands. We didn't know whether the Russians were coming to our aid, or whether they were occupiers. I was surrounded by a few Bolshevik soldiers on the street [and] taken to the elementary school building. We found a few hundred soldiers and officers already there. We were very disheartened. We were treated like prisoners of war. I didn't want to be imprisoned, and I looked for a way to escape. I went up to the guard, a local policeman, and asked him to let me go out for [my] belongings that were at my relative's place. The day before, I had noticed my surname on one of the signs in a local shop. I indicated [the sign] and presented my documents. He allowed me to go out and took away [part of text missing]. When I found myself out on the street, I burst into the apartment of the first Jew [I saw]. His name was Ajzen. Half an hour later, I walked out dressed as a civilian and left town. I traveled for two weeks toward Otwock. The entire road looked like a battlefield. Thousands of dead bodies lay alongside horse carcasses, cars drove over them, and no one was burying the dead. The Germans were already lording it over small towns and tormenting defenseless Jews in a horrible way. The situation in Otwock looked relatively better than in the towns I had visited on the way. I found [my] family at home, and there was no end to our joy. As I could not make a living in my profession, I took to bringing in food products to Warsaw. I was picked up for [forced] labor a few times. I worked in the Citadel, loading boxes of ammunition onto trucks. Another time, I transported furniture and items stolen from Jews to the Gestapo building on Szucha Avenue. I was not spared humiliations and beatings. Unable to stand all of this, I wanted to get over to the Russian side. I planned to carry out my conviction soon because of the experiences that befell me as I traveled from Otwock through Praga, next to the Paderewski Park. I was caught and taken to a building close to the Praga tollgate. A few hundred people were standing in line by a pump there, waiting for water. I was told to pump the water. I pumped for five hours, and when I couldn't keep up, was beaten horribly. I worked until dusk. Immediately afterward, I went to Otwock, said goodbye to [my] family, set off for Siedlce by train, [and] from there to Mordy on a cart, and one dark night, I crossed the Bug [River] outside Siemiatycze. I made it to Białystok. I couldn't find a place for the night in Białystok; I wandered from one place to another, [and] became covered in lice. I sold what I could in the market, and when [it] was closed down, got a job fixing cars in a mechanic workshop. I worked ten hours a day and could barely feed myself. I got a letter from [my] wife [saying] the situation [back home was] a bit better and that my clients were asking after me. I left the job in the workshop and went toward the border, hoping I would be able to cross it. I roamed the border zone for two weeks but did not manage to make it through the Russian cordon.

I abandoned [my] plan and went to Brześć. At that time, a registration of those who wanted to return home was taking place. I waited in line for the German commission for two days, and [managed to] register. I regretted it later, as it was said that those [who had] registered would be sent to Siberia. A few weeks later, on a Friday evening, NKVD-ers turned up at my apartment, told me to pack [my] things, and took me to the station, [where I was] loaded into a freight car. There were only single men traveling in this transport. We were watched closely, given bread once every two days, [and] a bit of soup at night. They were checking constantly [to see if] any of us had escaped. The train didn't stop until we were in the Sverdlovsk district, in the middle of a forest. I fared very badly at first. I lived in a *posiołek* located ninety kilometers from the train station and worked in a forest cutting down trees, never fulfilling the quotas and constantly starving. Later I was sent to the train station, to the workshops, where I worked as a mechanic, earning fifteen rubles per day. When the [German-Soviet] war broke out, our situation got worse. The workshops were stopped, there were no materials to work with, [and] I was sent to the forest. After the announcement of the Amnesty, I went to Sverdlovsk, in the hope of getting through to Tashkent from there. I got a job in a concrete factory there. I earned 1,500 rubles per month. I was happy, but when I heard about the formation of the Polish army, I left [my] good job, and having rented a carriage with a few refugees, went to Tacko.[533] As a Jew, I was classified as E category [by] the military commission, that is, unfit for duty. I went in front of a commission for the second time in Jang-Iuli,[534] but there too they did not accept me. I waited for a transport train and managed to get into one of the cars without being spotted. I found myself in Krasnovodsk and made it through to Pahlevi in the same manner. I spent a few months in Tehran, after which I came to Palestine.

533. Should be: Totskoye [original Polish correction: Tockoje].
534. Correctly: Yangiyul [original Polish correction: Jangi-Jul].

Protocol 210

Testimony of **Sara Broder**, age twelve, from Pułtusk, daughter of Aron and Józefa. Came to Palestine in August 1943 via Tehran.

My father was a boot maker. There were four of us children: Rachel, age eighteen; Fiszel, age sixteen; me; and Szlomo, age seven. My father ran a workshop at home; a few workers worked in it [and] we didn't fare [too] badly. When the war broke out and the Germans entered the town, I remember that Jews were afraid to go out into the street because the Germans were beating and killing [them], grabbing [them] for work, ripping [their] beards out. My sister, Rachel, and my brother Fiszel were afraid to go out into the street too, because it was said in town that the Germans grabbed young girls [and] ordered them to undress and to wash the floor with their undergarments. I don't remember how long the Germans were in Pułtusk. I only remember that one day all the Jews were told to gather in the market square and an order was given [for them] to leave town within a few hours. When we returned home, Father packed up some stuff—we made small packets out of it—each of us took a bundle on their back, and we set off across the bridge.[535] The bridge was half-destroyed [and] it was dangerous to walk on it. In front of the bridge, German tanks were standing in a row; [we] had to squeeze through between them. The German soldiers laughed at us and pushed us into the tanks with their gunstocks. When all of the crowd couldn't make it through [in between] the tanks, and some hesitated to go onto the broken bridge, the German soldiers started to shoot at them. Panic broke out, some [people] fell from the bridge into the water, many drowned. Mothers called for their children who had gotten lost in the crowd. Father didn't know what was happening to him. He threw [his] bundle to the side, grabbed [my] little brother with one hand and me with the other one; Mama took two of [my] siblings by the hand and we pushed ahead this way, [and] made it across the bridge. We ran on ahead, through fields and forests, to a village. We spent the night in the village. The next day, we set off again. The villagers didn't want to allow us into [their] barns, [so] we slept in the fields.

535. Bridge on the Narew.

We reached a small town where there was a rail station and set off for Białystok from there. We roamed around, without even a roof over our heads, until we got a corner in a synagogue, where we lived for two weeks. Because Father couldn't get work, and living in the synagogue became impossible too, we begged God to save us from this hell. Father signed up to go work in Russia; he was promised a job in his trade, good wages, and an apartment. We left Białystok a few weeks later and arrived in Homel, where we were welcomed with music; a number of speeches were made in our honor, and we were treated to a lavish meal at the station. We were taken to a workers' house where we got a small room for a home. There wasn't any furniture there [so] we set our clothes out on the floor. The next day Father went to the bureau where they were to show him the place he would work. He was told that there was no work and that he had to wait a few days. We had nothing to live on. We didn't have anything to heat a small pot of water on. And Father kept being promised work but not getting it. In the end, he was advised that we should go to a kolkhoz. Exhausted from hunger, we set off for the village, where we were greeted not so politely. We all worked in the fields [and] received rationed portions of bread, some potatoes, and a bit of soup for [our work]. The children got milk once a week. We worked hard, from sunrise to sunset, and were constantly hungry, and Mama, who worked in the field too, didn't even have the time to cook a spoonful's worth of warm food for us. After a few weeks the kolkhoz manager told us that there was no [more] work [and] that we had to go back to the city. Father started looking for work, wasn't finding [any, and] we were at risk of dying of starvation. We decided to return to Białystok. We bought the tickets. Mama and two children sat in one carriage, Father, with [the other] two—in another one. We were afraid of NKVD-ers, but God helped us, and we returned safely to Białystok. We lodged in the dirty synagogue again. Father and [my] older sister and brother traded and earned a little. Father didn't want to accept a Soviet passport; he registered to return home, like all of [our] neighbors in the synagogue.

A few weeks later, on a Friday evening, NKVD-ers surrounded the street, woke everyone up, told [us] to pack [our] things, [and] drove [us] to the station. [We were] loaded into freight cars and sent to Siberia. We traveled for four weeks and arrived in the Vologda Oblast. We got out of the car and set off on carts for the *posiołek*, which was located in the middle of the forest. At first,

Father, Mother, [my] sister, and [my] brother worked in the forest, [while] me and [my] little brother ran the household; later, Father got a job in his trade, [my] sister worked in a sewing workshop for the army in the summer, and only Mother and [my] little brother were going out to the forest. All of us together, working hard, earned so little that we constantly went hungry. Many people fell ill and died. We generally didn't fare [too] badly in the *posiołek* until the German-Russian war; however, after the war broke out things were much worse for us, because Father and [my] sister lost [their] jobs and had to go out to the forest [instead].

When the Amnesty was announced, we all set off for Tashkent. The journey was hard and long, the cars were crowded, and there was nothing to eat. The train would stop in a field, we would leave the car [and] pull up the grass in a field—and that's what we ate. In Tashkent, we could not [even] stand up on our feet. We couldn't find a place for the night; we slept outdoors, and in the end, had to all go to an Uzbek kolkhoz. We lived in a kibitka [and] slept on a damp clay floor. Everyone worked in the fields, for which we got a bit of grain that Mama made soup with. Father and [my] youngest brother fell ill with typhus[536] from [eating] this food. There was no cart [we could use] to take them to the hospital. They lay on the floor with us, had nothing to cover themselves with, and after a few days, Father and [my] brother died. The Uzbeks didn't allow us to bury them but grabbed the bodies instead, and I don't know where they buried them. Mama didn't want to stay in the kolkhoz anymore [and] we went to Turkestan. It was difficult to get on the train, [but] finally we found ourselves in the city. After long efforts, Mama managed to place us in a Polish orphanage. [My] older sister and Mama lived by trading. We didn't lack for anything in the orphanage; we were given clothing and food, but the Polish children bullied us terribly. We put up with all [of these] torments because we knew we couldn't go back home. Later we were taken to Ashgabat, [and] from there, a few months later, we were taken to Tehran. We stayed in Tehran until August 1943, [and] from there we came to Palestine.

536. Typhus is a bacterial infection spread by lice.

Protocol 214

Testimony of **Jakub Kalman** from Bochnia, age seventeen, deported to Russia. Came to Palestine via Tehran.

My father had a soap factory in Bochnia. We were well-to-do people. Father held a reputable position in town. My uncle, Józef Kestenberg, was the secretary for the council. There were two of us children at home. I had turned thirteen when the war broke out, and my sister, Gita—three. The Jews in town started running away on hearing about the approach of the Germans. We ran off toward Kongresówka[537] and stopped in the small town of Milanów,[538] near Rozwadów.

But the Germans moved faster than us and were soon in our town. There were [only a] few soldiers, but even so, they managed to cause a lot of damage and torment Jews. They caught them for [forced] labor, beat and humiliated [them]. Many Jews from Bochnia returned home. It was no different, after all, since the Germans were [in both places]. We received news from Bochnia [that] the situation was worse there than in smaller towns. Jews were being killed for no reason there. One of the Jews was called Szenfeld. They came upon him on the street and shot at him. Father decided not to go back to Bochnia, and we stayed in Milanów until the arrival of the Bolsheviks. They stayed in town for all of one week. When Father learned that the Russians were leaving town, we traveled to Lwów and lived there until the deportation to Siberia. Meanwhile, not-so-bad news was arriving from Bochnia. Well-known Bochnia tailors had their hands full with work, and Jews were being allowed to earn [money]. We also found out that our uncle had become an important person in the [Jewish] council, [that he] had set up a tailors' cooperative and was on good terms with the Germans. Refugees from other cities were being offered work there. A rabbi from Bochnia, Halbersztadt, a close relative of the rabbi from Bobowa,[539] was living with us. He was deported to Russia. The

537. Congress Poland. Even though the Kingdom of Poland ("Congress Poland") existed between 1815 and 1918, its territory was still often referred to as Kongresówka even after 1918 (when the Second Polish Republic was already established).

538. Likely refers to the town of Ulanów.

539. The rabbi of Bobowa was Bencjon Halbersztam (1874–1941) at the time.

journey to Russia was horrible. There were Poles and Jews in our group who constantly quarreled with one another. We were all starving equally, [and] even the Poles, among whom there were rich peasants and landowners, would sometimes offer us [food] products that they had brought with them. In the place [where we were] exiled, Jews and Poles were split into separate *posiołki*. In our *posiołek*, there were thirty Poles to six hundred Jews. Relations with them were very good. There was a high-ranking Polish official among us, a practicing Catholic and antisemite, who became very good friends with my father. They engaged in long talks and came to the conclusion that, in such a desperate situation, the only comfort left lay in religious life. That Pole helped the Jews get permission to pray on Rosh Hashanah.

Our *posiołek* was located in the Mari El Republic, not far from the Volga. The local people [were] very kind. Father worked as a logger but earned [very] little. I helped him stack the timber and made a few rubles per month. Later I helped Mother work the land and by the second year we had potatoes. Father's foremost interest was [his] religious life. He wouldn't work on a Saturday at any cost: he hired people to cover for him and gave away [his] last grosze in order not to violate [the sanctity of] the Sabbath. When the holiday of Rosh Hashanah [on 3–4 October 1940] was approaching, Father worried about where people would pray and where [they could] get a shofar. After some time, we learned that there was a young man in a *posiołek* forty kilometers from us who had worked in the manufacture of shofars in Poland—but where would we get the money for the [ram's] horn? Money was collected in the neighboring *posiołek*, and eight shofars were made in the space of a few weeks, and one of them was [part of text missing] brought in [to us]. During the holidays, thirty Jews didn't report for work. The Russian commissar executed a thorough search and caught those holding the illegal [religious] service. He chased the people away and threatened strict punishment. At first everyone dispersed, but then they gathered to carry the service through to the end. The next day the commissar punished the culprits. Among others, my father was sentenced to six weeks in jail. Finally, wages were decreased for six months. No one was scared by the punishment and people were readying themselves for the services on Yom Kippur [12 October 1940]. All the Jews in the *posiołek* stayed home from work, unafraid of punishment. Someone evidently informed the commissar about this, and he released the Jews from work on holidays from thereon. He was a wise man, that commissar, who avoided [fanning the flames of conflict]. We lived this way in the *posiołek* until the announcement of the Amnesty, when we were all moved to Samarkand. We fared worse there than in exile. After a short time, Father and Mother died of starvation. They were taken to the hospital, where Mother died after eleven days, and Father followed her. My little sister and I got into a Polish orphanage, from which we were taken to Tehran.

Protocol 215

Testimony of **Sara Halbersztat**, age thirteen, born in Siedlce, daughter of Józef and Masza. Came to Palestine via Russia and Tehran in August 1943.

From the first day of the war, terrible bombing of our city began. We spent days and nights in bomb shelters, and Mother was so scared of the air raids that I would break into tears on hearing the whirr of the engines from afar. Our home burned down completely. When the bomb fell onto our home, we were in a ditch, close to home, so that bricks and pieces of plaster flew over our heads. We thought we would be buried and never get out of the ditch again. Terrifying things were happing in the ditch: people were tearing their hair out, and lamenting, and sobbing. Mother didn't know what was happening to her. She pulled me in close and wouldn't let me out of her arms. She said that if we were to die, let us die together. When things calmed down a little and we got out of the ditch, we saw only the ruins of our house. Nothing was left of our belongings. We had only what we were wearing on [our backs]. We went to [see our] uncle Natan Halbersztat. [Our] uncle already knew about our misfortune and took us in. There was hardly a house in Siedlce that didn't suffer in the bombardment. The streets were covered in rubble. The homeless stayed with [their] families and friends. We lived with our uncle throughout all of the Germans' stay in Siedlce, and also during the Russians' stay in our town. When the Bolsheviks announced, on leaving town, that anyone who wanted to could go with them, we followed them. We went to Siemiatycze, to [be with] our grandma Bluma Awerbuch.

Siemiatycze was full of refugees. People roamed the streets, not having anywhere to stay the night. Every day new refugees from the German occupation would arrive, telling horrible [stories] about German cruelties. We lived near the rail station and lived off what Grandma gave us, since we had arrived without a penny to our name.

Father tried in vain to [find] work; they didn't want to [employ] him because they knew he had once been a merchant, and the Bolsheviks gave no work to people like that. Grandma was the owner of a house and a small stall with manufactures, but the Bolsheviks took away her merchandise, confiscated the house, threw [her] out of [her] apartment, and gave [her] a small room [instead]. We struggled a lot. Father asked that we be given a separate small room, but his request went unheeded. We had to squeeze in with Grandma in the tiny room. Grandma was left without [any] money too. We were all starving and would have surely died from hunger if it weren't for the help of our neighbors and friends. Father roamed the city and said it would be better to die from a German bullet than watch his family starve to death. Me and my brother Natan stopped asking for bread because we knew Mama had nothing to buy it with. We simply grew used to it, and hunger bothered us less and less. Father took up trading in the end. He traveled with goods from Siemiatycze to Białystok and back. He took foodstuffs to Białystok and brought back kerosene, salt, and other products from there. [My] brother helped him, and [soon] bread appeared in our home again. Mother cooked lunch every day and Grandma said that God would not forsake us.

Then the registrations began. The Bolsheviks were registering refugees and it was said that they planned to send them away from Siemiatycze. Father didn't want to become a Soviet citizen because he said he would never stay in Russia, and that's why he didn't go to the public office for [his] passport. He didn't register to leave, either, because he didn't believe he would be allowed to return home before the end of the war. During that period, Father was caught once when he was carrying a parcel with goods. [My] brother Natan was close by, also with a parcel of merchandise, but managed to escape. Father was taken to a police station, had his merchandise confiscated, and was threatened with deportation to Siberia if he was caught trading illegally one more time. From that time on Father was afraid to travel to Białystok and Mama would make the journey instead of him. But things were getting worse by the day. New and increasingly stricter regulations came out. Searches were being carried out all the time and Mother was afraid of falling into the hands of policemen. [Our] income stopped. Hunger [was a constant presence] again. But that didn't last long.

One Friday night, NKVD-ers knocked on our [door], told us to get dressed, carried out a thorough search of the house, and took everyone to the station. Grandma begged to be allowed to come with us. We wouldn't agree to it. Mama cried terribly when leaving Grandma, and I cried too, because Grandma said she would never see me again.

We were packed into freight cars, fifty people in each, the car doors were sealed, and we set off for Białystok a few hours later. There, other cars were attached to our train. Horrible things were happening in the station; [you] could hear screaming and crying. With their gunstocks, soldiers were pushing away those who had come to say goodbye. Thirty-six hours went by before we set off from Białystok. So we had been traveling for two days by then and had not been given anything to eat or drink. In vain did we bang on the locked door and beg the guards to pass us [some] water. We were [nearly] unconscious with hunger and thirst. Not until a few hours later, when we left Białystok, did we get a bit of hot food for the first time. We traveled for two weeks. We weren't allowed out of the cars, even to go to the toilet; we weren't given water to wash with, [and] two bucketfuls of drinking water every twenty-four hours had to be enough for fifty people. Lice bit [us]; many people were ill.

After two weeks' journey, we arrived at the station of Yemtsa, where the train stopped—by then, everyone was ill with dysentery. We were told to get out of the cars, but everyone was so weakened that no one had the strength to get up. We were in the Arkhangelsk district, where we were allowed to rest for a few hours. Then our belongings were loaded onto carts, and we were told to follow the carts on foot. We walked all night; people fainted from exhaustion on the way. The guards hurried us along, hit us with [their] gunstocks, and ordered us to walk right behind the carts. In the morning we arrived in a *posiołek* called Wola Ostrowaska [?] located in the middle of a deep forest. There were barracks there where we were accommodated, forty people in each. After a day's rest, we were told to go to work the next day. Father worked in the forest cutting up tree trunks and loading them onto trucks, but even though he worked hard, he couldn't fulfill [his] quota. We received two kilograms of bread a day for a family of four. Mama received a certificate of poor health from a doctor and didn't go to [work in] the forest, but she did work as a nurse in the infirmary. Mama's job was not difficult. She told [us] how the doctor complained about the lack of medical supplies, and about the resulting sense of helplessness in front of the patients. Work wasn't paused even during heavy frosts. People didn't have warm clothing and would return with frostbitten feet and ears. Many people fell ill and died. A cemetery was soon established where those who died from disease or unfortunate work accidents were buried. [My] brother and I went to school not far from our *posiołek*. We had neither notebooks nor pencils, [and] the classes were taught in Russian. We learned to read and write in chalk on a blackboard. We spent fifteen months in the *posiołek*. Our situation got a lot worse when the Russian-German war broke out. The school was closed down, and [my brother and I] and Mama had to go to work in the forest. We worked from sunrise to sunset, and the bread rations were becoming smaller by the day. We weren't even allowed to catch our breath, and our guards said that now, as allies, we should work more [to support] the war.

After receiving the news of the Amnesty, we went to Turkestan. We roamed around there, without even a roof over our heads [and] were only assigned a small room and food cards when Father found a job in a *valenki* factory. Father worked fifteen hours a day and earned so little that it wasn't enough for bread, which was impossible to get even with [ration] cards. The bakeries where the bread was supplied were besieged by thousands of people, and one waited for hours for a portion of bread. Mama was ill all the time and we children had to run the household. I tried to prepare some hot soup for Father when he returned from work. We cooked soup from various weeds. When an orphanage opened up in Turkestan, Father started to make efforts to have me admitted there, which he managed to do many months later. I lived in the orphanage for a few months. I was very happy there. There was enough food; I had clothes. Sometimes I would bring home a piece of bread. After some time we were moved to Ashgabat. Father and Mother cried terribly when we were separated. I spent ten months there. We didn't lack for anything at first, but later, when the Polish army left Russia and it was said that no more transports would be leaving, our situation got a lot worse. Our teacher would tremble [at the thought of seeing] us sent to a kolkhoz. One time, when we heard that the NKVD-ers would be turning up in a few hours to close down the orphanage and send the children to a kolkhoz, we barricaded [ourselves in] and put tables, wardrobes, and mattresses [against] the door, determined to defend ourselves and not let ourselves be sent away anywhere. Luckily a message came a few hours later that we were leaving Russia. We packed up our things in a hurry. [Our] joy had no bounds. We set off for Mashhad on buses, and from there to Tehran. After a few months' stay in Tehran, we went via Iraq to Palestine, where I arrived in August 1943.

Protocol 216

Testimony of Rabbi **Izrael Halbersztrom**,[540] age thirty-five, son of a well-known rabbi from Żmigród. Came to Palestine via Russia and Tehran at the end of 1943.

For five years, my father had lived in Kraków, at Starowiślna [Street] near the power station. On the Tuesday before the outbreak of the war, we set off for Zaklików, where my brother held the position of a rabbi. Immediately after the war broke out, German airplanes bombed Zaklików. We escaped to Janów [Lubelski]. Then on the night of the fourteenth [1939], Janów was bombed by tens of airplanes. We rented a cart at two o'clock at night and drove to the village of Gołkowice [?], where we stopped at a Jewish inn. On the night of Rosh Hashanah [14 September 1939], a group of bandits wearing masks attacked the inn and robbed it, taking everything. Two Jews who resisted were killed. One of the bandits stabbed me in the leg with a bayonet. At the end they tied us all up with rope so we couldn't raise the alarm. Robbed [of our belongings], we left the village and went to Turobin. Before we entered the small town, there was an air raid. We took cover in a cemetery, among the graves. Many other Jews were also hiding there. The airplanes noticed this, came down low over the graves and shot at those who were hiding. Many were killed. We survived by a miracle. We decided to go on to Krasnystaw, but all the villages and towns on the way were already on fire. Polish soldiers called to us to hurry because the German[s] were approaching. Our cart and the horse were taken away. We met a Jewish driver along the way, from whom we bought [another] horse and a cart, and we set off for Krasnystaw. We found the Germans there already. Panic had overtaken the city. The Germans killed twenty-five Jews for no reason. [Some] Ukrainians led the Germans through the Jewish district and riled them up even more [by] saying that Jews were hiding weapons. During the first search, the Germans shot dead the rich Bernstein family: the father, the mother, and [their] eight-year-old child. The Germans didn't spare a single Jewish home. They robbed [everyone] under the guise of looking for weapons and shared [the loot] with the Ukrainians. They didn't find anything in our

540. Izrael Halberstam, son of Sinai Halberstam, the rabbi of Żmigród, hailing from a well-known dynasty of Hasid Tzaddiks.

house, but they dragged us all outside and ordered us to dig graves for dead horses. We worked for a few days and were finally released in return for a large sum of money. Later we were arrested and accused of being spies from England, and [we escaped] only [because] the Hasids from Krasnystaw bought our way out for a huge sum of money.

We escaped to Chełm after Yom Kippur [23 September 1939]. When we got there, a pogrom that lasted eight days was taking place in Chełm. The Germans had to leave Chełm in the middle of the pogrom, because the Bolsheviks had arrived.[541] The Germans had been getting ready to destroy the entire Jewish neighborhood in Chełm. The neighborhood was surrounded by machine guns and cannons, but they didn't manage to carry out the [planned] destruction in time.

A few days after the arrival of the Soviet army, rumors spread that the Bolsheviks were leaving Chełm and the Germans were coming [back]. Many Jews left town along with the army, and we also moved, to Włodzimierz Wołyński. From Włodzimierz we went to Bobrujsk. There, my mother fell ill and died.

In Siberia

In Bobrujsk we lived with Rabbi [Dow Berysz] Wajdenfeld[542] from Trzebinia. Like other refugees, Father was well cared for by the local Jews. On 19 June [1940], a Friday night, NKVD-ers turned up at our house and drove us to Lwów on trucks. When I tried to leave the car to get my brother, I was beaten cruelly. Watching as they beat me and my father, Dr. Bernard Fiszer, a well-known Zionist activist from Kraków, had a nervous breakdown. Our train was stopped. The suffering man was taken away. I started shouting that we wouldn't allow ourselves to be sent away before a doctor came and certified that my sick and elderly father could not make the journey. Soon the station manager appeared with a doctor, and they agreed to have Father and me moved to a special car, which we paid for. As there were only six of us in the car, we took a few more Jews in with us. We traveled like this until Tyumen

541. On 25 September 1939, Chełm was occupied by the Red Army. Then, from 8 October 1939 until July 1944, the town was in German hands.

542. Rabbi of Trzebinia; founder of the Kochaw Mi Yaakow yeshiva. See also the footnote in Protocol 40.

in the Ural, and didn't run out of food on the way because we had brought in large supplies, not only from Bobrujsk but also from Lwów. It was worse when we got out of our carriage. We came upon 1,700 Jewish refugees who had been brought in from Lwów.

Everyone was deposited in a forest where there weren't even [any] barracks, nothing except the woods and the sky. Speeches were made to us promising that we would live in paradise so long as we worked. We were given axes and saws and told to start working. We were promised that nails would be provided, and we were supposed to build barracks ourselves. One refugee asked where we would sleep until the houses were ready; [the answer was that] we would sleep in the forest for now. There was nothing we could do. I wanted to file a complaint citing Father's old age. But Father categorically dismissed the idea of asking for special privileges. "I want to be treated like everyone [else]"—he said. It's difficult to describe what we suffered through in the forest. Hunger tormented us above all else. The food supplies [we] had brought with us were shared around, and by the next day, we started going hungry like others. We saw no way out of the situation; then we were told that they were sending us to a different place. We were loaded onto a ship and taken to the *posiołek* Larka in the Omsk Oblast. But things weren't any better there. Everyone had to work hard. My father, a seventy-year-old man, had to work too. The wardens, perpetually drunk, kept [trying to] convince us that we had to build a Soviet state. A well-known banker from Warsaw, Wacław Wawelberg, was working with us. Here everyone was equal and received an equally small portion of bread.

Father fell ill. Weeks later I got permission to take him to a hospital, where there were no doctors but a feldsher [instead]. The feldsher said that only bloodletting could save Father. But there were no leeches, and the feldsher suggested cutting into a vein on Father's arm or leg. I couldn't bring myself to [give the feldsher permission to do] it and the feldsher said [that] "[Your] father got worse and died in the end." He was conscious until the last moment and knew death was approaching. He asked that I myself look after his funeral, since there were no other Jews in the hospital. His last wish was for his body to be taken to Palestine. Immediately after the funeral I returned to the *posiołek*, where all the Jews and Poles had great sympathy for me. Straight after finishing work I gathered ten Jews[543] and wanted to say the prayer [for the dead], for which I was so [badly] beaten by the warden that blood was dripping from my nose. I protested. They sentenced me to two days in a punishment cell with no food.

The rule about not lighting [fires] in July is important in Siberia, because the dried-out wood burns easily, and fire can spread throughout the entire forest. However, since there were many bugs in our barracks that we could not [get] rid of except by lighting a fire, I planned to get rid of [them]. The warden brought a charge of sabotage against me. Witnesses who certified that a rabbi's son couldn't have set the forest on fire on Saturday, as was alleged in the indictment, were of no help. I was sentenced to six months in penal prison.

I served only fourteen days [and] was released because of the Amnesty. After leaving the prison, I understood that the Poles were starting to put an army together, and that rabbis would be needed in that army. I drove around *posiołki* and camps for three months with Rabbi Chaim Kaner to get rabbis released from them. We turned to the Polish outpost in Yangiyul [asking] that they take five hundred rabbis with them during the evacuation. Our request was endorsed by the delegate Professor Heizman and Colonel Szyszko-Bohusz. Eng. Jenicz,[544] who on the whole accomplished a lot of good [things] for Jewish refugees, defended us in a very bizarre way. One day, on a Friday, I was told to prepare to leave on Saturday morning. I obtained the correct pass. Everything I had, such as money, I shared with the rest of the refugees, because I was certain that I was going to [join] the army. Suddenly, before the train's departure, NKVD-ers arrived, accompanied by Polish military policemen, and started to call for Izrael Halberstat. I gathered that they meant me. They spotted me [and] put me in handcuffs. I felt I was lost. I made a scene. Colonel Szyszko-Bohusz, Consul Jenicz, Bishop Gawlina,[545] and the military attaché, Rudnicki,[546] arrived at the station. They started negotiating

543. [Traditionally, a group of at least ten (adult male) Jews, known as a minyan, is required to say Kaddish, the prayer for the dead.]

544. Andrzej Jenicz, officer of the consular department of the Embassy of the Polish Government-in-Exile.

545. Józef Gawlina (1892–1964): major general, archbishop, military bishop for the Polish army. After the Sikorski-Maisky agreement in 1941, he inspected Polish military centers in the USSR in Kyrgyzstan and Uzbekistan.

546. Klemens Stanisław Rudnicki (1897–1992): colonel of the Polish army, in 1940 chief of staff

and wanted to find out, first of all, why I had been put in handcuffs. It turned out that my only mistake was the fact that I had once agreed to become a Soviet citizen. While the Colonel and Bishop Gawlina carried out negotiations with the NKVD-ers and said that the transport would not leave without me, Consul Jenicz took off his gold watch and stuffed it into my pocket; [he] also gave me a leather case with thirty thousand rubles, advising that I smuggle myself to Tehran. I categorically refused. The NKVD-ers made telephone contact with General Zhukov.[547] The general said he would come to the station promptly. Meanwhile Bishop Gawlina said that I deserved my punishment because I had worn silk rabbi garments when visiting him, [but] dressed the European way [instead] when traveling. It [was] an insult to the rabbinic position, [according to him]. General Zhukov arrived, and he shouted at me [for] being a cheater, since it's not possible to have a Russian passport and leave as a Pole. Bishop Gawlina reacted sharply to [this] insult of a clergyman, stating that [it amounted to] insulting the entire clerical standing of all religions. This protest pacified General Zhukov, and I was allowed to leave. Consul Jenicz, Bishop Gawlina, and Colonel Bohusz brought my belongings to the train at the last minute, as it was starting up. Thus I left Russia and got to Tehran and Palestine via Krasnovodsk.

---

of General Michał Tokarzewski-Karaszewicz in ZWZ [Związek Walki Zbrojnej; English: Union of Armed Struggle]. He was arrested for attempting to cross the border and get to Lwów and was deported to Siberia. He was released after the Amnesty in August 1942. In 1943–45, he was deputy to the leader of the Fifth Carpathian Infantry Division in the rank of major general and was a participant in the battles of Monte Cassino and Ancona.

547. Georgy S. Zhukov [Polish: Georgij S. Żukow] (1907–?): major general of the NKVD, Soviet state commissioner for the affairs of foreign military formations organized in the USSR. After the evacuation of the Anders Army from the USSR, completed on 26 August 1942, he returned to the central office of his department in October 1943, then [supervised] the Kościuszko Division formed in the USSR on the initiative of the Union of Polish Patriots (de facto Polish Communists, fugitives from the occupied state). Later he was assigned to work in the leadership of the penal camps of the NKVD, the so-called Gulag. He was arrested for misuse [of power]; after discharge, he worked as the director of a hotel in Moscow.

Protocol 217

Testimony of **Abraham Lewi**, age thirty-two, from Jędrzejów Kielecki. Came to Palestine via Persia in June 1943.

During the first days [of the war], our town was bombed horrifically, because there were ammunition factories outside town that served as a target for the German airplanes. The civilians suffered too; many houses burned down, and the town inhabitants ran from one place to another looking for shelter. On hearing that the Germans were approaching, a few of us—a group of young people—decided to leave town. We planned to set off toward Kraków, where [some of] my relatives lived. The roads were full of cars, military and civilian carts, rushing ahead without a set destination. The roads became targets for German bombs. German airplanes [flew down] very low, and the people fleeing hid in ditches or in the surrounding fields, often still in reach of the German bombs. In the mid-part of the [route], we came upon a large group of refugees going in the opposite direction. From them we learned about the evacuation of Kraków, which is why we changed direction and headed for Lwów. Because we were very tired, we bought a horse and a cart in one of the villages and set off for Lwów in a group of eight. We only used this mode of transport for the first few hours: at one point we left the horse on the road when we went to hide from an air raid. On our return we found neither the horse nor the cart.

Walking toward Rozwadów and Rawa Ruska, we got to Lwów. Fighting was taking place around [the city]. The enemy had suffered his first defeat, which raised the spirits of the civilians a great deal. [People] believed that help from England and France was imminent. Civilians helped to build trenches; I also worked, not paying attention to the bombardment. Suddenly we saw Russian tanks go by. The remains of the Polish army were running away from the Russian border. The Germans retreated, and the Bolsheviks began [their] rule in town. The Jews breathed easy. The Ukrainians grew emboldened, but the authorities did not allow anti-Jewish or anti-Polish disturbances. Russian soldiers bought out everything from the shops. [People] did business with them; they had plenty of money.

With no news from home, where I had left [my] elderly parents and relatives, I became very worried. And despite the warnings of [my] friends, I set off toward the green border,[548] intending to go back to Jędrzejów. I wandered around the roads for eight days. I found evidence of total destruction everywhere. I finally made it home, where the atmosphere was gloomy. The Germans reveled as they wished. They caught Jews for work, cut off their beards, beat and humiliated them; and when the Jews [grew] fearful of going out in the streets, the Germans started coming into [their] houses and taking away everything they could get their hands on. I [understood] that it was pointless to stay like this any longer. Since I couldn't help [my] parents anyway, I set off for Lwów with [my] two sisters. You couldn't cross the street in Lwów—that's how many people there were—let alone get a room. I shared [a] room with [my] companions, and like them, took up trading. I traded in everything, mainly watches and currency. We earned good money. But this didn't last long. NKVD-ers persecuted us, and new laws came out every day.

When the passportization began, I refused to accept Soviet citizenship as I had no intention of staying in the Red country, and also because the refugee passports did not allow one to settle in a big city. When a German commission came to Lwów and the registration to return home began, kilometer-long lines formed in front of the bureau. Having had a taste of [being in] German custody, I didn't register, and I encouraged other people not to register [either]. I was arrested for this activity. Policemen came in the middle of the night; I was allowed to bring some stuff and the rest was taken away, and [I was] taken to the notorious prison in Brygidki. Forty-five people were housed in a small cell. I thought I wouldn't last long. I spent ten weeks in [these] awful conditions. [In the cell] with me there were social activists, Jews and Poles, ND-members and Communists. Every night a few [people] would be taken out for questioning, from which they would return beaten up. During the interrogation, I was accused of illegal border crossing. I had to sign a protocol of testimonies I had not given. Because I signed the protocol, I was no longer taken in for interrogation, but was driven to the station two weeks later. I didn't know I would be going and didn't manage to tell [my] sisters in time to bring my belongings to

548. A poorly protected section of the state border; typically terrain covered with vegetation: forests, thickets, or meadows.

the station. [I was] locked inside a freight car with fifty other prisoners, and we set off. In Homel we were taken to the local prison, where I spent a few weeks. I learned there that I had been sentenced to five years of labor camp, which was a light sentence. I then set off for Pskov and was locked up in prison again for a few weeks there.

The last leg of the journey finished in Rybinsk, in the Arkhangelsk Oblast. We went 150 kilometers on foot, all the way to the camp, which was located in the middle of a forest. There was a sawmill and a brick factory nearby, where we worked. There were ten thousand prisoners in our camp, Russians for the most part, mainly participants in the Russian-Finnish war who had fallen into captivity. When the prisoners returned home after the end of the war, they were sentenced to ten years in a camp, because a Soviet soldier was not allowed to surrender. The real reason for [their] deportation was the fact that the prisoners had gotten to know life in [a] civilized [country like] Finland. Those Russians robbed us of everything we had. Luckily, most of our belongings were in sealed coffers, looked after by the authorities. When I complained to the commandant one day that I'd had my jacket stolen, he carried out an investigation and didn't find anything. It turned out a few weeks later that the commandant himself was wearing my stolen jacket. When I pointed this out to him, he punched me between my eyes with his fist, and I collapsed, unconscious. From that moment on, he started bullying me horribly. I was told that if I wanted to live [on good terms] with him, I should sell him my gold Longines watch, which was in the locked coffer, for two hundred rubles. I replied that he would inherit the watch after my death. Even though I worked hard, not once did I manage to fulfill my quota and get a kilo of bread. I had to sell everything I had on me so I wouldn't starve to death. The situation worsened considerably after the outbreak of the war. We received four hundred grams of bread per day each. Working hours were increased; NKVD-ers watched us and wouldn't let us catch our breath.

After the announcement of the Amnesty, they tried to convince us that we should stay in Russia, promising us the moon. I got a pass and 122 rubles' worth of wages for the entire time I worked and went to Arkhangelsk. I looked for a buyer for my watch [and] finally got 430 rubles for it in a state consignment shop. With this money I rented a wagon with [some] others and went to Tashkent. Seeing the desperate situation of the people [there], who had no roof over their heads, I left the city and went to Bukhara. I attempted to find my two sisters [who had been] deported to a *posiołek* from Lwów, but did not succeed. In Bukhara I traded in makhorka, tea, and sugar. I couldn't get work and didn't want to go to a kolkhoz. A few times I tried to get accepted to the Polish army but did not succeed. I sneaked into a train car leaving with a transport and got to Krasnovodsk, and [the same] way, to Pahlevi. From there I went to Tehran, where I spent a year, and from there I came to Palestine after receiving [my] certificate.

Protocol 219

Testimony of **Cwi Landau** from Ostrowiec, age twenty-three.

I escaped from Ostrowiec, my hometown, before the Germans took control of it. I left on a bicycle (for which, on the way, I was offered a new car without gasoline), and went to Lublin, Chełm, Dubno, and Ostróg, all the way to the Soviet border. I arrived in Ostróg barely alive, and my only dream was a bed where I could sleep in peace. I don't know how long I slept. When I awoke, the Bolsheviks had taken over Ostróg. It was on the seventeenth [of September 1939] and all of the inhabitants of Ostróg, who had known nothing about bombardments until then, rushed out into the streets, Poles and Jews together. Polish policemen greeted the Soviet army with flowers. Local Communists brought posts on their backs and set them up in front of the city to mark the border. The joy did not last long. The Red Army surrounded the policemen carrying flowers and arrested them. The town got a taste of Soviet hunger. Food products disappeared from shops, [and] people were afraid of [what] tomorrow [would bring] . . .

It was said that the Bolsheviks would reach Warsaw and occupy all of Poland. We believed this, and a few refugees got on a train going to Poland, wishing to get home as quickly as possible. After seven days' journey, in Krasnystaw, we were told that the train would not go farther. Tired and hungry, we set off in search of food, and seeing the Polish army's supply car on a sidetrack, forced the doors open and found a lot of bread that the army had left behind during [their] escape. Although the bread was moldy, we didn't pay it [any] attention and we satisfied our hunger. We went on foot toward Izbica. We found [a state of] panic there. The Bolsheviks were leaving town. Young people didn't know what to do. The Bolsheviks were willingly taking civilians with [them] on their army trucks; they took me as well and brought me to Zamość. From there, I went to Lwów by train. I couldn't recognize Lwów. The streets were dirty and so full of people that one couldn't get across them. [Finding] a place for the night was out of the question, and like thousands of other people, I had to sleep in the station. Prices were unimaginably high. Within a few days, I ran out of money. I started to look for work. I was struggling [to find a job]. I went from office to office and finally got a job cleaning the streets for a few days. I earned around three to four rubles per day. The work was irregular.

I heard that registration of workers to go to Donbas had begun. I had nothing to lose and I registered, receiving fifty rubles as an advance for future work. Our transport soon left Lwów. We traveled for seven days, fifty people to one train car. We brought food from Lwów, and since it really was only young people who registered, had great fun in the car. We got to Stalino this way.[549] We were greeted with music at the station. Speeches were made, [but] we didn't know what they were about because no one understood Russian. We were taken to a canteen and fed generously. Then we were driven to a cinema where the film *Lenin in 1918* was being shown, and to finish the day, we were invited to a ballroom. I sat next to a Soviet girl in the cinema. I didn't know the language to communicate with her. But when I saw her in the ballroom, I asked her to dance. We danced without a pause, all evening long, until I noticed at some point that my companions had long since left the venue and I was on my own. I was distraught. While I did know the place [where] my companions were staying, I couldn't find it [alone]. There were two million people living in Stalino. I couldn't ask in Russian, but the girl comforted me, [saying] she would take me home. However, she took me not to my companions' place but to her room. She lived with [her] father, who began treating me like his daughter's fiancé. I spent a full six days and nights in Stalino. We were [finally] taken to a coal mine on the seventh day. We were given clothing [and] tools and lowered to the bottom of the coal mine. A few of us fainted during this ride down. We followed our guide down a corridor. A Soviet worker showed us how we were supposed to work, and we began working in incredibly harsh conditions. We worked at a depth of tens of stories and the elevator journey [down] to [our] place of work took an hour. We only worked for eight hours in the high temperatures, but with the descent and the [return] and getting changed, it took twelve hours [altogether]. I got five rubles per day for the work. I ate at the canteen, where a cutlet cost two rubles and soup fifty kopecks. To buy something to wear was out of the question. Even though the conditions weren't great, I kept on breaking the coal with a hammer and I

549. Stalino: current and former Donetsk.

placed supports under selected spot[s]. I pushed loaded wagons down tracks and worked for two weeks [in total] like this.

I would have carried on working were it not for an accident in which I almost lost my life. I was pushing a wagon with coal along with a Russian worker, when it fell off [the tracks] and almost buried us. I lost consciousness. A feldsher arrived and I was taken to a hospital by the mine. It turned out that my hip was broken, and I spent seven weeks in the hospital. The attitude of the doctors and nurses toward me was incredibly kind. [One] older nurse in particular, a Jewess, treated me like [her] son. I didn't lack for anything. After two months I got a certificate from the doctors [stating] that I was unfit for hard labor, and because I had completed a Red Cross course in Poland, I was made into a feldsher at the mine's polyclinic. My colleague, an older Russian feldsher, taught me in Russian, showed me how to treat the patients, and I soon became a good feldsher. I earned three hundred rubles per month, ate independently, lived separately, and was slowly growing used to life in Stalino.

The city was huge. The two main streets looked completely metropolitan. Omnibuses and trolleybuses ran in the city. Beyond this, the smaller streets looked more like a village and there were many houses thatched with straw. I spent five months in Stalino. I was the doctors' and the patients' favorite. I had many friends and grew attached to the city. But my longing for Father and Mother wouldn't leave me in peace, and when I received a letter from [my] uncle in Lwów [saying] there was a registration taking place of people who wanted to return to the German-occupied territories, I succeeded in getting leave [from work] and went to Lwów. I registered to leave and was soon arrested. Unmarried men, that is, single people, were arrested a month before the general deportation and sent to Siberia in July 1940. There were seventy of us in one car. Food was brought in every night. Water was rationed like a priceless liquid. We always kept [some] water supplies for those who lost consciousness, which happened often.

After a month's journey, we arrived at labor camp Sucha Bezwodna 17,[550] where 1,500 men and 50 women were accommodated in two barracks. Thanks to the protection of [my] friend from Donbas, I became the laundry supervisor. The work was hard: you had to pull the water up from a deep well,

550. Correct name: Sukhobezvodnoe [original Polish correction: Suchobiezwodnoje].

and I was responsible for the time [it took] to finish the undergarments. At any rate, I had a job. I slept separately next to the bathhouse [and] received better food. Twelve women worked in the laundry room. Their quotas were 120 pieces of undergarments per day, and those who fulfilled [it] got [their] meal from the canteen, while others ate from kettle number 3, where the soup equaled water. I was taught to forge the quotas [following] the bookkeeper's suggestions. No one noticed my machinations, while the warden flattered me generously, and [his] wife would bring me cigarettes when she came for a bath. I was considered the chosen one in the camp. Others were tortured. They were rushed out to work in the forest in the harshest frost, from which they returned sick, parts of [their] body frostbitten. They dropped like flies, and soon there were [only] five hundred people left out of a thousand. Suicide was common. One Jew, Rozen from Kraków, who had left [his] family behind in Poland, threw himself into the well from which we drew the water. I saved him by a miracle. Three times he tried to commit suicide. I locked him in the laundry room. He was sent to a hospital where he was watched closely. He sneaked out of the hospital one night and drowned himself in a huge kettle in the laundry room.

After many months, groups of Russian thieves were brought to our camp for hard labor. They considered themselves superior, bullied everyone, and denounced the Poles. I fell victim to them. One day the warden carried out a search in my corner, found a little pot I had bought from the peasants in the village, and as punishment, I was sent to work in the forest. I loaded timber onto wagons and overworked myself horribly carrying nine-meter-long tree trunks. For this hard work in −50°C [−58°F], we received laughable wages, and for a portion of bread, you had to pay twenty-five rubles. I sold my shirt, clothes, and shoes. After a month's work I was sent to the forest to chop [down] trees. We walked in deep snow, and it was seven kilometers to [our] work site. We were woken up at three at night, rushed to the canteen, [and] went to work at five o'clock. There wasn't a moment to rest. We didn't manage to achieve [our] quotas in time and received food from kettle number 3. I grew so weak and was so distraught because of lack of sleep and hunger that I almost killed our supervisor, who was a Pole. When I bent over to pick [some] berries in the woods and satisfy my hunger this way, he started shouting at me. I grabbed an ax, and were it not for my companions' intervention, would have killed him. I was sentenced to three days in the punishment cell and then sent to work in the care of the same supervisor. We slept on bare planks, covering ourselves with [our] work jackets. I lost [my] strength completely, was staggering on [my] feet, and only then was I given lighter work—which I couldn't do either. I lost thirty-five kilos in weight, and a doctor released me from work. I left the camp after the announcement of the Amnesty. I managed to cross the Russian border on 10 September 1942 and get to Palestine via Tehran.

Protocol 223

Testimony of **Mosze Zira**, age fifteen, from Zamość, son of Dawid and Szyfra. Came to Palestine from Russia via Persia in August 1943.

My father was the owner of a bakery, where a few workers were employed. [My] older brother Aron, age twenty-two, helped Father, and my younger brother Berysz and I studied. When the war broke out, there were long lines in front of our bakery. [People] tore bread out of each other's hands, and [we] couldn't keep up with the baking. The first two days of the war went by peacefully in our town, and the bombardments only started on the third day. Fighting between the Polish and German armies was taking place outside town. It seemed at times that the Germans were about to take the city, but then they would be pushed out. Many homes were destroyed because of the battles, and many people were killed. These battles lasted until the fourteenth of September 1939, when the Germans occupied our town. After taking over the town, they immediately gathered up the Jews and locked them in the barracks for eight days. They were not allowed food and water, and every evening the Germans would shoot at the barracks. Many Jews died.

It was said that the Germans would not let anyone out alive, but [they] left town on the eighth day and the Jews were saved thanks to the arrival of the Bolsheviks. The day after entering the city, the Bolsheviks requisitioned the bakery. It was forbidden to bake bread for the civilians, and Father had to use the flour for the army. When our flour supplies ran out, they brought in new sacks, confiscated from the peasants, and we continued to bake bread. Lots of arrests were carried out in that period; my uncle Gerszon Gewirman was arrested, among others. The Bolsheviks were in our town for two weeks, and when they were planning to leave, they put up posters with a message that civilians who wanted to leave town could come with them. They didn't forget to take with them all the people who had been arrested. Father, remembering what it had been like during the Germans' eight-day stay in the city, decided to follow the Bolsheviks, but the Bolsheviks didn't have enough space in the wagons and cars, [and we] had to find a means of transport on our own. We rented a car and went to Włodzimierz. Father rented an apartment there and we lived peacefully. Father and [my] brother didn't work. The Bolsheviks didn't want to give Father a job, viewing him as a former bourgeois, even though he was a [skilled] professional. We lived by selling things we had brought with us from home. Even though bad news was coming from Zamość, Father regretted leaving home where, as he said, he could always make do. Father was particularly worried about our education. As an observant Jew, he didn't want to let us go to a Soviet school and be brought up as Communists. We studied with a private teacher of Judaic studies. Every day new restrictions came out relating to passportization and registration. Father didn't want to become a Soviet citizen under any circumstances, but the time came when the Bolsheviks turned up at our house, arrested the whole family, and sent [us] to the station. We spent a month inside a sealed freight car, traveling in an unknown direction, hungry, dirty, and lice ridden. There were Poles in our car as well. I remember the surnames of [some of the] Jews: Englender and Figotner from Kraków.

After a month, we arrived in Assina,[551] Novosibirsk district. Because my brother Berysz fell ill on the journey, we were left behind in Assina, while others were sent to *posiołki*. We lived in a barracks that was a part of a group of barracks surrounded with wire, so we wouldn't be able to escape. We lived side by side with Russian exiles, both criminals and political prisoners. The criminals stole from us constantly and within a few weeks had left us with nothing. The political [prisoners] didn't want to speak to us at first, afraid of [making] contact with foreigners. Slowly, however, they began to tell us how they had been arrested and tortured in prisons. The barracks had been built by them, but it didn't count toward their work hours. They worked during the day and built at night. Many died from hunger and cold and diseases. After a few weeks, Father got a job in a bakery. We had enough bread, and there was [even] enough of it to exchange for other products. This situation lasted four months, after which Father was arrested, accused of consuming too much bread. He was taken to prison in Armak [?], close to us. At that time, a man named Rajman was also arrested for being five minutes late for work. He was put in Armak too, sentenced to a year in jail. Mother made attempts to see Father. It was in vain; we didn't see Father even once during his stay in

551. Correctly: Asino.

prison. [My] brother Aron was working in a sawmill in Assina. One day he was crushed by a tree trunk while at work. [My] brother was killed on the spot. We only found out about it a few weeks later.

Our situation was desperate. Father in prison, [my] brother dead, Mama ill—she couldn't go to work. We had no more belongings left to sell [and] were at risk of death from starvation. I went to the chief, asking for work. I was twelve at the time. I became a water carrier for officials and policemen. I received a skinny horse and a cart on two wheels, because you had to carry water from far away because the water in our *posiołek* was very poor quality. The tired horse would often stop on the way and I would have to pull the cart myself because I felt [too] bad to beat the starved creature. One day, however, I did have to hit it, at which point the horse bucked and tipped over the cart with the barrel of water. I was almost killed. I often wished I would die during this work, but the thought that I was supporting Mother and [my] younger brother kept me from [committing] suicide. I was a water carrier until the moment the Amnesty was announced. We didn't know about the outbreak of the war—only the decreased bread ration[s] and increased number of working hours showed us that something had happened. Even [my] sick mother was forced to work. Not until a high-ranking NKVD official told us did we learn about the war and the Amnesty.

We didn't want to leave the *posiołek* without Father. Mama was told that Father was ill, another time [she was told] that he had been sent away somewhere. Meanwhile, we were kicked out of the barracks and they didn't want to give us bread. We spent four days under the open sky, and realizing that we would die of starvation, set off toward the station, where we lodged in a small hut. Father was still in prison. Mama made efforts to have him released. Only two months later, after an intervention by the Polish delegation, was Father released. I didn't [even] recognize him: he was swollen up, had a limp, was hairy like a wild animal, and was dressed in rags like a beggar. He told [us] about his experiences. There were no cells in the prison, only earth pits, completely unfurnished. Father worked the winter and the summer there, all day long, and [had to] walk fifteen kilometers to work one way and fifteen [back]. On the way, the prisoners would try to steal from the fields out of hunger but would then be beaten over the head with gunstocks. Father said that [things] couldn't be worse in hell [itself]. He mentioned many well-known and respected people from Russia who were in that prison.

We rode the train south for two months, going hungry during the journey. The train would stop every few hours and wait for a few days. We begged for bread at the stations. Father passed away from hunger and exhaustion on the way. It was on the thirteenth of January 1942, at the station of Oryś,[552] one hundred kilometers outside Tashkent. He was taken away, and I don't know where he was buried. At the Kinel[553] station, [my] brother Berysz got off to look for food. The train started, and he [was left] behind. What happened to him I don't know; I never heard anything more of him. Out of the whole family of five, [only] Mother and I were left. We were supposed to go to Guzar, but I told Mother in Tashkent that we [should] leave the car and see the city. The train was waiting there all day. I left to look for food. When I returned toward evening, I found Mother dead. I started to cry and tear my hair out. Policemen took Mother's body away. I was left alone in the car. The train set off for Guzar the next day. They didn't want to let me off the car as there was a typhus epidemic there. We were told to go back. Representatives from the delegation gave us [enough] bread for three days, paid for our travel, and said that we would get food at the final station. We didn't receive anything, [and] no one was waiting for us. We ate oil cakes, caught cats and dogs, killed and ate them. After a month's journey, we arrived in Aktyubinsk. We were sent to a kolkhoz. They wanted to send me to a Russian orphanage, but I preferred to work in a brickyard. I thought I would share my family's fate as I worked in [these] horrific conditions. When I learned that there was a Polish orphanage in Akkemir [?], I went there and was taken in. I was sent to Ashgabat four months later. This was at the time when Polish-Soviet diplomatic relations were severed.[554] Our directors said that the Bolsheviks would send us to kolkhozes. How we rejoiced on hearing that, on 27 July 1943, we would leave Ashgabat and depart from Russia.

552. Likely the town of Arys.
553. The town of Kinel is in the Kuybyshev area.
554. That is, 25 April 1943.

Protocol 232

Doctor **Pilcer,**[555] lawyer, resident in Kraków before the war [and] currently in Tel Aviv, Hotel Ness-Ziona, testifies:

On the day of 2 September 1939, I left Kraków, going to Lwów the long way round. I found myself in Lwów on 17 September. I stayed in Warkowicze in Wołyń for some time, where the first news of the Soviet army's crossing of the Polish border reached me. That fact was generally explained as the army coming to help us in the fight again Germans. On the morning of 17 September, the manager of the local post office announced that the Soviet army was in Ostróg, and quoting the local authority's order, called on the townspeople to welcome the arriving Soviet divisions with loud acclaim. In accordance with this request, the residents of Warkowicze, Poles, Jews, and Ukrainians, gathered in large numbers at the time of the Soviet army's arrival. A *politruk* spoke to the gathered [crowd] with words that seem odd today: we're going to fight the Germans, Poland was [once] here—and here, a people's Poland will be.

At the same time, the Soviet authorities had already arrested the Senator Professor Doctor Schorr[556] in nearby Ostrów, and did not want to release him despite interventions.

When I arrived in Lwów on 17 October, the Soviet authorities already held complete power and were fully occupied with the Sovietization of political and economic life.

I have often come across the accusation that the Jews supported all of the Soviets' plans—an accusation as shallow as it is incorrect.

Among the Jewish, one must differentiate between groups: the first encompassed a small group of largely young worker-Communists [and] was, by its nature, the loudest and most active. Working in accordance with the intentions and suggestions of the Soviet authorities, it had the right and the duty to carry out propaganda. It was, therefore, everywhere. This group worked a great deal, and frantically, and was seen and heard all over the place.

555. Likely refers to Doctor Samuel Pilzer.

556. Mojżesz Schorr (1874–1941): professor at Warsaw University, senator of the Republic of Poland, rabbi of the Great Synagogue of Tłomackie [Street]. See also note in Protocol 171.

There was another group that wasn't politically active and didn't carry out any propaganda but wanted to survive. They were workers in various trades, factories, [and] workshops who had to adapt to the new conditions if they wanted to earn [enough] to support themselves and [their] families.

Finally, there was a third group, spanning a huge majority of the Jewish populace: the merchant class, owners of manufacturing businesses, owners of real estate, and a considerable part of the intelligentsia who were completely shocked [when] the Soviet regime was introduced. People in this group, broken and scared, hid in [their] homes, where they awaited the next orders with fear and worry.

And that same line of differentiation ran through Polish society, too.

Since only the Jews from the first group were seen, loud and active, on the streets, at demonstrations and marches and in new enterprises and workshops, and by the nature of things, one could witness neither the thoughts not the feelings of the Jews in the second and third groups—generalizations became common.

Within a few months, the entire merchant class was liquidated, all goods confiscated from the factory and real estate owners (which were nationalized), [and] the manufacturing circles closed down (their workshops turned into cooperatives). The legal profession (with the exception of a hundred people) was deprived of bread and work, and to a large extent, homes.

The first arrests began at that time. At that point, they affected only the most prominent political activists. One of the first was the MP, Doctor Sommerstein.[557]

The other tranche of deportees were refugees. That [deportation] took place after a few registrations [were] carried out, as announced in the official decrees, to register all refugees [who] wanted to return home. And indeed, a German commission arrived sometime later. Many Poles left then, mainly state and local officials, as well as a very small number of Jews.

At the end of May or the beginning of June, a registration with the aforementioned purpose was ordered again. But it turned out later one night that

557. Dr. Emil Sommerstein (1883–1957): lawyer, Zionist activist, MP of the Republic of Poland in the years 1922–27. After the war he was a member of PKWN [Polski Komitet Wyzwolenia Narodowego; English: Polish Committee of National Liberation] and chairman of the Central Committee of Jews in Poland [Polish: Centralny Komitet Żydów w Polsce]. He emigrated to the United States in 1946.

that was only a pretext. Around 20 June [1940], all or almost all single refugees, primarily men, were captured one night; and a few days later, the large majority of the refugee families. The first group was brought up on charges: so-called prosecutors carried out an examination of the "accused," and [the latter] had their sentences announced after some time without any trial. They were mainly accused of not accepting passport[s] (even though the relevant state regulations during the passportization, as it was known, in January 1940, contained provisions [stating] that only the permanent residents of a given locality were subject to passportization) and of espionage. The sentences amounted to between eight and ten years of prison; there were cases where the "culprits" received death sentences, which were, however, generally changed to prison time. Those sentenced this way were taken to *łagry*, forced labor camps with incredibly strict regimes, where according to consistent and unanimous descriptions by individuals who have stayed in various "gulags," life was, in every respect, hell on earth.

By contrast, the refugee families were captured in the days of 28–30 June 1940 [and] taken to the so-called work *posiołki* scattered across all of Russia, from the Volga regions to the farthest north and farthest east. Although these families were not [given] any sentences, the NKVD authorities announced uniformly everywhere that those families had been condemned to indefinite terms in those *posiołki*. Everyone was forced to work in those *posiołki*—in forests, mines, etc.; the work regime was immensely strict, the work conditions the worst one could imagine, the living and sanitary conditions very bad—with the exception of some *posiołki*—and under these circumstances, [and] despite the freedom of movement within the boundaries of the *posiołek*, life became unbearable due to the individual orders of the relevant NKVD commandants.

The economic conditions in the labor camps and the *posiołki* were lamentable. Almost everyone worked in the labor camps, with the exception of the temporarily ill. We received paltry, scant food. Everyone between sixteen and sixty years [of age] worked, [though] in reality, the upper age limit was [one's] ability to work. The wages were minimal. Young workers, women, and older people [doing] so-called light work didn't even earn enough to afford bread. The wages were between twenty and forty rubles. The men [doing] real work, e.g., in the forest, transporting the timber to the light rail line and loading [it] onto the cars, earned very little at first, but [a few] months later, the loaders in particular would earn amounts [that were] enough to live on—but the bonus system that was in place brought the wages back to the lowest level every six months. The result of these pay conditions was that we generally went hungry in the *posiołki*, or at least didn't eat a sufficient amount. The main source [of money] to cover the costs of a rudimentary upkeep was the sale of all of the belongings we had brought with us at deportation. And when, after some time, we had sold everything, we went around in rags. This led to a complete physical and nervous breakdown.

After the conclusion of the agreement between Poland and Russia in July 1941, a new era dawned for all Polish citizens who were in Russia. We were released from camps on this basis, and each of us received an *udostoverenie*[558]—a document stating that one was a Polish citizen, that they had been pardoned and had the right to reside across all of the territory of Soviet Russia, with the exception of the regions and towns listed in the document. Neither in the July [agreement], the document, nor [still] in the actions of the Soviet authorities, was there any differentiation according to faith or [one's] permanent place of residence on [either] the east or the west side of the border set between Russia and Germany in 1939. That differentiation came into being for the first time after the declaration of the Soviet government released in December 1941.

After various adventures, I found myself in Tashkent. A branch of the Polish authorities was operating there already whose aim was to extend social care over the masses of refugees coming in in the thousands from various *posiołki*. It is understandable that it was simply impossible to efficiently manage responsible assistance activities in [these] primitive conditions, particularly since the resources were highly limited. A certain lack in the functioning of this apparatus was seen in a notice put up in December 1941 on the gates of Hotel Nasional [Nacional], where the delegation operated, in which the funds were [declared to be] limited to only those people who had resided in kolkhozes, [while] tens of thousands of unfortunates filling up cities in search of paid work were excluded from using [these funds].

When the beginnings of a Polish army began to form in Soviet Russia in Totskoye, I reported to the Polish Military Mission in that matter on the basis of a voluntary draft—unfortunately without success. A few months later, the voluntary registration rule was abolished by the draft order announced in

558. *Udostoverenie* [original Polish correction: *udostwierenije*]: official [release] certificate.

Tashkent by delegate Kwapiński[559] on the orders of the army command, which stated: "Conscription only relates to Polish citizens of Polish nationality." The wording of the quoted order caused many an unnecessary misunderstanding.

From that moment on, masses of [people] who wished to do their duty by reporting for the Polish army began to flow in. During the first period of the organization of the Polish army, to which I bore witness, one road battalion stationed in Kermine numbered 240 people, including more than two hundred Jews. This battalion was then dissolved, and a large number of people were discharged. Because everyone had their *udostoverenie* taken away on reporting for the army, and didn't get the document back on discharge, those people found themselves in a desperate situation. They wandered around from town to town for months, unable to [find] either work or an apartment. One can imagine these people's destitution, bitterness, and anguish.

Parallel to the business of the organization of the Polish army in Russia there was the issue of evacuation. I made efforts, in the first instance, to get into the transports leaving Russia, going through various stages and phases of that one-of-a-kind epic [undertaking]. The first wave, in April 1942, came so suddenly and concluded so quickly that only those who lived in the towns where the departing units were stationed[560] knew about it. [As I] lived on a side route at the time, there was no way for me to join that transport. The army left then, [and] civilians concentrated in the towns where [their] sons, fathers [and] daughters had served. Those who found themselves on the route of the passing transport by chance, or who got to the route after hearing about the transport, also left without difficulties then.

During the organization of the second transport, which took place after the return of General Anders, a registration to leave was started, which I naturally [took part in] straightaway. However, right from the very beginning, such [serious] difficulties emerged—[difficulties that both] I and my friends encountered—that I simply fell into dark despair. The [issue] was that the evacuation authorities were applying with the utmost strictness a rule that excluded from the evacuation list[s] [any] persons who were present in the

559. Jan Kwapiński (1885–[1964]): PPS [Polska Partia Socjalistyczna; English: Polish Socialist Party; PSP] and union activist. See also note in Protocol 27.

560. [The original verb (*garnizować*) is flagged in the footnote, likely because it is not a widely used form. Interestingly, it is used in English (to garrison).]

territory annexed to Russia in the year 1939 during the [time of the] plebiscite in that [area]—that is, on 29 November 1939—invoking the position of the Soviet government on the matter.

I decided to turn to General Anders with a delegation on this matter, [and he] received me and Rabbi Hagler after some time. During the audience, General Anders said that he did not intend to hinder anyone's departure from Russia, even Polish citizens of the Jewish faith, [and the only thing that] stood in the way was the Soviet authorities, who kept a close watch over the acquisition of Soviet citizenship by persons who resided in the area annexed to Russia on 29 November 1939. We explained the sham of the plebiscite, as well as the fact that 99 percent of [people] who faced not being placed on the evacuation list were in the labor camps, precisely because they hadn't wanted to accept Soviet passports. General Anders decided to order that every Jew who submitted the correct certificate from the Soviet authorities be placed on the list, and authorized us to turn to those very Soviet authorities on this matter. We knew perfectly well what intervening with the general authorities of the NKVD meant. We didn't, however, have an alternative.

After much difficulty, we managed to contact Colonel Tyshkov, the permanent NKVD representative for the Polish command, and General Zhukov, representative of the Soviet General Staff for the matter of evacuation of the Polish [army]. During a special audience, General Zhukov presented to us an exhausting account of the Soviet point of view concerning evacuation, and then said that he had nothing against placing Jews on the evacuation list. In the course of the conversation, General Zhukov asked to see General Bohusz, General Anders's deputy, telling him more or less the same thing that he had told us. He also added that he would turn a blind eye to the lists and would sign [them] without checking.

The next day we reported to General Bohusz, who informed us that he was putting seventy departure places at our disposal. Although we knew that tens of thousands were waiting for [their] freedom, we had to accept that number, otherwise no one would leave.

Further formalities [before] departure were not at all pleasant, but [that meant] nothing compared to the feeling we experienced on realizing that we were finally leaving.

I came to Palestine on the basis of a certificate, on a sea transport, via Iran.

Protocol 235

Testimony of **Jehoszua Gertner**, president of the Jewish council in Kosów Huculski. Left Poland illegally in February 1943, escaping to Romania.

Bolsheviks in Kosów

When the Polish authorities left Kosów, the Jewish people were overcome with panic. The Germans were near, and news about their behavior in other towns came frequently. [Those] who wanted to escape across the border had [their] way blocked by the border guard. Meanwhile, news of the Russians' entry into Poland spread. At first, Jews took this news with a feeling of relief—it's always better to deal with those than with Germans. Everyone, however, grew disillusioned. We soon learned that antisemitism was not alien even to the Soviet authorities. Even though the Russians [themselves] didn't know it [antisemitism], they sent high-ranking Ukrainian officials from the Soviet Republic of Ukraine, who turned out to be outstanding antisemites. The local Ukrainians, who took revenge on Jews in any way they could, had a huge influence on [the newly arrived Ukrainians]. Officially, it was the merchant and the profiteer who were persecuted, not the Jew. There were many nationalists among the Ukrainians who had an influence on the new administration, members of the terrorist organization UNRO.[561] The Jews who had a Zionist past fared the worst. Those same Ukrainians who had flattered the Bolshevik authority became the Gestapo's trusted [people] after the Germans' arrival and started accusing Jews of [holding] Bolshevik sympathies.

561. Correctly: UNDO: Ukraińskie Zjednoczenie Narodowo-Demokratyczne [Ukrainian National Democratic Alliance]. Terrorist activity, however, was carried out not by UNDO but by OUN, Organizacja Ukraińskich Nacjonalistów [Organization of Ukrainian Nationalists].

Protocol 238

Testimony of Rabbi **Mordechaj Rokach**[562] from Białogóra, brother of a well-known rabbi from Bełżec,[563] who took refuge in Sokal when escaping the Germans. Left Poland in May 1943 and came to Palestine in January 1944, along with his brother.

At the time of the outbreak of the war I was in Białogóra and my brother, a well-known rabbi,[564] in Bełżec. Our town was bombed in the first days of the war. Panic broke out and people left their homes, going toward Wołyń. Knowing that my brother, the rabbi, was occupied only with the matter of his soul and was devoid of any practical sense, I decided to go to Bełżec, to be by [his] side in case we had to leave our old family residence. But the refugees were being directed toward Wołyń. I too went in that direction with [my] wife and daughter. In Poryck, I learned that the rabbi planned to leave Bełżec and go to the Borderlands.[565] However, he had no means of transportation, since carts and cars had been requisitioned for the army. The rabbi didn't change his way of life: he debated holy matters surrounded by a large group of his followers who had come there from various parts of Poland, keen to stay by their Tzaddik's[566] side in [these] tragic times. The front was getting close to the town. The Hasids bought a droshky and two horses, which waited on standby until the rabbi decided to leave Bełżec. The rabbi was an ascetic. He ate only once a day, in the evening, and during the day drinks only coffee every now and again. He knew that everyone around was busy with their business and wouldn't remember the hungry horses [and] while he was having his coffee he constantly asked if the horses had been fed yet. According to God's law, he said,

562. Should be: Rokeach (although the version "Rokach" is sometimes used).

563. Refers to the town of Bełz, not Bełżec as in the protocol.

564. Aharon (Aron) Rokeach (1880–1957): rabbi, Bełz Tzaddik (esteemed rabbi), descendant of a Tzaddik dynasty [of] Hasids from Bełz. After the outbreak of the 1939 war, he escaped from the Germans to Sokal, then found himself, successively, in ghettos in Przemyśl, Wiśnicz, Kraków, and Bochnia, from which he went to Hungarian Košice in 1942. He got to Palestine in 1944. He died in Tel Aviv. His followers established [Hasidic] communities in Europe and America.

565. Polish: Kresy.

566. Tzaddik [Polish: *cadyk*]: righteous man. Rabbi enjoying exceptional esteem due to the mystical spiritual connection with God attributed to him.

a herdsman is not allowed to touch food until the cattle have been fed. [This] situation carried on until 24 September, that is till the Day of Atonement.[567] The town was full of refugees, army [people], and thousands of Hasids who had come to see the rabbi. There was a noticeable lack of foodstuffs. There were still supplies of food in the home of the rabbi, which [he] ordered to be given out [and] shared among Jews and Christians, officers, soldiers, and civilian refugees, irrespective of faith.

As I said, a large number of troops were concentrated in Bełżec, expecting a battle to take place there; the army was later withdrawn. The first German patrols appeared two days later. The Jewish people were overtaken by panic. A patrol would stay in town for a few hours and leave, announcing that it would visit [again] on the following day. The Polish army present in the area shot those Germans dead. Bełżec was left without Poles and without Germans. This situation dragged on for a few days. The rabbi still did not neglect his daily duties.

I left Poryck during that time [heading] for Łuck, where the Russians already were at the time. I kept in touch with [my] brother throughout, sent him money, he sent his thanks, and it seemed to me that the storm of war would pass Bełżec by. After some time, the Germans arrived. Along with them—members of the Gestapo. And [so], on the holiday, the rabbi left town with [his] family, [his] whole court, and the rabbi from Złotopole, Wolf Twerski. Polish landowners from the Bełżec area who were acquainted with him managed to procure a car and made it possible for the rabbi to leave for Sokal. In Sokal, the rabbi was welcomed just as in prewar times. The Bolsheviks didn't interfere with the religious celebrations.

Germans in Bełżec

As I learned from a trustworthy person who left Bełżec later, the Germans took to demolishing the Tzaddik's manor and the magnificent synagogue built by our great-grandfather 170 years ago with particular cruelty. It was one of the most beautiful synagogue buildings in Poland. It had taken fifteen years to build it. It resembled a fortress. The Germans set fire to it twice. They tried to detonate bombs below it but did not succeed in destroying it. [Both] Jews and Christians confirm this information.

---

567. [The date is incorrect:] in 1939 the holiday fell on 23 September.

Out of revenge for not being able to destroy the synagogue, the Germans decided to expel all Jews from Bełżec. The smaller synagogues were turned into stables for horses. Later the Germans brought Jews to Bełżec from the surrounding areas, and even from Łódź. They lived not in town but in a ghetto built outside [of it].

As two members of the local Jewish council told me—one of them a man from Łódź and the other Dr. Tauber from Kraków—the Christians from the area told [stories] about how, every night, there appeared in the synagogue the ghost of an old man, and everyone was afraid to walk down that street. A Polish landowner turned up, too, and said that he had seen with his own eyes the old man crying. The landowner believed that it wasn't a ghost but a Jewish elder, and that he had to be saved. The Germans, keen to get rid of the temple, sold its bricks to Ukrainians, and [the latter] brought Jews in for the dismantling of the synagogue. The Germans didn't want to dismantle the holy place with their own hands, afraid of sorcery. I didn't receive any more information about the fate [of the synagogue].[568] I went to my brother to Sokal and stayed there for some time. Hasids from the area and from Eastern Galicia came to Sokal en masse. This lasted six months, until the Bolsheviks carried out a registration and the rabbi received an order to leave town, since as a refugee he was not allowed to live close to the border.

The rabbi moved to Przemyśl[569] with his court and didn't alter his way of life there [either]. Soviet officers sometimes sat at his table, Jews and non-Jews. By train, on carts, [and] on foot, Jews came to Przemyśl for the Tzaddik's blessing. We thought that we would stay there until the end of the war. Keen to stay close to [my] brother, I moved to Brzeżany, as I was afraid to live in the city. NKVD-ers, particularly Jews from the NKVD, started persecuting the rabbi, accusing him of engaging in religious propaganda. On Pentecost[570] 1940, NKVD-ers came up to the rabbi [as he] sat at the table with his Hasids and ordered him to leave town immediately. Panic broke out. It was possible to postpone the order to leave by two weeks. Then the rabbi went to Radziejów, was expelled to Busk

568. Translator's note: the original sentence is missing the subject, so it is not fully clear whose fate the author is referencing; the synagogue seems to make intuitive sense.

569. Likely refers to the town of Przemyślany.

570. [The Jewish holiday of Shavuot, which occurred on 12 June 1940.]

from there, wasn't allowed to stay long, set off for Gliniany, and only managed to return to Przemyśl after a long effort. I lived in Brzeżany with [my] family.

The new war that befell us caused panic. Before we knew it, the Germans occupied the city, on 1 July. [They] started off straightaway rounding up Jews for work. The rabbi was ill in bed. The Gestapo burst into [his] home, caught the rabbi's relative, Dr. Jehoszua Singer [and] beat him, thinking he was the rabbi. [Luckily], they stopped before killing him.

When the rabbi's eldest son, Mosze, known for his wisdom, saw the Jewish suffering, he started begging the rabbi to curse Hitler. The rabbi said that Hitler was only a tool in the hands of another force, and that he could not fight against God's will. [Hitler] would definitely be defeated in the end. But Reb Mosze kept insisting that [his] father [should] put a curse on Hitler.

On 8 July [1941], the Germans set fire to the synagogue in Przemyślany with the help of the Ukrainians and organized a hunt for Jews during the fire. Even though everyone went into hiding, [the Germans] managed to capture forty Jews, among them the rabbi's eldest son, Mosze Rokach, and throw [them] into the burning synagogue. The forty Jews burned to death. Only after an intervention by the Polish mayor was [the community] allowed to bury the charred remains. The Ukrainian police assisted with the persecutions of Jews, beating and robbing [Jews] anywhere they could. The Germans organized a spectacle at the police station with Jews fighting against Ukrainians, to rile up [the latter] even more. The rabbi stayed in hiding during that time under the name of Aron Zynger. He sent me a letter [asking] that I come to Przemyślany. I was living on my own in Brzeżany. My family had left for Kobryń before the war and I'd had no news from them. In Brzeżany there were twenty thousand Jewish families, whom I was trying to help. [Since I] hadn't received any news from [my] brother for some time, I was intending to go to [see] him. The Jews begged me to stay. The rabbi sent a car to get me one day. I found out that even his children didn't know where he was. He was living with [one of] his follower[s], Feffer, and was being waited on by a twelve-year-old boy who looked Aryan. Thanks to [that], the boy could go anywhere. The rabbi didn't allow anyone near him, not even his loyal assistant Aron Jehoszua Landau, who didn't [even] know where the rabbi was. I went to the rabbi. There I learned about the horrific slaughter of the Lwów Jews. The Germans had captured the best-known and most respected Jews—a number of rabbis among them, such as Rabbi Halberstadt, Rabbi Lewin, Icchak Lewin—doctors [and] lawyers, and killed them all. There were twelve thousand people altogether. The rabbi cried as he told me about it, but curiously, didn't mention the tragic fate of his eldest son, Mosze, who had perished in flames.

Our mother cried for days. Jewish women from the area would [come to her place] to tell her about their tragedies. I tried to reassure the rabbi. News was coming in about horrific slaughters, about the shameful behavior of the Ukrainians, particularly in Eastern Galicia. We received a message from Zborów, where our brother Rabbi Jehoszua from Jarosław was, [informing us] that the Germans had killed six hundred Jews there, and [my] brother had survived [only] by a miracle. Another brother was in Stryj, where a thousand Jews perished during the [Germans'] first operation. Many [of those] arrested were bailed out thanks to diamonds and foreign currency that were collected in town as bail for the victims. These slaughters took place in the towns occupied by the Germans after the outbreak of the war. In Western Galicia, on the other hand, in the regions occupied in the year 1939, there was relative peace. Jews were allowed to trade, and life went on there somehow. The Tzaddik's followers decided to move him to Kraków. The first courier who turned up, a Christian man sent from Kraków, took a large sum of money and didn't do anything for us. The Kraków Jews sent another man at that point. He was a Polish count, with a car from the economic branch of the municipal office at his disposal. The count demanded fifty thousand zlotys and came to Przemyślany to pick up the Tzaddik. This was in January 1942. The car waited all day because the rabbi said he wouldn't go without me. We had our beards shaved off and set off without documents. The servant came with us.

We traveled through Lwów. The city was lit up, full of German troops, tanks, heavy artillery. They were going east. We passed through Lwów in fear. No one bothered us. Close to Przemyśl, where the border ran between the lands formerly and currently occupied, the driver told us that we would not [be able to] avoid a check. At one point he called out: "Pray to God," but to our great surprise, the car drove across a bridge and only on the other side of [it] did the driver signal to us that the danger had passed. It turned out that the border guards were asleep. Out of great joy, we offered the driver vodka and drove on, toward Tarnów. We knew the Gestapo headquarters for Western Galicia was in Tarnów. It was nighttime [and] we fell asleep. The driver clearly took a nap too, and all of a sudden, we felt a tremendous blow. The car tipped over and we flew into a ditch with a cry of "Shema Yisrael." All four of us found ourselves under the car, among shards of glass and iron. [We] were lying on top of each other. [We were suffocating.] The rabbi started reciting the prayer for the dead. We thought this was the end for us. I don't know what happened then. We felt fresh air and started to dig ourselves out from under the car. When we were [out], the engine exploded. [All] that was left of the car was a pile of ash. We were all injured, covered in blood. This happened at three o'clock at night on a road full of military cars, close to Tarnów [and] the Gestapo headquarters. The driver left us and ran to town for help. We were left in the field. We felt we shouldn't stay there a moment longer. At one point we called out to a passing cart in Polish, to get it to stop, [and in response] we heard, in Jewish: "What are you doing here, close to the Gestapo?" The cart driver couldn't take us into town but gave us a lift to a nearby Jewish inn. On the way, the rabbi whispered to me not to reveal who we were. The inn belonged to the only Jew left in the area. He didn't want to let us in, but the cart driver told him that he had found injured Jews on the road. You won't regret allowing us in, I called. In the end, the innkeeper told us to go to the courtyard and let us into a storage cupboard full of wood. He himself went into a room and got into bed. We lay on the cold floor, whimpering because of our injuries. A woman who lived next to the inn heard our cries. She came into the room to see who was moaning. She immediately recognized the rabbi in the candlelight, and seeing him covered in blood, screamed loudly and fell unconscious.

It turned out that she was a Czech woman who had been sent to Poland along with many thousands of Jews. She was sent to Tarnów, but due to the shortage of apartments, had to live in the innkeeper's small house. Her parents were the owners of a restaurant in Marienbad, where the rabbi often came for treatments. This woman would go to the rabbi for a blessing, and that's why she recognized him now. The brother came running and alerted the owner of the inn. Iodine and gauze were fetched, we [had our wounds] dressed, beds were given up for us, we were given milk and coffee. Our servant, Hirsz, the most gravely wounded, was taken to town. A doctor was called in for us. Even though we asked that [our] secret be kept, news of the rabbi's arrival spread around Tarnów. Heedless of the danger, Jews came to the inn. We spent a day [there]. The rabbi blessed everyone who helped him, and the next day, the

Hasids brought a car and we drove peacefully to Wisznicz,[571] outside Bochnia. The situation in Western Galicia was almost perfect compared to Eastern Galicia. The Jews lived in peace, traded, did decent business, food did not run out. One could get anything with money, and restrictions were circumvented with the help of bribe[s]. The news of the rabbi's rescue spread fast. Hasids drove in on Saturday[s], feasts were thrown like in the old days. [People] in cities and towns continued to pray in synagogues, in Talmud Torahs, and in yeshivas. One would come across Jews with beards and peyot. Three yeshivas operated in Wisznica: a Bełz one, a Bobów one, and a Radom one. At the end of the winter of 1942, when the cold started to bother the German soldiers on the front, Germans issued an order for all fur [coats] to be surrendered. Many people were shot dead for wearing fur coats. Rabbis in particular were persecuted for wearing fox-fur hats. Rabbi Twerski was shot dead for it. Many women died for wearing coats decorated with fur.

When the German defeats began on the Russian front, the Jews were overcome with joy. The rabbi used to say, sighing: "Hitler needs a one-shot defeat, small[er] losses will raise his desire for revenge on Jews." We spent the holidays of Pesach [2–9 April] and Shavuot [22–23 May] in Wisznica, and this [stay] lasted until August 1942. Thinking that [they] would survive the war somehow, Jews [still] did business, bought their way out of trouble, and in the worst case, went to work. In August, a youth from Lublin came to see us and told us about the horrific fate of the Lublin Jews.[572] We thought they had been sent to the front to work. We received a letter from an acquaintance in Lublin at that time, asking the rabbi to pray for the Jews who were going along with the expulsion orders peacefully, not knowing that they were [actually] going to their deaths. The author of the letter begged [us] to alert Jews that they must hide and not let themselves be taken into the freight cars. We sent out a copy of this letter to sixteen towns. A German Jew, Sali Grajewer, director of many factories working for the Germans, was well known in our area. More than three thousand Jews worked for him. Grajewer helped Jews as [much as] he

---

571. Refers to the town of Nowy Wiśnicz.

572. Refers to the liquidation of the Lublin ghetto that began on 17 March 1942 and continued into April. [The ghetto's] residents were deported to [their] deaths in the gas chambers of the center for mass extermination in Bełżec. It was the first ghetto [whose residents were murdered] in Operation Reinhard, which extended to all of the General Government by autumn 1942.

could and was losing all of his riches bailing [them] out from the Gestapo. He was shot dead by the Gestapo during the last operation.

First Displacements from Western Galicia

The first displacements started at the end of August 1942. One day the Jewish council in Wisznica received an order for all Jews to move to Bochnia. We didn't wait until Saturday and left in a car procured for us by Grajewer. After arriving in Bochnia we learned that an operation was underway there.[573] We drove to Kraków in that same car. Before arriving in Kraków, we heard the news that the Germans had killed 1,200 Jews in Bochnia on Saturday, among them many rabbis, activists, and [members of] the intelligentsia.

In Kraków

Two ghettos already existed in Kraków: A and B. In one [of them], there lived Jews who were hired by the Germans, in the other one—[those] unable to work and children. We made our way to Ghetto A, to [the home of] a Hasidic friend. He received us without fear. We felt very sorry that he was risking his life for us, since we had no right to be in Ghetto A. We and our hosts were at risk at every moment. A certain Szymon Szpitz, a Jew [with] no small number of victims on his conscience, was well known in Kraków. Before every expulsion, he would extort a contribution from the Jews to prevent the disaster. [His promises], however, were of no use, and his appearance [was] only a sign of an approaching operation. With no other option, we turned to Szpitz to try to get us permission to stay in Ghetto A. We sent a man named Motel Erlich to Szpitz and asked if Szpitz would visit the rabbi. Szpitz replied that he would stop by. This response worried us. Szpitz came by the following day and behaved rather insolently. He said he had heard a lot about the rabbi. We told him about our situation. In response to our request, he said that he worked in the political division of the Gestapo, which, as was known, did no favors for any Jew. We responded that doing a favor for the rabbi would earn him respect and popularity. The next day, he brought us a permit under the name[s] of Aron Zynger and Motel Kaczynik, allowing [us] to live in the

573. German *Aktionen* were operations against "undesirables," in particular Jews, involving, among other things, mass deportations and murder.

ghetto and releasing us from work. From that moment on, Szpitz changed, and would gladly do favors for Jews. He managed to procure a residence permit for our servants and brought in an engineer who built a hut for the rabbi. Another [person] known [to be] helpful to Jews was a man named Landau, employed by the Gestapo, to whom thousands of Poles and Jews owed their lives. Landau was arrested and at risk of [the firing squad]. As he was the owner of a bank, one of the Gestapo officers asked him to procure foreign currency for him. From that moment on, Landau became the official supplier of currency. Having contact with high-ranking German officials, he often used [his] wealth to save Jews.

Expulsion from Kraków

On Monday, Szpitz called us [to say] that an operation was planned for Tuesday, and that he had prepared a hiding place for the rabbi and for me. We begged him to save the largest [possible] number of Jews. He solemnly swore to do it. On Tuesday morning, we were led to a hiding spot somewhere, with a small group of [other] Jews. The Gestapo posted a watch drawn from the Jewish police force, and made them responsible for our safety. The chief of the Gestapo came to us. We almost fainted. He asked how we had gotten to Kraków. We didn't answer him. He assured us that as long as the last Jew [in town] was in the ghetto, nothing bad would happen to us. A new [labor] camp for Jews was created on Jerozolimska Street,[574] and at its helm stood the infamous Ge[part of text missing],[575] former head of the camps in Majdan Tatarski outside Lublin. Since we knew what to expect from him, we decided to return to Bochnia. Szpitz and Landau procured a car. In Bochnia, we received worker IDs: the rabbi as a tailor, and I as a shoemaker. We received materials from the central office, and other Jews carried out the work for us. When a stranger appeared, we would grab [our] work tools: the rabbi an iron, and I a shoemaker's rasp. In February 1943, in the morning, a Jewish policeman alerted us that the Gestapo chief would be coming to see us shortly, because we had been denounced for not working and for holding meetings at our place.

574. Refers to the labor camp for Kraków Jews in Płaszów.

575. The testimony's author means Amon Goeth, commandant of the Płaszów camp from 11 February 1943 [onward], one of the cruelest torturers in the area. Executed in Kraków in September 1946.

I sat down on a chair with a shoe [in my hand] and the rabbi started sewing trousers. The Gestapo man arrived shortly, shouting: "You are sorcerers and liars." To this, the other Gestapo man replied: "What use is there for rabbis when soon there will be no Jews and no religion." We were in a cold sweat. We didn't know whether to ask him to sit down, or whether to take [our] hats off. Any careless gesture could be punished with death. We asked one of the workers for a chair. The Gestapo officer sat on the windowsill and asked: "What was happening at the rabbi's yesterday evening?" I replied that the rabbi was calling on the Jews to work diligently, since one should work for the one who provides [their] bread. This answer pleased the Gestapo officer. Finally, he told us that he was releasing us from work and that in addition to bread, he would allocate us two portions of horsemeat as a bonus. On meeting the old Rabbi Halberstadt in the street, he sent him for us.[576] On Purim, a Jew from Warsaw came to Bochnia.[577] He told us about the terrifying slaughters in Congress Poland.[578] I was so upset by those stories that I lost consciousness and only came to the following day. From that moment on, no one was allowed near me and even letters were hidden [from me]. That Jew told [us] that the Germans had murdered many rabbis out of revenge, among them Rabinowicz, with [his] wife, daughter, and [his] son-in-law Mosze Rabinowicz, a well-known gaon from Radomsk.[579] The Germans also shot dead a blind rabbi on the street—Dancygier—who was being led by [his] son. Afraid of being expelled from Bochnia, [people] started building bunkers, like [the ones] in other ghettos. The Germans would find [these] hiding places and blow them up with dynamite, killing [those who were] hiding. Partisans, too, Jews and Poles, who operated in the nearby forests, hid in the bunkers. They got money for weapons by attacking rich Jews, disguised as Germans, and [forcing] them to hand over their valuables at gunpoint. One of the leaders of the Jewish partisans was Rabbi Frenkiel from Jaworzno, son of the famous Tzaddik from Podgórze,

576. Meaning unclear.

577. Purim [Polish: Purym]: Jewish holiday celebrated in the month of Adar (February–March). In 1943 the holiday fell on 21 March. See glossary.

578. Congress Poland refers to the Polish territories included in the 1915 Russian annexation.

579. Szloma Chanach Rabinowicz (1882–1942): last Tzaddik of generation[s] of Tzaddiks from Radomsko. He was murdered in the Warsaw ghetto on 1 August 1942.

Symcha Frenkiel. Both he and [his] father were lost: the son in a clash with the Germans, the father in a ghetto.

A lot can be said about the attitude of the Poles toward the Jews. It is a fact that the relations were good in workers' districts. [Things] were worse in Kraków. Ukrainians took an active part in the operations and surpassed the Germans in [their] cruelty. They thought the Germans would return Ukraine to them, while Eastern Galicia would be annexed to the General Government, with a Polish administration and Polish schools.

Escape

Our friends abroad, particularly in Hungary, attempted to get us out of Poland. They put together a group that began to consider rescue methods. One day in May 1943, a Hungarian car arrived in Bochnia in which there were a Hungarian captain and a driver. The captain showed us appropriate papers and said that he wanted to move us to Hungary. A car with a Hungarian banner [was waiting] on the other side of the ghetto. We shaved off [our] beards, put on light[-colored] hats, colorful ties, [and] elegant clothes, and we walked out of the ghetto. We got into the car accompanied by one servant. The road to Hungary from Bochnia led through Slovakia. But the captain took us a roundabout way, across all of Eastern Galicia. Our car wasn't stopped a single time, even though all the other cars were being stopped because there were many partisans in the area. In Przemyśl, the driver stopped the car on the main street and went into a restaurant with the captain. We were on a street inhabited exclusively by Germans, but no one bothered us. Only at the Hungarian border did the border guard not want to let us through, claiming that the road was only for the military. The officer whispered something to the guard, who gave a salute and released us.

We traveled through Hungarian territory, planning to go to Budapest. Because Saturday was nearing, we [stopped] in Ungvár.[580] The car stopped, our servant got out, went up to an old Jew with a gray beard standing in front of a shop like in the olden days, and asked where the closest follower of the rabbi from Bełżec lived. A man named Zundelberger [Zundel Berger] was

580. Now: Uzhhorod.

passing by in the street and he turned out to be our ally. Our servant whispered into his ear that the rabbi from Bełżec was there, wishing to enter his apartment. Allowing a Jew from Poland into one's home [came] with serious punishment, but one couldn't refuse the rabbi. We drove up to Berger's home [and] were welcomed with curses, because Berger did not want to believe that we were who we claimed to be. The rabbi sat at the table and started to praise God in his [typical] way. He was immediately recognized. It was impossible to keep the secret. On Saturday evening, the room filled up with Hasids. The captain who was to take us to Budapest said what follows: "When the car set off from Bochnia it was immediately wrapped up in fog, and this way, almost invisible, we made it to the Hungarian border. That is why I allowed myself to leave [you] in the street in Przemyśl, certain that no one would bother you . . ." That same day we drove to Budapest and set off for Palestine from there seven weeks later.

Protocol 239

Testimony of Doctor **Jan Bader**, age forty-two, from Kraków. Came to Palestine via Russia and Tehran with [his] wife in October 1943.

I am a lawyer by trade. I did social work, was the president of Revisionist organizations in Kraków. A week before the outbreak of the war, a citizens' committee was organized in Kraków. Doctor Ignacy Schwarzbart, MP and current member of the National Council in London, became the president of that committee.[581] Doctor [Lejb] Salpeter, president of the Zionist Organization in Kraków, Doctor Szerman, Zygmunt Aleksandrowicz, I myself, and [some] others were [members] of the committee. The role of the committee was to care for the Jewish populace in the newly established situation. We issued an appeal to the Jewish people and called on all Jews to take part in the defense of the country.

When German airplanes started to bomb the city, a terrible panic broke out. There was no one to turn to for help; our committee was disbanded because all of [its] members had left town. On 4 September, I too set off in my car. My wife had gone to Torczyn to her parents' place a few days earlier. I set off in that direction. I drove through Przemyśl and Lwów, Żuków,[582] Włodzimierz to Torczyn, traveling only by night, as during the day, German airplanes bombed the roads. The roads were piled high with smashed-up cars, military vehicles [that were] sometimes full of corpses and injured [people]. People dragged themselves on foot or on carts; small children were carried in wheelbarrows. I had to travel on roundabout roads. And two days later, I was stopped in Zylków,[583] suspected of espionage. I was only allowed to go free after having my ID checked. There were no signs of the war in Torczyn [and] life was going on normally. Then on 13 September, when the news spread that the Germans were one hundred kilometers away from us, panic broke out. I had planned to travel in the direction of the Romanian border, but before I got

581. Ignacy Schwarzbart (1888–1961): lawyer, publicist, Zionist activist, MP for the Republic of Poland (1938–39), member of the National Council of the Republic of Poland in London, activist with the World Jewish Congress.

582. Likely refers to Żółkiew.

583. Likely refers to Żółkiew again.

there, the border had been closed. I set off farther on, and despite the danger on the road[s], made it to Aleksandria, a small town outside Równe. It was on 17 September when Russia unexpectedly occupied that part of Poland. The Polish army had left Aleksandria on 16 September, and the Bolsheviks had not arrived yet. The Ukrainian population armed itself with whatever was [available] and organized a Jewish pogrom. Luckily, a Polish police commandant was still present in town. This man, known for his liberal views, issued the Jews some weapons [and] a machine gun at the request of [their] representative, and organized a Jewish militia force, which defended the Jewish district. A battlefront formed. On one side, there stood the Ukrainians, on the other—the Jews.

It did not come to widespread disorder because the first tanks arrived in town that day. A Russian commandant gave a speech to the people, promising them all possible "blessings." The Ukrainians retreated to the country. The Russians arrested the Polish police commandant first of all, and it was said that they shot him [by firing squad]. Prince Lubomirski also lived in Aleksandria.[584] He was a man of liberal views, kind to Jews and Ukrainians, who did not believe that he would come to any harm. It was said that the prince had communicated with the local authorities in Równe the day before, asking what he should do. He was told to stay. The next day, the commissar who had so comforted the people, went to the prince's palace accompanied by the Red militia and picked up Ukrainians and Jews [he] met on the way. At the palace, he asked the people gathered there if they had any grievances against the prince. Everyone, even the Red militia, said no. The commissar asked if the prince had caused anyone harm. The [people] asked that the prince not be hurt. When [the commissar] turned to a Ukrainian youth and asked: "Does the prince owe any debts to you?" The boy replied that he owed him one hundred zlotys for a horse. The prince walked up to a cashbox to hand the money over to the boy, even though he did not remember that debt. At that point, the commissar gave the boy a gun and called: "Shoot him." And when the boy hesitated to carry out the order, [the commissar] himself shot at the prince. The prince collapsed, wounded, got up himself, and went to bed. The prince's

584. Hubert Lubomirski: husband of Teresa Radziwiłł, owner of the Aleksandria estate. Born 15 November 1875 in Równe; murdered on 21 September 1939.

wife wanted to help [her] husband but the commissar wouldn't allow it. The next day it was said in town that the prince would recover. He was helped by Doctor Dziewulski, an officer in the Polish army, who was later arrested. A few days later, that same commissar turned up at the palace and killed the prince on the spot.

As president of the Revisionist Organization, I was at risk of unpleasantness from the new masters, so I escaped to Równe, where it was easier to hide. It was difficult to find a place for the night. There was widespread hunger. The shops were closed. Only later did the Bolsheviks issue an order for all the shops to be opened and goods to be sold at prewar prices. Long lines formed, but the Soviet soldiers bought everything that was available in the shops. Synagogues and churches were full on holidays, but after a month, all temples were closed down. I spent twelve days in Równe, felt uneasy there, [and] went to Torczyn. I traveled on a truck. On the way, a military officer, a Kiev Jew, got into the truck. He told me that the Soviet army had been told that they were marching on Berlin and [that] the news of the German-Soviet Nonaggression Pact had shaken the Red Army to the core.

In Torczyn, rallies were taking place constantly. Soldiers-*politruki*[585] made speeches in Russian, Polish, Ukrainian, and Jewish. The elections for the Ukrainian council were taking place at the time. The candidates were chosen during meetings. [Each] candidate had to prove [their] Communist activism in Poland. Many voters, like me, put in blank papers. Thus 100 percent of the population took part in the elections. Then the arrests began. Poles and Jews, members of the Zionist committee, and members of our[586] Ukrainian national council were arrested. I went from town to town, afraid that I would be arrested [in Torczyn]. I knew about the arrests of all of the more prominent members of the Revisionist party. In Lwów, I met the lawyer Lejb Landau. He was completely broken and begged me [to end things for him]. He had been the defense lawyer for all the arrested Zionists. He [shared with] me a few details about the trial of the members of the Zionist Organization. The accused were so dejected after two months that they were close to taking their own lives. They all admitted to the charges brought against them to relieve themselves of

585. [Political commissars.]

586. That is, created through a bottom-up initiative of the Ukrainian people.

the exhausting nighttime examinations. Doctor Landau postponed the date of the trial, which [in the end] did not take place, as everyone was sent to camps in the meantime. Here's another fact, relating to a Revisionist activist who said that the Revisionists were fighting against England, as it did not want to create a Jewish state in Palestine. He was released [after] this statement, while others were convicted. The lightest [sentence] was eight years in prison, the most severe—death. The death sentence was pronounced on mag [?].[587] Chassid from Ostróg, who expressed himself in a hostile manner about the German-Russian pact during the trial. Sixty thousand people, Jews and Poles, were arrested at that time. Registration was [also] taking place at the time. All the Jews dreamed of leaving the Soviet paradise. On 10 February 1940, the arrests of settlers took place; they were deported to Siberia without trial. Many died on the way. The number deported was a quarter of a million.

In April, another deportation took place, [of] the women and children of Polish officials and the bourgeoisie. Ukrainians were not deported. The belongings of the exiles were put up for auction. I was in Łuck at the time and ran away to Lwów, since I was a wanted man. There were arrests taking place in Lwów. Russians were arriving from the depths of Russia to [settle in the] empty apartments. In June, there were arrests of bachelors and single men, and later arrests of families began. On 17 June at six o'clock in the morning, NKVD-ers ordered me and my wife to go to the station, where we were loaded into a freight car, forty people in each. We traveled through Równe and Zdołbunów to the station of Stołpce. There we were moved into Russians train cars, and via Homel, Orel, bypassing Moscow and Gorky, we got to Saria[588] outside Kirov. Only Jews were traveling in our car, as in the whole train. At that station the first five cars were unloaded, including mine.

We were taken three hundred kilometers north on trucks. After two days' journey, we arrived in Fermac,[589] Nikolsky district [and] walked for fourteen kilometers until we finally got to a forest [with] barracks that had been inhabited by Ukrainians and Poles before [us]. We worked in the forest. No one was able to fulfill [their] quota. Workers received a kilo of bread. Fortunately, we got potatoes, with which we [topped up our food intake]. The camp's

587. Unclear what this abbreviation refers to (perhaps manager, or magister).
588. Correct name of the town: Sharia [original Polish correction: Szaria].
589. Most likely refers to the town of Permas in the Nikolsk area.

commandant was a bad person. He put out guard[s] on holidays, who were to keep an eye out so that no one prayed and everyone went to work. We were so disconnected from the world that we lost track of time. We even worked on Sundays and gave that day's wages to the state. There were 280 of us in the camp. When someone fell ill, they [had to] rely on themselves for care. The outbreak of the [Russian-German] war made our situation worse; we were told to work for sixteen hours a day, bread portions were decreased, we were rushed during work. We thought we would not make it through. We were not notified about the Amnesty. Not until September 1941 were we told that we were free and given [travel] documents. We set off for Ustyug,[590] from there to Kotlas by water, [and] to Assina[591] via Tomsk by rail. I spent a few weeks in Assino. I met my wife's family there. We set off for Turkmenistan, where we fared well because that route wasn't known to the refugees. I stayed there until March 1942. I then set off for Guza[592] with [my] wife, where I was accepted into the Polish army. We stayed there until August 1942. We then set off for Tehran with the army. I served in the army until May 1943. I was discharged on 20 December,[593] and then, along with [my] wife, her mother and sister, left Tehran for Palestine.

590. Veliky Ustyug [Polish: Ustiuk].

591. Refers to Asino.

592. Correctly: Guzar.

593. Inconsistent with the introduction, which mentions arrival in October.

Protocol 240

Testimony of **Mosze Grajcer**, son of Sara and Dawid from Stoczek Łukowski. Came to Palestine via Russia and Tehran in August 1943.

My father was the owner of a bus line that ran between Stoczek and Łuków. On 24 March 1939, the government confiscated all private buses. We only received a compensation in the sum of twelve thousand zlotys in the summer, on the condition that we buy new buses with this money. It took a few months for the buses to be finished. They were sent to us a few days before the war, and on 4 September, Father had them taken away from him for the second time. The first days [of the war] went by peacefully [in our town]. My brother-in-law, Kuśnierski, [my] sister's husband, was mobilized for the Polish army. [My] sister [went to] live with [our] parents. Our family was made up of seven people: parents and five children. We had no news about [our] brother-in-law.

The Germans bombed our town for the first time on 7 September. The airplanes flew very low and dropped incendiary bombs, so that the fires could not be put out. Realizing that there was no end to the bombardments, Mama went to Gręzówka, taking a few [of the] children with [her], and Father stayed in town with [my] brother Meir. On the way to the country, the Germans bombed us again and we hid in a ditch. On 10 September, [my] brother Meir came to [see] us because [they] were saying in town that we had been killed. On the twelfth, we saw a huge glow in the sky. We didn't know where it was coming from. Not until morning did we see crowds of people. It turned out they were people running away from our town, my father among them. He told [us] that the Germans had occupied the town on Tuesday and set fire to all homes, not allowing anyone to save [any of their] belongings.

A few days later we went to Łuków, where father bought himself a horse with a cart and started trading. One day Father didn't return home, and we thought the Germans had shot him. We set off looking for Father. It turned out that he was lying sick with dysentery in Zołuchów.[594] Father came back a week later and we started to get ready to leave. It was in December. Father wanted to get across the Bug [River] with us, but it turned out to be impos-

594. Likely refers to the town of Żelechów.

sible. Father stayed, and we returned to Łuków. [He] returned a few weeks later, and we set off toward the Bug [River] again. We lost [track of] Father in the border village of Modliniec,[595] by Drohiczyn. We went to Siemiatycze on our own, and then to Baranowicze, where we lodged with Mother's brother, Szmul Estreicher. A few weeks later, Father arrived so exhausted and ill that he had to lie in bed. When he recovered, he rented an apartment for us. Father was a chauffeur and earned [a] decent [amount].

When the registration began and everyone was being forced to accept Soviet citizenship, Father registered to go back home. One day in June 1940, NKVD-ers arrested us and sent us to the [train] station. We were loaded into cramped and dirty freight cars, in which we traveled, hungry [and] lice infested, and weren't allowed out of the car until eight days later, at Tavda station. From there, we set off on the water, during which [journey] we received only salted herring to eat. We quenched our thirst with seawater.[596] Mosquitos bit us bloody, our faces were swollen. After getting off the barge, we were led through mud and sand all day long to [our] destination. Our feet were bloodied [and our] shoes torn when we reached Czasza,[597] Tawryski [?] district, Sverdlovsk Oblast. There was no glass in the windows in the *posiołek* Stabaraki, and [it was] in these barracks that we settled. Mosquitos, bedbugs, and fleas tormented us. We couldn't sleep and [spent] whole nights chasing after bedbugs, scaring [them] off with burning torches. We worked in the forest; no one could fulfill [their] quota. The workers received eight hundred grams of bread per day. Only Mama and I didn't work. Everyone was hungry; we couldn't buy ourselves soup from the canteen. [People] went to work with nets on [their] faces. When the [Russian-German] war broke out, we had our bread rations lowered and were told to work for twelve hours a day. After the announcement of the Amnesty, the commandant said that it did not apply to Jews. Only later did our documents arrive, [and] we set off for the river, waiting for the barge. Finally, we went to [the town of] Taba [part of text missing] [Tabory?], and from there, to Tavda, starving on the way. We made it to Chelyabinsk [only] after many difficulties. [They] didn't want to let us off the train. Father and [my] sister fell ill with typhus during the journey, and when we arrived in

595. Possibly Mielnik on the Bug River.

596. [Likely river water, since Tavda is a port on the Tavda River.]

597. Unidentified town in the area of the city of Tabory.

Chkalovo, both died. We buried them there ourselves, and after a few days' roaming around the town, set off for Turkestan. We had to go to the kolkhoz Urtak in Turkmenistan. We worked in the fields, lived in kibitkas, and received two hundred grams of bread per day for the work. Later, there was no [more] work for us; we returned to the city, roamed around for a few weeks, and went to Tashkent. On the way, Mother and [my] brother Jakil fell ill and both died. In Tashkent, I went to an orphanage on my own and was taken in. A few months later, I was sent to Ashgabat, from there to Persia, and finally, I got to Palestine.

Protocol 243

Testimony of **Icchak Lewkowicz** from Nieśwież. Came to Palestine via Russia and Tehran in January 1943.

In 1937 I graduated from a teaching course in Wilno and was planning to go to Palestine. Before that, however, I did military duty. In March 1939, when I was to be discharged, I was sent along with my company to the German border to build fortifications. At the time the war broke out, I was in the border town of Mława. We began to retreat two days later. We wandered the roads for two weeks until we reached Warsaw, which was defending itself bravely at the time. We were joined to a division stationed in the Jewish cemetery in Praga. We defended ourselves fiercely for two weeks there, until the surrender of the capital.[598]

According to the agreement made with the Germans, Polish soldiers were to be released.[599] Despite this, the Germans held us for two months in a camp in Mińsk Mazowiecki. When we were being led to the camp, we passed through the town of Góra Kalwaria. There I saw for the first time how the Germans tortured old Jews. The prisoners were locked in hangars. Polish soldiers captured alongside us started to incite the German guards against us Jews, and as a result the Germans started treating us differently from the Polish soldiers. We had our shoes [and] uniforms taken away and were told to carry out the dirtiest work. [The Germans] particularly enjoyed ordering us to clean latrines with our bare hands, and they beat us during this work and told us to sing Hatikvah.[600] Several times we Jews had to dance for them or pretend to be praying. After a few months, everyone was sent back to [their] place of residence. I returned to [my] parents' house in Nieśwież. The Russians were in Nieśwież at the time. I got into a teaching course there and studied for six months. I kept thinking about how I could get to Wilno. I

598. That is, 28 September 1939.

599. The act of surrender of Warsaw, signed on 28 September, assumed that officers would be taken prisoner, and the other soldiers would return home after disarmament. In practice, about 120,000–140,000 Polish soldiers who had been fighting to defend Warsaw were captured by Germany.

600. Hatikvah: The anthem of the Zionist movement and later the state of Israel. *Hatikvah* is the Hebrew word for hope.

tried to do so a few times but did not succeed, so I stayed with [my] parents until the outbreak of the Russian-German war.

A few days before [the war] broke out, the mood was tense despite reassurances from the official channels. On 22 June a German airplane appeared above town, and later, cars began to pass through carrying soldiers to the front. The officers' wives were leaving town. The Jews went into a frenzy; a mobilization was announced, and before we knew it, the first refugees from Grodno arrived. They had fled with [only] what they had on, [and were] telling [us] terrible things about the Germans' power. The next day, all those mobilized were sent to Baranowicze. The police fled with the Bolsheviks. The town was left in the hands of [some] shady elements, who started robbing the Jewish district. We decided to leave town. Since Father was not in town, I said goodbye to Mother [and] took [my] younger brother and [my] sister and [her] six-month-old child with me. I knew within an hour that [my] sister would not survive the journey and I sent her back home. We set off toward Mińsk. In Stołpce, we were told that the enemy was right behind us. We came across hundreds of injured people on the way, [some] fainting from exhaustion, [but] no one paid [any] attention to them. In Kojdynów [?] we rested, and only then realized that, out of our group of 250 people, there were only 50 left. After a few hours we continued on ahead. It was impossible to get anything to eat during the journey. We ran on.

As we were approaching Mińsk, we learned that the city was on fire. There was nothing to do except head to Mogilev. Things were relatively calm there. But the influx of refugees was increasing by the hour, and the authorities had started evacuating [them]. My brother and I and [some] others were loaded into a freight car and taken to Tambov. I was called up to the Red Army [and] became a *krasnoarmeyetz*.[601] Soon, on the basis of the Amnesty, I was discharged from the army. I didn't know where to go. My goal was [to get to] Palestine. I planned to go on foot through the Caucasus to the Turkish border. I went to Tashkent. I found out that it was difficult to cross the Persian border. On receiving the news that my brother was in Sverdlovsk, I went to see him [in order] to take him with me. Luckily I met a Polish artistic troupe on the way

601. Literally: Red Army man. The lowest military rank in the Red Army of the Soviet Union.

[and they] took me with them. In Sverdlovsk I found out that [my] brother was in a nearby town, I but didn't manage to make contact with him.

At the time, Poles who had been released from labor camps and *posiołki* were arriving in the thousands. People were dying from hunger and epidemics, and no one paid them [any] attention. Unable to stay in Sverdlovsk, I returned to Tashkent, where the situation wasn't any better, but where I found my brother. We decided not to split up. We couldn't get on any train going to Persia. They didn't want to accept us into the Polish army, and we went to Kermine, where a military commission assigned me to category E. In Kermine I met my cousin, a dental technician who had been accepted into the army. We walked him to the station when he was leaving, and [my] brother and I pushed our way into the train car. We traveled together. It was crowded. I lost [my] brother. I was on the train illegally. I was added to the manifest thanks to one woman, the wife of a Polish officer. In Krasnovodsk, to [my] great joy, I found [my] brother, but they didn't want to put us on the new list that had been put together. We got on the ship illegally, went to Pahlevi [and] from there to Tehran. In Tehran, I was helped by Mr. Szafar and Mr. Tartakower, and we soon received [our] certificates.

Protocol 244

Testimony of **Debora Bursztein**, age twenty, from Dolina [?]. Came to Palestine via Russia in July 1943.

My father was a merchant. He had a shop selling manufactures. There were four of us siblings: me, my sister Necha, and two little brothers. I studied in a Tarbut school. At the beginning of the war, the Germans dropped a few bombs on our town. People escaped to the country, thinking it would be safer there, [but] the German planes flew down low [over] the roads, firing machine guns. The Germans occupied our town on the holiday of Rosh Hashanah [14–15 September 1939] and killed 280 Jews on the first day [after] taking them outside of town. Those [still] alive they ordered leave [their] homes within ten minutes. We fled in a frenzy, taking nothing [with us] from [our] home. We got to Przemyśl. We experienced a horrific Jewish slaughter in Przemyśl but managed to cross the San River to the part of the city occupied by Bolsheviks. We lived in Przemyśl for nine months. Father wasn't earning anything [and] we had nothing to live on. A few friends of Father's, with whom he had done business before the war, helped us. I completed a nursing course [but] still could not find a job in my profession. I became a shop assistant in a cooperative. I earned decent money but still could not feed the whole family.

The registration was beginning at that time, but Father did not want to accept Soviet citizenship under any circumstances. My parents, afraid to stay [where we were], left for Lwów and took [my] youngest brother with them. They promised that they would bring us to join them soon [too]. But I never saw my parents again, because two weeks later, [my] sister and I were arrested. They didn't want to let our brother come with us, and he had to stay at home. I don't know to this day what the fate of my parents was, or what happened to my little brother in Przemyśl.

[A group of] 1,500 of us—Jews and Poles, women and men—were loaded into freight cars. The journey took three weeks. During the journey, we were given [only] a piece of bread and a bowl of watery soup. After three weeks' journey, we arrived at the station of Czermuszniki,[602] near Tomsk. We were

602. Likely: Cheremoshniki, Tomsk.

let out of the freight car. Our belongings were loaded onto carts. We walked for ten kilometers until we arrived at a place in the middle of the forest where there were barracks. The next day we were told to go to work. It was hard work, sawing wood. We worked between ten and twelve hours a [day], in two shifts. We received four hundred grams of black bread and soup that [we] bought in the canteen for the work. I grew so much weaker within a few months that I could not work in the forest, and after many attempts, got a job as a [nurse]. I tended to patients, [but] there was nothing to treat them with in the makeshift hospital.

I worked for a year, until the outbreak of the [German-Soviet] war and the announcement of the Amnesty. [My] sister and I joined a transport with a group of people and went to Tashkent. The train journey dragged on for weeks. We were covered in lice, collapsing from hunger. We didn't receive [any] bread. When the train stopped, we would go out into the fields to pick weeds that we ate. In Tashkent, they didn't want to let us into the city [so] we went to Kermine. I started to look for work and after some time found a job in a hospital. I fell so gravely ill with typhus that there was little hope that I would survive. After recovering, I had no strength to work and got sick leave for a month. During that time, a Polish military hospital was set up, and I got a job there. A doctor I worked with at the hospital advised me to say that I was Catholic, as I would [be able to] get out with the army that way. I didn't want to do that. Our hospital was soon evacuated and [my] sister and I were among the few Jewish women who were added to the transport. We reached Tehran from Krasnovodsk via Pahlevi. We were put in a refugee camp. We received a certificate but could not get a visa for Iraq before a military transport took us from Tehran to Palestine.

Protocol 245

Testimony of **Natalia Debolicka**, age twenty-five, from Chojnice, Pomorze. Came to Palestine via Russia and Tehran in 1943.

My father was a lawyer and had a large practice. I graduated from secondary school and started studying medicine at Lwów University. The war caught me in Lwów. Returning home was out of the question, because on the first day of the war, the Poles were already evacuating civilian people from the border towns. My parents were evacuated to Bydgoszcz. From Bydgoszcz, they went to Warsaw. I received letters from [my] parents under a fake name. They were telling me not to come to Warsaw but to stay in Lwów under the Soviet occupation. But I couldn't stop missing them. I continued to study at the university during the Bolshevik period. The situation of the students was difficult. Our past was constantly being examined [and] we were made to fill out questionnaires. There were many spies among us. Despite this, I continued to study, even though the program was changed and had Marxism studies added to it.

After a few months, a few students known to be Zionist activists were arrested. I was afraid for myself, as I too belonged to a Zionist group. I was looking for some way to go to [be with my] parents. It's no surprise [then], that when the registration to return home began, I was one of the first to register. As is [now] known, that registration turned out to be a trap. One night in July 1940, NKVD-ers arrested me, drove me to the station, and loaded me into a freight car. It was cramped and dirty [inside]. We were given a piece of bread during the day and a bit of watery soup at night. People fell ill from the filth and [from] hunger, and as a medical student, I tried to help them, but I had no medicines. We traveled for twenty-six days, until we arrived in Assino,[603] in Novosibirsk Oblast. We got out of the car. We loaded [our] belongings onto carts, and we ourselves went on foot through a forest that stretched for kilometers, [until] we reached a *posiołek* called Sosnowka. The *posiołek* was made up of fifteen barracks surrounded by barbed wire on all sides. Not far from us there

603. Correctly: Asino.

was a labor camp for exiled Russians. They were political exiles, [members of the] intelligentsia, most often with higher education. Their situation was no better than ours. They were rushed to work alongside us. We were forbidden to make contact with one another, [but] despite this, we made their acquaintance as we worked together in the forest. They had been living there for many years, were wearing rags, and had no hope of [ever] leaving the labor camp. I got to know one of them one day [when we were] sawing wood together. He had been a professor at Kiev University. He told [me] that he had a wife and two children, students at the university. One day he was arrested, and was tortured for so long during the interrogation that he confessed to [his] nonexistent crime. He was sentenced to fifteen years in prison and not allowed to correspond with [his] family. I took pity on the professor and brought him warm undergarments the next day.

I worked in the forest for fifteen months without missing [even] the most freezing days. I had no news of [my] parents. I fell into despair and didn't believe we would get out of there. We didn't have any medical help, or a hospital, or any medicines. The offer of my services as a doctor brought no response. The outbreak of the [German-Russian] war made our situation worse. Only the announcement of the Amnesty brought us freedom. I got to Kuybyshev after a long journey. I got a job in the local hospital but [then] had to leave town, as refugees were not allowed to live there. I went to Kyrgyzstan [and] was assigned to a department for health workers and doctors who were working Polish refugees. I got a portable medicine kit and went from kolkhoz to kolkhoz providing assistance to refugees. The work was hard. I dragged myself through snow, rain, and mud for kilometers on end. No one paid me for the work; I only got meal[s] in the kolkhozes. This was during a typhus epidemic and there was terrible mortality among children. The work exhausted me completely. I dragged myself [on, looking] like a shadow, but nevertheless I [felt] fulfilled because I was helping people.

When Polish military groups started being put together, I was sent to one of the units, where a mixed Russian-Polish commission dismissed my application because I was Jewish. I went on foot from town to town, from commission to commission, receiving the same answer everywhere. Resigned and dejected, I stayed in one town and roamed the street[s]. I fell gravely ill. A Jewish doctor in a Polish uniform found me by chance [as I lay] almost unconscious on the street, took an interest in me, and on hearing who I was, took me to his home. He treated me, and when I recovered, he got me into the army under his protection, and this way I got on a train going to Tehran. In Tehran I worked in a military hospital for people with infectious diseases. I then got a job in a local pharmacy. I lived with a Russian Jewish family who treated me like [their] own child. After a long stay in Tehran, I received [my] certificate and arrived in Palestine in August 1943.

Protocol 246

Testimony of **Jakub Rabinowicz**, age twenty-eight, from Grabowiec Lubelski. Came to Palestine in July 1943 via Russia and Tehran.

Until the outbreak of war, I was a member of the kibbutz in Grochów, outside Warsaw, and belonged to the youth organization Wolność, the right wing of Poale Zion.[604] On Friday 1 September 1939, when the radio reported the German attack, we heard the first alarm. An air raid took place at four in the afternoon, during which a bomb fell on the house I lived in. The house was destroyed. The police mobilized all the youth and organized help. Before evening we were sent to Falenica, where a few bombs had fallen on a school and we had to pull the victims out from under the rubble. During the siege of Warsaw, we intended to join up with the PPS to engage in the defense with them. It was already too late. When the authorities left town, we decided to go east with them. I wanted to say goodbye to [members of my] family who lived in town but I could no longer return to the kibbutz, as the bridge had been bombed out and there were no more transport connections to the right bank [of the river]. When I arrived in the courtyard of the kibbutz on 8 September [1939], I found no one there anymore. In the fields, Polish children were digging up our potatoes [and] picking [our] tomatoes; the adults were taking away our horses and cows.

I set off on my own, and this way, squeezed [in the middle of] the escaping crowd, reached the town of Ryki, [which was] completely destroyed. German airplanes pursued us. We had to hide from an air raid every fifteen minutes. I got to Lublin this way, where I found the Germans already there. I set off farther toward Chełm, [and] the Germans were already there, too. I was going in that direction as that's where my hometown of Grabowiec was. I met two companions from the kibbutz on the way, and together we set off for Brześć, where fighting was taking place between the Polish and Soviet armies at the time. One of my companions was killed in a street battle, the other got lost in the crowd.

604. Wolność (Hebrew: Dror) was the youth division of Poale Zion Right.

Left on my own, I decided to go to Grabowiec, to see my parents. The Russians entered the town. When they left town six days later, I went with the Bolsheviks to Włodzimierz Wołyński, [but] finding no place for the night, I set off toward Kowel to join the local kibbutz there. In the kibbutz, we suffered from hunger and anxiety about [the future]. All of [my] companions and I decided to go to Wilno. We were captured at the border. We went to Kowel after being released. Some of the [group] took up trading, but I found a job as a loader in a military kitchen. I earned six rubles per day, worked hard, [but] didn't get meals from the kitchen. I was fired from the job after some time because I didn't want to accept Soviet citizenship. Left with no job, I decided to make use of the agricultural [knowledge] I had acquired in the kibbutz and got a job as a qualified agricultural worker. I was sent on a five-month further-education course and became the district agronomist. The work wasn't difficult, but I risked deportation to Russia for any misdemeanor. At that time, [my] friends and acquaintances were coming back from Russia—some [of them] enthusiastic supporters of Communism who had voluntarily registered to go to Russia—now they returned disappointed and dejected. Ukrainian peasants were coming back too, and everyone told of the widespread corruption and bureaucracy in Russia. All the former Communists wanted to return to the German-occupied territories.

They didn't get to do so in time, however, as the infamous arrests began. During [the arrests] I hid in the attic. I continued to hide from the NKVD in a forest outside town, eating animals that I hunted and killed. I couldn't stand it any longer in the forest, however, [and] I returned home. That same night, a systematic search was carried out, but this time too, I hid in the attic. I knew, however, that in the end my freedom would not last, so I went [to get] a Soviet passport. I had to leave Kowel, like other refugees, but soon returned to the city and stayed [there] until the outbreak of the Russian-German war. I was mobilized alongside the rest of the young men. I was immediately sent to the front, even though I had never held a gun in my hand. The Germans surrounded us on all sides; we retreated, leaving masses of dead [behind]. The Ukrainians were shooting at the Soviet military, joining the Germans. We ran ahead all the way to Kiev in a panic. Our clothes were torn, we were covered in lice; we received a herring and a cucumber a day to eat. I planned to desert the army in Kiev but didn't succeed. I dragged myself on with the army to

Kharkiv, where I came upon a Jew I knew, who gave me civilian clothes. I got to Moscow by train, from there to Kuybyshev and Saratov.

I joined a kolkhoz. Things were hard there. The farm was deserted. Half of the crop was [left] out in the fields, unpicked. We started being mobilized for the Red Army again. I ran away from the kolkhoz and got on a train going to Tashkent by bribing the controller. This was after the Amnesty. I ran into many acquaintances who had taken up trading. I also became a merchant. Corruption, hunger, and epidemics were widespread in the city. I decided to give up trading and look for work [instead]. I found [a job] in a factory that was being built outside of the city. I worked ten hours a day and received half a kilo of bread and watery soup for it. I slept in a workers' house, where the sanitary conditions were poor and where a typhus epidemic soon broke out. We went hungry for weeks. One day I was told that they were selling soup at the railway station. We took a bucket and joined the line, where we got a bucketful of soup for eight rubles. We shared the soup among all the workers when we got home.

The situation in Tashkent was desperate. The intelligentsia and the formerly rich fought like feral animals over a piece of bread. During that time the Polish army started recruiting. There were three hundred of us Jews whom they did not want to accept. But we forced our way into a railcar and, waiting for three days and three nights without food, got to Krasnovodsk and then to Pahlevi. There we were told that we weren't Polish citizens and ordered to get out, despite [our] protests. We slept on the seashore, hungry, in the rain. An English officer who saw us took an interest in us and argued with the Polish officer. As a result, we were sent to Tehran and accommodated in a civilian camp. We spent a year there, and I left for Palestine after receiving [my] certificate.

Protocol 248

Drawn up on the basis of the testimony of **Samuel Rand**, age forty, resident in Bielsko before the war [and] currently in Tel Aviv.

I was mobilized at the end of August 1939 and assigned to my unit. I took part in a number of skirmishes and then eventually I found myself in the Jarosław area with my unit. We came upon a German patrol there, and during the battle I was wounded in the leg and lost an eye. I was transported to Radymno, where after recovering, I was arrested by the Gestapo. In the prison I was in, terrible events played out every day. I witnessed how the Germans took an industrialist from Kraków, Resenberg, out into the courtyard once, tortured him, and then shot him dead. The hostages [who were in the prison] with me, mainly Jews, were beaten in the morning and in the evening [and], one day, taken outside and exercised to death.

After a few weeks' stay in the German prison in Jarosław, I managed to escape. I sneaked out at night [and] got over to the Russian side in one piece, despite being fired on by machine guns. At a Soviet outpost [they] arrested me, handing me over to the Peter and Paul prison in Lwów. [My] stay in that prison was no better than the stay in the German [one]. As many "criminals" as could fit standing up were stuffed into the cell. The professional criminals who were in the same cell with us did not make our lives easier, and requests to be separated were unsuccessful.

Above all, we feared the NKVD examinations like hell. We weren't beaten during them, but sophisticated psychological tortures were used. The examinations took place at midnight as a rule—you were roused from sleep for them. For hours you were inundated with scores of tricky questions. To "soften up" the [person being] examined, [they] would show them tasty ham sandwiches [and] amazing cigarettes lying on the table. You would leave this examination half-mad. A few [people] who were in the cell with me really did return having lost their sanity. After several weeks of such torture, I was sent to Karelia one day, without a sentence. On the way, convicts sentenced for murder were added to our transport—we already had a taste of what was to come at that point. [When we arrived, it turned out] that this must have been the worst labor camp in existence in Russia. First of all we had to build ourselves hovels to live in with our own [hands], in –50°C [–58°F]. Anyone who didn't manage to make [them] in time—perished. Every movement of your hands was already torture.

Finally, when the hovels were ready, we were rushed—without being allowed to rest—to work. We worked cutting down trees. During the first few days, falling logs crushed a few people who were inexperienced in [this] new line of work. The guards stood by and laughed. We began work at three in the morning. Usually in –50°C [–58°F], [we] had to grope around almost blindly—it was deep nighttime still—toward the logging site and start working there without breakfast. Everyone had a set quota. If they didn't fulfill it, they didn't get bread after returning to the camp, and on top of that, were sometimes locked up in a special dark cell. They would either never come out of this dark cell again, or [would be] a cripple for the rest of their life.

There was a doctor in the camp, but his role was limited to declaring people unable to work, only [if they had] a fever above 40°C [104°F]. Apart from that he treated . . . dying people.

I survived for eight months in these conditions. Being a strong and well-nourished person by nature, I could handle it all. Hundreds of others, physically weaker, died. We envied them.

When the German-Russian war broke out, we were transported to the Arkhangelsk Oblast. We were run around day and night, without a [chance to] catch our breath. We often covered thirty kilometers a day in severe frost. When we wanted to stop to support [our] collapsing friends, the guards would use knouts and gunstocks to force us to continue marching. Naturally, those friends left behind in the snow perished.

In Arkhangelsk, we were placed in a camp where the conditions were not a change for the better. The work was probably even harder, as even higher quota[s] were assigned to us. We had to walk sixteen kilometers to [our] place of work. Even though our trousers and bast shoes[605] were in tatters, we didn't get new ones, so we had to rush to work through the snow almost barefoot. We were guarded by criminals chosen by the commandant, who took out their grievances on our backs.

---

605. Clogs, usually woven from linden, birch, or elm. They were put on wrapped feet and tied with a thong or string.

People were dying like flies. Pneumonia was the mildest illness. Dysentery raged with impunity as there was no doctor at all, nor medicines. No one took note of the fact that I was a war invalid—I had to fulfill the same set quota.

When I entered the camp, I weighed ninety kilograms, on release—forty-eight kilograms. I was released from the camp with others thanks to the Amnesty. I made my way to Lugovoy in the Ural, where I reported to the Polish army, was drafted, and was sent to Iran with a transport.

After I was discharged from army duty, I came to Palestine.

Protocol 249

Drawn up on the basis of the testimony of **Amalja Jollesówna**, schoolgirl, age seventeen, resident in Borszczów before the war [and] currently in Tel Aviv.

On 17 September the Russians entered our town. At first people said and thought that they were coming as allies, especially since the *politruki* attached to the Red Army units encouraged this view to begin with. Soon, however, we learned that this view was a mistake. The truth came out the moment the school's principal was arrested. He had ammunition planted [around] him and was then accused of counterrevolutionary agitation [and] taken away somewhere unknown. The pupils reacted with a revolt that lasted several days and involved taking serious measures. The NKVD "abolished" the action in a brutal manner, arresting a number of my schoolmates, including my brother.

The only section of society who were feeling good in the new situation were Ukrainians, who put themselves in the service of the NKVD without question, becoming a Communist-oriented force overnight. They ratted out Polish citizens—Poles and Jews—and thanks to their servility, [soon] occupied the highest positions in the city.

A plebiscite was conducted among parents, [asking] what language of instruction they wanted to see in the gymnasium. Even though the largest number of votes was cast for Polish, and then Jewish, Ukrainian was introduced. Speaking any language other than Ukrainian in school was prohibited. The entire faculty was replaced, [either with] professors brought in specially from the depths of Russia, or by putting pedagogical positions in the completely unqualified hands of the Ukrainians. And so, for instance, the position of principal was given to a man named Hejlo, a Ukrainian from outside Kiev, a carpenter by trade, who couldn't even read or write well. The teachers' objective was well understood of course, as even during physics and singing lessons they lectured [on] . . . the Soviet constitution.

The freedom to work in a [chosen] trade was abolished. Assignments from work bureaus were instituted, where it was not [one's] qualifications that were considered but the proletarian purity of the applicant's father and grandfather. Our apartment was soon requisitioned, leaving us—a five-person family—with one tiny room at our disposal. There was no method to the apartment allocation—chance played more of a part, or most often, the malice of an NKVD official.

After some time, private shops were closed down, leaving only the cooperatives. Naturally this resulted in foodstuffs running out within a short period of time, and lines forming [in front of the shops].

The real wave of terror, however, truly began with a series of arrests. First, large landowners were arrested and then deported: the Chortków *ordynat*,[606] Menkes, and others. My father and brother had so far avoided this fate, saving themselves by running away from Lwów.

On 10 February, I was arrested along with my [m]other as a member of a dangerous bourgeoisie class. We were taken to the rail station, not allowed to bring anything with us except a few tens of zlotys that Mother happened to have on her. At the station, we were loaded into freight cars, where there were already many of [our] acquaintances crowded in together. We waited for three days in the station. The townspeople brought us food and money. We learned from [some] friends that our home had been burglarized during our absence.

Finally the train set off toward Husiatyn. After [we crossed] the border, I could see just how many haggard and ragged people were roaming the Russian rail stations. Many came up to us and begged for a piece of bread or a grosz. Around eighty people were traveling in our car, so it's easy to imagine the conditions [during] the journey. During the three weeks of our journey, I was outside only a single time. We were given moldy black bread a few times and some soup that we weren't brave enough to try. It was horribly freezing in the car. One time when I took a nap, I noticed on waking that my braids had frozen to the wall of the car.

We were unloaded in the Altai Krai. We thought the worst was over—but it was only beginning. At the Troitsk station, we were loaded onto a sledge and driven into the woods. Every two sledges had the same carter so that every other pair of horses walked free. This resulted in calamitous situations: the horses were walking around a strange forest in ungodly frost, lost, [and] very often they would tip over the sledges with the people and [their] belongings. One time during a snowstorm, I fell off the sledge and no one even noticed.

606. Owner of an ancestral estate (in this case Chortków estate) that is indivisible and inalienable and passes automatically to an heir determined by the settlement.

It was only some time later that Mother realized, but the carter didn't want to agree to go back. Only the insistence of everyone [else] forced him to turn back. By the time we arrived in the *posiołek*, people's fingers and toes were frostbitten.

We were assigned barracks in the *posiołek*, one for every sixty people. They were full of holes and unimaginable filth. The first thing I noticed after entering [one] such barracks were the bedbugs crawling on the wall.

We weren't even allowed a proper rest after so horrific a journey, as on the third day, we were already ordered to report for work. Only men over sixty and women over fifty were exempt from this heavier work. Technically, children under sixteen were also to be exempt from work, but in practice, even twelve-year-old children were forced to do it.

Sawing and stacking the wood were considered the lightest [types of] work. One can imagine how people who were ill [as a result of their] experiences to date, [or] were unused to physical labor, fared doing this lightest work. Collecting resin was considered more difficult work. Many of us were referred for that; normally convicts sentenced for serious crimes were employed to do it.

There was no bread [in the *posiołek*]; it had to be brought in from beyond the forest. It was usually wet and moldy. We got sugar once every few months. Even worse times came in the spring, when the thaw came. We didn't have any spare clothing, so we had to walk around for weeks in wet and torn clothes that were rotting on us. Shoes would fall apart completely, and walking to work across the swamps in bast shoes was hell. Death lurked in our barracks more and more often; illnesses of all kinds ran rampant, which [still] didn't exempt anyone from work. There was no doctor—instead there was a feldsher, whose advice we preferred not to seek.

The commandant treated us with unheard-of brutality. He rushed [us] to work, unheeding of [people's] health. He was always assisted [in this work] by a knout. The only comfort in this situation was the solidarity of all the Polish citizens in the *posiołek*. Everyone helped one another however they could. Each of us had managed to bring some Polish books [with us], which were read a hundred times over. Once, the commandant ordered a search among us and a confiscation of all Polish and Jewish books.

When I fell gravely ill, the commandant allowed me, after numerous entreaties, to be moved to a nearby village where the hospital was. During

[my] stay in the hospital I had the opportunity to learn about the lives of the peasants. Their life was actually not at all different from ours in the camp. Generally, even though this wasn't said [aloud], there was a hostile attitude toward the existing regime. In almost all of the cottages one could see pictures of the saints. Even young people—with whom I talked very often—despite being heavily propagandized, were not enthusiastic about the Communist slogans. Admittedly, they belonged to the Komsomol, but that membership was more of an obligation. The village club was located in the [Orthodox] church.

The terror in the *posiołek* escalated further still after my return. [People were] arrested for any small thing. I myself spent a long time in a punishment cell—for what?—unknown. Such a punishment cell was the most sophisticated [form of] torture. [Just] a hole, without a floor of course, without a bunk [and] without light, that could bring many to suicide. In a few cases, too, corpses were pulled out of it.

When the German-Russian war broke out, our conditions worsened even more. We were working like automatons by then, unable to think, and moving as if in a dream. Our colony dwindled down to 40 percent [of the original population]—the rest lay in the cemetery.

We were supposed to be released in August as a result of the Polish-Russian agreement. Our commandant, however, did what he could to keep us as long as possible, first of all refusing us horses and carts that could have taken us out of the forest. There was nothing left to do, then, but continue working, and thus we made it to October. Finally those who still had enough strength decided to risk going to the station on foot rather than stay one more winter in the *posiołek*. The journey back through the forest was a torture a hundred times worse than the ride to the *posiołek* [had been]. Not only did we have to break through a thick wall of trees, but also had to carry [our] luggage. There were moments when we wanted to return to the camp; there were moments when, having lost [our] bearings, we were preparing to die from starvation—finally, by a miracle, we staggered through to the station.

Naturally, [getting] a train in a normal fashion was out of the question. One had to go through so many formalities, get so many certificates, that it would probably have taken us a month. We sorted it out in the normal Russian way—by giving a bribe to the station manager. He joined up [some] cars to a passing train, and thus we started our journey south.

We traveled for five weeks. We were all lice ridden, ragged, and hungry. Every few hundred kilometers, we had to unload someone gravely ill—or a corpse—from the freight car. Procuring food became somehow animalistic. At every stop we would sell off what we still had, and we supported ourselves this way, sharing with those who had nothing. Along the way, and particularly at the train stations, there lay corpses, which no one paid attention to anymore—we had fallen into a state of total numbness. Eventually we arrived in Foroba [?].[607] The NKVD authorities wanted to keep us there and send us to work again in a kolkhoz, but we managed in time to bribe the chief, who directed us to Georgia. There, too, they would not leave us in peace. The kolkhoz loomed over us again. We managed to escape to Kazakhstan, where we got off at the Shu station. The NKVD refused us the right to settle in this city, so we reached again for the tried-and-tested resource that had saved us so many times already, and for a few hundred rubles were left [undisturbed] in the city. The stay in that city was more hanging around just existing, waiting for a miracle.

Indeed, [the miracle] came. After some time the Tenth Division of the Polish army came. We left for Krasnovodsk with this army, with the first lot. By then, as a military family, we were under the care of the Polish authorities during the journey. We survived one more difficult event—a journey by ship. In Persia, we rested properly, and I came to Palestine from there.

607. This place has not been located.

Protocol 250

Drawn up on the basis of the testimony of **Chaim Fischer**, age thirty-five, resident in Oleszyce before the war [and] currently in Tel Aviv.

Around 11 September 1939 the first units of the German army entered the small town where I lived, Oleszyce near Jarosław. During the first days of the occupation, when the town was changing [hands] and the army ruled [it], relations were relatively peaceful. Only after a week did [the Germans] show what their rule would look like. At the time of their entry into town, we learned how their spy service was organized. There was an allegedly Polonized German, a man named Preisler, who had lived for years in Oleszyce, pretending—as it turned out—to be a good Polish patriot. The first German motorcyclist who arrived in town went straight to that very Preisler and then carried out inspections in his company.

After the first week, the Gestapo took control of our town. It started with rounding up Jews for labor and taking residents hostage. One time, the Jews most advanced in age were chased [around and] ordered to sweep the road with their beards. When some of them flinched at doing it, they were beaten unconscious with gunstocks. The younger ones were ordered to lift up huge logs on their own, which was impossible to do. Those [Jews] too were [beaten within an inch of their lives]. Only Poles and Jews were taken hostage, leaving the Ukrainians in peace. They received full power from the Germans [and were] the masters of life and death. They used this power, tormenting Poles and Jews cruelly and inhumanely. They prepared proscription lists, based on which the Germans would shoot [people]. My father and seventeen-year-old brother were shot at that time, among others. The pretext was their [alleged] saboteur activity.

On the eve of the Day of Atonement,[608] the Germans set the synagogue on fire. When the rabbi attempted to save the Torah scrolls from the burning building, he was shot on the spot, along with two other people.

The Russians entered Oleszyce around 25 September. Naturally the Ukrainians greeted them most enthusiastically. The Hasids and the Zionist

608. That is, 22 September 1939; the holiday of Yom Kippur fell on 23 September 1939. See also the glossary.

youth hid among [various] houses. The Ukrainians changed their allegiance and attempted to buy their new rulers' favor with flattery. There was total peace in town until mid-October. The reforms [implementing] the Soviet standard[s] hadn't yet been carried out in full. This peace, however, soon came to an end, when a special commissar of the NKVD, a Russian man from outside Kiev, arrived in town. The administration was staffed largely with Ukrainians, who, having been keen executors of Hitler's cruelties a mere few weeks earlier, now transformed themselves into dutiful followers of Communist slogans. The objects of persecution remained the same: Poles and Jews. It started with kicking [people out of their apartments] and requisitioning [the apartments] for Soviet officials and military personnel. [The Russians] would burst into shops, where they would "requisition" goods—without paying for the items taken of course—[and would] issue a worthless receipt at best. Homeowners were kicked out of their properties, industrialists deprived of their factories. The resulting chaos led to hunger overtaking the town in a short time.

When the elections were called for the highest Soviet magistracy,[609] it was announced that they would simultaneously serve to determine voters' wishes on annexing the occupied areas to the Soviet Union. A thorough registration of the town's residents was carried out, [the town] was divided into small wards, and the propaganda began. It was announced that the elections would be held under the most democratic regulations, according to the existing laws of the Soviet constitution. There [was] freedom to choose a candidate. Political agitators went from home to home, themselves not fully committed, and campaigning reluctantly. They had one significant argument, however: one had to take part in the vote because there was no alternative. On the day of the elections, that argument was supported by a blunt declaration from the NKVD that anyone who didn't take part in the election would find themselves herding polar bears in Siberia.

Naturally, there was only one list of candidates. Our electoral district's candidate, a Ukrainian woman [from Prypiat?] came to Rawa Ruska and announced in a public meeting that, even though she could not read or write, since she had had no opportunity to learn under the Fascist rule—she had

609. The author means the elections to the People's Assemblies of Western Ukraine and Western Belarus. See glossary: elections.

grazed cows [instead]—the Soviet authorities had told her to run for this high position, which was, perhaps, proof of democracy, and meant that every person had the right to hold high office in public life. During the elections themselves, the commission instructed [the voter] that in the next room he could cross out the candidates he didn't want to vote for. However, an NKVD-er [then] stood next to the voter giving his own instructions, that if [the voter] crossed out a candidate's name, he would be a counterrevolutionary. In that case his—the voter's—journey to the adjoining room could have unpleasant, and even fatal, consequences. We weren't surprised, then, by the election results.

Sometime after the assumption of power by the Soviets, a registration was called [in our town] of persons who had come from different parts of the country [and who wanted] to return to [their previous] places of residence. Simultaneously, the first deportations began. Property owners were deported first, as classic representatives of the bourgeoisie; then came the turn of state officials, foresters, etc. Also deported were peasants who had bought land during the parceling operation[610]—as equivalents of Russian kulaks.

The deportations peaked in the middle of April [1941]. [People] were being sent away en masse in that period. A simple denunciation was enough for one to be arrested and deported. It was enough to be suspected of patriotic activity, Zionism, [or] religious practice to find oneself on a list to go to Siberia.

I too was arrested during those deportations, as the son of an alleged bourgeois. One should remember that such a small-town bourgeois might have had wealth consisting of maybe a few thousand zlotys. Even someone like that passed for "bourgeois" [in our town]. My defense [arguing] that the Germans had shot my father and brother was in vain; I was loaded into a freight car in which there were already sixty people, the car was closed, and the train set off.

It's difficult to describe the atmosphere inside the locked railcar. It is a fact that we were pulling out the corpses of friends and relatives within the first twenty-four hours of the journey. Before [we got to] the border station of Podwołoczyska, people would crowd our cars from all sides, trying to help us in any way—however, this was made a lot harder because the guard[s] would not allow anyone near us. Even that illusory assistance ended the moment [we

610. [Parceling operation: a 1925 agrarian reform. Its essence was the division of public and private lands with an area exceeding 180 hectares (444.79 acres). Land buyers paid market prices.]

crossed] the Russian border, as here the people also crowded around our cars, but demanding provisions from us!

We traveled for around three weeks in these conditions. Finally, when we [had begun to] doubt that we would leave the cars alive, we pulled into [our] destination station of Alga, Aktyubinsk Oblast, Kazakhstan. Immediately after [our] arrival at the station, we were loaded onto trucks and split between the local kolkhozes. [Our group] was unloaded in one of the kolkhozes at twelve at night. The driver told us that we would be living there. He didn't say a word about homes or food—we were left on our own, under the open sky, hungry [and] ragged. The night was freezing. The next day, early in the morning, each of us began to look for some corner [to settle in] on their own. None of us found any lodging that day, as the peasants flatly refused, not having the NKVD's permission to take [anyone] in. After another night spent in the field, we were granted this permission, and the peasants, who treated us very warmly throughout [the rest] of our stay in the kolkhoz, helping however they could, took us in very gladly.

The [chief] of the kolkhoz called us in and read out the rules that would apply to us. We were not allowed to leave the kolkhoz. We must, under threat of serious punishment, take part in the May Day celebrations. A representative of the NKVD told the kolkhoz members gathered at a rally that the Poles had come here at their own request, completely unable to find work [in Poland]. For us, 1 May meant the start of work in the kolkhoz. We weren't split up according to trade, but everyone was assigned to work in the fields. We plowed and sowed, cultivated the land—a special official noted our *trudodnie*,[611] that is, the days [that we] worked. Now we had to wait until the harvest. If it was successful, then, after separating out the best crops as a tithe for the state, one could rest for a time. But if the harvest was not successful, [all] that was left was starvation. In the meantime, between the first planting and our first harvest—we went hungry. [We] lived by selling items or pieces of clothing [we] had. Outrageous prices were sometimes paid for a watch worth five zlotys. *Czasy*[612]—watches—were a hit in the kolkhoz.

611. Workdays. From Russian: *trudoden*; Polish transliteration: *trudodzień* [singular].
612. From Russian: *chasy*.

We petitioned to have everyone work more or less in their trade. We were told that we could not be self-governing at that time because we were in a correctional place. If any [member of] a family didn't turn up for work or transgressed in any way, the NKVD commandant would warn them that the family was currently "free," [but] could all find themselves in prison as a result of [any] further offenses.

[We] generally worked from sunrise to sunset, sometimes fourteen or more hours. Being late for work was punishable by *progóły*[613]—the most awful of punishments, as it resulted in starvation. The sanitary conditions were beyond any comprehension: there were no doctors and no pharmacy. A local folk healer treated [people] with methods that in a few instances—not even involving grave illnesses—caused death.

After the harvest was finished, everyone received twenty-five kilos of rye of the poorest quality, the same amount of rotted potatoes, and some cabbage leaves for 120 *trudodnie*. Everything of higher quality, on the other hand, was requisitioned for state needs. Naturally such an allocation could not be enough for a year's livelihood. As a result, theft occurred. Once, a teacher stole literally five potatoes for her child [and] was sentenced to three years in prison for it. It was a relatively lenient sentence, too.

Once a woman named Mrs. Tiegerowa, from Tarnów, having sold off all of the lesser-quality pieces of her wardrobe, went into town in her one last silk dress. She was arrested for it and sentenced to eight years in prison. In their explanation, the court stated that it was a case of counterrevolution, [of] wordless agitation. For lodging a complaint or a grievance, a person would usually be ejected from the kolkhoz [and] put into prison. I demanded my documents after leaving the kolkhoz, [and] by mistake the commandant released a file of complaints addressed to the highest Soviet authorities [about] me and others. It turned out then that he hadn't sent them at all, [but was] storing them [in his office].

At the same time, an issue of *Izvestia*[614] fell into my hands that [supposedly] proved that an English and an American worker lived in conditions a hundred times worse than a Russian one.

613. Russian: *progol*, from *progolodatsya* (to starve).

614. Main state daily newspaper in the USSR.

Many in our kolkhoz had been given prison sentences based on the accusation that they had stated that America or England was going to win the war.

I myself was sentenced for a similar offense. This was because I once said to the commandant that the German-Soviet pact was a worthless piece of paper. I was arrested, and after a long stay in jail, received notice in my cell that my trial had taken place and that I had been sentenced. Without [any] interrogation, defense, etc. Even [my] Mother wasn't allowed to [see] me.

I was only released as a result of the Amnesty related to the Polish-Russian pact. I worked in the [Polish] delegation set up in Aktyubinsk for some time. I reported to the Polish army [regiments] being newly formed, and after being ranked, left for Iran with my unit.

Protocol 251

Drawn up on the basis of the testimony of **Samuel Chmielarz**, age forty, industrialist, resident in Radom before the war [and] currently in Tel Aviv, 13 Zamenhof [Street]. He testifies as follows:

On Friday, 1 September 1939, I experienced the first bombardment by the German Luftwaffe in Radom. The bombings targeted primarily houses occupied by civilians. Bombs dropped in large numbers and one of them hit a house opposite [ours], killing a family of four people.

Relenting to my wife's pleading, I left for Warsaw a few days later, afraid of the approaching Germans. I witnessed the horrendous bombing and siege of that city. The Germans, with premeditation and sequentially, bombed hospitals, the fire station, and other public buildings. As a member of a [newly] formed citizens' vigilante [group], I stayed up all night, guarding the places assigned to me. One night, Mayor Starzyński called for six hundred men, ready for anything, to report [to him]. Thousands of people reported to the assembly point on the route through the DOK[615] at the agreed time. A hail of bullets was descending on Warsaw day and night. By day, the airplanes brought devastation; by night, the artillery buried the city with lethal missiles. On the eve of the [Jewish] New Year,[616] all hell broke loose in the city's Jewish district. Hundreds of airplanes dove in, flattening houses [and] murdering innocent people with machine-gun fire. There were thousands of casualties. Two horribly maimed boys lay on the pavement in front of my house. The entire life of the besieged city moved down to the cellars. People moved from the bombed streets into those still intact. Food ran out. There were notable instances of heroism on the part of the civilian population. In the building where I lived, one of the residents broke through the German iron cordon[617] and brought food for all from the countryside on his return. He was killed a few hours later by a bomb, when he could have stayed outside the perimeter of the besieged city. Living conditions became harder by the day; water

615. Dowództwo Okręgu Korpusu [Corps District Command].

616. That is, 13 September 1939; the first day of the holiday of Rosh Hashanah fell on 14–15 September 1939.

617. [Refers to the strong defensive position of the well-equipped German army.]

ran out, the lights—despite this, [people] did not grow disheartened [but] endured the horror of the siege with heroism and solidarity. Various fantastical pieces of news circulated during the siege: that Hitler had died, that the English were already outside Warsaw, that the Russians had joined together with General Sosnowski[618] and were coming to Warsaw's rescue.

Eventually, however, Warsaw had to surrender. During the first [period of time after] the Germans' entry, they handed out food among [all] the people, irrespective of faith. The famished population crowded [around] the trucks. No one suspected that this "German generosity" would later be used for the purposes of German propaganda. It turned out that the Germans were constantly filming the scenes of crowds in front of the trucks with food, and later released the photos into the world with appropriate notes. When the propaganda requirements had been sufficiently met, the Germans stopped the food handouts and began their bloody rule. First of all, they rounded people up to clean up the corpses, which were buried in garden squares and anti-aircraft ditches. The Germans didn't allow any ritual or liturgical rites; they ordered that the corpses be simply thrown into the ditches and buried. No crosses or markings were allowed to be placed [on them]. I witnessed the laying of the arms in Marszałkowski Square. Thousands of soldiers and civilians threw [their] guns and revolvers onto a pile, but [their] faces revealed the feelings suppressed inside. Despite the orders that threatened death for not surrendering weapons, large numbers of them were buried. In the courtyard of the house where I lived, a group of soldiers buried a large number of firearms one evening.

The Germans intensified their brutality by the day. Cruel street roundups began, during which the soldiers of the regular army attempted to one-up another in [their] cruelties. One day, a group of people was chased [under the blows] of gunstocks to a burning local gasworks. We were ordered to jump into the [flames] and pour water on the sources of the fire. Many died during this work. Throughout, the officers didn't stop hitting us with knouts. An old, seventy-year-old Jew fainted during the course of the work, [and] the guards took pity on him, leaving him in peace. An officer who arrived in the

618. General Kazimierz Sosnkowski (1885–1969): later commander in chief of the Polish army of the Government-in-Exile in London. In September 1939, commander of the Southern Front, which did not, in reality, manage to be set up in time.

meantime gave the soldiers hell [and] hit the unconscious elder and stomped on him with [his] boots, shouting that no mercy could be shown to a Jew. We worked under these conditions for twenty-four hours, without food.

People were captured on the streets [and] sent for labor outside Warsaw. One transport, on the way to [Góra] Kalwaria, was tied up to cars [?], some people died from gunshots, some were dispersed by the speeding cars. One day, we were led to clean the toilets and the stables of the Rakowieckie[619] [army] barracks. We asked to be given brooms and brushes for cleaning. In response, we received a serving of inhuman beatings and an order to clean with [our] bare hands. All night long, we picked feces out of the cesspit, [and] there was no shortage of beatings and jeering to go with it. The guards would pass [us] a piece of bread from time to time, in mockery, which we naturally could not even take into our hands [because of] the thick layer of feces we were covered in. We were released, foul-smelling, a few minutes before the curfew, so that we had to make it home in time, running—tired from the horrendous work.

Because the water pipes were not yet functioning, people obtained water from the Wisła. The Germans amused themselves by shooting at the people going to get water, or they would call a lucky person who had already managed to get the water to the barracks and order him to pour the water on the ground after beating [him].

The first restrictions applying to Jews came out. They took the form of confiscation of possessions, work quotas on households, etc. It was becoming more and more difficult to go out in the streets, as [people were] shot dead for nothing. The German cruelties increased as the Gestapo took over control. Once, a soldier came to my landlord, the owner of a leather warehouse, demanding that he hand over the leather. When [the landlord] asked for a receipt after handing it over, the soldier ordered him to come with him [and] promised that he would give him this confirmation at the station. We never saw the landlord anymore.

A member of the Gestapo turned up at my watchmaker friend's [workshop] once, demanding a watch. When the trader demanded payment, the Gestapo officer asked him to come with him. [The watchmaker] was found shot dead in Plac Broni the next day.

---

619. That is, on Rakowiecka Street in Warsaw.

I returned to my [home]town after some time. The conditions were the same there as in Warsaw. I learned in time that the Germans had prepared a list of hostages, and that my name had found its way onto the list. Knowing that this meant death, sooner or later, I went into hiding at my friends' [place]. [My] wife started making efforts to arrange my departure and managed to bribe a [local] German (*Volksdeutsche*) who placed a car at my disposal. Thus I found myself in Warsaw for the second time. I arrived at the time when the edict came out ordering the liquidation of Jewish apartments and the move to the ghetto. I pondered crossing the Soviet border before [getting] locked behind the walls of the ghetto. To this end, I made my way to the town of Drohiczyn, via Mordy. There, the Germans robbed us of everything, massacred people inhumanely, and then threw us across the Bug River.

I dragged myself to a Soviet post in Siemiatycze, where I was arrested. I was locked up, along with [some] others, in a pigsty and kept for thirty-six hours without bread or water. I was examined in the pigsty: asked if I was a Jew, a Zionist, why I had offended the Red Army. I was threatened with death by firing squad—with regard to this alleged offense. Luckily I managed to get through to the chief. During another examination it turned out that some documents had been switched, and I [had been] mistaken for someone else. After being released from the pigsty, I left for Brześć.

In Brześć, signs of the Soviet system were already visible. The only way to procure food products was to wait in line. Bread and other necessities ran out. I did not stay there long, aiming for Lwów [instead]. You had to wait for days for a train connection; [trains had been] so punctual only a few weeks earlier. Finally, however, I got to Lwów.

The mood in Lwów was the same as I had witnessed in small towns during [my] journey in June. The city, cheerful until then, [now] made a somber impression. Thousands of [new] arrivals—masses roaming the streets aimlessly—contributed to the strangeness. You would come across [those] typical lines at every step. [Only] a small number of shops were open.

When the registration to return [to German-held territories] began, a huge number of people chose the possibility to be reunited with their families, refusing to accept Soviet passports. As a consequence of this registration, deportations started taking place. Even before that time, the "bourgeoisie" had been sent away from the city, [as well as] homeowners, higher-ranking officials, and social and political activists. As a next step, mass arrests of single people were carried out.

One night an air raid alarm was called. During this alarm, an NKVD patrol came into my apartment, carrying out a search. They asked where my gun was and searched my pockets. Naturally, they found no gun, but they did take [my] money. After the search, I was loaded into a truck, [and] at the station, moved to a cattle car, where there were already fifty people squeezed [together].

We set off after a long wait at the station. The cars were tightly sealed, of course. Despite fierce heat waves, which would have been a struggle even under normal conditions, we were kept without water, sometimes for twenty-four hours. In desperation, we tried to force our way out of the cars [but] such an attempt was suppressed with buttstock [blows] each time. At first, the most aggravating problem was the issue of relieving ourselves: it had to be done in the car. As time went by, we grew used to it, began to grow indifferent. Lice bit us mercilessly; washing ourselves [or] tidying up our clothing wasn't allowed. A five-month-old child traveling with us was completely swollen up from the bites. We traveled like this for weeks, in complete numbness, until we finally arrived at our destination station, Sosva. There, without being allowed to rest, we were loaded onto barges and transported again on them for four days and nights. We lived off moldy bread we had hidden in our pockets. We were unloaded in a forest, in a clearing where there were more than a dozen[620] sheds [barracks] abandoned by criminal prisoners. The barracks were completely run down, the stoves broken, the walls riddled with holes, so that we had to take to repairs before anything else. Then we had to "scythe" [some] grass with a pocketknife, to serve as a pallet and a pillow. After two days' rest, we were sent to work. Billions of mosquitos descended on us; there was no way of fighting off this scourge. We walked around bloodied and swollen, but it was not possible to be excused from work. Because when someone objected, the warden would throw them into a dark cell, which was something worse than death. When the warden grew spiteful toward someone, he would bring a charge of espionage against them, sending them away somewhere where no one returned from. This happened to the five-person Lipschitz family, no trace

620. Translator's note: here and henceforth, where "more than/over a dozen" appears, it is used in place of the Polish word *kilkanaście*, which means a number between eleven and nineteen.

of whom were we able to find, despite our efforts. A man named Landau, from Kraków, fell ill with pneumonia. After long negotiations, he was allowed to leave for the hospital. When he improved, he was ordered to return to the *posiołek*. As it was freezing cold and often snowed, he asked the authorities [to provide transport], especially since he had just gotten out of the hospital. He was refused a cart, however, and had to return to the camp on foot, despite the lethal weather conditions. On the way he fell into snowdrifts [and], exhausted, could not dig himself out. He lay for hours like this in the snow. When he had dragged himself to the *posiołek* in a last-ditch effort, he relapsed with pneumonia. He died a few days later.

Once the commandant ordered a man named Pressler to travel over a dozen kilometers up the river in a boat. It was known that Pressler suffered from constant vertigo and it was explained to the commandant that the journey could end in tragedy. These arguments did not [succeed]. Pressler went, had an attack after a few kilometers, fell into the water, and drowned.

A man named Grunstein was sent by the commandant to fix a road at a section twenty kilometers from the camp during a terrible snowstorm. When he didn't return for a long time, we wanted to go rescue him—however, the commandant would not agree to it. We found Grunstein after some time, frozen to death.

When, after long months of waiting, a small shop was finally opened in our *posiołek*, we were able to each get a kilo of bread per day from it. Throughout our entire time in the *posiołek*, that is, fifteen months, we received four hundred grams of sugar.

When the Russian-German war started, [the authorities] pushed even more for work productivity. It was announced that [anyone] who shirked work or did not fulfill their quota would be considered a traitor and an ally of the Fascist enemy, and as such—[would be] punished. Once the commandant sent me to a station fifteen kilometers from the *posiołek* in order to fix [a section of a] road. I objected because I was sick. The commandant reported me, and consequently I was put [on trial]. The judge was a woman [and she] asked me, at the beginning, if I agreed to a red trial. Naturally, the question was a rhetorical one. With the sentence, 25 percent of my wages were taken away, which in a sense equaled a sentence of slow death from starvation. After leaving the court "building," I read a piece of news in the paper by chance about the conclusion of a Polish-Russian agreement. This news had such an effect on me that without waiting for the cart, I immediately made my way to the *posiołek* on foot to share this joyous news with the others. It was not without difficulty that our commandant acquiesced to the fact that we were no longer prisoners. He took [his] revenge on us by refusing to help or to organize [our] departure. Despite sizable difficulties, however, we managed through our own efforts to cover the distance of four hundred kilometers that separated us from the rail station of Sosva. [Then, we faced] the difficulty of getting hold of a train car. Only the right bribe worked; we received an allocation of our own two cars, in which we slogged on south for seven weeks. We finally made it to Wrewsko,[621] where the Polish army was stationed. I got across to Persia with an army transport.

621. Should be: Vrevskoye [original Polish correction: Wriewskoje].

Protocol 254

Testimony of **Miriam Kołdra**, from Warsaw, Czerniakowska Street, age sixteen. Came to Palestine from Tehran.

My father sold fruit. He leased orchards around Czerniaków and sold the fruit [in] Warsaw. At the outbreak of the war, Father, Mother, and we children were in an orchard outside Skolimów. We went to Warsaw on foot. On returning home, we found [our] home open and burglarized. Our neighbors fed us, but our situation was dire. It was impossible to get out of the Czerniaków area. The main battles for Warsaw were taking place not far from us. The largest number of bombs fell in our neighborhood, and the most people died. Only when the Germans arrived did the [truly] horrible times begin. Roundups of Jews took place in the streets; they were beaten and had [their] beards cut off. [My] parents decided to move to the Soviet side. The journey was hard. We had to wait for three days and three nights by the Bug River, as it happened to be a full moon at the time and they didn't want to take us across, fearing the Soviet soldiers. We hid with Poles in [their] peasants' homes, which German soldiers often visited to have fun with Polish girls. They [the Germans?] had boats at their disposal but did not want to take us across. They often organized raids on Jews, who had to pay generous ransoms [to save themselves]. They often actually hunted Jews, robbing and beating the unfortunate [people] who wanted to get to the other side. Finally a dark night came. Father took two hundred zlotys out of a pillowcase and gave it to a peasant, who had agreed to smuggle us to the other side. The leader of the German guard himself turned up in front of us and took the money from the peasant in our presence. When our boat was in the middle of the river, it ran into another boat in the dark, and two children fell into the water and drowned.

We made it successfully to Drohiczyn. Father went to a beth hamidrash and told [them] that he had come with [his] wife and seven small children. We were taken into a home, and a fair amount of money was collected for Father. We ate our fill for the first time in many months. That same day, we set off for Białystok via Siemiatycze. Białystok was full of people. We found many friends and neighbors from Czerniakowska [Street] there. We made our way to the beth hamidrash, to find a corner [to stay] there. We lay down on the ground and fell sound asleep. Father and the older children waited in a line for bread. We spent a few weeks like this. There wasn't enough room for everyone on the floor. During the day, Mother and the older children slept, at night Father and the younger ones. Father went to the magistrate looking for work. He got a job as night caretaker in a factory. He was paid [only a] little money but brought home bread for everyone. But Father grew weary of this life and one day told Mother and the children to get ready [to leave]. We were supposed to go to Lida and smuggle ourselves to Wilno from there. We set off without a ticket. We were told to get off in Wołkowysk. We spent the night in the station but got into the carriage again the following day without a ticket. We arrived in Lida. The NKVD was watching the outsiders. Father went to the rabbi for advice. But the rabbi didn't want to hear him out, and it was only a Jewish acquaintance who pointed him toward a young man with a cart, on which we set off for Raduń. Father gave the peasant all of his savings, that is, two hundred rubles, in exchange for which the peasant took on [the task of] getting us across to Wilno. Instead of Wilno, he drove us to a guard post and turned us over to the military police. We didn't have a penny. They locked us up in a cold cell for twenty-four hours without giving us anything to eat. We would have been held [even] longer, but Mama developed such pains that we started banging on the door with Father, screaming for them to release us. Late at night, an NKVD agent arrived and saw Mama lying in a pool of blood. We were [not] let out, and she was taken to the hospital on a cart, where, late at night, our youngest brother Benek was born. We continued to be held in prison and watched closely, lest we escape. In the hospital, too, a policeman was watching Mama so she wouldn't run away. On the eighth day, Mama and Benek were brought to prison. Father asked what would happen to us. He was told that we would be sent to the city for a trial. We were sent eleven kilometers on foot, and Mama got a hemorrhage on the way. She was taken to the hospital. She was then returned to us. We were put on trial and accused of espionage for a foreign state. The response to Father's question of which foreign state that would be was that all runaways were spies. We were sentenced to five years in prison and Father tried in vain to take the full blame upon himself. We were sent to Lida, and from there to Łuck, to prison. We were certain we would starve to death, because we got a piece of bread and a pot of bitter coffee only twice a day and were treated like criminals. After a few months, all the arrestees, including us, were sent away. We were loaded into freight cars, sixty-three people in each, and traveled for long weeks in a crush like that until we arrived in [the Autonomous Soviet Socialist Republic of] Komi, in the Sverdlovsk Oblast. We were very hungry and drank dirty pond water to quench our thirst. In winter, there were terrible frosts, and in summer mosquitos bit us until we bled. We couldn't stand it there and were sent to Frunze. Mother got brain inflammation from worrying, and without medical help, passed away. Father gathered ten Jews together to say Kaddish. For this offense, Father and [my] two little brothers were sentenced to the punishment cell. They were also tormented later for praying during the holidays. Half of our family perished in Frunze. [My] eldest brother, Abraham Kołdra, age eighteen, died of galloping consumption. [We] weren't allowed to bury him properly, and dogs were later seen dragging out his body. [My] little brother Zysel, three years of age, fell ill with brain inflammation and died. The youngest, Benek, born in prison, froze to death. When the Amnesty was announced, there were only five of us left: Miriam [me]—age sixteen; Jasza—age fourteen; Pesa—age twelve; Joséf—age ten; and Szlomo—age eight. We left for Ashgabat, then for Mashhad. We were all accepted into a Polish orphanage, sent to Tehran, and from there to Palestine.

Protocol 255

Testimony of **A. A.**, master of law, who was present in Tarnopol until the end of July 1943.

I was born in Kraków in 1912. During the Great War,[622] our entire family escaped to Górny Śląsk,[623] where I was raised in the Zionist spirit. I established an organization, the Hebrew Youth Association, during my time in gymnasium. I studied at the university in Kraków and received my master's degree in 1935. I began to work as a lawyer, but the lawyers' association did not want to accept me as a member, because Jews were not admitted. I played sports, too, and was the tennis champion of our district. In September [1939], I was mobilized. We set off to the East. On the way, we took part in small skirmishes with the Germans.

I fell into Soviet captivity, from which I was later released. I couldn't return to Katowice because the Germans were there. Many Jews stayed in the town of Maureta, where the Bolsheviks stopped us.[624] The local Jews, small merchants and craftsmen, treated us kindly. We later received permission from the Soviet authorities to go to Lwów. Lwów was full of refugees, who were being housed in all the public buildings. Many people slept under the open sky. The refugees traded in food and clothing, or anything they could. Illegal trading was punishable by strict penalties. To begin with, it would go no further than an arrest, but then people started being deported to Siberia. After three months' stay in Lwów, I left the city and made my way to Kałuszyn, where I got a job as a teacher in a Soviet school.[625] They paid well, we received housing, fuel, and five hundred rubles per month, as well as larger food rations than others. Only teachers were in this privileged position. At first, the Bolsheviks didn't bother Jews in carrying out services, but political organizations were persecuted, and the leaders of Zionist groups sentenced to deportation. I held a teaching post until May, and then, having received a passport with Article 11, had to

622. First World War.

623. Upper Silesia.

624. Likely refers to the town of Malorita.

625. This could not have been Kałuszyn. It's possible that [the author] is referring to the town of Krotoszyn.

leave the border town. The expulsion of refugees was to take place within two days. The possessions of the rich were confiscated during this registration. The bourgeoisie were expelled. I returned to Lwów, where a registration of refugees was taking place. One had to choose between going back to the Germans or [taking] a [Soviet?] passport. Holders of Soviet passports had to move deep into Russia. Those who didn't agree to these terms were deported to Siberia. During that time, Jews lived tolerable lives under the German occupation. I received letters from [my] parents and brother, sent from Górny Śląsk to Congress Poland. My parents had lived close to Cieszyn before the war. In 1939, they were sent to one of the towns in the General Government. In the year 19 [part of text missing], they were locked up in a ghetto. On 2 April 1943, I received a letter from them [with the news that] the ghetto had been liquidated and that they were hiding with [some] Christians. I was moved from Lwów to Brzeżany, where I attended a teachers' course organized by the Bolsheviks. My stipend amounted to 150 rubles per month, on top of accommodation. After the outbreak of the Soviet-German war, I tried to escape to Tarnopol. A Jewish Soviet officer wanted to take me to Kiev in his car. In Horodyszcze outside Tarnopol, German paratroopers attacked us. I jumped out of the army car, and severely banged up, got to Tarnopol on foot. I spent two weeks in the hospital. The Bolsheviks retreated from the city, [and] the Germans occupied Tarnopol. [They] started by plundering shops and homes. A few days later, the SS staged a Jewish pogrom with the Ukrainians. Five thousand people were killed. The Jews were ordered to put together a council. Three hundred people who reported [to be a part of] the council—and they were the cream of the intelligentsia—were shot dead. Women and children were spared during the pogrom. After the pogrom, a German announcement appeared [saying that] anyone caught stealing would be killed. The German administration began implementing its agenda. An order came out [that] all men and childless women between the ages of fifteen and fifty had to report for compulsory labor. Jews had everything they owned taken away from them. A ghetto was created, [and] a Jewish badge introduced. The council had to pay different contributions every day. A Jewish police force collected the contribution. Apart from this, a blood sacrifice was demanded from the council, that is, a list of Jews whom the Germans were to murder. The council gave a list of eight hundred sick and old [people]. This was in March 1942. A warning hung by the entrance to the ghetto, [announcing] that access to the ghetto for Aryans was forbidden due to a typhus epidemic. Crossing the gates of the ghetto was punishable by death. One couldn't cross the ghetto border without a special passport, [and] food smuggling was punishable by death. Meanwhile, the Germans organized systematic operations during which one thousand Jews were slaughtered. The Jews hid anywhere they could. The Jewish police were forced to carry out searches [and] find [those] hiding, who were gathered in a set place in groups of one or two thousand and rushed off to the rail station. Anyone who didn't walk fast enough was shot. The operations took place at night. Jews were dragged out of [their] homes. At the train stations, people were pushed into freight car[s], seventy people in each. Many suffocated in[side]. It wasn't permitted to bring anything to eat; nothing to drink was provided. Trains full of Jews from other towns ran through the station: from Trembowla, from Zbaraż, from Skole, from Podwołczyska. The cars traveled toward Bełżec. Jews from France and Hungary were also brought there. They were stripped naked and poisoned with gas. Many Jews from the first Tarnopol transport survived. During the journey, a few cars were opened at night with the help of Polish rail workers, a few Germans, and Hungarian soldiers. From the first transport that contained two thousand Jews, five hundred people were saved, [and they] returned to the ghetto in Tarnopol.

In the winter of 1943, a labor camp was established outside the ghetto, where the healthiest men and women were sent. They would leave for and return from work under the watch of the Jewish police. The camp chief was the vice leader of the SS, Rokita, and the supervisor a Jew, Miller. [People] didn't receive any compensation in the new camp, as the SS took it away. I worked in that camp and received four hundred grams of bread per day, a small pot of black coffee, a serving of soup for lunch, and sometimes a piece of horsemeat in the soup. Rokita opened a canteen in the camp, where he sold kielbasa, butter, marmalade, biscuits, etc. at speculative prices. [We] obtained money by selling [our] last clothes. Every day a few people were killed in the camp. At first no one wanted to go to the camp. Later, when it turned out that life there was more stable than in the ghetto, people paid large sums to be accepted there. All the towns around Tarnopol had been cleared of Jews. At that time, a group of young and healthy Jewish workers, as well as those who could get in for a lot of money, were brought to our camp. Older people, the poor, women, and children were not allowed into the camp. [That meant] death for them. The ghetto in Tarnopol was liquidated in the months of April and May 1943. To begin with, there were twenty thousand Jews living there. By that time, only eight hundred Jews remained. The remaining eight hundred were brought to designated places, robbed, and murdered. Many were buried alive. In a few instances, [those] more lightly injured got out from the common graves and made it to our camp. Our camp contained between 2,000 and 2,500 people. Grynfeld—the president of the Jewish council—his wife, daughter, [and] son-in-law were killed. He himself was killed in Tarnopol, and [his] family in Skole. After each operation, the Germans would come for the possessions of the murdered. Valuables and better pieces of furniture were sent to Germany after careful disinfection. Lesser items were sent to our camp. After the liquidation of the ghetto, the houses were blown up with dynamite and the bricks sold to peasants. Jews who came out of [their] underground hiding places met their end [at the hands of] Ukrainians. Tarnopol was proclaimed Jew free. The camps around Tarnopol were closed down. Only a few survived from those. Our camp was being shut down too. On the advice of a German engineer who worked in a road building company, I tried to escape. I sent [my] wife off to Skole. She received no help there. [Anyone who] harbored Jews risked the death penalty. [My] wife escaped from Skole to a small border village, and a week later, I found myself there as well. I had Aryan papers. Two Jewish engineers who were hiding like me were captured by the railroad military police and killed. On 1 August 1943, I found myself in hiding in the mountains with [my] wife. We crossed the border after five days of roaming around.

The members of the Jewish council in Tarnopol were: Grynfeld, Fleischman, and Doctor Pochoryłło. The chief of the Jewish Security Police was Chaim Helle, his deputy—Bergman. The worst criminal of the so-called Sonderdienst was the so-called [B]ig Miller. He was helped by: [S]mall Miller, Korow, Lachs, and Maja. The aforementioned storm troopers organized slaughters in Skole, Zbaraż, Trembowla, Jeżów, Zborów, Brzeżany, Czortków, and Podhajce. The slaughters in these towns were carried out with machine guns and hand grenades. Germans and Ukrainians would throw hand grenades into the cellars where the Jewish hiding places were. The cellars became communal graves. In the camp in Kamionka, they killed women and men separately, lay the bodies in a pile and set them alight. There were instances of strong resistance in Tarnopol. Before the liquidation of the camp, a gun cost between three and four thousand zlotys. Many camps had hidden weapons. In Tarnopol there were no Poles but Ukrainians, who turned out to be a lot crueler than the Germans toward Jews. I heard about incidents where rabbis would turn toward the Germans before their death and state that [the Germans] had won the war against children and defenseless women but lost it against England and Russia. [People] knew something was afoot before each operation. The Jews would come up with the most [creative] hiding places. Holes were dug in basements, [with] the basement entrance bricked in. In most of the hideouts, however, you couldn't survive longer than two to three days due to the lack of air, light, and water. The more well-to-do fitted out bunkers with ventilation and water supply as well as supplies for a few months for themselves. Bunkers like these were deep underground and had an exit into the Aryan part of the city via underground tunnels. People are hiding in such bunkers to this day. Only the partisans knew the access to these bunkers. They, like the Jews, were fighting against the Germans and the Ukrainian police. Many a time the bunker dwellers had to bury victims from the partisan [ranks]. In one incident, the number of [those] from the underground movement who were killed was forty. Many of us wanted to join the partisans but they didn't want to accept us because they were seeking specially trained people. The Jews in hiding believed that the war would end soon, and [that] they would live to see its end living in the bunkers. A certain number of Jews from Tarnopol were hiding among the Aryans.

The Jewish militia force was made up of volunteers. Most of them [were] Communists. They had reported for duty [with the Germans], wanting to save their lives this way. They didn't kill Jews, but some [of them] would rat us out and beat us. There was an incident where a member of the militia gave up sixty Jews to save his wife. Some of the Jewish property was hidden with peasants and [other] Aryans. In my opinion, there are three hundred Jews hiding in the Aryan district in Tarnopol.

The Gestapo explained [their] killing of Jews by the fact that [the latter] had caused the war. In the camp, Rokita killed Jews himself. He brought in the prettiest girls for himself from the local camps. They lived in his apartment. One of them—H—helped Jews however she could, and later escaped with a

Jewish doctor—B. During the first pogrom, many Jewish girls were raped by the SS; later, these incidents were rare. I saw [those] sentenced to death, walking to their doom, naked. They were beaten on the way. Sometimes German soldiers helped the victims and gave them something to eat. A German soldier is desperately afraid of the Gestapo. In the German company where I worked, some clerks were Party members. They received special instructions on how to treat Jews and conducted themselves accordingly. Despite this, some [of them] gave me cigarettes and bread. The worst tormentors [were] people from the SS and the Sonderdienst,[626] butchers and craftsmen by trade. I heard [stories] that the slaughter in Bełżec takes place in the following way: the starved people are [poisoned] with gas, and their bodies are made into soap.

---

626. The author likely refers to the Sonderkommando, a unit of Hitler's security police [and] part of [the] Einsatzgruppen [a Nazi paramilitary group], which carried out mass executions of the Jewish population in the initial period of the German occupation of Poland.

Protocol 257

Testimony of **Mrs. Aszkenazy**, age thirty, from Kołomyja. Left Kołomyja at the end of December 1942 and came to Palestine via Hungary in March 1944.

Out of forty thousand Jews who lived in Kołomyja, I am the only one who survived and got to Palestine. All of my relatives died. I can hardly believe it when I talk about it, and sometimes I myself don't believe what my eyes have witnessed. I survived thanks to the fact that I look like a Christian woman and managed to obtain Aryan papers. At the outbreak of the war, there were twenty thousand Jews in Kołomyja. Later Jewish refugees from Kosów, K[part of text missing],[627] and other small towns arrived. [As a result], there ended up being forty thousand residents [imprisoned] in the Kołomyja ghetto during the destruction operation, who were killed in batches. Kołomyja was occupied by the Bolsheviks at the beginning of the war, then by the Hungarians, finally by the Germans.[628] Throughout the various occupations, the Ukrainian population treated Jews in a hostile manner. [They] robbed, denounced, and murdered [them]. The Jews' hatred toward Ukrainians was so great that it was often asserted that Ukrainians were worse than the Germans. When the Russians occupied Kołomyja, they took away our home and sawmill and didn't give [us] any work in town. They sent all refugees to Siberia and arrested [those] politically suspect, among them Zionist activists. Those who worked for the Russians earned so little that they couldn't feed themselves. Most [people] worked in smuggling and black market trading or selling their old possessions. I moved to another town with [my] husband, where no one knew us. We got jobs and got by somehow. After the outbreak of the German-Russian war, we didn't want to go to Russia and went back to Kołomyja [instead]. The Hungarian army occupied Kołomyja. The Hungarians behaved decently. They

627. Likely refers to the town of Kuty.

628. In Kołomyja before the war, there were fifteen thousand Jews, and after September 1939, at least another [fifteen thousand] Jewish refugees from central and western Poland arrived. The city was occupied by the Red Army on 17 September 1939. On 30 June 1941 the Soviet administration left the city, pushed out by the German army. Three days later, the city was given by the Germans to be occupied by their ally: Hungary. During the few days before the arrival of the Hungarian authorities, Ukrainian nationalists murdered Jews in the city. On 1 August 1941, Kołomyja found itself under German occupation.

only confiscated radios. However the Gestapo had their representatives there, who would turn up from time to time and arrest [whomever] they wished. One Sunday a Gestapo unit came and took fifteen hundred Jews with them. They were taken outside the city and ordered to dig graves for themselves. The shooting order was ready. A young Hungarian city commandant found out about it. At the last minute, he went to the place of execution in a car and told the Germans that as long as the Hungarians were there, no killing would take place. Thus the Jews were saved.

But soon the Germans occupied Kołomyja. Operations began that were carried out in a diabolically methodical manner. Not straightaway, but slowly. Various registrations were carried out, giving [people] hope that certain categories of people would survive. The Jewish militia force looked after the registrations. The first large-scale operation took place in autumn 1941.[629] The Gestapo captured two thousand Jews and took them out to a forest outside Kołomyja. All were killed and buried in a common grave. In the city, [people] comforted themselves [by saying] that this was a one-time punitive operation and that it would end there. The police force in Kołomyja were [people from] Vienna at that time. They consoled us, [saying] that the Jews' situation wouldn't always be this desperate and that we should be patient. It often happened that a Viennese policeman would bring a Jewish child a piece of bread. But their fear of the Gestapo would not allow them to help us. At first they behaved cruelly only to men and didn't persecute women. One day [it was] the birthday of Geier, the chief of the Kołomyja Gestapo. He ordered one hundred small Jewish children to be brought into a local slaughterhouse and shot those hundred children dead himself one by one, later boasting in town that that was the way he celebrated his birthday. Then the second operation took place.[630] The registration of the intelligentsia, lawyers, teachers, and others began. Five hundred people were gathered and killed outside the forest. Then alien citizens—Jews—were registered, three hundred of them assembled and killed.[631] Those Jewish alien citizens never thought that registration would equal a death sentence for them.

---

629. 12 October 1941. Around three thousand Jews were murdered then.

630. 6 November 1941.

631. 23 December 1941.

Before Pesach of 1942,[632] the city was divided into three ghettos, an eviction committee arrived, and a horrendous operation of mass extermination of Jews began. Seven thousand Jews were deported in one day.[633] No one had any illusions [about] what this deportation meant. Jews attempted to avoid the registrations and hide. The Germans set fire to homes. When [those who were] hiding there tried to escape the fire, the Germans would grab them and throw them back into the flames. After Pesach of 1942, the Germans issued an order [stating] that all Jews had to register and all were subject to deportation. The council president at the time was Horowicz, the owner of a lace factory. He tried to commit suicide but didn't succeed. He only managed to take his life four weeks later, and was lucky this way not [to die] at the hands of the Nazis but by his own hand.[634] The greatest luxury was to own poison.

The German commission left, and we learned that, through various means, six thousand Jews had managed to avoid expulsion. They were concentrated in a small ghetto. I hid in an underground apartment, a so-called bunker, for some time, and saw with my own eyes how a mother suffocated her small child when it started crying, wanting to save the other bunker dwellers this way. Small children were given strong sleeping pills for the night. One child [started] crying. The bunker owner demanded that the mother calm the child down immediately. Soviet airplanes flew over Kołomyja and sitting in the bunkers, we prayed for bombs. We dreamed of a humane death. I decided to escape to Hungary. [My] Polish acquaintances sorted out Aryan papers for me. The Germans tyrannized the Poles. They killed the Polish intelligentsia and sent the youth to Germany. Many Poles escaped to Hungary. Until the last moment of the ghetto's existence, a secret committee of the Joint was operating in Kołomyja. There were soup kitchens where people would share their last piece of bread. The worst was the situation of the refugees from the provinces, who arrived naked and barefoot. Before killing Jews, the Germans took away their riches. This was carried out systematically. At first they demanded

632. Before 2 April 1942.

633. They were deported to gas chambers in Bełżec. This operation took place on 3–4 April 1942. Further deportations to the Jewish extermination center in Bełżec took place on 7 September and 11 October 1942.

634. The suicide of the leader of the Judenrat in Kołomyja, Mordechaj Horowitz, took place in the second half of October 1942.

that diamonds and jewelry be delivered, then—gold and silver. Later [they] ordered that furs and undergarments be brought in. Wearing fur was punishable by death. I had nothing to be afraid of anymore. With the remainder of [my] money and jewelry, [and] the help of a smuggler, I made my way to Hungary. The journey took four weeks. We walked by night. We finally got to Máramarossziget. There were fourteen of us. The Hungarians received us well. They issued us an official certificate [saying] that we were Catholics, [despite] knowing we were Jews. We also received permission to work, even though refugees did not have that right. This was also immensely important, in view of our mental state. We gave the smuggler a letter for our friends hiding in the Kołomyja bunkers. Another group tried to cross the border. They revealed to the smuggler that they had jewelry on them. That same smuggler killed [them] one by one on the way and robbed [them]. I learned how the last Jews in Kołomyja perished. The Germans brought in a few tens of Jewish craftsmen and a few doctors. Those craftsmen had to search the remainder of the houses, and then the entire group was sentenced to death. The doctors committed suicide. The thirteen Jews who arrived with me stayed in Hungary and are now in the hands of the Germans. I had always been religious. [These] experiences shook me so much that I believe in nothing now.

Protocol 258

Testimony of **Michał Lipnik**, musician by trade, age forty-five, from Wilno. Arrived in Palestine via Persia in the year 1944.

I was a volunteer in the Polish army in the year 1920. I managed to conceal this fact from the Bolsheviks during the occupation of Poland. I'm a musician by trade. When the war broke out, I was mobilized for the army in Wilno. Our garrison was in Lida. On 17 September [1939], I fell into Bolshevik captivity. We were sent to Gorky, not far from Moscow. We were kept in Gorky for six weeks. There were sixty thousand Polish soldiers there. Officers were kept separately. We lived in former convents. I was a sergeant major in the cavalry. Our camp was surrounded by wire but [we] could move around freely within [it]. We weren't given any work. We weren't allowed to engage in cultural [activities]. We read Russian papers. We were also allowed to correspond with the areas that were occupied by Germans. Our meal[s] consisted of six hundred grams of bread per day, two hundred grams of dried fish, and sour cabbage soup. After a few weeks, the Russians carried out a registration and freed everyone except officers, military policemen, and the police. I returned to Wilno. I learned that the Russians were deporting the volunteers from 1920 to Siberia. I escaped from Wilno to Białystok, afraid of denunciation. I was accepted into a Belarussian [Belarusian] theater. Later, I joined a Jewish troupe whose director was a man named Rokita. There were Warsaw actors who belonged to the troupe: Morewski,[635] Landau, Turkow,[636] Litan,[637] and others. Shakespeare's *The Tempest* was staged, directed by Leon Schiller. One day, after the first performance, the famous actor Landau died on stage. He had once been an actor on the Polish stage and performed alongside [Wincenty] Rapacki. His body lay on the theater stage[638] for three days, and thousands of people came to pay him their last respects. The funeral was magnificent. Delegations from various countries sent wreaths; many speeches were given at the grave. None of the Jewish actors to date had had a funeral like that. We performed in Białystok

635. Abraham Morewski (1886–1964): actor, director, writer, and essayist.

636. Icchak Turkow (1906–1970): actor, writer, and dramaturg.

637. Likely Jakub Litman or Pepi.

638. [The body lay in state on stage with respect to the actor's profession.]

until 7 May 1940 and then went to Mogilev. Arrests among refugees began. Actors were arrested too. It turned out that 90 percent of the actors and stage workers and musicians were refugees. The theater was closed down. The less dangerous were sent to kolkhozes, the others to prisons. I was arrested based on a denunciation regarding my volunteer [service] in 1920.

One day Mogilev was bombarded by the Germans. The bombardment lasted for two hours. The Germans dropped paratroopers during the bombing. The arrestees took advantage of the chaos and rebelled. I took part in the rebellion. The guard[s] allowed us to run away. We tore out the bars and rushed to escape. We ran through the bombed-out city. I escaped with a group of fourteen people. We destroyed [our] papers and joined a group of Russian refugees who were being evacuated from the south. We set off for Tashkent, where, it was said, there was enough bread. We were starving on the way. I gave away my jacket for a piece of bread. Finally we got to Tashkent, and from there to Frindze[639] in Kyrgyzstan. I had sold everything in the army, in prison, [and] on the journey, keeping my only treasure—a trumpet, which I even brought [with me] to Palestine. I could find work easily thanks to [having] my own instrument. In Fryndze, I was immediately hired by a Russian theater, Russkaja Drama. I earned six hundred rubles per month. Despite these earnings, I constantly went hungry, so I set off again. I decided to give up art [concert music] and work as a musician in a restaurant. I received twelve hundred rubles per month in the restaurant, playing from seven until twelve-thirty at night. The audience was made up of high-ranking military officials. The civilian population visited the restaurant only between four and four [*sic*]. The meals consisted of two hundred grams of bread and soup for three rubles. Outside of these hours, privileged [people] received the best available stuff in the restaurant. I witnessed an incident where a drunk Russian shouted: “Fight the Jews, save Russia.” He was asked to leave the premises but came back later as if nothing had happened. Drunkenness was a common occurrence.

One day I received a call-up for the Red Army. I had a Polish passport and a Soviet one, [and] got a placement thanks to the latter. I was sent to officer school. I lived there for a few weeks and had the opportunity to observe the [training] system of Soviet officers. Entry requirements were as follows: age

639. Incorrect name of the town of Frunze.

under forty, knowledge of the Russian language, and an initial familiarity with active service. Privates were not accepted into the school. The greatest importance was attached to the teaching of propaganda. Between six and seven, there was a breakfast consisting of bread and tea. Then we were taught how to handle arms. From twelve till one, lunch: meat, soup, potatoes. From one till four, we were taught contemporary Russian history and familiarized with the works of Lenin and Stalin. From four till six, marching exercises. From six onward we were free. Dinner consisted of soup and bread. [We] got as much tea during the day as [we] wished. One could even [stay out and] not return to the barracks all night long, from six [onward]. Our battalion's commandant was a Pole—Nowak. The school's commandant was a Jew—Mojsejew. After the announcement of the Amnesty, I moved from the Russian army to the Polish one, as I had been placed on the list of soldiers in the Polish army. I set off toward Turkestan. In Kuybyshev [and] in Chkalov[o], I waited in line for hours for a piece of bread. I bought myself food with my last grosze. I spent two weeks on the kolkhoz Krasnoje Znamia, made up of two hundred people, a few refugees among them. We received six hundred grams of bread per day. I saw Russian peasants praying in front of icons. A peasant could have his own cow but had to pay the state twelve kilos of butter per year and four poods of meat for it. There was a school for children in the kolkhoz. I finally got into the Polish army and [went] to Persia, where I became the manager of the officers' casino. I came to Palestine with the Polish army.[640] I'm now working in my trade as a musician. My family remained in Wilno and I've had no news of them.

640. [A military formation created by General Władysław Anders consisting mostly of people freed by the Amnesty from Stalinist labor camps, prisons, and places of exile. The army was evacuated from the Soviet Union in March 1942, going first to Iran and then to Palestine. See glossary: Polish army in the USSR.]

Protocol 259

Testimony of **Adela Gutman**, age twenty-eight, born in Warsaw and working as a health worker in Lwów. Came to Palestine via Tehran in 1944.

I worked as a health worker in a Jewish hospital in Lwów, also at the moment the war broke out. I lived through all of the Russian occupation and the period of the Russians' departure from Lwów as a health worker in the hospital. I know how numerous the casualties were from the very moment of the outbreak of the war. I can't forget the particularly tragic incidents. One bomb fell on the Hospital of the Infant Jesus, the children's annex. It killed twenty children. There were no men in that hospital [who had been] mobilized for duty, the entire personnel was made up of women. A second German bomb fell on an air raid shelter on Piłsudski Street and killed sixty people. The first bomb fell on Friday [1 September 1939] at twelve noon, near the station. It killed six people and wounded fifteen. The wounded were immediately transported to the hospital where I worked. Their bodies were disfigured and faces unrecognizable. Families identified the deceased through distinguishing marks.

The Germans bombed Lwów for three weeks, day and night.

We continued our rescue work.

Odd twist[s] of fate could be observed among the victims: one mother survived while the child she was holding in her hands was killed. After a week, the hospital was left with no water or electricity. The health workers brought in buckets of water from a well [located] one kilometer away, and patients were operated on only by day. The bombardment was so severe one day that the wounded were being brought in for two days nonstop. The sanitary conditions worsened by the day. You could see lice on the injured patients. I would clean the bugs from a wound with tweezers before surgery. Our hospital was bombed. Patients with their legs in casts jumped up and ran off to the shelter. We set up a gynecological ward in the hospital's basement. Five children were born during the bombardment, and all turned out to be healthy. A Polish hospital sent a request to us to move a few of our health workers [there]. I was present at difficult surgeries and witnessed excellent operations carried out on soldiers by the Polish doctors.[641] The hospital director officially stated that he could not force the sisters to work during the bombardment, but none [of them] evaded their responsibilities. The sisters were allowed to bring in [their] families and relatives so that they wouldn't have to be separated from their loved ones.

We worked during the surgeries without hot water or light. Out of the supplies, there were some groats left, which were split between the doctors and the sisters. From time to time I went up onto the roof and surveyed the area. The Germans were positioned on a hill. They wore navy blue [?] uniforms and were firing at the city from a short distance away. Many doctors, refugees from Warsaw and Łódź, came to our hospital. They immediately reported for work. The hospital could hold twelve hundred patients. We had quite a lot of bandages. Before the Russians took over the city, shooting could be heard—the Polish and the Russian [armies] were shooting at each other. A wounded *krasnoarmeyetz*[642] was brought into the hospital, [and] we provided assistance [to him]. The hospital operated as normal. After six months, the management of the hospital moved into Bolshevik hands, [and] they implemented their order. Our hospital had been built by the father of a Socialist MP, Dr. Herman Diamant.[643] The founder's bust stood in the hospital. The Bolsheviks ordered it removed. A bust of Lenin was put in its place. The Bolsheviks appointed their [own] management, their [own] doctors and sisters.

In April 1941, the Russians arrested refugee doctors and nurses and deported them to Russia. I was left [alone]. The wages were so low that one had to make money on the side by stealing in order to survive. A doctor earned three hundred rubles per month, half of which went to taxes. For six hours of work, a health worker received 170–250 rubles per month. The remuneration did not include food and lodging, and a kilo of meat cost sixty rubles. [People] even ate dogmeat, but that too was expensive. There was nothing left to do

641. "Polish" is used here in contrast with the Jewish hospital where the author worked initially.

642. [Red Army soldier.]

643. Herman Diamant [Diamand] (1860–1931): lead activist of the Polish Social Democratic Party [Polska Partia Socjalno-Demokratyczna; PPSD] and its MP in the Austrian Parliament, member of the International Socialist Bureau, MP for the Polish Republic [MP for the Second Polish Republic] in the years 1918–30, participant in the Geneva Conference.

but steal from the hospital. The winter was harsh; the central heating did not work. Lwów was swamped with refugees, whom the local people could not help as they themselves had nothing to live off of. The Russians took all the supplies away to Russia. Goods would be requisitioned, paid for with [mere] grosze, and huge trucks would leave from Lwów. They even took away wood. The NKVD-ers introduced the following scheme in Lwów: They would arrest people [and] buy their furniture from them after the arrest. One day a search was carried out at a Russian prosecutor's [place] and stocks of English fabrics were found [there]. People came in from all of Russia, happy when they got a job in Lwów. Some Bolsheviks ate several lunches per day.

At first the Bolsheviks only courted the Ukrainian writers, paying no attention to Polish and Jewish [ones]. One of the writers, [Jerzy] Putrament, was literally dying from hunger. Later, the Russians would support Polish writers. [Tadeusz] Boy-Żeleński, Brzoza,[644] [Włodzimierz] Słobodnik, [Leon] Pasternak, Wanda Wasilewska, and others were living in Lwów. Rooms were requisitioned for them and attention was paid so that the NKVD would not send them to Russia. Despite this, some were sent [away]. A Polish paper was published. Writers were invited for readings in factories and academies. A special canteen was opened for them. A Polish theater was formed as well. The painters' situation was worse. The head of the painters' group was a Ukrainian man, who later collaborated with the Germans. He told all the painters to adhere to the classical style and set Repin as the ideal. A conflict broke out. The painters gave up and eventually started painting portraits of Stalin and Lenin en masse, in the classical style.

The influx of refugees did not cease. [People] slept in theaters, on the ground. Bolsheviks propagandized the people to sign up for work in Russia, promising them the world. The local Communist Party was dissolved,[645] [and] new parties were formed.[646] There were Jewish intellectuals living

644. Jan Brzoza, actually Józef Wyrobiec (1900–1971): Polish novelist and communist activist.

645. Communist Party of Western Ukraine, illegal in the Second Polish Republic, was an independent faction of the Communist Party of Poland [Komunistyczna Partia Polski; KPP], which was also illegal. It was disbanded on the orders of Stalin before the war in the years 1937–38.

646. The only party permitted was the All-Union Communist Party (Bolsheviks).

in Lwów:[647] Szneur,[648] Bomza,[649] Perle,[650] Kacyzne,[651] Drekurs, Gruen,[652] Aszendorf,[653] Rachel Korn,[654] Ber Horowitz,[655] Imber,[656] and the painter Rei from Kraków, as well as Ida Kamińska[657] with her troupe. Arrests took place often. The opening of a Jewish theater was not authorized. Only later did a Jewish delegation from Kiev arrive to organize the Jewish intelligentsia. They worked slowly, rather looking for fun of their own. Then Perec Markisz[658] and Sholokhov[659] came to Lwów and organized a meeting with the intellectuals. The establishment of Jewish cultural operations went slowly. On the radio, [people] spoke in Jewish for only three hours. One received twenty-five rubles per show. Work in propaganda was offered. [Part of text missing] poetry. Jewish textbooks were printed, and writers were hired as copy editors. Jews in Lwów read a Jewish paper published in Kiev, which printed dispatches from Lwów. Twenty-one Jewish schools and a theater were opened. A Russian man from Dnipropetrovsk became [the theater] director, and the manager—Ida Kamińska. Russian plays were performed in Jewish; a play by Perec Markisz was also staged. Two months before the Germans' entry into Lwów, a Jewish paper[660] was published on the premises of *Chwila*[661] and cultural initiatives in the Jewish language were expanded. Various authors were translated into

647. The author is listing a group of authors who wrote in Yiddish.

648. Likely Mosze Szneur (1885–1942): conductor, composer, arranger, founder of the 150-person Jewish Folk Choir in Warsaw.

649. Nachum Bomze (1906–1954): poet writing in Yiddish.

650. Jehoszua Perle (1888–1944): writer, translator, critic.

651. Alter Kacyzne (1885–1941): poet, writer, playwright, publicist writing in Yiddish; translator, photographer.

652. Józef Grin (1905–1990): (after the war, Józef Zawadzki) economist.

653. Izrael Aszendorf (1909–1956): poet writing in Yiddish, author of poetic drama pieces and novels.

654. Rachela [Rachel] Korn (1898–[1982]): poet, novelist writing in Yiddish.

655. Ber Horowitz (1895–1942): poet, author, illustrator, painter, translator of Polish literature into Yiddish.

656. Samuel Imber (1889–1942): poet.

657. Ida Kamińska (1899–1980): eminent actress and theater director.

658. Perec Markisz (1895–1952): writer, poet, playwright writing in Yiddish. Murdered on the orders of Stalin.

659. Mikhail Sholokhov [Polish: Michaił Szołochow] (1905–1984): eminent Russian writer. Winner of the Nobel Prize in Literature in 1965.

660. A Yiddish-language paper, *Der Reuter Stern* was published for a very short period of time, only from 1 June 1941.

661. A [Zionist] Polish-language Jewish daily [published in Lwów from 1919 to 1939].

Russian and Ukrainian and many Jewish-language translations were published. Kacyzne became the leader of the Union of Writers. One had to have had a book published to become a member of the Union of Soviet Writers, but an order arrived from Moscow not to take into account writers' political leanings or [but?] their literary credentials. A policy encouragement was observed. Rachel Korn sat among the censors. Relations with Polish writers were ideal. They often took part in common meetings. Only the Ukrainian writers emphasized their nationalism. Many of them remained on the Germans' side. The Russian-German war broke out. A few Ukrainian families fled immediately. The Russians told [people] to work until the last minute. Newspapers [continued] being published. [On 22 June 1941] at six in the morning, Lwów was bombed, and the war was announced at twelve. The first battle took place outside Brzuchowice. On the second day, a fire broke out. Ethanol and oil refineries were burning. The ethanol burned for two days and two nights. The Germans bombed the city relentlessly. The Russians started running away but did not take the civilian population with them, even the Communists. The order to flee was only issued on the third day. Trains stood in the station ready to evacuate people, but no one knew about it because the stations were on fire. On the first day of the war, there was a meeting in the Jewish editorial departments. An order was issued: to stay [put] until the last moment. At twelve noon, four people in an editorial department were killed by a bomb. Rachel Korn survived by a miracle. We escaped on the third day. The NKVD was burning documents. There was a group of us: myself, Bomza, Aszendorf, and another young person also. We fled on foot to Podwołoczyska, covering 150 kilometers. We got on a train from time to time, which [however] would be shot at so much that we preferred to go on foot. We came upon many refugees on the way. When the Russians arrived in Lwów for the first time, they were greeted very enthusiastically by some of the people. The Bolsheviks leaving Lwów were shot at by the Ukrainians, [who] set up a provocation by placing machine guns in abandoned apartments in the Jewish district. The Russians drove into the Jewish district in tanks and destroyed the houses in Źródlana Street, Podzamcze, and Żychnicka Street. The Russians didn't know whether they [should] defend themselves from the bombs [falling] from the German airplanes, or from the bullets coming from the windows. The Ukrainians poisoned the wells on the way. Girls who had made friends with the Russians were given dirty looks. That is because the Bolsheviks, having left their wives and children in Russia, often married the local girls. The Russians were generally hated. Their women bought everything without [standing in] line and emptied out the shops. Later, [people] learned not to sell them goods. The Ukrainians organized Jewish pogroms. The Bolsheviks tried to help the refugees, but the Germans were bombing the runaways. [People] talked about German paratroopers. The Ukrainians excelled at helping the Germans. The Poles did not run away from the cities. They said: "One evil isn't better than another." From Podwołoczyska, we went to Kiev. There was no organized help [available]. Men were taken for the army along the way. Writers were mobilized this way: Aszendorf and Bomza. Alter Kacyzne was killed by a bomb on the way,[662] and his wife and daughter survived. I couldn't stay long in Kiev because the evacuation began. I set off with a group of Jewish writers. We traveled for two days in freight cars, without food. The writers went to Ufa, and I stayed in Kuybyshev. They didn't want to register me [for residence]. I got a place to sleep on the floor for a large sum of money. I went to Tashkent. I traveled in the company of [some] Russian women who had escaped from Moscow. They treated me kindly. In Tashkent, thousands of refugees were living under the open sky, without [any] assistance. I met the actress Ida Kamińska and her troupe. She had been in Równe at the time of the war outbreak. She had escaped to Tashkent without [her] belongings. One day when I was standing in the market [trying] to sell something, I had [my] purse with [my] money and documents snatched away. I was left with no money and no papers. A refugee woman from Poland took me in as a domestic helper but kicked me out later because I didn't have papers. I looked for work in a hospital but could not get it for the same reason. Eventually, I received a transcript of my school-leaving certificate by chance and was able to get a job in a cooperative thanks to it. [Some] writers came to Tashkent: Rachel Korn, Slobodnik, and Aszendorf. Five people slept on the floor in one tiny kitchen. Despite this, the poets read newly written poems to each other every day. Thanks to [my] school-leaving certificate, I was issued legal paper[s]. A Russian friend, a health worker, Senia Andrejewna, helped me get a job. The winter was rough; I swelled up from [malnutrition], received six hundred grams of bread per day and had to share

662. Alter Kacyzne died in Tarnopol during a pogrom.

it with other illegal refugees. From time to time, I would steal something from the hospital where I had gotten a job. Dawid Bergelson and Perec Markisz[663] came to Tashkent with their families. The writers created a commune and improved their situation this way. Gradually the writers left for small towns. I changed jobs [and] got a job in a laundry, where it was warm. I managed to get to Persia with the Polish army. I worked in a hospital. I fell ill with typhus, and when I recovered, came to Palestine.

663. Eminent Jewish writers, murdered in 1952 in the USSR on the orders of Stalin as part of an operation against Jewish writers and cultural activists as well as Jewish cultural institutions.

Protocol 268

Testimony of **Mosze F.**, from Sarny. Arrived in Hungary at the end of the year 1941.

The war caught me in my hometown, Sarny. The town was full of refugees [who suffered from] awful destitution. This destitution was so great that the refugees dreamed of returning home, even under the German occupation. When a Soviet-German commission arrived to carry out a registration of everyone [who] wanted to return home, long lines formed in front of [its] offices. The outcome of this registration was sad. In June and July [1940], the Bolsheviks sent huge transports of refugees to camps and *posiołki* [in] Siberia.

Protocol 270

Drawn up on the basis of the testimony of **Laura Beckmann**, age forty-five, resident in Kraków before the war [and] currently in Tel Aviv.

I left Kraków on Sunday along with [my] family, heading toward Bochnia. On the way, a throng of people running from the city essentially blocked the road, looking for shelter from bombardments. We successfully managed to get onto a platform [vehicle] passing by, on which [some] people we knew were traveling. We did not, however, manage to avoid the outcome of the bombing, because a German airplane dropped a bomb on our vehicle in one moment and then dropped down and started to shoot at us from machine guns. We survived this incident in one piece, hiding in ditches. The cart, on the other hand, was completely destroyed, and the horses and the person who stayed on the cart were killed.

Keen to avoid further encounters with German airplanes, we turned off the main road and traveled on rural tracks. People [we] met on the way claimed that the [section of the] road before Tarnów was already under fire from German guns. As a result, we went in a more northerly direction. We walked like this for entire days, left to the mercy of peasants. I wish to stress that [their willingness to] help never let us down—many a time both bread and a place to sleep were shared with us in a [peasant's] hut. A number of the villages I passed through were completely burned down. I once witnessed how a German airplane flew down very low over a field and shot at the young herders with machine guns. Another time still, German pilots set fire to stacks of dry hay with incendiary bombs.

We got to Zamość on a peasant cart almost at the time that we were getting closer to Zamość. [*sic*] We were in the suburbs, where we could observe the feats of the German "heroes" above the city. We then drove past a bombed-out rail station.

In Zamość, I lost [my] husband and child in the unbelievable crowding in front of the train. Tragedies of this kind often played out in front of my eyes, not always with a happy ending—like mine. I reached Równe by train, again at the time of the city's bombardment. If it weren't for the train stopping at the outskirts, we would have suffered inevitable doom.

I was in Równe for three weeks. It turned out that my husband was in the same city, [but] we didn't know anything about each other for a long time. Meanwhile, the Russians had settled for good in the city. Shops were closed down, leaving only co-ops, where one could get food in limited quantities [after] waiting in line for hours. Apartment[s] were confiscated, and one had to suffer [through] the nightmare of room allocation. Russians and Belarussians [Belarusians] assumed command in the city.

Although I had successfully found [my] husband, [our] child's fate remained unknown. As a result, we began a search to find some trace of [the child]. We traveled through Ukrainian villages, finding a hostile atmosphere everywhere. We often had the opportunity to learn how much the Ukrainians hated the Poles and the Russians but clung to the Germans. Knowing that we had escaped from the territory occupied by the Germans, they asked me detailed questions about [the Germans'] actions, and I could easily conclude from their reactions how great their joy would be if Hitler's invasion reached them too.

I successfully found a sign of [my] child in Zbaraż. An acquaintance notified me that he had seen [the child] with [some] friends heading toward Zaleszczyki.

[We] had to travel through the villages again in that direction. By a lucky happenstance, the Soviet authorities did not stop us, even though we were traveling by night. How great my joy was when, upon [our] arrival in Zaleszczyki, we indeed found [our] child. We arrived just in time, as the child was gravely ill with scurvy and required tender care. At that time a perfect opportunity to get across to Romania presented itself to us, [but] sadly, we could not take advantage of it due to [our] child's illness.

We stayed in Zaleszczyki, which was already fully Sovietized, for about three weeks. When the Russians began to expel the non-settled people from the border zone, we too were affected.

We moved to Lwów, where we stayed for a long time. In that short amount of time, Lwów had changed beyond recognition. A joyful and carefree city had become bleak and gray, and if humor popped up here and there, it was of the dark variety. One could see Russkis[664] sleeping in garden squares. All trade was speculative. A general anxiety about the future prevailed.

---

664. [Russians (in the original, Muscovites).]

I registered to return to Kraków. In the meantime, a Russian officer tried to [get] my apartment but did not manage to kick me out of it because I very actively resisted. On 28 June, he came to me accompanied by the NKVD, told me to pack, and informed [me] that we were to go back to Kraków. We were taken to a freight station, loaded into cars that were already completely chock-full, and after twenty-four hours, set off for Siberia.

The three-week journey has stayed in my memory until today. It was extremely hot, but it was forbidden to [bring] anything into the tightly sealed cars. A bucket of water, enough for a mere few people, was supposed to last fifty people a full twenty-four hours. No consideration was given to the fact that I was traveling with a small child.

Finally we got to the *posiołek*. We were assigned accommodation and work. I was exempt from it on account of [my] small child. The others worked all day, receiving [only] paltry food in return. We were, in fact, prisoners, cut off from the entire world. The realization that this imprisonment could be life-long killed [us in the worst way]. The peasants also foretold such a [future] for us—luckily, it turned out to be wrong.

We were released from the *posiołek* as a result of the Amnesty. We went to Kazakhstan.

In Buzuluk, my husband signed up for the army and was accepted. As [a member of] a military family, I was then evacuated from Russia to Iran, and left for Palestine from there.

Protocol 271

Drawn up on the basis of the testimony of **Mala Horowicz**, age twenty-eight, resident in Sosnowiec before the war [and] currently in Haifa.

When the Germans started to get close to Sosnowiec, I decided to leave town. With a whole wave of refugees, terrorized by air raids and terrified by deliberately spread misinformation, I walked toward Sandomierz. Throughout the whole journey, we had no peace [and were] constantly attacked by German airplanes. They didn't even respect the sign of the red cross, as proven by burning hospitals, or [those] already lying in ruins. In Kraśnik, where makeshift first aid stations were located, German airplanes organized a slaughter [of] the wounded. Walking day and night, I finally reached Sarny. [I came upon] the incoming Soviet army there.

In the first days of the "new order," [people] already understood [its] conditions. Completely innocent people started being kicked out of [their] homes [and] placed in hovels and mud huts. Valuables, tools, and even household equipment were spitefully destroyed or given away to the gawking mob. On the Silbermann estate, the land, horses, cows, [and] agricultural equipment were given away to the local peasants—Ukrainians—throwing the owner's family out on the street.

I got through to Lwów. I couldn't support myself there in any way and decided to return to [my] family. During a snowstorm, wrapped in a bedsheet to throw off the guard[s], I tried to get across to the other side of the San River. The trick would have worked were it not for a horde of dogs that picked up my scent and almost tore me apart alive. They were the dogs of the Soviet border guard. The guard led me to the station, where I was kept without food or drink for a day and night and was only examined later. Those examinations were worse than anything else. I had to stand upright for hours and answer exhausting questions. There were hours when the examiner did nothing but mock me in the cruelest way. Half-conscious, I was finally taken to a cell, for the same procedure to be repeated the next day. If this were to repeat for a third time, I promised myself solemnly that I would take my life. It didn't come to that, as I was moved to a prison in Przemyśl.

In the Przemyśl prison, I stayed in a cell with fifty other prisoners. The cell was so crowded that even standing up was difficult; beds were out of the question, and on account of the crowding, [we] slept on the bare ground in shifts. When some got up, others would lie down to sleep. Lice and bedbugs crawled over us, and all attempts at de-licing failed to bring any results. Food consisted of dry, moldy bread and some slop that reeked so [badly] I couldn't swallow it. I was there with professional female thieves and criminals, which naturally did not make [my] life easier.

Eventually it was decided to take us into Russia. When our train stopped at the station in Lwów, scenes played out [like] a flash of light, which I probably won't forget until the end of my life. Residents of Lwów began to gather in front of our cars and throw foodstuffs, cigarettes, and other items and useful implements inside. Everyone was overcome with sobs. The railway men were still attempting to assist us when the train was already in motion. It was a magnificent, and simultaneously macabre, farewell.

During the journey, we were deliberately fed thirst-inducing food. After some oversalted herring [and] stale kielbasa, we were dying for a drink [but] received nothing. From time to time we rebelled. Often when passing through larger stations, we straight up howled: "Water! [give us] water!" It was a horrendous journey. We were driven around Ukraine like this for three weeks. However no prison wanted to take us due to widespread overcrowding. Most of the passengers fell gravely ill, fatal accidents happened every day, and suicides were a daily occurrence.

We were finally unloaded in Dnipropetrovsk. We were put seventy people to a small cell. They took away our clothes, gave [us] prison rags riddled with holes, and later on, we went to Ural also wearing these [rags]. In the prison there was an "ironic" central heating that never worked, however. The food consisted unchangeably of boiling water and groats. Illnesses began to afflict us more often and more gravely still. Scurvy and general languor in our bodies sucked away our energy. The real curse was the strong electric light that shone all night long. [We] all suffered with eye [problems]. Neither protests nor rebellions helped; instead the situation would worsen after such actions. We were so exhausted that we didn't even have the energy to take part in the walks. Anyway, we had already gotten to such a state that fresh air became harmful to us. [This is because] we spent all [our] time in a cell, where even the small window was tightly boarded up. To walk around in circles in the courtyard for ten minutes, then, did not appeal to us at all. During this "recreation," our dream was to pick the green branches from a tree that grew in the courtyard. That, too, was strictly forbidden.

It's no wonder that not all personalities survived mentally in this situation. Some broke down, and that led [them] to [engage in] denunciations. [This], however, did not become widespread and there was generally a strong solidarity. None of the Jewish women ever denounced anyone.

Each bath was torture for us. [This is because] men led [us] for baths, and they were authorized to watch us during washing too. We tried to rebel against this, [and] unbearable punishments would [follow] then. Hunger strikes were a form of such rebellion; however, they made no impression as we were allowed to freely starve ourselves to death.

I was still under investigation. I explained myself however I could. During the investigation, it was the order of the day for the investigators to hit our faces and bodies, and [our] cellmates were very often brought in unconscious. Others still were led on, tempted with cigarettes and food. And here it must be stressed that [strong] characters endured. When the investigator told one of [my] friends, "You will never see Poland," she, without thinking, retorted: "I will." For this response, she was sentenced to an awful punishment of two weeks in the dark cell.

Finally, I had my sentence announced without a trial: five years. Women who had been sentenced were separated from the rest after some time, and we were taken farther out. We traveled in "*więźniarki*"[665]—railcars resembling cages for wild animals. We were sent to the prison in Kharkiv, where for a short time, we stayed in conditions even worse than in the previous prison. We were stuffed into cells with professional female criminals for whom human life held no value. Once one such criminal broke off a piece of a windowpane and cut off one of [her?] friend's ears with it. That cell, too, was so full that I spent most of the time in a standing position. I left some of my friends behind in this prison, [those] who died of typhus or scurvy.

665. Colloquial name for a vehicle used to transport prisoners, a feminine form of the word "prisoner."

Finally, we were loaded onto *więźniarki* again and went to Ural in them. It was an odd feeling to see the beautiful Uralian panorama out of the windows and to feel as sick as I felt at the time. The beauty of nature, however, was sometimes stronger than the pain [already] suffered and that which was still to come—I forgot about the real world, immersing myself in the magnificent spectacle of nature.

Soon, however, I returned to the horrific reality. We were unloaded in Maryjskaja.[666] We were put in *zemlyanki*[667]—tunnels dug underground whose levels were connected with primitive ladders. I spent months living underground in conditions that people on the lowest level of civilization probably lived under. If snow covered up the small windows, there was no more contact with the outside world. I encountered Russian individuals there who had been sentenced to long exile. They were the families of Trotskyists[668] sentenced during the purge in 1937. They treated us very decently; the behavior of the nuns in particular was full of sympathy. They took away our hope, however, when it came to one thing: leaving that labor camp. Next to us there was a camp for sexually perverted women.[669]

Each of us received three planks to use, for sleeping, etc. We were told that if we started working, we would get a blanket too. Because we were unbelievably exhausted after the journey, we had no energy to work. So [we] had to sleep on bare planks, covering [ourselves] with what we had. We were still wearing the ripped clothes from the first prison—ours had not been returned to us then. The food went hand in hand with the living conditions. Anyway, hunger made itself known much more quietly here, as the lack of air alleviated the sensation.

I worked haying for some time and chopped wood in the forest in winter. [We] worked from sunrise to sunset. We didn't get special remuneration for the work, or special food. We were not given any warm undergarments during work in winter. We had to work in deep snow almost barefoot. No wonder, then, that many of us fell ill with pneumonia and died. One could be excused from work with a fever of 39°C [102.2°F] [or more].

---

666. Likely refers to the Mari ASSR.

667. *Zemlyanki* [Polish: *ziemianki*, pl.]: dugouts.

668. Trotskyists were members of the Communist Party accused of forming an opposition faction.

669. Likely: lesbian women.

There were twelve places in the camp hospital. Even if there was a need, it wasn't possible or allowed to put more people in there. A habit had already been set that [the only people] taken to the hospital were [those] on their last legs, who were probably carried out in a coffin.

When the news of the Amnesty arrived, we were released from the labor camp. We were sent to Semipalatinsk, where the Polish authorities welcomed us incredibly warmly. We were put up in wonderful—to us—apartments, received special food.

I reported for the army after some time and was accepted. I was moved to Guzar. A cholera epidemic broke out there, which decimated the masses of refugees.

I left for Iran with a military transport, and then [came] to Palestine.

Protocol 272

Drawn up on the basis of the testimony of **Abraham Kudisz**, age forty-five, resident in Milan before the war.

I lived in Milan for a long period, working as an associate in a large hat factory. In August 1939, my wife went to visit her mother to Stryj, as [she did] every year, and as a result of the war that broke out, I was cut off from her. I decided to [join] her. The present consul in Bombay, [who was] then working in the same capacity in Milan, [managed to] procure Yugoslav and Hungarian visas for me, and I left Italy on that basis. I sneaked into Poland around Ławoczne, finally reaching Stryj, where I [re]united with the family. I found the Germans already in Stryj. There was no Gestapo or SS yet, and the army units behaved relatively well. On 22 September [1939], the Soviet army entered. At first it exhibited total inaction. Soon, however, power moved into the hands of the civilian administration, and everything changed abruptly then. The scum began to have a voice more and more often, sometimes carrying out bloody acts of revenge that the authorities did not respond to. People were kicked out of [their] homes and left on the street.

After a few weeks, the authorities began nationalizing manufacturing and trade. An inventory would be written up, and the owner sent off without any compensation, while the Soviet officials staffed or closed down the establishment. A few shops were left open, where [goods] were sold at set prices. It doesn't need to be added, naturally, that hardly anything could be [found] in those shops, where the Red Army soldiers had already bought everything earlier.

The saddest symptom was the lawlessness of individual[s], the nonadherence to orders, since each member of the NKVD could freely interpret the edicts himself. Once when one of my friends [who was] on trial asked the judge for the legal code, [the judge] looked at him, dumbfounded, and finally replied that one could probably only get that in Moscow. In the initial period, the Bolshevik authorities attempted to win over all sections of society, but when this eyelash batting not only brought no results, but even [brought about] a negative response in [terms of people] registering to leave for Germany,[670] a wave of exterminations and persecutions began.

670. [Refers to the part of Poland occupied by Germany.]

Generally speaking, some of the working classes sympathized with the actions of the Bolsheviks. Among the Ukrainians, too, who wanted to use the situation against the Poles, a friendly attitude could be observed. It was, however, remarkably two-faced.

When the Red Army marched into Stryj, elements who had been involved in Communism even before the war expected that they would be able to have a say in social and political matters, or would even become the ruling class. The first days of the occupation seemed to confirm these hopes. A number of declared[671] Polish Communists inserted themselves into the leading positions in the first days of the occupation—this didn't last long, however. Soon they met with disappointment, as during the ongoing organization of the administrative [structures], the Soviet authorities deliberately didn't allow these Communists a say, and even made it known to them more than once that they did not trust them. As a result, a number of Communists were arrested for Trotskyism, even those who had only just gotten out of prison.

In December a plebiscite combined with elections to the Supreme Soviet[672] took place. This plebiscite, or elections—it's difficult to find the [right] terminology—was void of any democratic characteristics. On election day, the voter would come to a polling station, receive a voting card from the leader of the commission, and drop it into the ballot box without looking, according to the instructions explained earlier by the NKVD during rallies. Despite incredible pressure, a large number of citizens did not take part in the electoral activities, [and] the later announcement that 100 percent of Stryj residents had chosen the Soviets was a blatant lie.

The inevitable consequence of the plebiscite was the passportization operation. Despite acts of violence and terror, a large part of the population did not want to accept Soviet passports. The Soviet administration categorized those as counterrevolutionaries and treated them appropriately later. The passport situation of the so-called bourgeoisie was interesting. The passports received by this category of people contained two clauses: [first,] that it was forbidden

671. Translator's note: the original text employs the adjective *prononsowani*. The word does not appear to be in use in modern Polish and was clearly unusual at the time of the first publication, as a footnote is included explaining it (*zdeklarowani*—declared).

672. The elections to the Soviet (Council) of Western Ukraine took place on 28 October 1941.

to settle in voivodeship-level cities; and second, that the holders belonged to a group of *neblagonadezhnye*.[673] With this second marker, the NKVD were to identify their future victims. Naturally, this system became the basis for all kinds of corruption and blackmail.

A citizen branded with the aforementioned clauses could easily bribe the relevant authorities with some amount of rubles and receive permission to stay permanently in a voivodeship-level city, and one could even exchange the passport for a "legitimate" one. Positively comical incidents would take place where a real bourgeois would be deliberately demoted to the role of a worker and carry on living freely—paying off the authorities regularly, of course.

The organization of labor was as follows: existing businesses were turned into collectives, or when they were larger, became the property of the state. The latter were given the name Sowtorg.[674] All collectives and state enterprises were, naturally, under the control of the NKVD, which gradually appointed its representatives to each of them. Such a representative, generally hired for the role of a small-time clerk, would rise to the top because of his character[istics] and eventually become the *spiritus movens* of the company. He hired and fired workers, managed production; he also shaped the political direction. This element of the NKVD's activities was very systematic and was, in fact, the basis of [its power].

The situation of the workers seemingly improved in the initial period, that is to say, no one had anything now. The equalization was downward.

The Russians technically kept the existing network of schools, except they put in their own [people] as leaders. They organized atheist clubs in each school. They already existed even in elementary schools, where small children were taught anti-religious principles. Moreover, in each school there was the position of a *politruk*. It has to be said that the Russians took care of libraries, but as time went by, they would remove "bourgeoisie"-minded books and replace [them] with Communist literature.

I worked in free trade for the first few months, selling goods to the authorities, even in large quantities. I would buy those goods from factories in the not yet nationalized areas.

---

673. *Neblagonadyozhny* [Polish: *niebłagonadiożnyj*]: untrustworthy.

674. Sowtorg, Sovetskaya Targovla [Polish: Sowieckaja Targowla]: state commercial network.

Later, I worked as a commercial clerk in a manufacturing collective in Stanisławów, made up of a candle factory, soap [factory], cosmetics [factory], etc. Then I was hired for a mechanical plant [producing] drilling tools in Stryj, [and] finally, the NKVD forced me to move to work on the construction of an aerodrome. One worked seven days a week there [and] the workday was ten hours long. I personally protested against these working conditions, declaring that I had to have one day off work per week. The authorities considered my demands sabotage, and suspicion against me grew because of it. [They] started baiting [others] against me and slandering me. In the end, to "finish" me, the implications of my stay in Italy were brought up and I was branded a dangerous Fascist. During a search, an ID from a business syndicate[675] in Milan was found at my place, which the NKVD took for a Fascist Party membership card. Based on this, [and] despite many explanations, I was arrested and put in prison in Poltava.

There were more than a dozen thousand prisoners in that jail, and it was one of the so-called model ones. Indeed, the living conditions were generally bearable there. Not the worst sanitary conditions, food the same—I imagine—as in all the prisons in the world, and above all, the opportunity to work, made a "model" impression indeed. As I learned from my fellow inmates, however, a stay in this "paradise" lasted a very short time; prisoners were normally moved to other prisons after a few weeks, where they lived in dumps, ate slop, worked until unconsciousness, and finally, died.

During the investigation of my case, the authorities came to the realization that the ID discovered at my place was not identical with a Fascist Party ID, and the case was put on hold. However, as I had a "dirty stamp," I was forcibly deported to a kolkhoz in Alba Szu[676] in Kuban, two hundred kilometers from the Turkish border.

When I was already in the kolkhoz, I learned from the residents that they had been enemies of the regime since the revolution of 1917, and that almost every year anti-Soviet uprisings broke out, bloodily suppressed each time. In 1936, the so-called counterrevolution was ultimately suppressed by deporting almost all the men between twenty and fifty years of age across different

675. Here: trade union.

676. Should be: Albashí [original Polish correction: Albaszi].

parts of the country. It was striking, too, that the only people one could see in Kuban were [either] very young [or] very old. There were hardly any middle-aged men.

Life in the kolkhoz was lamentable. Living standard[s] were considerably lower than in any other village. The situation was more confusing still because Kuban is probably one of the most beautiful and fertile lands I have ever seen. Grain grew in abundance across the boundless steppes almost by itself, the grass could [feed] countless numbers of cattle; while in the mountains were hidden unprecedented mineral riches. Whereas in the kolkhozes, [people] died from hunger because of the disastrous economy, caused partly by a suspicious and hateful attitude toward the authorities.

Kolkhoz residents had to regularly work for twelve hours a day, and during the harvest, in which I too took part, we worked even at night. Despite this intense work, one could still have fed a large European empire with what was left over in the steppes.

The payment for the work was calculated so that it could not be enough for a whole year's keep. [We] received paltry and unappetizing lunches in the canteen, some bread and honey, an egg once every two months—this was the compensation for my work. A kolkhoz member worked on the basis of *trudodnie*.[677] Very often, for some trivial reason, the supervisor would log only half a day instead of a full day for a kolkhoz worker. The [summary] calculations took place after the harvest. Normally a kolkhoz worker would not get what they were owed for various reasons. On the other hand, each of them owned a small house with a garden, kept pigs and cattle, and sold their products at discretionary prices, and this way, each of them kept their head above the water. One day, a newspaper fell into my hands from which I found out about the agreement between Poland and Russia, which was the basis for an amnesty for all Polish citizens living in the Soviet territories. I decided to leave as quickly as possible, which naturally was neither straightforward nor easy. I finally turned to the only effective method in Russia, that is, I offered a bribe in the form of worn-out clothing to the kolkhoz's prefect. This effort brought immediate results, and I soon found myself on a train heading for Kuybyshev.

677. Workdays.

On the way, I stopped in the capital of Kuban, Krasnodar (former Yekaterinodar) for a few days and was able to witness once more how strong the deeply rooted hatred toward the Soviet regime was in that area. I had the impression that Krasnodar was the hub of the Soviet counterrevolution. After a few weeks' travel, I got to Kuybyshev, [only] to come to the conclusion some time later that perhaps I shouldn't have left the kolkhoz so hastily. This was because hunger was widespread in Kuybyshev, and the street was the standard place to live.

I learned that the first units of the Polish army were forming in Buzuluk. I made my way to the station and waited so long that a transport heading in that direction finally came. I joined the army at the rank of lieutenant (I was the lieutenant of the reserve) and was sent to Totskoye, where the army mobilization was being completed. I then went to Uzbekistan. In Jangiull[678] we came upon thousands of Poles already there. Life in the civilian camps was hell, even though the military authorities did what they could to ease the plight [of their inhabitants]. Sadly, the behavior of the delegates was not always up to the task. Some [of them] contributed to many tragedies through their carelessness. I was shown a cemetery of twelve hundred people in Jangiul, which the Polish refugees had named after a delegate.

I was then evacuated from Russia with the army, and then came to Palestine via Iran.

678. An incorrect name of the town of Yangiyul [original Polish correction: Jangi-Jul].

Protocol 275

Testimony of **Jecheskiel Szternziem [?]**, age twenty-eight, from Warsaw, who came to Palestine via Russia and Tehran.

I was in Grudziądz when the war broke out. Immediately after the war broke out, we tried to defend ourselves against German airplanes that bombed our barracks. I was wounded in the arm. On Saturday, 2 September [1939], we escaped from Grudziądz to Jabłonowo. We fought battles against the German army along the way. It wasn't an equal fight. The enemy advanced, equipped with excellent weapons. We escaped to Żychlin, and from there to Warsaw. My wound, light at first, turned out to be dangerous and I had to go to the Marshall Piłsudski hospital. I was in the hospital during the heroic defense of the city, besieged from all sides. The civilian population and the army fought side by side on the barricades, and after three weeks, the capital surrendered because of lack of food. On 27 September, along with the other wounded soldiers, we were evacuated from the hospital to the barracks in the Citadel that were turned into a war camp.[679] Three hundred people were living in one building. Food ran out; we suffered from thirst. We begged for death. The Germans gave us coffee with rusks on the third day. We threw ourselves on it like starved animals. There was never enough water, and the taps were heavily guarded, so we could not get to them. Many people fainted. After a few days, we were led out of the Citadel to Służewiec, to the racetrack.[680] We slept in the open and set fire to the small wooden boxes in the field. The Germans issued an order forbidding setting fire to these boxes. We lay in the field for a few days, exhausted with hunger and assisted only by women who threw us beets and potatoes over the fence around the grounds. The Germans didn't allow the Jews to catch the beets being thrown. Realizing that I would starve to death there, I decided to plan my escape. And when the Germans allowed the local women residents to bring us a bit of food on the fifth day, I asked one woman to give me a bucket that I would help her take [back]. I told the guard I was going to get food and never returned to the camp. There was a German military

679. Prisoner of war camp.
680. Horse racing.

policeman next to the church on Piłsudski Street,[681] who was checking the passersby and he let me through, since I was carrying the bucket. I finally made it to my parents' home on Parysowska Street. I spent seven days in Warsaw. The Jews' situation worsened by the day. They were captured for labor, beaten, and robbed. My father, too, had his beard cut off. When my wound healed, I decided to leave Warsaw. During that time, a few tens of Jews were taken out of our area into fields and told to look for hidden mines. Many people perished during this work. I left Warsaw at the end of September. I went to Siedlce via Mordy, crossed the border by Drohiczyn, and from there, via Siemiatycze, got to Białystok. I spent four months in Białystok. I didn't get a job; I lived off what my brother, who had also fled Warsaw, gave me. Seeing no other way out of the situation, I registered to work in Russia. This was when there were posters in the streets of Białystok calling on young people to register for work. It was stated in the terms that the work was light and well paid. I registered to go to Magnitogorsk, to a local factory. When passing through Moscow, I decided to get out of the carriage and see [my] brother who had been there since before the First World War. My brother was very happy and decided to make efforts to allow me to stay in Moscow, saying that there was no way he would let me go to Magnitogorsk where I would not [be able to] deal with the hard work. My brother was a pharmacist by trade and worked in a laboratory [but] earned very little in spite of it. He and his family, made up of [his] wife and three children, lived in one room in a former hotel, now converted into a dwelling house. I was asked to speak quietly at home as they were afraid of the neighbors. Only after some time did I realize that the walls have ears in Russia. My brother's efforts achieved nothing, only that my route was changed from Magnitogorsk to Saratov, where we had friends. Even though I was received well, I understood that they were not happy with my arrival and I decided to go to the other side of the Volga, to the town of Engels, where I was supposed to get a job. It was a German colony. The German colonists fared very well, considerably better than other kolkhozes. Large tobacco plantations brought in big profits. Living there, I had the impression that I was in a German village in Western Europe. The Germans occupied high positions and felt at home. While they were no friends of the Jews, they were not hostile, and compared

681. Refers to Aleja Piłsudskiego [Piłsudski Avenue].

to the Nazis, were philosemites. I looked for work in my trade and got a job in a pharmacy, and a month later, became a pharmacist with full rights. There was little work, medicine ran out, substitutes[682] were used. In the end we put medicines together [using] what we had in stock. I went to Engels in April 1940. It didn't occur to anyone that the situation would soon change. The Germans believed in victory and in the strengthening of their influence in Russia. In June 1940, they were told that they had to leave their homes, taking five hundred kilos of luggage each and leaving the livestock behind. I spent a year and nine months in Engels. I earned three hundred rubles per month. Russians were brought in place of the expelled Germans, and after some time, the farms looked like [they do] in all of Russia. During the German-Russian war, the situation there worsened too. Mobilization began, and because an amnesty for Polish citizens was announced at that time, when asked which army I wanted to serve in, I said the Polish one. I went South to Kermine. I roamed the streets for months and had nowhere to lay my head. I didn't lose hope of leaving Russia. One day, I sneaked into a transport going to Krasnovodsk, and from there, made my way to Pahlevi and Tehran illegally, [and] from there I came to Palestine.

682. [The original uses a German word: *ersatz*, which is explained in the footnote as "substitute"; Polish: *namiastka*.]

Protocol 277

Testimony of **Joel Szrajber**, from Warsaw, age twenty-four. Came to Palestine via Russia and Iran.

During the outbreak of the war, I was serving in the Polish army. I was in the Modlin Fortress, where we defended [ourselves] against a much stronger enemy who surrounded us on all sides. The fighting went on until 29 September [1939]. We fought hard. German airplanes flew down low and bombed the fortress. Our defense [tried to] destroy the airplanes any way it could. A few times, the enemy burst through into the fortress, a few times we pushed him back. We were certain that Warsaw would stand, and that help would arrive from outside. On receiving the news of the surrender of the capital, we were so shaken that the fighting spirit deserted us, and we capitulated a few days later. The Germans took us prisoner, took away our belongings, money, and even blankets. They ripped [our] shoes off of us, took off the officers' boots, and gave us old bast shoes [instead]. Then they stuffed us into a boiler house and kept us without food for three days. We were lined up and ordered to walk sixty kilometers to Zegrze.[683] Germans on horseback convoyed us, beating [us] and not allowing [us] to rest. We were thirsty, hungry, and could barely stand up. In Zegrze, we were loaded into freight cars, seventy people in each, and sent to Horsztyn,[684] to East Prussia. During the journey, we received a slice of bread and a bit of soup each. Many died from exhaustion and hunger. In Horsztyn, we were accommodated in barracks made from thin wood, fifty people in each [one]. We lived in awful conditions. We slept on the bare ground; there were no sanitary [provisions]. In the morning, we got boiled beet water without sugar, and for lunch, sour cabbage soup and thirty dekagrams of bread. We lived with Poles at first, helping one another. A few days later, the Jews were separated, and our conditions were worse. We were starving horribly. We were given the hardest work. We worked from sunrise until sunset, were beaten and humiliated. Eighteen soldiers were killed. They were innocent people and

683. The distance between Modlin and Zegrze is approximately twenty-eight kilometers.
684. Likely to Olsztyn.

were killed because their work was not to the liking of the supervisor. A Polish sergeant was killed in front of my eyes because he walked up too close to the fence. On Sunday[s], the German population would come up to the barbed wires that surrounded us and throw pieces of bread and meat inside for us. They threw [this food to us] the way one throws food to animals in a zoo, enjoying the spectacle of us catching the food, famished [as we were]. They laughed watching Polish soldiers fighting over a piece of bread. These scenes were photographed. When the [reason for] the German sympathy became clear to us one Sunday, we decided not to accept the charity. They walked away, annoyed, deprived of an amusing show. After six weeks' stay in the camp, we were called in to the commandant's office in tens and told that we were free. Nonspecialist [workers] were released. The qualified workers were sent to Germany. [People] were not released from other camps. [Those] released were taken to the station in Działdowo, where we spent a few days under the open sky, in the rain. And we survived thanks to the fact that Polish people brought us food. I went to Warsaw. I spent two weeks in the capital. [Part of text missing] until the end of October 1939. Seeing the suffering of the Jewish population, I decided to move to the Russian side. I got to Białystok across the Bug River. I found the city full of refugees. Realizing that I would starve to death, I signed up for work and went to Homel, where I was received with great honors. Tables with food stood in the station. Between one course and the next, speeches took place, then we were taken to a workers' house where I spent a few days. After a few days, we were driven to work. During the registration for work, we had been promised work in our trade and accommodation. It turned out that we were given black work[685] and barracks instead of apartments. [We] bought food with our own money; the wages were so low that they weren't enough [to buy] soup. Our group, left leaning, was gravely disappointed. Complaining was not allowed. We looked for a way to escape. The work site was located in a village close to Homel, and one day, we set off for the city, looking for work on our own. Employment was not given without the Party's order. Seeing that I wouldn't achieve anything there, I left for Białystok. This was during the passportization. Because I didn't want to accept Soviet

685. [Unskilled labor.]

citizenship, I was sent to Kotlas. I worked in a forest, in terrible conditions. We suffered with hunger and cold, and from diseases. When the Amnesty was announced, I set off for Tashkent. On arriving in the city, I fell gravely ill with typhus, [and] later with dysentery. I spent six months in the hospital. I began to look for ways to get out of Russia. I learned that military and civilian transports to Persia were leaving from Krasnovodsk. I got on a train that took me to Krasnovodsk; there, I got onto a ship that took me to Persia. After a year's stay in Tehran, I came to Palestine.

Protocol 281

Testimony of **Icchak Fuksman**, age thirty-six, from Przemyślany. Came to Palestine via Russia and Tehran in August 1943.

I am a tailor by trade. When the war broke out, I was working in my trade. On the first day of the war, panic broke out in our small town even though [we] weren't suffering from bombardments—however, people were afraid of the Germans and expected them [to arrive] at any moment. The first tanks we saw were Bolshevik tanks. The Jewish population welcomed the Bolsheviks kindly, as it was expected that the Russians would help the Poles against the Germans. It turned out that they had arrived as occupiers. After a few days, they started introducing their order. Tenement houses were nationalized, goods in shops requisitioned, homeowners kicked out of their homes, and craft workshops became the property of the state, too. There was a noticeable lack of the most important food products, and long lines formed in front of shops. Arrests began. All political and social activists were detained, Jews and Poles.

Many refugees settled in our town. The situation of these refugees was much worse than ours. They had no roof over their heads; they slept in synagogues and batei hamidrash[686] and had nothing to live on. They sold the remnants of the [supplies] and clothing [they had] brought with them. Their situation was becoming so desperate that they were losing their minds, especially since their families were under the German occupation. The news coming in from [those areas] wasn't the worst. When the passportization order arrived, most of them registered to return home. That is when the mass searches and arrests began. The arrests took place at night. People were dragged out of their beds and sent to Siberia in freight cars. Desperate letters arrived from there, begging for food parcels and clothing. I continued to work in my trade as a member of a cooperative. I earned a good living and lived decently. Residents of the areas occupied by the Bolsheviks automatically became Soviet citizens. This lasted until the outbreak of the Russian-German war. We didn't know anything about it; the Russians were instructing people on how to behave during an alarm and declared that there would be no war, despite the concentration of armies at the

686. [Plural of beth hamidrash (see glossary).]

border. Before we realized it, our town was bombed by the Germans on 22 June 1942. Panic overtook not only the civilian population but also the military. Soldiers and officers were running around the streets like mad, and the panic was magnified by the women and children of Soviet officials. At nine in the morning, the Russians led a few tens of Ukrainians out into the main square and killed them, having accused [them] of espionage. Our town is located forty-five kilometers from Lwów. A few hours later, the retreating Soviet army had already appeared on the road. The army was mixed up with civilians and everyone was running ahead in a hurry. On 26 June, I received a mobilization card to report for the army. I showed up at the set time and was assigned to an extra battalion located outside Kharkiv. I was supposed to stay in town a few more days but received an order to leave within an hour. The order was so unexpected that the officers and soldiers didn't manage to bring their families in time. Evacuation of the civilian population was out of the question. We left Przemyślany in a panic and in haste and went toward Kharkiv. The Germans occupied the town the next day. We were rushed on like cattle, not an army, to Proskuriv. The journey took two weeks. We arrived ragged, with no military clothing, and famished. Machine guns rode behind us and shot at [anyone who] tried to escape. We didn't rest once in two weeks. We rested in Proskuriv and were sent to Kharkiv from there. We were sent to build an airport. While I was digging up an embankment, I heard an alarm and then was buried under the earth. I was only found many hours later and was taken to Penza to a hospital. After two months in the hospital, I was discharged from the army. All residents of Western Galicia, whom the Bolsheviks didn't trust, were discharged. After discharge, I was sent to a kolkhoz outside Tashkent. I worked building a canal for field irrigation. I received three hundred grams of oats per day. The work was difficult, from sunrise to sunset. The Uzbek kolkhoz looked like an Arab village. The houses were built from clay and you sat on the floor, where the fire was burning. There were many refugees from Poland in that kolkhoz, deported in 1940. Exhausted from yearslong exile, they were vulnerable to all [kinds of] diseases. I fell ill with typhus in the kolkhoz and stayed down for six weeks without medical help. Out of twelve [people] who were sick, eight died. On 10 March 1942, an order came out about Polish citizens reporting for the Russian [or] the Polish army. We all decided to go to the Polish army, and when we got there, after long suffering, we were told that Jews, Ukrainians, and Belarussians [Belarusians], inhabitants of the areas occupied by Russia, were considered Soviet citizens and weren't being accepted into the army. I procured a fake document and was accepted into the army along with five hundred [other] Jews. We were sent to Czabak,[687] where a Polish commandant, a major, told us that he could not accept us into the army because of the typhus epidemic, and told us to return to the kolkhoz. I didn't want to go back; I stayed at the rail station and waited for a chance to get on a transport going to Krasnovodsk. I got through to Tehran, where I stayed for a year, earning decent money. After receiving [my] certificate, I came to Palestine.

687. Incorrect name of the town of Chok-Pak [original Polish correction: Czok-Pak].

Protocol 286

Testimony of **Leon Parnes**, age forty-three, lawyer, born in Lwów and resident there until 9 July 1943. Came to Palestine via Slovakia, Hungary, and Romania in the year 1944.

Until the outbreak of war, I worked in Lwów as a lawyer, and when the war broke out, I started working for the Red Cross with [some] friends.

In Soviet Prison

I was arrested after the occupation of Lwów. I spent eight months in prison, then got a job in a Jewish council, which was still under the eye of the police and was forced to report to the NKVD daily. Soon the registrations and the pressure to accept Soviet citizenship began. As a result, the Russians deported tens of thousands of refugees to Siberia. Permanent residents of Lwów could not officially be deported, but the NKVD sent very many away in spite of it. Life worsened by the day. Food ran out.

Protocol 288

Drawn up on the basis of the testimony of **Jozue Finkielstein**, age thirty-two, from Rudnik on San, currently [resident] in Palestine.

I was in Kraków on the day the war broke out. I was awoken in the morning by powerful detonations, after which came explosions. I ran out in front of the house but the general consensus out on the street was that the bomb explosions were a false alarm, and that [we were] dealing with a test alarm. It wasn't until two hours later that the news spread that Poland was at war with Germany. The next day I packed [my belongings], and after [some] difficulties, got onto a train, which was already unbelievably packed. I got to Tarnów, but [any] further journey turned out to be out of the question. Tarnów then was already full of refugees, who would drive or walk on after a few hours' stay. German airplanes simultaneously bombed Mościce [688]and the city. It was widely believed that Mościce and Tarnów would be heavily defended. During the bombardment, a bomb fell on a passing tram, destroying it completely. The bodies of more than a dozen people, maimed and crushed beyond recognition, were pulled out from under the wreckage.

I managed to get onto a cart in Tarnów; we traveled by night toward Pilzno [and] then turned back toward Dębica. Dębica was already under heavy bombardment, particularly [its] factories. The streets were deserted, and [people] hid in the woods. Unburied corpses of people and horses were strewn across the pavements. In Zawada, I found myself at the estate of Count Raczyński,[689] which was severely bombed during my stay. Opposite the mansion, on the railroad track, stood evacuation trains. Horrific scenes played out during the air raids. I got to the outskirts of Przeworsk; it wasn't possible to get into town since the bridges were either blown up or damaged from the bombardment. The sugar factory was in flames, while many workers died during its bombardment. Faced with the impossibility of getting into town, I retreated to a nearby village, where I took cover in the badly damaged palace of the Lubomirscy. Taking advantage of the darkness, we set off further and got to Jarosław.

688. [The industrial district of Tarnów.]

689. At the time, the owner of the estate was Count Edward Bernard Raczyński (1891–1993), a diplomat, Foreign Minister in the Republic of Poland's government in London in the years 1941–43.

Beyond Jarosław, I ran into a military patrol leading six young Germans who had come down on parachutes close to where the Polish troops were concentrated. According to the patrol's account, they had been captured while they were informing the German pilots about bombing targets using small mirrors. These paratroopers were dressed as Polish peasants. Still in Jarosław, I heard that a well-known merchant of German nationality, who turned out to be a German spy, had been shot in the town square.

I planned to go to Przemyśl, but because of the news that the road to that town was being heavily bombed and was full of the military, I aimed for Niemirów and Rawa Ruska. I had not [ever] seen the kind of bombing that I experienced in this town. I tried to avoid towns and roads now, traveling by side roads. We hid in a hut not far from Radziwiłłówka,[690] but a peasant asked us to leave, as he was afraid that the German pilots had noticed our arrival. [This is how] confused the public perception was.

We wanted to aim for Brody [but] saw from afar that the city [was] on fire [and], as a result, we gave up that plan and aimed for Krzemieniec. There, too, we had no peace, as the Germans bombed this town closest to the border as well, attempting—unsuccessfully, anyway—to destroy the local power station. We spent the night in Krzemieniec, and when we went out into town the next morning, we noticed, to our astonishment, that a Soviet banner was waving from one of the small turrets of a lyceum. Soviet army units drifted through the streets nonstop, packed onto trucks or carts.

It was the Day of Atonement [23 September 1939]. The Jews were afraid to go to the synagogue because of the consequences that might follow from the Soviet [authorities]. But despite this, the synagogue was full, and the Soviet authorities did not disturb the prayer services.

A revolutionary committee made up of former prisoners took control of the town. During the expropriation operation, one of the local landowners resorted to force to oppose it [and] shot a Soviet *komandir*.[691] In response, the Russians warned the people and started using terror. There were a few thousand refugees in Krzemieniec at the time. A committee was formed, headquartered in the lyceum, whose chairman was a famous Socialist leader—Szumski.[692]

690. Likely refers to the town of Radziwiłłów.

691. *Komandir* (Russian): commander.

692. Romuald Szumski (1901–1964): PPS activist, publicist. In January 1942, delegate of the

Out on the streets, one could already witness scenes [heretofore] unknown in Poland—long lines in front of shops. It wasn't permitted to buy any products without prior permission. With my shoes completely destroyed, I turned to the committee asking for permission to buy new ones. The committee inspected my shoes closely and pronounced that I did not need new ones, since a repair would suffice. Naturally, one could get a lot of things [on the black market].[693]

I left Krzemieniec for Lwów after some time. We traveled for four days instead of a few hours.

In Lwów, the Soviet authorities had already [settled in] for good. Huge lines in front of the remaining shops were proof of [their] order. The cafés were full of refugees. In those cafés, too, underground trade blossomed, forbidden by the authorities. The refugees were administered by voivodeship committees. At the helm of the refugee committee of the Kraków voivodeship was Dr. Drobner. The main commander of the occupying army, Timoshenko,[694] lived in the George Hotel. At night, one could spot Soviet officers sleeping in garden squares.

Through listening to the radio, we learned that Wilno was to be annexed to Lithuania [and], as a result, we decided to go there. We managed to get on a train going in that direction; however, we only got as far as Baranowicze. There we made contact with [some] guides who, for a lot of money, took us toward Ejszyszki. The journey was very dangerous—on one side the Soviet guard kept watch, on the other the Lithuanian. A few kilometers before Ejszyszki, we were captured on the side [held by] the Soviets, who chased us into a hut [and] carried out a thorough search. We were then moved to Baranowicze for an investigation. The conditions we lived in for a few months [while] under investigation were unheard of. Eventually I had my [verdict] announced, sentencing me to a few years of hard labor in exile.

Embassy of the Republic of Poland in Kuybyshev for the then districts Kirov, Gorki, Molotov, and Mari ASSR.

693. [The original employs the term *pasek* to describe a system of black market trading, or profiteering—this comes from *paskarz*, which refers to a person involved in such activity (the activity itself is *paskarstwo*).]

694. Semyon Timoshenko [Polish: Siemion Timoszenko] (1895–1970): marshal of the Soviet Union. In the years 1940–41, people's commissar for defense of the USSR.

After the announcement of [my] sentence—I never received a copy of the text—I was moved, along with a larger group of professional criminals, to the Arkhangelsk Oblast. There we were ordered to dig out a shelter in the snow, given a few planks that [we] had to hew [ourselves], and I lived like this for more than a dozen months. Around me, people dropped like flies. I begged God for a quick death. However I survived in one piece, as if by a miracle.

I was released after the conclusion of the Polish-Russian agreement. I went south. I traveled for a few weeks until I got to Tocko,[695] where the first battalions of the Polish army were forming. I went in front of an army commission and was accepted without problems. After some time, our evacuation from Russia took place. [When I was] already in Iraq, I went in front of the commission for a second time and [was] discharged. Then, by sea, I came to Palestine.

695. Correctly: Totskoye [original Polish correction: Tockoje].

Protocol 289

Drawn up on the basis of the testimony of **Marceli Rosenberg**, age thirty, clerk, resident in Kraków before the war, currently in Tel Aviv.

On the day the war broke out I was in Kraków, working as a volunteer in a military hospital. Due to the general evacuation, I received an order to make my way east on foot. I receive a requisitioned cart in Mielec, on which I make my way to the Tarnobrzeg front. I am assigned to a sanitary convoy working in the section of the front between Tarnobrzeg and Rozwadów and transport the wounded within this section. I make my way further east then and come upon the Russians in Słonim.

On the day the Russians arrived, a militia force made up of local civilians took power in town. General chaos ensued, particularly among the merchant class and the bourgeoisie. Soon after, the first acts of terror began, combined with the requisitioning operation that was being carried out. I was sitting near the cathedral once and—drawing being my passion—was sketching its dome. Suddenly, a patrol turns up; I had my notebook snatched from my hands and was taken to the police station. There, after a long examination, I was listed as a Polish spy [and] tortured with tricky questions. Who knows what might have happened to me were it not for a successful intervention by one of my friends.

I decided to go to Lwów. Lwów was full of refugees in those days. The atmosphere [there] was one of general mutual mistrust. Everyone was afraid of the others, and even best friends stopped trusting each other. The other characteristic was the speculation madness. The lack of goods and products, even the essential ones, made for fertile ground for illicit trade. Oddly, the Soviet authorities did not react to this speculation for a long time; one almost had the impression that they were quietly supporting it. Then, when [people] began to be deported en masse for speculation—most often unfairly—it turned out that there had been a provocation, sui generis, in the former apparent lack of action against the speculators on the part of the authorities. In June [1940], the first general deportation of refugees took place. Around forty people were packed into one freight car, the doors were slammed shut and sealed, and [people were] sent deep into Russia like this, in very difficult conditions.

[People] traveled under a strict military escort, as prisoners. Even the most rudimentary health and sanitary care was out of the question. Food in an average prison was sophisticated compared to what we received.

Our journey took around fourteen days. After arriving at our destination, we spent another night in the freight cars. We were in a deep forest. In the morning, when the order to disembark from the cars came, many people could simply not get up because of swelling and [insect] bites. Those people had to be carried out. We were accommodated in barracks, which the previous inhabitants had left in an awful mess and filth. It was difficult to remove the insects and bedbugs since their nests were inside the wood. Not even fumigating helped. As a result, [our] first action was to build new units. After they were built, older people and families who excelled at industriousness were accommodated in them.

Already on the third day after [our] arrival, all people were assigned work. The work was very hard, and there was a quota [system] in place, whose fulfillment required maximum physical effort even from a qualified worker. The average level of the work we did was 12–16 percent in the initial period. Due to general exhaustion, awful climatic conditions, [and] malnutrition, this percentage fell even lower later.

When I tried to convince my superiors that working in my trade would benefit everyone more, I received an unchanging answer: "The state needs wood . . ." When we objected to the inhuman work, we constantly heard: "*Pryvyknesh*."[696] Work efficiency was pushed with force and special propaganda. Naturally, neither one nor the other was effective for a simple reason: to work in such harsh conditions one has to have a strong body and good nutrition. People who were already sick were brought into the *posiołek*, and the nutrition was below any standards.

Hard times came when the order about so-called *progul* came out, that is, the taking away of bread for not fulfilling quotas. The times [around] new decrees were among the worst overall. [That is because] they were not announced, [and] we generally found out about them only when the punishment was doled out. When the *progul* rule came out, nine people, including

696. *Pryvyknesh* [Russian; original Polish transliteration: *prywykniesz*]: "You will get used to it."

three women, were punished by harsh prison [time] and having their food rations cut for demanding that warm work clothing be provided. This was in February 1941, when the temperatures reached −45°C [−49°F].

The local people's attitude toward us was very friendly. They helped us in what they could, even though they didn't have much themselves.

The attitude of our superiors depended on the level of quota fulfillment, and because of the fact that we were constantly behind, we were treated ruthlessly and unforgivingly almost the entire time.

I fell ill with inflammation of the lymph nodes during work. Despite [my] serious condition, [they] didn't want to release me from work. One node after another became inflamed, but I had to continue working. Eventually wounds opened and began to fester; I continued to work with open and running wounds. Finally I was sent to a small makeshift hospital, also located in the middle of the forest, where rational treatment was, naturally, out of the question. When I was brought in, the hospital doctor, a young, maybe twenty-one-year-old Russian, complained that they sent him almost exclusively half-dead people, and then everyone was surprised that he had to report such a high mortality rate. Indeed, people who were already dying were sent to the hospital. Once one of the nurses said to the doctor, pointing at me, that [they] would soon be able to take out my corpse [and] then the air would be cleaner. The dedication of the nurses, however, saved me.

The conditions improved a little after the outbreak of the Russian-German war. September brought our full release—on the basis of the announced Amnesty.

For the appropriate payment, we had railcars placed at our disposal, in which we left for [our] chosen towns. When we arrived in Dzhambul we were, for unknown reasons, attached to a train with evacuated Russians. We arrived in the town of Czarczo;[697] from there we were to be transported all the way to the Aral Sea. We strongly objected to this, and were only unhooked from the train of the Russian refugees as a result of [our actions]. We slept in the cars for three more nights before we were taken back to Dzhambul.

697. Likely refers to the town of Chelkar (Shalkar) close to Aralsk [original Polish correction: Czełkar].

In Dzhambul, I found myself a hovel to live [in]. After some time a Polish delegation was formed, which assisted the refugees greatly in surviving the worst times by helping [them] financially and in kind.

That help, however, did not manage in time to prevent an awful epidemic of typhus and typhoid fever, which broke out in the spring as a result of the extreme living conditions. This epidemic resulted in thousands of casualties. People collapsed right in the streets. It was difficult to undertake any action because of the lack of medicines. In these circumstances, the natural end of the epidemic [had to be] awaited.

I reported to the military commission in Dzhambul. Unfortunately, I was not accepted. Captain Trojanowski told a group of people in the courtyard of the *voyenkomat*[698] that their requests could not be considered.

I went to Jangiul[699] then, where the army healthcare [headquarters] was located, [and] presented my papers confirming my voluntary health service during September, but the draft commission responded to my [application] negatively this time also.

So I returned to Dzhambul with nothing, to turn up again in the [army] headquarters three months later. As a result of various solicitations, I achieved a compromise: while they did not accept me into the army, I was put in uniform and included in the evacuation, and this is how I got to Tehran, and later to Palestine.

---

698. *Voyenkomat* [Russian; Polish transliteration: *wojenkomat*]: short for *voennyi komissar*. Local military authority agency of the Red Army responsible primarily for registration of conscripts and reservists. Equivalent of the Polish Regional Recruitment Command [Polish: Komenda Rejonu Uzupełnień].

699. Correctly: Yangi-Yul [original Polish correction: Jangi-Jul].

Protocol 290

Drawn up on the basis of the testimony of Dr. **Joachim Arnhold**, Kraków lawyer, currently resident in Tel Aviv.

I left Kraków on 3 September [1939] to find myself in Dąbrowica by Sarny on 17 September, after a rambling journey that was adventurous and full of risky ventures. When the Russians began to occupy the eastern swathes of the country, I made my way to Lwów via Równe. I arrived there in the first days of October.

In the first period of the Russian occupation, its initial stage, [we] didn't feel [any] strong pressure from the new administrative powers. This was because the authorities were either still setting themselves up or working on and preparing [their] economic plans for the future.

The mass deportation[s] of refugees began in June 1940. Although we had heard about deportations into Russia even before that period, this referred primarily to big property owners, famous political party leaders, etc. Only in June, in connection with the passportization that was ordered, did the issue of deportation of refugees come to the fore, as [only] a tiny percentage of [the refugees] asked for Russian passports. Deportation would take place after it was confirmed that the given person was a refugee and that they had not fulfilled the directives related to the passportization bill.

Single refugees, men and women, were the first in the line of fire. The Russian authorities promoted the message that the deportation order did not apply to families. Married men and women accepted this reassurance naively, and life went on normally for some time, since there was no need [for people] to hide. The authorities exploited this naivety at some point, entering [the homes of] the unsuspecting families at night and then deporting [them].

Members of Lwów's Communist Party who held positions [in the administration] and special units of the NKVD brought in from Kiev took an active part in the deportations. The [scale of] the deportations grew so much with time that even broken carts were requisitioned to be used in them.

A certain group of refugees saved themselves from deportation as follows: [some] members of the professional association of transporters who were hired for the operation would warn their friends about "the visit" that was to take place. Those forewarned would hide during the critical night and avoid deportation this way.

The Soviet authorities were strict about the deadline for the deportation operation to be completed. When the deadline passed, the refugees who had been spared were technically out of danger, could move around and work freely, etc.

Still during the deportations, the biggest danger was the house janitors. Knowing that a large number of refugees were hiding illegally around various homes, the Soviet authorities issued an order that every janitor was obliged to report to the authorities any persons who were hiding, and threatened that they would be held personally liable. This led to a scourge of extortions, terror, and denouncements. Many of my friends would still be alive today were it not for a Lwów caretaker giving them up to the Russian authorities.

I hid in the outskirts for around four weeks, in a hostel run by a man from Kraków. Around fifty people lived in two rooms.

After the last deportation, the Soviet authorities found that there were a large number of refugees left in town, despite it all. They called on them again, then, to accept Soviet passports, threatening to deport the stubborn ones at the first possible opportunity. A handful of people turned up; most remained passive. Nothing, in fact, happened to the latter, they still moved around freely, while [those who] accepted the passports had the clause with paragraph 11 put in them, concerning a ban on living in Lwów and larger cities,[700] and were forcibly moved to the provinces. Once again it turned out that respecting the rules in Russia is not always advantageous.

I left Lwów at the beginning of September 1940, planning to make my way through to Chernivtsi. It was a very risky and dangerous endeavor in those days. Although Chernivtsi, too, [was] under Russian authority at the time, [they] did continue to preserve the border between Poland and Bukovina. Illegal crossing of this strictly guarded border was punishable by a few years in prison upon capture.

I went to Kołomyja first, where I began to look for contacts [who could] allow me to get across the border. After some time I put together the right people and guides, and we set off on the dangerous journey through the

700. This paragraph forbade living in larger cities and their surroundings.

Eastern Carpathians. We walked mainly at night, on the ridges, until we reached the Cheremosh River. The border guard stopped us once [and] we, dressed as Hutsuls, explained that we were on our way to help with log driving. Luckily we did not arouse suspicion. We then crossed the border in the heart of the mountains without difficulty, and after some time, I found myself in Chernivtsi.

In September, the people in Chernivtsi were not yet familiar with the practices of the Soviet authorities and did not expect that repressive measures against them, in the form of deportations, would be coming. They responded to our stories about what had happened in Lwów [by saying] that this did not apply to Chernivtsi, because while the Russians had occupied Eastern Poland as an enemy state, they would enter Bukovina as their territory.

One could notice the change in Chernivtsi with the first [developments] after the arrival [of the Soviets]. In Lwów, the Russians had left the owners [to run] their shops and workshops during the first period, which at least allowed the merchants to sell off their wares and get cash. Having learned from this situation, the Soviet authorities issued an order immediately after crossing the border of Bukovina, nationalizing shops and factories, so that private property disappeared overnight and the residents became paupers on the spot.

The attitude of the Soviets toward the local people was [that of great suspicion]. They clearly didn't trust them. [They] made use of a whole network of secret agents and provocateurs, and filled the key political and economic positions with people from inside Russia.

In June 1941, the people of Bukovina learned for themselves how naive their beliefs about deportations were. In that month, the Russians began to deport the population of Bukovina to Siberia en masse, first the owners of huge companies, political activists, etc. Then they started up the factories under their own management.

Immediately after the outbreak of the German-Russian war, the Russians left Chernivtsi in a hurry. One could gather from the fact that [they] left behind huge [amounts of] supplies and stocks—particularly textile goods, brought in not only from Romania but also from Russia—that the Soviets' retreat was sudden and unexpected. They simply ran off.

The Russians retreated on the night of 3 July [1941], while the Romanian troops did not enter Chernivtsi until the morning of the sixth. During [this] period of abandonment, Ukrainian gangs rushed in, robbing shops and murdering residents irrespective of [their] faith. Only after the arrival of the Romanian army did the regular Jewish pogroms begin, and in that period, around two thousand people perished in the outskirts of the city. The soldiers entered apartments, took the residents out into the courtyard, and shot them there. The victims of these murders were not buried in the cemetery in Chernivtsi until a few days later.

After the Romanian units, the Gestapo entered the city. Their first action was to set fire to the big synagogue and murder around a thousand Jews, mostly the intelligentsia and wealthy people. At first, they picked one hundred people out of that group of a thousand hostages, took them outside of the city, [and] then all trace of them was lost. The rabbi, [Dr. Abraham] Mark, was among them as well.

As a result of a protest by the Romanian authorities, the Gestapo handed over the Jewish issue to the Romanians. The first Governor of Bukovina for the central government in Bucharest was a well-known antisemite, who also issued the first anti-Jewish laws. He ordered the wearing of armbands [by Jews], set curfews, and prohibited Jewish doctors from seeing Aryan patients. A bureau for Romanianization was created, too, whose aim it was to expropriate the Jewish property.

Not all of these orders could be acted upon because the Romanians were short on specialists, so they had to resort to [using] Jewish help. The work ban order was eventually annulled.

The second governor, a man who was honest but old and ailing, was being directed by his secretary, a Romanian army major with animalistic instincts.

That very major, along with a small group of his followers, began his rule by sending the government a memorandum on the matter of the deportation of all Jews to Transdniestrja.[701] This concerned around fifty-six thousand Jews present in Bukovina and Bessarabia at the time. The mayor of Chernivtsi

701. Transnistria [Polish transliteration: Transniestria]: name used at the time to describe the lands to the east of Dniester, which were taken from the USSR by the Germans and Romanians in summer 1941 and given by the Third Reich to the Romanian administration as spoils of war. Jews from parts of Ukraine (including Odessa), Bessarabia, and Bukovina were murdered in extermination centers in Transnistria, mainly at the hands of the Romanian army. Altogether around 275,000 Jews were murdered in Transnistria. Germans (including *Volksdeutsche*) and Ukrainians also took part in the murders.

strongly opposed this plan—[he was] essentially an honest man, even though he belonged to the Legionaria[702] himself. He argued that the Jews were an important economic contributor to the country and could work positively for the good of the state. A fight ensued, in which the mayor had the vast majority of the population behind him, and the major—the Germans. Naturally the Germans won, and against the wishes of the governorship.

The first preparatory step for the deportations was an order concerning the creation of a ghetto for the Jews, irrespective of nationality. They were given a short period of time before they were to be behind its walls, so that it wasn't even possible to empty out apartments or sell the furniture. It was a horrible sight when the Jews traveled to the ghetto at the appointed time, bundles on their backs. The Romanians, however, harbored many Jews; many were also kept in their workplaces as specialists. Around twenty thousand Jews managed to save themselves this way; the rest, that is around thirty-six thousand, were sent to Transdniestrja after some time.

A typical situation unfolded, verging on the farcical. Immediately after the Jews were locked in the ghetto, the German consul in Bucharest intervened on behalf of Jews [who were] German citizens, demanding their immediate release from the ghetto based on the fact that only the Berlin government could [have a say] regarding these citizens. Naturally, those Jews were immediately released.

Based on this precedent, Jews [who were] Polish citizens turned to an influential Romanian lawyer to have him intervene with the Chilean foreign mission, which took it upon itself to defend the interests of Polish citizens in Romania on the matter of [their] release from the ghetto.[703] Within three weeks, permission from the government was obtained, and this way, a thousand new souls were saved. They were saved by convincing General Janeczek, who held the power over the ghetto in his hands, to send the Polish citizens

---

702. Legionaria, or Legionnaire movement [Polish transliteration: Legjonarijja]: the antisemitic Legion of the Archangel Michael, created in 1927 by Corneliu Codreanu, which became part of the fascist Iron Guard in 1930.

703. [After the Nazi invasion of Poland in 1939, the Chilean embassies in Italy and Romania represented the interests of the Polish state in these countries. The consul of Chile in Bucharest issued around 1,200 Chilean passports in the years 1941–43 and contributed to the rescue of Polish Jews persecuted by the German Nazis.]

only at the very end. Because of this, that thousand people managed to be saved while there was still time.

After the deportation of around thirty thousand Jews, the ghetto was liquidated, and the remaining Jews were able to return to their apartments without trouble.

All this was happening in October 1941. After that period, there were still a number of anti-Jewish decrees issued; however, no one was sent to Transdniestrja anymore until May 1942.

In May 1942, deportations were talked about again; however, they could not be carried out without the permission of the governor himself. In reality, around a thousand Jews were sent away in June, including around two hundred Polish citizens.

To solve this problem once and for all, the Chilean mission was approached again, and they procured so-called protection passports for the [Polish] citizens, which were to protect them from further deportations. Soon, however, the governor began to interpret this issue according to his whim, stating that since there was no Poland, then there were no Polish citizens either. The Chilean embassy issued two notes to the government on this matter and eventually received a statement from the government's deputy prime minister, aimed at the governor, that he was not allowed to touch the Polish citizens during deportation[s].

It got to a point where, during the organization of the third transport, when the governor attempted to sabotage the government's edict, a special delegate came from Bucharest and pulled all the Polish citizens from the Makkabi [football] pitch, where the transport was being formed. This should be credited to the active campaign of the Jewish religious council in Chernivtsi.

At that time, too, the government ordered the abolition of armbands, and even entertained the idea of moving the Jews from Bukovina to Central Romania, to the so-called Regale. Efforts were also made to bring back the Jews from Transdniestrja, sometimes even with successful result[s]. Conditions improved even more when the old governor stood down and General Dragelin[704] took his place. He invited Jewish representatives to see him and

704. Cornel Dragalina: General Governor of Bukovina.

wished for—as a good host, he said—collaboration. He abolished the wearing of armbands, eased a number of anti-Jewish decrees, and even allowed Jews to earn [money] in special camps, in basically bearable conditions.

On the eve of the reentry of the Soviet army into Chernivtsi, a mass exodus from the town began. The conditions were so difficult, however, that a mere thousand people managed to get to Bucharest in time; I was among those, luckily.

After a four-week stay in the capital, I managed to leave for Constanța; there, I got on the ship *Milka*, on which I went to Turkey, and I got to Palestine from there.

Protocol 300

Testimony of **Jakob Hager**, age thirty-six, bookkeeper and social activist, born in Kołomyja.

With Bolsheviks

For twelve years, I worked as a bookkeeper in a large Jewish company that owned landed properties, breweries, mills—Bretler and Co.[705] in Kołomyja, where the company's headquarters were. I had been running its accounts since the year 1933, even when the Russians confiscated the firm's assets after occupying the city. Before the war, I belonged to the organization of Revisionists.[706] I took active part in the organization['s activities], and everyone in town knew about this. The Bolsheviks also knew that, and it [could have been] a [good] reason to take away my job and send me to Siberia. Despite this, as a good specialist, I not only stayed put but got the job of head bookkeeper of our company. Prices were incredibly high in the city during that time. The merchants hid the remnants of foodstuffs and goods and demanded huge sums for them. New products were not arriving. My relatively high earnings, 650 rubles per month, were not enough to live on, and if it weren't for the fact that there were barns with cows and pigs on the mill premises and we had meat to use ourselves, I would have had to go hungry. Changes occurred in the second half of 1940. The Bolsheviks brought in grain from Ukraine. We didn't have such grain in Poland. This grain was milled in our mill, to be used by hospitals and health resorts. They would often inject large supplies of white flour into the market. One could get as much white bread in the bakeries as one wished now. The purpose was to get the merchants, afraid of prices going down, to [release their] hidden supplies into the market. [Now] able to get leather and manufacture in the city, the peasants brought products from [part of text missing] into town. The effect of such an economy was astonishing. Not only did the prices fall, but also the value of the currency. The director of our company was a Jew from Kiev, Frachtenburg. The clerks and workers were friends with him. He didn't demand more than the terms of the contract. Before the Bolsheviks

705. [Polish: *i sp.*: *i spółka*]

706. That is, Revisionist Zionists, the right wing of the Zionist movement.

entered into war with the Germans,[707] one worked for six hours a day [at our work site] and every sixth day was free from work.[708] No one was prevented from carrying out their religious practices. Prayers were held openly in synagogues. On Simchat Torah,[709] [people] danced in synagogues, [and] we were certain that we would survive in this state until the end of the war.

Life was not smooth sailing for everyone. News reached us about the arrests of the former military [and] officials, and their deportation to Siberia. The same applied to Ukrainian nationalists and Jews. The fate of the refugees who registered to return to their homes and were sent to Siberia was tragic. The fate of the people sent away in freight cars, crowded and dirty, made one's blood run cold. But we, the residents of Kołomyja, were faring well.

Soviet-German War

This peaceful way of life of ours was the reason we did not realize what was ahead. Before our director left, when the Bolsheviks were evacuating the city,[710] he called us in for a meeting and suggested that we go with him. We couldn't bring ourselves to leave our native place and share the fate of the refugees. We had seen with our own eyes what being a refugee meant. Besides, we were receiving news from towns occupied by the Germans, [saying] that the situation wasn't too bad [there]. Some people smuggled themselves across the border to return home. The Germans, we were told, valued specialists highly and paid them well. The director left on his own. We regretted this decision in the morning. We saw young people leaving the city en masse and crowding the Soviet evacuation trains. Older Jews begged the officials to be taken to Russia. One older Jew, when I asked [him about it], told me: "I remember the Hitlerites in Vienna. I won't be able to stop myself from answering their insults. Not for all the world will I stay with the Germans." The Bolsheviks took all residents and even gave them seats in the railcars. But they did not let those who had thought [it] through and didn't want to go [anymore] get off

707. It is Germany who attacked the USSR on 22 September 1941.

708. This was the result of legislation in force in USSR at the time (from 1929 to 1940) regarding workdays and holidays. [The goal was] a so-called uninterrupted production process, on the basis of which a five-day workweek was introduced, where every sixth day was free.

709. Simchat Torah (Hebrew): rejoicing of/with the Torah. The last (seventh) day of the holiday of Sukkot, observed in the month of Tishri (September–October).

710. 30 June 1941.

the train. One of the Jews jumped out of the car when the train started; he was killed on the spot. We feared these trains. It was dangerous to travel on army trucks. They were bombed on the way. The Bolsheviks gave army uniforms to all army truck passengers—in case they fell into German hands, they would be treated like prisoners of war. Even that we couldn't bring ourselves to do. At the county council, the Bolsheviks gave out uniforms even to those who were staying. I didn't want to take such a uniform. I didn't know what was better: to be a Bolshevik soldier in German captivity, or a civilian Jew.

Ukrainian Nationalists

The first days of July went by in lawlessness in Kołomyja. The Russians had left, and the Germans had not yet taken over the city. We worried the most about those days. The Ukrainians grew emboldened.[711] They were certain that Hitler would proclaim a Ukrainian Republic, and [that] their bloody reign would begin. Ukrainian nationalists affiliated with Konowalec,[712] who was in Berlin at the time, were readying themselves to take power. A Ukrainian militia group was formed, military marching [songs] were sung, the magistrate [and] the county council were filled [with their people], roads were guarded, and a Ukrainian cooperative, whose headquarters were in London and which had only been a trading establishment before the war, assumed the Ukrainian state powers.

Magister Lewicki, former official at the district office in Kołomyja, became the political official, magister Paprocki—press official, Dr. Nataszek—health official, and Michaluk and Babiok constituted an economic committee. The meetings of the interim government took place in the national house. Twenty-two thousand Kołomyja Jews trembled with fear.

Our fear grew greater still when we heard that the committee had issued an appeal for peasants to come to the city with the weapons they had hidden, knives and scythes. News reached us from the village of Chlebiczyn, where the peasants had massacred fifty Jews, their neighbors. They threw small children into graves alive and buried them alongside [their] parents. We also heard

711. See footnote in Protocol 257.

712. Yevhen Konovalets [Polish: Jewhen Konowalec]: leader of the Organization of Ukrainian Nationalists (Polish: Organizacja Ukraińskich Nacjonalistów, OUN).

about the slaughter in the villages of Słobódka [and] Leszno, from which the few Jewish residents still alive came to us.

The press official, magister Paprocki, was my childhood friend. We went to the same school. Before the war, he had opened a flour shop with my help. I had slept at his place. As a management figure, he assured me that there would be no pogrom and that [fragment of text missing] would only come for the Jews in the economic sphere. They didn't want to stain the young Ukrainian independence, still being born, with Jewish blood. Dr. Kremer, who had many friends among the Ukrainian activists, was reassured in the same way. They explained the village massacres as old score settling between neighbors. Nothing [like that] would repeat itself in the city. This promise was kept to some extent. There was no pogrom [in our city]. The Ukrainians kept an eye on one another. Disturbances began when the Hungarians occupied the city.

Hungarians

Ukrainian guards were posted on the road used by the Hungarian army to enter the city. They shot at the army and killed three Hungarian soldiers. The Hungarians answered with [gun]fire. One Ukrainian was killed. The Ukrainians spread a rumor that [it was] the Jews [who] had shot at the Hungarians. Luckily, the Hungarians did not believe this hearsay. Despite this, when the occupying army found itself in the city, a Jewish pogrom was organized. The Hungarian commandant ordered all Jewish residents to gather in the town square. The Hungarians surrounded the Jews and drove them to clean the city of the posters and images the Bolsheviks had left behind. The Ukrainians were furious at having their power taken away, and when the Jews returned after finishing the "work," Ukrainian youths, armed with sticks, were waiting for them and beat them. No one was killed, however. The Jews thanked God that that was all it had come to. The Hungarian soldiers arrived with full rucksacks, bringing bread, kielbasa, soap, [and] cigarettes from Hungary. Trading began. For the products that were brought in, the Jews would offer leather [and] manufacture. On Wołowa Street, where the local authority building was, business transactions between Hungarian soldiers and Jews took place quite openly. The street looked like a market.

Germans in Kołomyja

After a week, the German Reichswehra[713] arrived in town. The Ukrainians were pleased. Ukrainian independence remained only a promise. In reality, the freedom the Ukrainians were given was to deal with the Jews. The Jews were ordered to gather in a square by the Ogród Miejski,[714] and a German officer did exercises there with them, ordering them, the old and the sick, to do unimaginable things. Old women were beaten mercilessly. This was not enough for the Ukrainians. The German officer said that this was a lenient punishment for Jews who had spat at German soldiers. Were this to be repeated, he would shoot everyone. The Ukrainian police gathered all the Jews on one side of the market square, where rows of Ukrainian youths armed with sticks were positioned. The [Jews] passing by were hit over the head mercilessly. I saw my former friends among the thugs. I called out their names. They grew embarrassed and lowered [their] sticks. For this impudence, other Ukrainians treated me with a double helping of blows.

Third Jewish Day

Those two Jewish days turned out to have been innocent play in comparison with the third day, organized for us by the SS who were passing by on the way to the Russian front. They were [well] trained in this work. They arrived in Kołomyja on 22 July [1941]. Relations between the Hungarians and Ukrainians were not working out well. The Hungarians were accused of trading with the Jews and destroying Ukrainian business. The Ukrainian Soyuz wanted to use the occasion to get richer, to confiscate Jewish possessions. The battle over the mills was particularly fierce. The owners of the Jewish mills took the transmission belts off the machines, and new ones were difficult to find. The Ukrainians, however, found a transmission belt and wanted to open up Goldberg's mill for their own use. The Hungarians turned up, took away the belts and sent them to Hungary. Ukrainians complained to the Germans. They accused the Hungarians of favoring Jews, and pointed out as evidence the fact that not one Jew had been killed to date. They presented a list of the names of 180 Jews accused of Bolshevism. The Ukrainian intelligentsia drove

713. Refers to the Wehrmacht.

714. Public Garden.

around the city in droshkies and brought those 180, under various pretexts, in front of the SS commandant. The German authorities were pleased with this work. They ordered that the Jews be taken outside of the city [and] told to dig their own graves, as was the common practice. Soon the city learned about this. A few well-known activists ran to the Hungarian commandant to ask [part of text missing.] Just then, the execution order was given. One Jew had already been killed. The Hungarian commandant halted the execution. He turned to the German and accused him of acting outside of his authority. "These are Bolsheviks," said the German. "Bolsheviks are not killed without being examined," replied the Hungarian, "information has to be extracted from each of them." The German had to agree to let everyone be taken to jail. Everyone was examined separately, and four weeks later, all were set free.

Soon, German pioneer groups[715] arrived, who were to work on alterations to the railroad tracks. The capturing of Jews for labor began. The work was hard and humiliating. People were beaten with gunstocks. [They] often didn't return home from work. After a day's work, the Germans would take the Jews to the clay pits outside the brickyard, [and] order them to get into the water, dance, sing, and dive there. To avoid [having to do] similar work, I hid outside of the city and didn't show myself in the streets.

Jewish Council

The first task of the Jewish council was the regulation of the conditions of forced labor. The council paid the nonwealthy for the work, and [those who] avoided work had to pay off the people standing in for them generously. For me and three other Jews the Jewish council found work in the management of the post office opened up to serve the ghetto. The post office manager, a German, promised to issue us appropriate documents so we wouldn't be picked up for [forced] labor. Despite this, the roundups did not stop. Despite the contingent of workers supplied [by the council], Jews continued to be picked up for [forced] work, and the Ukrainian youths helped to torment those captured. The hatred between Ukrainians and Hungarians grew, and the Ukrainians used all of [their] influence to get the Hungarian army recalled

715. Military engineers.

from [the area]. The Hungarians retaliated in kind. One day, they surrounded the home [part of text missing] and carried out a thorough search. All of a sudden, the Hungarians were recalled because of an order from Berlin, and the Ukrainians were dancing in the streets with joy. Their happiness did not last long. Eastern Galicia was annexed to the General Government.[716] They knew they couldn't expect anything from the Germans. The relations between them became hostile. The Germans became the only authority in the city, [thus] inviting upon themselves the hatred of all of the population.

716. District of Galicia [German: Distrikt Galizien] was annexed to the General Government on 1 August 1941.

Protocol 302

Testimony of **Szloma Beglikter**, student, age eighteen. Came to Palestine via Russia and Tehran.

I was a refugee even before the war. Before Hitler came to power, my parents had moved to Germany. We lived in Köln, where Father had a haberdashery shop, and in 1938, the Hitlerites moved us over to the Polish [territory] and we lived in the camp in Zbąszyń[717] for a long time. My father died in that camp, and I then left with Mother to go to [stay with our] relatives in Przeworsk. There was heavy fighting taking place there at the beginning of the war. The station was bombed, and the town suffered.

With the Germans

After a few days of fighting, the German army occupied Przeworsk. They immediately started capturing Jews for labor, torturing the older [ones] especially, who had their beards cut off and were mocked. The people had to pay huge contributions, and notwithstanding, the Germans went around to Jewish homes and took away everything that fell into their hands. After a few days, the Germans desecrated the cemetery, took away the statues [and] reserved them for street paving. The synagogue and the beth hamidrash were set on fire, and [the Jews were] not allowed to save the holy books from them. The Germans didn't allow the fire to be put out. The fact that the rabbi, heedless of the danger he was facing, burst into the burning synagogue and tried to save the Torah, made a big impression. He was badly injured in [the attempt]. Two Jews who ran after the rabbi burned to death. The Germans arrested the rabbi afterward and tortured him for the aforementioned crime. A huge contribution was levied then, too, which the Jews were not able to pay, but the Lwów [Jewish] council came to [their] rescue, and the contribution was paid.

717. From November 1938 to August 1939, there was a camp in the border [town] of Zbąszyń for around four thousand Jews, Polish citizens, who had lived in Germany [and] had been expelled by Hitler's authorities. The Polish authorities refused to accept them for many months. The camp was located in abandoned [military] barracks. This predicament was the impetus for Herschel Grynszpan (whose parents were among the stranded deportees) to shoot the German diplomat Ernst vom Rath, whose death in Paris on 9 November 1938 instigated the Nazi pogroms called Kristallnacht.

Expulsion

After a few weeks, the Germans issued an order for all Jews to leave town within one hour. The order was issued at eight o'clock and stated that if any Jew was left in town [after] nine, they would be shot on the spot. It's difficult to describe the panic that broke out. People didn't know where to run to. [They] grabbed whatever was there. Gangs were waiting outside town, accompanied by German soldiers, [and] robbed the Jews of their paltry belongings. We ran toward the San River. There were no boats. A group of Germans had requisitioned the boats and were demanding four hundred zlotys per head to transport a Jew. Only a small number of people had that amount on them. Many tried to swim across the river. The Germans shot at them; many people drowned. I got to the town of Kałoszyce[718] along with my mother. There was a lunatic hospital there from which the hungry patients had escaped, [and they] lunged at every passerby in the street. These scenes made a horrific impression on me. We escaped to Niemirów. We found the Russians there already. Mother and [my] older sister took up trading, and we fared all right.

In Siberia

We lived in Niemirów for five months. Prices rose by the hour, and the Soviet authorities persecuted traders. My mother was arrested because she was caught with a box of merchandise. A decree came out about passportization and registration. We didn't want to become Soviet citizens. News was coming in from the German-occupied territories that life had normalized there. We registered to leave. Soon afterward, NKVD-ers turned up in our home and drove us to the station. Along with thousands of [other] people, we made the horrific journey to Siberia, and were all sick when we arrived at [our destination]. We lived in barracks, working hard. Many people were ill, unable to stand the harsh conditions. The warden did not care about the high mortality, claiming that in Russia, all exiles had to die in Siberia. We suffered in the freezing temperatures. Mother received permission for us to go to Bukhara, where the climate was a lot better. With no apartment, we roamed around in the open for eight days, until we turned to the local authorities [and asked] to be sent to a kolkhoz. We fared all right in the kolkhoz: we worked and had food. One

718. Likely: Oleszyce.

day the kolkhoz chief gathered all refugees from Poland and told them about the Amnesty, and said that we were to go to England. Our joy was endless. We set off toward Turkestan, where the situation of refugees was hopeless. We had no roof over our heads, or food. The news about [being able to leave] Russia turned out to be a fairy tale. At our request, we were sent to the Kaganowicz kolkhoz, where Mother fell ill with typhus and died. [My] sister and I were ill too, but recovered. We turned to the Polish delegation [and asked] to be taken into an orphanage. [My] sister was already twenty, so they didn't want to accept her; she stayed in Turkestan and I haven't had any news from her since. I, along with other children, was sent to Tehran, [and] from there I came to Palestine.

Protocol 304

Testimony of **Jakob Berkowicz**, age thirty-eight, from Przemyśl. Came to Palestine via Russia in October 1942.

The Germans were in our town for eleven days.[719] During that time, however, they managed to empty all the shops, and used a tried-and-true tactic whose aim was to prove that it was not them but the mob who had organized the pogrom. They themselves took away large loads of goods on trucks, and left the rest for the hooligans, whose antics they then photographed. Immediately after the Germans' entry, roundups began in the streets. Six hundred Jews were taken out into the cemetery, ordered to dig graves for themselves, and killed. Among those killed were: the president of the council Herszel Glazer, Dobromilski, Rabbi Zajdel [?], Eng. Szefel. Among those killed were also many refugees whose names we didn't know.

Russians in Przemyśl

The Germans left town eleven days later, and the Russians entered. We breathed easy, as they didn't harm anyone. Everyone was allowed to trade [and] work, and it seemed to us that normal times were ahead. That lasted three weeks altogether. The Soviet regime started to be noticeable in town. The nationalization of homes, shops, [and] factories began, the bourgeoisie were kicked out of [their] homes, searches and mass arrests were carried out. Zionists, social activists—Jews and Poles—and also the intelligentsia, judges, lawyers, and state officials, were arrested. They were taken to a prison and kept in inhuman conditions—tens of people to a cell—until they were sent to Siberia. On the eastern side of the San were the Germans, on the other side the Russians. One day the Germans issued an order that Jews had to leave town within two hours and cross to the other side of the river, to the Bolsheviks. I was living in the Russian part of town and watched from afar how the Germans threw the Jews out of their homes, not allowing them to take even hand luggage. I saw, too, how those who didn't manage to leave [their] apartments in time were

719. Beginning 14 September. On 28 September, they handed the city over to the USSR. The city was split in two. The south (main) part of the city ended up in German hands, and the so-called Zasanie was in Soviet hands until the attack on the USSR by Germany on 22 June 1941.

killed. The Bolsheviks did not want to let the poor people in, [and] they were run around from one side to the other. On the Germans' side of the river stood machine guns, ready to shoot at returnees. Tens of people perished this way. Finally the Russians took pity on the Jews and allowed them into town. The Russian-occupied part of town was surrounded with barbed wire.

Passportization

The situation in Przemyśl worsened by the day. The most essential food products ran out. Shops were emptied out; people who used to have something were not given work and were not allowed to trade. A decree came out about the mandatory adoption of Soviet citizenship. Even though the Jews knew what was happening on the German side, 80 percent [of them] did not agree to the passportization and registered to return home in front of the Russian-German commission. Some citizens of Przemyśl did this too.

First Conscription

During the Russian-Finnish[720] war, the Russians ordered the forced conscription of twenty-two- and twenty-three-year-olds and sent them to the front. Later, they mobilized other age groups but did not manage to send them in time, because peace had already been made.

In Exile

As the owner of a shop with manufacture that was nationalized by the Bolsheviks, I hid, fearful of being arrested. And when the registrations began, I registered under a fake name. After a few weeks, along with a group of others, I was sent to Siberia in inhuman conditions. We traveled for twenty-six days, not knowing [our] destination. We suffered from hunger, overcrowding, and the filth [inside the car]. We stopped at the station of Suslonger in the Mari Oblast. When we got out of the cars, I counted that our transport was made up of 33,000 [?] people. We were split into groups and led through a thick forest. Completely exhausted from hunger, tiredness, and dysentery, I dragged myself after the group to [our] destination, where we found a few barracks that were

720. The Soviet-Finnish war, started by the USSR, lasted from 30 November 1939 until 12 March 1940. As a result, Finland was forced to give up a part of its territory to the USSR.

to be our home. The barracks were surrounded with barbed wire. We couldn't move around freely. The next day, we were ordered to build new barracks. Two hundred people were to live in each. We slept on bunks, on pallets, covered with our own rags. The quota was twenty-five trees per day, and we managed to cut down five at the most. Since no one fulfilled the quota, we received four hundred grams of bread per day and watery soup. Later we would bribe the supervisors and they would log a [fulfilled] quota for us. A typhus [epidemic] broke out in the camp, which kept spreading, claiming tens of victims. Finally they brought a doctor in for us. A battle began against the epidemic, which only stopped when frosts of –60°C [–76°F] came. We worked 46 [16?] hours a day. It was better to work than sit in the stuffy barracks. For many months, we didn't undress, wash, [or] shave, as water was hard to come by. We were allowed to wash once a month and were given a tiny bowl of water for it. We stopped believing in the existence of a free world. We looked like feral animals. We didn't know about the outbreak of the war between Germany and Russia. We only learned about the Amnesty in December 1941. The commandant wouldn't hear of [it]. We started thinking about an escape. The area was so wild that we were afraid to set off. A few of us simulated illness [and] were sent into town. They didn't want to accept us into the hospital. The commandant designated the apartment of some Russian woman who had been exiled for counterrevolution as a place [for us] to stay. I escaped, having gotten on a train going to Bukhara. That train traveled only to Kazan,[721] and I only got to Tashkent after a few weeks' wandering. I was ill a few times, stayed in a hospital, had my right arm paralyzed, and was unable to work. I worked trading and received assistance from the Polish delegation. Thanks to [my] friends' help, I snuck onto a train traveling with a Polish soldier transport, and this way, [I] got to Tehran.

721. Likely refers to the town of Kagan.

Protocol 305

Testimony of **Michał Honigman**, born in the year 1913 in Sosnowiec. Came to Palestine in February 1940.

I escaped from Sosnowiec on 3 September 1939, on the eve of the occupation of Zagłębie by the Germans. Battles were taking place around the town, but the Polish army had to surrender because of the enemy's dominance and [they] retreated to the defense line [in] Częstochowa. People left [their] homes in a panic; the roads were overrun with cars, carts, and pedestrians; some went toward Kraków, others [toward] Lublin or Warsaw, thinking that the enemy would not catch up with them there. I walked toward Kraków. There was panic there no less than in other cities; airplanes bombed the city. It went on like this until 8 September. The Germans occupied Kraków that day. With the exception of street roundups, Jews did not experience [any] special discrimination. The council provided laborers to the Germans and paid them from its own coffers. The council also looked after tens of thousands of refugees, who were accommodated in all the empty buildings, in schools, and in synagogues. Soup kitchens were opened. As the arrival of the Gestapo was expected, I decided to leave town and return to Sosnowiec. Here, too, I arrived to roundups, stealing, and shooting of defenseless people. I remained in Sosnowiec until October 1939, and seeing that the situation was getting worse, decided to cross over to the Soviet side. [I] set off along with a few companions. After a few days, we found ourselves in the village of Żurawica, outside Przemyśl, on the Soviet side, where I was arrested and taken to Przemyśl. I spent eight days in an overcrowded prison. The conditions were awful; we were fed meagerly. On the fifth day, we were awoken at night and taken out for interrogation with other prisoners. [The interrogation] took place in a huge hall, where there were many tables, one prisoner being examined at each. I recognized one of the judges to be a Communist from Sosnowiec with whom I had often had discussions. He pretended not to recognize me, but chance meant that I had my interrogation with him. I was accused of illegal border crossing. I admitted guilt. My judge called me a Fascist, and after [I] signed the protocol, ordered me to be taken back to the cell. Eight days later I was told that I was free and that I wasn't allowed to live closer than 150 kilometers from the border. I set off for Lwów that same day—[it was] so overrun with refugees that you couldn't move about in the streets. The housing [situation] was terrible [and] we couldn't get a roof over our heads.

In Exile

I stayed in Lwów until June 1940. During that period, the registration and passportization took place. Since I didn't want to accept Soviet citizenship, and I was caught a few times [committing] the crime of trading, I was sent to Siberia one day. It's difficult to describe the horrendous conditions of [that] journey. When we got out of the car at a small station in Ural, I could not stand on my feet. It turned out that we were in the Sverdlovsk Oblast. Our transport was made up of twelve thousand people. Most were Jews. There were many rabbis among them, like the rabbi from Jarosław—Steinberg,[722] the rabbi from Sosnowiec—Hager,[723] and the rabbi from Podgórze—Chudy [?]. We were accommodated in barracks and sent to work in the forest the next day. The quota turned out to be disproportionately higher than our capacities. We received a minimal [amount of] bread, that is, four hundred grams a day, and watery soup. As a result of the hunger, epidemics broke out, which claimed new victims from our transport every day. If it weren't for the food products we received from [our] relatives, no one would have survived. The religious Jews suffered a lot, [as they] were ordered to work on Saturday[s] and were forbidden to pray. Later on, the rabbis were exempted from work in the forest and given lighter work. The outbreak of the [German-Soviet] war worsened our situation: the bread portions became smaller, but the working hours increased. We found out about the Amnesty. We set off on trucks and arrived in Bukhara three weeks later. The area was full of Polish citizens; there was nothing to eat and nowhere to sleep. I got a job in a suitcase factory. Realizing that [my] earnings would not be enough to live on, I set off for Tashkent, and from there, to Iang-Iul,[724] where I registered for the Polish army. I was classified as category D because of [my] poor health. Despite this, I did not give up [my] plan of leaving Russia, and I smuggled myself to Persia. After a year's stay in Tehran, I received a certificate and came to Palestine.

722. Izaak Halewi Steinberg: until 1921, rabbi of Halicz, then a rabbi in Jarosław. He left for Israel in 1951 and died in Tel Aviv in 1967.

723. Menachem Mendel Hager: from 1930, rabbi of Podgórze. He died in Israel in 1954.

724. Correctly: Yangi-Yul [original Polish correction: Jangi-Jul].

Protocol 307

Drawn up on the basis of the testimony of **Michał Zakszapine [Załszupin?]**, age nineteen, resident in Warsaw before the war [and] currently in Tel Aviv.

The outbreak of the war caught me in Warsaw. I experienced all of the horrendous siege of the city. Despite the lack of water, electricity, and food, people did not lose their spirit. In our block, a few people left every day to report as volunteers for work in the defense. Throughout the whole period of the siege, one could sense that one was dealing with a consciously organized defense and not an amateurish undertaking. The anti-aircraft defense was taken over by the young people because of the absence of older [ones], who either were at the front or had left the city earlier. The last two [days] of the siege were the worst, when the Germans took turns bombing and shooting the city for forty-eight hours. Then suddenly, an incredible silence fell; in the morning, you could already see German patrols buzzing around in Marszałkowski Square.[725] Warsaw capitulated after resistance.

In the first days, the German reign expressed itself through roundups of people for work, which consisted of removing corpses and rubble from the squares and streets. The regular army went around to homes and took away radios. For as long as the army ruled the city, the conditions were still bearable; however, when the Gestapo arrived in town one day, the [horror] began. We felt it immediately in [our] family. [That was because] Father was taken from the street for labor one time [and] returned home with a broken jaw. The Gestapo patrols entered apartments [and] took furniture [and] valuable items out of them, often leaving corpses behind.

We decided to escape from this hell. With the [help] of a guide, we reached the border zone. Here the [real] tragedy began. We were shot at from both sides. The Germans did not want to let us back in. The Russians, on the other hand, banned us from entering their territory. We suffered from hunger and thirst. Women were committing suicide. Already during an examination by the Germans, where women were examined so thoroughly that even [gynecological exams were carried out], a few [of them] took their own lives. Finally,

725. Refers to either Marszałkowska Street or the Marszałek [Marshall] Józef Piłsudski Square.

driven to the edge, we stormed through the Soviet border, not paying attention to the drawn bayonets and the whizzing bullets.

We reached Białystok. Conditions were still largely normal there, the situation made easier by the fact that the zloty was still in circulation. In the first days, the entering Soviet army had already bought out all the goods that were in the shops, so that in order to get them, you had to either stand in line for hours outside the cooperatives or buy them [on the black market].[726] Of course, the second option was generally chosen.

Our chaotic life forced [us] to make a decision. We decided to "push through" to Lwów, which was a serious undertaking at the time. You had to try to procure a permit to leave by rail, then [came] the problems of obtaining a ticket, [and] when everything was ready, you could wait for hours in the station for rail connections. After two days' journey, we finally got to Lwów.

Lwów looked like a million-strong city at the time. The streets were swarming with roiling masses of refugees from all areas of Poland. Even though the authorities were generally still passive, one could feel the nervousness and the uncertainty regarding the future. It expressed itself in the frenzy of merriment and joy, to which the people applied themselves with delight. At two or three at night, it was bustling and lively, like at midday, not only on Akademicka [Street], but also on the side streets. The residents drowned the[ir] desperate fear of an uncertain future with apparent lightheartedness and amusement.

When the registration was announced, the authorities began pressing [people] to collect [their] passports. The merriment died down; it was immediately understood that the expected tragedy was approaching fast. It was not yet known what form [it would take], and because of that, a wave of various rumors enveloped the desperate residents.

Things slowly began to come clear in January. One night the sirens suddenly cried out an alarm. In accordance with the regulations in force, it was forbidden to go out into the streets then. The next day, we learned that the goal of the alarm was to make the deportation of the first [group] to Siberia easier. [The group] was made up of, first and foremost, higher-ranking state officials, the owners of large real estate holdings, town house owners, etc.

---

726. See footnote in Protocol 288.

I went to school throughout my whole stay in Lwów. With the exception of installing a Russian supervisor, the teaching staff remained generally the same. The curriculum was also hardly changed, although Latin was replaced with Russian. Lectures were extended [to include] hours of the history of the Bolshevik revolution, of course.

In June [1940], further deportation[s] took place. The Russians had been driven to despair by the Polish citizens' negative attitude toward the idea of changing their citizenship to Russian. Ninety-nine percent of Jews refused to accept Russian citizenship.

One night a few armed NKVD members knocked [on our door], told us to get dressed, and not allowing us to bring even the most essential items, they loaded us into cars, transported us to the freight station, and then moved us into cattle cars. At that point we simply ceased to be [human] subjects, becoming objects [instead]. The first indication of what awaited us was already noticeable at that same station. We were held at the station for three days, inside tightly sealed, impossibly overfilled cars. When we finally started, the draft and the air from the fresh meadows and fields brought many a person to. During the journey, we slowly grew numb to the moral and physical pain—and that was perhaps our luck. We were generally fed at two o'clock at night [while] the train was stopped in the middle of nowhere. [The food] consisted of some scraps and moldy bread. To relieve ourselves, we would go [out] under bayonet point, in a [set] and timed order.

Finally, after a long journey, we reached our destination in the Mari El Republic.

The conditions in our *posiołek* were bearable compared to what I later heard about others. We generally had decent supervisors and this, perhaps, affected [our] situation. The work was hard: we [worked] cutting down and loading trees. The sick, however, were made exempt from this work; it was qualified very liberally. Mothers were exempted from work too. In instances of more serious illness, [people] were sent to rather well set-up—by Russian standards—hospitals.

We languished like this for more than a year. When the Amnesty came as a result of the Polish-Russian agreement, we received *udostoverenia*[727] and could

727. Certificates [protocol text: *udostrowiejenia,* corrected in the original footnote to *udostwierenija*].

pick a place we wanted to go to. Everyone went south, for two reasons: because it was warmer in the south, and because persistent rumors had begun to circulate about an evacuation that was to take place via Persia.

Our journey south probably was among the most horrific moments [I] lived through in Russia. We would stand for days on end in the overcrowded aisles; it was [our] dream to get a place on the train's roof—although a few people fell from there, killing themselves—still [it] was a chance to at least gulp down [some] fresh air. There was nothing to eat. Every day corpses would be thrown out of the train, even through the windows.

When we disembarked in Bormak,[728] for a long time we couldn't find a place [to stay], until we finally managed to settle in some basement. I had a bit of luck as I fell ill with typhus and was put in a hospital.

Winter came, and with it, heavy frosts. Because [we] could not protect ourselves from them with warm clothing, we decided to save ourselves by leaving for warmer Uzbekistan.

We settled in a small town close to Fergana. It was indeed warmer there, but there was terrible hunger. People died right on the streets after a few days—or even a few tens of days—without food. As a rule, one received four hundred grams of bread per day, but there were weeks when it was not possible to get anything. Moreover, the attitude of the Uzbeks toward Polish citizens was worse than bad. They didn't want to sell [us] anything, unless [it was] at very high prices, they refused to rent out apartments, and woe unto the daredevil who dared to set foot over [his] doorstep at night. He would be found the next day dead and naked in the middle of the street. During my journey across Russia, I often noticed the astonishing lack of any organizational sense in Russians. There were incidents among us where someone would board a Tashkent-bound train and learn a few days later that, despite [having] carefully checked the information, they were en route to Leningrad. There was no universal food card system: they were different in every city, and this led to a lot of confusion.

In the city streets, you would see people with faces somehow gray, resigned, numb—and this was typical of Russia.

728. Refers to the town of Borma in the Kuybyshev district.

In large cities, the disparity between the stunning modern buildings and the lack of food was often jarring. The prisons were normally the most impressive buildings. I was told that, during the establishment of any kind of housing development, the first building erected was normally a prison. The attitude of the average person toward the regime: the older people carefully concealed their hostile stance, the youth were enthusiastic supporters. In village huts, one could very often find an icon and pictures of saints, but the young were already being raised in a godless spirit.

News arrived about the organizing of Polish army divisions. Indeed, a short time later, a unit began to form nearby. We would go to the barracks then, where we were given food, and this saved us from dying. [This is because] the army had enough food in Russia, and there were special canteens at every station where soldiers, including Polish ones, could get whatever they wanted.

The procedure of admitting [people] into the Polish units was not complicated at the time. I was accepted into the army as a *junak*.[729] After [I had stayed for] a short time in a camp, an evacuation from Russia took place, via Krasnovodsk.

Then, via Iran and Iraq, I came to Palestine.

729. A young cadet. See glossary: Polish army in the USSR.

Protocol 308

Drawn up on the basis of the testimony of **Izrael Ganzweis**, age thirty-four, clerk, resident in Bielsko before the war [and] currently in Tel Aviv.

On 1 September 1939, so on the first day of the war, panic was already noticeable in Bielsko. [People] started passing various rumors [from one to another] and [part of text missing] the rapid march of the German army. The result of this was that, that same day, the exodus of Bielsko's residents began. [By] Saturday, the town was almost deserted; one could still see the last refugees—including myself—heading east. We walked toward Kraków, the whole group. In every town we passed, the same story repeated. When we entered the town, there would be relative calm, which soon, however, turned into panic, [and] eventually our group would swell with a few tens of people from the town [in question].

In Skawina, we were subject to strict control by the military authorities. A map of Poland was found on my brother; he was arrested but was soon set free after an adequate explanation.

We didn't stay long in Kraków. The bombardment of the city, as well as a wave of rumors, drove us out. We headed for Kielce. The scenes [we] witnessed during that journey were fundamentally different from those we had left behind. There wasn't even anyone left to startle in the towns, as some of them were burned down to their foundations, while others were [still] burning like torches. Those burning signposts saved us in a way, because we avoided bombardments—for the simple reason that there was nothing left to bomb [there].

We didn't, however, get to Kielce. That's because a group of young scouts we came upon explained to us that Kielce was already in German hands, and that bloody fighting between Polish and Hitlerite units was taking place in the area. We turned off, then, toward Sandomierz. There was a guard posted before the bridge on the Wisła, warning [people] against crossing, because the bridge might be blown up any moment. Heedless of the danger, we set off across the bridge in a mad gallop. The [second] we stopped on the other side, an awful explosion told us that the bridge behind us was no more.

After eight more days of journeying, we reached Lublin. The city was in flames after a series of air raids. Entire streets lay in ruins. Corpses littered the pavements and roads. We ran farther away from those scenes.

Outside Chełm, we passed an improvised airfield while an air battle was taking place above it. We saw the Polish fighters shoot down two German airplanes, which plummeted down in front of our eyes like columns of fire. I managed to notice the white [dome] of a parachute, [then] quickly ran on away.

In Chełm, news reached us about the occupation of Kresy by the Red Army. We had been expecting Germans in town. The situation was odd there for a bit. The town was free of both occupiers; they clearly could not agree on its fate. After some time, however, a demarcation line was finally established, and the Russians entered the town. The residents organized, or rather improvised, a defense of Chełm. [They] defended themselves fiercely all night, and when the dominant Soviet forces pushed the defenders out of the main streets, they locked themselves in a church, continuing the defense. Finally, silence enveloped the town. The next day, an ostentatious funeral was held for two slain Soviet officers. Many soldiers died; it was difficult to find out [how many?].

Just two days later, however, the bodies of the killed Soviet officers were exhumed, which led the residents to believe that the Bolsheviks were retreating from town. The Russian authorities officially denied that rumor; however, just an hour after that repudiation, the Soviet retreat began. Afraid of the Germans, I too set off. Completely exhausted, on the road near Równe I met a Polish officer, already in civilian clothing, naturally, who took care of me and put me up [at his home] in Luboml. Thanks to the fact that my caregiver became a director at the Soviet Tax Office, I fared all right. I decided, however, to go to Lwów. The conditions [there] were generally bearable in the first days; however, they worsened with every day the occupation lasted. The issue of passportization came up, which was a decisive influence on the fate of refugees. The consequence of refusing to accept a passport was deportation to Siberia. And acceptance of a passport was normally combined with the addition of paragraph 11 [to it], which meant the inability to settle in the zone stretching one hundred kilometers around Lwów.[730]

730. This paragraph forbade living in the larger cities and their surroundings.

During my stay in Lwów, two [things] happened to me that illustrated the conditions at the time. When I was returning home one time, two Russian officers came up to me and dragged me forcibly to a nearby gate. There, at gunpoint, they demanded that I show them where I was hiding [my] gold. I got out of this dangerous situation by seemingly agreeing to identify the place. However, instead of taking them to my house, I aimed for the closest police station, where, by shouting, I lured out the NKVD agents, who seized the disoriented officers. Another time, an NKVD agent came up to me in the street, demanding a bribe. He took me to the nearest gate, where he set my price at four rubles. When he noticed that I only had two rubles in my wallet, he took them, setting me free.

A number of people managed to hide in connection with the deportations that were taking place. There was general confusion, as some claimed that the Russians were sending [people] back to Germany, and others already knew about the deportations to Ural, or to Siberia.

I hid for two weeks with a group of forty people. We lived in cellars and in attics during that time, not sleeping and not eating. After two weeks, we came out into the open air—and no one touched us. The Soviet authorities themselves proclaimed that whoever had been cunning enough and managed to hide during the purge, could later, after its conclusion, show themselves on the street in peace.

I was harbored for a long time, at night, by a Polish bookseller. He would lock me in the book depository at night, where I was quite safe, since it didn't occur to the Soviet authorities to carry out a search there.

At that time, the mutual relations between the Polish and the Jewish people were beyond reproach. [People] helped one another and came together in [their] misery. It was typical for the Zionist youth to still carry out Zionist activities despite the risk of severe punishment, and I myself was even present at an illegal commemoration in honor of Żabotyński.[731] When the Russians occupied Bessarabia and Bukovina, a group of refugees who had been hiding from deportation in Lwów for three months decided to get to Chernivtsi at all costs. The goal was twofold: to get in front of the German commission

731. Vladimir Yevgenyevich Zhabotinsky (Ze'ev Jabotinsky) [Polish: Włodzimierz (Zeew) Żabotyński] (1880–1940): Zionist activist, founder of the Revisionist movement in Zionism, [which was] considered right wing by the other strands of Zionism.

holding office in Chernivtsi at the time, or to get out of that town [and] carry on. Getting across the former Polish-Romanian border was not an easy undertaking. One had to lay in wait at night for a suitable opportunity to cross the Cheremosh. The consequences of falling into the hands of the border guard were worse than death.

When we successfully got to Chernivtsi, there were no signs of Soviet terror there yet. Generally speaking, people did not believe that mass deportations [would take place], and indeed, [deportations] were limited to political, even radical, leaders.

When we learned about the outbreak of the German-Russian war, we thought ourselves safe. After such a long period of gloomy days, the moment of the Soviet army's departure from town seemed most beautiful to us. Soon, however, we were to learn that even worse times lay ahead. In the period between the departure of the Soviet army from town and the entry of the German and Romanian troops, the mob ruled Chernivtsi bloodily. The first [act] of the German and Romanian armies after the[ir] entry was to carry out a search. Around five hundred people were taken away during it, [and] disappeared without a trace. Men were herded to carry out hard labor; it was known that work assigned outside town generally equaled death. Concentration camps were established, where [people] were locked up for the slightest indiscretion. There was no returning from them. During the period when the Romanians ruled the city by themselves, conditions were still bearable. However, when the units of the Stabspolizei[732] appeared—there was no regular German army in the city almost the entire time—the conditions became awful. A person could no longer keep themself safe with a baksheesh.[733]

Special badges were introduced for Jews, [as well as] curfews, a work ban, separate bread cards—in other words, the methods of the Gestapo were planted on Romanian soil. Even then, however, the Romanians found a way to help the Jews. This was because a decree came out [stating] that every company had the right, in the case of urgent need, to hire Jewish specialists. Very many people survived this way, and they even had the opportunity to make significant fortunes.

---

732. The author likely means the Gestapo or the Einsatzgruppen, special police units, intended primarily for the murder of Jews.

733. Bribe.

At one point, a rumor began to circulate more and more often that a Jewish ghetto would be established in Chernivtsi. This rumor eventually turned out to be true, and one Saturday, without any special order being issued, and with only a few hours' warning, all Jews were ordered to gather in one place, where they were locked up. Some of the Jewish population resisted at first, but [that resistance] was cruelly nipped in the bud.

In accordance with the German plan, the people locked in the ghetto were to be sent to Transdniestrja,[734] which equaled death. Indeed, two transports were sent in that direction; however, as a result of a fitting intervention, further deportations were halted. A registration of people according to their professions was carried out in the camp, and necessary specialists could get a so-called authorization, which protected [them] from deportation. In a short time, it [proved] possible to obtain authorization for around six thousand people. Naturally, money was the best authorization.

Eventually, after the intervention of Mayor Popowicz,[735] the ghetto was fully liquidated. He issued an authorization of his own accord, known as the Popowicz Authorization. For now, the regulations around wearing [arm]bands, curfews, [and] a separate allocation of bread and sugar for Jews remained in place. Jews worked in factories and companies, not in the worst conditions. Jews who were foreign citizens generally made use of the right to asylum—officially, none of them were deported; however, it did happen [once] that four hundred foreign citizens were found to be missing—as the Romanians said: deported by mistake. During the assembly of the transport in the Makkabi [football] pitch, they had their passports torn up, for example Polish ones, so that no [foreign] statehood could be proven.

Generally speaking, the attitude of the Romanians toward the Germans was negative. The intelligentsia in particular cursed the Hitlerites and did not hide their hatred in conversations with Jews. Until Stalingrad, the Romanians were afraid of their de facto occupiers; however, with Germany's defeats, they began to stand up to them more and more brazenly. I didn't see organized resistance anywhere.

---

734. Also known at the time as Transniestria [Transnistria]. See [Protocol 290].

735. Traian Popovici: mayor of Chernivtsi in the years 1941–42.

During my time, large amounts of food were sent away to Germany, [with noncompliance] punished severely. However, the harvest had been so abundant lately that [the effects of] those transports were not noticeable at all.

When the new governor, General [Cornel] Dragalina, took power, the situation began to improve. Curfews were abolished; it was possible to work and buy [things] freely. He even allowed Jews to take off their armbands, and ordered Jewish schools, previously closed, to be opened again.

When, with the outbreak of the German-Russian war, the front began moving closer to Chernivtsi fast, the issue of evacuation came up. This was because people were afraid of a transition period, which they had already experienced once.

In the meantime, a new wave of refugees arrived from Poland, and with them came the first real news about what was happening in the areas under Russian and German occupation. Messengers of the underground movement in Poland, Poles and Jews, turned up, making contact with the Romanian refugees. Poles from Chernivtsi responded to the Jewish tragedy with full understanding, helping however they could. A common Polish-Jewish kitchen was opened for legal and illegal refugees. A common committee was established, too, whose aim was to deal with the business of the refugees.

There were around 250 illegal Polish refugees in Chernivtsi at the time. The procedure applied to the capture of an illegal meant that an illegal Jew was sent to Poland, [and] a non-Jew legalized. The committee did a lot of good in this matter. Polish citizens were under the care of the consul of Chile at first, and then of Switzerland. Unfortunately, passports issued by them were not always recognized.

In December 1943, five illegal Polish refugees were sent to Bucharest, where [the process of] legalization was not as difficult as in Chernivtsi. However, as the result of a denunciation, they were arrested at the station in Bucharest, and following a proper interrogation, gave up the entire committee in Chernivtsi, including myself. Our activity in Chernivtsi consisted of sending the illegals to the Polish YMCA[736] in Bucharest, which, having the right contacts, sorted out the matter further.

---

736. YMCA: Young Men's Christian Association.

In one night, the whole committee in Chernivtsi was arrested, and therefore me as well. They tried, above all, to get out of us where our funds [came] from. We underwent elaborate tortures, were beaten and tormented, but did not reveal the secret. Two weeks later, we managed to get out of prison.

When the Soviet army was nearing the city, everyone pulled out all the stops to get farther away. A decree came out [stating] that all attempts to leave Chernivtsi would be punished with deportation to Transdniestrja—these threats were fruitless, however, [and] everyone saved themselves however they could.

I managed to get through to Bucharest in time through various routes. There I made contact with the Zionist authorities, who dealt with the matters of [the] remaining journey, and with the Polish YMCA, which dealt with the matters of legalization and financial aid. The rescue of many people from certain death can be credited to the YMCA's activity. The [people in charge of] the YMCA very often asked the applicants to give Aryan surnames, as this helped it with the legalization [process] with the Syguranza.[737]

Life in Bucharest in the initial period before the bombing was almost normal, except that the city was crowded with refugees from all of Romania. Large sums were paid for the opportunity to get to Bucharest; the irony of the war meant that just a few weeks later, huge sums were being paid for the opportunity to get out of that bombarded hell.

The first bombardment came. It lasted nearly fifteen minutes and claimed around ten thousand casualties, just those killed. During the first three days after the bombardment, there was no electricity [or] water in the city; the trams and train did not run.

The second bombardment, which happened ten days later, did not claim as many victims, because people took cover in air raid shelters. Because of the bombardment[s], a state of affairs became established where every day at eleven, before midday—so at the time of an expected air raid—all shops would be closed, [and] people would run home quickly to get into the shelters in time. In front of the Banca Nationala, where the best shelter in town was located, at eight in the morning one could already see hundreds of people waiting for the moment of the alarm.

737. Syguranza [Romanian: Siguranța]: Romanian security service.

During the first air raids, the Jewish neighborhoods survived. The Romanians explained this [by claiming] that the Allied pilots spared the Jewish people. At that point, the Germans moved their offices to the area of Vacaresti (a Jewish district) [and], a few days later, the entire Jewish neighborhood was bombed flat.

The Romanians complained loudly that the Germans had brought misfortune upon them, and had grown to hate them intensely, especially in the past year. It was spoken about completely openly at the end of 1943 that the Germans had lost the war.

After a few weeks' stay in Bucharest, I managed to get on a ship going to Turkey.

Protocol 310

Drawn up on the basis of the testimony of **Mojżesz Spieler**, graduate of the Faculty of Chemistry of the Jagiellonian University in Kraków, age thirty-four, currently resident in Tel Aviv.

I was marching through the forest. One day I came upon a group of Poles camped [there] who warned me against further travel, because the Russians had already killed two of them.[738] As a result, I returned to Chernivtsi. Soviet rule was already in full force there. Larger companies and factories were nationalized, apartments requisitioned, private shops closed down. I already knew, from experience, the outcome of all this—black market[739] and lack of food. Only those who could prove that their parents could not have been bourgeoisie were allowed into the university. I got a job—everyone got work and there were no real unemployed—in a Landesspital,[740] as a chemist. The work would have been fairly nice were it not for the fact that every two weeks a new manager was sent from Kiev or Moscow, who would normally turn the old order upside down. I got a kind of a Nansen passport[741] in Chernivtsi. At the time, the Soviet authorities decided to issue so-called *widnażytielstwo* [*sic*] for the *bezgran*,[742] for people who didn't want to accept Soviet citizenship but who came from areas not occupied by Russia. One day, all of a sudden, a thousand agents came to the city from Russia and they began to purge the city of the bourgeoisie and political leaders, sending them to Siberia. This did not apply to the average citizen. One day, explosions rang out. The next day we learned that the Germans had bombed the airport and declared war against Russia. Immediately, too, the Russians started evacuating the town. They would induct the locals into [their] military ranks by sheer force on the way. Before leaving town, the Russians set it on fire. The entire Postgasse burned, and it was not permitted to save anything or to put out the fires—the patrols would shoot then.

738. The Red Army occupied Northern Bukovina in June 1940.

739. See footnote in Protocol 288.

740. *Landesspital*: district hospital. Chernivtsi belonged to Austria-Hungary until World War I and the German language was still widely used there.

741. Passport of a stateless person.

742. *Wid na żytielstwo/vidnazhitelstvo*: residence permit. The term *bezgran* should be understood as an abbreviation from the Russian *bez grazhdanstva* [Polish transliteration: *bez grażdanstwa*] (those without confirmed citizenship).

Protocol 311

Drawn up on the basis of the testimony of **Debora Szulwerk**, from Katowice, who came to Palestine from Tehran.

I escaped from Katowice with [my] husband and child on the first day of the war. We were the owners of a manufacture warehouse. Eight days before the war, the German civilians had already become emboldened and were behaving impudently toward the local people. Some of our German employees, too, behaved insolently toward us. I had a foretaste of what awaited us should the Germans occupy the city. We took what we could and left the rest of [our] belongings to the will of God. My husband managed to [convince] his Polish friend, a doctor, to take him by car. We set off on the way. The Germans bombed us, flying low over our heads and shooting from machine guns. We drove until the gas ran out. We left the car and set off to Złoczów on foot. I was so sick and devastated that I could not move [any] further, even though the goal of our journey was the Romanian border, where—we knew—all the officials and the entire Polish intelligentsia were rushing. I was ill for two weeks in Złoczów, and before I recovered, the Russians occupied the town. We lived in Złoczów for three months and watched the Russian state of affairs. [My] husband didn't want to accept Soviet citizenship, afraid that he would lose contact with the outside world this way. We hid in a field for two weeks, afraid to spend the night at home. [My] husband got pneumonia from sleeping out in the open and had to return to town.

In Exile

When, after two weeks, I lay down in a bed for the first time, NKVD-ers knocked on our doors and told us to get dressed. My [protests] that [my] husband was gravely ill were in vain. He was carried out on [their] shoulders and taken to the station. It was terribly stuffy inside the car, cramped and dirty. Dangerously ill, [my husband] couldn't even lie down on the floor, and naturally, didn't receive any medical assistance. Despite this, he recovered, and when the car was opened after six weeks' journey, my husband got out of it by himself. It was at the station of Ufa, in the Yakutsk Oblast.[743] We were loaded into trucks and taken to

743. Ufa is located in the Bashkir ASSR. Yakutsk had no rail connections. The author of the testimony has confused geographical names [here]. [This] likely refers to the town of Uk in the Irkutsk Oblast [Uk has not been located].

a *posiołek*, to Nirendza.[744] The *posiołek* was located in a deep forest. We were accommodated in barracks; there were barracks with Russian exiles nearby. The *posiołek*'s commandant was an exile. We worked in the forest for twelve hours a day. No one could fulfill their quota, and that is why no one received more than four hundred grams of bread and one ruble per day. Soups were served in the canteen, but it was rare that anyone could afford them. In that region, the summer lasts two months, and the winter is long and hard. We suffered from various insects as well, bedbugs in particular. At night, the mice wouldn't leave us in peace. The commandant was an antisemite and didn't allow us to go beyond the perimeter of the *posiołek*. Because of this, we were deprived of the opportunity to sell our belongings, which had to be sold through the commandant. The freezing temperatures prevented the spread of epidemics, but we suffered with *cynga*, a horrific disease which meant that various body parts would fall off.

War and Amnesty

The outbreak of the Russian-German war worsened our situation considerably. Our bread rations were lowered, and the regime became stricter. We had already accepted [that] our lives were over, when the news of the Amnesty came. We set off toward Tashkent. The horrendous journey took two months. Lice-ridden, dirty, and sick, we arrived at the destination, but the NKVD didn't want to register us for residence and we had to roam the streets, sleeping in an Uzbek teahouse. The attitude of the Uzbeks toward Jews was hostile. They were true antisemites, who persecuted us. We introduced ourselves as Aryans. At that time, a Polish delegation was opened in Tashkent, thanks to whose assistance many people were saved from death from starvation. Realizing that the chances of getting an apartment in Tashkent were slim, we set off for Samarkand. The situation was no better there. After weeks of roaming around, my husband fell ill with typhus. There was no space in the hospital; he wasn't admitted until the eighth day. It was too late by then. He died the day after being admitted to the hospital. I couldn't even afford to bury him in a funeral robe. I was left alone with [my] small daughter and was literally dying from hunger. I made efforts to be put on the list for military families. I succeeded thanks to my connections. We were sent to Kermine, and from there, via Krasnovodsk and Pahlevi, I came to Tehran.

744. The *posiołek* was probably called Nirezna, in the Irkutsk region.

Protocol 312

Testimony of **Abraham Lewenstein** from Warsaw, age twenty-eight, came to Palestine via Russia and Persia.

I am an electromechanic by trade, and two months before the war, I accepted a job on a construction project. On 1 September [1939], I went out to work, like [all the] others, unaware that war had broken out. The first bombardments caused a frenzied panic in the city. People ran around like mad, everyone was looking [to stock up on products], and work—naturally—was halted.

On 7 September, when there was a call over the radio for young men to leave the capital, carried away with the current, I found myself—along with others—in a crowd of people in Praga, and then outside the city. We survived a few heavy bombings along the way. Not until the third day did we find ourselves in Siedlce, but the city was already in ruins. The bombardment was still going on. I was wounded in the leg.

Journeying onward was out of the question. I spent three weeks in a tent outside the city. During that time, the Germans occupied the city [and] began the persecutions of Jews. Many [Jews] they rounded up in the streets were sent away to camps, from which they never returned again. But the Germans soon left the city, which was taken over by the Russians.

According to the new border, however, Siedlce belonged to Germany. Many Jews were leaving town with the departing Bolsheviks. I, too, found myself among them. I got to Białystok. The city was full of refugees; it was impossible to find a place for the night for any price. I threw myself into a search for a job in my trade, but to no avail. Realizing that I might die from hunger, I registered for voluntary work, to leave for Russia.

After registration, we were told to report to the station, were seen off with music and speeches, fed and watered, and loaded into freight cars. We thought we were going to paradise.

At all the stations, we were welcomed with banners, white bread rolls, and tea. This is how we reached Homel. There, again, a parade with music, and speeches, as well as food, were organized in our honor. We were accommodated in a local workers' home. The next day, we were taken to work. We had been told during the paperwork that everyone would work in their trade. Despite this, we were taken outside of the city, put up in tents, and told to carry out the hardest [possible] unskilled work, like carrying loads [and] loading trucks and railcars. We thought that this was only temporary work; however, after two weeks, it turned out that nothing was changing. The work became increasingly harder; we were collapsing from exhaustion. Our supervisors, at first incredibly polite, became strict and demanding. We were shouted at, threatened with accusations of sabotage, called names [such as] "Polish lords." I am physically weak, [and] I felt I would not be able to stand this work for long. Without thinking too long, I escaped to Homel, and heedless of the danger that loomed in traveling by train without permission, returned to Białystok. Luckily for me, there was no document check during the journey. I started looking for work again in Białystok. I hid around [friends'] apartments, afraid that I would be arrested. Finally, I found a small corner for myself in the synagogue and settled there, along with other refugees.

I took up trading. I earned all right and thought I would settle down somehow. After some time, a registration began of refugees who were interested in returning to the lands under German occupation. I didn't register, afraid of any contact with the authorities, and for [that same] reason, did not want to report to [get] a Soviet passport.

One night, in April 1940, NKVD-ers surrounded the synagogue, told the refugees to gather their belongings, and we were taken to a prison in Białystok. In a cell intended for eight people, sixty were placed. We were called for an interrogation every night. One day, everyone was taken to the station and sent to Siberia inside freight cars. We traveled for four weeks in horrific conditions, starving on the way, dying of thirst. The train stopped at some forest station, and when we got off, we were told that we were in the Arkhangelsk district. We were chased on ahead, on foot. After many hours' exhausting journey, we found ourselves in a deep primeval forest, in the labor camp number 30.

A few barracks stood there. The camp was surrounded with barbed wire. Our group was made up of six hundred men and eighty-six women. We lived separately. The next day after arriving in the camp, we were taken to work.

We were told to cut down trees [and] load them onto wagons. The women worked cutting off branches. There was a camp for Russian exiles nearby. They were, for the most part, political exiles, involved in the affairs of the year 1937. They told us during work that their sentences amounted to between eight and fifteen years of exile. They were very bitter. They talked about their abandoned families with longing. They envied us our past and "comforted" us [by saying] that we would never get out of there.

The mortality in our camp grew by the day. There was a funeral almost every day. Young women died particularly often, unable to deal with the climate, the work conditions, and the hunger. Out of the eighty-six women, soon [only] thirty-six were left. Out of the 600 men, 150 perished.

We were cut off from the world. We found out about the Amnesty a month later than everyone. We set off toward the rail station on foot, spent a few days at the station, out in the open, until we got on a train that was to take us to Tashkent.

We roamed the streets of Tashkent for entire months, without a roof over our heads and without work. I fell ill with typhus. When I got out of the hospital in one piece six weeks later, I reported to the military commission and was classified as category C. With assistance, however, I got into a railcar traveling toward the Caspian Sea. From Pahlevi, I got to Tehran in the same way. After a year's stay in Tehran, I came to Palestine.

Protocol 315

Testimony of **Szmul Cackiewicz**, from Chełm, who came to Palestine via Russia and Tehran.

Our town was bombed in the first days of the war. German airplanes bombed military sites and barracks, and the destruction was so horrendous that the authorities ordered the evacuation of women and children. There were only men left in town, who were mobilized to put out the fire[s]. The bombardment lasted two weeks; we didn't understand what it meant. Suddenly, three days later, Russian tanks appeared. The Polish army was convinced that the Bolsheviks were arriving to help. Meanwhile, the Russians were taking Poles prisoner. The Russians did not stay long in our town. After eight days, a notice was issued that the Bolsheviks were leaving town, and [that] anyone who wanted to could go with them. A small number of people joined them; most of the residents stayed in Chełm.

The Germans occupied Chełm two days later. Things were very peaceful at first. Only the Ukrainians became emboldened and started taking revenge on Jews and Poles. A vigilante force prevented riots, [and] only when the Gestapo arrived did anti-Jewish laws and roundups in the streets begin. Jewish property was stolen from homes and shops, Jews were kicked out on the street, and the Ukrainians denounced [them] any way they could. One day, all the Jews were ordered to gather in the main square and were chased toward the Soviet border. Along the way, those who didn't run fast enough were shot at. Around six thousand Jews were killed that day in the cruelest way.

I found myself among the exiles and got to Kowel. The city was full of refugees; long lines stood in front of shops [selling] bread. Mass arrests were taking place. Officials, social activists, policemen, and their wives were arrested. They were taken to prison and then deported. I looked for a place to sleep. I finally found it outside the city. I am a boot maker by trade. After long efforts, I got a job in a workshop that still had leather supplies. I earned so little that I was never full. The Bolsheviks persecuted independent workers, and my foreman didn't want to join a cooperative where one had to give up [one's] machines, which became the property of the cooperative. He eventually sold his workshop and thus I was left jobless. I could not join a cooperative without a machine. I took up trading. Then, the registrations and passportizations began. I didn't want to accept Soviet citizenship, and I hid outside the city. I was so weakened from this roaming around that, dejected, I returned to [my] apartment.

In Exile

One night, at the end of June 1940, NKVD-ers turned up at my apartment, told [me] to pack [my] things, and took me to an assembly point—to the synagogue, where we were kept prisoner for eight days, without food or drink, and then loaded onto a train, sixty people in each car, and set off on the way. Before the train set off, NKVD agents carried out body searches on the deportees, taking away all of their documents and valuables. We tried to resist but it was in vain. After two weeks' journey in horrific conditions, we arrived in the Komi ASSR. We were split into two groups. One group, which I was in, was sent to the White Sea. We went on foot through swamps; our legs swelled; we dragged ourselves like this for a few days until we reached a place a few kilometers from Ukhta, in a deep forest. There were around a thousand of us. We built huts for ourselves and settled [in them]. During rainfall, the huts were half-submerged in water. We cut down trees, never able to reach the work quota or the bread quota. We were threatened with the punishment cell and jail. Later we were sent to build roads. The ground was frozen, and it was difficult to work. Our hands and feet were freezing; there was a frost even in April. There was no doctor or even a bandage to tie around the frostbitten limbs. We wore rubber footwear, which we'd often take off with pieces of [our] body [attached to it].

War and Amnesty

After the outbreak of the [German-Soviet] war, the number of working hours was increased, and so much was demanded from us that we didn't think we would make it. We soon learned about the Amnesty. We set off for Kotlas [and] from there to Tacko,[745] which we reached after weeks of an immensely

745. An incorrect name of the town of Totskoye [original Polish correction: Tockoje].

taxing journey, during which we suffered a great deal from hunger and diseases. There was a Polish army commission in Tacko, where they didn't want to accept me into the army due to my poor health. I didn't want to go to a kolkhoz as I knew I would not last long there. I decided to get onto a transport traveling to Krasnovodsk. I waited for a few weeks there until I managed to get on a ship going to Pahlevi. Sick, I arrived in Tehran and spent four months in the hospital. Later, I received a certificate and came to Palestine.

Protocol 316

Testimony of **Jakub Medrowskie [Mendrowski?]**, from Kraków, who came to Palestine in October 1942.

We did not believe, in the beginning of the war, that the city would surrender so easily. During the first bombardment, which was thought to be an air raid drill, a few tens of people were killed, and panic broke out in the city. On 3 September [1939], it became clear that the enemy was near. People left [their] homes and ran. Everyone spilled out into the streets. A human current carried me off. After a few days' journeying, I got to Lwów. Lwów was under siege by the Germans. Along with a few refugees, we pushed through into the city. The Polish army was defending itself heroically on the streets of Lwów. The fighting lasted until 22 September [1939], when the Russians arrived. There were no official battles between Russians and Poles. The Russians took away the Poles' weapons. There were many cases of suicide among the officers, who preferred to die rather than be taken into captivity. No one went out into the streets. It was forbidden to come close to the windows. The Bolsheviks were afraid that [people] would shoot at them from [their] windows. This order didn't help much, because on some streets, like Karmelicka, Wyspiański, and Legiony, people were indeed shooting at the army and tossing bottles [filled] with gasoline at the Russian tanks. The Russians carried out searches of homes and killed the suspects. The army [marched on] through the city for a few days. The Russians introduced their rules. [They] started to nationalize homes, shops, [and] factories, threw out the former owners of town houses or apartments. During the mass arrests, former social activists, officials, writers, and officers were hunted particularly zealously. Dr. Sommerstein and Rabbi Schorr, who hid from the Bolsheviks in Lwów, were arrested.

Elections

Then came the time of the registration and the elections, which were called a plebiscite. As is known, the elections had nothing to do with democratic elections. The city was divided into districts, and in each district, five homes made up a unit which was under the care of a commissar. Everyone over eighteen voted, including refugees. On the day of the elections, the commissar checked whether everyone had made their way to the ballot box, and since abstaining [from voting] was punishable, [it's] no wonder that 100 percent of people voted. There were neither Jews nor Poles on the electoral list, only Ukrainians and Russians. After the elections, the passportization order was issued. I was a philosophy student. I interrupted [my] studies because of the war and was not able to continue them at the Lwów university, as they didn't want to accept me there as the son of a bourgeois. I attended mechanics courses, but was kicked out of [those] too because I didn't want to accept Soviet citizenship.

First Deportations

The first mass deportations took place in February 1940, when the NKVD surrounded the whole neighborhood, arresting the former capitalists, wives of officers, political activists, lawyers, etc. Around twenty thousand people were arrested and deported then. Among them were holders of foreign passports. After those arrests, it was said that all refugees would be deported. I looked for a way to escape from Lwów. People were registering to return to the German-occupied territories, to which only one transport left. One night I was arrested. We were taken to [army] barracks, where we stayed for a few weeks in awful conditions, without food. At night, we would be taken for interrogation and tortured until the morning. A few weeks later, we were sent to Siberia. We traveled for four weeks. Many people fainted from hunger. Two passengers died from exhaustion. Finally, we got off at the station of Fari-Bari [?]. After five days spent out in the open, we were loaded onto a ship and sent to Parsek [?], in the Yaroslavl Oblast.[746] Another twenty kilometers' journey on foot later, we found ourselves in a labor camp surrounded with barbed wire on four sides, and lit up by floodlights at night, so no one could escape. We were led to work under convoy. We worked for ten hours a day, but none of us were able to fulfill [our] quota. We couldn't stand up straight. The mortality grew in a terrifying manner. Between fifty and sixty people died every month. It got to a point where the NKVD ordered the regime to be relaxed. This didn't help much. None of us would have survived if the Amnesty hadn't saved us. We all

746. The place-names listed by the witness are illogical and difficult to identify.

set off toward Samarkand. We traveled by train for many weeks, hungry, sick, and lice ridden. Things were not better in Samarkand. People were dying in the streets from hunger and from typhus. The NKVD was [trying to] banish us to a kolkhoz, where the situation was even worse. I tried to get out of Russia. I met a few friends from the student council, now officers in the Polish army, who, seeing my sorry state, took pity on me and [managed to] have me added to the list for military families. This is how I got to Tehran, [and] from there, after going through a serious lung illness and many months in the hospital, I came to Palestine.

Protocol 326

Testimony of **L. B.** from Lwów, who escaped to Hungary in August 1943.

Lwów was bombed for three weeks[747] at the beginning of the war. On 17 September [1939], the first Soviet airplanes appeared, dropping leaflets [that said that] Galicia had always belonged to Ukraine, and the moment of its liberation from the hands of the lords and the bourgeoisie was coming. The Polish police force left the city, and power was assumed by a citizens' militia. They soon transferred it into Bolshevik hands. The Soviet army pounced on the shops and started emptying them. The Bolsheviks began the nationalization of homes and mass arrests. [They] disbanded Jewish councils and all organizations. The official line was that they had nothing against religion; in reality [however], synagogues were closed down and turned into apartments for refugees. The allocation of work began. The bourgeoisie, Zionists, [and] Bund members did not get [any]. Workers received work cards, which were later exchanged for Soviet passports. It was not allowed to live in Lwów without a work card. There were 150,000 Jews living in Lwów at the time. In June 1940, a registration began to return home, and more than half the refugees stated [their] readiness to return to the German-occupied territories. They were later sent to Siberia. The elections to the Ukrainian Soviet took place with great fanfare. People were forced to vote. The sick had the ballot boxes brought to their homes. Failing to vote was punishable by sanctions. I had been a law student until the outbreak of the war. After entering Lwów, the Bolsheviks established a lawyers' cooperative, to which twenty lawyers belonged. There was a lot of work, because even the slightest offense was punishable by many years in prison. Once we defended a group of young Revisionists[748] who were sentenced to eight years in prison for carrying out illegal political activity. One of them died in the Lwów prison.

747. The bombardment lasted around two weeks.

748. See the glossary: Revisionist Zionists.

War Outbreak

On 22 June 1941, at two at night, the city was shaken by the news of the outbreak of a Russian-German war, which was no less of a surprise for the Russians than for us. A few thousand Jews left the city with the army; others thought that the Germans would not do anything bad. Lwów was bombed heavily; the Russians blew up a number of buildings; the Ukrainians helped to expel the Russians. It's difficult to [describe] the joy of the Ukrainians, who simply danced in the streets, dreaming about the coming pogrom.

Protocol[749]

Chaim Besser, born in 1927 in Łuków, Lublin voivodship. Father: Izchak, mother: Miriam, brothers: Lejb, Szlojme, and Aron, sisters: Chaja and Itte. Father owned a shoe shop in Łuków.

On a Friday morning, German planes bombed the Łuków rail station. Many people died. A few days later, the Jewish district was bombed as well.

After a week of war, I left with my family for the town of Stoczek, where we stayed for six days. When we heard gunshots, we hid inside apartments. We thought that fighting between the Poles and the Germans was taking place nearby. Soon, the Germans arrived in town, and shooting at the homes, shouted: "*Juden heraus*!" We went out into the street [and] lined up. A few Jews were shot. We were told to gather the most essential things and go outside of town.

The town was burned down after we left. We spent all night in a barn and returned to Łuków in the morning. The Germans took us from Łuków to Mińsk Mazowiecki; two weeks.

When we heard that the Muscovites were coming to Łuków, we returned. The Soviet army arrived a few days later. When the Russians left Łuków after another six days, we went, with [my] father and brothers, to Brześć. In Brześć, we were asked if we wanted to go to work in Russia. We agreed. We left for the town of Tołoczno in the Vitebsk Oblast, where we worked in a shoe factory for six months. We couldn't make ends meet there so we returned to Baranowicze. In Baranowicze there operated a German commission. We registered to return home.

After two months, one Friday night, we were woken up, a search was carried out, [then] we were driven out of town and loaded into dark train cars. We traveled like cattle for five days. [We] weren't given food. The train only stopped in Sverdlovsk. We were given bread and tea. From Sverdlovsk, we

749. This is the only protocol that has been preserved as a manuscript. The unnumbered protocol at the beginning of the testimonies is a slightly redacted version translated from the typescript. For additional information on the transcription and translation of the protocol, see the introduction to this volume by Maciej Siekierski.

traveled to Tavda on the same train. And from Tavda, by river, it took five days to the Tos camp, Sverdlovsk Oblast, Taberinskij district.

We stayed in barracks, fifty families to one, for two days, and were then taken to work. Father went to the forest and received four rubles after eight days. One of my brothers mowed hay fields for pennies. [Anyone] who asked how we were to make ends meet was arrested. In the winter, we worked in the forest in temperatures of −50°C [−58°F]. Anyone who had anything sold it to survive. The answer to our complaints was: "Work." One [of the people] who worked with me died. We cried at assemblies and the commandant shouted: "You're staying here forever. Forget about Warsaw."

After fourteen months a commission arrived, we were given Polish passports and released. We had no money for travel and walked the three hundred kilometers to Tavda on foot. In Tavda, we registered with the authorities and went to the city of Turkestan. Work began again in Stalin's kolkhoz. We worked all day for three hundred grams of black flour between five people.

My brothers: Szlojme, age twenty, and Aron, age eighteen, lay ill at home for five days. Then the hospital took them away. One of them died on the way to the hospital, the other one passed, too, in the hospital. I was left in the kolkhoz with one more brother and our father. We knew we would die. And we went back to Turkestan and carried bricks in a brickyard. We earned two rubles and three hundred grams of bread per day.

I was then taken to a Polish orphanage where they gave me food and clothes. After two weeks, I was taken along with the others to Ashgabat. I stayed in a Polish children's home for four weeks.

And then we left for Iran with the Polish army.

Chaim Besser

Appendix

London, 10 November 1942

MINISTRY OF FOREIGN AFFAIRS

The Ministry of Foreign Affairs sends in attachment for the embassy's information and potential use a copy of the memorandum by Professor Sukiennicki on the subject of "The Issue of Jews, Polish Citizens" in Soviet Russia.

* * *

Embassy of the Republic of Poland in Moscow

THE ISSUE OF JEWS, POLISH CITIZENS

in light of official documentation and the practices of the Soviet authorities

Position in Principle of the Polish Authorities

The Polish authorities in the USSR, in accordance with the constitutional principles of the Republic of Poland, have not and do not differentiate between Polish citizens (from the date of 1 September 1939), regardless of their nationality, faith, or race. This position appeared to have been held by the USSR authorities also, at least in the initial period after the establishment of relations in August 1941. Among the Polish citizens released from prisons and camps on the basis of the Decree of the Supreme Soviet from 12 August 1941, there was a sizable number of Jews and other non-Polish nationalities. They were treated equally with Poles and considered Polish citizens at the time, clear proof of which is a note of the NKID[1] No. 13 from 23 September 1941, in which the NKID, [in a report] about the release of ten [persons] (from among a hundred and a few tens people, whose release was requested in the first instance by the embassy), listed among them Wiktor Alter and Henryk Erlich[2] as Polish citizens.

Jews in the PSZ in the USSR

A large number of [those] released from prisons and camps made their way directly to the ranks of the Polish Armed Forces being mobilized in the USSR. Among them there were also many Jews. On 8 October 1941, representatives of the Revisionist Zionists turned to the commander of the PSZ[3] in the USSR with a petition for the creation within the PSZ of a separate legion made up of Jews. This petition brought about serious objections from other Jewish groups, and General Anders, after meeting with the representatives of the Jewish population (Bund and Zionists) on 24 October 1941, rejected the proposal to create a separate Jewish region, taking the position that Jews, like all the other Polish citizens, would carry out military duty on an equal footing within a uniform Polish army. At the aforementioned meeting, General Anders announced a fight against all signs of antisemitism in the army, and on 14 November 1941, issued a special order in which, aiming to "clearly specify the unified and unambiguous attitude [to be] assumed by my subordinate commanders and [by] the Polish soldiers on the Jewish issue in our army" and

1. Narodnyi Komissariat Innostrannykh Del, NKID [Polish: Ludowy Komisariat (Ministerstwo) Spraw Zagranicznych; LKSZ]: The People's Commissariat of Foreign Affairs.

2. Henryk Erlich (1882–1942): lawyer from Lublin, from 1903 an activist of the Jewish Labor Bund, member of its leadership, participant in the Russian February Revolution in 1917. After the October Revolution, he protested against the abolishment of the Provisional Government [of the Republic of Poland] by the Bolsheviks. From 1918, active in Warsaw; 1919–39, one of the leaders of Bund in Poland. From September 1939, he was imprisoned by the Soviet authorities, and later released as a result of the Amnesty for Polish citizens. In December 1941, he was arrested again, along with Wiktor Alter (see also footnote in Protocol 45), and with him, sentenced to death by Stalin. In May 1942, according to the official line, he committed suicide in prison.

3. Polskie Siły Zbrojne, PSZ: Polish Armed Forces; PAF.

"to put an end to all malicious insinuations and rumors conceived behind our backs about the alleged antisemitism in the army, likely coming from sources that are hostile to us," he categorically stated:

1. That Jews, Polish citizens, had the same rights and duties to serve in the Polish army as other Republic citizens.
2. They are to be treated equally with others in the army, genuinely and cordially, and given the same trust as other soldiers of the PSZ.
3. To avoid any misunderstandings, he clarified that during the current stage of recruitment for the PSZ in the USSR, Jews are subject to the same restrictions in being accepted for active duty as Poles, that is, an immediate draft applies to: officers, professional NCOs, privates on active duty, and volunteers who had undergone training in the Polish army and been accepted by the draft committee. All others are sent to the southern republics of the USSR, where their registration will take place as an additional reserve for enlistment. I announce the above so that the commanders have a background to dispel the rumors being spread by the enemies, [claiming] that Jews who wish to join the Polish army have obstacles created for them.
4. I order all my subordinate commanders to categorically fight against all signs of racial antisemitism and not to allow any violations in this matter. It should be explained clearly and explicitly to the subordinates that Poland has always stood on democratic and tolerant foundations and that it will not leave this path now. Any infractions against a Polish citizen—a Jew—only because he is a Jew, are unacceptable. We will apply the same laws to a Jew in the army as to a Pole.

Difficulties Made by the Soviet Authorities in the Joining of the PSZ in the USSR by Jews

While the Polish authorities held the position of the full equality of Jews, Polish citizens, in the Polish army, the Soviet authorities began to cause all manner of difficulties for non-Pole Polish citizens wishing to enter the ranks of the PSZ in the USSR. Due to the information coming in about this matter, on

10 November 1941 the embassy issued note No. D-740/41 to the NKID, in which it announced, among other things:

> According to the information received, the war commissar of Kazakhstan, General Shcherbakov,[4] issued an order in Alma-Ata for all Polish citizens displaced by the Soviet authorities from the occupied lands of the Republic who had Ukrainian, Belarusian [or] Jewish nationality marked in the documents issued by [the Soviet] authorities, to be sent to the Red Army, as long as they fulfilled the age and health criteria. In response to an intervention by the people concerned and the embassy social welfare representative (*homme de confiance*), General Shcherbakov stated that he acted on the basis of instructions from the central authorities, who were to have ordered that all Republic of Poland citizens of a non-Polish nationality who held Soviet passports be treated like USSR citizens. . . . [5] That same segregation of Polish citizens according to their nationality or race, based on no objective premise and contradictory to the Polish-Soviet agreement from 30 July 1941, is used by the military authorities in Alma-Ata who, also in this case, hide behind the instructions of the central bodies as regards Polish citizens who report [to them] in order to take care of the formalities associated with joining the Polish army in the USSR. Only Polish citizens of Polish nationality receive permission to pass through to the place of formation of the Polish military units, while Ukrainians and Jews [who are] Polish citizens are allegedly met with a categorical refusal on the part of the aforementioned authorities. In the conclusion of this note, the embassy requested from the NKID the "unprejudiced application" to all Polish citizens of the rules resultant from the agreement of 30 July 1941, as well as the military agreement from 14 August 1941, and "consisting of guaranteeing each Polish citizen capable of carrying arms the right to serve in the Polish army in the USSR."

---

4. Aleksandr Shcherbakov [Polish: Aleksander Szczerbakow] (1901–1945): Soviet politician and general. In 1938–45, First Secretary of the Moscow Committee of the All-Union Communist Party (Bolsheviks); in 1941–45, Secretary and Deputy to the Member of the Politburo of the Central Committee of that same party. In 1942–45, Deputy to the People's Commissar for Defense and Chief of the Main Political Administration of the Red Army.

5. As in the text. Here and henceforth where an ellipsis is used, the author of the memorandum omits fragments of the Soviet documents not relevant to his edit.

The Soviet Argument on the Issue of Restricting the Right to Polish Citizenship Exclusively to Poles

The above note brought about a statement on the part of the NKID on the issue of conditioning Polish citizenship on the nationality of individuals. During the talks in the first days of September 1941, as well as on 14 October 1941, representatives of the NKID already stressed, when quoting the number of Polish citizens released from captivity on the basis of the decree from 12 August 1941, that that number did not include "former Polish citizens who, pursuant to the Soviet decree of 1 October 1939, attained Soviet citizenship," however, they did not clarify their position further. In response to the embassy's note from 10 November 1941, meanwhile, the NKID reported the following in a note from 1 December 1941: "The Embassy of the Republic of Poland, in reference to the facts of the mobilization in the Kazakh SSR to the Red Army, as Soviet citizens, the citizens of Ukrainian, [Belarusian], and Jewish nationalities who had left the oblasts of the Western Ukraine and Western [Belarusia], questions the validity of this order, being of the mind that it is contradictory to the rules of the Soviet-Polish military agreement from 14 August 1941. The People's Commissariat cannot concur in this point of view of the Embassy of the Republic of Poland. Neither the agreement of 30 July, nor the agreement of 14 August 1941 gives a basis for putting forward the point of view laid out in the aide-mémoire of the Embassy of the Republic of Poland. In accordance with the Decree of the Presidium of the Supreme Soviet of the USSR from 29 November 1939, all the residents of the western oblasts of the Ukrainian and [Belarusian] SSR who were present in the territories of said oblasts on [the days of] 1–2 November 1939, attained, according to the law "of citizenship of the Union of Soviet Socialist Republics" from 19 August 1938, USSR citizenship. The readiness of the Soviet government to consider as Polish citizens the persons of Polish nationality who lived on [the days of] 1–2 November 1939 in the aforementioned territories testifies to the goodwill and obligingness of the Soviet government, but can in no way form the basis of a corresponding recognition as Polish citizens of persons of a different nationality, in particular the Ukrainian, [Belarusian], and Jewish ones, since the issue of borders between the USSR and Poland is not settled and is subject to consideration in the future."

The position of the Soviet government was rejected by the Embassy of the Republic of Poland with note Dz.D-902/41 from 9 December 1941. In this note, the embassy stressed, among other things, that "1) Polish legislation is built on the basis of equality before the law of all citizens irrespective of their nationality or race. Neither are there provisions in Soviet law known to the Embassy of the Republic of Poland which would introduce or sanction this kind of discrimination or differentiation. The agreement of 30 July 1941 and the military agreement of 14 August 1941 do not introduce the concept of nationality or race in any of their resolutions related to Polish citizens (the Amnesty, army duty), [and] therefore, apply to all Polish citizens. As it stands, the Embassy sees no possibility of changing its position expressed in note D-740/41 from 10 November 1941. . . . 2) the fact of the possession by a given person of Polish citizenship is regulated by Polish law, in particular the legislation from 20 January 1920 regarding the citizenship of the Polish state. Due to this, and because of the reasons stated above in point 1), the Embassy has the honor of announcing that it does not see a possibility of accepting the statement included in the NKID note from 1 December 1941, that the Soviet government is willing to consider as Polish citizens, from among the persons resident between 1–2 November 1939 in the territory of the Republic of Poland temporarily under military occupation by the Soviet Union, only persons of the Polish nationality."

The above arguments did not convince the Soviet government who, in note No. 2 from 5 January 1942, announced that "the People's Commissariat, after familiarizing itself with the point of view on the issue of former Polish citizens from among the residents of Western Ukraine and Western Belarusia—Ukrainians, Belarusians, and Jews—presented in the Embassy's note from 9 December 1941, sees no reason to change its position laid out in the note from 1 December 1941." . . .

The fundamental difference of opinion between the Polish and Soviet authorities as regards the issue of citizenship of the persons resident in the territories of the Republic occupied by the Red Army in September 1939 came to light many a time in the course of many talks; however, so far a common position could not be established in this matter. The Soviet authorities, exploiting the factual situation, imposed their point of view despite the categorical objection and resistance on the part of the Polish authorities.

The Case of Erlich and Alter

A few days after the NKID note from 1 December 1941, there took place an arrest by an NKVD apparatus of Henryk Ehrlich [Erlich] and Wiktor Alter, whose release, as Polish citizens, was announced to the embassy by the NKID with note No. 13 from 23 September 1941.

During verbal interventions by the ambassador on the issue of their release, Vyshinsky[6] initially brought up a charge of collaboration with the Germans (a discussion from 6 December 1941), and thereafter, in a note from 26 January 1942, the NKID, referring to the above-mentioned position on the matter of the citizenship of the persons of non-Polish nationalities (note from 1 December 1941), questioned their Polish citizenship, and ignoring the logical and legal arguments referenced in the embassy notes from 7 March 1942, refused, with a note from 12 April 1942, any further discussion on this subject. Since Misters Alter and Ehrlich [Erlich], both councilors of the capital city of Warsaw, had not been permanently resident in the territory occupied by the Soviet army, the position of the Soviet authorities was practically inconsistent with the argument formulated in the note from 1 December 1941, and challenged the Polish citizenship of all persons of non-Polish nationality, and particularly Jews.

Issue of Departure Visas for Polish Citizens–Jews

Indeed, when the embassy vigorously supported, in note No. D-941/41 from 8 December 1941, the request by Mr. Dawid Aleksandrowicz, known to the ambassador, and his family, permanently resident in Kiev, to be issued departure visas from the USSR to Palestine, the Deputy Chief of the Consular Department of the NKID, Mr. Belaev, in a conversation with the first secretary of the embassy from 20 December 1941, referenced the note from 1 December 1941, and the NKID ultimately refused the Aleksandrowicz [family] the departure visa on 29 December 1941, viewing them as Soviet citizens.

---

6. Andrey Vyshinsky [Polish: Andriej Wyszyński] (1883–1954): in the years 1933–39, procurator general of the USSR, the main prosecutor in the show trials (so-called Moscow trials) in the 1930s. In the years 1939–44, he was deputy chairman of the Council of People's Commissars of the USSR. Simultaneously, beginning in 1940, he was deputy people's commissar of foreign affairs. In the years 1949–53, he served as foreign minister.

The Embassy of the Republic of Poland, fundamentally disagreeing with the position of the Soviet authorities, not only created no obstacles, but on the contrary, supported all efforts of Polish citizens–Jews to leave the USSR. Overall, around four hundred foreign passports were issued by the embassy and departure and transit visas for partner countries were obtained. According to the information held by the embassy, in only one case did the Soviet authorities issue a departure visa from the USSR to an interested person. The rest, despite their possession of valid Polish foreign passports and transit and entry visas issued for a short period of time, were not issued departure visas by the Soviet authorities, which, according to the legislation in force in the USSR, the interested persons themselves had to apply for. Departure visas are neither obtained by those among the Polish citizens of Jewish origin who specify Polish nationality in the visa questionnaire. The case of Misters Knoebel and Geller, who held visas for Iran and Palestine expiring on 30 April, can be used as one of many examples. As a result of an intervention by the deputy of the embassy delegate with the chief of the Oblast Directorate of the NKVD, they were promised [that they would] be issued departure visas within two days. Both of the departure applicants made their way to the local visa department and received there a questionnaire to fill in, in which they specified Polish nationality. They found themselves accused of giving false information in the questionnaire and threatened that, should they fail to change the declarations, their case would not be considered at all. Since the Polish citizens in question had already declared their Polish nationality in official documents in Poland and were in possession of military identity cards specifying [their] Polish nationality, they refused to change the information in the questionnaire. As a result, they had their passports returned and were not issued departure visas.

In light of the fundamental refusal of the right to Polish citizenship of persons of Jewish origin, the promise to release all rabbis and rabbinical candidates from the USSR to Palestine, given in America and England by the resident USSR representative [bodies], acquires a peculiar flavor.

Issues of Interventions for the Release of Jews–Polish Citizens from Prisons and Camps

In view of [the fact that] the Decree of the Presidium of the Supreme Soviet of the USSR about the release from captivity of all Polish citizens had not, in practice, been actioned to date, the embassy lodged many interventions, on behalf of individual persons, for the release of Polish citizens, listed by surname and address, about whose continued imprisonment it received messages. Overall, the embassy personally intervened [in the cases of] 5,100 persons in a year, including 745 with Jewish-sounding surnames. In 76 percent [of cases], (that is, 565 people), the NKID provided no response to the intervention. [In the case of] 124 (around 20 percent), it reported that they were not Polish citizens. [In the case of] twelve [people, it said] that they had not been found, and [in the case of] only about twenty-five, that they were already free, having clearly been released in the first period after the conclusion of the Polish-Soviet agreement. It can, however, be ascertained that, as of December 1941, Polish citizens of non-Polish nationality are treated as Soviet citizens, to whom release does not apply. This also applies to the persons who were rearrested under charges of various crimes, even after the day of the Amnesty from 12 August 1941. As such, for example, [in response to] a verbal intervention of an embassy representative from 21 February 1942 on the matter of eleven Polish citizens arrested in Alma-Ata, the NKID representative refused all talks, stating that they were Soviet citizens. Most of the arrestees were Jews and had been arrested for keeping in contact with the embassy's delegation, since, according to the legislation in place, contact by Soviet citizens with agents of a foreign state is a crime. When, on 11 March 1942, the first secretary of the embassy interpellated the NKID on the matter of sixteen-year-old Mieczysław Wajsman, sentenced to eight years' forced labor for willful abandonment of work, an NKID representative started a discussion about nationality and would not accept the intervention, stating that, already due to the sound of [his] name, Wajsman was a Jew, and so could not be a Polish citizen.

When the embassy informed the NKID, in note No. D-2853/42 from 10 July 1942, that it had "received, by telegram, a note that a number of Polish citizens, Jews, were to be expelled from Kirovabad, Azerbaijan SSR, on 4 July in an unknown direction" and requested that [it] be told "for what reasons and to where the Polish citizens, Jews, have been displaced" and that further displacement of Polish citizens be stopped, it received a response from the NKID from 19 July of that year, No. 137, containing the following: "In response to the note of the Embassy of the Republic of Poland No. D-2663/42 from 10 July 1942, the NKID has the honor to inform that the issue raised in the aforementioned note lies exclusively within the remit of Soviet bodies as it pertains to Soviet citizens. The relevant point of view of the People's Commissariat has been presented to the embassy to an exhaustive [extent] in notes No. 84 from 1 December 1941 and No. 2 from 5 January 1942."

Issue of Polish Citizens–Jews, Embassy Social Welfare Representatives (*Hommes de Confiance*)

As a result of an agreement between the embassy and the NKID, a procedure was set out in January 1942 of appointing social welfare representatives of the embassy for the care of Polish citizens in the USSR. The surnames of [such] social welfare representatives were to be reported to the NKID by the embassy in order to [pass onto] the local authorities the instruction to provide them with help and support. The Embassy of the Republic of Poland, making no differentiation between Polish citizens based on their faith or nationality, often appointed to the positions of social welfare representatives, [or], alternatively, delegation employees, persons of Jewish origin. On one of the lists of the new social welfare representatives of the embassy reported to the NKID in line with the newly set-out procedure, the surnames of Rozencwajg and Lustgarten could be found. The following day, after the sending of the note containing the above surnames to the NKID, one of the officials of the Fourth European Department of the NKID telephoned the embassy asking, on the orders of the director of that department, what was the nationality the representatives Rozencwajg and Lustgarten, reported the day before. The following conversation ensued:

Embassy representative: "Both are of Polish nationality."

NKID representative: "And not Jewish?"

"They are Polish citizens of Polish nationality."

"And their surnames, are they Polish?"

"The surnames demonstrate nothing."

After the conversation with the representative of the department was concluded in this manner, the director of the department, Novikov, called the embassy again a few hours later. The conversation took place as follows:

"I would like to clarify the issue of the nationality of Rozencwajg and Lustgarten, already brought up at noon."

"Both of the social welfare representatives registered by me are Polish citizens of Polish nationality."

"They are not Jews?"

"They are not Jews, they are Poles."

"But mind you, there can be Poles and Poles. When someone's named Smogorzewski for example, then he's a Pole, but Rozencwajg and Lustgarten—they're surely Jews."

"This, categorically, demonstrates nothing. I, for example, don't have a Polish surname, and as you know, Mr. Director, I'm a Pole."

"This issue, however, must be clarified. It is not about these people's citizenship, but nationality."

"The Polish legislation is not led by racial considerations. If someone is a Polish citizen and states that they consider themselves a Pole, we don't prove it to them that they're a Jew. Anyway, this is beside the point for the staffing of the social welfare representative positions."

"There can be no talk about racial considerations. You know, Sir, of our position on the matter of Polish citizenship. I ask that you might further clarify the matter of the nationality of Rozencwajg and Lustgarten, as the processing of the embassy's letter directed to the Narkomindel[7] depends on it."

"I will explain this issue to Mr. Ambassador, but I don't think he will take a different stance."

In light of the fact that the embassy did not deem it possible to take a position discriminating against Polish citizens based on their nationality, director Novikov returned to the case of Lustgarten and Rozencwajg in a conversation

---

7. NKID.

with the first secretary of the embassy on 21 February 1942, stating "that in view of the lack of a clear answer by the embassy, he was forced to halt the case, and that he had made no steps to register them as social welfare representatives. In the future, we would ask that the embassy might avoid appointing as social welfare representatives persons who might arouse these kind of doubts."

Since without the NKID's clear instruction to the local authorities to provide assistance and support to the embassy's social welfare representatives, their work was practically impossible, the embassy was forced to indeed restrict the appointment of social welfare representatives from among Polish citizens [who were] non-Poles.

Issue of Celebration of Easter by Polish Citizens

In due course, the Soviet government issued a decree on the request of the Embassy of the Republic of Poland exempting Polish citizens from work during the Christmas holidays. Referencing this precedent in a conversation with the deputy of the leader of the Council of People's Commissars on 24 March 1942, the ambassador asked that Polish citizens, Christians, be exempted from work on 5 and 6 April of that year, and Jews on 2 and 3 April that year. In light of the above, the following discussion ensued:

Director Novikov: "One thing is confusing here, what is it actually with the holidays for Jews? What is this date of 2 and 3 April this year?"

Amb.: "It refers to Polish citizens of Jewish nationality."

Wysz.:[8] (picking up Novikov's thought) "Well, if it were about persons of Jewish nationality who lived in the areas of Western Ukraine and Western Belarusia on 2 November 1939, then they are Soviet citizens, in accordance with our note from 1 December 1941."

Amb.: "I, here, as the ambassador of Poland, represent all Polish citizens. We do not differentiate between Jews and non-Jews. When I request holidays for the Christians, I have to request the same for the Polish citizens of Jewish faith."

Wysz.: "When it comes to Poles, there is a precedent—Christmas holidays. When it comes to Jews—the situation complicates the matter of citizenship."

8. Likely short for Wyszyński (Vyshinsky)—see footnote in "The Case of Erlich and Alter," above.

Amb.: (laughing) "I couldn't very well ask for Christmas for the Jews, who don't recognize this holiday at all. If Mr. Chair considers the existence of Polish citizens, Jews, possible, then I seek a holiday for precisely them."

Wysz.: "This matter is complicated by the issue of citizenship. How are some to be separated from others? It's better to have the holidays without the Jews."

Amb.: "Too bad, I represent all Polish citizens here."

Issue of Polish Citizens–Jews, and Soviet Censorship

As a side note to the above issue, one can note down the following typical episode: one of the foreign correspondents, mistakenly informed about the positive result of the intervention for both faiths, wrote a fitting telegram with the information that "the ambassador intervened for Polish citizens, Jews and Christians." From that text, the censor crossed out the word *Jews*, leaving a text from which one might gather that the intervention (not the result) applied only to Christians. The correspondent claims that, in light of this, he never sent that telegram at all, which the embassy could not check, naturally. When a correspondent from *Everybody's Daily*[9] in Buffalo (USA) declared a telegram at the Narkomindel [which said] that the delegations of the embassy provided help to Polish citizens irrespective of nationality and faith, the [phrase] "irrespective of nationality and faith" was erased by the censor. Similar erasures were also repeated in other analogous telegrams. When an associate of the embassy, the well-known Jewish journalist Singer,[10] was to give a radio address to Jews, Polish citizens, a representative of the NKID Press Department, Petrov, said that he would allow an address to Jews who were under German occupation, whereas he could not allow an address to Jews [who were] Polish citizens in the USSR, since there were none of those at all, or there was a small handful of them at most.

---

9. [*Dziennik Dla Wszystkich*, Polish-language daily newspaper published 1907–57 in Buffalo, NY, USA.]

10. Bernard Singer, pen name Regnis (1893–1966): journalist, publicist. During the war, he was arrested by the NKVD in Riga [and sent] to a labor camp. Released as a result of the Amnesty, he was employed by the Polish embassy in Kuybyshev in the press department. In 1942, along with the army of General Anders, he left for Iran, and from there to London, where he worked in the Ministry of Information and Documentation.

Issue of Selection of Jews, Polish Citizens, to the PAF in the USSR

After obtaining, during General Sikorski's stay in the USSR, the permission of the Soviet authorities to expand the Polish Armed Forces in the USSR through the creation of a few new divisions, a draft of Polish citizens into the Polish army was to take place. The Polish military authorities issued an instruction for the draft committees not to discriminate in any way in the matter of nationality. In accordance with the Polish-Soviet agreement, however, representatives of the Soviet military authorities were to also form a part of the draft committee. The draft was carried out in a few republics and oblasts; it was not carried out in the remainder of the territory in light of a renewed restriction on the numbers of the PAF in the USSR in March 1942.

Even before the start of the draft, the Polish military authorities were informed, unofficially, that the Soviet liaison officers had received instructions from their headquarters, in line with which "to the new divisions there is allowed the draft of Poles from all of Poland, also from Western Ukraine and Western Belarusia; other nationalities are not to be included in the draft." Despite the objection of the Polish authorities, the representatives of the Soviet military authorities in the draft committees for the PSZ managed to action their [stance] in practice. During the draft, the embassy received tens of telegrams and letters from various parts of the USSR in which Polish citizens of Jewish, Ukrainian, and Belorussian [Belarusian] nationality protested against not being accepted into the ranks of the Polish army. It emerged from the reports of the Polish members of draft committees received later that the Soviet members of those committees would not allow anyone who[se Polish nationality] they doubted to be drafted. There were instances of an applicant being rejected based only on the sound of [their] name or [their] appearance, and as a rule, in doubt-arousing situations, the Soviet committee members would ask the applicant not only about their nationality but also about [their] faith, and they were interested in the faith of the parents too, or even grandparents. In individual cases, [they] even resorted to such a drastic method of confirming "nationality" as a doctor's examination ([of] circumcision). As a result of the categorical refusal of the Soviet members of the army committees, only a very few individuals of Jewish origin ended up in the ranks of the Polish forces in the USSR from the draft that was carried out.

Issue of the First Evacuation to Iran

In light of the order by the Soviet authorities to decrease the numbers of the Polish army in the USSR, they agreed for a few divisions to be evacuated to Iran. At the same time as the military personnel, permission was obtained for the evacuation of the part of the civilian population who were being fed by the army, and of military families. Because the evacuation took place in a very hasty manner, it was impossible to put together a list of persons being evacuated according to a plan. [Efforts] were made on the part of the embassy for the evacuation to include some of the Jewish population, in particular the more eminent and representative. They managed to achieve this in part, despite the objection of the Soviet authorities stemming from their fundamental position on the matter of the citizenship of persons of non-Polish nationality.

Issue of Passportization

Polish citizens released from captivity on the basis of the decree from 12 August 1941 were issued special "Amnesty certificates," with a note that they were to be exchanged for passports within three months. Polish citizens of non-Polish nationality released from prisons and camps as a result of the conclusion of the Agreement from 30 July 1941 (see above page 1 [?]) also received such certificates. Technical issues around the printing of the passport applications resulted in the issue of Polish passports starting only in March 1942. In the meantime, the NKID informed the embassy in note No. 18 from 7 October that the local authorities had received advice about the extension of the validity of the certificates held by Polish citizens until the time that they were given temporary Polish passports. More or less at the same time as the start of the issuance of the Polish passports, news began to come in to the embassy from various parts of the USSR of the taking away by the Soviet authorities of the certificates issued at one point to Polish citizens. This applied in particular to persons of German nationality. In note No. D-1088/42 from 16 April 1942, the embassy, pointing to the fact that the aforementioned certificates were, in very many cases, the only basis on which the Soviet authorities could establish the Polish citizenship of their holders, and that they were the basis for the issuance of Polish passports, requested that the operation of taking away the certificates be stopped. Simultaneously, in the same note, the embassy stressed that, according to the information it had received, during the operation of the revoking of the "temporary certificates," Polish citizens "are given some forms to fill out in which, among other things, there is alleged to be a section about the renunciation of Polish citizenship by the signer. In [certain] individual cases, representatives of the local authorities allegedly encourage Polish citizens to fill in the above section affirmatively, while in others [they] question the nationality declaration supplied by the applicants, ask about [their] faith, question the sound of the names supplied by them, etc." The embassy also pointed to the fact that individuals who had their certificates taken away were then called up to the Red Army, or incorporated into the Soviet army list, against which they could not defend themselves, having been deprived of the evidence of their Polish citizenship.

In a response from 6 May 1942, No. 85, the NKID informed the embassy that "the citizens released on the basis of the Decree of the Presidium of the Supreme Soviet from 12 August 1941 . . . had their temporary release certificates collected only to check the citizenship of those persons, [and] by no means taken away, as stated in the aforementioned note. The embassy's claim that in the questionnaire [that had to be] filled out to receive a residence permit there is a point about the renunciation of Polish citizenship by the [person] completing the questionnaire is based on some kind of misunderstanding. In the aforementioned questionnaire there indeed exists point 18 concerning the matter of regularizing citizenship. However, the content of this [section] is different from what the embassy's note claims. Nevertheless, to avoid any misunderstandings, the competent authorities have been advised to remove point 18 from the questionnaire . . . The embassy's information about the alleged regional army committees' incorporation of Polish citizens into the army list, with all the consequences that follow, has not been confirmed by an inspection carried out by the relevant bodies. Only persons who are Soviet citizens are added to the list."

[This is] despite the fact that it followed from the NKID's response, in no uncertain terms, that the "checking of citizenship" of the persons released from captivity on the basis of the decree from 12 August 1941 was intended to [add] all non-Poles to the [ranks] of Soviet citizens, with all the consequences that followed (inclusion on the army list). The embassy, in note No. D-1937/42 from 8 June 1942, pointed to the pointlessness of checking the citizenship of persons released from captivity as Polish citizens, and again stressed that the aforementioned release certificates were essential evidence for the Polish authorities of the possession of Polish citizenship, on the basis of which interested persons were issued Polish passports; it pointed out that "the possibility, due to the operation of citizenship-checking that was ordered, of a change in the Soviet authorities' perception of the citizenship of the individuals released as Polish citizens, would bring about confusion in the entirety of the activities of the embassy and its local branches" during the issuing of passports and the provision of assistance in cash or in kind. The above note by the embassy brought a response by the NKID from 19 June 1942, No. 119, in which the NKID asserted, in an offended tone, that a "campaign of revoking certificates" of the Polish citizens had never been undertaken, and instances of checking the citizenship of individual persons could in no way be considered a "campaign," and thus the embassy's request that a special instruction be issued to cease the "campaign" [that was] allegedly started is clearly based on a misunderstanding.

While the above diplomatic correspondence was taking place, very many Polish citizens—Jews, Ukrainians, and Belorussians [Belarusians]—were deprived of the Soviet authority–issued documents confirming their Polish citizenship. Although some of them managed to obtain relevant Polish passports at the embassy or its respective delegations on the basis of previously issued certificates, in many cases those passports were confiscated from them when they reported to the [People's Militia] to register, having it stressed to them that, as Jews, and [as] others, they could not hold Polish passports, and that they were Soviet citizens. In individual cases such persons reported to the embassy again, where they reported the loss of the Polish passports they had been issued, and as a result, received duplicates in place of them.

It should be noted that given the vast area of the USSR and the various [ways of] working of the Soviet administration, a fully uniform mode of operation was a difficult thing [to achieve]. The approach to the issue of Polish-nationality citizens was stricter in certain oblasts and less [so] in others. Evidently, in order to ultimately settle the entirety of the matter, and to impose a uniform stance of the Soviet authorities on the issue of citizenship, the People's Commissariat of Foreign Affairs sent, on 9 June 1942, note No. 107 to the embassy, in which it advised that the appropriate Soviet bodies, in order to settle the matter of issuing Polish passports, "consider it necessary that alphabetically ordered lists of the Polish citizens to whom the embassy intends to issue national passports be sent to the NKID in four copies, according to each oblast where the Polish citizens are residing, with the inclusion—to speed up the regularization—of a Russian translation." [It demanded] that the nationality, faith, citizenship, and place of residence prior to November 1939, [and] the citizenship and place of residence of the parents of the applicant, and so on, be provided in the above lists among other things, as well as indicating, "[if they] are not a permanent resident of Western Ukraine and Belorussia, then when and under which procedure [they] arrived on the territory of the USSR." "The NKID asserted that all persons against whom the appropriate Soviet bodies raised no objection would, on supplying their Polish passports, be issued residence certificates for foreigners." "The NKID also has the honor to inform the embassy of the need to provide the aforementioned lists in relation to persons who had already been issued Polish national passports as well."

The embassy, aware of the fact that the aim of imposing the procedure for issuing Polish passports in such a drastic way was to eliminate from among Polish citizens all persons of non-Polish nationality, deemed it necessary to turn to the Polish government for instructions on this matter, and at the same time, to avoid possible conflict with the Soviet authorities, ordered a total suspension of the issuance of Polish passports.

After receiving appropriate instructions from the government, the embassy announced, in note No. D-2362/42 from 24 June 1942, that "in line with the basic regulations of international law, the Government of the Republic of Poland asserts that it adjudicates matters of Polish citizenship within its own remit and does not deem it possible that the nationality of Polish citizens who had resided on the territory of the Republic of Poland, and found themselves—involuntarily, as is known—in the territory of the Soviet Union in the years 1939–41, should be decided by the Soviet authorities during the inspection of the lists of Polish citizens [that are being] demanded from the embassy. . . . The issuance of passports to Polish citizens by the Embassy of the Republic of Poland and its delegations is carried out on the basis of the Polish legislation and regulations in force. In line with the Constitution of the Republic of Poland and the Polish legislation, nationality, faith, or race, or place of residence within the borders of the Republic of Poland, have no influence on the Polish citizenship of the given person. Taking into account that the above-mentioned NKID note seeks to impose a procedure for the issuance of passports that is not practiced in relations between sovereign states, the Government of the Republic of Poland sees no possibility of a relevant discussion on this matter based on the proposed procedure."

In note No. 129 from 8 July 1940, the NKID asserted that it "insists on the procedure for issuing Polish national passports communicated to the Embassy in the NKID note, and it brings to the Embassy's attention that only with the [adoption] of this procedure is the issuance of Polish national passports in USSR territory by the Embassy bodies, as well as the issuance by militia of residence certificates to the holders of the aforementioned passports for foreigners, possible."

A few days after receiving the embassy's note from 24 June 1942, the Soviet authorities began arresting the embassy delegates (a delegate in Arkhangelsk on 29 June, a delegate in Vladivostok on 30 June). On 3 July of the same year, the NKID sent an aide-mémoire in which it advised of a unilateral decision to shut down four of the twenty delegations of the embassy. And on 20 July of that year, the deputy of the President of the Council of People's Commissars submitted a statement to Minister Skolnicki, [claiming that] the delegates of the embassy, as well as their associates, rather than loyally carrying out their duties as regards the provision of help to Polish citizens, in close cooperation with the local bodies of the Soviet authority, were practicing activities hostile to the Soviet Union and carrying out intelligence work. As a result of the above, the People's Commissariat deemed the further existence of the embassy's delegation impossible, in accordance with which appropriate instructions had been issued to the local bodies. In the meantime, all the embassy delegates were arrested by the Soviet authorities, along with most of their associates, including passport officers, to start with. During the searches [that were] carried out, the Soviet authorities collected, in the first instance, lists of issued passports and passport applications, and during the investigation they made it clear to the persons being examined that the USSR-hostile activity included, among other things, dealing with the business of Soviet citizens and issuing them Polish passports.

The fierce conflict that arose with regard to the arrest of around one hundred delegates, delegation employees, and social welfare representatives of the embassy between the Polish and Soviet government[s] has not yet been resolved.

Issue of Polish Citizens, Jews, with regard to the Evacuation of the PSZ in the USSR

[Given] this state of affairs, it is difficult to expect the possibility of evacuating a larger number of Jews—Polish citizens—as part of the contingent of civilian persons, numbering more than a dozen thousand, whose evacuation alongside the army the Soviet authorities had agreed to. Efforts were made on the part of the embassy for the evacuation of the civilian persons to be carried out in a more organized and expedient way this time. A list containing around 350 surnames of the more eminent and valuable-to-society Polish-citizen Jews was developed in the embassy. The above list was sent to the command of the PSZ in the USSR with [the instruction] that the military authorities take all possible steps to bring the above-named people to the places [where] the Polish units were stationed and evacuate them alongside the Polish army outside of the USSR borders. According to recently received reports, the Soviet liaison officers pay special attention to the issue of the evacuation of Jews—Polish citizens—and demand to be presented the list of persons intended for evacuation for a strict inspection. According to the statement by General Zhukov, the Soviet authorities will agree to the evacuation of only those Polish-citizen Jews whose immediate relatives (father, son, or husband) serve in the Polish division within the territory of the USSR and are [designated] to be evacuated outside of its borders. Because of the general line of the Soviet authorities on the matter of allowing Jews into the ranks of the Polish army in the USSR, the number of persons of Jewish nationality who can expect to take their families abroad is minimal. This agreement will undoubtedly provide arguments for the hostile-to-Poland propaganda on the international stage and for the accusation of Polish agents of "racial antisemitism."

Use of the Nationality Policy of the Soviet Authorities in Propaganda within the USSR

It would make sense, in order to illustrate the use in internal propaganda of individual actions of the Soviet authorities toward Polish citizens, to reference two testimonies submitted by Polish citizens of Jewish origin who were kept in labor camps for a number of months after the Amnesty, and who eventually managed to convince the Soviet authorities that, despite [their] Jewish origin, they should be considered Poles and be released on that basis.

1) Mr. Roman Fajans,[11] in the memorandum "On the Republic of Poland citizens heretofore imprisoned in the Ukhtizhem penal-correctional camp," writes, among other things: "the lower camp authorities make it known to the citizens of the Republic of Poland at every step that they are simply societal outcasts, whom the Polish side does not wish to claim, and who are rejected by the Soviet side, unwanted by anyone. If you were truly full-fledged Polish citizens"—[the authorities] remind them continually—"you would have long since been freed as equals to the thousands of Poles who have already been free for several months."

2) A legal apprentice from Warsaw, Mr. Wiktor Brandes, released from a camp in the Arkhangelsk Oblast on 2 June 1942, writes even more vividly in the note entitled "How the camp authorities and prosecution representatives attempt to sow discord among Polish citizens—Poles, Jews and Ukrainians, and kill the patriotic feelings inside them": " . . . at the end of November 1941, the chief of the Third Division of the 'Kargopollag'[12] said in a conversation with me: if we are holding you all, then it is taking place with the knowledge and permission of your legation. You can repeat this to your friends. I know, after all, that you have written to the Polish Ambassador [with the help of] the released people, so if I were worried about that, I would have ordered that everyone leaving the camp be searched. . . . Your embassy has known about everything for a long time and does not intervene, as you see, because there exists a kind of agreement that complements the one that was [released] for public information."

The chief of the subcamp of Yertsevo, Samochwałow, put it [like this]: "You have been sold out by your government." The prosecutor, Safronow, said the following (at the end of March 1942): "Ukrainian nationalists (not only of the OUN kind) are an undesirable element on the outside; both from the Polish

11. Roman Fajans (1903–1976): well-known Warsaw journalist, prisoner in Soviet labor camps, emigrated to France after the war.

12. The management of the penal camps located around the town of Kargopol in the Arkhangelsk Oblast.

point of view and from ours, this is a special enemy. . . . Jews do not come under the blessing of the Amnesty either. (When I pointed out: why did you release over a thousand Jews?) You understood the agreement in an honest way: that in accordance with the text, it applied to all citizens of the former Polish state. I received a clarification (*razjaśnieno*) later; had I had it earlier, I would of course not have released the Jews. This should not surprise you; it is, after all, in line with the history of Polish-Jewish relations and the politics practiced by your governments. After all, you cannot accuse the Soviet government of such an antisemitic interpretation of the agreement."

At one of the camp sites (number 37, if I'm not mistaken), the *obłastnoj*, the deputy prosecutor, answered the Jews' question about release during an inspection: "It isn't we who are holding you, it's your government. It's not our fault that Sikorski doesn't want you."

Given the astonishing consistency of these statements by camp authorities and prosecution, as well as representatives of the higher powers, one cannot help thinking that they are not expressions of personal views but rather blatant, insidious work carrying out the instructions of the central authorities—this is the conclusion reached in his note by a Polish citizen of Jewish origin, released ten months after the Amnesty.

Kuybyshev, 11 August 1942

Glossary

agreement (Polish: *umowa*): here, the so-called Sikorski-Maisky pact. An agreement signed on July 30, 1941, in London between the prime minister of the Polish Government-in-Exile, General Władysław Sikorski, and the USSR ambassador in London, Ivan Maisky [Mayski]. The most important articles of this agreement are as follows:

> Art. 1. The Government of the Union of Soviet Socialist Republics acknowledges that the Soviet-German treatises from 1939 related to territorial changes in Poland are no longer in force. The Government of the Republic of Poland declares that Poland is not tied to any third state by any agreement aimed against the Union of Soviet Socialist Republics.
>
> Art. 2. The diplomatic relations between both governments will be reinstated after the signing of this agreement, and an exchange of ambassadors will take place immediately.
>
> Art. 3. Both governments commit to mutual provision of all types of assistance and support in the current war against Hitler's Germany.
>
> Art. 4. The USSR agrees to the creation of a Polish army in the USSR territory, whose command will be appointed by the Government of the Republic of Poland in consultation with the Government of the USSR. The Polish army in the USSR territory will report to the High Command of the USSR on operational matters, which will include a representative of the Polish army.

Amnesty (Polish: *amnestia*): here, *release*. Based on the Decree of the Supreme Soviet of the USSR from August 12, 1941, the Amnesty released Polish citizens present in prisons, labor camps, and other places of forced deportation within the territory of the Soviet state. It was the result of an agreement between the government of the Republic of Poland and the Soviet government (see *agreement*), concluded in London on July 30, 1941, which contained an additional protocol negotiated by the Polish Government-in-Exile. It stated: "At the moment of restoration of diplomatic relations the government of the Union of Soviet Socialist Republics will grant amnesty to all Polish citizens who are currently deprived of freedom within the territory of the Union of Soviet Socialist Republics either as prisoners of war, or for other relevant reasons."

Anders Army: see *Polish army in the USSR.*

***artel* (Russian)**: term for various types of work cooperatives, primarily craftsmen and small manufacturers, in the former USSR.

beth hamidrash (pl. batei hamidrash; Polish: *bet-hamidrasz*): house of teaching and study of Jewish religious texts.

brit milah (Polish: *brith-mila*): ritual circumcision. A ritual surgical procedure carried out on the eighth day after the birth of a boy. See *mohel.*

Bund: General Jewish Labor Bund in Poland, a socialist political group created in Vilnius in 1897. It was active mainly in the areas of the Russian partition, as well as in the so-called Pale of Settlement (the Western and Southwestern guberniyas of tsarist Russia and areas of the Eastern Borderlands of prepartition Poland). In the early days of the Second Polish Republic, the Polish Bund became the largest Bund organization in the world. In the 1930s it also became the largest Jewish social democratic organization in Poland.

***bytoviki* (Russian; Polish: *bytowicy*)**: common criminals; persons convicted of nonpolitical offenses.

cantor (Polish: *kantor*): singer in a synagogue who leads the prayer services.

CENTOS: Centralne Towarzystwo Opieki nad Sierotami (Central Society for the Care of Orphans), a Polish-Jewish social organization created in 1924 to aid Jewish orphans following World War I. CENTOS provided aid to families and ran orphanages and schools.

cheder: religious elementary school for Jewish boys.

COP: Centralny Okręg Przemysłowy (Central Industrial District), the largest industrial complex in the interwar period, a grouping of arms industry factories located in south-central Poland (Rzeszów, Stalowa Wola, Mielec areas).

***cynga* (Russian)**: scurvy, an illness caused by vitamin deficiency. Scurvy causes inflammation of the gums, and as a result, tooth loss. Many Siberian exiles and prisoners suffered from it, and in the extreme conditions in the labor camps, it took considerably more dangerous forms: various types of subcutaneous and suppurative exudate and the falling off of whole pieces of flesh from the areas where wounds had formed.

delegation (Polish: *delegatura*): here, a field representation of the embassy of the Government of the Republic of Poland in exile. Delegations were set up in areas where there were large numbers of Polish citizens returning from places of confinement, exile, prisons, labor camps, and other places of forced labor.

***Der Moment* [The Moment]**: Yiddish-language daily newspaper published in Warsaw 1910–39, published by Noach Pryłucki (1882–1941), the leader of the Jewish People's Party.

***Dobry Wieczór–Kurier Czerwony* [Dobry Evening–Red Courier]**: *Kurier Czerwony* was a pro-Jewish afternoon journal published 1922–39 by Warsaw-based Dom Prasy SA. It merged with *Dobry Wieczór* in 1932.

Donbas: Donets Coal Basin.

elections (Polish: *wybory*): here, the elections to the People's Assemblies of Western Ukraine and Western Belarus, that is, the eastern voivodeships of the former Second Polish Republic occupied by the USSR. The elections took place at the end of October 1939. Both assemblies ratified the annexation of their territories to the USSR.

eszelon: a train used for special purposes, usually military.

evacuation of the Polish army (Polish: *ewakuacja armii polskiej*): an evacuation from the Soviet Union to Iran that took place in two stages: in

March–April and August 1942. The evacuation covered around 114,000 persons in total, including 25,000 civilians (see *Polish army in the USSR*).

gaon (Hebrew): venerable. A title of honor awarded to rabbis of two Talmudic academies in Sura and Pumbedita in Babylonia from the end of the sixth century. Here: a title bestowed upon eminent rabbis known for [their] authority and learnedness.

German-Soviet war (Polish: *wojna niemiecko-sowiecka*): war initiated by Hitler's attack on the USSR on June 22, 1941. In the first phase of the war, the Germans sustained immediate victories over the Red Army and advanced quickly into the USSR. The Battle of Stalingrad (July 22, 1942–February 2, 1943) turned the tide and the war ended with Germany's defeat and its unconditional surrender signed on May 7, 1945.

GPU: Gosudarstvennoye Politicheskoye Upravleniye (State Political Directorate). The Soviet security service in the years 1922–34; a political police force. Superseded in 1934 by the NKVD (see entry).

***gruzchik* (Russian; Polish: *gruzczik* [also *gruzownik*, *gruzowszczyk* in the testimonies])**: loader.

Haggadah (Haggadah shel Pesach; Hebrew; Polish: Hagada szel Pesach): Jewish text that tells the Passover story and sets the order of the Passover Seder (see *Seder*). The story of the Israelites' departure from Egypt under the leadership of Moses, read aloud during the Seder, represents a link between the biblical and modern periods.

***hakhsharah* (Hebrew; Polish: *hahszara*)**: professional training program for future Jewish pioneers in Eretz Israel led by the Zionist Hashomer Hatzair (see entry).

Hashomer Hatzair (Hebrew; Polish: Haszomer Hacair [Young Guard]): international Zionist Jewish youth organization formed in 1916 in Vienna, modeled on the British Scouting movement. Janusz Korczak was one of the founders. Hashomer Hatzair stressed a cooperative lifestyle and immigration to Palestine, and many members settled in Mandate Palestine as workers and farmers.

Hasid (Hebrew; Polish: *chasyd*): observant Jew following the ultra-Orthodox tradition, normally tied to the "court" of his Tzaddik. Hasidic Jews seek full communion with God through song, dance, and prayer.

Hatikvah (Hebrew; Polish: Hatikwa): lit. the hope. *Hatikva* is the title of the anthem of the Zionist movement and later the State of Israel.

HeHalutz (Hebrew; Polish: He-Chaluc): lit. the pioneer. HeHalutz was a Polish youth movement that brought together around forty thousand young Jews by 1939. The organization provided training in agriculture and skilled trades to prepare members for emigration to Palestine.

Jewish Agency (Polish: Agencja Żydowska; Sochnut): nongovernmental organization created in 1922 through a mandate of the League of Nations to represent Jews to the British mandate powers in Palestine and to the League of Nations. Currently the executive arm of the World Zionist Organization on matters of emigration to Israel.

Joint: commonly used name for the American Jewish Joint Distribution Committee, a charitable organization formed in the United States in 1914 that supported the social and economic activities of the Jewish people in countries afflicted by poverty.

Kaddish (Hebrew; Polish: Kadysz): a prayer that is part of all traditional Jewish communal prayer services. The Mourner's Kaddish is recited in memory of a loved one. *Kaddish* is an Aramaic word meaning *sanctification* and is related to the Hebrew *holy*.

kibitka (Russian): here, a type of primitive hut in Uzbekistan and other Soviet republics of Central Asia.

kolkhoz (Russian; Polish: *kołchoz*): collective farm; an agricultural cooperative in the USSR.

***komandirovka* (Russian; Polish: *komandirowka*)**: business trip or a pass allowing one to travel.

kosher (Yiddish; Polish: *koszer*): food that is chosen, processed, and prepared according to Jewish dietary laws. Kosher laws govern, among other things, the slaughter of animals and the production, processing, and preparation of foods.

Kownoer Zeitung **[Kowno Times]**: German-language daily of Kowno (Kaunas), Lithuania, from 1916 to 1918, published by the Kowno Soldiers' Council.

Kuczki **(Polish)**: see *Sukkot*.

Kurier Warszawski **[Warsaw Courier]**: daily newspaper printed in Warsaw from 1821 to 1939, with two editions daily.

lepyoshki **(Russian; Polish: *lepioszki*)**: Central Asian flatbread similar to naan, typical of Uzbek cuisine.

lesozagotovka **(Russian; Polish: *lesozagotowka*)**: industrial logging enterprise.

lesprotarg **(Russian):** Soviet state enterprise for the timber trade.

makuchy **(Polish)**: see *oil cakes*.

mixed Russian-German commissions for resettlement: commissions appointed on the basis of the agreement between the USSR and the Third Reich at the end of 1939. Their main aim was to resettle the Germans residing in the Soviet occupation zone to areas under German rule.

mohel: person who performs ritual circumcision (see *brit milah*).

NKVD (Polish: NKWD): Naródnyy Komissariát Vnútrennikh del (the People's Commissariat for Internal Affairs). Political police of the USSR, operating under this name in the years 1934–46. Successor to the OGPU, antecedent of the KGB.

Nowy Dziennik **[New Journal]**: Zionist Polish-language journal that appeared daily in Krakow, 1918–39.

oil cakes (Polish: *makuchy*): solid residue resulting from the extraction of oil from rapeseed or other oil plants. Used as cattle feed.

paragraph 11 (Polish: ***paszport z nr*** **11;** ***paszport z paragrafem*** **11)**: a type of Soviet passport that forbade the holder from living in or near the larger cities or in a one-hundred-kilometer zone at the western border.

passportization (Polish: ***paszportyzacja*****)**: an operation to force the Eastern Borderlands residents to accept USSR passports. Passportization was carried out twice: in the first half of 1940 and in March 1943.

Pesach: Passover. A Jewish holiday observed on the fifteenth day of the month of Nisan (March–April), which is the first full moon in spring, to commemorate the Jewish people's exodus from Egypt.

plebiscite (Polish: ***plebiscyt*****)**: see *elections*.

Poale Zion (Polish: Poalej-Syjon): workers of Zion, a radical Jewish Social Democratic party, formed in 1905 in the Russian Partition. Poale Zion strove to build a socialist society in Palestine.

Polish army in the USSR (Polish: ***armia polska w ZSSR*****)**: often referred to as the Anders Army or Anders' Army. A military formation created by General Władysław Anders pursuant to the Sikorski-Maisky agreement of July 30, 1941, which established diplomatic relations between the USSR government and the Polish Government-in-Exile. The army consisted mostly of people freed by the Amnesty from Stalinist labor camps, prisons, and places of exile. Siberian youths ages fourteen to eighteen were also admitted to the army. The first goal of the operation was facilitating the troops' departure from Russia; the second, providing the Polish army with future educated personnel. The army was evacuated from the Soviet Union in March 1942, going first to Iran and then to Palestine.

Polish children's homes in the USSR (Polish: ***ochronki polskie w ZSSR*****)**: orphanages created in various areas of the USSR by representatives of the Government of the Republic of Poland in exile.

Polish citizenship in the territory of the USSR (Polish: ***obywatelstwo polskie na terenie ZSSR*****)**: establishment of citizenship for refugees and residents in Soviet-occupied territories, governed by two decrees: one from November 29,

1939, which deemed all persons present on November 1–2, 1939, in territories that were occupied by the Red Army after September 17, 1939, to be Soviet citizens; and one from August 12, 1941, which reinstated Polish citizenship to the persons who had held it until November 1–2, 1939.

***politruk* (Russian)**: officer for political matters.

***posiolek* (Russian; Polish: *posiołek*; pl. *posiołki*)**: settlement, colony. Here, it refers to a settlement called a *spetsposiolek* (special settlement; pl. *spetsposelki*), the name given to unofficial forced labor camps created by the Soviet political police in places of exile. The settlements were located in uninhabited woodland areas of the Siberian taiga, where the exiles themselves often had to build primitive barracks or dugouts from materials acquired in the forest. The main activities of the exiles in these camps were most often logging, to produce lumber for the needs of the Soviet economy, and road construction.

***Prawda* [The Truth]**: newspaper published by the Front for the Rebirth of Poland, a clandestine anti-Fascist organization formed in 1941 by a group of secular Catholics.

***progul* (Russian; Polish: *progul*)**: lateness or absence from work. In the Soviet forced labor camps, *progul* was punished by the reduction of food rations or even imprisonment.

Purim (Polish: Purym): Jewish holiday observed on the fourteenth day of the month of Adar (February–March) to commemorate Queen Esther's thwarting a plot to exterminate the Jews organized by Haman, chief minister of the Persian king Ahasuerus.

registration (Polish: *rejestracja*): here, the operation carried out by mixed Russian-German commissions for resettlement (see entry) to register refugees for a return to their former places of residence. As a result of the registration, some refugees from central Poland, including a small number of Jews, returned to their towns, along with Germans who had been living in Soviet-occupied territory. Jews who registered to return to the German-held territories were generally sent to labor camps in Siberia instead, as punishment.

resettlement (Polish: *przesiedlenie*): see *mixed Russian-German commissions for resettlement.*

Revisionist Zionists (Polish: Syjoniści-rewizjoniści): revisionist faction of the Zionist movement, led by Vladimir Ze'ev Jabotinsky (Vladimir Zhabotinsky), which called for Jewish statehood, mass immigration to Palestine, and the establishment of a Jewish fighting force.

Rosh Hashanah (Hebrew; Polish: Rosz Haszana): Jewish New Year, observed on the first and second days of the month of Tishrei (September–October). The holiday is marked by celebration, prayer, and sounding the shofar, a trumpetlike instrument made from a ram's horn. In Poland it is called the Feast of Trumpets.

Seder: festive ceremonial meal consumed on the first two days of the holiday of Pesach (see entry), recounting the story of the exodus of the Jews from captivity in Egypt.

Shavuot (Polish: Szawuot): the Feast of Weeks or Harvest Festival (known as Pentecost on the Christian calendar). Observed in the month of Sivan (May–June), Shavuot celebrates the giving of the Torah to the Jewish people at Mount Sinai. It is one of the three pilgrimage festivals (alongside Pesach and Sukkot).

Shema Yisrael (Hebrew; Polish: Szma Israel): "Hear, O Israel," the first words of a Jewish prayer recited in the morning and in the evening, and considered to be the most important part of every prayer service.

shochet (Polish: *rzezak*): person trained and certified to perform the ritual slaughter of animals according to Jewish law, to obtain kosher meat.

shofar (Polish: *szofar*): wind instrument made from a ram's horn that is sounded to remind the faithful about the need for forgiveness and penance. Used during synagogue services on Rosh Hashanah (the Jewish New Year) and Yom Kippur (the Day of Atonement).

Sochnut: see *Jewish Agency.*

sovkhoz (Russian; Polish: *sowchoz*): state agricultural holding in the USSR.

Soviet-German war: see *German-Soviet war*.

Stakhanovite (Polish: Stachanowiec): top-performing worker. The term comes from the name of A. G. Stakhanov, who was the inspiration for the Stakhanovite movement to increase worker productivity in the USSR.

sukkah (Polish: *kuczka*): temporary hut built for the holiday of Sukkot (see entry), where observant Jews often eat, sleep, and otherwise spend time during this holiday.

Sukkot (Polish: Kuczki): weeklong celebration of the harvest observed in the month of Tishrei (September–October). Sukkot commemorates the divine protection afforded to Jews when they fled Egypt. Sukkot is celebrated by dwelling in a foliage-covered hut (see *sukkah*) and by reciting special prayers during synagogue services while carrying the Four Species: citron, palm frond, myrtle, and willow.

***tallit* (Polish: *tałes*)**: Jewish prayer shawl covering head and shoulders during the prayer.

Talmud (Hebrew): lit. instruction, learning. A collection of treatises, commentaries, legal articles, and religious tradition that is the primary source of Jewish law and theology. The Talmud is made up of the Mishnah (oral traditions) and the Gemara (rabbinic commentaries).

Talmud Torah (Polish: Talmud-Tora): religious elementary school supported by the Jewish council.

Tarbut: lit. culture. Jewish Cultural and Educational Association for the development of secular Hebrew-language schooling. Active in Poland, Romania, and Lithuania prior to 1939.

tefillin (Polish: *tfilin, tefilin, filakterie*): a pair of black leather boxes containing Hebrew parchment scrolls, worn on the head and the arm by the observant during weekday morning prayers.

Torah scroll (Polish: *rodały*): parchment scroll containing a handwritten text of the Torah. The scrolls are kept inside the Torah ark and retrieved during prayer services for the reading out of the appropriate section of the Torah.

treif **(Yiddish; Polish: *trefne*)**: food that is not kosher; inconsistent with Jewish dietary rules (see *kosher*).

Tzaddik (Hebrew; Polish: *cadyk*): a righteous man. A rabbi given special respect by the faithful, who believe him to have a mystical spiritual connection with God. Among Hasidic Jews, Tzaddiks maintained "courts" made up of their most important pupils and their families. The Tzaddik, along with his court, was provided for by his supporters.

udostoverenie **(Russian; Polish: *udostowierenije*)**: official [release] certificate.

Vid na zhitelstvo **(*vidnazhitelstvo*; Russian; Polish: *Wid na żytielstwo*)**: residence permit; a USSR residence permit for a foreigner.

yellow badge (Polish: *żółta łata*): a marker consisting of a black Star of David on a yellow background that Jews were required to wear in Nazi-occupied Europe. It was a revival of church decrees in Catholic Medieval Europe requiring Jews to wear special clothing.

yeshiva (Polish: *jeszybot*; *jeszywa*): Jewish religious secondary school.

Yom Kippur (Hebrew; Polish: Jom Kipur): Day of Atonement, celebrated in the month of Tishrei (September–October). The holiest day of the Jewish year.

Zionism (Polish: *syjonizm*): political movement formed at the end of the nineteenth century with the goal of creating a Jewish state in Palestine. Its conception came alongside a wave of Jewish emigration to Palestine in the wake of Jewish pogroms in the southern Russian Empire (now Ukraine).

About the Editors

Dr. Maciej Siekierski, a former research fellow at the Hoover Institution, is curator emeritus of the European collections at the Hoover Institution Library & Archives, where he spent thirty-six years specializing in Poland and Eastern Europe, with principal responsibility for acquiring European archival materials. From 1991 to 1993, Siekierski directed Hoover's Warsaw office, overseeing the collection of tons of publications and documents released in the wake of Eastern Europe's revolutions and transitions to democracy. Among his publications, he edited Jerzy Kwiatkowski's memoir *485 Days at Majdanek* (Hoover Institution Press, 2021), *Helena Paderewska: Memoirs, 1910–1920* (Hoover Institution Press, 2015), and Wiktor Sukiennicki's two-volume *East Central Europe during World War I: From Foreign Domination to National Independence* (New York: East European Monographs, 1984); and compiled *Polish Independent Publications: Guide to the Collection in the Hoover Institution Archives* (Hoover Institution Press, 1998). Siekierski is or has been a member of the American Historical Association, the American Association for the Advancement of Slavic Studies, and the Polish Institute of Arts and Sciences of America. He received fellowships from the International Research and Exchanges Board and the Kosciuszko Foundation. In 2001, Polish prime minister Jerzy Buzek honored Siekierski with the Laur Award for his work in preserving Polish historical records. In 2013, he was recognized by the Lithuanian Ministry of Culture for his contributions to the restoration of Lithuanian cultural and archival heritage. And in 2019, he was awarded the Medal of the 75th Anniversary of Jan Karski's Mission, a distinction earned for his work in guarding Polish history.

Dr. Feliks Tych (1929–2015) was an eminent Polish historian and director of the Jewish Historical Institute in Warsaw (1996–2006). After surviving World War II, he studied history in Warsaw and Moscow and went on to work at the Institute for the History of Science of the Polish Academy of Sciences. Purged from this post in the anti-Zionist campaign of 1968, he continued his scholarly work and lectured at the universities of Göttingen, Darmstadt, Freiburg, Kassel, and Berlin. He also participated in an international group of scholars and representatives of Jewish scholarly institutions to plan the creation of the POLIN Museum of the History of Polish Jews (Muzeum Historii Żydów Polskich), which opened in 2013 on the site of the former Warsaw ghetto. Tych served as a member of the museum's council as well as on the Council of Science of the Polish Academy of Sciences and as a member of the editorial committee of the Polish Biographical Dictionary. Among his many publications are a biographical study of the Polish revolutionary Julian Marchlewski, coauthored with Horst Schumacher, *Julian Marchlewski: Szkic biograficzny* (Warsaw: Książka i Wiedza, 1966); a three-volume edition of the correspondence of Rosa Luxemburg and Leo Jogiches, *Róża Luksemburg: Listy do Leona Jogiches-Tyszki 1893–1914* (Warsaw: Książka i Wiedza, 1968–71); and a major study of the Holocaust, *Długi cień zagłady: Szkice historyczne* (The long shadow of the Holocaust: Historical sketches, Warsaw: Żydowski Instytut Historyczny, 1999).

Index of Names

Note: Bold type indicates biographical note.

Index of Places